The Handbook of Contemporary Clinical Hypnosis

The Handbook of Contemporary Clinical Hypnosis

Theory and Practice

Edited by

Les Brann, Jacky Owens and Ann Williamson

WILEY Blackwell

This paperback edition first published 2015
© 2012 John Wiley & Sons, Ltd.

Edition history: John Wiley & Sons, Ltd. (hardback, 2012)

Registered Office
John Wiley & Sons Ltd, The Atrium, Southern Gate, Chichester, West Sussex, PO19 8SQ, UK

Editorial Offices
350 Main Street, Malden, MA 02148-5020, USA
9600 Garsington Road, Oxford, OX4 2DQ, UK
The Atrium, Southern Gate, Chichester, West Sussex, PO19 8SQ, UK

For details of our global editorial offices, for customer services, and for information about how
to apply for permission to reuse the copyright material in this book please see our website at
www.wiley.com/wiley-blackwell.

The right of Les Brann, Jacky Owens and Ann Williamson to be identified as the authors
of the editorial material in this work has been asserted in accordance with the UK Copyright,
Designs and Patents Act 1988.

Library of Congress Cataloging-in-Publication Data

The handbook of contemporary clinical hypnosis : theory and practice / edited by Les Brann, Jacky Owens,
and Ann Williamson.
  p. ; cm.
 Includes bibliographical references and index.
 ISBN 978-0-470-68367-5 (hardback) ISBN 978-1-1190-5727-7 (pbk)
 1. Hypnotism–Therapeutic use. I. Brann, Les. II. Owens, Jacky. III. Williamson, Ann, 1950–
[DNLM: 1. Hypnosis–methods. 2. Mental Disorders–therapy. WM 415]
 RC495.H357 2011
 616.89′16512–dc23

                                    2011015214

A catalogue record for this book is available from the British Library.

This book is published in the following electronic formats: ePDFs 9781119950912; Wiley Online Library
9781119950905; ePub 9781119979920; eMobi 9781119979937

Set in 9/10pt AGaramond by SPi Publisher Services, Pondicherry, India

1   2012

Contents

This book has been written by members of the British Society of Clinical & Academic Hypnosis (BSCAH).

National Office

Tel: 0844 884 3116
Email: natoffice@bscah.co.uk
Web: www.bscah.co.uk
Charity number 1108372
Registered in England 5120862

Incorporating the British Society of Medical & Dental Hypnosis (BSMDH), founded 1952, and the British Society of Experimental & Clinical Hypnosis (BSECH), founded 1977.

About the Editors

Dr Les Brann BSc, MBBS, MRCS, LRCP, DRCOG, MRCGP, MMedSci, ECH, BSCAH Accred

Dr Les Brann originally qualified as a biochemist but retrained in medicine and has been a general practitioner for 27 years. He has had a career-long interest in medical hypnosis and became an accredited member of BSMDH in 1985. He was in the first cohort of students to undertake the post-graduate diploma in clinical hypnosis and subsequently the masters degree at Sheffield University, obtaining both with distinction. A keen member of BSCAH, and its predecessor organisations BSMDH and BSECH, he is currently president of BSCAH. He has been involved with the setting up of an NHS Hypnotherapy Service and is a strong advocate for its inclusion as an adjunct in many areas of mainstream medicine. As a GP, his interests within hypnotherapy are wide ranging, including psychosomatic conditions, chronic pain, depression, obstetrics, infertility and psychosexual problems. He continues to teach hypnotherapy to health professionals.

Mrs Jacky Owens SRN, BSc, MSc, Dip Onc Nur, ECH, BSCAH Accred

Jacky Owens qualified in 1968 as a registered nurse and worked within the NHS for over 40 years, during which time she specialised in cancer care, was involved in teaching nurses at university level and still guest lectures in cancer care and hypnosis on some nursing MSc courses. Now she runs her own independent company offering a complementary nursing service for cancer sufferers and their carers. Jacky has an MSc in clinical and applied hypnosis from University College London (UCL). She is an accredited member of BSCAH; currently she is a member of BSCAH Council and serves as honourable secretary as well as serving as honourable secretary of the Northern Counties Branch. Jacky is president of the Section of Hypnosis and Psychosomatic Medicine at the Royal Society of Medicine. Her professional interests are in holistic support for cancer patients with a particular interest in immune function.

Dr Ann Williamson MB ChB, ECH, BSCAH Accred

Dr Ann Williamson has been a general practitioner for 32 years and has used hypnosis for more than 15 years to help her patients deal with stress and anxiety and to help them facilitate change in how they live their lives. She is an accredited member of BSCAH, is a certified neurolinguistic programming (NLP) master practitioner and has had training in brief solution oriented therapy and other approaches. She has been involved for many years with teaching health professionals how to use hypnotic techniques both for themselves and within their own field of clinical expertise. She runs stress management, personal development and brief psychological interventions workshops on request, as well as seeing private clients for therapy. She has also lectured at Manchester, Chester and Salford Universities. She has written three books: on stress management, smoking cessation and brief psychological interventions in clinical practice.

About the Contributors

Mrs Phyllis Alden BA, AFBPsS, CPsychol, BSCAH Accred. is a consultant clinical psychologist specialising in oncology, palliative care, pain and post-traumatic stress disorder (PTSD). She is on the Board of Directors of the European Society of Hypnosis.

Dr Kottiyattil K Aravind MB, BS, FRCS is a fellow of BSCAH and was born and qualified in medicine in Kerala, India. He has lived in the United Kingdom since 1965 and was a GP in Rotherham for many years. He was co-author of the 4th edition of *Hartland's Medical and Dental Hypnosis*.

Dr Les Brann BSc, MBBS, MRCS, LRCP, DRCOG, MRCGP, MMedSci, ECH, BSCAH Accred.

Dr David Byron AFBPS, DEdPsy, MA, MEd, BAHons, CertEd, DipAppHyp, BSCAH Accred. is a chartered psychologist, an *eye movement desensitization and reprocessing* (EMDR) Europe practitioner and an associate fellow of the British Psychological Society. He has taught extensively on post-graduate courses and uses hypnosis in his therapeutic work with young people and adults to address anxiety, depression and trauma related difficulties.

Dr Michael E Y Capek MB ChB, MRCGP, MSc in health psychology, BA, BSCAH Accred. is a GP with a special interest in mental health (GPwSI) and specialises in long term medical or psychological conditions and psychosomatic disorders.

Ms Lucy Coffin BSc (Hons) in clinical nursing is a nurse specialising in complementary therapies with an interest in infertility and pregnancy/childbirth.

Dr Barry Cripps CPsychol, CSci, FBPsS is a founder member of the BPS Division of Sport and Exercise Psychology. He is particularly interested in personality, assessment, psychometrics and sport psychology. He has produced two books and has lectured extensively at universities in the United Kingdom and China.

Dr Alastair Dobbin MBBS is a GP in Edinburgh. He is the past president of the British Society for Medical and Dental Hypnosis Scotland, and is a director of the Foundation for Positive Mental Health.

Dr Mike Gow BDS, MSc, BSCAH Accred. has used hypnosis extensively within the dental field.

Dr Adrian Hamill BDS, BSCAH Accred. has used hypnosis over many years with his dental patients.

Dr Peter Hawkins BSc, MSc, Clin Psych, PhD is a counselling psychologist; professor in psychotherapy, Instituto Superior da Maia (ISMAI), Portugal; co-director, Erickson Institutes of Madrid and Porto; and president of the European Institute of Integrative Psychotherapy. His special interests include sleep and psychosexual problems.

Dr Geoff Ibbotson BSc, MB BS, DObstRCOG, BSCAH Accred. was a GP for many years and then worked as a psychological therapist in a clinical psychology department. He is a fellow of BSCAH and a master practitioner in neurolinguistic programming, and has trained in many different approaches to therapy. He has been involved in training health professionals in the use of hypnosis for over 15 years and has a special interest in PTSD and trauma.

Mrs Gardenia Imber BSc Psychol holds post-graduate diplomas in psychotherapy, applied hypnosis and post-traumatic stress counselling. She works in private practice as a psychotherapist, and uses hypnosis and the creative arts to enable people to overcome a wide range of traumatic experiences and psychological problems.

Dr David Kraft BA, PhD, DipClPsy is a psychotherapist working in private practice in London.

Mrs Karen Mackrodt RGN, BSc, MSc, ECH, BSCAH Accred. holds the post-graduate diploma in clinical hypnosis from UCL. She is a former clinical nurse specialist in pain management and is now a practice nurse working in the Chelmsford Medical Hypnosis Unit.

Dr Mhairi L McKenna MB ChB, ECH, BSCAH Accred. was a GP who has had a special interest in dermatology and is president of the European Society of Hypnosis and a fellow of BSCAH. She has contributed to published works and lectured extensively on hypnosis.

Mr David Medd BA, BAPsychol, MSc, PGCE with diplomas in counselling and psychotherapy specialises in treating anxiety, depression and those suffering with movement and neurological disorders.

Dr Caron Moores MBChB, FRCA, DCH, DRCOG is a consultant in paediatric anaesthesia at Alder Hey, Liverpool whose main specialist interests are anaesthesia for paediatric oncology and urgent surgery.

Dr Peter L N Naish BSc, DPhil, AFBPsS, CPsychol, BSCAH Accred. is a visiting reader in psychology at the University of Sussex, and has spent many years as recorder to the British Science Association's Psychology Section. He has spent many years researching the theoretical aspects of hypnosis and has taught and lectured widely. He chairs the Scientific Advisory Board of the British False Memory Society and is frequently called as an expert witness in cases involving the misuse of hypnosis and possible false memories.

Mrs Jacky Owens SRN, BSc, MSc, Dip Onc Nur, ECH, BSCAH Accred.

Mr Cliff Robbins BSc, MSc, is a chartered psychologist and associate fellow of the British Psychological Society and holds the diploma in applied hypnosis from UCL. He has many years of experience working in the NHS across mental health services, forensic services and learning disability and autism. He is currently based in Canterbury as an independent consultant psychologist.

Dr David Rogerson MB ChB, MMedSci, FFARCSI, DA is a consultant in anaesthesia and intensive care medicine in Derby who has used hypnosis for many years as an adjunct to anaesthesia and in an outpatient clinic.

Dr Duncan Shrewsbury FHEA, MAcadMEd, MBChB, MMEd, BMedSc (Neuro) is an academic foundation doctor in North Staffordshire and holds the advanced diploma in clinical hypnosis from Staffordshire University.

Mr David Simons MA, LDSRCS (Eng.), BSCAH Accred. is a retired dentist and a director of Cavendish Cancer Care, a cancer care charitable trust.

Dr Grahame Smith MB BS, D ObstRCOG, DA, BSCAH Accred. holds the diploma in clinical hypnosis from the University of Sheffield. He is a GP and a former GP trainer and educational supervisor. He works in Pontefract, West Yorkshire using hypnosis and related techniques to help patients with a range of problems as seen in general practice.

Dr Sobharani R Sungum-Paliwal MD, FRCPsych, DTM & H, DipSocLT is a consultant in child and adolescent psychiatry at Birmingham Children's specialising in autism spectrum disorders and neuropsychiatry. She is also an honorary senior clinical lecturer in paediatrics and child health at the University of Birmingham, and teaches hypnosis to specialist registrars as well as being an examiner for Birmingham Medical School and for the Royal College of Psychiatrists.

Mrs Diana Tibble SRN, RM, holds post-graduate diplomas in counselling and in applied hypnosis from UCL, and as a former midwife has a particular interest in hypnosis for fertility, pregnancy, childbirth and the post-natal period.

Dr Leslie G Walker MA, PhD, DipClinPsychol, CPsychol, FBPsS, FSB and emeritus professor of cancer rehabilitation at the University of Hull. He serves on a number of national cancer-related committees and carries out research in the field of psycho-oncology.

Dr Martin Wall BDS, BSCAH Accred. teaches at the Peninsular Medical and Dental School, and has been involved in training and the use of hypnosis in dentistry for many years. He is currently on the Board of Directors of the European Society of Hypnosis.

Dr Ann Williamson MB ChB, ECH, BSCAH Accred.

Foreword

David Spiegel, MD

Willson Professor and Associate Chair of Psychiatry and Behavioral Sciences
Stanford University School of Medicine
Past President, Society for Clinical and Experimental Hypnosis
Past President, American College of Psychiatrists
November 21, 2010

Hypnosis is the oldest Western conception of a psychotherapy, yet generation after generation forgets and then rediscovers it. Hypnotic techniques have been oddly dissociated from the canon of mainstream medicine, despite their efficiency and effectiveness. The aura of purple capes and dangling watches haunts hypnotic history and daunts practitioners. Yet the phenomenon of hypnosis touches on something central in the healing arts: getting the patient's full attention, mobilizing an alteration in awareness, sensitizing the patient and doctor to the importance of clear and empathic communication and honing therapeutic strategies. Hypnosis is not a treatment, but rather a mental state that can facilitate a variety of treatment strategies. It is a form of highly focused attention coupled with an ability to dissociate – put outside of conscious awareness – things that would ordinarily be in consciousness. Hypnosis is to consciousness what a telephoto lens is to a camera – what you see you observe in great detail, but you are less aware of the context. This means a reduction in critical scrutiny and an emphasis on doing rather than thinking about what you are doing. Such a state of mind offers special therapeutic opportunities – the patient is really paying attention. But it also confers special responsibilities on the clinician using it – to assess the problem well, think through therapeutic strategies carefully, evaluate the patient's response, be clear when the hypnotic experience is over and teach the patient how to mobilize and make good use of their own hypnotic abilities.

Thus the material in this book, written by leading clinicians and practitioners of hypnosis, is important to clinicians entering into and practicing with the uses of hypnosis in medicine and related disciplines. Hypnosis involves trust, and that trust is rewarded by clinicians who understand the phenomenon, along with its assets and limitations, and who use it artfully to help patients master problems. There is widespread misapprehension that hypnosis poses a threat of losing control. Practiced appropriately, it is a powerful means of helping patients enhance control over symptoms like pain and anxiety, aspects of somatic function and psychological distress. The chapters in this book provide a firm clinical basis for helping patients to help themselves.

There is a growing evidence base, including sizeable randomized clinical trials, demonstrating effects of hypnosis on problems such as chronic pain, procedural anxiety and pain, irritable bowel syndrome, migraine headaches and asthma. The side effect profile for hypnosis is favourable compared to that of virtually any medication. So the risk-benefit profile is favourable. Despite this, there remains concern that hypnosis is either ineffective or dangerous. We are accumulating more evidence that it works and how it works, with neuroimaging studies using event related potentials, PET and fMRI demonstrating changes in brain function associated with hypnotic instructions and symptom reduction. We have plenty of evidence, and should and will accumulate more. What is needed now is educated use of hypnosis to help people suffering from pain, anxiety, smoking and other medical and psychiatric problems. Read this book and enhance your ability to help your patients. They will thank you. And remember, it is a smart hypnotist who knows who is hypnotizing whom.

Preface

This book is the culmination of a decision made at the BSCAH Council meeting in February 2008 to produce a definitive textbook to assist in our teaching programme and as a basic reference for all health professionals and academics interested in hypnosis. The decision was easy, but producing the text has been hard work, not only for the contributors and for ourselves as authors and editors, but also for our families and colleagues who have had to endure our focused attention on this mammoth task over the last 18 months.

There was a need for the book to be so much more than a comprehensive trawl of the literature and a subsequent regurgitation of what, in reality, is already in the professional domain. Notwithstanding the above, research findings are included, but the student is reminded that, by its very nature, hypnotherapy does not fit easily into the 'controlled trial' model of clinical evaluation. Consent and co-operation of the patient, the development of rapport and the skill and experience of the therapists are prerequisites of hypnotherapy, and this cannot be reproduced with the use of set scripts or videoed programmes. Also, during therapy, the very nature of the diagnosis may change (e.g. from irritable bowel syndrome [IBS] to victim of childhood abuse), and this underlying problem may never have been uncovered in the control arm of a trial. Randomisation, therefore, is likely to be at best speculative. It is reassuring, however, that despite the above reservations, research evidence does exist and is of huge importance, especially in the area of neurophysiology, but in clinical trials it is likely to significantly undervalue the hypnotherapeutic intervention. Thus results of clinical outcome audits will be a better guide for health service commissioners.

The current obsession with evidence based medicine has inevitably led to the commissioning of restrictive, protocol driven services in the mistaken belief that this will provide 'cost-effectiveness' for the health economy. As a consequence of this approach, there has been a decline in the practice of treating a patient as an individual exhibiting a set of problems unique to their own genetic make-up and its interaction with the environment in which they grew up. We hope that this book will become a resource for commissioners who will be required to take a more holistic approach to service provision. It is eminently suited to integration with other aspects of health care being compatible with pharmacological, surgical, medical and psychological programmes of therapy in a time efficient manner.

Some sections are unashamedly clinical where the content is based on years of experience and observation in the clinical setting. Much learning of hypnotherapy, however, goes on from a mixture of formal study and clinical discussion such that the experienced therapist evolves a methodology that is an amalgam of techniques and styles absorbed from a variety of often forgotten sources, which have been adapted to suit the specific personality and clinical orientation of that therapist. The text, therefore, will not be interrupted unnecessarily with a plethora of references, and we hope our colleagues in the Society and worldwide will forgive us if they recognise their own ideas but without any due acknowledgement.

Throughout the book we have made repeated reference to the need for therapists to work within their field of competence, and this competence relates to their background health professional status as much as it does to their hypnotherapy expertise.

Techniques, treatment regimes and verbatim scripts are included to give the student ideas and confidence to begin. They are not intended to imply that this is the 'must do' approach. There is no such thing as 'the' technique for any particular problem, and the student must follow the 'learn it, try it, adapt it' approach to these different methodologies. Outcome audit and personal development are fundamentals of best practice.

What to include or exclude in a book on hypnosis has been difficult. The chapter on informal techniques demonstrates the usefulness of the hypnotic approach without formal induction and is a reminder for us all to think 'hypnotically' in our ordinary consultations. Similarly, utilisation of the broader concept of 'trance' has enabled the inclusion of reference to areas such as dance and art therapy. Overlap with other therapeutic areas is obvious, and the student new to hypnosis will soon recognise that many of the 'active ingredients' of treatments have their true origins in hypnotherapy.

Permission has been obtained to use various case examples; all have been anonymised to avoid identification and all names given are fictitious.

Whilst we appreciate that there is a lot of academic debate about the exact definition of certain terms and concepts, throughout this book we have used the terms 'unconscious' and 'subconscious' synonymously and interchangeably. In the clinical sections this interchange equally applies to 'hypnosis' and 'hypnotherapy'. We have chosen to use 'patient' rather than 'client' and have used the masculine form where the gender could be either. Similarly where we have used the terms 'medical' and 'clinical', we intend these to refer to the wide ranging disciplines encompassed by medicine, psychology and allied health professions.

We have been privileged to have been entrusted by BSCAH to produce this work and thank the Council members for their support and encouragement. We would like to thank, of course, all our contributors and apologise if at times we have been difficult to satisfy. Particular thanks are due to Karen Mackrodt and others who have helped with the proof reading. There are many others who, perhaps even unknowingly, have given help with this project and who deserve thanks – it would be impossible to list them all but we hope they will accept this global message of gratitude.

Les Brann, Jacky Owens and Ann Williamson
October 2010

Part One

Hypnosis: The Fundamentals

1

Hypnosis: The Theory behind the Therapy

Dr Peter Naish

Introduction

There seems to be a tendency for people using hypnosis therapeutically to be surprisingly uninformed about the science behind the process. There are doubtless a number of reasons for this, not least that a busy therapist will feel there is little time for keeping up to date with the latest research. This may be so, but imagine consulting a surgeon who said, "*Yes, I've got a vague idea of how the body works and I gather they have scanning and so on nowadays, but I just do what I picked up when I first started this. It seems to work for me!*" One would have to ask, "*But does it work for the patient; could it be made to work better?*"

Therapists who have 'been around a while' do actually have a reason for turning their backs on hypnosis research in the past; a few decades ago, that research appeared to be investigating a very different phenomenon from the one they used every day in their practices. As will be explained, the message coming from the laboratory seemed, in effect, to be that hypnosis was not 'real'. Meanwhile the therapists were using these 'unreal' procedures and getting very real therapeutic effects – something was wrong somewhere!

Nevertheless, even from the seemingly uninviting scientific landscape of that era there were gems to be mined. For example, it was shown that merely instructing people to relax and imagine could produce quite convincing hypnotic effects. However, giving precisely the same instructions, but preceding them with the information that this was hypnosis, produced stronger effects (Kirsch, 1997). It was possible to draw a number of conclusions

The Handbook of Contemporary Clinical Hypnosis: Theory and Practice, First Edition.
Edited by Les Brann, Jacky Owens and Ann Williamson.
© 2012 John Wiley & Sons, Ltd. Published 2015 by John Wiley & Sons, Ltd.

from this, including the observation that since simply speaking the word 'hypnosis' can hardly do anything very dramatic, the enhanced performance seemed unlikely to have involved any impressive change in brain state. A therapist may not be very concerned whether there is a change in brain state or not, but he or she should note that an important element in getting people to behave 'hypnotically' seems to lie in defining the situation as 'doing hypnosis', rather than in the precise instructions spoken. Many people starting to use hypnosis therapeutically try to learn so-called induction scripts verbatim, as if, like some necromancer's conjuration, a single wrong word will bring catastrophe. Clearly this is untrue; whatever words work for the hypnotist should work for the clients – as long as they believe it is all in the cause of hypnotizing them. Even better of course is to choose words that are well suited to the particular client; that is where the skill lies, not in remembering a script.

Magic or Medicine?

It has been mentioned above that hypnosis produces very real therapeutic effects – but does it? Many members of the general public attribute almost magical powers to hypnosis, and with expectation of that sort there is bound to be a significant placebo effect. Could it be the only effect? A conspiracy theorist might postulate that therapists deliberately ignore the science, because they believe that if simply saying 'hypnosis' makes things work better, then it is clearly a placebo. If that truth leaked out it would be like GP patients learning that a pill was only sugar; the magic would evaporate and the cure would cease to work. In fact therapists need have no fear, because good, laboratory based research has shown that hypnosis is more than just a placebo. One of the most impressive and effective uses of hypnosis is in the treatment of pain. Non-harmful pain can be produced in the laboratory, making it possible to research the impact of various forms of analgesic. One thing that can be done is to apply a pharmaceutically inactive cream, along with the message that it will help the pain: it does – clearly a placebo effect. The pain relief is due to the release of endorphins, which are endogenous morphine-like substances that block the neural pain signals. Naloxone is a morphine antagonist – a compound that prevents the action of morphine and thus permits pain to resurface. It has exactly the same effect on endorphins, so that the administration of Naloxone undermines the pain reducing qualities of a placebo cream. So much for placebos; what of hypnosis? Well, it turns out that Naloxone does not block the analgesic effects of hypnosis (Spiegel & Albert, 1983). Hypnosis must be something more than just a placebo.

Hopefully this brief introduction has convinced you that anyone intending to use hypnosis in a therapeutic setting should understand something of the science behind it. Theory should inform practice, just as clinical observation should be part of the seed-corn of research. It is hoped too that the preceding paragraphs offer a sufficient taster for you to see that the science need not be dry and dull; it offers the tantalizing promise of explaining the paradox that while hypnosis has none of the magic that many people imagine, in fact it seems capable of far more than many trained scientists once believed. So, now we must make a very brief exploration of the path science has trodden and consider the vistas that have only recently started to unfold.

A Quick Look Backwards

It is something of a tradition in books on hypnosis to begin with Franz Anton Mesmer (1734–1815); one could say that was when science first took an interest in hypnosis like processes. Mesmer practiced in Paris in the days before the French Revolution, and also the days before it was called hypnosis or even (subsequently in his honour) Mesmerism – it was then called magnetism. This episode of history is instructive because it picks up two themes raised in the introduction of this chapter. We need not be concerned with the finer details of Mesmer's theories; it is sufficient to say that he believed cures could be effected by correcting the flow of a kind of magnetic fluid through the body. Even in those days theory influenced therapy. Thus, when Mesmer became too popular to deal with so many people on a one to one basis, he devised a table-like drum called the Baquet, filled with iron and appropriate magnetic paraphernalia. A whole group of people could sit around this and receive the healing power simultaneously. Of course Mesmer's beliefs were wrong, as demonstrated very effectively and scientifically by a French royal commission, so eventually the theories as to what was going on evolved, as did the way in which they were implemented in therapeutic practice. That is as it should be: no one claiming that the final, 'right' answer has been found, but practitioners keeping up with current thinking. Unfortunately, even then the signs of a disconnection between science and practice were apparent. The French scientific team showed convincingly that magnetism was in no way involved in whatever was going on in these mesmeric sessions. Nevertheless, many people clung to the idea that the wonderful effects (that we would recognize today and call 'hypnotic') could all be attributed to the power of magnets. It was Thomas Wakley, founder of the journal *The Lancet*, who made a dummy magnet from wood (that could not be magnetic, of course) and showed that it was just as effective.

Wooden 'magnets' seem to be getting us back to the realm of placebos again – it is what you believe that counts. In Mesmer's day it was believed that recovery could not be attained without passing through a kind of internal struggle, referred to as the crisis. Mesmer's patients expected to have this experience, and they duly exhibited it. Fortunately for today's patients there is no such expectation, so they are spared that little episode. Nevertheless they still tend to follow expectations, and the fact that they do so, rather than just sticking to 'basic hypnotic behaviour', is something that science must explain. In fact, truth be told, there is little that could count as a basic behavioural hallmark of hypnosis. People simply do what they are told to do, so that a hypnotic induction involving relaxation just makes them look relaxed. Nothing much happens after that, unless a specific suggestion is given for a particular behaviour. This absence of a clear hypnotic hallmark was one of the factors which made it difficult for researchers to accept that hypnosis was in any sense a 'thing apart'; the brain, it was concluded, must be doing much the same as in many other situations.

Scepticism and Social Effects

Before considering explanations for hypnotic behaviour, we must note that some of us do not exhibit any such behaviour at all. People vary in their responsiveness to hypnosis; some seem untouched by it, while others respond dramatically; most lie between the extremes. In research it is common to assess experimental participants, to get a measure of their responsiveness; to do this, hypnotic susceptibility scales are used. These comprise a series of graded suggestions that may or may not produce effects in the person being tested. The suggestions cover a range of potential experiences, for example motor effects such as *"Your arm is getting lighter and will begin to lift"* or sensory ones such as *"There is sugar dissolving on your tongue and it tastes sweet"*. People are rated by the proportion of the test items that 'work' for them. In the clinical field it is often considered a waste of valuable time to carry out a test on someone who is to be treated anyway, whether of high or low susceptibility. However, while a complete formal assessment may be inappropriate, using just one of the test items can give a helpful hint as to the sort of person being treated. Moreover, if there is any degree of 'working' this can be fed back to the patient as indicating that hypnosis really can 'do things'; never miss the chance of enhancing the hypnosis with a good placebo effect! At the same time, note that the experienced practitioner does not permit the absence of an effect in the test to undermine the effectiveness of the treatment.

It will be observed that both the examples of test items given above could be faked; someone could lift their arm and say that it felt light, and they could claim to taste sugar when in truth they did not. This applies to all test items – if a non-susceptible subject wished, they could behave as if they were responsive to everything. We assume that they do not wish to fake it, and as with so many situations of human interaction, we take their responses at face value. However, this is a little unsatisfactory for science, where it is considered better to be sure. Psychology is the science most familiar with trying to research the hidden, subjective experience and finding objective handles by which we can gain some grasp of what is going on. An early researcher in this field was the American T. X. Barber (see e.g. Barber *et al.*, 1974) who used a hypnotic susceptibility test with two groups of people. One group had been conventionally hypnotized, but the other had not. Instead they had been exhorted to do the best they could in the series of tests they were about to be given; they were told that the tests were not hard, and if they didn't make an effort the experiment would be a failure, which would be an embarrassment to the researcher. Clearly, this was rather pressuring (as was intended) and it may not be surprising to learn that the non-hypnotized group passed more of the hypnotic tests than the hypnotized group!

We have a good explanation for the pressured group's performance – they faked it, because they thought they should. Now, science prefers parsimony; it does not like multiple, complicated explanations when one will do. So why postulate some invisible process called hypnosis, when we know that people raise arms and taste sugar if they feel social pressures to do so? Well, this 'social' explanation might serve for the hypnosis group too, but only if we could identify social pressures acting upon them also; it turns out that pressures are easy to find. We are a social animal and behave very much like other group-living primates. Most of us do not like to stand out as too different or awkward, and we tend to want to please someone perceived to be of higher status. A university professor carrying out experiments on the students (the situation for much psychological research) is of higher status. The students know what is expected of them, because we all have a broad idea of what hypnosis is supposed to be like; what they do not know is supplemented by what is implicit in the suggestions given. If a participant finds to their concern that nothing seems to be happening they may think something along the lines of *"Oh dear, what's wrong with me? I bet everyone else gets hypnotized properly."* The only solution is to act the part. Not everyone would be so compliant as to respond in that way, but then not everyone scores high on the tests.

One may well wonder how the above picture was supposed to map onto clinical experience. Did 'cured' patients fake their recoveries? The title of Wagstaff's (1981) book *Hypnosis, Compliance and Belief* gives a hint of his sceptical stance, but others adopted more of a compromise position. They still emphasized the social aspects of the situation that led people to behave 'hypnotically' (and the inverted commas were often used) but acknowledged that some people actually went on to convince themselves that they were having the experience – they were not deliberately lying. Spanos was a Canadian researcher who seemed to spend much of his research career (sadly cut short in a flying accident) devising experiments to show that hypnotized people did only what they believed hypnotized people do. He used the term 'socio-cognitive' to label these 'middle-ground' theories; the label derives from two fields within psychology: social and cognitive. Where social psychology is concerned with the interactions between people (including between hypnotist and hypnotized), cognitive psychology is a branch of the discipline seeking to understand the hidden mental processes giving rise to conscious experiences within the individual. Spanos (1991) did not expand greatly upon the nature of the cognitive processes that might enable a person to alter their conscious experience. That it did alter was taken by some to justify referring to hypnosis as an 'altered state of consciousness', but for the socio-cognitive school that was to go too far; they saw no evidence for a significant change in brain state. The ensuing controversy became known as the 'state versus non-state debate' (see chapter 2), and it is only quite recently that the arguments have become more muted (see Kirsch & Lynn, 1995 for a helpful review).

Cognitive Processes

Whether or not social factors are especially important in hypnosis, if people's experiences are genuine (i.e. they are not faking) it is indisputable that rather unusual cognitive processes are taking place. Take moving an arm for example. As I pause in the typing of this chapter I reach for a cup of tea. Because I am concentrating on what I want to say I am only half aware of wanting to take another sip; I am not at all aware of the arm movement that makes that sip possible. So, there is nothing unusual in having an arm move without knowing that one is doing it. However, now that I have chosen arm moving as my example, I have become entirely aware of it. Not only that, but I am aware of intending to cause that movement. That is all exactly as one would expect; it would only become odd if I was aware of my arm moving, but had no sense of being the agent of that movement. That is the experience of people who pass the arm levitation test of a hypnotic susceptibility scale. The work of Spanos showed that people get the effects that they expect, so it cannot be claimed that the hypnotist's suggestions are somehow acting directly on some part of the participant's brain and bypassing conscious control processes. Clearly the hypnotized person hears the suggestion, then presumably uses fairly normal channels to set things in motion. The unusual element of this must be in the failure to recognize that they are using those 'channels'.

Intention and awareness

A number of theories have suggested that there must be some kind of disconnection between intention and awareness (e.g. Bowers, 1992; Brown & Oakley, 2004; Woody & Sadler, 2008), and they draw to a greater or lesser extent upon the idea that our monitoring and control systems are hierarchical in nature. Thus with my cup it is sufficient to wish to pick it up; I do not need to know anything about the precise movements of arm, hand and fingers to achieve this. Nevertheless, I can attend to those if I wish, for example if trying to extricate a very full cup from a cluttered desk, without spilling tea on the other things. Usually our level of awareness is at the same level as that at which intentions are made, but it is conceivable that one might issue commands at a high level (e.g. 'Have another sip') while monitoring at a lower ('I can feel my arm moving').

A variation on this theme has been proposed by Dienes and Perner (2007), who based their ideas upon the concept of higher order thought (i.e. self-awareness of awareness). Our human consciousness, it is suggested, derives from our ability to think about our experiences and even to think about that thinking (I feel the cup; I am aware that I am feeling the cup; I notice that I am having that awareness about the sensation of holding the cup). Dienes and Perner suggest that in hypnosis we abandon those higher order thoughts that have to do with the intention to act, and hence simply have conscious awareness of the result. Brain scanning had previously identified a frontal region of the left hemisphere that appeared to be involved in the higher order thinking process. Hence, Dienes and Perner reasoned that if this region were unable to work effectively, a person would be more likely to experience hypnotic behaviour as happening by itself. Sure enough, after using a technique known as transcranial magnetic stimulation to disrupt the region, they found that people rated their hypnotic responses as feeling more automatic.

Time distortion

It is possible to approach the notion of disconnection (or at least some form of neural disruption) from a different perspective: that of its impact upon time judgements. It is a common observation that a person who has just had a session of hypnosis will produce a striking underestimate if asked how long they feel the session lasted. In fact this effect might qualify as the only true example of spontaneous hypnotic behaviour, since people do not expect it and the hypnotist does not suggest it. A series of experiments (Naish, 2001, 2003) has shown that, over a range of different timing tasks, hypnotized people behave as if their 'internal clock' is running slowly. While the exact nature of the inner clock remains unclear, it is generally assumed that it involves oscillatory neural circuits, with evidence that these may be linked to our sense of conscious awareness (Naish, 2007). From such a link it would follow that disruption to these circuits might simultaneously modify both the sense of time and the nature of conscious experience. Perhaps that is what hypnosis achieves.

Brain scanning and the psychosis dimension

The fact that a hypnotized person can experience auditory hallucinations, or feel that limb movements are taking place outside their control, is reminiscent of the experiences of the schizophrenia patient. In fact this would seem to be more than a passing resemblance, because there are several other factors in common. Many people who would never be diagnosed with schizophrenia will nevertheless score relatively high on a scale of schitzotypy. These scales ask questions such as whether the person ever feels that they look different, or whether they sometimes think they heard a voice when they knew no one could be there. There is a correlation between schizotypy scores and hypnotic susceptibility; put another way, if you are inclined to have 'odd' experiences anyway, you are more likely to respond to suggestions in hypnosis (Gruzelier *et al.*, 2004). Brain scanning reveals further parallels between hypnosis and schizophrenia, but it should be stated categorically that hypnotic responsiveness is in no way an indicator of schizophrenic illness and has little clinical significance.

The advent of advanced brain-scanning techniques has rendered theorizing about brain behaviour rather less speculative. Although a full understanding remains a distant dream, scanning results can at least constrain theories and point to basic mechanisms. It would perhaps be helpful to break off from the description of similarities between hypnosis and schizophrenia, just to outline the brain-scanning techniques available and the kinds of information they are revealing. The earliest window onto brain activity was electroencephalography (EEG). By attaching electrodes to the scalp it is possible to detect the tiny voltage changes caused by neural activity in the brain. The firing of one neuron would produce an effect too small to detect, so only the activity of many brain cells firing together can be monitored. This inevitably rules out the possibility of getting a fine-grained picture of what is going on, a failing which is exacerbated by the insulating properties of the skull. As a result, it is not possible to identify the locations of neural activity in anything other than a rather general way. Thus, Gruzelier (2006) describes EEG experiments that showed a shift from predominantly left frontal brain activity to rather more posterior, right hemisphere activity (an observation discussed below). Where EEG does come into its own is in the ability to show precisely when activity takes place. For example, when different brain regions are working together their activity patterns become 'phase locked', rather like different musicians following the same conductor. Fingelkurts *et al.* (2007) used EEG to demonstrate a weakening of this synchrony during hypnosis, a finding that has parallels with schizophrenia, where equivalent effects occur.

What might be called the first of the modern scanning techniques is positron emission tomography (PET). Unlike EEG, this methodology is very poor at revealing the exact timing of activity, but it is a good deal better at showing where it is taking place. It does so indirectly, because an active brain site has more blood delivered and it is the blood flow that is monitored. This is done by injecting mildly radioactive substances into the blood stream. For that and other reasons PET is not an ideal technique, but it did begin to reveal a lot more about the hypnotized brain. Szechtman *et al.* (1998) used hypnosis as an analogue for schizophrenia, because it was not easy to PET scan patients while having a hallucination. In contrast, hypnotized subjects were able to 'hear' a voice that was not there while being scanned, and that revealed activity in the auditory cortex, just as if a sound were present. This paper was one of the first to report that hypnotic experiences were associated with activity in the anterior cingulate cortex, a frontal region of brain that appears to be involved in many processes, including those associated with attention and consciousness. Activity here appears to be a common feature of hypnosis.

The last technique we will consider is functional magnetic resonance imaging (fMRI). This uses the same MRI scanners that might be used to detect a tumour, but they are set to respond to magnetic field changes brought about by the presence of oxygenated blood (oxyhaemoglobin has magnetic properties). Since more oxygen is delivered to regions of the brain that are active, the scanner is able to identify those regions. Both the time-measuring and spatial resolution of fMRI are better than those of PET and are improving with each new generation of machine. As these scanners and their associated computing software become more sophisticated they are able to reveal more, including the tracing of major fasciculi (connecting tracts) through the brain. This function will be mentioned in what follows as we return to our discussion of the brain, and the parallels between hypnosis and psychosis.

Inhibition

One important factor in all aspects of brain activity is the process of inhibition: signals from one set of neurons 'dampen down' the activity in another set. It was mentioned above that hypnosis can produce auditory hallucinations; scanning has shown that brain regions responding to speech are easily activated, to the extent that our brain behaves as if it is 'hearing', even when viewing speaking lips in the absence of sound. In spite of this sensitivity, the activity is muted when we think to ourselves in words, as when speaking under our breath. The low activity is the result of inhibition; because we are aware of what we are saying to ourselves, we do not need to hear it too. A similar process reduces the brain's response to changes in arm position when we decide to move our own arm. In contrast, if someone else moves the arm for us there is a strong neural response: we cannot normally inhibit the unexpected. This inhibiting of self-initiated responses occurs in healthy individuals, but less so in those suffering from schizophrenia. When they believe they are hearing voices, there is not only activity in the speech-generating regions (they are talking to themselves), but crucially there is also activity in the auditory regions: they are actually 'hearing' a voice. It may be that because there should normally be inhibition of internally generated signals, any signal that escapes inhibition is automatically interpreted as coming from somewhere else. Patients sometimes believe that the television is talking to them, or that neighbours are beaming messages into their room. This failure to inhibit may be due to problems with the connectivity within the brain; Lawrie *et al.* (2002) report discontinuities in major interconnecting fasciculi.

Startlingly, scanning people who are experiencing hypnotic movements 'happening by themselves' has revealed that they too are not inhibiting the associated activity. In other words, rather than responding as if they are causing the movements themselves (which of course they are) their brains show the sort of activity that would be observed if someone else caused the movement (Blakemore *et al.*, 2003). Apart from anything else, this certainly shows that they are not faking the experience. The hypnotized person obviously does not have a breakdown in connectivity, as in schizophrenia, but the anterior cingulate appears to modulate inhibition (Fletcher *et al.*, 1999) and so may mimic the psychotic connectivity problems.

Perhaps the most surprising parallel between hypnosis and a psychotic condition, such as schizophrenia, is that such patients have been shown (Elvevåg *et al.*, 2004) to be very poor at making time judgements. This finding is consistent with the earlier suggestion that changes in connectivity in the brain can lead to changes in both conscious experience and also the sense of time. The observation prompts one to look to see whether there are other conditions that combine an impact upon time perception with hallucinatory experiences.

Timing, hallucinations and the hemispheres

There are two other consciousness-changing conditions that have an impact upon time perception that deserve mention. A much researched group of patients, from the point of view of temporal judgements, are those with Parkinson's disease; they display a 'slow clock' effect, very much like that of the hypnotized person. These patients are well known for their tremor and movement difficulties; less well known is that a significant proportion experience hallucinations (Fénelon *et al.*, 2000). It is harder to find an explanation for this intriguing parallel than it is for schizophrenia, for which 'disconnection' is the plausible link, but there is evidence that the same general neural circuitry may be involved in both conditions. In fact overdoses of L-dopa, the treatment for Parkinsonism, can result in psychotic effects like schizophrenia.

L-dopa is used for treatment, because it boosts levels of dopamine, the neurotransmitter that is depleted in Parkinson patients. It is known that the depletion occurs within a deep brain region, whose elements are collectively termed the basal ganglia. Because raising the levels of dopamine improves timing in patients, it has been assumed that the neural apparatus for the inner clock is located in the basal ganglia. However, studies of hypnosis using brain scanning have never implicated the basal ganglia as key structures in the hypnotic process. Hypnosis appears to involve frontal cortical regions of the brain, especially, as mentioned earlier, the anterior cingulate cortex. This is as would be expected in a process with a large voluntary element involving changes to attention and conscious experience.

How then can hypnosis impact the clock? Using fMRI scanning during a timing experiment, Lewis and Miall (2006) identified a region in the right dorso-lateral prefrontal cortex which appears to be involved. Since there are neural connections (via dopamine-using neurons) to this region from the basal ganglia, we may have a plausible way to bring together the disparate components of this story. There is one element of the Lewis and Miall observation to highlight: the evidence that timing is, at least in part, a right hemisphere process. The potential relevance of this observation will emerge when we have considered the final example of timing and consciousness modification.

Sufferers from post-traumatic stress disorder (PTSD) experience 'flashbacks' of the precipitating event. Flashbacks are hallucinations that can be so vivid as to make the victim feel that they are actually back in the trauma scene. They also experience foreshortening of retrospective time. What is more, PTSD patients are more than averagely susceptible to hypnosis (Yard et al., 2008), a fact that makes hypnosis a useful tool in the treatment of the condition.

There is some evidence that these PTSD sufferers have a higher than normal level of activity in the right hemisphere (Hans et al., 2002). It is believed that this hemisphere is more involved with the processing of 'global' information, whereas the left hemisphere is specialized for the finer detail. For a person experiencing heightened arousal and a constant state of anxiety (which is the case in PTSD), it is indeed plausible that they would direct their attention towards the 'big picture' rather than the minutiae of their surroundings – in effect, they are too occupied with looking out for danger to spend time on detail.

It can be hypothesized that the change in right hemisphere activity in PTSD impacts the time-related region mentioned above, which is also located in the right hemisphere. Thus we may have an explanation for the time distortion effects of PTSD, but we are yet to provide the hallucination link; a comparison with schizophrenia may provide one. Caligiuri et al. (2005) has suggested that there is poor connectivity between the hemispheres in schizophrenia, so that the left hemisphere is less able to exert an inhibitory influence upon the right. As a result, the right hemisphere, they propose, becomes unstable and generates hallucinations. It is certainly the case that there is a high incidence of 'mixed laterality' in schizophrenia; in other words, patients tend not to have a clear left or right hand preference. This can be taken to imply an absence of dominance between the hemispheres.

We are now in a position to postulate that in PTSD the shift of brain activity towards the right hemisphere not only interferes with the timing processes based there, but also facilitates the formation of hallucinations. Could this be the case in hypnosis? Gruzelier (2006) did indeed cite evidence for a rightward shift during hypnosis, and his findings have been extended (Naish, 2010) to show that highly hypnotizable people are normally strongly left hemisphere focused but swing to an equally strong right focus when hypnotized. Using the same measurement technique with PTSD sufferers (in a study which is ongoing at the time of writing) is producing data which seem to round off the

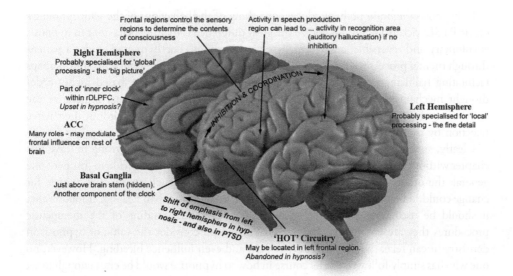

Figure 1.1 The two hemispheres of the brain (separated for clarity) showing key areas associated with hypnosis. © Peter Naish.
Key: ACC: anterior cingulate cortex; HOT: higher order thought; PTSD: Post-traumatic Stress Disorder; rDLPFC: right dorso-lateral prefrontal cortex.
Note: A possible explanation for hypnotic phenomena is that the ACC decreases the amount of inhibition of predicted (self-initiated) sensations, hence leading to hallucinations or feeling of things happening by themselves. A shift of emphasis from left to right hemisphere processing may facilitate the 'by themselves' sensation by ignoring the left-based HOT region. Moving to the right may support hallucinating by accentuating 'big picture' formation. The shift may also interfere with clock circuitry in the right hemisphere.

account very well. It turns out that the patients have a hemispheric asymmetry exactly like that of a hypnotized person.

A clinical observation is relevant in this context. Although in the calm conditions of a laboratory many people turn out not to be especially responsive to hypnosis, front-line medical staff report high levels of success in using hypnosis with most patients. These patients are frequently anxious, which may well be nudging them into a greater use of their right hemispheres. (See Figure 1.1.)

Summary, Conclusions and Cautions

This brief overview has necessarily omitted an enormous volume of research and theorizing about hypnosis. Nevertheless, it has shown clearly that hypnosis is associated with distinct changes in brain operation. Moreover, the fact that some people seem able to achieve this rather more easily than others appears to be paralleled by underlying differences in their everyday brain function (McGeown *et al.*, 2009; Naish, 2010).

In hypnosis the brain perhaps adopts something of the behaviour of the schizophrenic's or the PTSD victim's brain. Of course the great difference is that the behaviour in hypnosis is voluntary and reversible, and normally entirely benign. The hypnotist guides a patient through mental processes that are not fully grounded in reality, the rightward shift perhaps facilitating hallucinations or leading to the abandonment of the left-based higher order thought mechanisms (Dienes & Perner, 2007). By muting the rational imperative the patient may become able to engage in new thoughts and experiences without their fierce rejection by the intellect.

Clearly, such processes offer powerful possibilities, but it would be wrong to leave this chapter without mention of their potential dangers. Reference will be made to just two; one general, the other specific. The first is the observation that such an effective vehicle for change could, if inappropriately employed, lead to harm rather than healing. It follows that it should be used only by people with an adequate understanding of the therapeutic procedures they are employing. By way of illustration, consider the value of hypnosis in dentistry: it can relax the patient, alleviate pain and even influence bleeding. However, no one who has simply followed a brief course in how to hypnotize would be crass enough to set themselves up as a dentist – one hopes! The brain is a good deal more complex than the jaw, yet many people, with minimal psychological knowledge, do consider it proper to study hypnosis and launch themselves upon an unsuspecting public as psychotherapists.

These delusions of adequacy are dangerous, and every opportunity should be taken to warn the public not to consult hypnotherapists who are not first and foremost health professionals.

Of the different kinds of damage that might be caused during hypnosis, one stands out as especially pernicious: the creation of false memories. Many therapists value hypnosis for its role in re-vivification: not infrequently, the problems a client presents today have their roots in the past, so a vivid 'working through' of the precipitating events can be useful. What is not useful is to follow the following line in faulty reasoning.

- All problems are caused by past events.
- If an event is not remembered, the memory must have been repressed, being too painful for conscious awareness.
- Resurrecting the memory will facilitate a cure.
- Hypnosis is the perfect tool for finding the buried material.

This could even be expanded to imply that the problem-causing past events almost certainly involved childhood sexual abuse, because there are many so-called therapists who hold that belief. In fact, every assertion in that list is at best questionable and probably downright wrong. This is not a chapter on memory, so suffice it to say that the Freudian notion of repression is far from proven, whereas the ability of hypnosis to facilitate the generation of pseudo-memories is very well established, to the extent that the Home Office has issued guidelines to police forces not to use hypnosis to 'refresh' eyewitness memories.

The author (PN) has encountered many cases of troubled people who have 'recovered' memories of past abuse, but the uncovering seems to have done nothing to alleviate their unhappiness. Rather, they become estranged from their families (generally the accused) and lead lonely, even unhappier lives. Meanwhile, the families are devastated and break-ups often ensue. Not everyone appears to be vulnerable to the creation of false memories, but unfortunately the qualities that make a person more hypnotizable actually make them more prone to these erroneous recollections. It is important to note that whilst high hypnotizability predisposes a patient to false memories, this is not exclusive to hypnosis but can occur in any poorly managed counselling or psychotherapeutic encounter. Nowadays, many therapists pay lip service to the need to guard against false memory, but that is not enough. Guidelines issued by the British Psychological Society (BPS) are instructive, as for example:

> Hypnosis does not have any special property for enhancing memory in therapy...using hypnosis in this way carries a real risk of producing substantial pseudo-memories...some can be so plausible as to beguile the therapist and client alike into accepting them as accurate. (Heap *et al.*, 2001, p. 12)

And the following:

> For a therapist merely to claim awareness of the problem and to be guarding against it provides insufficient protection against the dangers of false memory. Research has shown that simply to label a situation 'hypnotic' will cause people who are attempting to recall their earliest memories to produce [so] many more...as to make it virtually certain that the recalled memories are false. (Heap *et al.*, 2001, p. 12)

A recent court case involved a middle-aged man accusing a much older man of having sexually abused him many years before, when the accuser was a young boy. As a grown man he had lost a job and apparently turned to drink; he then consulted a lay hypnotherapist for help with his depression. Questioning in court established that the therapist had followed a part-time on-line course, enabling him to go from having no qualification of any sort (not even a General Certificate of Secondary Education [GCSE]) to being a 'qualified hypnotherapist' in the space of three months! It was also established that this woefully ignorant (but doubtless well-intentioned) man had 'helped' the client over a series of sessions to build up a 'memory' of the alleged abuse. The police were taken in by this piece of fiction and initiated proceedings, but the judge was not so gullible. Having been informed of the nature of memory and of hypnosis, and made aware of those BPS guidelines, she ruled all the evidence acquired during hypnosis inadmissible. As that was the total of the evidence, the prosecution had no case, so it was dismissed without the jury ever hearing a word of it. Justice of a sort had doubtless been done, but the man who should have been in the dock, the therapist (or better, the man who received money for the so-called training), got off free. The accuser is doubtless in a state of angry confusion, and the poor accused may be haunted by the anxiety of the false accusations to his dying day.

Anyone intending to use hypnosis in a psychotherapeutic role would do well to read the full BPS document, but the basic message is simple. If, in the absence of hypnosis, during history taking for example, a client refers to issues in the past, then these may well be worth exploring. However, the temptation to use hypnosis to carry out an active search for a putative repressed memory should be resisted: the all too real risks outweigh by far any slight chances of benefit.

Having sounded that very strong warning note, it should be pointed out that later in this book you will encounter a process often called 'uncovering'; it is important to appreciate the difference between this and the kinds of dangerous practice described above. The distinction is perhaps best illustrated with an imaginary example. A person comes complaining of being terribly stressed at work. Questioning reveals that this started when a new boss came; he is not bad and others seem to like him, but he has a rather forceful manner. This seems especially scary in group meetings, when he will pick on people to give verbal reports. Within hypnosis the patient is asked to let his mind go back and find another time when he had those feelings (using affect bridge; see page 127). He remembers a teacher at school, who often shouted, and once embarrassed the patient dreadfully, by making him stand up and explain something to the whole class. He could not do so, and was treated to a loud verbal dressing down. Once this episode is 'uncovered', the parallels are obvious and the patient is surprised never to have spotted them before. Once the link has been made, the therapist is able to find appropriate therapeutic strategies to deal with the problem. Note that the memory itself does not come as a surprise; it had not been repressed, and certainly had not been invented in hypnosis. In fact 'uncovering' is probably not a very good term for finding the significance of a memory in this way, but it is quicker to say than the 'never-noticed-the-connection technique'!

If you are reading this book it is probably because you firmly believe in the therapeutic value of hypnosis. The hope is that, after reading this chapter, you will also recognize that hypnosis is a fascinating phenomenon in its own right and an exciting field for research. The hope is also that you will make time to continue to dip into research findings occasionally, and when they are relevant allow them to influence your practice. There is still much to discover about hypnosis, but we do now know that it produces real changes in the brain. As the following chapters will show, by combining hypnosis with traditional procedures, these changes can result in significant therapeutic enhancement.

References

Barber, T. X., Spanos, N. P. & Chaves, J. F. (1974), *Hypnotism, imagination and human potentialities.* New York, Pergamon Press.

Blakemore, S. J., Oakley, D. A. & Frith, C. D. (2003), Delusions of alien control in the normal brain. *Neuropsychologia*, 41, 1058–67.

Bowers, K. S. (1992), Imagination and dissociation in hypnotic responding. *International Journal of Clinical and Experimental Hypnosis*, 40, 253–75.

Brown, R. J. & Oakley, D. A. (2004), An integrative cognitive theory of hypnosis and hypnotizability, in Heap, M., Brown, R. J. & Oakley, D. A. (Eds.) *The highly hypnotizable person.* New York, Brunner-Routledge.

Caligiuri, M. P., Hellige, J. B., Cherry, B. J., Kwok, W., Lulow, L. L. & Lohr, J. B. (2005), Lateralized cognitive dysfunction and psychotic symptoms in schizophrenia. *Schizophrenia Research,* 80, 151–61.

Dienes, Z. & Perner, J. (2007), The cold control theory of hypnosis, in Jamieson, G. (Ed.) *Hypnosis and conscious states: the cognitive neuroscience perspective.* Oxford, Oxford University Press, 293–314.

Elvevåg, B., Brown, G. D. A., Mccormack, T., Vousden, J. I. & Goldberg, T. E. (2004), Identification of tone duration, line length, and letter position: an experimental approach to timing and working memory deficits in schizophrenia. *Journal of Abnormal Psychology,* 113, 509–21.

Fénelon, G., Mahieux, F., Huon, R. & Zigegler, M. (2000), Hallucinations in Parkinson's disease, *Brain,* 123, 733–45.

Fingelkurts, A. A., Fingelkurts, A. A., Kalio, S. & Revonsuo, A. (2007), Cortex functional connectivity as a neurophysiological correlate of hypnosis: an EEG case study. *Neuropsychologia,* 45, 1452–62.

Fletcher, P., McKenna, P. J., Friston, K. J., Frith, C. D. & Dolan, R. J. (1999), Abnormal cingulate modulation of fronto-temporal connectivity in schizophrenia. *NeuroImage,* 9, 337–42.

Gruzelier, J. H. (2006), Frontal functions, connectivity and neural efficiency underpinning hypnosis and hypnotic susceptibility. *Contemporary Hypnosis,* 23, 15–32.

Gruzelier, J. H., De Pascalis, V., Jamieson, G., Laidlaw, T., Naito, A., Bennett, B., *et al.* (2004). Relations between hypnotizability and psychopathology revisited. *Contemporary Hypnosis,* 21, 169–76.

Hans, S., Weaver, J. A., Murray, S. O., Kang, X., Yund, E. W. & Woods, D. L. (2002), Hemispheric asymmetry in global/local processing: effects of stimulus position and spatial frequency. *Neuroimage,* 17, 1290–9.

Heap, M., Alden, P., Brown, R. J., Naish, P. L. N., Oakley, D. A., Wagstaff, G. & Walker, L. G. (2001), *The nature of hypnosis.* British Psychological Society report. Leicester, British Psychological Society.

Kirsch, I. (1997), Suggestibility or hypnosis: what do our scales really measure? *International Journal of Clinical and Experimental Hypnosis,* 45, 212–25.

Kirsch, I. & Lynn, S. J. (1995), Altered state of hypnosis: changes in the theoretical landscape. *American Psychologist,* 50, 846–58.

Lawrie, S. M., Buechel, C., Whalley, H. C., Frith, C. D., Friston, K. J. & Johnstone, E. C. (2002), Reduced frontotemporal functional connectivity in schizophrenia associated with auditory hallucinations. *Biological Psychiatry,* 51, 1008–11.

Lewis, P. A. & Miall, R. C. (2006), A right hemispheric prefrontal system for cognitive time measurement. *Behavioural Processes,* 71, 226–34.

McGeown, W. J., Mazzoni, G., Venneri, A. & Kirsch, I. (2009), Hypnotic induction decreases anterior default mode activity. *Consciousness and Cognition,* 18, 848–55.

Naish, P. L. N. (2001), Hypnotic time perception: busy beaver or tardy timekeeper? *Contemporary Hypnosis,* 18, 87–99.

Naish, P. L. N. (2003), The production of hypnotic time-distortion: determining the necessary conditions. *Contemporary Hypnosis,* 20, 3–15.

Naish, P. L. N. (2007), Time distortion, and the nature of hypnosis and consciousness, in Jamieson, G. (Ed.) *Hypnosis and conscious states: the cognitive neuroscience perspective.* Oxford, Oxford University Press.

Naish, P. L. N. (2010), Hypnosis and hemispheric asymmetry. *Consciousness and Cognition*, 19, 230–4.

Spanos, N. P. (1991), A sociocognitive approach to hypnosis, in Lynn, S. J. & Rhue, J. W. (Eds.) *Theories of hypnosis: current models and perspectives*. New York, Guildford Press, 324–61.

Spiegel, D. & Albert, L. H. (1983), Naloxone fails to reverse hypnotic alleviation of chronic pain. *Psychopharmacology*, 81, 140–3.

Szechtman, H., Woody, E., Bowers, K. S. & Nahmias, C. (1998), Where the imaginal appears real: a positron emission tomography study of auditory hallucinations. *Proceedings of the National Academy of Sciences*, 95, 1956–60.

Wagstaff, G. F. (1981), *Hypnosis, compliance and belief*. Brighton, Harvester.

Woody, E. Z. & Sadler, P. (2008), Dissociation theories of hypnosis, in Nash, M. R. & Barnier, A. J. (Eds.) *The Oxford handbook of hypnosis: theory, research and practice*. Oxford, Oxford University Press.

Yard, S. S., Duhamel, K. N. & Galynker, I. I. (2008), Hypnotizability as a potential risk factor for posttraumatic stress: a review of quantitative studies. *International Journal of Clinical and Experimental Hypnosis*, 56, 334–56.

2

Hypnotic Phenomena and Hypnotizability

Dr Ann Williamson

Introduction

As has been mentioned in the previous chapter exactly what constitutes hypnosis and how it arises has been the subject of much debate over the years. Controversy between the state and non-state theorists raged, especially during the twentieth century, with the state proponents convinced that hypnosis was 'an altered state of consciousness' and the non-state theorists being equally convinced that hypnosis could be totally explained by socio-cognitive models. In the twenty-first century the margins have become more blurred as most would now agree that both arguments have merit and that the truth lies somewhere in between. Hypnosis is certainly much influenced by socio-cognitive factors but would also seem to be a particular 'state' or form of processing in the brain (see chapter 1). There is evidence for a genetic trait but hypnotic ability can also be enhanced by training (Gorassini & Spanos, 1999).

Some people have a greater ability to enter hypnosis than others in the same way as some people have greater musical ability. We may not all have the ability to become a concert pianist but most of us could be taught to play a simple tune and we would improve with practice.

Hypnosis can be thought of as an increased attentional focus on one experience whilst the focus on other things decreases. This leads to a suspension of various thought processes such as reflection and critical thinking. A decrease in self monitoring and arousal networks in the brain has been shown in common with other meditative states (Gruzelier et al., 2006; Rainville & Price, 2003). Also the distinction between self and others is weakened in hypnosis as parietal lobe function is diminished (Rainville et al., 2002). Hypnosis requires

The Handbook of Contemporary Clinical Hypnosis: Theory and Practice, First Edition.
Edited by Les Brann, Jacky Owens and Ann Williamson.
© 2012 John Wiley & Sons, Ltd. Published 2015 by John Wiley & Sons, Ltd.

some capability of both concentration and imagination and can be seen as a bio-psycho-social capacity that we all possess (Spiegel & Spiegel, 2004).

It is possible to classify hypnosis into three types; spontaneous hypnosis, self hypnosis and hetero-hypnosis. Spontaneous hypnosis can arise when a patient becomes very anxious or is in shock, and this will be referred to later when we talk about suggestion and post-hypnotic suggestion or imprints (see page 23). We maintain that all patients should, if at all possible, be taught self hypnotic techniques that they can then utilize when appropriate to help themselves. Hetero-hypnosis refers to induction of hypnosis with a therapist and whilst the therapist is merely facilitating the patient to access a hypnotic state many find it easier to do this when led by a therapist. Especially in the early stages of therapy it may be useful to give the patient a recording of an induction to follow when they do their self hypnosis practice until they become familiar with doing it for themselves.

Many inexperienced practitioners think that using hypnosis will take up too much time within the consultation but once taught (which can be done in groups or within a short consultation with an information handout and a short demonstration) it often takes only a matter of seconds for a patient to enter trance on subsequent occasions.

Suggestibility

There is a difference between suggestibility and hypnotic susceptibility, although suggestibility is said to increase with hypnosis (Dienes *et al.*, 2009). The variability in responsiveness to suggestion follows the normal distribution curve.

There are various kinds of suggestibility:

Primary: this is typified by ideomotor response and related to that measured by hypnotic susceptibility scales.

Secondary: this is more complex and concerned with direct or implied changes in sensory modalities. This does not correlate with hypnotic susceptibility scales and is linked to ease of persuasion.

Interrogative: this is the proneness to change account of events (and memory) with leading questions or adverse feedback.

Hypnotizability is a genetic trait and has many correlations and therefore is probably composite in nature. It remains fairly constant over time and has a high test–retest reliability (Nash & Barnier, 2008) Many ways of measuring hypnotic responsiveness have been used over the years, and just a few will be mentioned here.

Hypnotizability Scales

The Stanford Scales of Hypnotic Susceptibility (SHSS) (Weitzenhoffer & Hilgard, 1959), and Harvard Group Scale (Shor & Orne, 1962) were developed in the 1950s and 1960s.

The problem with these is that they are very lengthy to administer and score. The Stanford Hypnotic Arm Levitation and Induction Test (SHALIT) takes less than ten minutes to administer and correlates well with the SHSS (Hilgard *et al.*, 1979). A shorter version of the Stanford Scale, the Stanford Clinical Scale, was devised (Morgan & Hilgard, 1978/ 1979a) together with one suitable for children (Morgan & Hilgard, 1978/1979b).

The Hypnotic Induction Profile (HIP), developed by David and Herbert Spiegel, is an induction procedure in itself, shorter than the SSHS but with only a weak correlation to it (Orne *et al.*, 1978). It is scripted precisely and starts with an eye roll induction. A score is given for the amount of sclera visible between the iris and the lower lid (which is said by some to be a biological marker for hypnotic susceptibility), and an extra mark is given for convergence as the eyes close. This is followed by arm levitation and a post-hypnotic suggestion, and the client's responses are scored (Spiegel & Spiegel, 2004).

The Creative Imagination Scale (CIS) (Barber & Wilson, 1978) uses ten items that the client is directed to imagine and then rate as to how realistic their response was on a five point scale. This takes 30 minutes to administer and score and measures different qualities than the SHSS (McConkey *et al.*, 1979), so it is not often used in a research context but may be useful clinically. A low score on the CIS may indicate that imagery needs to be more tailored to the individual, whereas a high score may mean more standardized imagery could be used. Council (1999) gives a clear explanation of the available assessment tools.

As clinicians we need to know whether high hypnotic responsiveness leads to improved outcomes. It would appear that there is only a weak relationship and other factors are influential, but high responsiveness is said to be more likely to influence outcome on unconsciously driven problems such as pain and psychosomatic disorders rather than more self instigated problems such as smoking and obesity. Conversely high hypnotizability has been associated with certain conditions such as post-traumatic stress disorder (PTSD), although it is not certain whether this is causal or consequential (Bryant *et al.*, 2001).

Kirsch and Braffman (1999) did an interesting study on response to suggestion with or without a hypnotic induction and found only a small increase in responsiveness in the induction group with many showing no increase at all. This highlights the main problem with experimental hypnosis in that as many variables as possible need to be removed. This usually entails a script which is delivered to all participants whose main motivation is money or university credits. This is very different to the clinical context where motivation is usually high, with the clinician being highly unlikely to use a single induction method and where the hypnotic interventions are tailored to the patient. Many use hypnotic techniques with no formal induction, however to suggest that induction is unnecessary would fly in the face of years of clinical experience.

Hypnotic susceptibility does not correlate well with any major dimension of personality or cognitive style; it peaks at ages 9 to 13 years and then shows a slow decline and has no significant gender difference. Those who score high on scales that measure absorption and fantasy proneness tend to be more highly hypnotizable, but these do not seem to be key factors. Vividness of imagery has a weak and unreliable correlation (Groh, 1989), although it has been said that those with poor visual imagery tend to be poorer subjects. This may be a reflection on the type of induction used, and such people may do very well with an auditory or kinaesthetic induction.

Dissociative ability as measured by the Dissociative Experiences Scale only has a weak correlation with the Stanford Scale (Frischolz *et al.*, 1992). Cognitive flexibility, however, the ability to switch quickly from one state of mind or mental activity to another, does have a positive relationship to hypnotic susceptibility (Evans, 1991).

A positive attitude to hypnosis and an expectation of being a responsive subject are definite predictors of hypnotic susceptibility. So time spent preparing the patient and building expectation is time well spent. We know that rapport is essential for the successful use of hypnosis, as it is for any psychotherapeutic intervention, so the first session is often of paramount importance as it sets the scene for subsequent therapeutic outcomes.

Hypnotizability scales were devised originally to try to determine a definition for hypnosis but are now a pre-requisite for any credible hypnosis research. In the clinical context, time is usually at a premium and such scales are usually too lengthy to be used routinely. Shorter scales such as modifications of the HIP and CIS and explorations of a patient's imagery capabilities such as in the lemon test (see page 22) may be thought to be more useful. Determining a patient's hypnotizability may colour the expectations of both patient and therapist, which will affect outcomes. Framing any hypnotizability test as an experiment or an exploration removes any sense of possible failure; all responses give information helpful to the therapeutic encounter.

Hypnotic Phenomena

Hypnosis is known to modify perception of sensory input, motor and autonomic output and psychological processes. Although commonly labelled 'hypnotic' phenomena, all can occur in the 'waking' state. Few people will demonstrate all the phenomena all of the time, but this is seldom important when using clinical hypnosis.

The individual response depends on their innate hypnotizability and the context, for example someone may be unable to demonstrate hypnotic analgesia experimentally but be able to utilize these suggestions in a painful emergency situation. Other factors include the ability of the therapist and the patient to be creative and flexible and the acceptability of any suggestions given by the therapist.

Trance logic

An important factor that the hypnotherapist needs to be aware of is the tendency for patients in trance, whether this has arisen spontaneously or been induced formally, to take the literal sense of whatever has been said. In one instance, a woman developed unexpected morbidity following a simple surgical procedure. She was seen by a hypnotherapist who discovered she had been in a quasi-hypnotic state as the anaesthetic wore off and she had heard the surgeon exclaim, "Well, she's finished!" This she had misinterpreted as a statement that she was about to die. This may be an apocryphal story but the therapist would do well to remember to listen to the literal sense of their words. Patients in hypnosis will also find objects and associations quite matter of fact that in the normal waking state they would find strange. This is due to the patient displaying a greater tolerance of logical incongruities when in hypnosis.

Post-hypnotic suggestion

A post-hypnotic suggestion (PHS) is a suggestion given in hypnosis to be acted upon following the intervention when the subject is out of hypnosis. This may be simply a suggestion that *"Each day you will feel calmer and more in control"* to actual actions such as *"When you hear 'x' you will be unable to remember the number five"* or *"When I say 'x' you will get an overwhelming desire to go and open the window"*. This type of PHS is more commonly used in stage hypnosis and with highly hypnotizable subjects may be very effective. When challenged as to why they did the action prescribed in the PHS the person will rationalize, for example, *"I thought it was getting hot in here so that is why I opened the window"*. Some therapists use a post-hypnotic suggestion for amnesia, although the author (AW) prefers the suggestion *"You will remember whatever is necessary for you to remember and remember to forget whatever is necessary for you to forget"*.

It is said that a person will not do in hypnosis anything against their values and beliefs, and this is generally the case with post-hypnotic suggestions also. However if a patient has high hypnotic ability it is possible that unethical and inappropriate suggestions may be acted upon. However, the vast majority of people are aware of having an active 'observer' position even whilst being in hypnosis and will ignore any inappropriate suggestion, change it or come out of hypnosis. It should be remembered that our mind is the most powerful tool we possess and anything powerful can be used for good or ill.

Perception of sensory input

All the senses, visual, auditory, taste, smell, kinaesthetic and balance, may be subject to alteration in hypnosis. The typical stage hypnosis utilization of this effect is to get a participant to smell ammonia as a fragrant scent or to eat a lemon whilst believing it is an apple.

Alteration of smell and taste may be important tools with clinical usage when unpleasant-tasting medicines need to be administered or smells encountered. More often negative affect becomes linked to certain smells as in feeling anxiety and nausea when smelling disinfectant in a hospital or dental setting thus setting up a negative link or 'anchor' (see page 145). A positive link or anchor can be constructed by repetitively linking pleasant feelings of comfort and calmness to a scent that the patient can easily access such as scents via a small pomander.

Utilization of the ability to alter these sensations lies at the heart of imagery work with such conditions as pain, tinnitus, flashbacks and nausea. Development of local anaesthesia such as in 'glove anaesthesia' is a good example of this as is 'turning down' the volume control in tinnitus (Attias *et al.*, 1993). Such alteration can be demonstrated neurologically where hypnotically induced blindness is associated with attenuation of the visual evoked potential (Spiegel *et al.*, 1985). Similar findings have been reported with auditory evoked potentials in hypnotically induced deafness (De Pascalis & Carboni, 1997). Szechtman *et al.* (1998) and Kosslyn *et al.* (2000) have demonstrated that hallucinated visual and auditory stimuli generate neurophysiological changes in a similar way to the 'real' thing.

Temperature change may also be effected in hypnosis by way of suitable imagery suggestions such as *"You may notice how warm your right hand is getting as you sit with your right side turned to the fire. It might be interesting to notice any difference in sensation between that hand and your left hand that is resting in the snow"*. This ability to alter temperature sensation can be used combined with alteration in 'weight' of the hands to demonstrate to a pain patient that they have the ability to alter their sensation of pain. Such imagery together with imagery of increased blood flow has been successfully used by the author (AW) in a case of Reynaud's phenomena.

Modification of motor and autonomic output

Physical relaxation of facial and other muscles usually accompanies hypnosis (unless an active alert induction is used; see page 118), and this is usefully employed with anxious patients.

The ability to control smooth muscle tone is utilized when suggestions are given to reduce bleeding or blushing, to reduce dysmenorrhoea or help in labour (including premature labour) and to reduce bronchospasm in asthma or abdominal cramps in irritable bowel syndrome (IBS). It may also be utilized when giving suggestion to help resolve urinary frequency.

In all the above, whilst some patients may be able to develop some remarkable control over more usually perceived 'unconscious' processes, usually work is also needed on the psychological underpinnings of the symptom. However, often patients may be able to reduce the 'bothersomeness' of a symptom rather than or as well as its intensity.

Use of hypnotic cataleptic rigidity was documented during and after the Second World War with plastic surgery patients in the Guinea Pig Club (Andrew, 1994). It was noted that not only did patients with pedicle grafts which necessitated keeping, for example, their arm up to the face feel more comfortable with maintaining the position with hypnotic rigidity rather than having a cast, but also there was not the same degree of muscle wasting.

Ideomotor signalling   This is a motor response that follows some suggestion such as *"Your arm will feel lighter and lighter and begin to float up all by itself"* or where movement of a finger or arm is linked to unconscious processing such as *"Your hand will gradually begin to float up as your unconscious mind gathers up the resources it needs to..."* The patient feels that the arm or hand is moving 'by itself' rather than under their conscious volition. The mechanism of this 'perceived involuntariness' is discussed in chapter 1. Ideomotor movement tends to be slow and hesitant rather than smooth and continuous, and is most commonly used in exploration of a symptom when ideomotor finger signals are set up for 'yes' and 'no' (see page 129). This non-verbal communication may be useful when verbalization may be thought to lighten the hypnotic state, and it is generally thought to give a more accurate reflection of unconscious processing.

Similar 'involuntary' type movement can be seen when arm levitation is used as an induction (see page 113) or a Rossi type technique is used such as described on page 241.

Effect upon the immune system

Psycho-neuroimmunology is the study of how psychological factors can influence our neurology and our immune functioning. This is covered in more detail in chapter 23 and is the basis of working with various auto-immune disorders, cancer and other chronic illnesses. It could be argued that the use of regular self hypnosis leads to increased wellbeing and optimal functioning of our immune system.

Modification of the inflammatory response is also utilized in hypnosis especially when working with skin conditions, asthma and burns when suggestions for cool comfort are often surprisingly effective (Ewin, 1983).

Modification of psychological processes

The ability to effectively work with emotions rather than just cognitions is one of the strengths of hypnosis. There are numerous ways, some of which will be described later, where imagery is used to help patients deal with their negative emotions, access positive emotions, connect with their goals and work to resolve issues from their past that are impinging on the present. Amnesia, even if not specifically suggested, will often occur for part or all of a hypnotic session. Memory recall, as has been stated elsewhere, may be enhanced but the veracity of such information is always questionable.

Hallucination

The ability to have both positive hallucinations (to see what is not actually there) and negative hallucinations (not to see something that is actually there) is utilized in hypnotic analgesia and also to enable a patient to connect with their desired goals as in positive mental rehearsal. Ideosensory response, where the patient has a physical feeling rather than a movement (ideomotor), may be utilized to engage unconscious processing.

Time distortion is an almost universal experience in hypnosis (see page 8) where people often greatly underestimate the time they have been in hypnosis (see also chapter 1). This can be a good indication of how deeply hypnotized they have been and could provide interesting audit data if enough therapists recorded it.

The effect of time distortion can be utilized in analgesic techniques (see page 304) where the suggestion is given that the time of comfort seems much longer and the time when the patient experiences discomfort seems very much shorter. In anticipatory anxiety, time distortion can also be used such as in the time capsule metaphor on page 325.

Age regression is a phenomenon whereby the person, in effect, relives a time in the past as though it were taking place in the present. They 'become' how they were at that age with the associated speech patterns and mannerisms. Because they are 'associated' (see page 43) and not merely looking at themselves they also feel all the emotions of the time that they are accessing. Age regression is used, to some degree, in any work on past events, although dissociative techniques whereby the patient is looking at the event from a distance rather than re-living it are recommended by the authors when working with past trauma (see page 401). Some patients and therapists believe that it is possible to regress to 'past lives' and find working with this concept useful. The issue of false memory has already been discussed.

Age progression is when the person sees themselves in the future and is utilized whenever the therapist suggests solution oriented imagery. In goal setting or a positive mental rehearsal the person first sees themselves the way they want to be and then 'steps into' the image in some way (becoming associated) in order to really feel and experience their goal. It is also utilized in crystal ball techniques whereby the therapist may suggest that the patient in hypnosis looks into an imaginary crystal ball and discovers whatever they need to know for the resolution of their problem. This future orientation may also be used in post- or pre-state anchors (page 242) where the patient accesses a time when their problem has been resolved or alternatively a time before they had the problem.

All these phenomena can be found outside of hypnosis but within hypnosis they are utilized for therapeutic intent and the experiences are more intense than in the waking state. Importantly it is through this utilization that therapeutic outcomes are achieved.

The uses of hypnosis are tabulated below for ease of reference.

Uses of hypnosis

Communication
- More effective communication – with others – with your 'inner self'
- Improved ability to comply with treatment
- Facilitate life style changes
- Observation and interpretation of minimal body language cues

Personal development
- Enables internal motivation and goal setting
- Gives more control over emotions
- Increases self confidence
- Increases coping skills
- Enhances performance

Anxiety management
- Reduces stress response
- Allows release of negative emotion
- Enhances effect of positive suggestion
- Reduces anxiety related to future stressful events
- Management of insomnia

- Reduction or stopping psychotropic medication (with the support of the responsible physician)

Utilizing alteration of perception
- Reduces acute pain (especially in shock)
- Used in chronic pain to give control and reduce bothersomeness and intensity
- Reduces problems with uncomfortable interventions such as venepuncture
- Useful in obstetrics during labour
- Can be helpful in tinnitus

Utilizing increased access to unconscious processes
- Management of past traumatic memory, dealing with the emotions
- Investigation and treatment of psychosomatic symptoms
- Increased awareness of intuition
- Modification of behaviour in habit disorders

Modification of physiology
- Alteration of smooth muscle tone, IBS and hypertension
- Optimization of skeletal muscle tone and sports performance
- Reduction in inflammatory response in burns, eczema and asthma
- Optimization of immune response
- Reduction of bleeding
- Reduction of salivation
- Regulating hormonal cycles, irregular periods and dysmenorrhoea

---

References

Andrew, D. R. (1994), The Guinea Pig Club. *Aviation, Space and Environmental Medicine*, 65 (5), 428–33.

Attias, J., Schemesh, Z., Sohmer, H. & Gold, S. (1993), Comparison between self-hypnosis, masking and attentiveness for alleviation of chronic tinnitus. *Audiology*, 32 (3), 205–12.

Barber, T. X. & Wilson, S. C. (1978), The Barber Suggestibility Scale and the Creative Imagination Scale: experimental and clinical applications. *American Journal of Clinical Hypnosis*, 21, 84–108.

Bryant, R. A., Guthrie, R. M. & Moulds, M. L. (2001), Hypnotizability in acute stress disorder. *American Journal of Psychiatry*, 158, 600–4.

Council, J. R. (1999), Measures of hypnotic responding, in Kirsh, I., Capafons, A., Cardena-Buelna, E. & Amigo, S. (Eds.) *Clinical hypnosis and self-regulation*. Washington, DC, American Psychological Society.

De Pascalis, V. & Carboni, G. (1997), P 300 event-related-potential amplitudes and evoked cardiac responses during hypnotic alteration of somatosensory perception. *International Journal of Neuroscience*, 92, 187–207.

Dienes, Z., Brown, E., Hutton, S., Kirsch, I., Mazzoni, G. & Wright, D. B. (2009), Hypnotic suggestibility, cognitive inhibition, and dissociation: consciousness and cognition. *American Journal of Clinical Hypnosis*, 18, 237–47.

Evans, F. J. (1991), Hypnotisability: individual differences in dissociation and the flexible control of psychological processes, in Lynn, S. J. & Rhue, J. W. (Eds.) *Theories of hypnosis: current models and perspectives.* New York, Guildford Press.

Ewin, D. (1983), Emergency room hypnosis for the burned patient. *American Journal of Clinical Hypnosis,* 26 (1), 5–8.

Frischolz, E. J., Braun, B. C. & Sachs, R. G. (1992), Construct validity of the Dissociative Experiences Scale: II. Its relationship with hypnotisability. *American Journal of Clinical Hypnosis,* 35, 145–52.

Gorassini, D. R. & Spanos, N. P. (1999), The Carleton Skill Training Program for Modifying Hypnotic Suggestibility: original version and variations, in Kirsch, I., Capafons, A., Cardena-Buelna, E. & Amigo, S. (Eds.) *Clinical hypnosis and self-regulation.* Washington, DC, American Psychological Society.

Groh, M. D. (1989), Correlates of hypnotic susceptibility, in Spanos, N. P. & Chaves, J. F. (Eds.) *Hypnosis: The cognitive-behavioural perspective.* Buffalo, Prometheus.

Gruzelier, J., Gray, M. & Horn, P. (2006), The involvement of frontally modulated attention in hypnosis and hypnotic susceptibility: cortical evoked potential evidence. *Contemporary Hypnosis,* 19 (4), 179–89.

Hilgard, E. R., Crawford, H. & Wert, A. (1979). The Stanford Hypnotic Arm Levitation and Induction Test (SHALIT): A six minute induction and measurement scale. *International Journal of Clinical and Experimental Hypnosis,* 27, 111–24.

Kirsch, I. & Braffman, W. (1999), Correlates of hypnotizability: the first empirical study. *Contemporary Hypnosis,* 16, 224–30.

Kosslyn, S., Thompson, W., Constantine-Ferrando, M., Alpert, N. & Spiegel, D. (2000), Hypnotic visual illusion alters colour processing in the brain. *American Journal of Psychiatry.* 157, 1279–84.

McConkey, K. M., Sheehan, P. W. & White, K. D. (1979), Comparison of the Creative Imagination Scale and the Harvard Group Scale of Hypnotic Susceptibility, Form A. *International Journal of Clinical and Experimental Hypnosis,* 27, 265–77.

Morgan, A. H. & Hilgard, E. R. (1978/1979a), The Stanford Hypnotic Clinical Scale for Adults. *American Journal of Clinical Hypnosis,* 21, 134–47.

Morgan, A. H. & Hilgard, E. R. (1978/1979b), The Stanford Hypnotic Clinical Scale for Children. *American Journal of Clinical Hypnosis,* 21, 148–55.

Nash, M. R. & Barnier, A. J. (Eds.) (2008), *The Oxford handbook of hypnosis: theory, research and practice.* New York, Oxford University Press.

Orne, M. T., Hilgard, E. R. & Spiegel, H. (1978). The relation between the Hypnotic Induction Profile and the Stanford Hypnotic Susceptibility Scales, Forms A and C. *International Journal of Clinical and Experimental Hypnosis,* 27, 85–102.

Rainville, P., Hofbauer, R., Bushnell, M., Duncan, G. & Price, D. (2002) Hypnosis modulates activity in brain structures involved in the regulation of consciousness. *Journal of Cognitive Neuroscience,* 14 (6), 887–901.

Rainville, P. & Price, D. D. (2003), Hypnosis phenomenology and the neurobiology of consciousness. *International Journal of Clinical and Experimental Hypnosis,* 51 (2) 105–29.

Shor, R. E. & Orne, E. C. (1962), *Harvard Group Scale of Hypnotic Susceptibility Scale: Form A.* Palo Alto, CA, Consulting Psychologists Press.

Shor, R. E. & Orne, E. C. (1962) *Harvard Group Scale of Hypnotic Susceptibility Scale: Form A.* Palo Alto, CA, Consulting Psychologists Press.

Spiegel, D., Cutcomb, S., Ren, C. & Pribram, K. (1985), Hypnotic hallucinations alter evoked potentials. *Journal of Abnormal Psychology,* 94, 249–55.

Spiegel, H. & Spiegel, D. (2004), *Trance and treatment: clinical uses of hypnosis.* 2nd ed. Washington, DC, APA Press.

Szechtman, H., Woody, E. Z., Bowers, K. & Nahmias, C. (1998), Where the imaginable appears real: a positron emission tomography study of auditory hallucinations. *Proceedings of the National Academy of Sciences, USA,* 95, 1956–60.

Weitzenhoffer, A. & Hilgard, E. (1959), *Stanford Hypnotic Susceptibility Scale, Forms A and B.* Palo Alto, CA, Consulting Psychologists Press.

3

History of Hypnosis

Dr Ann Williamson

Introduction

There have been many good discourses on the history of hypnosis such as that in *Hypnosis and Communication in Dental Practice* (Simons *et al.*, 2007), so this chapter is not focused solely upon the traditional history of hypnosis. Rather it will show how hypnosis and other psychotherapeutic approaches gradually arose in a historical context and how the cultural norms of the time can be seen to be reflected and instrumental in how hypnosis evolved to its current form as described in this book.

Trance States and Healing

Over every culture and in every age, a 'trance state' has been linked to healing. This was usually associated with rituals that invested it with great importance and set such healing at a different level from normal day to day activities. This of course also served to increase the expectation of the people who came to be healed. Ritual was also important in cultures where there was little if any written history and where such matters were passed on to initiates by word of mouth and practice and a set routine or format was more easily remembered. Although labelled differently in different cultures and contexts, an altered state of awareness from our usual active and alert 'consciousness' is common to healing with peoples worldwide, and the similarities to what we are labelling 'hypnosis' are obvious.

The Handbook of Contemporary Clinical Hypnosis: Theory and Practice, First Edition.
Edited by Les Brann, Jacky Owens and Ann Williamson.
© 2012 John Wiley & Sons, Ltd. Published 2015 by John Wiley & Sons, Ltd.

Pre-modern man

In earliest times man viewed himself as part of the whole of creation rather than as a separate entity and looked at the world with wonder, awe and gratitude. All living things had a 'soul' or spirit, and animistic religions are found worldwide as was shamanism. Shamanism viewed illness as personal disharmony with the universe, arising from being out of balance. Different shamanistic traditions certainly existed during the Palaeolithic era (50,000–30,000 BC) in North Asia and somewhere around 25,000 B.C. in Europe, although it could have been much earlier (Eliade, 2004).

Ancient civilizations

Four thousand years ago in ancient Egypt under the high priest Imhotep, 'sleep' temples were used for healing. Here the patient, having first ceremonially bathed and fasted, was induced into a trance state by chanting. Their dreams were then interpreted by the priests to help resolve their problems.

The ancient Hebrews used something similar where a trance state was induced by chanting, breathing exercises and using the word for the name of God as a visual focus.

The ancient Celts induced Druidic sleep which has many parallels, and shamanistic trances used for healing were used over nearly all the known world.

In early civilizations illness was thought to be a visitation by the god or gods, and little distinction was made between physical and mental illness. Treatment was based on appeasing the deities involved, and hence spiritual practice and healing were inextricably linked within the beliefs and lives of these peoples.

Induction

These trance states, whether utilized with a healing intent or not, were induced with some way of focusing attention. Psychotropic substances were sometimes used. There were many ways utilized to focus attention; chanting, singing, drumming, dancing or using visual symbols. During this time the person's awareness of external reality diminished as they became more focused on their internal reality. As brain studies have recently shown us, these meditative states are reflected in changes in the attentional and arousal networks of the brain (Rainville *et al.*, 2002). Sounds and symbols become anchors to trance (see chapter 12). This can be seen to be similar to the ways we induce the hypnotic state whereby a person may be focused on sounds, such as the sound of the therapist's voice, the sound of the sea, whale noises or music; or on something visual such as a candle flame, a pendulum or internal visual imagery; or with a kinaesthetic focus such as breathing, progressive muscular relaxation or dancing.

Use of ritual

Healing was, as mentioned above, often surrounded by ritual which added to the mystique. Both initiates and patients would bathe, which may be seen as a metaphor for both physical and mental cleansing before entering a realm they believed inhabited by their God. Fasting, sleep deprivation and endurance trials were also often used to encourage an altered state of consciousness. Ritual dress would be worn to mark out the solemnity and importance of the occasion.

Rituals inspire confidence in the participants, increase expectation of a positive outcome, denote safety and promote unquestioning obedience. The various forms of induction of hypnosis can be seen as rituals facilitating access to the hypnotic state. We know from research that the greatest predictors of a successful outcome in psychotherapy including hypnosis is expectation and the therapeutic relationship built up between patient and therapist (Assay & Lambert, 1999; Frank, 1971; Hubble *et al.*, 1999).

Ritual may also help engender active participation in the process of healing by the patient, as is seen to be necessary in modern psychotherapeutic approaches. Within the western medical model, patients are more often passive receivers of treatment rather than active participants in their care. The patient's intention, motivation to heal and willingness to work towards their psychotherapeutic goals are the key to successful psychotherapy, and the symbolic surroundings facilitate this. For instance, modern psychological therapists still often use a couch or have ornaments, symbolic objects or quotes visible in their consulting rooms. The patient's expectation of hypnosis and their perception of what hypnosis is are therefore hugely important in the successful use of hypnosis. To take time at the beginning of the first session building rapport and explaining about hypnosis is crucial to a successful outcome.

Greek and roman civilizations

The ancient Greeks were the first to distinguish mental illness as a medical condition, but from the time of Homer onwards humankind's focus turned towards a celebration of war and death rather than a celebration of life. The belief grew that illness was due to a physical problem within the body rather than being a reflection of imbalance between the person and his environment or within the person themselves.

Christianity

With the rise of Christianity healing was seen as a miracle or a gift from God, trance states as evil and practiced by witches and illness and suffering as part of humankind's payment for being born with original sin – just punishment for wrongdoing. However, in the eleventh century the person of the king of England, as a direct representative of God on earth, was thought to be able to heal by touch (from Edward the Confessor onwards).

In medieval times in the western world there was a resurgence of the belief that mental illness was linked with demonic possession, and the afflicted would be required to undergo ritual exorcism or tortured to expel the demons involved. Conversely, in the Middle East until relatively recently, people with mental illness were often thought to be possessed but were treated with tolerance or even reverence as being especially 'holy'.

Treatments at this time were commonly blood letting or medicines derived from plants, but even in the sixteenth century Paracelsus (1493–1541) advocated psychotherapy for treatment of the 'insane'. Within this context where learned men explored chemistry, alchemy and the natural sciences there gradually arose more knowledge about the functioning of the body. Descartes's (1596–1650) ideas of mind–body dualism took hold and are still prevalent today.

In the second half of the eighteenth century a Viennese doctor, Franz Anton Mesmer (1734–1815), used hypnosis but was discredited by a committee of influential thinkers set up by Louis XVI to investigate the phenomenon. Mesmer's theories that hypnosis was done with 'animal magnetism' were disproved and hypnosis was therefore thought to be nothing but hysteria. But it continued to be used and researched in France, and in the nineteenth century John Elliotson (1791–1868), a professor of medicine in London, tried to interest the medical establishment of the time in the use of hypnosis. At this time hypnosis was also being practiced successfully in India by James Esdaille (1808–1859), a Scottish surgeon who performed many operations under hypnosis at a time when the only anaesthetic agents were alcohol or opium.

By the latter half of the nineteenth century hypnosis was regarded more as a curiosity and an entertainment than anything worthy of serious study, but a Manchester doctor, James Braid (1795–1860), became interested and postulated that hypnosis was a form of nervous exhaustion and sleep induced by concentration on a bright object. In France Dr. Ambroise-August Liebeault (1823–1904) and Professor Bernheim (1840–1919) from Paris set up the Nancy School and propounded the idea that hypnosis was a special type of sleep where suggestion was acted upon more powerfully than normal. Another view, held by Professor Jean Martin Charcot (1825–1893), who worked with nervous diseases in Paris, was that hypnosis was a form of hysteria; although he had his followers at the time, his ideas were in conflict with those of the Nancy School and did not endure. A physician from Vienna, Josef Breuer (1842–1925), worked with Charcot and was the first to use hypnosis to 'uncover' past traumatic events which he believed underpinned the symptoms displayed. The patients would have a cathartic release of emotion once the event was recalled and talked about – the first example of a 'talking cure'.

The Dawn of Psychology

It was commonly thought that the mind and thought could not be measured so therefore psychology could not be thought of as a science, but this had to be revised when learned men of the time such as Ernst Weber (1795–1878) and Gustav Fechner (1801–1887) demonstrated that psychological events could be tied to measurable physical experiences. Sir Francis Galton (1822–1911) in England and Alfred Binet (1857–1911) in France both explored how one might measure intelligence, and this resulted in IQ testing that we know today.

Psychology as the science recognizable today arose from this background in the early twentieth century together with the psychoanalytic theories of Sigmund Freud (1856–1939). Sigmund Freud had studied with both Charcot and Bernheim but later rejected the use of hypnosis.

Psychoanalysis and psychodynamic approaches

Psychoanalysis arose from the ideas of Sigmund Freud, who believed that mental illness arose from repressed memories which if brought back into consciousness would resolve the problem. He also was the first to explore transference (and counter-transference), defined as where the patient develops feelings towards their therapist (and vice versa) that are in reality reflections of feelings they hold towards someone, such as a parent, in their past (see page 85). Because of his great influence in the psychological field Freud's eventual dislike and disregard of hypnosis led to it again being regarded as either fraud or hysteria, and it was only in the latter part of the twentieth century that this view started to be modified.

Jung (1875–1961) and Adler (1870–1937), who originally followed Freud, developed their own approaches, but therapy was extremely prolonged (often having no endpoint as such) and so was only available to the privileged few. As a backlash to the pre-eminence of the schools of psychoanalytic thought, psychodynamic approaches developed, focusing on the dynamic relationship between the mind (psyche) and life events. Jung's ideas of active imagination underpin much of the work done with imagery today. He believed that the imagination acted as a bridge between the conscious and unconscious parts of our mind and that the images that arose from the unconscious were relevant to the person and could be worked with therapeutically. Jung used imagery in very much the same way as we use hypnotic imagery today suggesting that the person acts as an observer waiting to see what image might arise rather than consciously 'trying' to generate an image. Work using dream imagery (see page 419) and utilizing the expressive arts (see page 64) also draws on these ideas (Chodorow, 1997).

Humanistic approaches

In the 1940s Carl Rogers (1902–1987) was instrumental in developing humanistic approaches where the patient was viewed with non-judgmental positive regard. Approaches such as psycho-drama (Jacob Levy Moreno, 1889–1974), gestalt (Fritz Perls, 1893–1970) and those using guided imagery also began to develop early in the twentieth century with their emphasis on use of imagination and imagery.

Cognitive-behavioural therapy

Behaviourism as a philosophical idea was around early in the twentieth century alongside Freud's psychoanalytic theories and was developed further with work on animal conditioning and learning theory by the American psychologist Burrhus Frederic Skinner

(1904–1990). The importance of cognitions became recognized with the advent of cognitive approaches in the 1950s and 1960s with figures such as Albert Ellis (1913–2007) and Aaron Beck (1921–). This recognition that thoughts, feelings and behaviour are interlinked and jointly influence our functioning in the world has been incorporated, to a greater or lesser extent, into many other psychological approaches. Cognitive-behavioural therapy or CBT is currently one of the most popular forms of psychotherapy today.

In Victorian times medicine was viewed with great respect and doctors generally were supposed to act with confidence and authority. Patients were expected to be passive recipients of treatment and to obey the doctor's instructions. Within this context hypnosis, as practiced in England prior to the 1960s by John Hartland (1901–1977) and others, was necessarily authoritarian. Patients were told that they were getting sleepier; they were instructed to close their eyes and go into hypnosis, and direct suggestions were given for removal of symptoms. Even today with stage hypnosis the view of hypnosis that implies that it is something 'done' to one causes problems with people thinking that entering hypnosis means giving up control, whereas in fact the person is gaining more control as they learn how to utilize their mind and the hypnotic state to help themselves. For differences between the more current, so-called maternal hypnotic language with its emphasis on permissiveness and facilitation rather than the so-called paternal authoritarian style, see page 108.

Solution focus

Most approaches, however, were still problem focused, and it was not until the 1970s that solution focused approaches began to appear. At the same time economic issues began to play their part and briefer therapies that were more centred on the patient's goals began to become more popular. These have resulted in the solution focused hypnotherapy that we expound in this book as well as solution focused brief therapy and the human givens approach.

Neurolinguistic programming

Milton Erickson was influential in showing how powerful hypnosis and utilization of the patient's resources could be in facilitating change. He was also, together with Fritz Perls and Virginia Satir, instrumental in modelling for Richard Bandler and John Grinder what makes different therapeutic interventions effective. Bandler and Grinder analysed the different language patterns used by patients and therapists to try to uncover the internal mechanism by which we develop and maintain unhelpful and dysfunctional functioning. These ideas became popular in both psychotherapy and advertising and have a huge market under the title 'Neurolinguistic Programming' (NLP) (Grinder *et al.*, 1981).

(*Note*: Milton Erickson, 1901–1980, was a psychiatrist and innovative hypnotherapist; Fritz Perls, 1893–1970, was the founder of gestalt therapy; Virginia Satir, 1916–1988, was a family therapist; Richard Bandler, b. 1950, is a mathematician; and John Grinder, b. 1940, is a linguist.)

From Milton Erickson to the twenty-first century

With Milton Erickson and others, permissive approaches gradually developed and these sit more easily with most therapists today. From the middle of the twentieth century with the cultural and political focus being directed towards apparent individual choice and with the rise of the media driven cult of the consumer, permissive language became more acceptable than direct command. In conjunction with more solution based thinking, hypnosis became more overtly patient focused, utilizing the patient's strengths and resources to help them achieve their therapeutic goals. Permissive, open language used within the context of a good therapeutic relationship can be shown to facilitate suggestion, and this will be expanded upon throughout this book.

The State Versus Non-State Debate

This debate polarized thinking about hypnosis for much of the latter half of the twentieth century. The state theorists preferred the view that hypnosis was an altered state of consciousness, whilst the non-state protagonists explained the observable phenomena of hypnosis in socio-cognitive terms of 'compliance', 'role-play' or 'suggestibility'. The majority of the published evidence for the non-state view came from laboratory studies and was extrapolated to cover hypnosis in general. Although it was not the intention of the researchers, the non-state view tended to be interpreted as being synonymous with 'hypnosis is nothing' (and therefore not worth doing!). Unfortunately this debate was continuing as clinicians were being pressurized into only using 'evidence-based' therapies, and given the lack of a sound theoretical basis, clinical research into the clinical uses of hypnosis waned. Much the same thing had happened when the French Royal Commission found the animal magnetism theory to be flawed and the observable clinical benefits were ignored. Fortunately, the advent of neuro-imaging techniques has made it possible to examine the neurophysiological changes associated with the use of hypnosis. The changes observable following hypnotic induction (see chapter 1) along with work such as the unifying theory (Oakley, 1999) which can accommodate both points of view have tended to make the state versus non-state debate obsolete. Hopefully, it will herald the beginning of a resurgence of interest in the clinical benefits of hypnosis especially as the modus operandi of clinical practice is shifting from process to outcomes.

The laboratory approach to hypnosis with volunteer subjects and fixed standard inductions and assessments is vastly different from the hypnotic situation constructed by the therapeutic alliance between patient and therapist. The main lesson to be learnt from this (destructive) debate is to encourage research into the features of hypnosis associated with positive clinical outcomes rather than getting bogged down with unhelpful and artificial theoretical constructs.

Reading chapters 2 and 3 of this book, it can be seen that hypnosis in its present form has developed over many years, although theories about what hypnosis actually is have changed from ideas of magic and mystery, through magnetism and hysteria, to a normal function of the human mind.

Table 3.1 details some of the most important stages in the history of hypnosis.

Table 3.1 Summary of the important theories and their authors in the history of hypnosis

In the beginning, trance states were used generally for healing. In Egyptian, Greek and Roman times sleep temples were common. Hypnotic like processes are mentioned in the Old and New Testaments of the Bible.

1770s	Franz Anton Mesmer	Mesmerism	Theory of animal magnetism	Disease due to blockage of universal magnetic fluid
1785	Marquis de Puysegur		Artificial somnambulism	Skills and abilities of the participant, *not* the hypnotist Role of psychological factors
1819	Abbé de Faria	Pre-hypnotism	Lucid sleep (believed to be hypnotic state)	
1791–1868	John Elliotson	Mesmerism in the United Kingdom	Discredited by medical fraternity	Founded a 'mesmeric' hospital and a magazine, *The Zoist*
1845–1853	James Esdaille	Mesmerism in India	Performed surgery under mesmerism in India	
1840s and 1850s	James Braid	Hypnotism Monoideism	Analogy to sleep	
1870s and 1880s	Jean Martin Charcot Ambrose-August Liebault	Neurological theory	Linked hypnosis to hysteria	Both aspects of the same neuropathological condition
1884	Hippolyte Bernheim	Acknowledged a 'base rate' of hypnotic behaviour	Hypnosis activated and intensified suggestibility	
1885	Sigmund Freud	Discredited hypnosis within the medical field	Worked with Charcot but later decided that hypnosis was a fake and not worth scientific study	

1925	Pierre Janet rejected Charcot's ideas	Concept of dissociation	Hypnotic suggestions could produce dissociated streams of consciousness		
1900 to 1950	Decline – no one wanted to research hypnosis or use it in clinical practice for two reasons	Reason 1: Freud's rejection of it and the emergence of psychoanalysis	Reason 2: rise of behaviourism within the field of psychology		
1930s	Clark Hull	Initiated an experimental approach	Introduced quantification – used controlled experiments and statistical analyses		
1950–1970s	Milton Erickson	Ericksonian hypnosis	Utilization		
1970s	Ernest Hilgard	Neo-dissociationist theory	The 'hidden observer'		
1999	David Oakley	Unifying theory – incorporates 'state' and 'non-state' factors	Hypnosis acts at the level of the 'executive control system'	The patient has the resources within to effect change	Socio-cognitive factors influence response

References

Assay, T. P. & Lambert, M. J. (1999), The empirical case for the common factors in therapy: quantitative findings, in Hubble, M. A., Duncan, B. L. & Miller, S. D. (Eds.) *The heart and soul of change: what works in therapy*. Washington, DC, APA Press.

Chodorow, J. (Ed.) (1997), *Jung on active imagination*. Princeton, Princeton University Press.

Eliade, M. (2004), *Shamanism, archaic techniques of ecstacy*. Princeton, Princeton University Press.

Frank, J. D. (1971), Therapeutic factors in psychotherapy. *American Journal of Psychotherapy*, 25 (3), 350–61.

Grinder, J., Bandler, R. & Andreas, C. (1981), *Tranceformations: neurolinguistic programming and the structure of hypnosis*. Newcastle, Real People Press.

Hubble, M. A., Duncan, B. L. & Miller, S. D. (1999), Directing attention to what works, in Hubble, M. A., Duncan, B. L. & Miller, S. D. (Eds.) *The heart and soul of change: what works in therapy*. Washington, DC, APA Press.

Oakley, D. A. (1999), Hypnosis and consciousness: a structural model. *Contemporary Hypnosis*, 16, 215–23.

Rainville, P., Hofbauer, R., Bushnell, M., Duncan, G. & Price, D. (2002), Hypnosis modulates activity in brain structures involved in the regulation of consciousness. *Journal of Cognitive Neuroscience*, 14 (6), 887–901.

Simons, D., Potter, C. & Temple, G. (2007), *Hypnosis and communication in dental practice*. New Malden, Quintessence.

4

Imagery and Visualization

Mrs Jacky Owens
with contributions from Dr Ann Williamson

Introduction

This chapter explains why imagery is such a powerful tool and why the use of imagery within hypnosis can be so effective. The use of all the senses within imagery and some guidelines for using guided imagery with patients are described with some sample scripts.

> *The soul is the source, imagination the tool and the body the plastic material.*
>
> Paracelsus (1493–1541)

Hypnogogic and Hypnopompic Imagery

We all experience imagery even though some people may not recognize that they do. In our waking state we have a generalized reality orientation (GRO), that is, we know where we are in time and space. There is a window of time, however, prior to sleeping when there is an absence of GRO and hypnagogic imagery occurs. During this time period a subject may be, and often is, elsewhere, else-when and else-who; so each and every one of us is able to let go of reality without fear or anxiety as a very natural thing. It is this same state that we are aiming for when we begin to enter a hypnotic trance. Another window of time when there is an absence of GRO occurs prior to waking, the state between sleep and full wakefulness, and this is when hypnopompic imagery is present. Both hypnopompic and hypnagogic images may be very distinct and provide for vivid experiences (Martin, 1994).

The Handbook of Contemporary Clinical Hypnosis: Theory and Practice, First Edition.
Edited by Les Brann, Jacky Owens and Ann Williamson.
© 2012 John Wiley & Sons, Ltd. Published 2015 by John Wiley & Sons, Ltd.

A hypnotherapist helps a subject create a trance state, then develop this type of processing and use it for therapeutic benefit.

Imagination and Imagery

'Imagination is more important than knowledge' (Einstein, 1931) for without imagination man would not seek knowledge. Everybody has an imagination, and using the power of the imagination in imagery, especially within a hypnotic context, can lead to profound beneficial changes. Heap and Aravind (2002) argue that the capacity for imaginative involvement, absorption and fantasy proneness may have clinical significance when working with hypnosis.

Imagery (visualization) is basically an exercise in imagination, using the 'mind's eye' to create new mental pictures or change existing ones, and it is possible to achieve a profound relaxation using imagery techniques. Hypnosis can greatly enhance a person's powers of visualization and therefore the therapeutic effectiveness of the technique; thus it is important that those who use hypnotic techniques understand the basic principles of imagery. A study by Liggert and Harbor (2000) in which athletes used imagery both in and out of trance found that hypnosis substantially enhances imagery intensity and effectiveness.

An image is not a photograph held in your mind's eye, indeed for many people an image is just a thought that brings with it a feeling. The saying 'It is your mind that creates this world' has been attributed to the Buddha, but more likely this is a simplification of 'We are what we think. All that we are arises with our thoughts. With our thoughts we make the world' (Byrom, 1993).

> *Nothing is good or bad tis thinking makes it so.*
> W. Shakespeare (*Hamlet*, Act II, sc. ii, 1. 255)

Most people, when they get into a car to travel, think and believe that they will arrive safely. Similarly most people, when they go to bed to sleep, think and believe that they will awake refreshed some time later. Yet car accidents and home fires are all too common. It is our thought patterns that keep us comfortable whilst travelling or sleeping. Obviously these activities may present difficulties for those who may have previously been involved in a car accident or a fire, but the acts themselves are neutral.

Types of Imagery

There are differing aspects to imagery; for some people images are visual, for some auditory, gustatory, kinaesthetic or tactile (Sodergren, 1992); and for those who wish to know the structure and quality of their patient's images, the Creative Imagination Scale provides rich information (see page 21). The Creative Imagination Scale emphasizes cognitive ability and self control, and it places the responsibility for hypnotic experience with the subject (Heap & Aravind, 2002). Knowledge of patients' imagery helps to inform the language patterns (see page 90) that will be most useful to the patient in bringing about a therapeutic change.

Images may be formed in response to emotions, images may express emotions and images may evoke emotions. Imagery provides communication between perception, emotion and physiological processes (Achterberg, 1985). This is why it can be extremely powerful especially when used within hypnosis. Thus there is a fundamental need for therapists to understand the possibilities, both good and bad, in order to maximize its usefulness. Hypnosis can greatly enhance a person's powers of imagery. It bypasses the conscious mind's logical editor and 'critical faculties', shuts out distractions and removes inhibitions on the imaginative processes. This enables the therapeutic effectiveness to be increased as evidenced by Derbyshire *et al.* (2004) using functional magnetic resonance imaging (fMRI) to show that hypnotically hallucinated pain activates the pain matrix whereas simple imagination of pain does not.

Guided imagery

Many relaxation techniques depend upon guided imagery and yet this can be problematic for some patients. The person guiding the imagery may introduce elements or use semantics that create anxiety rather than relaxation. This can be damaging to the therapeutic relationship that should exist between therapist and patient and be counterproductive in terms of benefit for the patient. Whilst some people find entering the relaxed state emotionally releasing, some find it scary and it may even precipitate a panic attack. This is especially likely in those patients suffering from chronic anxiety states when an induction that utilizes their high levels of adrenalin such as re-vivification may be preferable (see page 116).

It is also possible to do harm; we need to be careful in the use of imagery and hypnosis, for their inexpert use could have the effect of making people feel needlessly guilty about disease progression viewing it as a failure on their part (Spiegel & Moore, 1997).

In the United States there is a widespread movement towards imagery techniques alone without hypnosis. This may have something to do with US law in which testimony produced from hypnosis is prohibited, but, undoubtedly, many there believe that imagery alone is a powerful tool with which to create therapeutic change (Rossman, 2000; Rossman & Bressler, 1998). Some might argue that merely closing one's eyes and using imagery is in itself hypnosis. However it should be noted that according to the American Psychological Association definition a formal induction is necessary to call any procedure 'hypnosis'. Worldwide this view may not prevail.

Associated and dissociated imagery

It is important to bear in mind that a dissociated image (seeing yourself in the event) reduces the associated emotion and hence is used when working with traumatic memories.

An associated image (imagining actually being in the event) enhances the attached emotion, and therefore it is useful to check that the patient is associated with the event when accessing strengths and resources or imagining a special, safe place (see page 121).

Experiential Approach

An effective way to demonstrate imagery is to ask the patient to focus on something good in their lives – notice how and where they feel the pleasure – then get them to focus on something awful (perhaps use the 9/11 Twin Towers event with non-cancer patients and the cancer if relevant) and see how the feelings change. Always put them back into pleasure before ending the exercise.

To demonstrate just how thoughts affect feelings, ask the patient to:

- Close their eyes and remember a time or event that they enjoyed.
- Draw them into this memory by encouraging them to remember the location, the sights, sounds and smells associated with the event and the people they shared it with.
- Let them play with this memory for a minute and then get them to attend to the feelings in their hands, feet, tummy, chest and head.
- Now ask them to let the memory fade and to be once again with their doctor giving them their diagnosis or bad news and once again draw them right into the memory (personalize this to the particular patient you are working with)
- As soon as they exhibit signs of distress, ask them once again to attend to the feelings in their hands, feet, tummy, chest and head.
- Return once more to their pleasurable experience and keep them there until they are obviously calm and relaxed.
- End the exercise by drawing their attention to the feelings in their hands, feet, tummy, chest and head.

Patients are made aware through this exercise of how powerfully their cognitions create the feelings in their body and whereabouts in their body they hold those feelings. Demonstrating this concept to patients can be very useful especially when working with treatment regimens.

Use of Imagery

Imagery is used powerfully in hypnosis for many reasons, for example to create a place of safety, rehearse a desired behaviour, anchor a feeling or mitigate a symptom. It is preferable to have the patient generate their own imagery and work with that, for when utilizing patients' self generated imagery there is less risk of suggesting an external locus of control and the images generated by their own unconscious will be more powerful for them. That said, there is a role for guided imagery. For instance, when devising a research protocol, it is usual to have all the participants working with the same images.

Safe place imagery

It is important in the work we do that patients can access a place of safety, and therefore the therapist should check that the images invoked are actually safe ones to hold. This is especially important for cancer patients. A patient who said that the cancer could stay so long as it behaved itself was not generating safe imagery for it is not in the nature of cancer cells to behave; they live at the expense of normal body tissue. Imagery that patients describe in the waking state is often not congruent with that which they generate whilst in hypnosis; this occurs especially when accessing safe place imagery. Imagery generated in trance has a much greater potential to facilitate change in the patient.

Positive mental rehearsal

There are many occasions when patients can be asked to rehearse in the safety of trance a desired behaviour, and modern sports psychology is now utilizing this premise; for example David Beckham scoring a goal in imagery before taking a free kick. Indeed many sportsmen and women are now encouraged to rehearse and perfect their technique in imagery prior to actuality. Newmark and Bogacki (2005) describe the use of imagery and hypnosis techniques to enhance athletic performance, as do Pates *et al*. (2001).

Imagery in hypnosis can appear more vivid and be more effective (Liggett & Harbor, 2000), and some people have what is termed 'eidetic' imagery: that is visual or auditory imagery that is exceptionally vivid and allows for detailed recall of a previous experience. This quality of imagery is more common in children but when it occurs it can facilitate beneficial change.

Many patients present with low self esteem and confidence levels (see chapter 14), and imagery techniques used in trance can be a powerful mechanism to create a more pleasing self image and raise confidence levels and then anchor them such that the patient can always access the good feelings they produce.

Much research evidence now exists to show that imagery in hypnosis is a valuable tool for the mitigation of symptoms but in this chapter we shall use only two examples, pain and a psychosomatic symptom whereby behavioural change is desired, although many others occur throughout the book in relevant sections.

Use of imagery in pain

Pain is dealt with extensively in chapter 21, however there is a wealth of material supporting the use of imagery with or without hypnosis to mitigate physical pain and restore physical comfort (Alden *et al.*, 2001; Spiegel & Moore, 1997; Syrala *et al.*, 1995; Van Fleet, 2000; Walters & Oakley, 2006). As stated previously both imagery and the therapeutic effect are enhanced in hypnosis, and what may seem odd in the waking state can produce real and lasting effects when used in hypnosis.

Giving the following information in trance will set the scene:

> *These sensations are all subjective phenomena but as you know only too well it is difficult to consciously ... modify these ... feelings. ... We usually find it easier to modify concrete objects ... so the purpose of this image is to ... change your unpleasant sensation into an object that is a symbol of this sensation.*
>
> *Take your pain and discomfort and give it a shape by imaging or visualizing the first shape ... that comes into your mind ... the shape ... may be abstract ... or concrete. It can be an object ... an animate form ... or a geometric design. ... The first shape that comes into your mind is the ... appropriate one ... to work with ... anything else tends to be conscious ... judgemental effort.*

For those who are visual in their imagery, one might suggest changing the parameters of the shape in a way that eases the pain little by little (changing colour, brightness, clarity, size, distance and whether the shape is framed or unframed), until a desired level of comfort is achieved.

For those who hold kinaesthetic imagery, again changing the parameters can be the key to achieving comfort, noting if the pain is continuous or intermittent, noting its density and texture and determining whether it is sharp or dull plus also changing the temperature. Working with these aspects can, for some patients, have a remarkably beneficial effect.

It is also possible to work with audible imagery. For instance the sound of an angry sea can be softened to calm, gently rippling waves. Often giving voice to a pain can facilitate the patient being able to dialogue with it, discover why it is there and see what it needs to reduce or leave.

It can be helpful, at times, to encourage the patient to simply get rid of their pain in imagery in whatever way feels right to them; but for those who get stuck with this, perhaps suggesting that they can kick it, throw it away, send it off in an aeroplane or balloon, bury it or drown it may get them started.

Another very successful way to deal with pain in imagery is to ask the patient on a scale of one to ten, with one being comfortable and ten being the worst pain, the number of their current pain. Help the patient work down through the numbers suggesting at each change that the patient can let go of just the corresponding amount of pain until they have complete comfort in their body.

One of the authors (JO) finds this sort of scripting (patter) useful (starting with whichever number their pain is at): *"Just see if you can let that (for example) nine curl into eight, letting go of just a little of that pain, working slowly and gently until you have the right amount of pain for the number eight ... work in whatever way feels right to you"*. Use ideomotor signalling or head nods to signify that specific points have been reached. This is then continued moving down through the numbers: "... *which now straightens into seven: seven curls into six: six bends into five: five straightens into four which curls into three: three straightens out into a swan's neck (two): two straightens into one (a candle or a tree): zero becomes the sun or smiling face."*

It is a good idea to have the patient work up through the numbers to prove to them that they have absolute control over what is happening in their body and how powerful their mind is. Success in itself encourages the patient to continue developing this skill. Some therapists occasionally begin by going up higher first (thus increasing the pain, which some patients find easier to do) before bringing the numbers down for this very reason.

Ipsative imagery is that used by the patient in describing their symptom, and the hypnotic intervention is to transform their image into something more tolerable or manageable (Oakley, 2004; Oakley *et al.*, 2002) (see page 304). For example, one lady whose pain appeared as an old and holey jumper unravelled her pain as she unravelled, in trance imagery, the jumper.

Experience shows that if the emotional or psychological issues in someone's life are not dealt with, physical pain may and often does result. Pain experienced in the waking state that vanishes in trance is an indicator that the pain does not have a current physical cause, although it is no less 'real' for that.

Imagery in anxiety

A commonly experienced psychosomatic problem is that of anxiety, dealt with extensively in chapter 14. It is possible to have physical, emotional, cognitive and behavioural effects due to anxiety; some examples appear in Table 4.1.

Table 4.1 Some physical, emotional, cognitive and behavioural effects of anxiety

Physical	Emotional	Cognitive	Behavioural
Breathlessness	Crying	Amnesia	Aggressive
Diarrhoea	Deflated	Difficulty in decision making	Clingy
Dry mouth	Defeated	Forgetfulness	Drinking (alcohol)
Frequency	Depression	Frequently changes mind	Always early
Headache	Frightened	Hypercritical of self and others	Hyperactive
Hypertension	Helpless	Unable to cope	Hysterical laughter
Indigestion	Immobilized	Lack of objectivity	Illogical
Palpitations	Insecure	Nightmares	Insensitive to others
Squeaky voice	Sad	Overestimates abilities	Always late
Stomach ache	Self pity	Puts self down	Shouts
Sweating	Upset	Suppression of feelings	Stuttering
Tense muscles	Vulnerable	Tunnel vision	Takes pills
Wobbly knees	Worried	Unable to plan	Withdrawn

If we take, for example, someone who is about to undergo an interview, perhaps a student applying for a university place, an unemployed person seeking a job, a young man asking for a hand in marriage or someone preparing to give a lecture or sitting an examination, these are all situations in which it is possible to feel anxious even if you are not naturally an anxious person. Using imagery skills, with or without hypnosis, one can do work in preparation for the event, rehearse the event, address possible differing responses and above all engender self confidence. An event that, for some people, is traumatic in the anticipatory period can be transformed into a comfortable and even possibly an exhilarating experience through the use of imagery.

Mind–Body Links

Demonstrating mind–body links allows the patients to see and understand that they can create physical changes in their body using their mind. Walker and colleagues (Walker 2004; Walker *et al.*, 2005) have researched widely in this field and provide a rich source of information to underpin this work. The use of the Creative Imagination Scale can achieve this when assessing hypnotizability, however when time is short the following simple imagination exercise is quick and simple to do.

Ask the patient to engage fully with you – to use their imagination to make the scene as vivid as possible. Ask them to:

- *"Bring an image of a fridge into your mind . . . any fridge but it is plugged in and working."*
- *"Go towards it and open the door . . . a waft of cold air comes to meet you."*
- *"Inside on one of the shelves is a fresh lemon . . . it may be yellow or green . . . it may be smooth skinned or pitted . . . it may be knobbly at the ends . . . it does not matter . . . it is your lemon . . . but you are aware that it is a very fresh lemon heavy with juice."*
- *"Take it out and roll it in your hands . . . feel its coldness . . . feel its weight . . . heavy with juice."*
- *"Take it over to a chopping board, and in a moment you are going to chop through it with a knife . . . when you do, you will see some of the juice spurt out . . . it is such a fresh lemon . . . you may see a pip spurt out, and you may even hear the juice as you slice through the lemon."*
- *"Cut through the lemon now."*
- *"See that juice . . . perhaps a pip . . . perhaps you hear it."*
- *"Cut a piece from the lemon and rub it on your fingers so that the oil in the peel is transferred to your fingers."*
- *"Put your fingers to your nose and smell the lemon . . . breathe in that fresh clean smell."*
- *"Cut another piece from the lemon. . . . This time you are going to put into your mouth and taste it. . . . If you don't want to put into your mouth directly, you might like to imagine that it is a warm summer day and a glass of lemonade would go down nicely; or perhaps it is the right time of the evening for a gin and tonic. In whatever way is right for you,*

take the lemon into your mouth and taste it now.... Taste that clean, sharp almost springtime taste."

Invite the patient to open their eyes and orient themselves back to the room. Then ask the patient:

- Could they see the lemon? Was it in colour?
- Could they feel it as they picked it up?
- Were they aware of any movement throughout the exercise?
- Could they smell the lemon?
- Could they taste it?
- Did they salivate?

The Psychoneuroimmunology (PNI) Perspective

Especially for those patients who do salivate during this exercise (i.e. those who produce a physical response to an imagined object), it allows them to see that by working with their mind and following the clearly defined pathways of psycho-neuroimmunology (PNI) (see chapters 23 and 24) they may be able to facilitate change, for this approach connects the mind, body and spirit into an integrated whole. One can connect their experience to the way unconscious processes affect feelings, the effect the mind can have on the body and the physiological effects of the imagination.

Plato wrote, 'For this is the greatest error of our day, that physicians separate the soul from the body'. Yet working from the PNI perspective not only facilitates the interconnectedness of the person but also empowers them to tap into innate sources of healing.

In summary, the key concepts of imagery are:

- The patient and not the therapist should generate the imagery, as self generated imagery has more meaning and potential for therapeutic benefit than therapist presented imaginative ideas.
- Imagery generated in trance has greater potential for therapeutic change.
- There is not always congruence between waking state and hypnotically generated imagery.
- Guided imagery can produce distress in some.
- There is a need to check out cancer patients' imagery as to its safety in cancer terms; cancer patients often hold unhelpful imagery.
- Imagery may afford unexpected insights.
- Imagery uses all the senses and is not just visual.
- Imagery helps access mind–body links.
- Associated imagery increases emotion.
- Dissociated imagery reduces emotion.

References

Achterberg, J. (1985), *Imagery in healing shamanism and modern medicine*. Boston, Shambhala.

Alden, A. L., Dale, J. A. & Degood, D. E. (2001), Interactive effects of the affect, quality and directional focus of mental imagery on pain analgesia. *Applied Psychophysiology and Biofeedback*, 26 (2), 117–26.

Byrom, T. (1993), *Dhammapada – the sayings of the Buddha*. Boston, Shambhala.

Derbyshire, S. W. G., Whalley, M. G., Stenger, V. A. & Oakley, D. A. (2004), Cerebral activation during hypnotically induced and imagined pain. *Neuroimage*, 23, 10.

Einstein, A. (1931), *Cosmic religion: with other opinions and aphorisms*. New York, Covici-Freide.

Heap, M. & Aravind, K. K. (Eds.) (2002), *Hartland's medical and dental hypnosis*. Edinburgh, Churchill Livingstone.

Liggett, D. & Harbor, G. (2000), Enhancing imagery through hypnosis: a performance aid for athletes. *American Journal of Clinical Hypnosis*, 43 (2), 9.

Martin, E. A. (Ed.) (1994), *Oxford concise colour medical dictionary*. Hong Kong, Oxford University Press.

Newmark, T. S. & Bogacki, D. F. (2005), The use of relaxation, hypnosis, and imagery in sport psychiatry. *Clinics in Sports Medicine*, 24 (4), 5.

Oakley, D. A. (2004), Hypnotic imagery and pain. Paper presented at the Anglian Pain Society Spring Scientific Meeting, Royal College of Physicians, London, September.

Oakley, D. A., Whitman, L. G. & Halligan, P. W. (2002), Hypnotic imagery as a treatment for phantom limb pain: two case reports and a review. *Clinical Rehabilitation*, 16 (4), 368–77.

Pates, J., Oliver, R. & Maynard, I. (2001), The effects of hypnosis on flow states and golf-putting performance. *Journal of Applied Sport Psychology*, 13, 4.

Rossman, M. L. (2000), *Guided imagery for self-healing: an essential resource for anyone seeking wellness*. Belvedere Tiburon, CA, H J Kramer.

Rossman, M. L. & Bressler, D. E. (Eds.) (1998) *Interactive guided imagery: clinical techniques for brief therapy & mind/body medicine*. Los Angeles, Academy for Guided Imagery.

Sodergren, K. M. (Ed.) (1992), *Guided imagery*. Clifton Park, NY, Delmar.

Spiegel, D. & Moore, R. (1997), Imagery and hypnosis in the treatment of cancer patients. *Oncology*, 11 (8), 17.

Syrala, K. L., Donaldson, G., Davis, M. W., Kippes, M. E. & Carr, J. E. (1995), Relaxation and imagery and cognitive-behavioural training reduce pain during cancer treatment: a controlled clinical trial. *Pain*, (63) 10.

Van Fleet, S. (2000), Relaxation and imagery for symptom management: improving patient assessment and individualizing treatment. *Oncology Nursing Forum*, 27 (3), 501–10.

Walker, L. G. (2004), Hypnotherapeutic insights and interventions: a cancer odyssey. *Contemporary Hypnosis*, 21 (1), 35–45.

Walker, L. G., Green, V. L., Greenman, J., Walker, A. A. & Sharp, D. M. (2005), Psychoneuroimmunology and chronic malignant disease: cancer, in Vedhara, K.& Irwin, M. R. (Eds.) *Human psychoneuroimmunology*. Oxford, Oxford University Press.

Walters, V. J. & Oakley, D. A. (2006), Hypnotic imagery as an adjunct to therapy for irritable bowel syndrome: an experimental case report. *Contemporary Hypnosis*, 23, 141–9.

5

Use of Language and Metaphor

Dr Ann Williamson

Introduction

Language reflects our reality and can be a powerful tool for good or ill. This chapter shows how the words we use when someone is in shock or anxious can have an even more powerful effect than usual. It will describe how our brain processes story and metaphor, making it the most effective communication tool we possess. Different types and styles of metaphor, as well as ways of using experiential, patient generated, empathic and constructed metaphor, will be described with case examples.

Language reflects our internal reality and therefore is probably the most important tool we have to help people change. Much of our communication is non-verbal and both mediated and understood at an unconscious level. However our internal thoughts are usually represented as language, and we use language to consciously communicate ideas to each other. How we use words can have a profound effect on the meanings we wish to convey and on how likely someone is to do whatever we are suggesting that they do.

Frames of Meaning

As we hear language we process it using our own internal imagery. This is 'coloured' by our previous experiences, our imprinted beliefs, our culture and the context, which gives a meaning to the word. These meanings or frames are specific to each individual and the

The Handbook of Contemporary Clinical Hypnosis: Theory and Practice, First Edition.
Edited by Les Brann, Jacky Owens and Ann Williamson.
© 2012 John Wiley & Sons, Ltd. Published 2015 by John Wiley & Sons, Ltd.

patient's frame may be totally different from that of our own. Some 'frames' are useful; others are not. Those that are restrictive and unhelpful we may wish to help our patients change by altering their words to something more resourceful.

Common 'frames'

Migraine = incapacitating headache necessitating bed rest and sleep
         = (unconsciously) time out
Cancer = dying a painful death very soon
MS   = becoming confined to wheelchair

'Alcoholism/depression/smoking is an illness' – therefore:

1   it is genetic
2   it is not my fault
3   I can do nothing about it
4   I take tablets to correct the problem
5   the doctor is powerful
6   the patient is powerless

Verbal Reframing

To reframe is to help the patient to see the situation or symptom from a different angle, or to disrupt a preconceived idea. All therapy could be seen as re-framing in that in therapy one tries to lead the patient to taking a different perspective on themselves, their problems and their life. Once the meaning is changed the associated feelings, thoughts or actions also change.

Example of Reframes

Instead of talking about a rebellious and stubborn teenager, direct attention to the fact that this may be partly because they have ideas and feel they know their own mind – a beginning of independence.

When you hear 'must', suggest 'prefer' in order to reduce the attached emotion.

For other examples of re-framing, notice how the feelings of anxiety and panic can be re-framed as an adrenalin rush (see page 176) and how pain can be reframed as discomfort (see page 310).

Suggestions are used both in and out of trance. Understanding some of the ways we can use language will make your suggestions more effective.

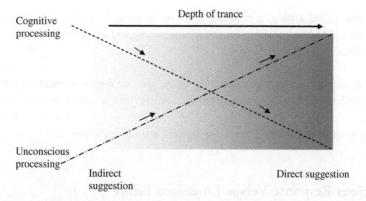

Figure 5.1 This figure shows how processing and type of suggestion vary with depth of hypnosis.

Direct and indirect suggestion

When someone is deeply in hypnosis their cognitive processing is less than in their normal 'conscious' state (see Fig 5.1) and direct suggestion can be given quite successfully.

"Just allow that socket to bleed just the right amount for healing to occur."
"As you listen to the sound of my voice you can become more and more relaxed."

In lighter levels of hypnosis more indirect suggestion may be more effective. An indirect suggestion could be seen as a direct suggestion that has been 'gift wrapped'.

"I know you don't know how you can turn off that bleeding, but your unconscious mind can turn it off just as you can imagine turning a tap off."

The choice of direct or indirect suggestion also depends upon the patient's style of learning and their personality. (See Figure 5.1.)

A post-hypnotic suggestion is a suggestion given in hypnosis that will be acted upon later, out of hypnosis.

"When you visit your dentist next week you will be pleasantly surprised at how calm you feel."

Embedded Command

Sometimes an effective way of giving suggestion is to mark out or emphasize the words of the suggestion with your voice tone when they are embedded in a conversation; in this way the direct suggestion appears to be indirect.

This is also called analogue marking and can be done by either changing voice tone slightly or changing head position on the specific words to be emphasized, which will have the same effect.

*"I wonder if, as you listen to the sound of my voice, you can **begin to relax** and as you listen and understand with your conscious mind . . . maybe your unconscious mind can help you to **relax** . . . or maybe your conscious mind can help you to **relax** even further while your unconscious mind understands the things I am talking about. . . ."*

Unconscious Response Versus Conscious Effort

Endeavour not to use the word 'try'. To consciously try implies failure – how many times have you tried to do something and failed? It is much better to *"Allow the conscious mind to wonder . . ."* while you ask the unconscious mind to produce a response. How often have we just tossed a screwed up ball of paper into the waste basket accurately without thinking about it whereas if we took aim and threw it would miss!

In hypnosis it is very important to encourage the unconscious response rather than conscious effort. For example when talking about special place imagery consciously the patient may wonder whether the best place would be the beach on holiday, in their back garden or curled up on the sofa in front of the fire and have difficulty choosing. If they *"Allow the conscious mind just to wonder . . . what image might come into your mind's eye of a place that is safe, relaxing, happy, "* their unconscious will almost certainly come up with a perfect place for them. Talking about the conscious and unconscious doing two different things, wondering and finding an image, also encourages dissociation which facilitates hypnosis.

Experiment or Exploration

At no time do you want to seed the idea of failure, so to suggest an exploration or experiment, which does not imply success or failure, is a much better way to frame any intervention. Phrases such as *"I wonder . . ."* or *"You might wonder whether . . ."* or *"Your conscious mind can wonder . . ."* can be usefully employed.

General Principles of Suggestion

When we induce hypnosis it is very important to feed back to the patient whatever response you notice they produce. Do not be in a rush – allow them time to respond and use a confident reassuring tone even if you do not actually feel very confident yourself. If you are giving a suggestion of a response which you want to occur in trance, then it is much more likely to happen if you *"Wonder when . . ."* rather than *"Wonder whether . . ."* it will happen.

As you can see from chapter 4, imagery is an extremely effective way to communicate. When 'painting' a word picture it is important to remember that the patient's image may be different from the one you are imagining. As well as directing experience through all the different senses, using descriptive words (adjectives and adverbs) in any guided imagery is important, so long as you are not prescriptive but give choices to the patient (more on this later). Remember also that the images created by the patient will be more meaningful for them than any the therapist describes.

When giving suggestion it is clearly important to draw on and utilize the patient's own past experiences. The health professional can also, if it seems appropriate, relate their own experiences or utilize truisms, those stories or facts that are of general experience and held to be 'true'. (Examples appear later in this chapter.) Another useful tool is to describe another patient's experience, real or imaginary, in order to seed an idea.

"I would like to tell you about someone who came to see me last week who had a similar difficulty to yourself. He told me that he had found . . . very useful to him and I just wonder whether you might consider that. . . ."

Acknowledging and marking response

Always watch your patient and utilize any feedback, both verbal and non-verbal (see chapter 9 on induction). If you notice your patient swallow, mark it maybe with a *"That's right"* or an *"Hmmm"* so that at an unconscious level they know that you are with them; this helps to increase rapport. Remember that your patient can speak when in hypnosis and do not be afraid to ask for feedback, especially if you are unsure about what is happening. *"What are you feeling now?"* or *"Would you like to tell me what is happening just now?"* are often useful questions to use.

The 'yes set'

When giving suggestion it is useful to build on what you already have. If you direct your patient's attention to feelings and occurrences that are obviously true they will, consciously or unconsciously, agree. Once someone has agreed to three or four things they are more likely to agree to the next. This is well known to sales representatives and is often called the 'yes set', but it is really only pacing and then leading (see page 89 on building rapport).

The 'Yes Set'

"And you may begin to be aware of the support of the chair at your back, of your feet resting on the floor, of your hands resting gently on your lap and as you notice the sounds from outside this room you can allow yourself to become even more comfortable and relaxed. . . ."

Positive orientation

Suggestion tends to be more effective if couched in positive terms. The unconscious (or right brain, if you like that model – see page 98) does not process negatives–to "*. . . not feel anxious*" you first have to think about feeling anxious. Perhaps you could *not* think about a pink elephant?

Encouragement

We know that encouragement is associated more with praise than criticism (see page 164) so always give positive reinforcement, praise for what they have accomplished so far. This is utilized in compassionate friend imagery (see page 161).

Permissive language

Give choices and use permissive language; words such as 'may' and 'perhaps' are useful here. Be permissive also as regards the timing of the response rather than the response itself.

The double bind

The double bind, or apparent choice, is also a good language pattern to utilize: "*Do you want to take your glasses off before you go into hypnosis or do you want to keep them on?*" The patient by responding in either way agrees to go into hypnosis.

Assumption of response

Implication of response, assuming that the response will happen, is another useful pattern.

It is important however not to be too directive or if the response fails to occur you will lose some rapport and credibility, so give choices: "*I wonder which hand will start to feel lighter and begin to float up and up?*" or "*I wonder whether that feeling of numbness will start in your thumb or your fingers? Maybe in your palm or in the middle of your hand. . . .*"

Linkage

Using linkage is one of the most important tools in giving suggestion. One observes a response and links the next suggestion to that response: "*As your arm and hand begin to float up, feeling lighter and lighter . . . so you can become deeper and deeper relaxed.*"

It is important to actually wait for the response (in this example, of the hand beginning to move) before linking it to what you are hoping to achieve.

W	O	R	D	S	W	O	R	D	S	W	O	R	D
O	R	D	S	W	O	R	D	S	W	O	R	D	S
R	D	S	W	O	R	D	S	W	O	R	D	S	W
D	S	W	O	R	D	S	W	O	R	D	S	W	O
S	W	O	R	D	S	W	O	R	D	S	W	O	R
W	O	R	D	S	W	O	R	D	S	W	O	R	D

Figure 5.2 Words can become swords depending upon your perception.

Repetition

In giving suggestion, especially in hypnosis it is important to use repetition. It is a good idea to repeat suggestions two or three times; maybe using different words or images as it has long been known that repetition increases the memory and hence the effectiveness of the suggestion (Smith, 1896).

Negative Suggestion

Remembering the above, one can see how often we unintentionally give negative suggestions to our patients or patients and also to ourselves! Medical staff may say, "*This won't hurt!*" rather than "*You will be surprised at how quickly we can do this.*" (See Figure 5.2.)

When someone is in shock they are already in a quasi-hypnotic state and inadvertent words can easily become imprinted (see page 237) as negative suggestions. Some well meaning person saying "*You might have been killed*" after a road traffic accident has resulted in post-traumatic stress disorder in some patients (personal observation).

Equally direct positive suggestion can be surprisingly effective in these circumstances to reduce pain and bleeding (see page 53).

Informed Consent

When obtaining informed consent for procedures it is very easy to give negative suggestion, and with the patient being in a vulnerable and suggestible state this can give rise to avoidable anticipatory anxiety and increased morbidity. Obviously side effects and possible negative outcomes need to be explained to the patient but there are ways to do this that can leave the patient with positive feelings about the procedure.

Risks need to be put in a context that the patient can understand. For example, a risk of one in 1,000 could be described as ten people out of the population of the author's (AW) home town which has a population of around 10,000.

How a choice is worded has an influence on the decision then made, as evidenced by the work of Tversky and Kahneman (1981), who showed that choices involving gains are often risk averse whilst those involving losses are often risk taking.

For example if there is a decision to be made whether to enter a trial for a relatively new drug regime or whether to go for a standard best treatment option this may be influenced by how the choice is put. The physician could say that there is an 80% chance that the new regime would be successful and the ten-year survival rate was 70%. Or he could say that there would be a 20% chance of the new regime failing and even if it was successful 30% failed to achieve a ten-year survival. This gives the same information but framed in very different ways.

Talking about the possible risks could be prefaced by a phrase such as *"I am really pleased that I am required to tell you about the possible risks involved with this procedure because that gives me the opportunity to tell you how safe it is."*

It may be useful to talk first to the patient in a general way about risk. Everything carries an element of risk; we could slip in the shower and fracture our neck, or burn or cut ourselves whilst cooking in the kitchen, but we are not required to put up 'danger' signs in the home. In a hotel it is rather different; because of the risk of litigation such signs are often displayed although the danger might be presumed to be obvious.

It is important to 'sandwich' any discussion about risks and negative outcomes with future orientated positive suggestions such as *"When you look back on today you might be pleasantly surprised at how easily everything went."*

Suggestions against post-operative nausea and vomiting and for normal bowel action can be incorporated and could take the form of *". . . and you can look forward to that trickle of water over your tongue, down your throat, welcomed by your stomach and moved on in just the right way . . ."* or *"I wonder whether you can imagine your favourite meal and look forward to eating it. You can look forward to having a good appetite for your favourite food and drink."*

Having described the risks a useful suggestion may be *"You will be pleasantly surprised by how comfortable you will be as long as normal healing is continuing and when you look back on all this, you can remember how calm and comfortable you were."*

In summary:

- Give general positive future oriented perspective.
- Put risk in context.
- Describe risks.
- Put risks in context – a reminder.
- Give positive suggestions and positive future oriented perspective.

Metaphor

Throughout time, story, parable and metaphor have been used to convey information clearly and effectively. When we think of any great teacher we find that they use metaphor and parable. They tell a story that invokes images, and thereby emotions, within the listener. They take something that is unknown and graft it creatively onto something familiar.

Telling a story is a more powerful and a more memorable way of communicating than a simple statement of fact. In a therapeutic context, patterns of behaviour and relationships often need a language other than logic.

Word pictures such as are generated in stories and metaphors integrate right and left brain modes of processing; conscious and unconscious; linear verbal and non-linear sensory, imaginal forms of processing. This integration of logical cognitive processing and sensory imaginal processing helps to link intellectual rationality with emotional knowledge.

Content (imagery) of metaphor is processed within the right hemisphere whereas the structure and form contained in the words are processed in the left hemisphere (Danesi, 1989). Therefore metaphors need the functioning of both right and left hemispheres to be decoded both abstractly and conceptually so that their meaning can be understood.

Subjects typically make a link between their sensory and perceptual experience and metaphoric statements (Verbrugge & McCarrel, 1977) so you do not need to explain the metaphor or story. One should simply incorporate it into what you are saying and ensure that there are enough connections between the story and the patient's situation for the patient's unconscious mind to make the associations.

Another possible reason for the power of metaphorical communication is that it can bypass a patient's conscious defences or resistance to change and allow the suggestion of change to be accepted as it is presented in a non-threatening way as a story.

Styles of Metaphor

Verbal metaphor

There are three forms of verbal metaphor:

1   Patient generated metaphor
2   Intuitive empathic metaphor
3   Constructed metaphor

Patient generated metaphor.   The metaphors our patients use can often give us, as therapists, a powerful way of communicating with our patient and helping them to access the changes that they desire.

This can be how the patient views a problem: for instance *"... a can of worms," "... a pain in the neck,"* or *"I feel trapped ..."* Patient generated metaphor can also be generated by such questions as *"If I were seeing it, what would I see?"*

These metaphors can be explored to good effect with further (non-leading) questions: *"What do you see as you have that feeling of being trapped? What else do you see, what else is going on?"* Other senses are then introduced: *"What does it sound or feel like to be ...*" and then a beneficial change is suggested: *"If you could change it in some way what would you do?"*

Patient generated metaphor can be one of the principal tools used in treating psychosomatic symptoms or pain. All imagery techniques are basically metaphorical as they represent the problem, resource or symptom rather than being the thing itself.

> A depressed patient said that she saw herself as being in the bottom of a very dark pit. She was asked to stay with that image and describe what she was aware of as she was in the bottom of the dark pit. She said that very far away she could see a slight paleness as though there was the opening to the sky. She was then asked to look around and see whether there was anything there that might help. She found a torch and reported that there were ledges reaching up out of her pit but she could not reach them. Over the course of her therapy various stones and bricks appeared which represented things she had done or resources she could use and she built them up so that she could reach the ledge and begin her climb upwards and out of her pit. Metaphorically as she began to feel an improvement she began her ascent from the pit.

Intuitive empathic metaphor.   Often when in good rapport with a patient, the therapist may find a story, metaphor or idea popping into their mind and this can also be utilized. *"May I tell you the story that occurred to me while you were saying ...?"*

It may not be effective, but it very often is and should not be ignored because the therapist or health professional is too embarrassed to share their sudden thought.

Constructed metaphor.   Stories, fairy tales, myths and legends can act as a bridge to help us access a child's ability to learn; they can remind us of possibilities and options and show us different perceptions.

Constructed metaphor combines layers of meaning, inherent in the words and metaphors used, with a story that allows the message to be a communication to the patient at the level that it is needed. The therapeutic power is increased by allowing less precision in assigning meaning to the story by the therapist, allowing the patient to choose the most useful interpretation for themselves (Kopp, 1995).

Constructed metaphors may be:

1   Stories from the therapist's own background and experience
2   Truism metaphors – about nature or types of experience that are so universal that the patient cannot deny them
3   More complicated stories designed to make a point that are either metaphors that the therapist constructed previously, especially for a particular patient, or ones 'off the shelf' as it were

Jane – overwhelmed with emotions

Jane said that she was terrified of being overwhelmed by her emotions which was why she had not been for help previously. It was suggested to her that it was a little like repairing a dam wall; if one was about to do so, one would lower the level of the water first by finding the sluice gates. These might be rather rusty as they may not have been used for some time but with a little oil and some effort they could be successfully opened and allow some water to drain anyway in a safe and controlled manner.

Susan – everything changes

Susan was suffering from depression and felt that things would never get better. It was important for her to connect with the thought that everything changes, so metaphors were used from nature such as the changing seasons, how each season has different qualities, all of which can be experienced in different ways, how there is an endless cycle of death and renewal, how the caterpillar changes into a butterfly, how a seed grows into a great tree. . . .

The constructed metaphor needs to reflect the patient's problem in some way and point to some solution or experience that would be useful for the patient to access.

There are two main types of constructed metaphor: naturalistic and isomorphic.

Naturalistic metaphor. This is the simplest type of metaphor to construct. Firstly one determines the problem state of the patient and what they want to achieve, the solution state. One then thinks about the quality of the experience needed and develops a metaphor to engender it.

Present state	*Desired state*
Unsteadiness when walking	Walking more confidently

Quality needed
Balance

Develop stories about times when the patient had balance: as a child learning to walk, ride a bike, walking along on the top of a wall or fallen tree trunk or dancing.

Isomorphic metaphor. With this type of construction one determines the *elements* of the presenting problem and the *relationship* between them and then reflects these in the metaphor as in the example below.

Sarah – the cracked pot metaphor

Sarah thought she was a failure. She had an elder sister whom she felt was much more attractive and clever than she was. As she was speaking the well known tale of the cracked pot came to mind and I shared this with Sarah whilst she was in hypnosis to demonstrate to her that we all have different abilities and talents, even if sometimes we are unaware of them. *"There was once an old woman whose job it was to fetch water from the well each day. She had two earthenware pots suspended from a wooden pole that she carried on her shoulders. One pot was perfect but the other had a crack, so that each time the old woman came home from the well it was only half full. The cracked pot felt very ashamed of itself and very much admired the perfect pot. One day the old woman heard the cracked pot apologizing yet again for not being 'perfect' and said, "On our way home I want you to look along the path and tell me what you see." As the cracked pot looked she saw that alongside one edge of the path there were beautiful flowers growing. The old woman said to the cracked pot, "Everyday as we walked back from the well you watered the seeds from the crack in your side and now you can see the result. Your sister pot may hold more water than you but she didn't help the flowers grow on her side of the path."*

In this example of an isomorphic metaphor the two pots of course match with the two sisters.

The aim of any therapeutic intervention is to connect the patient with a different, more helpful perspective than they originally had, and imagery and metaphor can be a powerful way of doing this in an unthreatening but highly effective manner. For those who are interested in learning more about constructed metaphor, we can recommend the *Handbook of Hypnotic Suggestions and Metaphors* (Hammond, 1990).

Experiential metaphor

Experiential metaphor may use simple everyday objects to make the point experientially to the patient so that they have a visual rather than just an auditory input.

Life history paper (Beaulieu, 2004). This is useful when a patient's perception is that they have always had the problem. A piece of paper is taken to represent their life to date and a line marked off depicting the start of the problem to the present day, as in the example shown below. The black area in this example represents three years. The paper is then folded so that only the black area shows and the patient asked whether this is the way they wish to define themselves rather than by the whole (as the paper is unfolded).

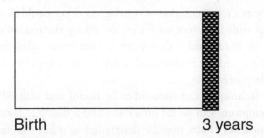

Birth   **3 years**

Plastic cups. This is a technique that is particularly useful in patients who have multiple problems in order to allow them to gain perspective. The props needed are up to ten plastic cups, a marker pen and some water. Prior to commencement one cup is filled with water.

The patient is asked to name the things that consume their energies or that they spend energy in worrying about. A cup is labelled for each item named and the patient places it on a table in whatever position they choose. This continues until they have described all the important factors for them. Some patients are very specific in exactly where on the table these are placed.

The patient is then given the cup full of water and asked to put the appropriate amount in each named cup to represent the amount of energy they give to each activity or person. They are asked to adjust the amounts until they are satisfied with the distribution. Once finished it is often found that they have not chosen a cup for themselves and have no water left anyway. It may be appropriate to point this out and ask them to use the cup that was filled with water for this purpose and to label it. If they have no water left they are asked if they wish to re-distribute the water in order to have some for their own cup.

The point of this process is for the patient to explore things of which they may not previously have been aware. Hence it is important to be non-directive.

When they are satisfied with the water distribution as a representation of their present situation they are asked if this is how they want it to continue, or do they want to make some changes. If they wish to make changes they re-distribute the water. It may be appropriate, when they have finished, directing them towards working out specifics of how and when they are going to make these changes.

It may be that they realize that they have not got enough water (energy). If this is the case they are asked to describe what they could do to generate more energy. This may be through sport, relaxation, time out and so on. Another cup of water could be used to represent the energy they would obtain in this way and they then decide how they will distribute it.

The labelled cups become externalized representations that can be talked about and moved. Some patients may wish to take the cups away with them. It is important to show respect for the cups; you do *NOT* pick them up and throw them into the bin and go on to the next part of the session. Usually the rest of the session is continued with reference back to the process and the cups.

In the case of grief following a death, once they have worked through and resolved any issues, it may become obvious to the patient that it is a 'waste' of energy pouring into the cup of a deceased loved one. It is possible to suggest that when they are ready, they up end the appropriate cup gently as a representation of moving on. They could be asked whether they wish to leave that cup with the therapist if they are taking the rest away. In this case it is agreed where it is to be stored and if they want to take it out again for the next session.

Respect for the patient and their values and beliefs must be kept in mind by the therapist throughout the whole process.

Empty chair type techniques can sometimes be useful and utilized metaphorically in various ways. The 'symptom' can be sat on a chair and a dialogue encouraged between it and the patient. Sometimes chairs may be designated as other significant people in the problem and the therapist facilitates dialogue between them and the patient, often with the patient (or sometimes the therapist) taking the part of the various people involved. Sometimes when the author (AW) is 'stuck' she has found it useful to sit the patient in the 'therapist's chair' and elicit some ideas from the patient as to what they need to hear. In all these role plays the patient will automatically enter a light trance state and often gain access to hitherto undiscovered insights.

Use of expressive arts in therapy

All the creative arts can be used as forms of experiential metaphor. These approaches have become specialist therapies in their own right, and their usefulness should not be judged by the brevity of these paragraphs – the interested student should seek out appropriate texts and training.

Dance (movement), music and art are all used in therapy to explore a difficulty metaphorically and then to connect the patient with their strengths, their desired state and inner ways of helping. By externalizing the problem the patient steps automatically into an observer position which may facilitate alternative insights and solutions. By utilizing the expressive arts the patient also enters a 'right brained' state which consequently enables greater access to their internal resources (Edwards, 1993).

In its simplest form, encouraging a patient who is emotionally distressed or suffering with depression to do something such as cross stitch embroidery, colouring in pictures or mandalas can act as a distraction from their feelings and at the same time facilitate a shift into a right brained state which is linked to the resting phase of the body or the relaxation response.

Sometimes patients have difficulty verbalizing their feelings, and using art, music or dance (movement) to represent their problem can be helpful. Having focused on expressing the problem the therapist can then suggest that they focus on how they would like to feel and express that also through their chosen modality. The patient can then be focused on how intuitively they could change the picture, sound or movement creatively to begin to feel better. This draws on Jung's concept of active imagination whereby if we allow the unconscious to present images to us, either in imagination or through authentic movement, we can access our unconscious resources to resolve emotional difficulties that our conscious rationality is unable to solve (Jung, 1935).

It is important that the patient realizes that the drawing/sound/dance is not being judged as a performance but that it is the process that is important. A perfectionist, for example, might need to be guided to simply doodle rather than produce a work of art! Encouraging patients to dance or utilize some other form of representation at home when no one is watching allows for full expression, but care must be taken to ensure that they spend only a short time representing their problem otherwise this will act as a negative rumination – time must be spent rehearsing the desired state.

Creative writing such as writing letters to express feelings (with the caution of not actually sending them) has been found helpful in anger management, grief and loss. Writing a letter from a future perspective (a year or two into the future) can be useful in helping someone determine what is really important to them and what goals they really want to work toward.

Ideomotor modelling using Playdoh or Plasticine is another example of a way to externalize the emotional difficulty so long as this is done without conscious thought; utilizing a light trance state here can be helpful and an example utilizing this is given below.

Ideomotor Modelling

After establishment of ideomotor signals (IMS) for 'yes' and 'no', say:

In a few moments I am going to ask you, the unconscious mind, to take control of your hands. I am doing this so that the unconscious mind can create a model to explore the problem you have been having. Are you prepared to do this?

IMS response.

In a few seconds I am going to ask you, the unconscious mind, to take over control of your hands. In a few moments time when I say the word NOW your unconscious mind can take over control of your hands so that they become detached and no longer under conscious control. Maybe you will lose feeling and sensation, or maybe they will feel somehow different, perhaps lighter, perhaps that they no longer belong to you. Do you, the unconscious mind, agree to this?

IMS response.

Thank you. I would like you to imagine, just pretend, that you are looking down at yourself from somewhere above. Take a position somewhere above us so that you can see yourself sitting there. As I say the word NOW in a few moments time you will see the hand you have chosen reach out to take the Playdoh from me. Then you will see your hands shaping the Playdoh without any conscious knowledge of what is being created. Maybe you will notice your eyes opening, or maybe they will remain closed, but your hands will model without any conscious control, and this will be linked in some way to the problem you have been having. And when your unconscious mind has finished your eyes will close and you will sink down into a very relaxed state, even more deep than you are right now.

NOW . . . NOW.

Watch the modelling activities.

Thank you . . . well done! Has your unconscious mind finished its work in shaping the model?

IMS response.

That's good. So your unconscious mind has modelled something which is in some way related to the problem you have been having. If you are still looking down at yourself from above, just gently drift back down and in a few moments time I will ask you to open your eyes. When you open your eyes you are looking down at the model you have made and seeing in it just what it means as far as your unconscious mind is concerned. You are seeing in that model some part of your unresolved problem. But, remember, your unconscious mind is your guardian, and you will experience no more hurt than you need to, in order to begin to resolve your problem. And when you have seen in the model all you need to see, you can close your eyes and let yourself enter into whatever feelings it produces within you. And you can let yourself feel those feelings secure in the knowledge that you are perfectly safe. However, can I check first with your unconscious mind that you ready to look at the model in order to explore the problem?

IMS response.

Okay – open your eyes.

When the eyes close again:

Staying as you are, if it would help, you can talk to me.

Wait for any response.

If not and you are ready to proceed give me a 'yes' signal.

IMS response.

So now I would like you to take that position again somewhere above us so that you can see yourself sitting there. And as I say the word NOW in a few moments time you will see your hands again shaping the Playdoh without any conscious knowledge of what is being created. Maybe you will notice your eyes opening, or maybe they will remain closed, but your hands will model without any conscious control, and this will be linked in some way to a creative solution to the problem that you have been having, a solution that is right for you as a whole person. And when your unconscious mind has finished your eyes will close and you will again sink down into a very relaxed state, even more deep than you are right now.
NOW . . . NOW.

Watch the modelling activities.

Thank you . . . well done! Has your unconscious mind finished its work in shaping the model?

IMS response.

> *That's good. So your unconscious mind has modelled something which is in some way related to a creative and satisfactory solution to the problem you have been having. If you are still looking down at yourself from above, just gently drift back down and in a few moments' time I will ask you to open your eyes. When you open your eyes you are looking down at the model you have made and seeing in it just what it means as far as your unconscious mind is concerned. You are seeing in that model some part of your solution to the problem. And when you have seen in the model all you need to see, you can close your eyes and let yourself enter into whatever feelings it produces within you. And you can let yourself feel those feelings secure in the knowledge that you are perfectly safe. However, can I check first with your unconscious mind that you ready to look at the model in order to explore some solution?*

IMS response.

> *Okay – open your eyes.*

When the eyes close again:

> *Staying as you are, if it would help, you can talk to me.*

Pause.

> *Does your unconscious mind think that you have seen and felt all you need to experience from this session?*

IMS response.

> *Does your unconscious mind feel that this session has been helpful in resolving the problem you have been having?*

IMS response.

> *Will your unconscious mind put these new learnings and perspectives into effect over the next few days, and so allow the problem that you were having begin to resolve?*

IMS response.

> *In a few moments this session will be over, and when you bring yourself back to the here and now you will remember or forget just as much as you need to remember or forget, in order for you to begin to resolve the problem you have been working on.*

Below are two case studies contributed by Gardenia Imber where making a picture collage, and the use of walking (a spatial metaphor) was used as a basis for the therapeutic interventions.

The cases outlined below describe therapeutic work using 'Naturalistic Hypnosis' or 'The Common Everyday Trance' (Rossi & Lippincott, 1992). This is therapeutic hypnosis without the use of a formal, recognized hypnotic induction: what Erickson called 'The General Waking Trance' used when he 'dared' not use obvious hypnotic induction (in Rossi *et al.*, 2008). The general waking trance involves 'intense response attentiveness' and 'intense mental absorption' on the part of the patient. Rossi proposes that these states are functionally related to 'novelty, enrichment and exercise (both mental and physical) that can turn on activity dependent gene expression and activity-dependent brain plasticity; that are the molecular-genomic and neural basis of memory, learning, consciousness, and behaviour change' (p185).

Novel experiences were used to enrich the therapeutic work. In the first instance, pictures selected by the patient were utilized; in the other, physical movement through the therapy space was employed. Zeig (2008) refers to hypnosis as a 'symbol-drama of change' presented to the patient as a method where "*. . . by living this experience you will be different.*" He encouraged the use of dramatic methods in therapy 'to promote change and make understandings more memorable'.

Additional hypnotic methods were included. Ego-state therapy (Watkins & Watkins, 1997) focuses on issues that divide the self and on the development of more integrated functioning and re-nurturing scripts (Murray-Jobsis, 1990), weaving various types of possibilities into age regression. Such methods 'invite the patient to use their imaginative capacities' and 'to re-experience a more complete life beginning, adding nurturing experiences that may have been missed or inadequate' (Phillips, 2004).

Picture method.   The first case involves a woman of 55 years. She was a 'compliant' child who never 'answered back' for fear of distressing consequences. She could 'lose herself in books', creating rich inner realms of mental imagery and bringing stories to life, therein experiencing pleasure.

She described presenting a 'false front', seeking to fit in. When attempting leisure activities she had discomforting tension and anxiety. Her goal was to relax and enjoy herself with others and in leisure pursuits of her choosing, rather than experiencing this as wrong, or less important, than accomplishing domestic or work tasks.

The patient had mentioned she could not "*even sit and relax with a magazine.*" This expressed desire was utilized to create a bridge between 'required tasks' and leisure.

It was suggested that she produce a collage of images, taken randomly from magazines, in her own time, at home. It was explained that the pictures would be the basis of future therapy sessions. The aim of the activity was to disrupt her usual pattern of experience with magazines by making it into a 'task'. This was explained to her to encourage motivation and as an invitation to 'collaborative' rather than 'compliant' engagement. She agreed to make a collage to represent her past, present and future to bring to the next session. The pictures lent themselves to being used for hypnotic experiences.

'The picture has its own reality and even creates its own chemical flow in the body like a real event does'. In the ISM theory of imagery, the ability to mentally see a picture is said to be natural for each of us. 'Every important image (I) creates bodily or somatic feelings (S) with vague or clear meanings (M)' (Ahsen, 1984). Taktek and Hochman (2004) found that individuals 'did not have to first imagine the chemicals' (feelings) in the body, instead seeing the mental picture involved them without the person even being aware of it. Following the verbal instruction to engage with the image, the person could immediately use pictures in order to create emotional states and come to know how the mind and body work together.

The pictures she produced were utilized to enable relaxation, re-nurturing and ego strengthening.

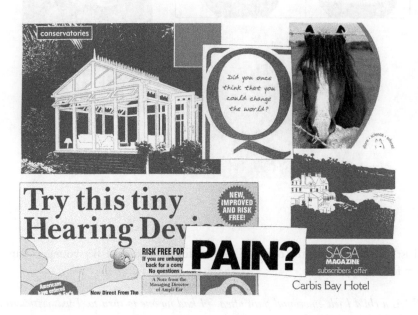

Past

The 'Past' pictures and words provided a focus for discussion of her younger years and pointers for therapy:

'Pain?' *"As a child I felt emotional pain often – I had no one to turn to. I was criticized and punished frequently."*

She had internalized the harsh mother who never let her be.

'Nature' *"I used to enjoy walks with my father in the countryside."*

Nature pictures could induce relaxation and ease.

'Horse' *"My Grandmother took me riding. She was the only one who let me play."*

Her Grandmother could be suggested as an ally in her quest for enjoyment.

Present

'The Garden' *"I've had my garden landscaped; I'd like to be able to potter and relax in it, yet I pull back."*

Step into the picture.   It was suggested that it was possible to step into the picture and to feel the sensations of being in the garden, to feel whether it is warm or breezy, to find a spot that pleases her. To see what she can see, hear what she can hear and feel what she can feel as if she is in the garden right now.

> *"How does it feel?"*
> *"It feels soothing, peaceful."*
> *"Now step into experiencing what it is to be the hedge, with its firm lines, still and unmoving. How does that feel?"*
> *"Steady, a bit serious."*
> *"And if you leave the hedge and step into being the plant with small flowers that tumbles onto the pathways? How does that feel?"*
> (She smiled.) *"This feels much lighter, like I can explore."*

Ego-Strengthening suggestion

> *"Not even the paths can stop these flowers flowing, doing what it is they wish to do. Whenever you want to feel free to do as you please, all you need do is step into the plant and remember you too can do as you wish."*

(Patient nods.)

> *"Step out of the picture when you are ready, bringing the good feelings with you to take into the day ahead. How do you feel compared to when you arrived today?"*
> *"More relaxed, less tired."*

For homework she was encouraged to continue stepping into the picture exercise. Also to be sure she can feel her feet firmly on the ground after the exercise here or at home.

To counter the impact of the internalized disapproving mother, the picture of the garden was also used to introduce re-nurturing. She was invited to step into the picture and to meet her younger self there, to be her own best parent and encourage her child-self to explore and play. In daily life she went to a botanical garden and imagined supporting her child self to engage in the 'children's greenhouse activities'. In order to keep negative thoughts at bay, she created the 'bad parent police' coming to take her forbidding mother away.

When the patient wanted to go swimming for the first time with friends, it was suggested that she step into the picture of the horse, to meet with her Grandmother and invite her to accompany her to the swimming pool to 'spur her on'. She was then encouraged to imagine her Grandmother with her when she went swimming and was gradually able to enjoy herself more with each visit.

The 'Warning!' picture was stepped into with the suggestion that she and her younger self could treat the exclamation marks as bowling pins or sculpt them into totem poles with funny faces.

The Future images were representative of her aim to reveal her inner self (the opening pods) and to feel carefree and light (the butterfly). At the end of her sessions she felt more able to relax both in company and alone. She had started dance lessons and was experiencing more pleasure in life.

Walking method.   This case concerns a man, aged 30. He had grown up in a rural area and enjoyed a rich fantasy life, playing alone as an only child. He was experiencing anxiety when procrastinating. He put off doing things that were important to him and believed he was deluding himself regarding his aspirations as a writer. Deadlines increased his anxiety yet he was better able to complete study or work tasks under pressure. The idea of presenting himself to the world in any way that was not as perfect as he wished to be had him hold back and feel frustrated. His goal was to manage his anxiety and his time, so as to commence writing.

Erickson's (1990) visual hallucination screen technique for dissociation (see chapter x) and Watkins's (1971) affect (somatic) bridge (see page 127) were combined and adapted into a walking process for this person.

It was suggested he would experience the therapy space as a store of memories he could walk through. He would be able to step into an illustrative memory, identify the event, fully experience the sights, sensations, sounds and emotions and then step out of the event to watch himself, as if watching a performance on a screen. It was explained that we would be able to use this memory as a 'blueprint' to step further back in time to find the first ever time he had experienced this emotion and accompanying bodily sensations.

The process was demonstrated to further focus his attention, explaining it again as the therapist walked it out. He was asked if he would be willing to move through the space thus, so we *"would be able to explore and understand what originally happened to cause this feeling?"* He agreed. It was suggested he stand to begin walking through the memory store with the assurance that the therapist would walk with him. A pleasurable experience was first sought to enable him to become familiar with engaging in the process. Thereafter his discomfort was worked with.

> *"I would like you to find a younger self, experiencing the anxiety of not getting anything done, to walk, here or there* (I point) *in this space that holds all your memories and to stop when you've stepped into a memory."* I join him in walking to find the memory. *"Can you let me know where you are, what you are experiencing and how you feel?"*
>
> *"I'm at a party, a few months ago. I didn't finish the fancy dress outfit I was making in time. I'd imagined going in an amazing costume and having great conversations with people. But I'm the 'boring me' instead. I feel sick, and disappointed; I don't want to talk to anyone."*

(*Note:* This matched the patient's description of not wishing to present himself in a less than perfect way to others and holding back regarding his creative expression as a writer. In order to explore underlying factors, age regression using affect [somatic] bridge was chosen.)

"I would like you to let the context drop away, the room, the people, let it fade, until just the sick feeling and disappointment remain and to nod when you've done that."

He focuses and nods.

"Now, let us step back in time, through the memory store, walk to find an earlier, important time, when a younger and perhaps smaller you felt similarly. A time that can help you be free of putting things off. Once you have found the experience, step out of it" that is, take one step, *"to watch your younger self and tell me what is happening."*

We walk together. He walks, pauses and steps aside.

"I'm searching for fake ammunition from the museum. I want it for the castle I'm building. I'm about seven. It's not in my toy box, I think my Mum's taken it; she doesn't approve of war games. I look upset."
"What is younger you most upset about?"
"He's disappointed, in his head it was going to be great, now it's ruined."

(*Note*: As the severe distress in the initial 'party' scenario was due to not having completed the task of making an outfit to wear, it is likely that the patient will benefit more from successful completion of the castle as a younger self than from distracting younger self.)

"How do you feel about younger you?"
"I want to distract him, so he's not sad and tell him although he hasn't had the great outcome he'd imagined – that's just the way it is sometimes. Older me behaves like younger me. He may be wasting his life away chasing dreams. I feel concerned about him."
"Step out one more step and as 'observer', look at older you, what do you see? What does 'observer' (from two steps away) think of younger him?"
"I want him to snap out of it and tell him he can build a different, better thing."

At times a further step away from the scenario allows the patient to become more compassionate, as this was not the outcome he was asked:

"Is there anybody who really understands seven year old you who could be with him and ask him what he would like?"
"My Granddad."
"Can you invite Granddad to join him, and step into older you and into scenario with him. What does younger you tell Granddad?" (Steps forward two steps.)
"He'd really like to find the ammunition to put on the castle but Mum's too busy to ask her."
"Let Granddad ask whether seven year old you prefers for Mum to tell Granddad where it is or for her to find it and be with him when he puts it on the castle?"
"He wants Mum to come, and he's looking excitedly at the castle again."

"Let things unfold as younger you would best like. Step into younger you. Let all the good feelings of having Mum help you be felt and have Mum tell the younger you how great the castle is or anything you would most like to hear."

"Granddad tells Mum it's important she get the ammunition because they need it to defend the castle. Mum brings the ammunition; she's giving it to me. Granddad's giving me a military cap to wear." (A broad grin is on patient's face.) *"Mum looks happy too because she's taken a break."*

"How do you feel as younger you?"

"I'm excited; I want them to go now. I want to play with the castle on my own."

"I would like you to get ready to step into older you again, bringing all the good feelings with you, and to say goodbye to younger you and Granddad and Mum as you bring all the good feelings back with you." (Steps to the side.)

"Younger me is too engrossed to say bye, we're leaving him to it." (Laughing.)

"So taking the good feelings with you, let us sit a while before you carry them with you into the days ahead. . . . How are you feeling now as older you?"

"I feel really good, relieved."

We sit until he is ready to leave the session, alert and associated with the here and now.

Following therapy he was making longer term plans and taking small steps towards them. He had asked someone to help him create a writing den. He no longer made changes 'for the sake of it', an active way of putting things off. He said he used to shut himself off in his room, moping. Now, he tells himself *"You are not a kid anymore, you can go outside and do something; you don't have to sit alone in your room."* He was feeling more positive and purposeful.

Both of these individuals were highly motivated to overcome their difficulties. The methods employed with these patients were chosen specifically because in a motivated subject it is possible for a therapist to create the expectancy that hypnosis will allow the subject to have certain experiences and responses. This response expectancy was considered the essence of hypnosis by Kirsch (1991). Also, the individuals had expressed a capacity for fantasy proneness and a capacity for vivid sensory experiences, traits that suggested they would readily engage in and benefit from hypnotic interventions (Wilson & Barber, 1982).

This chapter describes how important are the words that we use and also how non-verbal communication may be utilized to help patients express and deal with their feelings. Paramount in any therapeutic communication, whether verbal or non-verbal, is the ability of the health professional or therapist to listen to their patient. They will often tell you metaphorically, either verbally or through their non-verbal behaviour, what the difficulty is and how best to approach resolution. Rapport developed between patient and therapist needs to take account of both verbal and metaphorical communications for effective suggestion.

Principles of suggestion: a reminder

- Repetition increases effectiveness.
- Vividness increases effectiveness.

- Strong emotion increases effectiveness.
- Positive phrasing increases effectiveness.
- If you think you can't – trying won't succeed!

References

Ahsen, A. (1984), ISM: the triple code model for imagery and psychophysiology. *Journal of Mental Imagery*, 8 (4), 15–42.

Beaulieu, D. (2004), Workshop on using experiential metaphor, Scarborough, UK.

Danesi, M. (1989), The neurological coordinates of metaphor. *Communication and Cognition*, 22 (1), 73–86.

Edwards, B. (1993), *Drawing from the right side of the brain*. London, Harper Collins.

Erickson, M. H. (1990), Erickson's age regression techniques, in Hammond, D. C. (Ed.) *Handbook of hypnotic suggestions and metaphors*. New York, W. W. Norton.

Hammond, D. C. (Ed.) (1990), *Handbook of hypnotic suggestions and metaphors*. New York, W. W. Norton.

Jung, C. G. (1935), *Analytical psychology: its theory and practice*. The Tavistock Lectures. London, Tavistock.

Kirsch, I. (1991), The social learning theory of hypnosis, in Lynn, S. J. & Rhue, J. W. (Eds.) *Theories of hypnosis: current models and perspectives*. New York, Guilford Press.

Kopp, R. R. (1995), *Metaphor therapy: using client-generated metaphor in psychotherapy*. New York, Brunner/Mazel.

Murray-Jobsis, J. (1990), Re-nurturing: forming positive sense of identity and bonding, in D.C. Hammond (Ed.) *Handbook of hypnotic suggestions and metaphors*. New York, W. W. Norton.

Phillips, M. (2004), Joan of Arc meets Mary Poppins: maternal re-nurturing approaches with male patients in ego state therapy. *American Journal of Clinical Hypnosis*, 47 (1), 3–12.

Rossi, E., Erickson-Klein, R. & Rossi, K. (2008), Novel activity, dependent approach to therapeutic hypnosis and psychotherapy: the general waking trance. *American Journal of Clinical Hypnosis*, 51 (2).

Rossi, E. & Lippincott, B. (1992), The wave nature of being: ultradian rhythms and mind-body communication, in Lloyd, D. & Rossi, E. (Eds.) *Ultradian rhythms in life processes: a fundamental inquiry into chronobiology and psychobiology*. New York, Springer-Verlag.

Smith, W. G. (1896), The place of repetition in memory. *Psychological Review*, 3 (1), 21–31.

Taktek, K. & Hochman, J. (2004), Ahsen's triple code model as a solution to some persistent problems within Adams' closed loop theory and Schmidt's motor schema theory. *Journal of Mental Imagery*, 28 (1-2).

Tversky, A. & Kahneman, D. (1981), The framing of decisions and the psychology of choice. *Science*, 211, 453–8.

Verbrugge, R. R. & Mccarrel, W. S. (1977), Metaphoric comprehension: studies in reminding and resembling. *Cognitive Psychology*, 9, 494–533.

Watkins, J. G. (1971), The affect bridge: a hypnoanalytical technique. *International Journal of Clinical & Experimental Hypnosis*, 19, 21–7.

Watkins, J. G. & Watkins, H. H. (1997), *Ego states: theory and therapy*. New York, W. W. Norton.

Wilson, S. C. & Barber, T. X. (1982), The fantasy prone personality: implications for understanding imagery, hypnosis and parapsychological phenomena, in Sheikh, A. A. (Ed.) *Imagery: current theory, research and application.* New York, John Wiley & Sons, 340–87.

Zeig, J. K. (2008), The (dramatic) process of psychotherapy. *American Journal of Clinical Hypnosis*, 51 (1), 41–55.

6

Safety

Mrs Jacky Owens

Introduction

In this chapter, guidelines as to who might be a suitable patient for hypnotherapy will be discussed. Contraindications and limits will be stated. The difference between hypnosis in an emergency setting and within a more formal setting will be discussed, and safety issues highlighted. This chapter will also cover the problems inherent in the use of hypnosis for entertainment and the need for proper training in the field in which hypnosis is being used.

Suitability for Hypnosis Interventions

As we said in chapter 1, hypnosis is a consent state requiring co-operation (Waxman, 1989; Yapko, 1995), and those who could benefit must first and foremost agree to it; people who do not wish to experience trance will not use it. It does not however necessarily follow that all those who would agree to its use are suitable candidates for this type of technique.

Whilst babies obviously are not suitable, young children usually are and those skilled in paediatrics can use hypnosis with some as young as two years (Olness & Kohen, 1996).

Age is not a barrier to hypnosis work but the ability to focus and concentrate is needed. These skills are often impaired with age, and each potential patient needs to be assessed.

For most therapists psychosis is a reason to avoid hypnosis, and where mental illness is concerned hypnosis should be carried out only with the cooperation of the caring

The Handbook of Contemporary Clinical Hypnosis: Theory and Practice, First Edition.
Edited by Les Brann, Jacky Owens and Ann Williamson.
© 2012 John Wiley & Sons, Ltd. Published 2015 by John Wiley & Sons, Ltd.

physician. Some therapists with the necessary expertise may work with those prone to psychosis, including schizophrenia, using hypnosis (Hart & Spiegel, 1993; Santiago & Khan, 2007), but it is important to realize that the use of imagery may lead to a loosening hold on reality in some cases and should only be used by those used to dealing with such patients.

Those with some forms of dementia may not be able to engage in the process, although more recent research supports the use of hypnosis with this group (Duff & Nightingale, 2007). Others with diminished mental capacity (e.g. head trauma) also may not be suitable for hypnotic interventions, although the expertise of the hypnotherapist and the individual case need to be considered in each patient. There is emerging evidence that some stroke victims can be helped through the use of hypnosis (Diamond *et al.*, 2006).

At one time it was deemed unwise to use hypnosis with depression, and although this is no longer considered to be the case (Yapko, 1997), caution should be exercised especially with anyone known to be at risk of suicide. The danger period for suicide is always just as the patient is beginning to respond to therapy whatever approach is used.

Normally one would expect that patients and therapists share a common language, and for the bulk of work this is so. It is possible however to work through an interpreter; the inherent difficulties in such circumstances are addressed in chapter 39.

Being deaf does not preclude the use of hypnosis, but some creativity is necessary on behalf of the therapist. Lip reading can be a mechanism to achieving successful hypnosis since eye closure is not required for alert hypnosis (Isenberg & Matthews, 1995; Wark, 2006).

Hypnosis in a Formal Setting

A formal setting is used here to describe therapy that takes place in a planned manner often in a surgery or designated therapy room. It is necessarily a calm and structured intervention where the 'norm' is to follow the tenets of best practice, as successful outcomes are deemed to be dependent upon:

- Providing an *environment* conducive to the delivery of therapy
- Taking a *history* that leads to an understanding of the patient and the patient's needs
- Establishing a *rapport* with the patient, 'rapport' defined in the *Oxford English Dictionary* as a sympathetic relationship or understanding
- Where indicated, assessing the subject's *hypnotizability* using one of the recognized hypnotizability scales
- Checking the *motivation* which is deemed to be crucial to a successful outcome (Waxman, 1989)
- Increasing *expectancy* (of both patient and therapist) that encompasses a positive attitude and a belief that they are a responsive subject (Heap and Aravind, 2002)
- Gaining *consent* to the use of hypnosis, usually simply a verbal consent
- *Explanation* of the procedure

Hypnosis in an Emergency Setting

There are many occasions when people can be helped where it is not possible to follow the above described norm. Such instances could include:

- At the roadside helping someone who has been involved in a road traffic accident
- Acute pain such as with sickle cell anaemia, patients in crisis or presenting with sore mouth as a consequence of chemotherapy especially in those undergoing a bone marrow transplant, or chest pain (N.B.: it is important not to mask the diagnostic value of acute pain: see chapter 21.)
- In casualty departments during potentially painful procedures such as manipulation of a dislocation or fracture
- Breathing difficulties such as in an asthma episode
- Acute anxiety regarding an intended procedure such as venepuncture, lumbar puncture, bone marrow aspirate or (breast, liver, nodule) biopsy
- Intractable nausea, commonly due to chemotherapy, radiotherapy or anti-biotic treatments
- A labour which does not occur at the expected time or in a safe environment
- Burns

The practical approaches used in these situations will be described elsewhere in this book, but in these situations the patient is already in a hypnotic like state and not behaving in their normal rational way.

> Spontaneous trance is a common phenomenon in medical and dental situations, where a strange environment, combined with fear of pain or discomfort, disrupts a patient's usual state of consciousness and makes it easier to slip into an altered state. (Pratt *et al.*, 1988)

In an urgent or emergency setting, it is perfectly possible to achieve successful outcomes working against the norm described above, that is:

- The *environment* for such therapy is often noisy, public and uncomfortable but will not necessarily detract from achieving trance.
- The *history* elicited is often partial, scant or arrived at non-verbally. Patients in distress want their distress relieved as quickly as possible; attempting to draw out a full history is usually counter-productive.
- Establishing a *rapport* with the patient: 'You have rapport when your patient feels understood and he or she feels you have an appreciation for the value and complexity of his or her personal experience' (Yapko, 1995).
- *Hypnotizability* is not known or assessed.
- The desire to relieve a distressing symptom is highly *motivating*.
- *Expectancy* can be measured by the reaction a patient gives when a therapist introduces themselves.

- *Consent* to be helped is often all that is required. To ask for consent for the use of hypnosis requires also that one gives *explanations* of hypnosis; but this is counter-productive in the emergency setting. A precedent has been set by esteemed exponents of the medical use of hypnosis, in particular Dabney Ewin, who describes simply holding out his hand to a man with a dislocated shoulder in an emergency room and saying, *"I'm Dr Ewin. I can help you. Will you do what I say?"* and, on getting a 'yes' response, proceeded to hypnotize him for the corrective manipulation (Ewin, 1999).

Informed Consent

We feel that it is best practice to gain informed consent if hypnosis is specifically planned; however this is not as straightforward as it may appear. Often gaining consent is deemed to interfere with the therapeutic alliance and is time consuming, in which case we suggest sending the patient a consent form along with any other necessary questionnaires and have them bring them back to the planned session. When treating patients in hospital, verbal consent only may be required. Heap and Aravind (2002) posit that if you are only using suggestions of eye closure, easy breathing and relaxation, you may prefer not to describe your technique as hypnosis; indeed, Ewin (1999; and see above) does not elicit formal consent or give explanations when working in the emergency room.

Written consent is required if you wish to use patient case material, including photographs and anonymized outcome data, in case presentations or publications.

The Use of a Chaperone

Whether hypnosis is used in the formal or informal situation, the use of a chaperone should be considered. Such use offers a safety net for both the therapist and the patient. Video recording is now common in the formal setting and obviates the need for a chaperone whilst there are usually several people attending in the emergency setting. Many therapists are comfortable working with a patient companion in attendance, although Heap and Aravind (2002) do not agree.

Touch

When using hypnosis it is important to be aware that if touch is used, for example in setting an anchor (see page 145), then this should be discussed beforehand and permission obtained. When in hypnosis it is good practice to warn the patient if you are going to take their hand or touch their shoulder so that they are prepared for this and not startled.

Problems Inherent in the Use of Hypnosis for Entertainment Purposes – Stage Hypnosis

Hypnosis for entertainment purposes is usually referred to as 'stage hypnosis', and as such it is governed by the Hypnotism Act of 1953. This act applies to the premises in which the entertainment is to take place, not the hypnotist who performs therein. These hypnotists are usually very skilled in inducing trance and obtaining compliance from subjects since their livelihood depends upon their skill. In stage presentations of hypnosis the subjects have all volunteered to be there, and there are many examples of people exhibiting strange and extreme behaviour in public with no hypnosis, such as in the TV show 'The Generation Game', some of the American and Japanese game shows and, more recently, the plethora of reality television shows.

Stage hypnosis keeps alive the various misconceptions around the subject. The general public's belief seems to be that in hypnosis people will tell the truth about things they would normally lie about. Because this is not true, many countries do not allow the use of hypnotically retrieved information to be stated in a court of law. With particular relevance to the law is the misconception that hypnosis can improve memory. The phenomenon of false memory syndrome emerged due to the inexpert handling of hypnotized people being led to believe inaccuracies about their past; commonly this would relate to some form of abuse, often sexual in nature. There is also a belief that what occurs during a hypnotic session cannot be remembered. Whilst it is possible to plant a post-hypnotic suggestion (PHS) for forgetting and many stage hypnotists do, the usual purpose of therapy is to bring about change and for that to happen the subject needs to be aware of what has occurred. In certain circumstances, however, for instance when using techniques to reframe material, the patient maybe unaware consciously of the alternatives their mind has generated (see page 443).

Watching a stage presentation leads many people to believe that hypnosis occurs effortlessly and indeed one of the qualities of trance is that the subject feels it is effortless, yet those who practice hypnosis know that the subject is following given suggestions. Many believe that hypnosis cannot be faked yet research evidence shows that it can be, sometimes duping very experienced practitioners. Perhaps the most damaging to the medical use of hypnosis is the misconception that a hypnotized person can be made to do something they would not ordinarily do, for when a person is hypnotized control is not relinquished to the hypnotist (McConkey & Jupp, 1985–1986). In stage hypnosis the show is designed to make it seem that the hypnotist is in control and has 'power' over the subject. In reality stage hypnotists are expert at filtering their audience so that only highly hypnotizable people are kept on stage. These are expecting to perform and are either extroverted or psychologically hide behind the label of hypnosis, perpetuating the myth that the hypnotist is 'making' them perform. This context also enhances the role of social compliance.

A young man was experiencing great anxiety about his diagnosis of leukaemia. On being introduced to the hypnotherapist, he immediately said, *"They screwed everything else up in here, you're not going to screw my mind up as well – go away"*. Initially in the hospital this was not an unusual response. It was only after some time when the therapy had proven to be beneficial and the medical and nursing staff openly encouraged patients to see the therapist that this type of response lessened. Many patients expressed concern about being in control, and it was found that saying, *"If I could control another human being, I should not choose a sick patient but rather my bank manager"* often produced a wry smile and an agreement to work hypnotically.

Stage hypnotists do not always counter the suggestions they give to their subjects, and some suggestions if not removed before alerting the subject present a very real issue of safety. A PHS (see page 23) should be given to remove all the suggestions given in the stage show, but this is not always done.

The Need for Proper Training

The cause of medical hypnosis has been and is still being hindered by stage hypnosis, but also sometimes by the lay sector. This is a thriving, financially productive area, and these hypnotists, who make hypnosis their source of income, tend to be skilled in the art of hypnotism, but sadly the science, therapeutic skills and understanding are often lacking.

Here we have to take a look at the lay and medical training debate. Lay schools, of which there are many, often train all comers, some with professional qualifications but many who have none. The medical societies train people already qualified in some form of health care, usually to degree standard or an equivalent. (See Table 6.1 for a comparison.)

The divide between the medical and lay societies is still wide, and there is little meeting of the ways. The medical societies believe that to treat illness using any modality you have to understand first the illness and all its ramifications. This is the prerogative of medicine – the term 'medicine' is used here in its broadest sense to include all health care trained professionals. The key protection rests in there being an accountable body who register people in order to maintain standards and afford protection for patients. For health care professionals (doctors, dentists, nurses, radiographers, psychiatrists, psychologists, coun-sellors etc.), their registering bodies are this safeguard. The lay registering bodies may not have the same ability to protect patients.

The most concerning part about stage and lay hypnosis is the possible harm people may suffer. Several high profile cases have been brought against stage hypnotists where a volunteer subject has claimed consequential untoward effects and even a death (Heap, 1995; Leninhauz, 1981; Perry, 1979; Wagstaff, 2000) Many practitioners of medical hypnosis will have met or have patients whose problem at worst has been exacerbated and at best has not been resolved due to the inexpert handling of their problem by their therapist.

Table 6.1 Some of the similarities and differences between medical and 'lay' societies

Medical societies	Lay societies
View hypnosis as a tool to be used within an established discipline – an adjunct to other treatment modalities.	Tend to view hypnosis as a therapy in its own right and as able to be used to treat any problem.
Train those already qualified in some health care discipline that has a regulatory body governing their work.	Train all comers whatever their background and then affiliate the students to a lay body which may or may not be effective.
Members agree that they will only use hypnosis within their own area of expertise and level of hypnosis competency.	Often allow their members to treat all conditions and in many instances teach how to deal with lots of medical conditions.
Demand that members engage in regular clinical supervision.	Often make no stipulation regarding ongoing clinical supervision.
A condition of membership is to continually engage in updates (continuing professional development, or CPD).	Good ones encourage updating skills and practice.
Have a vetting system to oversee all applications.	Variable standards of vetting applications.

Clinical governance is provided through regulatory bodies, and with the government decree that all those working in health care need to be registered with one of their approved regulating bodies the protection for patients becomes stronger.

There is another issue that should be addressed in this chapter: that of guided imagery. Imagery has an important role to play in hypnotherapy and this is addressed in chapter 4. Increasingly guided imagery is being used to facilitate relaxation in both individual and group sessions. It is really important that the therapist understands the potential for harm, for it is all too easy to inadvertently trigger an abreaction. To serve an as example, consider the following: many guided imagery scripts will include water in some way, either a lake or beach scene or pool. If someone in the group has had a near death experience due to drowning, then that person is very unlikely to be relaxed at best and is likely to be in considerable distress at worst. Since in group therapy the therapist usually has no idea of the individuals' personal history, they do need to understand the potential for harm their words can have and tailor their language accordingly.

Before closing this chapter, we need to make mention again of false memory syndrome. Therapists using regression techniques risk eliciting strongly held but factually incorrect memories. Inexperienced therapists or those who have not undergone appropriate training may possibly implant a false memory in a patient resulting in a distressing and harmful outcome.

Dr. John F. Kihlstrom, professor of psychology at Yale University, has suggested the following definition of false memory syndrome:

> A condition in which a person's identity and interpersonal relationships are centered around a memory of traumatic experience which is objectively false but in which the person strongly believes. Note that the syndrome is not characterized by false memories as such. We all have memories that are inaccurate. Rather, the syndrome may be diagnosed when the memory is so deeply ingrained that it orients the individual's entire personality and lifestyle, in turn disrupting all sorts of other adaptive behavior.

False memory syndrome is also often characterized by the person avoiding or denying anything that might challenge their beliefs. The false memory may have very far reaching effects, disrupting both relationships and lives.

Hypnoanalysis, often used to explore the psychological underpinnings of problems, presents some safety issues to be noted. It is vital when undertaking this work that the patient is provided with a safety anchor and that they are held in a dissociated state (this is covered in greater detail in chapter 26). It is important the therapist does not probe for details after re-alerting but allows the patient to volunteer whatever information they remember from the session. Information accessed in hypnosis needs to be worked through therapeutically even if it is not historically true (see chapter 1).

Alerting From Trance

Care is needed in guiding patients into trance to ensure that they are safely held, even when difficult emotional issues are being dealt with; care is also needed on alerting the patient from trance. They should be guided to their full waking state and allowed to fully re-orientate into the present environment, ensuring that they are fully alert and all sensations are returned to normal.

Some patients show reluctance to alert, and this may be for a variety of reasons: perhaps they are feeling the best that they have felt in a long time and do not want it to end, or perhaps they are, in imagination, spending time with a departed loved one. To the novice this can be quite a worrying situation but we know that if left, eventually the patient will either naturally wake or fall asleep, and if time permits it may be wise to explore why they are not alerting using uncovering techniques. If the patient is in a hospital bed, you can suggest that when they are ready they drift into a restful, peaceful sleep, however if in a therapy room it is imperative that you have them re-alert. Elman (1964) suggests saying in a sharp tone that unless they alert they will not be able to reach this wonderful state again, however perhaps it is kinder to simply acknowledge their deep state, reassure them that they will be able to reach it again whenever they want or need to and count them awake in a fairly loud voice. If this does not work the first time, simply repeat it all and perhaps clap your hands together as you count. In reality this happens very rarely, and more commonly the patient has drifted into sleep.

Transference and Dependency

Transference occurs when a patient starts feeling towards their therapist emotions that have been engendered by some significant person (often a parent) in their past and suppressed. The dynamics of the therapy situation or something about the therapist may have triggered this feeling quite unconsciously in the patient, and it always has an important bearing on the presenting problem. It is important for the therapist to be aware of this when it occurs as it can be utilized to help the patient gain new insights. The patient may express love or hate, and the best way to safely deal with it is to continually refer it back to its source. Counter-transference occurs when the therapist's feelings and reactions to the patient also have their roots in their past relationships.

People seeking or referred for help are often in a vulnerable state and depend upon the therapist for help and care. The ultimate goal for the therapist has to be that of helping the patient establish self reliance and independent living, having addressed the referring issue. It is therefore important that the therapist gives a clear explanation of what hypnosis is and what may possibly be achieved with its use. It is equally important to dispel common myths, especially the myth that leads people to believe the hypnotist is in control. The patient needs to be really aware of how empowering this therapy can be. Thus by the therapist establishing boundaries at the beginning of therapy and teaching self hypnosis, they are unlikely to have to deal with issues of dependency.

Whilst there are many safety issues that need to be considered, the novice therapist should not be daunted. Mindful of the need to work within one's field of competence, the health professional already has the patient's safety as paramount and their existing clinical integrity should act as a sound basis for progress. As a further safeguard for both patient and therapist, it is essential that the hypnotherapist holds indemnity insurance for this additional specialty.

References

Diamond, S. G., Davis, O. C., Schaechter, J. D. & Howe, R. D. (2006), Hypnosis for rehabilitation after stroke: six case studies. *Contemporary Hypnosis*, 23 (4), 173–80.

Duff, S. & Nightingale, D. (2007), Alternative approaches to supporting individuals with dementia: enhancing quality of life through hypnosis. *Alzheimer's Care Today*, 8 (4), 321–31.

Elman, D. (1964), *Hypnotherapy*. Glendale, CA, Westwood.

Ewin, D. (1999), Hypnosis in the emergency room, in Temes, R. (Ed.) *Medical hypnosis: an introduction and clinical guide*. Edinburgh, Churchill Livingstone.

Hart, O. V. D. & Spiegel, D. (1993), Hypnotic assessment and treatment of trauma-induced psychoses: the early psychotherapy of H. Breukink and modern views. *International Journal of Clinical and Experimental Hypnosis*, 41 (3), 191–209.

Heap, M. (1995), A case of death following stage hypnosis: analysis and implications. *Contemporary Hypnosis*, 12 (2), 11.

Heap, M. & Aravind, K. K. (Eds.) (2002), *Hartland's medical and dental hypnosis*. Edinburgh, Churchill Livingstone.

Isenberg, G. I. & Matthews, W. J. (1995), Hypnosis with signing deaf and hearing subjects. *American Journal of Clinical Hypnosis*, 38 (1), 27–38.

Leninhauz M & Beran, B. (1981), Misuses of hypnosis: a medical emergency and its treatment. *The International Journal of Clinical and Experimental Hypnosis*, 29 (2), 148–61.

McConkey, K. M. & Jupp, J. J. (1985–1986), A survey of opinion about hypnosis. *British Journal of Experimental and Clinical Hypnosis*, 3 (2), 87–93.

Olness, K. & Kohen, D. P. (1996), *Hypnosis and hypnotherapy with children*, 3rd ed. New York, Guilford Press.

Perry, C. (1979), Hypnotic coercion and compliance to it: a review of evidence presented in a legal case. *The International Journal of Clinical and Experimental Hypnosis*, 37 (3), 187–218.

Pratt, G. J., Wood, D. P. & Alman, B. M. (1988), *A clinical hypnosis primer expanded and updated.* New York, John Wiley & Sons.

Santiago, A. I. D. & Khan, M. (2007), Hypnosis for schizophrenia. *Cochrane Database of Systematic Reviews* (4), art. no. CD004160.

Wagstaff, G. F. (2000), Can hypnosis cause madness? *Contemporary Hypnosis*, 17 (3), 14.

Wark, D. M. (2006), Alert hypnosis: a review and case report. *American Journal of Clinical Hypnosis*, 48 (4), 291–300.

Waxman, D. (1989), *Hartland's medical and dental hypnosis.* London, Bailliere Tindall.

Yapko, M. D. (1995), *Essentials of hypnosis.* New York, Brunner/Mazel.

Yapko, M. D. (1997), *Breaking the Patterns of Depression.* New York, Broadway Books.

Part Two

The Stages of Therapy

Dr Les Brann

With contributions from
Dr Geoff Ibbotson
Mrs Jacky Owens
Dr Ann Williamson

7

Initial Steps

Establishing Rapport

Rapport is the most fundamental part of the entire therapy and has been defined as 'sympathy, harmony between individuals, an emotional bond or a connection'. Interestingly, the *Oxford English Dictionary* quotes an 1848 definition as 'a state in which a mesmeric action can be exercised by one person on another', and whilst we would argue that rapport is a shared experience and not something done by one person to another we would recognize its special nature and its importance in therapy. Indeed it is suggested that whenever two people are deeply involved in communication they are in an 'altered state' of awareness, and this shared altered state is the 'therapeutic relationship' which is seen as a major factor in any successful therapy (see Drisko, 2004; Frank, 1971; Frank & Frank, 1991 for more details of this concept).

Thus, establishing rapport is so much more than simply putting your patients at ease. But it has to start somewhere, and it is very difficult to repair a consultation if you get off on the wrong foot. Learning how to put your patients at ease is a lesson which must be learnt. There are no hard and fast rules, but a few fundamental points are useful to take on board.

- Ensure a polite welcome. If you have a receptionist, ensure that they are expecting the patient and take the trouble to point out the toilets – it is difficult to relax with a full bladder!
- Invite the patient into the consulting room whilst smiling and making eye contact. Shake hands and introduce yourself in whatever way you feel comfortable, but it is

The Handbook of Contemporary Clinical Hypnosis: Theory and Practice, First Edition.
Edited by Les Brann, Jacky Owens and Ann Williamson.
© 2012 John Wiley & Sons, Ltd. Published 2015 by John Wiley & Sons, Ltd.

suggested that you include your Christian (first) name. It may be appropriate to use your title, but there is no need to emphasize it.

- It may be useful to break the ice by making brief but polite chat about the journey, and it is important to establish the name by which the patient wishes to be called.
- Show respect. There is no need to wear a three piece suit and a bow tie, but make sure you are presentable.

Rapport often occurs naturally, and we have all experienced feeling very comfortable with someone we have just met. With others however things may seem hard going, and it takes time before that comfortable feeling evolves. With friendships and social interactions the time frame and possibly the outcome are less crucial. In the therapeutic setting there is inevitably a constraint on the number of sessions available, and so it is important to be aware of the need to deliberately build rapport. The experienced therapist probably is not aware of how they actually build rapport; they have subconsciously learnt to respond to the wide variety of different personalities, moods and situations and can do so without any conscious plan. The student and novice therapist however need to be aware of the major factors which can be utilized to accelerate the development of rapport particularly with an individual with whom you would not normally, easily and naturally communicate.

We utilize both verbal and non-verbal communication at both a conscious and an unconscious level within any social interaction (Mehrabian, 1971). Thus it can be seen that there is not going to be a simple verbal script that guarantees rapport!

Many attempts have been made to analyse the critical components of successful rapport and therapy. Grinder *et al.* (1981) analysed the work of revered masters such as Milton Erickson, Fritz Perls and Virginia Satir which led to the development of neurolinguistic programming (NLP). Such constructs rely heavily on the observation of subtle aspects of verbal language patterns and body language.

One premise is that we have preferential ways of communicating using, at any one time, visual, auditory or kinaesthetic language. If a patient is communicating using visual words such as *"It seemed to me quite clear that . . ."* or *"I see what you mean . . ."* then it does not aid rapport for the therapist to respond with auditory or kinaesthetic language such as *"I hear what you say"* or *"I understand that this was a heavy burden for you"*.

For more details on language patterns, see chapter 5; or for a more advanced and detailed exposition of NLP, see Burton and Bodenhamer (2000).

Whilst the student is encouraged to be aware of all these approaches and suggestions, it must be stated clearly that there is not a single formula for building rapport. Each therapist must find their own recipe for each particular patient. The formula will need to be dynamic as the degrees and levels of rapport change throughout the therapeutic process, especially if the therapy has involved or requires the exposure of highly intimate and sensitive material. Stanton (1985) summarizes the qualities of the therapist as:

- Genuineness: showing himself as he is
- Acceptance: of the patient as he is
- Empathy: the ability to see things from the patient's viewpoint, sharing an overview of the illness

- Skill and professionalism: the therapist's belief that he can help – and confidence to say if he can't!

The therapist's body language and general demeanour will, therefore, set the scene, and a calm, friendly, caring approach will guide the patient into the receptive mode for therapy. Sometimes, however, the presenting problem prevents the natural drift into that mode. High levels of anxiety can inhibit the rapport building, and if the patient fails to naturally fall into step with the therapist then it can be useful for the therapist to fall into step with the patient. Increasing the speed of your chat to 'match' the speed of the patient's speech or adopting a similar posture may have the effect of creating the subconscious connection sufficiently to allow the therapist to then 'lead' the patient away from the anxiousness by gradually slowing the rate of speech and settling back into a more relaxed and open posture. This is termed 'pacing' and is a useful tool as long as it is done subtly and not in an obviously mimicking way. Do not be fooled, however, into thinking that *all* you have to do is 'match', 'pace', then 'lead' – sometimes you do not get the response you were hoping for and you may have to work with the anxiety rather than try to reduce it.

Similarly the use of the so-called double bind appears to give the patient an option whilst agreeing to something else, for example: *"Would you like to relax in this chair or on the couch?"* By agreeing to stay in the chair, they have apparently agreed to relax! Be careful with this type of approach as it has been adopted in all sorts of aggressive marketing techniques, and many people now spot them and immediately have the sense of being 'conned' and credibility is lost. Equally, just because they have answered the bind does not mean that they will follow it!

So whilst these tools are important parts of the therapist's armamentarium, none are guaranteed to build rapport; sometimes it just takes time, sometimes you never feel comfortable with that patient and sometimes you have to behave as though you feel you have rapport. Despite your own reservations it is possible that the patient feels more comfortable with you than they have with anyone else – you have to start from where you are, not from where you would like to be.

Taking a History

It is worth remembering that history taking is the first part of therapy, and the manner in which it is done can continue to build or ruin rapport. Usually you have some sort of idea what the patient's problem is from the referral letter, but it breaks the ice to get them to tell you briefly the reason for their referral, and not infrequently what the patient says bears little resemblance to the referral information. Perhaps, then, the best approach is to direct the questioning to their past medical history. Whilst this is always important, its purpose here is to establish (early on) whether they have any contraindications (absolute or relative) to hypnosis, in particular:

- A history of psychosis. This is generally regarded as an absolute contraindication unless it was a clearly drug induced episode with no long term sequelae.

- Severe depression: depression was originally classed as a contraindication for hypnosis, but there is now ample evidence that hypnosis is a very effective therapy in depression. Nevertheless if somebody is actively suicidal or has severe retarded depression such that they are unable to engage in treatment it is essential to withhold hypnotherapy until the patient is stable and receptive to therapy. Even then it is essential to work with the permission of and in conjunction with the patient's psychiatrist or general practitioner.
- Dementia: Patients with significant dementia may simply not be able to engage in the therapeutic process. Hypnosis can be used in these cases for relaxation, although induction may take more time and imagery must be kept simple and clear.
- Mental capacity: Patients with significant learning difficulties or significant damage following head injury, stroke or tumour may not be suitable for hypnotherapy. Much depends on the residual mental functioning and the problem for which the hypnotherapy is being considered – most, if not all, could benefit from learning to relax – and, therefore, all such patients should be considered individually. However, it is not uncommon to be approached by relatives of, say, a stroke patient to ask if hypnosis can be used to bypass the damaged area of the brain, and whilst there may be case study evidence (e.g. Mackrodt, 2007) to suggest there may be some functional gain, the therapist is strongly advised not to make unrealistic claims for hypnosis.
- Deafness: This is purely a practical problem. It is impossible to shout in a relaxed tone! It is possible to use headphones and a microphone, but for most therapists treating such patients will be difficult although not impossible (see page 78).

At this point the hypnotherapist should ask, *"Am I straying outside my area of competence?"* If the answer is *"Yes"*, then refer on to a more appropriately experienced colleague or recommend an alternative form of therapy.

Having established that there are no contraindications to hypnotherapy, it is often useful to gather a bit more detail about the patient and their particular problem. There is no right amount of detail, and each therapist must decide for themselves when they have gathered enough information to proceed. As all hypnotherapists should be first and foremost health professionals and all only working within their field of expertise, their history taking should fulfil the requirements of their specialty. Notwithstanding the above it is important to remember that information can be gathered at any time during therapy, and if it becomes apparent that salient points are missing then those questions can be asked at that time – whether the patient is doing hypnosis or not! The following areas of questioning may be of use:

- What is the problem, and when, why and how did it start?
- What investigations have they had and with what results?
- Has a formal diagnosis been made and by whom? For example: *"The doctor at the hospital said the X-ray showed my spine was crumbling and nothing could be done"*.

- What are their views on the problem?
  - What makes it better – or are there times when it seems better or not so bad or when the problem was expected but did not occur?
  - What makes it worse – or are there times when it seems worse?
- What have other people said about the problem?
- What treatments have they already had – including medication?
- A brief history of their childhood, parents, siblings and schooling. Details can be expanded upon if the brief history (such as in the Life History Inventory in appendix 1) exposes potentially important information.
- Relationships, past and present
  - The effect of the problem on these
  - The effect of these on the problem
  - Depending on the nature of the problem it may be necessary to take a more detailed psychosexual history, but unless this is overtly the problem it may be better to leave this very personal detail until a later session for fear of making the patient uncomfortable.
- Jobs, past and present
  - The effect of the problem on these
- Sickness record
  - The effect of the job on the problem

History taking not only is about gathering factual information but also gives the therapist a clue as to how the problem fits into the patient's life. As Williamson (2008) points out, history taking is part of the 'therapeutic interview' and is a golden opportunity to instigate the shift in attitude from being problem focused to solution focused.

Patients become experts on their problems, and if allowed they may wallow in the problem throughout the interview and, therefore, continue to reinforce it (this is particularly so if there is a significant element of secondary gain). Interrupting such a negative history needs to be done subtly and can be achieved by 'accidentally' dropping your pen or coughing, sneezing or so on. The interview is then recommenced in a more solution focused way: "*You mentioned that you always seem better on holiday – have you any idea how you managed to do that?*"

Such 'pattern interrupts' must not get in the way of validating the patient's distress, and for some it is essential to allow the patient to 'tell their story' as this can be, in and of itself, therapeutic. It is only with experience and through case discussions during clinical supervision that the student will learn which approach is appropriate. The view of the author (LB), however, is that where there seems to be a need to 'tell the story' or catalogue a series of life events (especially abuse), this is best done during formal hypnosis.

Assessing the relative importance of life events can also be useful, and Williamson (2008) uses a timeline chart to allow the patient to plot positive and negative events both temporally and qualitatively. (See Figure 7.1.)

The Life History Inventory (see appendix 1) enables a 'score' to be obtained to assess the complexity of someone's history. It is suggested that events early in a person's life have more of

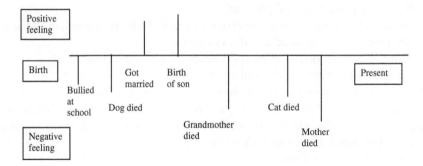

Figure 7.1   Timeline chart demonstrating important events with degree of positive or negative affect.

an impact than later events, and the scores are weighted appropriately. The maximum score is 130 (very poor), and those with scores below about 50 may be suitable for short therapy regimes whereas those above are likely to need more complex and longer term therapy.

A very useful final question to ask when taking the history is *"Is there anything else I need to know?"* Any reply to this almost always is of greatest importance, and it is advisable to write it down verbatim for future reference.

Collection of Baseline Audit Data

It is important to document your pre-treatment audit data – see chapter 40 for suggestions and details. Some data can be collected prior to the initial appointment, but any patient centred data is perhaps best collected after taking the history. At this stage some therapists define aims and goals with respect to the patient's hopes and expectations. Unless there are any clearly false expectations, this may be best left until there is a clearer picture of the depth and complexity of the problem.

References

Burton, J. & Bodenhamer, B. G. (2000), *Hypnotic language – its structure and use*. Carmarthen, Wales, Crown House.

Drisko, J. W. (2004), Common factors in psychotherapy outcome: meta-analytic findings and their implications for practice and research. *Families in Society*, 85 (1), 81–90.

Frank, J. D. (1971), Therapeutic factors in psychotherapy. *American Journal of Psychotherapy*, 25 (3), 350–61.

Frank, J. D. & Frank, J. B. (1991), *Persuasion and healing: A comparative study of psychotherapy*. Baltimore, John Hopkins University Press.

Grinder, J., Bandler, R. & Andreas, C. (1981), *Tranceformations: neurolinguistic programming and the structure of hypnosis*. Newcastle, Real People Press.

Mackrodt, K (2007), Case presentation at the Joint BSMDH/BSECH Conference, York, UK, April.

Mehrabian, A. (1971), *Silent witness*. Belmont CA, Wadsworth.

Stanton, H. (1985), Conference presentation at the BSMDH Conference, Cheltenham, UK, April.

Williamson, A. (2008), *Brief psychological interventions in practice*. Chichester, John Wiley & Sons, Ltd.

8

Explanation of Hypnosis: The Working Model

Introduction

Having taken the history and collected the baseline data (which in itself may give a clue as to the relative merits of each aspect of the problem), it is necessary to give an explanation of hypnosis to the patient. A working model is a representation of the process, often using metaphor, in order to improve understanding. It is virtually impossible to communicate concepts without the use of models and metaphor. It is important to stress that these are only models and to describe ways in which hypnosis seems to work without the necessity for them to be actual 'truth'. Each therapist develops their own way of giving that explanation and its content. It is important to give sufficient time to this part of the initial session, and it will often need about twenty minutes. It is recommended that the explanation be written on a whiteboard or flip chart as you are talking as it will be impossible for anybody to remember the details to which you will be referring as you proceed. Alternatively or in addition, previously prepared information sheets may be given to the patient.

Before starting any explanation, it is necessary to ask what the patient may already know or if they have had any previous experience of hypnosis. Even if they have had training in or previous experience with hypnotherapy, it is probably wise to run through your explanation as inevitably your explanation will contain clues as to the possible mechanism of their problem and pointers to mechanisms of resolution. Even if your patient is a fellow health professional, do not assume they will know – work through the explanation anyway.

The Handbook of Contemporary Clinical Hypnosis: Theory and Practice, First Edition.
Edited by Les Brann, Jacky Owens and Ann Williamson.
© 2012 John Wiley & Sons, Ltd. Published 2015 by John Wiley & Sons, Ltd.

The Hemispheric Specialization Model

What follows is a virtual transcript of such an explanation, and, remember, this is being summarized up on a whiteboard at the same time.

Let us assume that the brain works as a very sophisticated computer. The upper part of the brain has two separate sides which we call the hemispheres. In computer terms it seems that each hemisphere is programmed differently. The left side is our logical side and seems to be responsible for our logical, rational, critical, analytical, abstract and mathematical type functions – the important thing is that it is not programmed to understand emotions. The right hemisphere is our emotional side and is programmed to be responsible for our emotions, feelings, instincts, intuition and imagery, and aids in the understanding of such things as metaphor.

It seems as well that the right – emotional – side has many more connections with our bodily control centres (autonomic) compared with the left hemisphere. These control centres are responsible for our bodily functions, such as heart rate, breathing, appetite, bowels and all our separate emotions including fear, anger and happiness. We can easily recognize examples of this as our intellectual functions rarely affect our body but if we are doing something emotional such as an examination or interview we experience palpitations, butterflies and frequent trips to the loo, so we know that emotional things affect our bodily functions.

Each hemisphere seems to have its own type of memory – the left is the intentional memory which, as the name implies, is concerned with recording and recovering the things we wish to remember. The right side by contrast is our involuntary memory and records things without our conscious effort. An example is music; we have all experienced getting a new CD and finding that after playing it a few times the end of one song leads us automatically to sing the first few bars of the following track. There are, or course, many other examples of this. The important thing about our involuntary memory is that it records the emotions attached to that memory as well – most of such emotions are fairly neutral, but we become aware of the extremes of good or the extremes of bad. An example would be that after experiencing a road traffic accident, we might feel frightened when we pass the same place (or somewhere similar). In reality highly emotional events seem to press the record button on the right side and may give us a clue as to the mechanism of such things as PTSD (post-traumatic stress disorder).

Each hemisphere also has its own method of communication – the left is verbal. Language, it seems, evolved alongside our ability to think logically and in evolutionary terms is recent – we seem to be the only animal to have evolved such a sophisticated language system. The right hemisphere however uses non-verbal communication – body language. This involves eye contact, facial expression, body postures, gesticulation intonation and we should probably include here natural scents and odours. Normal communication is a synthesis of the two, but occasionally there is a conflict. Imagine the scenario where someone at home is moping around and if you dare ask the question, 'What is the matter?' invariably the gruff reply is 'Nothing'. Nobody takes any notice of the actual word 'Nothing', but note is taken of the manner in which it is said and the accompanying body language. So, when there is a conflict the right hemisphere is the correct one. (Using this as an example together with other observations of human function, we can demonstrate that.)
... We like to think of ourselves as the logical, rational person ... in reality, we are governed by our feelings. Indeed, the well known philosopher Emile Coue noted that when the will and the intellect are in conflict, the will always wins!

Observation of people in hypnosis seems to show that it is as though there is a shift in function from left to right, and using the computer metaphor it seems that in hypnosis we have 'logged on' to

the right hemisphere. This, therapeutically, gives us access to the emotional memories and our feelings
but more importantly the actual (autonomic) control centres.
 Thus hypnosis is a specific utilization of those right hemisphere functions.

During such an explanation there is often interaction with the patient – many women for example point to the left side and exclaim *"That is my husband!"* and immediately the therapist gets a clue as to the likelihood of significant emotional support at home. It often helps patients to understand why all their logical and rational efforts have failed to bring about a resolution to their problems and reassures those for whom cognitive-behavioural therapy (CBT) has also been found wanting!

But the explanation can be expanded or contracted as necessary. If, for example, you know your patient has presented with PTSD, it is possible to dwell on the involuntary memory and give a further explanation of how highly emotional memories do not seem to have been 'filed away' properly and so give rise to flashbacks and intrusive thoughts – symptoms with which they are all too familiar (see chapter 26 for more details). So not only are you offering a reason for their symptoms but also you are indirectly suggesting a mechanism by which they can be resolved.

It is often useful to give imagery special emphasis. Thomas (2005) highlighted the importance of imagery in thought and the construction of our inner reality.

Jung says that the 'emotionally infused image is the primary organizer of the human psyche' (qtd in Young-Eisendrath & Hall, 1991). According to Jung, thinking in images (rather than words):

- Is developmentally prior to mastery of syntax and language
- Is more motivating and powerful than language (think of the parables and stories told by all the great teachers of the world)
- Has meaning that cannot be fully encompassed in language
- May lead to emotionally based organization of thought

Although the visual component of imagery is often predominant, imagery may also be auditory, olfactory/gustatory and kinaesthetic and we would also include here spatial awareness. Sometimes patients have an 'awareness' of whatever they are thinking about and know where in space it seems to be without actually having a visual image. When using imagery in therapy, all forms of processing need to be utilized. Patients need to be made aware of this during the explanation.

Some therapists will feel uncomfortable giving the left-right hemisphere model as though it were gospel truth. It is important to qualify the explanation by noting that it is obviously a simplified version and that in reality those different functions are not necessarily restricted to each hemisphere, but clinically those two ways of processing are observable and the model fits with the way hypnotherapy seems to obtain its results. This model is also broadly supported by such tools as functional magnetic resonance imaging (fMRI) and positron emission tomography (PET) scans, however in hypnosis the right brain activities also tend to be associated with a shift towards the frontal areas (Ray & Oathes, 2003; Woody & Szechtman, 2003). Levi-Agreasti and Sperry (1968) showed that the right brain processing is rapid, complex, whole-pattern, spatial and perceptual, whereas the left brain processing is verbal and analytical.

Models Referring to the Conscious and Subconscious Mind

In the medical context 'conscious' has the meaning of being aware of and able to respond to one's surroundings and stimuli. Following injury or disease there can be a spectrum of decreasing consciousness which may result in coma and the patient is said to be 'unconscious'. However the words 'unconscious' and 'subconscious' can also be used to describe a part of the mind. This nominalization divides consciousness into 'the conscious mind' and 'the subconscious (or unconscious) mind'.

Hartland (1971) stated,

> The conscious mind is that part of the mind which feels thinks and acts in the present . . . the unconscious mind is a much greater part of the mind, and normally we are unaware of its existence. It is the seat of all our memories, all our past experiences, and indeed all of that we have ever learned. In this respect it resembles a large filing cabinet to which we can refer in order to refresh our memory whenever we need to do so. (p. 13)

It has been calculated that the conscious mind can only process a very limited number of things at once and can be seen to be analogous to left hemispheric functioning in that it is verbal, analytical, abstract, rational, digital, logical and linear in its processing.

The unconscious mind is believed to have massive capacities of correlation and control (Miller, 1956). It is non-verbal, synthetic (puts things together to form wholes), analogic (sees likeness between things), non-temporal, non-rational and logical, spatial (sees how things fit), intuitive and holistic. Thus our conscious mind (left brain processing) is concerned with detail, whilst the unconscious (right brain processing) is more global in its application.

Thus models of hypnosis utilizing the conscious and unconscious minds postulate that hypnosis gives us access to the subconscious. Indeed Heap and Aravind (2002) have summarized it thus:

> The following claims are being made for hypnosis. Hypnosis facilitates the hypnotist's and subject's ability:
>
> 1   To communicate with the unconscious mind
> 2   To ask or direct the unconscious mind to do certain useful things
> 3   To receive communications from the unconscious mind

Aspects of the two models are often combined with the subconscious being linked to right hemisphere functions and the left being linked to conscious activity. The above models have the benefit of helping the patient understand why their logical (conscious, left hemisphere) attempts to solve the problem have failed. Conscious rationality does not

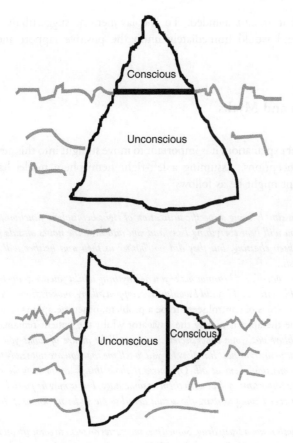

Figure 8.1   The iceberg model.

easily modify emotions. Hence simple logic cannot modify, for instance, a desire to smoke. In a similar way, telling yourself to stay calm when you are becoming panicky does not often prove effective.

Another simple model to demonstrate how hypnosis increases access to subconscious processing is the iceberg model. Our usual waking state is analogous to the iceberg floating on the sea when only the small area above the surface of the water is accessible (our conscious awareness). In hypnosis it is as though the iceberg tilts over, allowing greater access to normally hidden areas of the iceberg (the unconscious). (See Figure 8.1.)

Other models and explanations are often given perhaps describing hypnosis as a form of 'deep relaxation'. Whilst all models are only 'models' it seems sensible to maximize the benefits of using hypnotherapy, and as hypnosis is so much more than 'deep relaxation' confining one's explanation to this level is likely to underutilize the benefits. Gandhi and Oakley (2005) have shown that labelling something as hypnosis produces a more profound effect, so it is important not to undo such positives by 'dumbing down' the explanation. Similarly, although theoretical psychology considers the concept of suggestibility significant in understanding the phenomenon of hypnosis, most patients would misinterpret the concept and it is best avoided. To the lay person, suggestibility is synonymous with gullibility and would immediately undo the positive rapport and the shift into solution focus.

Allaying Fears and Myths

Having given your explanation, it is important to move straight into this next phase and pre-empt any misconceptions. Assuming a left-right hemisphere model had been used, a verbatim transcript might be as follows:

> *So, with hypnosis simply being a specific utilization of right hemisphere functions, you do not lose consciousness. You will hear everything I say and you will hear the noises outside just as you have whilst we have been chatting, but they did not bother us then and neither will they whilst you are doing hypnosis.*
>
> *You do not lose control. . . . I cannot make you do anything whilst you are doing hypnosis that you are not comfortable with . . . if I could I would have stopped all my smokers from smoking but, sadly, I cannot!* (Where issues of control seem to be a problem, other metaphors can be added here. For example, the therapist is merely the navigator whilst the patient remains the pilot.)
>
> *You do not 'blurt out' your inner secrets . . . you will be aware of what you are saying and whether you want to say it or not. It is okay for you to tell me that you are not ready to discuss certain things or not to mention them at all. Of course if those things are or may be relevant to your problem it will be important to deal with them at some stage, but it may be possible to deal with the problem without ever having to share the actual detail so please let me know if there is something troubling you.*
>
> *Equally, hypnosis is not a truth drug. Sometimes memories do seem to come up under hypnosis that you have not been aware of before and they MAY be true but . . . just because it has come up under hypnosis it does not mean that it is historically true. All memory is reconstructed in some way, and although, from a therapy point of view, we may need to treat it as though it is true, corroborative evidence would be needed to substantiate it further.*
>
> *You will be wondering what it feels like to be doing hypnosis. Well, probably not a lot different from how you are feeling now. There is not a sudden point, there is no flash on the road to Damascus, after which you can say, 'This is it, I'm in hypnosis!' Your thought processes are continuous . . . if you stop and think about a daydream, you never know you are going to go into it, you don't know you are in it, but you do know when you come out of it and you get that 'Wow! I was "miles away" type feeling'.* (It is always possible to add other examples such as getting absorbed in a good book or film.) *Those feelings are similar to hypnosis . . . your thought processes are continuous and it is important that you 'go with the flow'. Please do not analyse or get sidetracked wondering why I am saying certain things . . . just go with the flow. You do not have to listen . . . your ears will hear me anyway and if anything I say is not relevant to you just now you may ignore it or keep it to use at another time.*
>
> *How do we get you to start doing hypnosis? That is easy. All we need to do is to get to be aware of feelings, for example what it is like to feel yourself breathe. You can feel the air flowing in . . . and flowing out. Now you have been breathing in and out a dozen or so times a minute all your life, but you rarely stop to feel it. As you concentrate on that feeling you will be aware that breathing out is a relaxation of your muscles and we can then add to those feelings some images . . . so if we have*

feelings and imagery we must be working in your right hemisphere which is exactly where we want to be.

　　Anything goes under hypnosis . . . if you are happy you will laugh, if you are sad you may cry – and there are plenty of tissues so do not worry if you do. If you become uncomfortable you can move or if you have got an itch on the end of your nose you can scratch it without coming out of hypnosis. You can speak without coming out of trance . . . so it is all very easy.

That sort of transcript seems to cover the major myths and concerns, and by pre-empting their questions you have covered all the things that you need them to know for your style of working. Obviously, you must ask if there is anything specific they wish to ask and answer accordingly.

So to summarize the common myths:

- You do not lose consciousness.
- You do not lose control.
- You hear everything.
- You can speak, laugh or cry.
- You remember as much as you do with any conversation.
- You do not blurt out your inner secrets.
- Hypnosis is not a truth drug.

Consent

Having gone through the history, explanation, answered questions and allayed myths it is important to once again get their consent to begin doing the actual hypnosis. In the author's (LB) unit, patients bring their signed consent form to the first session but despite that it is essential to confirm at this stage that they are still happy to continue and that they have no further questions before you start the hypnosis. Some therapists are happy with 'implied consent' by virtue of the patients presenting themselves for hypnotherapy, but those working with NHS contracts may be expected to obtain written consent. This needs to include agreement to allow recording the session and for using their 'anonymized' data for outcome audit, case reports or research. Some therapists obtain consent for utilizing outcome audit at the end of therapy rather than at the beginning.

Chaperones

Generally speaking one to one therapy is just that and nobody else is present during the sessions, but in these days of litigation it is important to make sure certain safeguards are in place. It is not advisable to do any therapy without someone else in the building, and the patient should be aware that, in an emergency, the nurse, receptionist or secretary could quietly come into the room without disturbing the hypnotherapy. This is protective for both the patient and therapist. Recording the session is also a safeguard. In some circum-stances the patient may ask if their partner or friend can sit in, and if that is their wish then that must happen. It may, however, be useful to suggest that the other person does not speak unless invited to do so and that they sit out of the eye-line of the patient.

In reality this might be appropriate for the initial explanation and introductory session but once the patient has experienced hypnosis and seen that there is no loss of control it is probably wise to suggest that it might be better if they were on their own, but remember it would be unwise to insist as it might break rapport. There are differences in this respect when working with children – parents will often accompany them, at least in the initial stages (see chapter 34).

When dealing with known psychosexual problems, it is sensible to ask the patient to tell their partner that they are going to have therapy – the impression is that this is not always done but if you have recorded your request in the notes you have covered yourself in the case of any complaints from the partner. Other safeguards useful when dealing with this group of patients are specifically discussed in the relevant chapter.

Goal Setting

Some therapists advise planning therapy and setting goals at this stage during the first session. Whilst it is important to be firm about what hypnosis cannot achieve, in the opinion of the author (LB) it may be inappropriate to do any goal setting before the full nature of the problem becomes clearer as therapy progresses. Goal setting should be seen as a dynamic, something to be regularly reviewed and modified as each nuance of the problem (and possible solutions) becomes revealed as therapy continues.

Even if no specific goals are being set, the direction of therapy needs to be established at the start of therapy. Questionnaires such as Measure Your Medical Outcome Profile (MYMOP) (see page 586) and the scaling question (see page 163) are useful to facilitate the therapy focus as sometimes the patient's needs are different to the therapist's preconceived expectations. Unrealistic ideas need to be sympathetically explored for their underlying message, and more realistic, perhaps interim, goals can be negotiated with the patient. One author (AW), having taken a history and completed questionnaires (usually problem based), directs the rest of the first session towards discovering what the patient wants to achieve and how they might begin to do this.

It is important to realize that this process applies to planned therapy – sometimes hypnosis is used in the emergency setting where work is focused on the immediate issue.

However, much planning and goal setting take place within each hypnosis session and become integral parts of the wider processes of resolution. The goals set in hypnosis may well be greater than those set in the waking state because self-limiting beliefs are less operational. If the goal intuitively feels 'right' to the patient when they imagine experiencing it, then it is achievable by them (see page 163). All goals set hypnotically involve first 'seeing' the goal achieved and then 'stepping into it' and experiencing it. This with some patients is too difficult in the early stages of therapy, and intermediate stages need to be accessed as in the scaling question (see page 163). Sometimes the therapist has to 'carry hope' for the patient until such time as they are able to believe for themselves that they can achieve their goals.

The Special Place (Also Known as a Safe Place or Safe Haven)

One of the most important tasks before starting the hypnosis is to establish the outline details of the patient's special place. This is somewhere where they can feel relaxed and safe. It can be a real place or somewhere purely imaginary. At this stage general terms are all that is necessary – for example the beach, the garden or a favourite armchair. Some therapists merely introduce the concept of a 'special place' and suggest that the patient's subconscious mind will find the right place for them – some people who find it difficult to relax may have problems using their conscious mind to locate such a place. Others may elicit detailed description both before and during hypnosis to generate an almost virtual reality. What is essential, however, is to make a note of any specific fears the patient may have (such as fear of water) so that you do not inadvertently stray into these situations.

References

Gandhi, B. & Oakley, D. A. (2005), Does 'hypnosis' by any other name smell as sweet? The efficacy of 'hypnotic' inductions depends on the label 'hypnosis'. *Consciousness and Cognition*, 14, 304–15.

Hartland, J. (Ed.) (1971), *Medical and dental hypnosis and its clinical applications*. London, Balliere Tyndall.

Heap, M. & Aravind, K. K. (Eds.) (2002), *Hartland's medical and dental hypnosis*. Edinburgh, Churchill Livingstone.

Levi-Agreasti, J. & Sperry, R. W. (1968), Differential perceptual capacities in major and minor hemispheres. *Proceedings of the National Academy of Sciences*, 61, 1151.

Miller, G. A. (1956), The magical number seven, plus or minus two: some limits on our capacity for processing information. *The Psychological Review*, 63, 81–97.

Ray, W. J. & Oathes, D. (2003), Brain imaging techniques. *American Journal of Clinical Hypnosis*, 52, 97–104.

Thomas, N. (2005), Mental imagery. *The Stanford encyclopedia of philosophy*. Stanford, CA, Stanford University Press.

Woody, E. Z. & Szechtman, H. (2003), How can brain activity and hypnosis inform each other. *International Journal of Clinical and Experimental Hypnosis*, 51 (3), 232–55.

Young-Eisendrath, P. & Hall, J. A. (1991), *Jung's self psychology: a constructivist perspective*. New York, Guilford Press.

9

Induction and Deepening

Introduction

Many of the myths and fallacies about hypnosis stem from the mystique surrounding the hypnotic induction. The historical concept was that the hypnotist possessed or had developed some sort of power which they exerted over their subjects; hypnosis was something *done* by the hypnotist to the subject. Even as medicine became more scientific, experts still implied that hypnosis was some sort of quirk that could only be brought about by a fairly rigid process of induction. Gindes (1953) published an equation:

$$\text{Misdirected Attention} + \text{Expectation} + \text{Belief} = \text{Hypnosis}$$

Such a view implies that hypnosis was a result of some sort of trickery which enabled the state of hypnosis to develop in the mind when its attention was focused elsewhere.

In contrast, when the state versus non-state argument was raging (see chapters 1 and 3) much emphasis was based on the notion that the observed hypnotic phenomena had nothing to do with the induction of a 'hypnotic state' but to a social compliance with an expected behaviour pattern. Meanwhile the humble clinician continued to observe that good results were obtainable following 'induction' and that expectation and compliance were only a part of the process. Indeed many, if not most, patients report that it was *"Nothing like I expected"* indicating that they were not simply being compliant with an expected, preconceived idea!

Whatever the theoretical arguments the important thing is to help the patient into an appropriate state of mind (trance) where the observable benefits of hypnosis can occur. Traditionally this is divided into two parts: induction and deepening. In reality this division is probably unnecessary and, perhaps, it is even impossible to separate the two. Thus, trance induction is a process by which we assist the patient to enter an altered

The Handbook of Contemporary Clinical Hypnosis: Theory and Practice, First Edition.
Edited by Les Brann, Jacky Owens and Ann Williamson.
© 2012 John Wiley & Sons, Ltd. Published 2015 by John Wiley & Sons, Ltd.

state of consciousness known as 'hypnosis' and there are as many techniques as there are therapists.

Deepening is a process which follows induction and improves the quality (depth?) of trance. There are a wide range of responses, and some patients seem to easily enter a very deep state whereas in others there seems very little change from the normal 'waking' state. It is important to realize that this seems to make very little difference to outcomes in the clinical setting. It is true, however, that the therapist (probably subconsciously) utilizes different styles and techniques according to the response of the patient, and this emphasizes the value of having a wide range of techniques at hand.

Tables 9.1 and 9.2 summarize the differences between older and more modern approaches. It must be stressed that just because a technique is old does not mean it has lost its usefulness, and the student is advised to learn as many as they can. What is important is to completely dispel the view that the hypnotist has any special power, so this point always needs to be stressed.

Table 9.1   Differences between traditional and modern induction techniques

Hypnotic induction techniques	
Traditional	*Modern*
Something the hypnotist did to the patient.	Hypnotist as an instructor: patient induces hypnosis following instructions from the hypnotist.
Misdirected attention + expectation + suggestion = hypnosis.	Alteration of the focus of the patient's attention from external to internal stimuli.
Often physical: swinging watch, eye fixation, Mesmeric passes, etc.	Utilizes mental imagery.
Uses direct suggestions: *"You will listen to my voice. . ."*	Uses indirect, permissive suggestions: *"You may find yourself listening. . ."*

Table 9.2   Differences between traditional and modern deepening techniques

Deepening techniques	
Traditional	*Modern*
Tend to be physical	Tend to use visual imagery
Hand clasp, arm levitation or heaviness	E.g. imagery of walking down steps
Progressive muscular relaxation	E.g. breathing away tension

Whilst there is no specific physical physiological state that defines the hypnotic trance there are important non-verbal clues that indicate responsiveness and the drift towards a trance like state. If you are using an eye fixation technique the first clue you usually notice is that the eyes defocus but for all techniques the main changes are those of muscle tone. You can see the muscles 'letting go'. It is important to feed these things back to the patient *"As your arm relaxes you may find that . . ."* Perhaps the most important group of muscles to observe are those of facial expression; frowns disappear, the jaw and lower lip relax and the lips sometimes appear larger. These facial expressions change as you guide the patient through the various stages. Eye movements can sometimes be seen accompanying the visual processing. Eyelid flicker may be seen as the sympathetic muscle tone is reduced in hypnosis before the parasympathetic is affected.

Breathing generally settles into a relaxed rhythm, but a small group of patients, particularly those with anxiety who tend to habitually hyperventilate, tend to use their accessory muscles of respiration and need to be reminded to use a gentle shallow diaphragmatic breathing pattern. With general relaxation skin colour changes can be noted, particularly a faint blush. Sometimes a small tear can be seen at the inner canthus. It must be stressed that not all patients exhibit all of these signs and the student is advised not to get worried if they do not appear. The novice hypnotherapist is often frightened to proceed *"What if they are not in hypnosis?"* The advice is to proceed 'as if' signs of trance have occurred. Otherwise the patient will soon pick up a sense of failure in the therapist and this is unhelpful. Lots of reassurance and positive murmurings such as *"That is really good . . ."* are helpful. Remember it is your tone of voice that is most important.

So, whilst the non-verbal signs are variable the therapist must concentrate and observe these changes not so much for an indication of trance but for clues as to changes of emotion that take place during therapy.

Despite the fact that the actual words used account for only part of the communication the choice of words remains important. Choose words which in an onomatopoeic sense naturally imply the mood which you wish to convey. Use words such as wander, drift and soothe, and words such as fragrance rather than smell. Avoid intellectual words which are left hemisphere, so you would use 'tummy' rather than 'abdomen'. Absolutely central to the practice of hypnosis is the concept of a suggestion of a response which can then be linked to another phenomenon such as trance deepening. Linkage words such as 'as' and 'then' are used (e.g. *". . . as your whole body relaxes . . . then your mind can focus on the fragrance of the flowers . . ."*). The alliteration simply adds to the rhythmical effect. The student can be reassured, however, that it is not necessary to be word perfect.

If you have used a left-right hemisphere model of hypnosis the patient will be aware that utilization of right sided functions is all that is required; so that once they are aware of feelings, physical or emotional, and using imagery, they must be accessing the right hemisphere pathways required for hypnosis.

What follows is a series of different induction methods written largely in script form so that you can use these verbatim. The list begins with the older style induction methods and progresses towards the more modern approaches. It is preferable, of course, to personalize them and use your own phraseology, but they can be used exactly as written.

The Raised Arm Technique

For this method the patient sits with their arm raised above their head, the elbow slightly bent and the head tipped back so that there is an element of eye strain as the eyes focus on the fingers.

> *I want you to keep your eyes fixed on your fingers which are quite straight and the thumb is held down . . . fingers quite straight and close together . . . now you can take your time relaxing . . . by closely watching your fingers . . . when you are ready to start relaxing . . . you will notice some movement in one or other of your fingers . . . it may jerk slightly at first and then spread apart from the next finger . . . I will bring this to your notice . . . and you will see how you begin to relax . . . more . . . and more . . . all right . . . good . . . now keep your eyes glued to your fingers . . . fingers close together . . . thumb apart. Breathe slowly and deeply . . . in . . . and . . . out . . . in . . . and . . . out. Soon you will notice slight movement in one or other of your fingers and a space will appear.*

This last sentence can be repeated once or twice, and if you notice their eyes getting tired draw their attention to this but you do not want their eyes to close yet.

> *There! Your* [for example] *index finger has moved slightly all of its own accord . . . and . . . there is space between it and the next finger . . . now all the fingers are separating and your eyes feel very tired . . . your eyelids are very heavy . . . but do not let your eyes close yet . . . just keep watching your fingers . . . and . . . as you do . . . you notice . . . that your arm is very slowly bending . . . so that your hand is coming . . . nearer . . . and nearer . . . to your face . . . as though a magnet was attracting your hand . . . as your hand comes nearer to your face . . . you will blink more . . . and more . . . and soon . . . your hand will touch your face . . . and that . . . will be the signal . . . for your eyes to close . . . for your arm . . . to flop down into your lap . . . and you sink down in the chair very . . . very . . . deeply relaxed . . . there . . . your fingers touch your face . . . your eyes close . . . you feel beautifully relaxed . . . warm . . . and comfortable. . . .*

Sometimes, if the arm seems to be taking an eternity to touch the face it is possible to modify it by saying something like "*. . . you are so relaxed . . . your arm seems to be just floating in space . . . and like in space . . . a gentle push . . . is all that is needed . . . to get . . . things moving. . . .*" As you say that, gently take the arm by the wrist, and slowly move it to gently touch the cheek or forehead and then say "*. . . just close your eyes . . . let your eyes close . . . let yourself relax completely. . . .*"

The Dropped Coin

> *I am going to place this coin in your hand . . . then I ask you to close your fingers gently over it and turn your hand over . . . hold it only tightly enough so that the coin does not fall to the ground. All right? Good! . . . Now stretch your arm out straight in front of you and you keep it there, please. You will find that very simple to do . . . your thumb is extended right away from the hand. Now here is the first instruction. You are to keep your eyes fixed on that thumbnail . . . right through*

the exercise until I suggest otherwise. Your eyes are going to be glued to your thumbnail all the time, right?

I am going to start counting now . . . and . . . with each count . . . you will feel . . . changes in the fingers of your hand . . . while your eyes are occupied with this thumb . . . your mind can pay attention to the feelings in your fingers . . . to the relation of your fingers . . . to the coin . . . how the fingers feel against the coin . . . and the feeling of relaxation and looseness that follows . . . now as I count . . . allow your fingers to relax and straighten out . . . with each count . . . so that eventually the fingers straighten out to a point where the coin drops to the floor . . . when the coin drops that is the signal for two things to happen . . . firstly for your eyes to close . . . secondly for your whole body to go limp . . . and melt right down into the chair . . . just as if you were going to sleep . . . into a deep . . . deep . . . sleep. Sometimes though, your eyes get so heavy and tired from being glued to your thumbnail . . . so tired . . . that they close long before the coin drops . . . that is fine if it happens . . . if your eyes close before the coin drops . . . let them stay closed . . . then you can pay all your attention to the way your fingers feel . . . and . . . the way they are relaxing with each count . . . I am going to repeat these instructions so that you can follow them exactly . . . you keep your eyes glued on the thumbnail . . . I count . . . and as I count . . . you pay attention to your fingers and feel them straightening out and relaxing. They relax more and more with each count . . . until the fingers have opened to a point where the coin drops. Then unless your eyes are already closed, they close now and you go deeply relaxed. The thud of the coin on the floor makes you go into an even deeper relaxed state. I will hold my hand under your arm so that you do not have to fear to relax. Now I think you have understood these instructions thoroughly, so we will just go ahead and you can do your part.

One . . . pay attention to your fingers and feel the nice relaxation that is going to come into them . . . with each count . . . a little bit more . . . your eyes are glued to your thumbnail and your fingers relax a little bit with each count . . . they are relaxing a little now and . . . your eyes . . . are getting tired . . . and heavy . . . looking at your thumbnail . . . soon they will want to close . . . they are starting to blink . . . it is perfectly all right to let them close. . . . Two . . . eyes getting heavier . . . fingers straightening out . . . you're doing very well. . . . Three . . . eyes are beginning to water a little now . . . your eyelids are blinking and your fingers have opened a little more round the coin . . . you are doing very well . . . you are making an excellent subject. . . . Four . . . you can hardly keep your eyes open . . . fingers straightening out more and more. . . . Five . . . eyelids closing . . . fingers opening . . . it is perfectly all right for you to close your eyes any time you want. . . . Six . . . fingers straightening right out . . . your eyes closing and your eyeballs are rolling up . . . you're doing fine . . . let your eyes close now . . . very good. . . . [The coin drops to the floor and the eyes have closed.] *Breathe slowly and deeply . . . with each breath that you take feel yourself relax more and more* [catch arm as it drops] *now when I let go of your arm you will feel the heaviness of it pulling it down onto your lap . . . it just flops down into your lap when I let it go and it takes you down into a deeply relaxed state . . . there . . .* [let the arm drop] *. . . just sit there and enjoy the calm comfortable feeling of complete relaxation.*

This technique demonstrates par excellence the utilization of natural physiological responses to fatigue. Of course the eyes will tire, water and blink; of course the fingers will tire and relax the grip on the coin; of course the arm will fatigue and feel heavy having been held out straight. The therapist can, therefore, confidently predict that these things will happen yet the patient seems blissfully unaware of the inevitability of it and has a sense of involuntariness.

The drawback of these techniques is that to the novice it seems as though the verbalization has to be word perfect, for if the instructions are not clear the patient gets confused. In fact it does not seem to matter, and whatever has been said (remember tone is more important than words) the fingers relax and the coin drops!

Another drawback of using a script is that it may lead to a mismatch if the student does not match the words he is saying to the response of the patient – if their eyes are shut one should not be talking about how heavy their eyelids feel and how nice it would be for their eyes to close!

Another version of the coin drop is when the coin is held very lightly between the tips of the thumb and finger and the gaze is directed at the coin. As relaxation occurs the coin slips from the fingers.

Eye Roll Technique (Adapted From Spiegel & Spiegel, 1978)

Check your patient is not wearing contact lenses as this method would not then be suitable. It can also be used without the challenge of the eye lock.

I would like you to roll your eyes up to look at an imaginary spot on top of your head and while your eyes are in that position, close your eyelids down. Your eyes will relax so much that you will find it impossible to open them, and the harder you try to open your eyes the tighter they will close, as the little muscles in your eyelids relax so much that they really cannot work at all. You can try and see how difficult it is to open them and each time you try it will become harder and harder as those little muscles in your eyelids relax more and more. . . . [Wait for this to happen, then proceed.] Then as you bring your eyes into a comfortable position you can notice how comfortable your eyelids can feel resting gently on your eyes . . . and now that relaxation can spread. . . .

Continue with a progressive muscular relaxation down the body, then take the patient to their special place, give some positive suggestions and invite them to come back to the here and now by counting backwards from five in their head so that by the time they have reached one they are wide awake and refreshed. This can of course be adapted to be used without the challenge of trying to open the eyes.

Eye Fixation and Distraction

I want you to lie back comfortably in the chair . . . look upwards and backwards at the tip of the pencil . . . can you see it? . . . good! . . . Do not let your eyes wander from it for a single moment . . . now start counting backwards from three hundred . . . mentally, to yourself, not out loud . . . keep on counting . . . slowly and rhythmically . . . and go on counting until I tell you to stop . . . you need not make any effort to listen . . . any more than you can help . . . your ears will still hear everything I say . . . but try not to listen . . . just stick to your counting . . . just let yourself go, completely limp and slack . . . breath quietly . . . in . . . then out . . . and, whilst you are breathing quietly in ... and out ... you can feel that your eyes are becoming very, very tired ... they may feel a little watery ... the pencil may look a little blurred ... already your eyelids are beginning to feel very, very heavy and tired ... presently they will want to blink ... as soon as they want to blink ... just let them blink as much as they like. ...

You see they are starting to blink now ... just let everything happen ... exactly as it wants to happen ... do not try to make it happen ... do not try to stop it happening ... just let everything please itself ... and presently your blinks will become slower ... and bigger ... as they do so ... your eyes will become more and more tired ... so tired they feel they are wanting to close ... as soon as they feel they want to close ... let them go ... just let them close ... entirely on their own ... your eyelids are becoming heavier and heavier ... they are wanting to close, now ... let them close ... closing tighter and tighter ... relax completely ... as deeply relaxed as you want to be ... give yourself up completely to this very pleasant, relaxed, drowsy feeling ... stop counting now ... just relax ... as deeply as you want to. ...

You would then take the patient to their special place, give some positive suggestions and invite them to come back to the here and now by counting backwards from five in their head so that by the time they have reached one they are wide awake and alert and all their sensations are back to normal.

Using Sensation: Arm Heaviness and Levitation

I would like you [or "I wonder if you can begin"] to concentrate on your right arm and hand and to imagine that as you become deeper and deeper relaxed that that arm and hand is becoming lighter and lighter. You could imagine a large brightly coloured balloon filled with helium tied to your right wrist ... tugging at your arm, pulling it up and up ... what colour is your balloon? ... Maybe your hand will float up quickly ... or maybe it will take a little time ... and as your arm gets lighter and lighter ... so you will become deeper and deeper relaxed ... more and more comfortable ... as the pull on your arm gets stronger and stronger ... as it floats up and up, floating up and up just like a feather floating gently in the air ... and that can just continue. ...

... And as you begin to focus your attention on your left arm and hand. ... I would like you to imagine that your left arm and hand are getting heavier and heavier as you become deeper and deeper relaxed ... pressing like a lead weight on your thigh ... feeling heavier and heavier. ...

... And you can become really interested in the difference in sensation between your right hand and your left hand ... your right hand floating up and up and your left hand getting heavier and heavier ... as you go deeper and deeper into that comfortable relaxed state ...

... Maybe your arm will float up to reach your face and as it does so you can feel the pull towards your face getting stronger and stronger ... as though there were two magnets attracting each other ... and the closer they get the stronger the pull ... as you become deeper and deeper relaxed.

And when your hand touches your face, you will become twice as deeply relaxed as before and gradually the sensation will return to normal in your arms and hands and as your hand gently comes back to your lap you can become just as deeply relaxed as you want to be. ...

You would then suggest that the patient went to their own special place, enjoying it while you give some positive suggestions, and then bring them back to the here and now by counting back from five to one in their head so that by the time they reach one, they are fully awake and alert, feeling refreshed and calm.

Breathing Focus

I would like you to begin to focus on your breathing, to become aware of the rise and fall of your chest, of the flow in and out of your breath. Do not try and change it in any way, just be aware of your breathing. Follow the flow of air in and out through your nose and you may begin to notice the slight temperature difference between the air you breathe in, which is slightly cooler than the air you breathe out, because the air you breathe out has been warmed by its journey through your lungs. Just be with your breathing . . . you do not have to do anything at all. Just let go with each breath out to feel as comfortable as you wish. If any part of you feels uncomfortable, then breathe out into that part, direct your out breath into that part and let it go. If a stray thought comes into your head, let it flow out again, you don't need to follow it, just focus back onto the rise and fall of your chest, the flow of air in and out, the difference in temperature. Maybe then imagine a calm, relaxing place and really be there, seeing, hearing, smelling, and feeling the place you have chosen. . . .

Progressive Muscular Relaxation

I invite you to make yourself comfortable, place your feet firmly on the floor, and let your hands rest comfortably on your lap. . . . I wonder if you could look up to a spot on the very top of your head and while you are looking up allow your eyes to close. Feel the tension in your eyelids and then let it go . . . bringing your eyes to a comfortable position . . . and feel how comfortable your eyelids can be just resting gently on your eyes . . . maybe you could begin to let that comfort drift into all the little muscles of your head and face and neck . . . maybe become aware of the space within your mouth, the position of your tongue . . . you could imagine that comfort flowing down into your neck and shoulders . . . maybe as a colour . . . maybe just as a really pleasant feeling . . . let that comfort drift down your arms right to your fingertips . . . you might notice a tingling feeling or a feeling of warmth in your hands as you feel more and more comfortable . . . let the comfort flow into the muscles around your chest . . . and down into your back and tummy . . . let the muscles of your tummy go loose and slack as that comfort drifts down . . . let any outside noises recede into the background contributing to a feeling of safety and comfort . . . let that comfort drift down your legs . . . right the way down to your toes . . . and you can begin to notice just how this comfort feels for you . . . maybe you will feel really heavy, as you sink deeper and deeper into that comfort . . . or maybe you will begin to feel light and floaty as you drift deeper and deeper . . . or maybe you will begin to lose awareness of just where your arms and legs really are . . . but however you experience it, it is perfect for you . . . just enjoy that lovely comfortable feeling . . . and as your conscious mind notices how your body is responding, your unconscious mind can help you to double that calm comfortable feeling . . . letting go with each outgoing breath to become just as deeply relaxed as you want to be. . . . I would like you now to go to a very special place . . . a place where you can feel completely relaxed and safe and calm . . . it might be a place you have visited or it might be a place that your mind finds for you . . . it may be inside or outside . . . but when you are there in your own special place just give me a nod. . . . Good. . . . I want you to look all around you, see all the colours, all the shapes . . . smell any smells that might be there . . . hear any sounds associated with the place you have chosen . . . feel any feelings . . . the texture of whatever you are resting on . . . the temperature of the air . . . this is your own special place . . . a place where you can come when you need to relax . . . to re-charge your batteries . . . a place where any suggestions you give yourself will sink straight down into your unconscious mind and begin to exert an effect on how you think . . . and how you feel . . . and how you behave . . . so that each time that you use these techniques it will become easier for you to become even more relaxed . . . even more quickly . . . now, in a few moments . . . when you are ready. . . . I would like you to come back to the here and now . . . knowing that you can always come back to this special place . . . so you can begin to count back in your head from five to one . . . taking all the time you need . . . so that by the time you reach one . . . you are fully awake . . . feeling refreshed and alert. . . .

Using Imagery and Metaphor

Therapeutic imagery is a very effective, non-challenging method to assist people to change; *"Just close your eyes and imagine."* Provided that all types of imagery, visual, auditory, kinaesthetic, olfactory and perhaps gustatory, are utilized then there are very few individuals with whom this approach cannot be used. If using guided imagery it is very important that prior to the technique you discuss the imagery that you intend to use (see page 43). If they have past negative associations with that situation, then this will clearly cause problems.

Metaphor to get rid of negative emotions and to give positive suggestions can be interwoven into the imagery. Here is an example of such imagery using a beach although it can be adapted to any other place (see page 397). After the first experience, it is important that the patient is advised that they may wish to change the 'location' or even vary it on a day by day basis, according to their needs on that particular day.

Remember you are using your words to stimulate the patient to make their own imagery, not imposing your imagery on them.

Beach imagery script

Maybe you would like to let your eyes close gently, allowing your breathing to settle down in its own time, maybe taking three slow deep breaths and then breathing at just the right pace for you. You need not make any great effort to listen to what I am saying . . . your ears will hear anyway . . . and your unconscious can take from my words anything that is useful . . . disregarding anything that is not appropriate for you at this time.

I would like you to imagine you are on a beach . . . perhaps a beach you know . . . perhaps a beach that your imagination finds for you . . . or perhaps a mixture of the two.

I wonder what you can see. As you look around notice the things you can see . . . perhaps the sun glinting on the sea . . . the colour of the sea . . . the colour of the sky . . . any clouds . . . maybe seagulls soaring effortlessly in the sky . . . how the shore line looks . . . whether there are trees or cliffs at the edge of the beach.

Smell the smells of the sea . . . the seaweed, the sea air.

Hear the sounds . . . perhaps the waves . . . perhaps the seagulls calling.

Be aware of the feeling . . . is it a pebbly beach or a sandy beach? . . . If it is sandy, be aware of whether the sand is smooth and damp or dry and soft . . . maybe wriggle your toes into the sand . . . if it is pebbly or rocky . . . notice what colours and shapes you can see . . . what does it feel like under your feet?

This is your beach and you can either stay here or make your way around a headland to another smaller bay where you can be completely alone. But as you look around I would like you to notice some pebbles lying nearby.

Maybe you can watch as waves break on the pebbles. As the water recedes, watch how it froths. Listen for that special sound as the pebbles roll about as the waves come in and go out – that chinking sound of the pebbles.

I would like you to look around and you will find that there is one pebble that takes your notice. I do not know whether it will be its size, shape or texture, but you will know that it is the right pebble.

I want you to become aware of something you want to get rid of, perhaps a memory, perhaps a feeling, perhaps a behaviour and just squeeze that pebble in your hand and squash all that which you want rid of right into that pebble. When you have done that, throw that pebble as far as you can, right out to sea. You will see it land in the sea, maybe making a splash, but any ripples will not reach back to the shore. Perhaps you can see it, as it sinks down through the water, until it rests on the bottom with the millions of other pebbles on the sea bed and you can feel really pleased to be rid of those things that you have just got rid of with the pebble.

And now, I would like you to move slowly along the beach and again look for a special pebble, you will know which one it is and when you have found it. Pick it up and use it to give you something you want, some sort of feeling or resource. Squeeze that pebble and as you do so, feel the feeling flowing up your arm, around your body and into your mind.

And you can know that, any time you come back to your beach and squeeze that pebble, you can top up that feeling; so you want to find somewhere safe on your beach to keep that special pebble. There will always be pebbles on your beach for any particular feeling or resource that you need.

So now, spend as long as you want on your beach and then when you are ready just make your way back around the headland if you went that way, and then count backwards in your mind from five to one, in your own time, to get back to the here and now, feeling refreshed and alert.

Re-vivification

This is a technique that is particularly useful for those patients who worry about control issues. To begin with, one agrees with the patient on a particular experience that they have enjoyed. This needs to be a physical activity such as skiing, running, horse-riding, sailing etc. The patient is asked to choose a specific time when they really enjoyed this activity and then let their eyes close and re-experience it, ensuring they use all their senses, seeing, hearing, feeling and possibly smelling. When they have finished they should open their eyes. This is a minimalist induction, and all of the control is clearly with the patient because the therapist simply sets the scene and then says nothing. As the patient is undergoing this re-vivification the therapist should observe the body language and minimal cues in order to be aware of how the process is going. They may use tonality or phrases such as *"That's right"* to encourage the process.

It is possible for the therapist to guide the patient through a re-vivification. However the language and approach should be carefully chosen. The point of the intervention is to enrich the experience but the imagery and pace must be dictated by the patient (by non-verbal feedback), rather than the imagery being suggested by the therapist.

This approach can be very useful in a very anxious patient in that the physical activity matches the physiological adrenalin state of the patient. The activity can then be slowed down as they begin to relax.

An example of this would be swimming. One could have the patient start with re-vivification of swimming very fast and then suggest they gradually slow down until they are enjoying just floating freely in the water. The suggestions of the therapist should be very indirect; setting the scene of gradual slowing down rather than attempting to impose their imagery of what they feel the patient is experiencing.

A 'here and now' or 'mindfulness' trance

I would like to invite you to make yourself comfortable (take your glasses off if you wish), to place your feet firmly on the floor, and let your hands just rest comfortably on your lap. I would like you start to direct your attention to any feelings of touch or pressure where your body is touching the floor or seat. Become aware . . . of the feel of your feet on the floor . . . of the support of the chair along your back . . . of the pressure of your bottom on the chair . . . of the feel of your hands on your lap . . . of the sounds around you [mention whatever you can hear] *. . . you can become aware of your breathing, not changing it in any way . . . just being with your breath . . . noticing the slight movement in your tummy as you take a breath . . . in and out . . . noticing the movement of your chest with each breath . . . in and out. And if you notice that your mind has wandered . . . don't be cross with yourself . . . that is just what minds do . . . you can be pleased that you noticed your mind had wandered . . . and then you can gently bring it back to attending to those sensations . . . of touch and pressure . . . breathing your breath . . . if you become aware of some other sensation you can gently acknowledge it and then decide whether to focus your attention on that sensation or bring it back to what you were doing before . . . not having to do anything at all . . . just observing with kindly attention the sensations of touch and pressure . . . the sounds . . . your breathing. . . .*

You would then suggest that the patient went to their own special place, enjoying it while you give some positive suggestions, and then bring them back to the here and now by counting back from five to one in their head so that by the time they reach one, they are fully awake and alert, feeling refreshed and calm.

An Orientation to Trance

I would like to invite you to make yourself comfortable . . . maybe take a few deep breaths . . . allowing yourself to relax with each outgoing breath . . . and allow your eyes to close . . . begin to notice just how comfortable your eyelids can feel . . . gently resting on your eyes . . . and as your body begins to relax . . . your mind can begin to wander to other times when you have felt comfortable and relaxed. . . .

Introduce some examples: maybe lying in the sunshine listening to the birds, maybe floating, rocking gently up and down on the water, or maybe an occasion when they had a little 'quiet time' to themselves. . . .

> *As you are sitting here, listening to my voice, you can take from my words whatever will help you and be useful to you . . . we all lead such busy lives it is good to have a little time now and again to 'be' rather than have to be doing . . . and you don't consciously need to 'do' anything at all . . . you can just enjoy noticing just how relaxed you can feel as your unconscious mind drifts into thoughts and feelings and you begin to have that communication between your conscious and your unconscious mind that we are usually too busy to notice. . . .*
>
> *I do not know quite how quickly you can <u>go into trance</u> but as you begin to become more and more focused . . . and as you begin to become more and more absorbed . . . in your internal experience . . . your conscious mind can begin to notice just how you experience trance so that it is even easier to return to this state when you next decide to do so . . . we are all unique and special individuals and I cannot know exactly how you feel in trance . . . but some people notice a feeling of heaviness as they sink comfortably <u>deeper and deeper</u> . . . whilst others feel a sensation of lightness as they float gently and easily into that state of <u>relaxation</u> . . . whilst still others start to lose awareness of quite where their arms and legs are . . . and however you experience trance . . . it is perfect for you. . . .*

In the above paragraph, the underlining relates to examples of embedded commands (see page 53).

Active Alert Hypnosis

All the inductions described above tend to focus on relaxation, but it is perfectly possible to induce hypnosis whilst the patient is undertaking physical activity such as walking on a treadmill or using an exercise bicycle (Bányai *et al.*, 1993). Suggestions are given for alertness rather than relaxation, together with increasing energy and focus.

Malott (1984) compared levels of hypnotic responsiveness in 48 undergraduate students resulting from four induction procedures: (a) verbal active-alert induction alone (just using imagination), (b) bicycle pedalling alone, (c) verbal active-alert induction plus bicycle pedalling, and (d) traditional relaxation induction. No difference was found between (c) and (d), both of which were significantly more effective than (a) or (b).

An Amalgam of Techniques

This has become the author's (LB) usual induction and deepening process which has been found useful for the majority of patients and allows a natural drift into therapy. It takes about six minutes to administer but can be lengthened or shortened as appropriate.

> *Get yourself comfortable and . . . when you are ready . . . let your eyes close. Spend a few moments getting in tune with your breathing . . . you might find it useful to take a few, slightly deeper*

breaths . . . then . . . let your breathing settle down . . . into a nice relaxed rhythm . . . and as your breathing settles into a nice relaxed rhythm . . . you become aware that breathing out is pure relaxation . . . so, as you breath out . . . just let that word . . . relax . . . drift through your mind . . . some people hear it as though there is a little voice inside their head saying . . . relax . . . some see it as though it is written up inside their mind . . . and some do both . . . but whatever happens for you . . . just let that word . . . relax . . . drift through your mind with each breath out . . . and each time that word . . . relax . . . wanders through your mind . . . allow waves of relaxation to spread right through your body . . . drifting down through your tummy . . . to your legs . . . and feet . . . and toes . . . through your arms . . . to your hands . . . and fingers . . . and through your neck . . . to your head . . . and your mind . . . imagine you've taken yourself to the beach [or wherever the special place is] . . . remember . . . this can be somewhere you know well . . . or purely imaginary . . . but wherever you are . . . imagine you are there . . . on a glorious day . . . sun shining . . . blue sky . . . not a cloud in the sky . . . not a care in the world . . . as you are lazing there . . . the warmth of the sun . . . just melts away the remaining bits of tension in your body . . . and . . . as your whole body relaxes . . . it allows your mind to focus . . . on the fragrance . . . that fresh, salty fragrance of the sea . . . which . . . clears your mind . . . and . . . helps your mind to listen to the sounds . . . the sounds of the waves . . . lapping gently upon the shore . . . and each time . . . a wave laps gently upon the shore . . . so waves of relaxation spread through your mind . . . and through your body . . . and soon . . . you find yourself . . . in that lovely . . . dreamy drowsy state . . . where your thoughts can drift into any direction you wish . . . without any . . . effort whatsoever. . . .

Having suggested that thoughts can go in any direction, you can move seamlessly into looking at the problems. You have also involved the special place, so that is there for support whenever needed.

Deepening

Many of the above techniques involve opportunities for deepening and so separate methods may not be required, at least at the beginning of a session. It is not unusual, however, to 'pause' from therapy during a session and 'prepare' the patient for the next phase by using a deepening sequence. The experienced therapist will notice when a patient has lightened their trance and automatically give suggestions to deepen the trance. A complex formal method is not always necessary; maybe use a simple phrase such as *"Just let yourself drift down deeper and deeper."* There is also a commonly held view amongst therapists that suggests that the patient will naturally drift to the depth that is required at each phase of the therapy.

Notwithstanding the above, the following methods are examples of deepening techniques which can be used whenever needed.

If using an arm levitation induction using helium balloons

I would like you to imagine untying that balloon from your wrist . . . and as you watch it drift away . . . you can become more and more deeply relaxed . . . more and more comfortable . . . as the balloon becomes smaller and smaller . . . as it floats off into the distance, until it is just a tiny speck on the horizon. . .and you are completely relaxed inside and out. . . .

Counting

As I count up from one to ten you can allow yourself to become more and more relaxed with each number, deeper, and deeper . . . One, allowing all the outside noises to recede into the background. . . . Two, more and more comfortable. . . . Three, four, five, and as your body relaxes you can let your mind drift. . . . Six, comfortable inside and out. . . . Seven, floating down through the chair/ couch. . . . Eight, nine, deeper and deeper. . . . Ten. . . .

Counting can be either way; some people find counting up works for them whilst others find deepening is easier when you are counting down.

Stairway

I would like you to imagine some steps or stairs . . . and as you walk down step by step . . . you will become more and more deeply relaxed . . . and as you become more deeply relaxed you can walk down another step . . . deeper and deeper . . . step by step. . . .

Deepening bind

I am now going to stop talking . . . and in a few moments . . . when I start to talk again . . . you will be even more deeply relaxed.

Fractionation.   It has been found that facilitating someone to repeatedly go in and out of trance deepens the trance state.

In a moment I am going to count from five to one and as I count you will feel yourself waking up and . . . when I get to one you can open your eyes . . . but, as soon as your eyes are open I will start counting from one to five and as soon as I start counting your eyes will close and you will feel yourself drift back into an even deeper state of hypnosis . . . so that when I get to five you will be deeper than you ever thought was possible . . . five, four, three, two . . . one . . . open your eyes . . . one . . . close your eyes, two, three, four, five. . . .

This can be repeated several times until you feel you have achieved your goal. It is very useful, especially in obstetrics, where it helps the mother to realize she can go in and out of trance very easily *". . . with each contraction . . . such that as labour progresses you can become deeper and deeper relaxed and more and more comfortable."*

Lift technique.   Be aware of your patients' fears and do not use such imagery with someone who is phobic of lifts.

I want you to imagine . . . that you are wandering through the corridors of your mind . . . and at the end of the corridor there is a lift and you notice you are on the fifth floor. In a moment the lift will arrive and when you get in it will take you down floor by floor. As you go down you will feel yourself drift deeper into hypnosis . . . such that by the time you reach the ground floor . . . you will be deeper than you ever thought was possible . . . as you pass each floor I want you to say the number of the floor you have passed . . . as you get deeper . . . because you are so relaxed . . . you will find it harder to say the number . . . but I want you to try really hard to tell me which floor you are passing . . . even though it might come out no more than a whisper . . . get into the lift and press the down button . . . and remember to tell me which floor you are passing. . . .

Just as they are about to get to the ground floor where they are to be deeper in hypnosis than they ever thought was possible, you say, "*. . . And the lift goes straight down past the ground floor to the basement. . . .*"

This technique can produce some of the deepest trances especially in somnambulistic patients. In therapy, however, this is not always as useful as it might seem and patients may be so deep they are reluctant to speak. But, if this happens, you can always reverse the process and take them back up in the lift to a depth sufficient to access the benefits of hypnosis without the somnambulism.

General Considerations

As was intimated in chapter 3 the trance state is commonly utilized for healing and many complementary therapies access a trance state with the healing intent either intentionally or as a 'side effect' of the procedure such as massage or reflexology.

Whatever induction and deepening technique you have used, it is always sensible to use the 'special place' as the platform from which to launch into therapy. The easiest way to do this is to incorporate 'going to the special place' as part of the deepening process.

Some therapists seem to spend an eternity gathering and establishing the finer details of the special place and whilst this may be appropriate it is often unnecessary and has the potential to put undue pressure on the patient. Certainly it is important to suggest the use of all the sensory modalities but to ask someone to describe the fragrance when they cannot smell it creates a sense of failure and the therapist's approach should be to avoid those situations as much as possible. Do not unnecessarily give your patient a chance to fail.

It is of paramount importance to be aware of your patient's non-verbal feedback as this can be the only indication that your words may have inadvertently triggered a negative response. It is the responsibility of the therapist to be creative and flexible in their approach.

References

Bányai, E. I., Zseni, A. & Túry, F. (1993), Active-alert hypnosis in psychotherapy. In Rhue, J. W., Lynn, S. J. & Kirsch, I. (Eds.) *Handbook of clinical hypnosis*. Washington, DC, American Psychological Association.

Gindes, B. C. (1953), *New concepts of hypnosis: as an adjunct to psychotherapy and medicine*, London, George Allen and Unwin.

Malott, J. M. (1984), Active-alert hypnosis: replication and extension of previous research. *Journal of Abnormal Psychology*, 93 (2), 246–49.

Spiegel, H. & Spiegel, D. (1978), *Trance and treatment*. Washington, DC, APA Press.

10

Establishing the Problem

Introduction

Although you are aware of the presenting problem from both your referral letter and your previous history taking it is necessary, early on, to review this under hypnosis. What you know is the logical appraisal of the problem, and sometimes this is not the true underlying issue. There is no magic in this; you can just ask the subconscious mind to see what it feels is the major problem, or if you have used a computer metaphor in the explanation it is even easier. Ask the patient to imagine they have shrunk themselves down so small they can go into their control centre in their mind and ask the computer what the problem is. This approach is sometimes best as it inherently has involuntariness about it and can take away any blame or guilt that the patient may feel regarding the problem or lack of understanding of the important issues. It should be said that frequently there are no surprises and the presenting problem is just that, but a different slant on the problem is common enough to warrant using this with most, if not all, patients. Having established the main problem, it is then necessary to look at causes and resolution.

Uncovering Techniques

These techniques are used when a cause for the problem is unknown, or to enable the emotional links of the problem to be accessed. It is important not to imply that there has to be a cause so as not to create a false memory.

There are many uncovering techniques, but they all tend to follow the principal that the subconscious mind is somehow aware of the life events and sequelae that have led up to the symptom complex. Older techniques seemed to try to 'trick' the mind into revealing

The Handbook of Contemporary Clinical Hypnosis: Theory and Practice, First Edition.
Edited by Les Brann, Jacky Owens and Ann Williamson.
© 2012 John Wiley & Sons, Ltd. Published 2015 by John Wiley & Sons, Ltd.

this information as though the answer would come as a surprise, whereas newer techniques just assume that the information needs to be sought. Whatever method is used, the principles are the same and they can all be adapted to suit your own style. Methods should be flexible and therapists able to respond to a whole variety of answers and situations that may occur. When searching for causes there are two important points to remember: one is that most, if not all, of these causal events are likely to be upsetting and so some sort of dissociation is needed to protect the patient from being re-traumatized by re-living the memory. More will be said about this in the chapter on PTSD. Notwithstanding the above, the second point is that despite the attempts at dissociation, abreaction can occur at any time.

Abreaction

This is an unpleasant response that can occur in any therapy interaction. It may occur at any time in hypnosis due to accessing areas in the mind beyond conscious awareness and unwittingly triggering uncomfortable memories or feelings which are then brought to conscious awareness. Patients may become very distressed within moments of this occurring, and it can be a response to a real or an imagined experience.

This re-living can be so realistic, as far as the patient is concerned, that their body will actually reproduce the physical changes that occurred at the time of the event; if there was an element of suffocation, for example, your patient may suddenly find great difficulty breathing or may even stop breathing for a few moments. If they were physically abused in some way, then they may well feel that same abuse or the results of it whilst in your chair, just as if it were happening to them right at that very moment. A patient may scream, shout, sob, sweat, shake violently, curl up into a foetus, gag... it can be a truly unnerving experience for the unwary! On the rare occasions that this occurs, and if the patient comes out of trance, it may be useful to take the patient straight back into the hypnotic state to resolve the difficulty or to access calm.

Abreaction happens primarily in trauma survivors. It is a phenomenon which seems to be a powerful part of healing, although, if not handled well, it may re-traumatize. If it occurs, the important thing is to stay calm and reassure. Say things such as *"It is okay, just let those tears flow ... let all that feeling out knowing that you are safe now in the here and now"*. Do not try to hurry them, but as they settle take them back to their 'safe place'. They may wish to talk about it and recount the details in a dispassionate way either then or after the session, but it is important not to imply that they should.

In reality, however, most abreactions are mild and just consist of a few tears – but they still need to be handled sympathetically.

There can be three separate, though intimately connected, facets of any recalled memory: the perception of the event (usually visual), the physical sensations and the emotional response. They are entirely separate memories and each may 'surface' together or individually. The emotional part of any abreaction (often unwarranted guilt, shame or vulnerability) can be the most important, and once this has been 'surfaced' and worked through, it is not unusual for the patient to display little or no interest in further investigation of that particular memory. Occasionally the emotion is released without ever discovering the cause; this appears to matter little, for catharsis will still be affected and symptoms still alleviated.

In the vast majority of cases abreaction does not occur and the therapist is left trying to help the patient uncover the emotional links to past events which have led to the present symptom complex. It is important not to be overly elaborate, but in complex cases you may find you use a variety of techniques within one session allowing the patient to explore emotional links with a variety of situations. Below are a number of uncovering methods. None are guaranteed to work all of the time, so having a range of options is essential; only experience will help in deciding which to use with which patient, and probably that choice becomes intuitive rather than analytical.

Computer Technique

If you have used the computer analogy and left-right hemisphere model in your explanation, this will be a very simple and useful tool to use time and time again. Induce hypnosis by whatever method you choose and then proceed:

> *Imagine you have shrunk yourself down so small that you have gone inside your mind. Inside your mind, remember, there are lots of things... all your memories... all your feelings and... most importantly your control room. I do not know what your control room will look like in your mind... but I am going to talk as though it was like the captain's chair in Star Trek... controls at your fingertips, screen in front of you and all the help you could ever need close at hand. But your control room can be whatever you wish it to be.*
>
> *Ask your computer to do a 'Google' search on your problem... find out everything there is to know, when did it start, what caused it... and tell me what it comes up with... however silly or unconnected it may seem....*

Hilary – a woman who bit her nails

Hilary was a 22 year old woman who presented to her GP feeling 'crap'. She also bit her finger nails and had done so for as long as she could remember; she even bit them in her sleep. This and her general worrying nature were making life difficult for her especially in her work at an estate agents. She was referred by her GP for hypnotherapy and after induction and deepening was asked to go into her 'control room'. She asked her computer what was the cause of her problem, and Hilary said, rather incredulously, *"Well it's saying my sister's name!"* It transpired that this sister had died at the age of two from what initially had seemed like a 'cold'. This was before Hilary was born; her mother was pregnant with Hilary when the death occurred. At about the age of five Hilary began to worry about other members of the family dying: *"If my sister died from a cold..."* She would not sleep, in case something happened to them; or if she did, she had nightmares and this was when she started to bite her nails!

This simple technique has many different applications, and in this age of computer literacy is easy and well received by the patients. Hilary's case is a good example of the 'never-noticed-the-connection technique' (see page 16).

Finding the 'Problem' Room

This technique can be used with well defined problems such as phobias or with generalized disorders such as anxiety or depression. Having induced hypnosis:

> *Imagine you are wandering through the corridors of your mind . . . wandering down floor by floor into the depths of your mind . . . until you are below your 'should and ought' level . . . and there . . . right in the deepest part of your mind is a room named 'Problem'.* (It can be specified if known, such as 'x' worry room.) *In a moment . . . I want you to go into that room . . . you will be okay . . . you are only looking . . . so you will be able to see the problem without it bothering you . . . go into that room and tell me what you find there. . . .*

The beauty of this technique is that it can begin to unravel complex problems as well as simple ones. For complex ones it is often necessary to move on to secondary uncovering methods from this base (within the room perhaps) or to chip away at problems that seem so big to the patient that they are insurmountable. It also affords the therapist an opportunity to use trance logic (see page 22), intuition and metaphorical imagination to its full. Sometimes the subconscious seems to put all sorts of obstacles in the way, and it is not uncommon for the patient to go into the room and say, for example, *"It is too dark to see anything"*. Students should not be fazed by this and should offer a solution in a very matter of fact tone: *"Maybe you could turn the light on"* or *"Shine the torch"*. Speak as though it is totally normal for there to be a light or for them to just happen to have a torch with them. Or, if the door is locked, *"The key is usually hanging up"*. With practice the therapist gets used to being instinctive, intuitive and imaginative.

Barbara – a girl with eczema

Barbara was 16 years old and presented with a flare up of her eczema which always got worse when she was stressed. This flare up was associated with her forthcoming GCSE examinations. Her mother reported she seemed to worry about everything. She also had a needle phobia which was a problem as she tended to suffer from anaemia and needed fairly frequent blood tests. After induction she was taken down to her 'worry room': *"It is manic in here, too much, they are all flying round"*. It was suggested she just grab one as it flew past, and she was then asked, *"Which worry have you got?"* Her arm actually moved in trance and she said, *"Needles, blood, hospitals"*. Searching further on this, it transpired that when she was about three, Barbara was taken to hospital and needed to have lots of tests, and the doctors and nurses held her down and stuck huge needles in her!

The case below shows how the room titles can be interpreted in different ways by the patient yet can still be used positively.

Claire – a woman with irritable bowel syndrome (IBS)

Claire was a 26 year old worrier with irritable bowel syndrome and a bit of a perfectionist personality. In trying to locate the cause, source and origin of her worry, Claire was taken into her 'worry room'. Surprisingly, it was calm and quiet and she said *"I think this is the room where I come to worry, to go over things in my mind"*, so this did not appear to tell us anything causal. It was suggested to her that she must have opened this room at the time she had begun to worry so if she looked at the date plaque by the door (trance logic, and matter of fact tone!) it would tell us when this all started. *"When was the room opened?"* *"October 1985"*. *"And what happened in October 1985?"* Claire smiled, the sort of smile which accompanies a sudden realization: *"My sister was born!"*

As can be imagined, the 'problem room' can be modified in a number of ways. It is not necessary to direct them to rooms within their mind but to let their mind wander to a house or cottage in the woods (for example). Their description of the house or cottage becomes a representation of themselves and their problems, with rooms in the building revealing various problems. The 'problem room' can be used when the problem is known; for example, with chronic pain, the pain room will give a clue as to how the patient is interpreting it: *"It's so hot in here, it's all going too fast – I can't control it!"*

Thus, it can be seen that 'uncovering' is more about being flexible and supporting the patient in locating the source or cause of their problem and there is no one technique which will do the job. The experienced therapist will often used an amalgam of techniques within one session merging them as appropriate and not worrying about any seeming incongruity that happens when shifting from one metaphor to another; the patient in trance copes with it all without batting an eyelid! Some other methods (e.g. time road and cinema) will be described in other sections of the book when details are given about using hypnotherapy for specific conditions; be bold, however, look at the overall principles and tweak existing methods to suit your own personality.

Affect Bridge

Sometimes, we have only a 'feeling' to work with. Patients will find it difficult to describe it in words except as a feeling (affect) which has bedevilled them for a long time. Throughout our lives events occur where we, for one reason or another, do not express, deal with or come to terms with some emotion (affect).

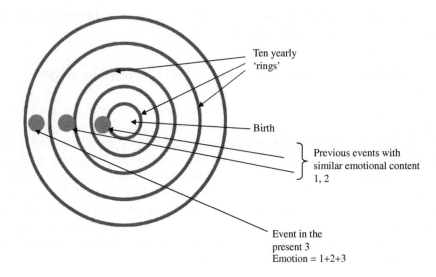

Ten yearly 'rings'

Birth

Previous events with similar emotional content 1, 2

Event in the present 3
Emotion = 1+2+3

Figure 10.1   Model showing how events in the past can influence the present.

In Figure 10.1, the late Pat Browne (a psychiatrist from Cork) showed how the negative emotion from past events is 'trapped' under successive memories that are laid down like layers in an onion. Each one of those memories carries an amount of potential energy insufficient on its own to cause a major upset but enough to create a persistent 'niggle'. Gradually the total amount of energy builds up to a point when an event (perhaps even apparently trivial) in the present can link back to those somehow related events and all the energy is released, so that the person experiences not just the affect from the present but all that from the past as well.

Another metaphor that may prove useful here is that of a bottle of champagne (or some other fizzy drink). The negative emotions build up, like bubbles in the champagne, until the pressure is such that they leak out or the bottle explodes.

The affect bridge (Watkins, 1971), then, is a technique that can allow the patient to regress, often in stages, to the sensitizing experience and open it up to psychotherapeutic intervention.

The principle of the affect bridge is that one first gets the patient to experience the emotions (affect) of the most recent event which triggered the emotion. Then they use that affect to track back (bridge) to a previous time when they felt the same affect. They are then able to deal with the earlier experiences that were linked to the later experience by the similar affect.

On some occasions there may be a chain of events which one travels along, using the affect bridge, clearing the past trauma at each event. A modern day metaphor for this approach is linked files in a computer; a change in one file results in the same change being made in all the linked files.

An example of the use of an affect bridge is presented here courtesy of Dr G Ibbotson.

Tracey – a woman who presented with flight phobia

Tracey presented with flight phobia although she had never travelled by plane. This was causing problems because her daughter lived in France and Tracey had been unable to travel to see her for several years. Upon taking a history she was not aware of why she was flight phobic. In hypnosis she was asked to go back to look at the time when her problem started. It transpired that she had travelled on the ferry just after the *Herald of Free Enterprise* disaster and had suffered from a severe panic attack. Using an affect bridge she took the feeling she had on the ferry back to a previous occasion and suddenly realized that what had triggered the panic attack had been a buzzer that the crew used to communicate, which had the same sound as the apnoea alarm she had had to use with her daughter when she was a baby. Once the link had been made, she was soon able to resolve her feelings of fear and travelled happily to France by plane.

Ideomotor Signalling

Ideomotor movement is a seemingly involuntary movement that is engendered by intention, focusing on an idea such as "Your arm is getting lighter and lighter." The patient is directed to other types of 'unconscious' movement such as head nodding in agreement or gesticulation whilst talking, and it is explained that their unconscious mind is perfectly able to produce movement which seems to 'happen all by itself'. In a way all body language is ideomotor movement and as such needs to be noticed and responded to by the therapist.

Ideomotor signalling is a technique whereby finger signals are set up for 'Yes', 'No' and sometimes 'I don't know' or 'I don't want to tell you'. It may be useful on occasion to set up such signals when the lethargy of trance makes speech more difficult, and it may also serve to deepen the trance state by giving a greater sense of dissociation. Ideomotor movement tends to be 'flickery' and slower than the smoother more 'conscious' movement. Head nods can be used to monitor how a hypnotic process is progressing with a patient, but finger signals allow for a more 'unconscious' exploration of any difficulty or psychosomatic problem. One way of setting up ideomotor finger signals is described below.

Setting up ideomotor finger signals

Rose came for help with her nail biting. It was explained that in everyday life we communicate using our bodies as well as words; we use hand gestures and head movements unconsciously without thinking. In hypnosis we can use fingers to allow the unconscious (or back) parts of our mind to do this. After a brief induction Rose was asked, *"Your unconscious mind can choose a finger on your right (or left) hand to mean 'yes'.*

Just allow yourself to think of the word 'yes', see the word 'yes', hear the word 'yes', feel the word 'yes' and as you do so allow your unconscious mind to choose a finger to represent 'yes'. When it has done so, one of your fingers, or your thumb, can lift into the air, all by itself, to let me know which one has been chosen".

This was repeated for a 'No' finger signal: *"So, now I would like you to keep thinking to yourself 'no, no, no' and as you do so allow your unconscious mind to choose a different finger to represent 'no'. When it has done so, another of your fingers, or your thumb, can lift into the air, all by itself, to let me know which one has been chosen".*

If the movement is slight, then it may be useful to suggest, *"If that slight movement is a 'yes' signal, then maybe your unconscious mind could repeat it and enhance it so that I can be sure that we have clear communication between us".* Sometimes there does not appear to be even slight movements of the finger, and in this case it may be useful to say, *"Sometimes the unconscious response is to give you a feeling in one of your fingers that is different from the others, and if this is the case then your conscious mind can notice that feeling and move the finger consciously so that I can have clear communication with your unconscious mind".* Sometimes even this does not get a response, in which case other methods might be needed to explore the difficulty.

The Cognitive Interlude

Sometimes during hypnotherapy especially after a problem has been uncovered, the therapist realizes that there is significant misunderstanding or lack of knowledge. It is essential that this is corrected as soon as possible and this can be done whilst the patient remains in trance. It is not uncommon for the patient to have misunderstood a poorly worded explanation given by a health professional: *"You have got a crumbling spine"* or *"You have got heart failure"* are classically misinterpreted. The case example of Hilary (page 125) is an example where she, as a child, felt responsible for the safety and wellbeing of her parents and required appropriate explanation. By giving the explanation during hypnosis, it allows the linked emotion to be modified at the same time.

Reference

Watkins, J. G. (1971), The affect bridge: a hypnoanalytic technique. *International Journal of Clinical and Experimental Hypnosis*, 19, 21–7.

11

Resolving the Problem

Introduction

Having identified a problem, it is clearly important to resolve it. Sometimes it appears that once things have been brought to conscious awareness, then that is enough. Certainly it is important for the patient to have reached the 'Ah ha' moment when feelings and events seem to fall into place, but it is essential to confirm that all is now well. In the vast majority of cases some sort of resolution procedure is required. Once more there are many different methods most of which have been adapted from a common theme, and it is important not to fall into the trap of believing that one type of resolution is needed for one type of problem.

Before one looks at various examples, there are two major points to consider:

1 Real events in patients' lives have happened, and no amount of therapy can ever lead to them not having happened!

2 Many problems are brought about by a persistence of an age appropriate response to a situation or event and thus the feeling or response was 'appropriate for then but not appropriate for now'.

Any method, therefore, needs to have considered both the above points, although not necessarily in that order. For the most part the method used in uncovering the problem is a guide to the resolution process but, as with the uncovering process, it is usual to use an amalgam of methods.

The Handbook of Contemporary Clinical Hypnosis: Theory and Practice, First Edition.
Edited by Les Brann, Jacky Owens and Ann Williamson.
© 2012 John Wiley & Sons, Ltd. Published 2015 by John Wiley & Sons, Ltd.

Computer Technique

If this was used and the 'search' identified the problem, then this analogy can easily be extended to act as the method of resolution. It can be introduced at this stage whatever the uncovering methodology used. It is based on the principle that your mind's computer has all the most sophisticated features possible. Thus problems can be deleted, edited, archived, minimized and so on. It is absolutely necessary that it is the patient who chooses what to do.

By all means suggest some possibilities, and although it is tempting to suggest to all that problems be deleted be mindful of point 1 above. Ewin (2005) introduced the concept of the 'personal museum'. This is the repository for things which you wish to store but are not to remain active or even remotely influential on a day to day basis. The option to move some of these events to the 'personal museum' is sound, and it gives credibility to the positive fact that the patient has coped despite the problem. The patient remains in control and can revisit the problem again should they ever wish, but they control access to the museum. Thus, 'archive in your personal museum' is a frequently used and highly successful method of resolution.

Those who are computer literate are well aware of the constant reminders we receive when we log into the internet to 'update' our programmes. The concept is sensible – why run on an old outdated programme? – yet point 2 above reminds us that we rarely update our own programmes (particularly those that are long established and highly emotional). The patient is invited to press the update button on the mind's computer and replace the old with the adult response and feeling to that event or situation. It can be as sophisticated as appropriate for the patient. The persistence of the outdated programme will have caused ramifications at various stages throughout the patient's life, and it is possible to use the 'search and replace' facility to search out these milestones and amend the response accordingly.

Having archived or deleted the problem, it is important to replace it with something positive.

> *Now that you have moved the problem to your personal museum you have got loads of space in your mind and you can see just how much space and emotional energy you were using for that problem. I want you to think of a time when you felt really good and happy, it needn't be anything special . . . perhaps just a lovely afternoon or a day out . . . but a time when you felt really good . . . I do not need to know the details but just nod or tell me when you have got that lovely feeling in mind . . . that's good. Now the magic of hypnosis is that you can take that lovely feeling and make lots and lots of copies . . . and I want you to go on copying that lovely feeling until you have got a pile big enough to fill all that space in your mind . . . tell me when that pile is big enough . . . that's good . . . now press the file button and that good feeling will be filed into every one of those spaces in your mind . . . so now wherever you are in your mind . . . you are close to that good feeling and you only have to stretch out your hand and it will be there . . .*

Occasionally, a patient will not have any happy memories and you may have to change the words to 'the best you have ever felt'. These patients are rare but are often abuse victims or from war ravaged areas and you will perhaps have a clue that happiness has so far eluded them. If you suspect this might be the case, do not use this approach as it will add to the patient's sense of failure and helplessness.

The Older Wiser Self

This technique acknowledges that the present adult now understands the origin of the problem and (with the benefit of hindsight) can reassure the child part of their mind which is still harbouring the problem. It can be used with a wide variety of problems.

A typical version for Hilary (page 125) for example might be: *"Imagine that you, as you are now ... your older wiser self ... has gone back in time to you as you were then. Give yourself a cuddle, tell yourself everything is okay, I'm okay ... you are not going to die ... I'm here ... Mum and Dad are okay ... there is no need to worry".* Then after a moment, ask how that feels. In the majority of cases they smile and report that they feel so much better. If they do not, always ask what was preventing them feeling better; the likelihood is that there is some previous or outstanding issue to deal with first.

Just occasionally, you do not get any response for any obvious reason. Do not worry and do not worry the patient; move on, with plenty of reassurance, to another technique.

Destroying the Problem

There are numerous techniques, all variations on a theme, whereby the problem is collected up as a pile of rubbish, on videos or some such, and the patient is invited to get rid of the pile in whatever way they wish. A common method is to burn it on a bonfire, but smashing it up and tipping it over a cliff also seems to be regularly chosen. As with the above methods, it is important to always replace the problems with some good feelings. It is also important to note that throwing away or destroying a problem does not necessarily equate with having dealt with it but may facilitate further work towards resolution.

The special place of bliss (after McCarthy, 2005)

A particularly nice metaphor to help offload is where the problems are envisaged as stones which are being carried around in a rucksack.

> *I would like you to imagine you are wandering in the corridors of your mind ... right in the depths of your mind ... as you walk along the corridor, there are doors leading off to the left and to the right ... the end of the corridor is a door ... a very inviting sort of door with a large nameplate which says the 'Special Place of Bliss'. Just the name has an effect on you ... and your imagination begins to ponder ... bliss, an old fashioned word ... yet full of awe and wonder. Bliss ... a*

beautiful state of mind . . . so much more than just the absence of negatives . . . the absence of worries . . . the absence of problems, concerns, difficulties, traumas and upsets. Bliss is more than that. As well as the absence of negatives, bliss is also the positive presence of such concepts as freedom . . . peace . . . comfort . . . joy . . . happiness . . . relaxation and rest . . . absolute pleasure . . . sheer and utter . . . bliss. So, in order to experience this sense of bliss . . . we have to let go . . . of all of our problems . . . and worries . . . and concerns . . . as this drifts into your awareness . . . you become conscious of the rucksack on your back. . . . You take the rucksack off and place it in front of you. Inside you find a collection of stones . . . special stones . . . all sorts of shapes and sizes but all . . . special. These stones are special because . . . in hypnosis they are very symbolic . . . they represent all of your problems . . . every problem . . . every concern . . . and . . . because these stones represent every problem . . . not just the ones that you have told me about . . . only you know what particular issues these stones represent . . . only you know how many stones are in the backpack . . . and perhaps most importantly of all only you know the weight and size of each particular stone . . . of each particular problem . . . and . . . unless you need to or want to . . . you will never have to share any of those details. . . .

These stones represent all of the problems that you have in your mind . . . there are the problems of now, the present . . . the issues and concerns that are on your mind now, today, this very day. But . . . there are also stones about the past . . . and the past includes yesterday . . . last week . . . last month . . . last year . . . ten years ago . . . many years ago . . . all the way back to your earliest memories of problems from childhood.

And . . . there can also be stones from the future . . . these are called the 'what if ?' stones. Some people carry around stones that represent worries about what might happen in the future . . . what could go wrong . . . what might not change. Sometimes these stones are possibilities . . . sometimes . . . remote possibilities. But . . . some people carry them around like rocks of probabilities . . . or even as huge boulders of certainties. . . .

In a moment it will be time to start emptying the rucksack . . . take out the stones . . . one by one . . . as you look at each stone . . . you will instinctively know what problem it represents . . . as you take it out, briefly feel the weight . . . and then place it down on the ground beside the door . . . then identify the next stone, feel the weight of that stone and then put it down beside the door. Some of the stones are the ones you expected to find there . . . others might be a bit of a surprise . . . some of the stones may be heavier than you had expected . . . some may be surprisingly light . . . some of the stones may have been there for a long time . . . some may no longer have any relevance. . . .

Keep doing this till the rucksack is completely empty. Take your time . . . there is no hurry . . . but when your rucksack is completely empty let me know by saying yes or lifting a finger.

Start unloading all your problems . . . stone by stone . . . issue by issue . . . problem by problem . . . until the bag is completely empty . . . take all the time you need.

Good, now that the rucksack is empty you are ready to go into the 'Special Place of Bliss'. . . .

Take some time to absorb the . . . joy . . . the enchantment . . . some people like to describe what they see in their 'Special Place of Bliss' . . . others just like to wander in silence . . . whatever you wish to do . . . but note how good it feels . . . to be unburdened . . . free. . . . (Give a few minutes to allow time in the room.)

It is now time to leave your special place of bliss . . . but . . . now you have found it you can wander there any time you like.

As you come out of the room you can see your stones lying beside the door. Sometimes the pile has got smaller . . . those which have lost their relevance have gone, those formed from pessimism have melted away . . . those stones left in the pile represent your remaining problems . . . past . . . present . . . and even future. Only you know what these stones represent . . . only you know how many stones there are. As you pass those stones some choices drift into your mind . . . you can pick all the stones up, put them in your rucksack and continue to let them burden you . . . you can leave them where they are in that pile . . . or you can move them . . . to . . . your personal museum . . . some stones represent real past events . . . those events cannot be changed . . . but those memories need not remain active . . . safely stored in your personal museum, they are out of harm's way. . . . I don't need to know what you have done with any of those stones . . . but you can tell me if you wish . . . but when you have done with them whatever you want to do . . . just nod or lift your finger so I know you are finished . . . so as you wander back along the corridor you can still feel the pleasure of the special place of bliss . . . and there is a spring in your step as you taste the joy of being freed of your burdens. . . .

The beauty of techniques such as this is that they can be modified to suit your particular patient. The 'Special Place of Bliss' does not have to be accessed through a corridor; it can be a 'Garden of Bliss' for example. Knowing your patient's likes and dislikes means that you can help guide them to maximize their own desires.

One useful addition that can be used especially with abused (especially sexually abused) patients is to add in a 'cleansing' sequence. Many such patients feel dirty and contaminated, and this method affords an opportunity to 'wash away' that feeling. One such patient described a fountain in her place of bliss, and as she stood close she could feel the cool spray. She was guided to let that spray represent the cleansing. As the cleansing began she said the water was black and horrible, but within a few moments this had become clear and she felt 'cleansed and pure'. Whilst it could be argued that such an addition would have had the effect of introducing negatives into the 'Special Place of Bliss', the experienced therapist can often sense (and often the patient will volunteer) that these negatives are preventing this lovely place becoming magical. It is in these cases that this sort of addition is beneficial.

This sort of technique can also be extended to aid relapse prevention. Having off-loaded one lot of stones, what is to stop the rucksack being filled again? It is useful to point out that some people have become 'habitual stone picker-uppers'. No one is born a stone picker-upper, so this habit is learnt and most commonly this is from a parent. This is particularly so where there is poor self esteem and a high level of social conformity where 'ought to' and 'should' feature greatly. Now that they have learnt that these stones can be put down again, their rucksacks need not become burdensome and they can soon learn not to pick up so many in the first place.

But some people with a lot of stones are not 'habitual stone picker-uppers'. They are usually very generous people, warm hearted and giving. They sometimes leave their rucksacks wide open and this allows other people or events, but particularly other people, to dump some of their stones in the open rucksack. Suggestions about keeping the rucksack closed can be very helpful.

The perfumed pebbles metaphor (courtesy of Mr D Simons)

Often past events are not wholly negative and this variation on the above metaphor can be used to preserve the positive emotional part of the memory. The patient imagines walking beside the sea or a lake, carrying a rucksack filled with pebbles that represent past negative events. They sit down comfortably, open the rucksack and take out the pebbles one by one. The pebbles have a perfume that represents the positive feelings attached to the negative event and as they roll the pebble in their hand, the perfume rubs off as this positive feeling flows into them. When they are ready they can throw the pebble, which now only represents the negative feelings associated with the event, into the water in order to be rid of it.

The Silent Abreaction

Another popular variation on the general theme of letting go of one's problems has become known as the silent abreaction. Many people have feelings of anger or frustration that, for whatever reason, they find inappropriate to express. They then begin to emulate a pressure cooker and as the pressure builds something has to blow! Helen Watkins was responsible for the initial development of silent abreaction, a technique that allows people to deal with powerful emotions such as anger in a safe and controlled way (Watkins, 1980). As with most hypnotherapeutic techniques it has since been adapted by many therapists to suit their own style and work with different patients (Krakauer, 2009).

Following induction and deepening (preferably a relaxing induction) and after spending a moment or two settling down in their relaxing place, one can proceed:

> *I would like to invite you to close your eyes and visualize a place such as a quarry or a mountain, miles away from anywhere or anyone. There you find a rock that is suitable to represent your anger. I would like you to imagine projecting all the anger that you want to be rid of just now into the rock, so that it becomes your anger, maybe marking it in some way. You can adapt it in any way you wish in order to link it to your particular situation. Give me a nod when you have done this.*
> (Wait for nod.)
> *I would then like you to look around your rocky place to find some way of smashing up your rock. You can deal with that rock in any way that you think fit. Maybe you will find a sledge-hammer, a pick or even a pneumatic drill. Enjoy really smashing that rock to smithereens. If you want to hurl verbal abuse at it in your head, then do so, no one will be disturbed. When you are satisfied with the end result and the rock is in tiny pieces, give me a nod.*
> (Having obtained a nod, one continues.)
> *Decide what seems right to do with the dust that is left and then allow yourself to imagine going to an appropriate place to feel calm again, maybe by a mountain stream or in a woodland glade, and to get in touch with those feelings of calmness. When you are ready, bring some of that positive emotion back with you as you open your eyes and return to the here and now.*

It is very important to suggest that the patient gets rid of as much anger as is appropriate at the time rather than 'all' their anger and not to open their eyes as soon as they have finished smashing up their rock but to go and connect with calmness before re-alerting.

As always there are alternatives, for example, instead of a stone in a quarry the therapist can suggest felling a dead tree in a wood (see page 399). The image must involve a physical action but need not be violent. One patient decided to knead dough to make bread, projected her anger into the dough, then imagined returning to the imagery of a bridge over a river and throwing the bread into the water, watching whilst the ducks eat it up. The therapist and patient are limited only by their own imagination.

Although the 'silent abreaction' was developed for use with anger, its use has extended way beyond this and all sorts of feelings or problems can be attached to the object, including problems about which the therapist needs to know nothing. This can be very useful where problems are too painful or embarrassing to openly discuss initially.

Corrective Imagery

So far the techniques for resolution have largely related to past problems or events that have caused subsequent problems. Much of the work of the hypnotherapist relates to dealing with physical symptoms (with or without a psychological cause), for example, chronic pain, migraines and irritable bowel syndrome (IBS). Corrective imagery can be a useful tool with these conditions as well, the concept having a wide range of applications for the hypnotherapist.

The method utilizes the link between feelings and images: a feeling or symptom is often represented in the patient's mind by an image which becomes fixed. If we change the image, we change the associated symptom.

Following induction and deepening the patient is asked to imagine they have shrunk themselves down so small that they can go inside their body. Once inside they are asked to wander down to where the problem is. Once there they are asked to describe it in detail.

Lucy – a woman with infertility problems

This 32 year old lady had presented with dysmenorrhoea. It had been an ongoing problem but with no underlying pathology. She was hoping to start a family so the usual options of the contraceptive pill or Mirena coil were not appropriate. Whilst doing hypnosis: *"I want you to wander down into your womb and imagine you are there during a period.... What does it look like in there?... What does it feel like?"* *"It is awful, dirty...it is disgusting...red, hot, tight...so tight I'm going to suffocate".* *"Change it then so that it feels better...cool it down...open some windows...make some more space...clean it up...take your time...there is no hurry...but tell me when you have done that. Is that better? Good!"* (Spontaneous comment from patient:) *"I remember my mother saying it was dirty when my periods started."* *"It doesn't have to be like that...it is just nature preparing your womb for the egg."* (This was the unspoken understanding that this is what she was wanting.) *"Is your womb ready for the egg now?"* *"Yes...that's lovely, soft, warm, cosy."*

This method also allows the use of trance logic and metaphor – opening windows in the womb!! Again this allows the therapist and patient to be as inventive and innovative as they are able.

One modification of this is a technique called the 'split screen' (Graham, 1988) whereby the patient imagines the problem state displayed on one screen and next to it another screen with the solution or desired state. As the patient watches, they bring the desired state screen towards them and push away the problem into the distance. The important aspect is to connect the patient strongly with their desired state so that their focus is not on the problem.

Ecological Check

Just as there are consequences from living with problems, so there can be (unforeseen) consequences from resolving them. Without being aware of it, we all adapt and modify our behaviours and responses to maintain the comfortable status quo.

Imagine a family in which the husband has been out of work as a result of chronic pain, where the wife has changed her role to become the major breadwinner and the husband has had to become the children's supervisor. The children's role within the day to day environment would have changed to accommodate their parents' situation. This pattern had been well established and had become the norm. The constant pain (and psychological sequelae) had led to the husband becoming grumpy, angry and unpleasant to live with. His wife found solace with a male colleague, and the children survived but were treading on eggshells all the time and spending lots of time away from home with 'friends' some of whom were rather unsavoury characters. Whilst no one would argue that it would be a very good thing to sort out this unfortunate man's pain, it is obvious that the consequences of this for the family would be far from simple.

The vast majority of cases do not have the same intricate web to unravel, but nevertheless it is important to allow the patient to review the effects of therapy in order to prepare themselves for the less obvious consequences so that change can be modified to keep pace with the effects for other people.

The methods are relatively simple. The patient is asked to imagine that they have progressed in time to some point in the future and they are asked to do two things: firstly, to see how they are coping without their problem and, secondly, to see how the rest of the family and their close friends and colleagues are faring with the 'problem free' person. It is important to do both of these things together.

There is no need to make this complicated and imply that there is some special magic required to get them to go forward in time. If you have used the time road metaphor in an earlier part of the therapy, then this is simply utilized to move ahead rather than back and the patient acts as an observer from his dissociative position in the helicopter, balloon or whatever was used originally (see page 401).

Equally, if you have used a computer metaphor, then the patient can be asked to 'check for bugs' with the new problem free person. Mentally rehearse what it would be like going through ordinary day to day routines without the problem; what has the effect been on others? If problems are identified, then these can be tackled by whatever method seems suitable. Often it is a question of simply slowing the progress so that others can get used to the idea.

References

Ewin, D. (2005), Workshop given at the European Society of Hypnosis Conference, Gozo, Malta, September.

Graham, G. (1988), *The happy neurotic*. Newcastle, Real Options Press.

Krakauer, S. Y. (2009), The therapeutic release of anger: Helen Watkins's silent abreaction and subsequent elaborations of the anger rock. *International Journal of Clinical & Experimental Hypnosis*, 57 (1), 47–63.

McCarthy, P. (2005), Workshop given at the joint meeting of BSCAH, RSM and BSMDH, Glasgow, Scotland, May.

Watkins, H. H. (1980), The silent abreaction. *International Journal of Clinical and Experimental Hypnosis*, 28, 101–13.

12

Ego Strengthening, Anchoring and Re-alerting

Introduction

As the name implies, ego strengthening is anything which boosts the patient's positive beliefs in themselves, increases self esteem and helps the patient tap into inner resources. It should be used as a basis for all communication during hypnotherapy where positive ideas can flourish.

It is said there is one possible contraindication and that is with a depressive patient who is expressing suicidal ideation (see page 196). In reality this accounts for a very small number of cases, and with that possible exception ego strengthening should be used in all hypnotherapy sessions.

Ego strengthening works in trance because of the increased suggestibility that occurs when left brain activity decreases (i.e. a reduction in the so-called critical faculty).

Ego strengthening need not be complex and be no more than a positive attitude from the therapist during the session: *"That's good"* and *"You've done a lot of good work today"* are examples. Care must be taken, however, not to come across as patronizing or cynical. Incorporating a specific ego-strengthening section in your session is good practice. The novice is perhaps advised to begin with a script which can be read out to the patient. This can be modified to suit your own style as you gain in confidence. With greater experience scripts will not be necessary and ego strengthening will become a spontaneous part of your verbalization. However a few suitable scripts are reproduced below. These can be used at any stage during the session but perhaps best towards the end so that the patient is 'dehypnotized' from a highly positive state.

The Handbook of Contemporary Clinical Hypnosis: Theory and Practice, First Edition.
Edited by Les Brann, Jacky Owens and Ann Williamson.
© 2012 John Wiley & Sons, Ltd. Published 2015 by John Wiley & Sons, Ltd.

Hartland's Ego Strengthening (Waxman 1989)

You have now become so deeply relaxed...so deeply asleep that your mind has become so sensitive...so receptive to what I say...that everything that I put into your mind...will sink so deeply into the unconscious part of your mind...and will cause so deep and lasting an impression there that nothing will eradicate it.

Consequently...these things that I put into your unconscious mind...will begin to exercise a greater and greater influence over the way you think...over the way you feel...and over the way you behave.

And...because these things will remain...firmly embedded in the unconscious part of your mind...after you have left here...when you are no longer with me...they will continue to exercise that same great influence...over your thoughts...your feelings...and your actions...just as strongly...just as surely...just as powerfully...when you are back at home...or at work...as when you are with me in this room.

Every day...you will become physically stronger and fitter. You will become more alert, more wide awake and more energetic. You will become much less easily tired...much less easily fatigued...much less easily depressed...much less easily discouraged.

Every day...you will become...so deeply interested in whatever you are doing...so deeply interested in whatever is going on...that your attitudes will become much more positive and your mind will become much less preoccupied with yourself, your problems and your own feelings.

Every day...your nerves will become stronger and steadier...your mind will become calmer and clearer...more composed...more placid...much more tranquil.. You will become much less easily worried...much less easily agitated...much less fearful and apprehensive...much less easily upset. You will be able to think more clearly...to concentrate more easily...your memory will improve...and you will be able to see things in their true perspective...without magnifying them...without allowing them to get out of proportion.

Every day...you will become emotionally much calmer...much more settled...much less easily disturbed. Every day...you will feel a greater feeling of personal wellbeing...a greater feeling of personal safety, security and control than you have felt for a long, long time.

Every day...you will become...and you will remain...more and more completely relaxed ...and less tense each day...both mentally and physically and as you become...as you remain ...more relaxed...and less tense each day...so you will develop much more confidence in yourself...much more confidence in your ability to do...not only what you have to do each day...but much more confidence in your ability to do whatever you ought to be able to do without fear of consequences...without unnecessary anxiety...without uneasiness. Because of this...every day...you will feel more independent and more able to stand on your own feet and to comfortably hold your own...no matter how difficult or trying things may be.

Because all these things will begin to happen exactly as I tell you they will happen...you will begin to feel much happier...much more cheerful and much more optimistic. ...

Hartland's ego-strengthening script has stood the test of time and can be used on its own or as a precursor to some other ideas that you may wish to float.

From Dr G Ibbotson:

Now relax and go deeper, deeper, even deeper and in a moment I will talk to you and you will be even more deeply relaxed.

(Then wait for about 15 seconds before speaking again.)

There are four things we are going to accomplish as a result of these suggestions. I call them the four S's: symptom relief . . . self confidence . . . situational control . . . and self understanding. First your symptoms will be less and less upsetting to you. You will pay less and less attention to them because they will bother you less and less. You will find you have a desire to overcome them more and more. As we work at your problems you will find that your self confidence grows and expands. You will feel more assertive and stronger and will enjoy moving towards a healthier lifestyle. You will be able to handle yourself better in any situations that come along, particularly those which tend to upset you. (Give examples.) *Finally and most importantly, your understanding of yourself will improve.*

We have worked hard here today, and we have stirred up lots of things inside your unconscious mind. I want you to be particularly alert and sensitive to those changes in behaviour which will occur over the period of time until we get together again . . . which will be the direct result of the marvellous work that you have done here today. Do not be surprised if these changes appear radical . . . they will always be appropriate to your particular needs.

Brief Ego Strengthening

While you are in your special place . . . any suggestions I give you . . . or you decide to give yourself . . . will sink straight down . . . into your unconscious mind . . . where they will remain . . . having an effect long after you have left here . . . . Each day . . . you will become . . . more relaxed and calm . . . more confident . . . more in control . . . you will become so deeply interested . . . in whatever you are doing . . . or whoever you are with . . . that your problems will bother you less and less . . . this feeling of calmness and peace . . . this feeling of confidence . . . will mean that you have more energy . . . to do the things that you want to do . . . you will see things more clearly . . . without distortion . . . more in perspective . . . and each day . . . this feeling of confidence and calmness will grow . . . having a positive effect on how you think . . . and how you feel . . . and how you behave . . . so that as each day passes . . . you will feel and act with more confidence . . . you will feel more calm and relaxed . . . you will feel fitter and healthier . . . and be able to use your inner resources . . . to help you to do . . . whatever is right for you.

Ego Strengthening Using Imagery

You could use the imagery of a small, still pool that represents your 'pool of internal resources'.

Give me a nod when you have found your pool . . . the air above the pool represents your conscious mind whilst below the water represents your unconscious mind . . . the surface of the water is calm and unruffled . . . and as you look below the surface of the water you can notice that there are crystal stones of various colours on the bottom of the pool. These represent all the strengths, abilities and resources you already have, and you can feel pleased and encouraged as your unconscious mind identifies them, even though your conscious mind may not know exactly what they are. Some you may have forgotten about and others you may not have realized you have. Around the edge of your pool are various other coloured crystal stones that represent other positive feelings or resources.

Pick up a stone that represents 'x' (e.g. physical relaxation, calmness, confidence to be the way they want to be, optimism) *...and your unconscious mind will let you know which stone is the right one. What colour is it?... Then drop it gently into your pool, and as you do the sunlight catches the (whatever colour) crystal and the pool and yourself are bathed in that lovely (colour)...and as you sense that glow, that 'x' feeling fills your mind.* (This is repeated with different coloured crystals representing all the resources the patient wishes to add. If the clear crystal has not been linked with any special quality, then use that last as follows.)

As you let that clear stone glide into the pool, it splits the sunlight into all the colours of the rainbow...and as you are bathed in all those colours, you realize you have become fully in touch with all those resources within you. ...

An alternative is to use pebbles or stones and then suggest the patient makes connection with the pool once the stones have been added. This could be by paddling in it, swimming in it or anything else the patient prefers.

The Resource Room

Before using this technique it is important that you know enough about your patient to be able to list some achievements about which the patient should feel proud. If you do not know any, it is probably best not to use it. However, it can be a very powerful and enabling method.

Imagine you are wandering...along the corridors of your mind...in the depths of your mind ...there are doors off to the left...and the right...but at the end of the corridor...is a room named 'inner resources'. In a moment...I will ask you to go into that room...and when you do...you will find all your resources...some you may have forgotten about...some you may not realize you possess. So wander into that room...and tell me what is there.

From here on the therapist must think on their feet, but there are three common scenarios:

1   The room may be empty. If this is the case, it is imperative to use your knowledge of the patient to provide some resources to put in the room.

Are you sure it is empty? It can't be. ....I am aware of lots of things you should be proud of. .... (Then list some of the things, e.g. you have got two lovely children, both doing well at school, you coped brilliantly with your mother's illness.) *So if they're not in your inner resource room...where have you put them?* (Gradually get them to fill the room with achievements.) *That is good...now you have started to find them, put them on show...Does that feel better? Good! Now all that resource is available for you to use at any time...instead of hiding it away in the depths of your mind...leave the door open...let those resources circulate right through your mind. ...*

2 The room may have some things in but often not on show and hidden away in cupboards covered in dust.

> *It looks as though you haven't been in here for a long, long time? . . . Better give it a spring-clean . . . what have you found?*
> *(Usually they smile as they discover things, old school or college certificates, a letter of an appointment to a job, photographs of an event and so on. Listen and encourage, and if necessary do the same as above to fill the room.)*
> *Leave the door open. . . .*

3 Occasionally the room is full and pristine yet the patient has very poor self esteem. A close look at the resources frequently reveals high academic achievement but very little in terms of social or relationship success. What was meant to be an ego-strengthening method has turned out to have uncovered a problem. No matter; the patient has plenty of resource and this aspect needs to be acknowledged and used. From there, however, without pointing out the negative, one moves on to explore the identified problem, often high achieving parents with high social conformity.

Anchoring

This technique is a useful way of learning to access a good memory by using a simple cue and is based on the right hemisphere state linked memory (see page 98) and is summarized in the equation:

$$\text{Memory} = \text{Event} + \text{Emotion Attached to It}$$

Smells, sounds or images can trigger memories and the good or bad emotions attached to them. These are called 'anchors'. According to Lankton (1980), 'An anchor is any stimulus that evokes a consistent response pattern from a person'.

In the same way as certain external stimuli (inadvertently) become associated with past experiences (thus recalling the past experience), it is possible to deliberately associate a stimulus to the memory of a past experience. Once this association has taken place, one can then trigger the memory of that experience at will, together with the corresponding emotion that is attached to it.

This is done by deliberately adding a specific new stimulus whilst a person is re-living (or associated with) an experience, so that the new stimulus then becomes associated with the recalled experience.

The new stimulus could be a touch, a sound or a visual image. If the timing is good, reintroducing the same exact stimulus brings back into consciousness the feelings of the recalled experience. This procedure is known as 'anchoring', and the inserted stimulus is referred to as the 'anchor'. Its purpose in therapy is to enable the instant recall of a particular feeling at a time when it is needed (e.g. to enable the recall of relaxation when about to do something which previously has caused anxiety). The triggered positive feeling is sometimes called the 'resource state'.

Physical objects can be used to trigger happy memories such as good luck charms and talismans. The problem with this is that objects can get lost or broken so a visual, auditory or kinaesthetic anchor is often preferable.

For anchoring to be effective:

1   The patient must have a memory of the sought after emotion.
2   The person must be associated with the event, that is, re-living the experience as though it was happening to them now . . . seeing, hearing, smelling and feeling the accompanying strong emotions.
3   The timing needs to be right in that the anchor needs to be set as the affect peaks rather than as it diminishes.
4   The anchor must be definite, precise and easily reproducible.

It must be said that not all patients can vividly recall or re-live a suitable feeling and although there is ample anecdotal evidence for rapid responses, with the general patient population results often fall short of the expectation (Gibson & Heap, 1991). Notwithstanding the above they are useful techniques to learn, and the clenched fist method (Stein 1963) has stood the test of time.

Clenched Fist Method: Calvert Stein Technique (Stein 1963)

The patient during hypnosis is asked to recall and re-live a time when the problem was bad, for example, anxiety during an interview. The patient is then asked to make a fist with their non-dominant hand and let this feeling collect into that fist. When all the feeling is being held in the hand, the patient is instructed to open it and *"Let the feeling go"*. Following this, the patient is then asked to recall and re-live a time when they felt good, relaxed and with the resource to cope with the particular problem. This feeling is then collected in the dominant hand. The clenched fist becomes the anchor for that good feeling. Calling up the good feeling by clenching the dominant hand is then practiced until the patient feels confident that they can do this outside of the therapeutic setting.

The theoretical concern with this technique is that a negative anchor has been set up with the non-dominant hand which could inadvertently be triggered, and although it is true that this can be immediately alleviated by opening the hand and letting go, the potential for a negative cue persists. Bandler and Grinder (1979) claim to have resolved this by the simultaneous triggering of both negative and positive anchors when it is said that the anchors have been collapsed and, if the strength of the positive anchor outweighs the negative one, the negative feeling is abolished. To avoid confusion, many therapists now use only the positive part of the Calvert Stein technique.

The clenched fist is only one of many anchors, and squeezing the thumb and forefinger together is a common alternative. Some therapists touch the patient on, say, the wrist to set up the anchor, but touching patients during hypnosis without prior discussion is not recommended. Another way of achieving the same thing is to get the patient to metaphorically wire a switch to some easily accessible part of the hand or wrist, and when needed this 'switch' can be activated to produce the good feeling.

Often visual anchors can be used such as starlight, fireworks or coloured auras, as can auditory anchors such as the imagined sound of the sea. If the strength of the anchor is not very high, say less than eight out of ten, then it is worth enhancing. There are various ways of doing this; one is by suggesting that the patient stands up and imagines in front of them someone (real or fictional) who has the feelings they want to anchor (e.g. confidence); they then step forward into the person and imagine feeling their confidence and at the same time fire their anchor. Another is by building up the affect in imagination and anchoring it when it reaches a level of eight or nine out of ten. Anchors can also be 'stacked' by linking several different but complementary feelings to the same trigger.

Post-Hypnotic Suggestion

Post-hypnotic suggestion (PHS) as a phenomenon has been discussed in chapter 2. A post-hypnotic suggestion is a suggestion given under hypnosis that will be carried out 'automatically' after the hypnosis session has finished. This has obvious applications in therapy, and there is a place for the use of this in every hypnotherapy session. In fact much of the ego strengthening is delivered as a form of post-hypnotic suggestion: *"You will find that each day you seem calmer and more able to use your own resources to look at things in a helpful way."*

Many such suggestions are presented in implied form, but within the therapeutic session it is useful to consider the general approach and what is hoped will be achieved. Specific examples will be given in other chapters, but the following points may be useful.

- Induction: it is useful to give a PHS to the effect that *"The next time you attend for therapy you will easily drift into a deep state of hypnosis on the simple instructions I will give you at the time"* or *"As with any skill, as you practice you will find it easier and easier to enter hypnosis whenever you want to."*

Note that the suggestion relates to the therapy sessions and not *". . . every time you hear my voice."* This clearly adds safeguards to scenarios where the patient may hear your voice in another context. Similarly, by not defining the instructions there can be no inadvertent cuing of the trance state until it is appropriate. Common sense applies, and there is no need to include caveats for every conceivable situation.

Some therapists will give a PHS for a very quick induction and set up cues such as a shoulder tap, and although impressive to the casual observer it tends to be rather gimmicky and perpetuates the old-fashioned 'power' of the hypnotist. Deepening is usually carried out afterwards, and in reality very little is gained.

- As an aid to uncovering and understanding the problem: *"... between now and the next session your subconscious mind can be working on the problem, without upsetting you in any way ..."*
- As an aid to resolution and ego strengthening: *"... you will find that your pain does not bother you so much ... so you can do more things ... and because you can do more things and your pain does not bother you ... you feel so much happier and more confident."*
- As an aid to self-hypnosis and homework: *"... as you practice your self-hypnosis each day ... you will be able to become more and more relaxed ..."*
- At the dehypnotizing stage: *"... enjoy those lovely feelings in your relaxing place ... and those lovely feelings will remain with you ... even after you come out of hypnosis ..."*

Termination of Hypnosis (see also page 28)

Try not to be in a hurry when it comes towards the end of the session. At some stage before you begin to 'wake up' the patient, it is necessary to ask, *"Is there anything else you wish to tell me today?"* Just occasionally they tell you something so important and urgent that you simply have to deal with it there and then, even if it means being late for the next patient. Fortunately this is rare, and even if it is highly important it is possible to acknowledge the problem and agree to put in on the back burner with a promise to deal with it next time. In these events the use of imagery where the problem can be placed in a box to which the patient has the key can be very helpful.

Most patients come out of hypnosis easily, but some patients, particularly after a long and emotional session, will take time to 'come to' and re-orientate themselves into the waking state. Traditionally the therapist has taken control of this timing by counting backwards from, say, three to one; with instructions to *"Open your eyes"* or *"Wide awake now"*. The preferable alternative is to allow the patient to 'wake up' in their own time. A suitable verbalization would be: *"It will soon be time for you to come out of hypnosis ... and when you do, you will feel very pleased with yourself for making progress with (the problem) ... you will find that between now and when we meet again for hypnosis, your subconscious mind can continue to work on the problem without any conscious distress ... and when we do meet again for hypnosis ... you will very easily and quickly drift into a lovely state of hypnosis on the simple instructions I will tell you at the time ... so ... when you are ready ... you can wake yourself up ... and open your eyes ... and note how good you feel."* Never miss the opportunity to end on a positive note.

Occasionally a patient will alert and abreact which may indicate a problem that needs resolution.

David was working on grief resolution following the death of his wife and as he alerted he started beating his chest with both hands, saying, *"Guilty, guilty"*. He was taken back into hypnosis, where he revealed that he had started having a relationship 12 weeks after his wife had died. Work was done on helping David resolve his feelings of guilt.

Sometimes the unexpected happens:

Alison alerted from hypnosis extremely distressed with a severe headache. She reported that this felt exactly the same as the headache she had experienced for five days following an epidural. Alison was taken back into hypnosis and the degree of headache 'turned down' with the suggestion given that it would become less bothersome and any ramifications from it would be dealt with at the next session. Interestingly, Alison's headache lasted five days in a mild form before disappearing.

Sometimes a patient will complain of a headache and this may well be because they have not spent long enough re-alerting. If they are taken back into hypnosis, and alerted more slowly, the headache will usually disappear.

As will be mentioned in later chapters, all sensations should be returned to normal before re-alerting apart from any positive feelings generated during hypnosis which, especially with calmness in the anxious patient, should be continued into the waking state by using a post-hypnotic suggestion.

During the first few minutes after a hypnosis session, the patient will still be more open to suggestion and so a quick resume of the salient points of the session may be appropriate.

Some patients will need longer to re-orientate than others, and suggesting that they move around, stretch and maybe drink some water can be useful to ensure that the patient is completely grounded again.

Post-Hypnosis Chat

It is important to find time to have a few moments of chat at the end of each session. It is not necessary to go over the whole of the hypnosis but necessary to find out how the patient felt in general terms; were there any problems, anything that could help next time? They may want to chat about specifics, and this should be allowed although it is sometimes better to try to delay those discussions until next time to allow the subconscious to settle things; but if the patient clearly needs to chat, it is important to do so. It is also important to check that the patient feels that they have addressed their concerns and that the patient is honest about how they felt the session and their rapport with the therapist progressed. It has been shown (Miller 2005) that doing this reduces the drop-out rates considerably as the therapist knows early on whether the session was in accordance with the patient's comfort and expectations.

Frequently during a session the therapist gets to understand – the 'Ah ha' moment – before the patient. It is absolutely paramount that this is not detailed to the patient. It is only when the patient realizes the 'Ah ha' factor for themselves that resolution begins.

Before the patient goes, ensure that arrangements for the next session are clear.

Pre-Hypnosis Chat

It might seem strange to end this section at the beginning of another session. Many experienced therapists feel that this is one of the most important parts of the therapeutic process. There are many questions that could be asked, but the main themes, although perhaps obvious, are worth listing:

- How have they been?
- How did they feel after the last session?
- Are things any clearer or better?
- Have they practiced any relaxation or self hypnosis?
- What did they find most useful from the last session?
- What has changed? (This implies that something has!)
- What do we need to do today?

It may be useful to enquire as to what has prevented completion of any 'own work' tasks (see page 151) if the patient reports that they have not done these. Sometimes it is because they have felt very much better but sometimes it is because they expect the therapist to do the work or wave a magic wand. Exploration of any 'self saboteur' can be therapeutically useful.

Some patients seem to want to chat and chat. Do not be in too much of a hurry to proceed with hypnosis – if the chat is relevant and positive, let them talk. Sometimes, however, you get the sense that they are skirting around the problem, and then it is worth making encouraging noises to continue with the hypnosis – but, remember, you can only do this if they are ready to move on. Sometimes it is worth reminding both yourself and the patient that if their conscious deliberations could have solved their problems, they would have done so already, so using hypnosis may be useful sooner rather than later – they can still talk in hypnosis.

References

Bandler, R. & Grinder, J. (1979), *Frogs into princes*. Moab, UT, Real People Press.

Gibson, H. B. & Heap, M. (1991), *Hypnosis in therapy*. Hove, Lawrence Erlbaum.

Lankton, S. (1980), *Practical magic*. Cupertino, CA, Meta Publications.

Miller, S. D., Duncan, B. L., Sorrell, R. & Brown, G. S. (2005), The partners for change outcome management system. *Journal of Clinical Psychology*, 61 (2), 199–208.

Stein, C. (1963), The clenched fist technique as a hypnotic procedure in clinical psychotherapy. *American Journal of Clinical Hypnosis*, 6, 113–9.

Waxman, D. (1989), *Hartland's medical and dental hypnosis*. London, Bailliere Tindall.

13

Self Hypnosis and Other Homework

Introduction

It has been argued that all hypnosis is self hypnosis; the patient simply follows the instructions of the therapist. Self hypnosis is, therefore, where the patient knows the instructions and is following them!

As with the novice therapist, initially the patient can use scripts which they read and visualize or listen to pre-recorded programmes on CD. With practice the patient can generate their own narrative but still often 'hear' it as though it is being spoken by the therapist. Sometimes the patient can record themselves reading the script, then listen when they have an opportunity to relax. This way they have added their own syntax to the script so that points of emphasis will be immediately recognized.

The importance of practice cannot be overemphasized, but any homework should be under the ownership of the patient and could more properly be termed 'own work'. It can also be useful to discuss scheduling self hypnosis practice with the patient.

Traditionally seven reasons for using self-hypnosis have been given (Gibson & Heap, 1991):

1 As an anxiolytic. Benson (1975) reported that a daily period of simple relaxation (15 to 20 minutes) has been shown to significantly reduce stress indices.
2 Can help to 'regain control' when stress levels are increasing. Winding down stress levels in this way is useful in psychosomatic conditions such as irritable bowel syndrome (IBS), for migraine, and in sleep onset insomnia.
3 As a useful way of rehearsing goal-directed affirmations: "*Smoking is bad for my health*" "*Exercise will keep my body healthy*". Such repetition helps keep up the motivation.
4 Offers an opportunity to mentally rehearse (for example) anxiety and anger management procedures.
5 Gives the patient a method of self help in conditions such as chronic pain.

The Handbook of Contemporary Clinical Hypnosis: Theory and Practice, First Edition.
Edited by Les Brann, Jacky Owens and Ann Williamson.
© 2012 John Wiley & Sons, Ltd. Published 2015 by John Wiley & Sons, Ltd.

6   Can help to facilitate learning: relaxation helps to focus the mind.
7   Enables the person to get in tune with inner emotions; helps increase self esteem and feeling of being in control.

As before, common sense should prevail as to the content of the suggestions, but it is important to avoid dangerous, irresponsible or unrealistic suggestions such as to be happy all day long and never to feel guilty, to feel no pain in a damaged joint until the race is over or to need only two hours of sleep whilst swotting for exams.

Self hypnosis is best taught in trance as a post-hypnotic suggestion. The patient is taken through the process during hypnosis with the suggestion that they will be able to do this for themselves when appropriate. It is advisable to use the induction procedure that they choose and feel comfortable with and agree on the purpose of the self hypnosis.

Before doing self hypnotism the patient must decide on the purpose and set the intent of the session. It may be simple relaxation, using trance imagery for calmness, confidence or energy or some other purpose. They need to decide how long they wish to remain in hypnosis so that their internal clock will mentally 'give them a nudge' when it is time to re-alert. If they are very tired or sleep deprived, it is a good idea to set an alarm in case they fall asleep. Hypnotic suggestion and ego strengthening should be planned in the waking state; suggestions need to be kept short, simple and positive.

When teaching self-hypnosis in trance, it is important for the therapist to build in safety with hypnotic suggestions such as the patient will only do their self hypnosis when it is appropriate, and if any emergency should arise whilst they are practicing they will come out of trance immediately to deal with it. Self hypnosis should *not* be done in the driving seat of a car. It is worth giving the suggestion that the patient will not do this for entertainment but only for their own self as training in hypnosis may make them more susceptible to the abuse of stage hypnotists.

Post-hypnotic suggestion to trance is given by linking the trance state to a cue or 'anchor' such as taking three deep slow breaths or *"When you decide to do your self-hypnosis you can tell yourself how long you wish to remain in hypnosis and, taking a deep breath in, count to three in your mind. On the count of one, your eyelids will feel heavy; on the count of two, they will close; and on the count of three, you will instantly feel this comfortable feeling as you slip into hypnosis"*.

It can be suggested that the patient re-alerts by counting backwards from five to one in their head (or whatever dehypnotizing process is used) to become wide awake, feeling refreshed and alert.

The process is summarized below:

1   Induce hypnosis.
2   Suggest timing and use only when appropriate.
3   Suggest the trigger to the trance state.
4   Give safety suggestions regarding emergencies and stage hypnosis.
5   Repeat instructions (3) regarding entering hypnosis.
6   Re-alert.

7   Repeat instructions out of hypnosis (2), (3) and (4).

8   Suggest the patient tries it out there and then for a couple of minutes.

It is useful to have the patient practice in the consulting room so as to build their confidence, and it may be useful to suggest that they enter self-hypnosis a few times that day so as to strengthen the link they have made.

It is useful to teach a short and long method for use in different situations. A shortened version of Spiegel's eye roll technique can be used whereby the patient rolls their eyes up and takes a deep breath in. As they breathe out they let their eyes relax, let their whole body relax and pass their hand across their forehead collecting up the hassles of the moment which they discard with a short internal affirmation as they let their hand down. An alternative can also be done in a busy office quite unobtrusively by suggesting that the patient rest their head on one hand whilst staring at the point of a pencil on the table held in their other hand. They take a deep breath in, let go any unnecessary tension as they breathe out and for a few moments take themselves to their special place before re-orienting to the office. As their special place has become linked with calmness over time as they use it during their hypnosis and self hypnosis practice, they can access that calmness by being there for a few moments. Their special place is used as an anchor to calmness.

This is particularly useful in situations such as when the patient is about to go into an interview or some other stressful situation and they feel the need to regain control.

Most patients report that they never feel as deep when using self hypnosis compared to when they are with the therapist. This is completely normal but does not mean that it is not effective.

Below is a script routinely given out in the author's (LB) unit.

Self Hypnosis Exercise

1   Find two periods of time during the day for a 'time-out'. This period can be as brief or as long as you find helpful. Ideally find a comfortable chair where you will not be disturbed or conversely practice whilst in bed before going to sleep at night time. Should you be disturbed by the telephone, door bell or any other signal that takes precedence over your current exercise, then immediately, and without any problem, attend to the situation.

2   Allow your eyes to look up at the top of your head, take a deep breath and then as you slowly breathe out allow your eyes to close and stay closed. Take three more deep breaths and slowly breathe out, and as you do so become aware of how you feel and just allow yourself to become cosy and relaxed and at ease with yourself.

3   In order for your muscles to become more at ease with themselves focus on muscle groups, starting with your toes. For example, clench your toes and release them, then your leg muscles, your pelvic muscles, your arm muscles, your shoulder muscles and your facial muscles. Having done this, perhaps you would care to focus on a particular part of your body, give this a particular colour, and on the next breath allow the tension and anxieties to just blow away on a breeze and notice how it feels.

4   Following on from the muscle relaxation, allow your mind to become even more at ease with itself by thinking of a 'mental holiday'. This can be the same or different each time. It can be either real or imaginary. The place can be in the past, present or future, and if you have difficulty coming to a particular place maybe you could imagine such a place. Having done this, use all your senses to experience this place in a very special way. Allow yourself to become aware of your emotions particularly satisfying ones such as love, contentment, confidence, warmth and general feelings of wellbeing. You will find it helpful to anchor some of these feelings having concentrated them in the corner of your mind by capturing them. To do this bring your finger and thumb together touching the tips to make a circle, knowing that in appropriate circumstances whenever you bring that anchor into place you will immediately feel as you did.

5   Having been through the routine, when you feel it is the time to come back to the present just allow your eyes to open bringing back with you as much of those pleasant feelings as are needed to allow you to continue with the rest of the day. Conversely, if you are practicing this at night time you will be able to drift off into a very deep and refreshing sleep allowing your subconscious to just do whatever work is necessary to put things in order. When you wake the following morning you will feel refreshed, full of energy, ready for the day and will notice as the day passes by how things just fall into place with yourself becoming more and more confident about your abilities to achieve those things that are important to you.

References

Benson, H. (1975), *The relaxation response*. New York, William Morrow.
Gibson, H. B. & Heap, M. (1991), *Hypnosis in therapy*. Hove, Lawrence Erlbaum.

Part Three

Specific Disorders

14

Self Esteem and Self Confidence

Dr Ann Williamson

Introduction

Self confidence is a quality many of our patients lack, and poor self esteem underpins many emotional problems. It is worth taking a little time to understand what we (and our patients) understand by these terms. *Self esteem* relates to how we value ourselves whilst *self confidence* relates to how we behave. Self esteem is to do with being and self confidence with doing, which builds on a positive feedback loop of successful action. It is important that therapists do not acquiesce with the patient's belief (expressed or not) that they lack potential and inner resources (Barnard, 1994).

People are born with genetic predispositions to certain personality traits such as introversion and extroversion (Jung, 1923), and these may become accentuated by the contexts in which they develop. Our early years have a huge influence on the adult we become, but personalities are not set in stone (Hall *et al.*, 2001), and with work and commitment people can and do change.

Published Evidence

Because any work with patients so often includes helping to boost self confidence and resilience, there is little in the way of evidence in the literature solely working with esteem and confidence issues. Building confidence in performance enhancement is covered in chapter 37, and there are many case studies to be found where hypnosis has been used to

The Handbook of Contemporary Clinical Hypnosis: Theory and Practice, First Edition.
Edited by Les Brann, Jacky Owens and Ann Williamson.
© 2012 John Wiley & Sons, Ltd. Published 2015 by John Wiley & Sons, Ltd.

enhance self confidence in patients with fear of public speaking (Schoenberger *et al.*, 1997) or with burnout (Ruysschaert, 2009). Improvement in self esteem has been found in studies involving cancer patients who were taught relaxation (equivalent to self hypnosis) and other coping skills (Fawzy *et al.*, 1990), and Taylor (1995) reports increased self esteem levels in a treatment group using hypnosis compared with controls. As with many other conditions, hypnosis is usually combined with other approaches for a successful treatment programme (Crouch & Straub, 1983).

The first part of this chapter concerns self esteem and how we can help our patients build self worth so that they value themselves (and hence others) more.

Self Esteem

There are six foundation stones to good self esteem (Branden, 1994), as shown in Table 14.1. The first is to be able to live consciously in the present rather than focusing on the past, as is common in depression, or continually worrying about the future, which happens in anxiety states. Teaching our patients mindfulness techniques whereby they notice their current sensory inputs without evaluating them can be very helpful (Fortney & Taylor, 2010; Hofmann & Asmundson, 2008). Mindfulness can be practiced at any time by deliberately focusing attention on what one is seeing, hearing, smelling, tasting or touching at any one time without labelling it either good or bad. Practicing this can facilitate our patients' abilities to step back from thoughts and feelings rather than being swamped by them.

Table 14.1   The six foundation stones of good self esteem

The six foundation stones of good self esteem
1. Living consciously
2. Being assertive
3. Self responsibility
4. Personal integrity
5. Having a purpose
6. Self acceptance

People with good self esteem are able to be assertive. This does not mean aggressively trying to get one's own way but rather allowing that we all have needs and accepting our own needs as well as those of other people. Often patients say that they are afraid or have some other negative emotion that stops them from communicating with someone. It can be useful in this situation to suggest that they start by telling the person how they feel, which immediately helps them to be more in control of the communication. Positive mental rehearsal in hypnosis can facilitate patients practicing more assertive communication.

Assertive Communication

'I feel' – own your feelings.
'I would like you to' – describe your desired action.
'And that would help me feel' – describe how that would help you.

Self responsibility, where we understand that we own our emotions, thoughts and actions and likewise cannot control those of someone else, is another key element of good self esteem.

Personal integrity is also important; being true to what one really believes and being in touch with one's intuition, thereby not doing something contrary to one's gut feelings or instinct. It is also necessary to be aware of and work with one's own values in mind.

Another foundation stone is that of having a purpose; not only short term goals but also having a sense of why one might exist, of one's purpose in the world. This can, but need not, be a belief in some sort of benign life force or God. Obviously atheists and agnostics believe in a different kind of purpose.

Most important of all is the idea of self acceptance, accepting all parts of oneself, good and bad, in the knowledge that no one is perfect but we can all strive to improve. Even those parts of ourselves that we may regard as failures or negative in some way should be appreciated as they may have been instrumental in driving us forward.

A useful metaphor is that of a tapestry; where the individual threads are interlinked to make a whole picture that cannot be appreciated until one is a distance away. Any thread, however seemingly insignificant, once cut will lead to the beginning of a hole in the tapestry. Each thread has its purpose within the whole.

We are what we think we are

Often, with patients who have poor self esteem and low resilience, it is found that they have a background of early trauma or come from a dysfunctional family. The use of an experiential metaphor here can be very effective. The patient is handed a ten pound note and asked how many one pound coins they would give in exchange for the note. Obviously they will answer, 'Ten'. The therapist then takes the note and screws it up, throwing it on the floor and stamping on it. The crumpled note is handed back to the patient with the same question. As the patient again answers, 'Ten', the point is made (Beaulieu, 2006, p. 27).

If our patient thinks of themselves as lacking in confidence they will, at some level, be making an internal image of themselves as looking, feeling and behaving in this way which will act as reinforcement of poor self confidence. Using hypnosis and imagery can help our patients connect more strongly with their goal or desired emotional state. By utilizing associated imagery the patient not only sets the goal at an emotional as well as a cognitive level, but also helps access those unconscious resources that are not so readily available to consciousness.

The 'mirror exercise' following can be done without any prior hypnotic induction and can be usefully done each morning to set the goal of the desired state or whenever motivation needs boosting (Graham, 1988).

Mirror exercise.   The patient first closes their eyes and imagines a full length mirror behind them in which they quickly put an image of how they do not wish to be. This may be a visual image or could simply be an 'awareness' of how they don't wish to be. They then imagine a full length mirror in front of them and spend a little time developing the image or 'awareness' of how they would like to be, and then decide which way they want to step. This gives apparent choice but it is unlikely that they will choose to step backwards. The patient then steps into and associates with the desired image and feels how good it would be to be this way. They say something encouraging and appropriate to themselves internally and then open their eyes again. The whole cycle should take no more than a minute or two. The first time this is taught, it is worth checking at this stage that there are no difficulties in doing the exercise, and then the whole cycle is repeated four or five times. After repetition in this way, the negative image is much less compelling and has often faded away.

Mirror exercise

1   Start with eyes closed.
2   Image behind – the negative state.
3   Image in front – the desired state.
4   Step into the desired state.
5   Feel how it feels to be 'x'.
6   Say something appropriate internally.
7   Open eyes.
8   Repeat four or five times.

Once the therapist knows the patient a little, it can be useful to use an experiential metaphor such as the playing cards (Beaulieu, 2004).

Playing cards metaphor.   For this, you can use an old pack of cards as it does not matter if a few are missing. The patient is asked to select a card which they think represents them (Ace high, two low). The therapist lays this card face down on a table or desk. If the patient has low self esteem, the card picked will be low (e.g. a three). The therapist then asks questions about roles and activities that they know are relevant to the patient and on which they suspect the patient will score higher or that they have previously said that they enjoy (for instance, how do they rate themselves as a friend, as a daughter, cooking a meal, gardening, dancing and so on?). These cards are added to the pile; for instance a Jack, a ten, a Queen, an eight and another ten. The therapist picks up the cards with the original three showing and confirms with the patient that this is the right card to represent them. The therapist then fans out all the cards and asks the patient, 'Well, what about all these then?'

Compassionate friend exercise.   Often low self esteem is driven by self critical negative dialogue. This can be disrupted such as described on page 176, or compassionate friend imagery (Gilbert, 2009) can be used. This latter is based upon eliciting from the patient the fact that they act as a good and compassionate friend to someone they know. How they respond to their friend when this friend faces difficulties or is distressed is determined, as is the fact that they do not respond in this way to themselves in a similar situation.

The patient is then asked to close their eyes and imagine something or someone that represents their self critical dialogue. A particular time when they criticized themselves is selected, and they are asked to listen to the self criticism and then open their eyes. The feelings that this engenders are discussed, as is the positive intent behind self criticism (i.e. to get the person to do better). The image may be a wagging finger or an angry or disappointed face, and the self critical voice usually sounds angry, contemptuous or disappointed and the feelings produced are usually those of discouragement and failure.

This is contrasted with how they previously described their response to their friend in trouble. The second part of the exercise involves the patient closing their eyes again, imagining what that compassionate, caring part of themselves would look like and returning to the incident that they looked at previously, but this time listening to what this part of themselves says about it. Often the image is that of light or a smiling face or someone putting an arm around their shoulder, and feelings of encouragement are usually accessed.

This can be a useful exercise to suggest as daily homework so that each evening the patient decides on one time when they had self critical dialogue and listens to what their 'compassionate friend' has to say about it. After doing this deliberately a number of times, it tends to then become an automatic response rather than the self criticism. This exercise would not however be appropriate if the patient was having difficulty imaging the compassionate part of themselves and is 'trapped in negativity'. It must also be remembered that being compassionate and supportive does not mean minimizing the fact that a mistake may have been made, but it does allow a more balanced view of the difficulty. The patient is more able to dissociate and view the difficulty dispassionately rather than getting overwhelmed by feelings of failure.

This ability to stand back from situations and not get completely swallowed up by the emotions of the moment is a skill that many patients need to practice. Many patients need to be encouraged to utilize their innate ability to step into 'observer' position and also sometimes into someone else's shoes in order to gain needed insights (see page 183).

Remaking the day

A useful variant of the above, which is best taught in trance then used during a self hypnosis session, is to ask the patient to review the day. When they find, in retrospect, situations where they would have preferred to have acted, behaved or felt differently, they are asked to edit that event and 'remake it' so that they acted, behaved or felt as they would have liked to have done. At first they find themselves remaking the same sort of thing regularly but in time 'as the days and the weeks go by', they discover that they have actually begun to mould themselves into the person they wish to be. This method has the advantage that there is a real time assessment of how that change has affected others and offers an opportunity to vary the 'moulding' to minimize difficulties to others and maximize the benefits.

Understanding where they developed their ideas about themselves can be helpful in building self esteem. By looking at their younger self and understanding that the people around were operating from their own stage of emotional development and difficulties, the patient can begin to realize that some of their ideas about themselves were based on opinions rather than facts. Beliefs that originally were thought to be true can be changed, such as common childhood beliefs in Father Christmas or the Tooth Fairy.

Use of a time road metaphor in building self esteem

The therapist needs to first discuss memory (see page 396) with the patient and talk about the possibility of belief change. It is useful to talk the patient through the process prior to actually doing it in hypnosis, seeding or priming the patient with these ideas.

The therapist describes to the patient a simplified version of self development; the idea that when born the patient had no idea of themselves as a separate identity, and that this develops as they grow, influenced by the words and actions of significant people around them. Their ideas about themselves are formed in this way and lead to a self belief that either they are valuable and valued or not.

The patient is asked in hypnosis to imagine their time road (see page 401) with their past in one direction and their future in another. Permission is obtained to review where their self beliefs arose. Having received agreement, dissociation is achieved by asking the patient to float up above their time road and look down on it from a distance.

Once there the therapist asks the patient to float back to above the time they were born and to begin, as they come towards the present, to review where their beliefs about themselves were generated and why. As they begin to understand this they can decide whether the belief still serves them well or not, in which latter case it is 'archived' and a more appropriate belief generated. This is continued until the patient is back above the present and feels the work is completed. As the patient does this review it may be suggested that the younger part of themselves may need help in understanding why people were responding in a less than ideal way and may need comforting, support and reassurance. This can be given by the older, wiser self, some real or imaginary friend or maybe a higher self or compassionate friend. All these 'parts' are of course projections of the person concerned and part of their inner resources.

To end the exercise it may be suggested that the patient floats to a time in the future where they have a sense of their own value as a human being. As the therapist talks about the six foundation stones of good self esteem, they can really connect with a sense of self worth as they associate with that image and make the internal adjustments necessary. Once they have really connected with a good feeling of self worth, they are directed to re-alert bringing back the resources they need with them. Alternatively they could be directed to their pool of resources (see page 143) and add a pebble to their pool for the work they have just done before re-alerting.

Building self esteem depends not only on an internal shift but also on action. Self confidence builds on success, and to have success one has to take action. A useful way to build action is to use the scaling question from brief therapy approaches in hypnosis.

Scaling Question in Hypnosis

The therapist asks the patient, whilst in hypnosis, to imagine their goal at ten, the opposite state at zero, and to determine what number they are at now. Patients rarely have difficulty being quite specific about where they are on this scale. The patient is then asked to look at what they need to do to move one step further towards their goal. If they are one step nearer their goal, what specific things are they doing differently? Once these have been determined, a positive mental rehearsal can be done before re-alerting. The specific goals are then discussed out of hypnosis and can form the basis for some homework.

A maintenance plan can be devised by suggesting that the patient uses the scaling question each day when they do their self hypnosis and writing down the answers to not only what they need to do tomorrow but also what they are doing today that is stopping them from being even lower on the scale than they are at present. They will then build up a written list of small steps that they can review and implement as necessary.

Goal Setting in Hypnosis

Hypnosis can be used very successfully to enhance goal setting. We all know that goals set normally need to be specific and measurable, manageable by one's own efforts, realistic and timely but often patients have limiting beliefs that mean they do not even think they can achieve something let alone set it as a goal. As can be seen below, in hypnosis, if the patient can comfortably associate with the goal and intuitively it feels 'right', then setting the goal in the hypnotic state can be amazingly effective.

Amy was a secretary of a local branch of an organization, and postgraduate centres would sometimes phone up to request a speaker to give a talk. She had been very shy and still felt she was completely unable to do this so she used to pass on the requests to others. At a workshop, a method of goal setting was described and she went into trance and did the process which involved (in her case) seeing an image of herself standing calmly and confidently in front of a roomful of people giving a talk. Once this was established as the desired image, she floated up above a time road (with the past in one direction and the future in another) and with the desired image in her hands, breathed energy into it with three deep breaths and inserted the image into the relevant time on her time road, wherever it felt 'right' to do so. She then forgot all about it until several months later a postgraduate centre phoned and *she heard herself* saying that she would be happy to come and give a talk. Almost the strangest part about this was that in the few weeks before the talk she kept expecting to feel really anxious but did not! She duly gave the talk and now, several years later, runs workshops and training and has often given talks to large audiences.

Sometimes the end goal of therapy seems too distant to connect with directly and feel real, and in this case using the scaling question can be very useful. Occasionally it may be that the therapist has to believe in the patient and carry hope for them until such time as they are able to see for themselves that they can achieve hitherto undreamt of goals.

Criticism and Praise

Patients with low self esteem often have great difficulty in both taking criticism and accepting praise. We often need to encourage our patients to practice taking that step backwards internally when someone criticizes them; to remind themselves that it is their behaviour, something they have done, that is being criticized. This separation of self from behaviour is important in order that negative feedback can be evaluated; after all, criticism is an opinion rather than the 'Truth'.

So whilst taking criticism to heart at the level of identity someone with poor self esteem will conversely discount any praise or compliment given to them. The therapist can usefully here employ a metaphor. If someone were to give the patient a beautifully wrapped present, how would they react? They would not reject it rudely but accept it gracefully. This is how they should accept praise.

Often our patients do not acknowledge to themselves when they have done something praiseworthy and need to be encouraged to acknowledge this to themselves.

Maureen was a deeply depressed 42 year old woman who had poor self esteem and had come from a very dysfunctional family. She felt a complete failure as she had been unable to work for several years and recently had been too depressed to help herself. She had begun taking some antidepressants and had decided that she would also come for counselling. On her first visit she related how awful things had been and what a failure she felt. She had totally disregarded the fact, until pointed out to her, that she had got out of her bed, washed and dressed herself, made herself a drink, driven herself to the surgery and turned up for her appointment. She was encouraged to acknowledge these positive actions which acted as useful ego strengthening.

As well as utilizing hypnosis for positive mental rehearsal it can used to build a confidence anchor as in the case study below.

Paul – a singer who lacked confidence

Paul was a 20 year old English student who was beginning to become well known in his community as a singer. He had had singing lessons and was fast becoming a leading light in the local operatic society as well as performing in productions at his university. He had always suffered from some examination 'nerves', but this was becoming more of a problem as his finals approached. The event that precipitated his request for help was that he had become so anxious prior to his last performance that he had been vomiting and had nearly cancelled.

He came from a professional background; his father was a university professor, and his mother had been a teacher in the past. He described his childhood as reasonably happy, although he had hated games at school and had suffered a certain amount of bullying. He loved singing but felt he was probably not good enough to make it a career which is why he was doing an English degree.

It was pointed out that whereas anxiety could be protective, in his case he was generating anxiety too well. When he became anxious he experienced a sinking nauseous feeling in his stomach, and he then built this up into a full blown anxiety attack with catastrophizing thoughts. The first intervention suggested was that, when he became aware of his negative self talk, he could imagine the voice tone changing to that of someone breathing helium or to some cartoon character. This would disrupt it and make the dialogue less believable (see page 176). It was important for him to experience the feeling in his stomach as a message that he needed to do something to help himself.

It was suggested that he close his eyes and just allow his focus to be on his breathing, not changing it in any way, but just noticing the rise and fall of his chest, following his breath in and out, maybe becoming aware of the slight temperature difference between his in breath and his out breath. It was suggested that he could imagine the colour or sound of calmness flowing into him with each breath, letting go of any unnecessary tension with each out breath.

Paul was then asked to imagine walking down five steps, each step allowing him to feel more comfortable and at ease. At the bottom it was suggested that he might find a rubbish chute that he could use to off-load any worries or anxieties before he went to his special place. This would be a place, real or imaginary, that his mind could find for him, where he would feel completely relaxed, calm and at peace.

We had talked before the hypnosis session about this and the fact that his conscious mind should just 'wonder' what place his unconscious would find for him, so he was 'primed' to respond rather than 'trying' to find a suitable image. When he demonstrated with a head nod that he was in his special place he was directed to really experience the place he had chosen through all his senses; seeing, smelling, hearing and touching things there, without suggesting what he might be experiencing. Paul was then asked to look around for something that could represent this feeling of calmness and relaxation, maybe a pebble or a flower, that he could 'bring back with him' to connect him to those feelings.

At the second session he reported feeling much better in himself and was practicing self hypnosis regularly. A progressive muscular relaxation was used, and then Paul was asked to allow his unconscious mind to take him to a time when he had sung really well and to really re-experience how great that had felt, using all his senses to connect with the event. As Paul did this he was asked to press his right thumb and index finger together and also to imagine a colour or a sound to connect him with those good feelings.

This was repeated with two other occasions when he had felt successful and confident. It was then suggested that whenever he felt a need he could press his right thumb and index finger together and immediately recapture those feelings of confidence. The suggestion was given that it was like a muscle: the more it was used, the stronger the link would become.

It was then suggested that whenever he had an examination or a performance he could spend a few minutes doing his self-hypnosis and imagining the end result, coming out of the examination or performance feeling he had done his best. It was important that he associated with this image so that he did not see just himself but actually imagined being in the image, maybe telling someone else how well it had gone.

Paul was asked to return to the here and now, and it was re-iterated how he could use his confidence link whenever he wanted. It was further suggested that he did the positive mental rehearsal whenever appropriate.

Happily Paul passed his finals and is looking set to make his singing more of a career than he thought possible way back when he first came for therapy.

It is important to be aware that patients with poor self esteem may feel so appreciative of the unusual attention given them that transference may occur and dependency issues may arise (see page 85). Notwithstanding this possibility, poor self esteem underpins many of the emotional difficulties that patients have and so needs to be addressed, even if only by simple ego strengthening.

References

Barnard, C. P. (1994), Resiliency: A shift in our perception? *American Journal of Family Therapy*, 22 (2), 135–44.

Beaulieu, D. (2004), Workshop on using experiential metaphor, Scarborough. UK.

Beaulieu, D. (2006), *Impact techniques for therapists*. New York, Routledge.

Branden, N. (1994), *The six pillars of self-esteem*. New York, Bantam.

Crouch, M. A. & Straub, V. (1983), Enhancement of self-esteem in adults. *Family Community Health*, 6 (2), 65–78.

Fawzy, F. I., Cousins, N., Fawzy, N. W., Kemeny, M. E., Elashoff, R. & Morton, D. (1990), A structured psychiatric intervention for cancer patients I. Changes over time in methods of coping and affective disturbance. *Archives of General Psychiatry*, 47 (8), 720–5.

Fortney, L. & Taylor, M. (2010), Meditation in medical practice: A review of the evidence and practice. *Primary Care*, 37 (1), 81–90.

Gilbert, P. (2009), *The compassionate mind*. London, Constable and Robinson.

Graham, G. (1988), *The happy neurotic*. Newcastle, Real Options. p. 57–9.

Hall, L. M., Bodenhamer, B., Bolstad, R. & Hamblett, M. (2001), *The structure of personality*. Carmarthen, Wales, Crownhouse.

Hofmann, S. G. & Asmundson, G. J. G. (2008), Acceptance and mindfulness-based therapy: New wave or old hat? *Clinical Psychology Review*, 28, 1–16.

Jung, C. G. (1923), *Psychological types: or the psychology of individuation*. Oxford, Harcourt, Brace.

Ruysschaert, N. (2009), (Self) hypnosis in the prevention of burnout and compassion fatigue for caregivers: theory and induction. *Contemporary Hypnosis*, 26 (3), 159–72.

Schoenberger, N. E., Kirsch, I., Gearan, P., Montgomery, G. & Pastyrnak, S. L., (1997), Hypnotic enhancement of a cognitive behavioural treatment for public speaking anxiety. *Behaviour Therapy*, 28 (1), 127–40.

Taylor, D. N. (1995), Effects of a behavioral stress-management program on anxiety, mood, self-esteem, and T-cell count in HIV positive men. *Psychological Reports*, 76 (2), 451–7.

15

Anxiety and Panic Disorder

Dr Ann Williamson

Neuroanatomy by Dr Alastair Dobbin, Also contributions from Dr Les Brann and Dr Geoff Ibbotson

Introduction

Anxiety can be thought of as fear, usually developed either through past previous experiences that were perceived as a threat or by learning the fear response (anxiety) from significant others when young. Some people have character traits of anxiety through their genetic inheritance but, as with all our emotional states, anxiety is multi-factorial with bio, psycho and social influences.

Anxiety of itself is not a bad thing although most people and patients regard it as such. We were not born anxious but learnt the set of responses, both behavioural and cognitive, as we learnt about danger and also copied those who were influential in our upbringing. Anxiety is on a continuum from appropriate to extreme. Anxiety leading to the safe crossing of a busy main road and adequate preparation for a presentation or exam is protective and appropriate. The upper continuum can lead to more extreme anxiety states and panic disorder.

Anxiety may be triggered by some stressful life event such as bereavement or an examination, or following being involved or witnessing some traumatic event such as a road traffic accident. In many cases this sort of anxiety will lessen after a few weeks and is only considered to be an anxiety disorder if the feelings are severe, long-lasting and interfering with daily life.

The Handbook of Contemporary Clinical Hypnosis: Theory and Practice, First Edition.
Edited by Les Brann, Jacky Owens and Ann Williamson.
© 2012 John Wiley & Sons, Ltd. Published 2015 by John Wiley & Sons, Ltd.

Specific anxiety disorders or illnesses are present in around 5% of the population at any time, and for one in ten people in the UK anxiety interferes with normal life (Office for National Statistics, 2000). GPs know that many of their consultations involve anxiety symptoms to some degree and we all experience anxiety symptoms in certain contexts that we (hopefully) have learnt to deal with.

Excessive anxiety is often associated with depression and may be a symptom of other mental health problems, such as obsessive compulsive disorder or alcohol dependence (Alonso *et al.*, 2004). It can also be caused by substances such as LSD or ecstasy, and GPs not infrequently encounter patients who imbibe excessive amounts of caffeine from coffee and other drinks, whose anxiety symptoms have subsided as they gradually cut their intake, and it is common knowledge that tranquilizers need gradual withdrawal so the patient becomes accustomed to the lowering levels.

Chronic anxiety with the concomitant activation of the hypothalamic-pituitary-adrenal (HPA) axis has been linked to hypertension, cardiac disease, peptic ulceration, type 2 diabetes, asthma, arthritis, dental problems, viral diseases and malignancy (Chrousos, 1995).

Stress and chronic anxiety during pregnancy may cause adverse effects on the developing baby. Huizink *et al.* (2003) have shown that babies exposed to higher levels of cortisol in the womb have delayed motor and mental development when tested at eight months. Of course many other factors may influence this such as the child's personality and surrounding environment.

Sometimes anxiety symptoms can be mimicked by physical illness, such as hyperthyroidism, and this needs to be borne in mind when seeing a new patient. For diagnostic purposes, anxiety can be divided into specific anxiety states such as phobias (which are covered in Chapter 17), anticipatory and procedural anxiety (see Chapter 22) as well as performance anxiety (addressed in Chapter 37) and more generalized anxiety and panic disorders. So-called free floating anxiety can become 'attached' to particular fears and contexts in patients who have more chronic anxiety problems sometimes giving rise to phobic responses.

Neuroanatomy of Emotional Disorders: Anxiety and Depression

Through conditioning by past experiences, fearful stimuli trigger activity in the *amygdala* which connects to the *hypothalamus*. This controls our body's response to fear (Ledoux *et al.*, 1988) by nervous and hormonal means, prepares us for 'fight or flight' and brings about all the bodily sensations of fear, such as the racing heart, the tight muscles and the nausea. It is these sensations that give us the perception of fear; the body is the theatre where fear is experienced. Information from the body is fed back to the brain through the autonomic visceral and muscular afferents, and it is this which alerts the brain to danger and makes us hypersensitive to external triggers. Anxiety and depression are characterized by over activity of the amygdala (Dannlowski *et al.*, 2007; Whalen *et al.*, 1998). There are two pathways for fear, one from the thalamus to the cortex (the conscious visual or auditory cortex) and a faster, pre-conscious one to the amygdala (Ledoux *et al.*, 1986). This latter is the pathway that kept us alive throughout evolution, and that creates the automatic sympathetic response. If cut, there is no reaction to conditioned fear. When exposed to danger the most important thing is *not* that we recognize it consciously, but that we react to it quickly *without conscious reflection*; this leads to the situation when 'being emotionally aroused and not knowing why is all too common for most of us' (Ledoux, 1996, p. 203).

Emotional distress is difficult to verbalize; it happens in 'some neural space not easily accessed from consciousness', and 'psychiatrists and psychologists waiting rooms are kept packed for this very reason' (Ledoux, 1996, p. 71). Hypnosis may allow access to 'hidden' memories; certainly this is the daily experience of many hypnotherapists, and many of the techniques in this book can be used for resolving trauma memories. But there are ways to deal with distress without knowing the source, and in the early stages of treatment such techniques provide safety and stability, which once established may pave the way for later exploration of memory if required or appropriate.

The functions of the *prefrontal cortex* (PFC) are executive planning, reappraisal, active generative visualisation, speech and abstract thought (Ranganath, 2005; and see Figure 15.1). PFC activity has a direct inhibitory effect on the amygdala; these functions serve to inhibit fear activity. When Pavlovian conditioned fear is set up by playing an auditory tone (conditioned stimulus) and giving a painful shock (shock unconditioned stimulus, or UCS), subsequently if the tone is played the animal will freeze (conditioned response, or CR) but if played without the shock a new memory (of CS without UCS) overrides the fear memory, and this new memory is set up through this inhibitory PFC – amygdala circuitry (Quirk & Gehlert, 2003); this process is called *extinction*. 'The amygdala's emotional memories, as we've seen, are indelibly burned into its circuits. The best we can hope to do is to regulate their expression. And the way we do this by getting

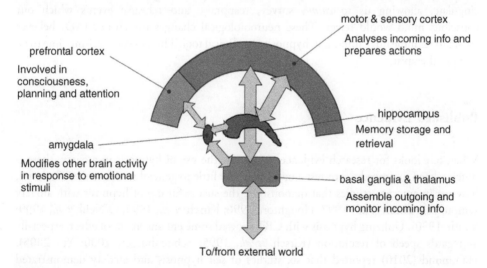

Figure 15.1   A schematic diagram of some principal elements of the brain, with their connecting pathways. Not shown are the extensive interconnections between prefrontal areas and the more posterior regions that they monitor and control. © Peter Naish.

the cortex to control the amygdala' (LeDoux, 1996, p. 23). This regulation can come through PFC activity, thus practicing visualisation (using a 'safe place' in regular self hypnosis) is particularly helpful for anxious and depressed people, inhibiting the amygdala and extinguishing fear conditioning.

Abstract thinking encompasses the planning of object manipulation and thus mathematics, but also encompasses reappraisal, which is similar to seeing a new solution to a mathematical problem, such as loss of job + spending more time at home arguing with family about money = disaster or, with reappraisal, loss of job + spending more time at home learning a new skill = opportunity. Reappraisal is an idea extensively interwoven into Buddhist philosophy, and the prefrontal cortex is thicker and more active in regular meditators (Lazar *et al.*, 2005). This increased thickness has also been shown to decrease sensitivity to pain (Grant *et al.*, 2010), and it is established that physical and emotional pain share the same central pathways in the brain (Eisenberger and Liebermann, 2004). It is likely that regular self hypnosis may have the same benefits as regular meditation given the learned experiential focus (see 'thinking styles', page 198).

Reappraisal is a method of changing the emotional impact of a situation by reformulating its meaning, and is one of the most effective ways of dealing with stress (Goldin *et al.*, 2008). Reappraisal has been shown to share the same pathway as simple extinction (Delgado, 2008) through the PFC. Such reappraisals can be put into ego-strengthening scripts (i.e. *"Every day you will find more ability to see things differently, to see failure as a learning situation, to see problems as challenges, hindrances as opportunities"*).

We thus have many ways that hypnosis helps with the fear and dread of anxiety and depression. One is through the implicit suggestion of reappraisal (significantly more effective than explicit: see Shih *et al.*, 2002), and the other is the dissociation between the affective (emotional) and cognitive aspects of processing (Gruzelier, 1998) in the cingulate, allowing us to *calmly* survey, reappraise and rehearse events which our conscious mind would reject. These neurobiological changes the author (AD) believes are set to rekindle huge interest in hypnosis as a clinical tool. This is a very exciting time to be a hypnotherapist.

Published Evidence

When one looks for research evidence to support the use of hypnosis in anxiety, there is much related to procedural or test anxiety and very little to general anxiety state. There are, however, many case studies that demonstrate the successful use of hypnosis with anxiety symptoms (Ashton *et al.*, 1997; Houghton, 1996; Kirsch *et al.*, 1995; O'Neill *et al.*, 1999; Smith, 1990). Utilizing hypnosis with CBT showed some enhancement of effect, especially as regards speed of resolution (Kirsch *et al.*, 1995; Schoenburger, 2000; Yu, 2005). Hammond (2010) reported that six studies of self hypnosis and anxiety demonstrated changes in trait anxiety but that there was a need for further research. O'Neill *et al.* (1999) reported in a group study ($n = 20$) over a 28 day period that teaching patients self hypnosis for anxiety management, as well as being effective, increased their sense of treatment efficacy when compared to a group only given relaxation. Mindfulness which teaches meditation skills allied to self hypnosis has also been shown to be effective in the treatment of anxiety disorders (Hofmann *et al.*, 2010).

The Chelmsford Medical Hypnosis Unit (Brann et al, 2010) has routinely recorded scores from the Hospital Anxiety and Depression scale (HADs; Zigmond & Snaith, 1983) for all patients referred regardless of the nature of the problem. The HADs questionnaire was developed to help identify clinical cases of anxiety or depression. Although the score is divided into normal (0–7), mild (8–10), moderate (11–14) and severe (15–21), a clinical 'case' of anxiety is usually taken to be a score of 11 or more. Of 323 completed forms, 217 (67.2%) recorded scores of 11 or above, and of those there were 102 and 115 in the moderate and severe bands respectively.

Looking closer at the 217 patients with clinical anxiety, following the hypnotic intervention 160 (74%) were no longer clinically anxious. A further 51 patients (23.5%) improved but remained in the dysfunctional range, and only 6 patients failed to show any reduction in their HADs scores after therapy. Table 15.1 summarizes the data. It should be noted that 72 (33%) also had clinical depression. Despite the heavy burden of psychological morbidity, these results were obtained in an average of four one hour sessions.

Table 15.1   Summary of Hospital Anxiety and Depression scale – Anxiety (HADs A) results

	Initial mean HADs A score (SD)	Final mean HADs A score (SD)	`Mean reduction in HADs A score (confidence)	Effect size	Statistical significance t-test	Mean number of sessions
Moderate (n = 102)	12.7 (1.1)	7.7 (2.6)	5.0 (+/– 0.53)	4.52	P = 0.00 (1.7×10^{-34})	3.9
Severe (n = 115)	17.1 (1.7)	9.4 (3.5)	7.7 (+/– 0.67)	4.53	P = 0.00 (1.3×10^{-43})	4.1
Total (n = 217)	15.1 (2.6)	8.6 (3.2)	6.4 (+/– 0.47)	2.43	P = 0.00 (7.1×10^{-71})	4.0

Patterns of Anxiety

When someone starts to become anxious, they are usually first aware of anxious thoughts or bodily sensations due to the rising level of adrenalin. With any perceived threat, real or imaginary, the HPA axis that controls stress hormone levels, including cortisol, becomes activated. Every anxious thought provokes an output of adrenalin and cortisol which contributes to the negative spiral. In the chronically anxious these high levels of adrenalin and cortisol last for days, weeks and months so it is not surprising that a common complaint is *"I feel tired all the time, doctor."*

Table 15.2   Some signs and symptoms of anxiety

Physical symptoms	*Emotional symptoms*	*Behavioural symptoms*
Headaches, sweating	Poor concentration and memory	Increasing mistakes
Palpitations	Inability to relax	Clumsiness and accidents
Shortness of breath	Losing sense of humour	Insomnia and tiredness
Hyperventilation	Difficulty in making decisions	Procrastinating
Dry mouth	Increasing irritability	Increasing nervous habits
Indigestion	Mood swings	Obsessional behaviour
Increased bowel and urinary frequency irritable bowel syndrome	Not feeling in control of your actions	Interrupting conversations
Difficulty swallowing Muscular aches and pains Dizziness, shaking Skin irritations Constant minor illnesses	Feeling detached from your surroundings (de-realisation)	Using more palliatives, e.g. tobacco, alcohol, food, or drugs

As clinicians we are all aware of the numerous symptoms associated with anxiety listed in Table 15.2, and it is useful to note that people tend to express anxiety in different bodily feelings. One patient may predominantly complain of head and neck tension and pain, whereas someone else may get predominantly abdominal symptoms or those associated with heart or lungs such as palpitations or feelings of tightness in the chest. These symptoms are not medically dangerous, but they tend to be frightening, and this in turn causes an increase in anxiety and the further development of the anxiety spiral (see Figure 15.2).

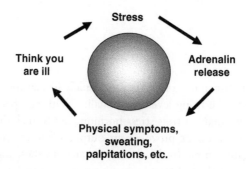

Figure 15.2   The vicious circle.

Some patients, because of their personality and background, are far more resilient in the face of life events than others, and so, apart from determining whether any practical precautions need to be taken, the 'why' that triggers the anxiety is less important than determining 'how' the patient develops and maintains their anxiety response. When a patient says *"I am anxious,"* they are taking on their anxiety at the level of identity which does not easily allow for change. If as health professionals we can lead our patients into looking at the behaviour patterns behind their anxiety, this enables movement and the possibility that they can change this behaviour pattern. There will be occasions when the patient has not been anxious or times when their anxiety levels have been lower. These exceptions need to be examined. What were they doing differently at these times? By determining 'how' the patient generates their anxiety, their pattern of how they build their anxiety spiral can be determined and therefore interrupted. We need to explain to our patients the interplay between our thoughts, feelings and behaviour and show them that interrupting a specific thought, behaviour or internal image can begin to lead to changing the feeling.

Working with Anxiety

Imagination

People who suffer from anxiety states have good imaginations! One of the key factors in any anxiety is the use of the imagination to paint negative scenarios internally (Dads *et al.*, 1997; Glisky *et al.*, 1991). This is often displayed as catastrophizing thought patterns, but at some level the patient is making internal images of the dreaded outcome and this leads effectively to negative suggestion. Such catastrophisation allows for no other possibilities, and of course each anxious thought injects further adrenalin into the system. Anxious patients interpret everything pessimistically so ordinary reassurance is ineffective, but determining such thoughts, and then interrupting and challenging them, is an important part of any anxiety management programme. Hypnosis may facilitate and speed up the therapeutic intervention needed (Kirsch *et al.*, 1995).

When a patient is suffering with high levels of anxiety, they are not functioning in their 'normal' rational consciousness but rather from their emotions. This is often from a 'younger' version of themselves that learnt and developed the anxiety response as a method of coping with anxiety provoking events in their earlier life. They feel out of control and buffeted by their current surrounding situations. It is not a resourceful state to be in, but when someone is drowning is not the time to give them a swimming lesson. Throwing a life belt may be more appropriate, such as showing them how to do diaphragmatic breathing (see page 474) or how to change their internal imagery of how they see themselves or others (see page 159, 400).

Changing negative self talk

Those suffering from anxiety states and low self esteem often drive these problems by negative self talk, and thus modification of their internal dialogue may be extremely useful.

Most people tend to have both positive and negative internal dialogue, but some seem to be aware of only the negative. Those suffering from mood disorders such as anxiety states and depression help drive these states with negative internal dialogue without any check being kept by positive dialogue. This can be addressed by using 'compassionate friend' imagery (see page 161).

Negative internal dialogue tends to be very believable and usually is not a helpful or encouraging response. Changing the voice tone as described below may serve to lessen this believability and hence the impact of such a response. It is important to discuss the ecological sense in negating internal dialogue; sometimes negative dialogue is useful, but usually it is not.

The first stage is the calibration of internal dialogue. The patient is asked to close their eyes and access a time when they were using negative internal dialogue. Once they can access that state, they give a nod. They can then be asked to describe where the sound seems to be coming from: left, right, top or bottom. They can also describe how the voice sounds and whose voice it is.

The patient is then asked to open their eyes, and the process is then repeated for positive dialogue. Almost invariably, the positive and negatives come from different apparent sources and the character of the voices are different.

The patient is then asked if they have ever heard what someone sounds like when they talk after having inhaled helium. Most find that the sound is amusing and has no credibility.

The patient is asked to close their eyes and access a time when they had negative internal dialogue. They then focus on the negative dialogue and 'heliumize' it. Hence the negative dialogue becomes a source of amusement rather than a driver of fear and panic. Some patients find it easier to change the sound into that of a cartoon voice. It is sometimes useful to ask them to be aware of an amusing visual image of the adjusted dialogue.

The arousal state

We have only one arousal state – that mediated by adrenalin, and whether we label it as excitement, an adrenalin burn, a panic attack or being in love depends on the context. Reframing anxiety in this way can be helpful as can general education about adrenalin and its effects.

Reframing Adrenalin

Sympathetic arousal

We have many contexts in which adrenalin produces an 'arousal state'.
    Panic attack   Adrenalin burn   Excitement   Fear   Being in love

---

Picking up on cognitive distortions and gently challenging them whilst taking the history can turn the history taking into a therapeutic encounter (see page 91). Some words that should not pass unremarked are 'never', 'always', 'must', 'should', 'ought' and 'can't'. Such challenges should be made gently and in rapport, rather than in a confrontational way which would cause hostility and break rapport. This facilitation of alternative insights can be re-iterated during hypnosis to good effect. Some examples are given in Figure 15.3.

Practical skills such as time management strategies may be usefully taught as one of the first symptoms of increasing stress is feeling time pressured.

Setting the Goal

Having taken a therapeutic history it is necessary to facilitate the patient to define their goals in a positive and specific way. The scaling question (page 163) can often be most effective when asked whilst the patient is in the hypnotic state. Setting the scaling question as homework to be done each day during self hypnosis can not only help focus on the desirable outcomes but also help develop a maintenance plan as the patient makes a written note afterwards of their responses to the questions asked. This then acts as an aide memoire of useful actions that the patient can take if relapse threatens.

Use of imagery techniques such as the mirror exercise (page 160) and positive mental rehearsal (page 45) facilitates a focus on what the patient wants to achieve and enables them to access the internal strengths and resources that they need to do so.

Thought-stopping techniques can be taught such as snapping an elastic band on the wrist, saying an internal 'No!' or utilizing some internal image that the patient brings to mind when catastrophizing or negative thoughts are noticed to become persistent. Having become aware (the first step) the patient needs to develop ways of challenging and changing the negative. This could include changing the language used in the thought (instead of 'must', use 'prefer'), allowing that there are other possibilities that actually may be more likely than the worst case scenario they have thought of or developing a positive counter-argument.

Use of Hypnosis

One of the first things that comes to mind when someone mentions hypnosis is that it is usually (although not always; see page 118) associated with relaxation (Bányai & Hilgard, 1976; Wark, 2006).

Having taken a therapeutic history and having explained about hypnosis and addressed any concerns, it is usual to introduce the patient to hypnosis, which of course can be done in many ways. If the patient has had any previous experience, then this should be utilized if positive and avoided if negative. The patient may already be using a way to relax such as

Cognitive distortions and some alternatives – developing other perspectives

I feel (or do) = I am - taking actions or feelings on at level of identity – change 'being' to 'doing'

> *"I am depressed"* to *"I am doing (or visiting) depression at the moment"*

Black and white thinking or generalization – change 'always/never' to 'sometimes'

> *"Boys always scare me"* to *''Boys always scare me, except when they don't!"*

Explore exceptions to the belief that all men are scary – brother, work colleague, father, etc.?

> *"I can never do anything right"* to *"I can never do anything right except when I do"*

Explore exceptions to belief – e.g. making a meal, running a household, etc.

Mind reading or crystal ball

> *"I know they don't like me"*

Explore how this is known and whether there are other possibilities

> *"They are out to get me"*

Explore how this is known and obtain more information *"Who, precisely, is out to do what?"*

Attribution of blame

"He makes me feel so angry!"

Questions such as *"How does that seem to happen?"* and *"Has there ever been a time when you did not feel angry at what he says? What was different then?"*

Explore separating the behaviour or action from the person and facilitating the realization that we make our own feelings.

Personalization (also see chapter 14 on self esteem)

> *"It's all my fault ..."*

Explore what other factors may also be involved.

Must, should, and ought

> *"I must go to work"*

Explore *"Who says you must?"* and why.

Can't

> *"I can't ask her out" "I can't say no"*

Explore possibilities: *"What would happen if you did?"* and *"What stops you?"*

Sometimes if the patient is locked in 'can't' mode, a response *"Can't or won't?"* shakes them out of this fixed, concrete negative thinking.

Try – implies failure

Try not to use the word!

Figure 15.3   Cognitive distortions.

Some time management strategies

The three 'D's: ditch it, delegate it or do it

Decide whether something really needs doing or not and if so can you enlist help?

The three 'P's: prioritize, plan and premium time

Plan and prioritize – write a list but tick off one task a day; anything else is a bonus!

Motivation – imagine the end result rather than getting stuck in the process.

Premium time

     Protected time – if something is really important and needs doing, define when you are going to do it and do not allow interruptions (take the telephone off the hook, or post a 'do not disturb' notice).

     Lark or owl? – some people are at their best in the early morning or the evening; if this is you, then do more difficult and important tasks at that time.

Breaks and leisure time – it is false economy to ignore these. Our concentration and work are much enhanced if we take regular breaks of ten minutes every couple of hours or so.

The big 'N':

Say NO … but say it with a smile. Do not play 'Persuade me' or rationalize your decision.

If you are someone who finds yourself automatically saying "Yes," it can be useful to practise asking for time to consider: "I'll have to think about that … I'll get back to you later."

Figure 15.4   Some time management strategies.

playing a musical instrument or singing internally. If so, then this is a bonus and can be utilized.

Some people like to administer some form of hypnotic susceptibility test but if this is done it must be remembered that if either the health professional or the patient thinks the patient is of lower than average hypnotic ability then this can doom the intervention to failure before you start. We are all capable of altering our focus of attention and entering common everyday type trance states such as getting lost in a good book or day dreaming; some people are just better at doing this than others. For therapeutic purposes we do not need deep somnambulistic trance states, merely a shift into a right-brained state (if you use that model).

There is, however, one intervention that can be used quite usefully that on the surface purports to be an exploration of someone's hypnotic abilities to use imagery but because of the therapist's responses is actually an expectancy enhancer.

The McCarthy Teapot Test (Adapted from McCarthy, 2005)

Ask the patient to sit back in the chair, make themselves comfortable and close their eyes and then ask them to imagine that they are in their very own kitchen.

I want you to imagine that you are picking up the kettle … and taking it to the tap. Turn on the tap. SEE the water pouring from the tap, into the kettle.

As the water pours into the kettle, LISTEN to two distinct sounds. The sound that the water makes as it leaves the tap, and also the sound that the water makes as it fills the kettle.

Then notice the kettle getting heavier with the weight of the water as you FEEL the weight of the kettle filling.

When there's enough water in the kettle, turn off the tap. Notice if the tap makes a noise or a squeak as you turn it off, or if it is silent. Then put the kettle on to boil.

Then CHOOSE a mug, any mug. It can be any size of mug or cup, any shape, any weight. It might be your favourite one, or your least favourite one.

NOTICE the shape of the handle. It might be semi-circular shaped or shaped like the letter D or it might be more like a question mark.

HEAR the sound the mug makes as you put it down on the worktop.

Then open the fridge and take out the milk container. NOTICE the kind of milk container. It might be cardboard, glass or plastic. How full is it? It might be full, half full or almost empty.

Then HEAR the sounds coming from the kettle as the water starts to heat up.

Then get out a teabag and place it in the mug.

HEAR the sound of the kettle boiling now and SEE the steam coming out of the spout. Then, carefully, pick up the kettle and pour the hot water into the mug.

SEE the steam rising from the mug. Then put the kettle back down and wait for the tea to infuse and become ready.

Then off to the RIGHT, SEE a bowl of fruit. At the front of the bowl there are two oranges and a banana. And at the back there is a lemon.

Pick up the lemon and NOTICE if the lemon is completely yellow or still has some green colour.

FEEL the lemon and notice if it is a smooth shiny skinned lemon or whether the variety you have chosen is more crinkly in texture.

NOTICE the shape of the end of the lemon. Some lemons are rounded at the end; others have a little pointed bit at the end.

Then SMELL the lemon. Notice the tangy, lemony smell. Then take the lemon over to a chopping board and CUT the lemon in half.

SEE the spray of juice in the air. And SMELL the lemon more clearly. Pick up half of the lemon and SEE the cut, wet, glistening surface, of this juicy, juicy lemon.

Bring the lemon up to your nose and SMELL that lemon smell more clearly.

Then BITE into the lemon and TASTE the lemon juice.

Then take out your teabag and add milk or sugar to taste. Take a sip of the tea and wash away the TASTE of the lemon.

Notice the TASTE of the tea and FEEL the WARMTH of the tea. Take another sip of the tea.

Then OPEN your eyes and let's talk about your experiences.

Post-test questions are asked such as: could you SEE the things I described? Could you HEAR the sounds? Could you get a sense of the FEEL of the lemon or weight of the kettle? Could you SMELL the lemon? Did you get the TASTE of the lemon or the tea?

The patient is congratulated on their positive responses, and their positive responses are turned into an expectancy of success when using hypnosis.

If, for example, the patient gave more visual responses then more questions could be asked about other visual observations in the kitchen, and this could also inform the type of induction and intervention used.

If the patient reports that the imagery did not 'fit', then what they did needs to be explored. Did they comply with the suggested imagery anyway, in which case this demonstrates that they are 'flexible', or did they ignore you and 'do their own thing,' in which case they demonstrate an ability to know their own mind and take control? Both responses can be framed as success.

One format for a first session is to introduce various hypnotic inductions for the patient to explore and determine which is easier and most enjoyable. An attitude of exploration and experiment is essential to remove any preconceived ideas of the right way to do it and to enable the conscious mind to 'allow' rather than 'try'. A useful metaphor is that of throwing a ball of screwed up paper into a wastebasket – easily done unless you become 'aware' and try, when it often misses!

If someone has been highly anxious for a long time relaxation is usually perceived as difficult, and the patient may be so unaccustomed to the bodily feelings of relaxation that they produce a feeling of fear. In this kind of patient with high levels of anxiety, the best approach may be to use re-vivification (re-experiencing in an associated way using all the senses) of some physical activity (see page 116). It can be suggested that the patient starts off doing their activity in their imagination at a fast speed which they then slow down as they feel able until they are resting.

Once the patient has become familiar with doing this, they may then be introduced to a breathing focus exercise (see page 114) or a progressive muscular relaxation (see page 114).

There are some points to remember when using these inductions. It is important to use awareness of how they are now, rather than 'trying' to relax or change their breathing pattern. It is useful to warn the patient that if their mind wanders, rather than berating themselves, they should simply gently acknowledge to themselves that they have noticed and re-focus their attention.

It is often better to use the word 'comfort' or 'ease' rather than 'relaxation', and an initial eye roll to begin a progressive muscular relaxation may be found useful as it gives a focus of tension that can then be released. The feeling of comfort that ensues can then be 'spread' around the body. It may also be useful to remind the patient that they might like to imagine comfort spreading down their body as a colour or simply as a feeling, maybe like a warm glow; and any tension can *"drain out of the feet into the floor."*

It is important that the patient is given an opportunity to metaphorically 'get rid of things' and replace them with positive feelings. Suggestions for the future ease of obtaining this state of comfort and relaxation can usefully be given together with any ego-strengthening suggestions that are appropriate. Also a trigger or anchor (see page 152) to trance may be given as a post-hypnotic suggestion.

There are many ways that self hypnosis can be taught as an ongoing tool that the patient can take away, become more proficient at and use to help to cope with day to day life. It may be that they simply practice some of the inductions and imagery that has been used in the session, or a trigger can be used as mentioned above.

Mindfulness

When someone is anxious their focus of attention tends to be the future, worrying about things that have not yet happened. Being in the present with non-judgmental awareness, which is what mindfulness techniques entail, can be a very helpful exercise especially for the anxious. By learning to observe thoughts and feelings as they arise, the patient can begin to gain a different perspective rather than being 'stuck' in their emotional state.

Once a patient begins to take up an observer position to their emotional state they can begin to discover their patterns and then do something different. One small change in a pattern can change it completely. We have already talked about interrupting thought patterns and rumination; self hypnosis can be used to interrupt the build up of adrenalin, and imagery in the self hypnotic state can be used to interrupt feelings.

Anchors have been described and discussed in chapter 12, and calmness anchors can be very useful in helping an anxious patient access calmness when anxiety or panic start to be triggered.

> A young woman with agoraphobia utilized colour as her anchors. When she was practicing going out and started to feel anxious she would imagine a glowing aura of blue flowing down herself and if she felt she needed more confidence she used a red aura. She had successfully linked these feelings to these colours during her sessions and found she could access the feeling of calmness or confidence as necessary.

Metaphor and its effectiveness have been discussed in chapter 5, and metaphor can be used with anxious patients to facilitate a different perspective or to reframe problems.

Ego strengthening (see page 141) is something that should be done at every opportunity, as failing to do so could be likened to giving someone an anaesthetic without performing any surgery. Ways of utilizing imagery for ego strengthening, throwing away unwanted thoughts and feelings and replacing them with desired thoughts and feelings should be taught to every patient along with ways of entering the self hypnotic state so that they learn these lifelong skills to help themselves, not just with current difficulties but also in their future.

Panic Disorder

Many people with anxiety states suffer panic attacks which are sudden and disabling episodes which may last from a few seconds to half an hour or more. DSM-IV (American Psychiatric Association, 2000) describes a panic attack as a discrete period of intense fear or discomfort that develops abruptly and has four or more of the following which peak within ten minutes: palpitations, pounding heart or accelerated heart rate; sweating; trembling or shaking; sensations of shortness of breath or smothering; feeling of choking; chest pain or discomfort; nausea or abdominal distress; feeling dizzy, unsteady, lightheaded or faint; derealization (feelings of unreality) or depersonalization (being detached from oneself); fear of losing control or going crazy; fear of dying; parasthaesia (numbness or tingling sensations), chills or hot flushes. Such episodes often seem to arise suddenly and for no reason apparent to the sufferer. Many who experience a panic attack for the first time fear they are having a heart attack or a nervous breakdown. Those who have repeated persistent attacks or feel severe anxiety about having another attack are said to have panic disorder.

Panic disorder tends to be viewed as a separate problem diagnostically from an anxiety state but could usefully be seen as merely one end of the spectrum. Interventions as described above for anxiety can all be used and general ego-strengthening, relaxation and self hypnosis training are non-specific tools that can help (Iglesias, 2005).

Usually the patient is terrified of experiencing another panic attack because either they think that they might die or they are embarrassed to be seen in such a state. This leads to avoidance of the possible trigger situations or places. Teaching perceptual positions and encouraging the patient to imagine and evaluate the situation as an observer can lead to helpful insights.

Emily avoided going to her local supermarket because she had had a bad panic attack whilst shopping there some months before and she felt people would be looking at her and thinking she was mad or drunk. One of the interventions used was for Emily to imagine being in a supermarket when someone else was having a panic attack and to observe what was happening and how she felt as an observer. Upon questioning she reported that she felt that she wanted to help and reassure the person having the attack and that she did not feel judgmental towards them. What might happen if Emily had another panic attack whilst shopping and what the likely outcome would be for both Emily and any bystanders were then explored.

Someone such as Emily in the example above may have a panic attack while in a supermarket, and subsequently the same supermarket will become associated with the negative experience of the panic attack so that entering the supermarket again will give rise to feelings of fear. This can then spread by association to other supermarkets, standing in check out queues and so on. As they feel the feelings of fear (= danger), the panic attack is triggered and then spirals. Often the fear around the initial panic attack needs to be resolved, maybe using time road imagery (see page 401). The patient needs to understand at an emotional as well as a cognitive level that however unpleasant it was, they survived, and that they now have tools to help themselves should they start to feel panic arising again.

Anxiety reduction requires that the person re-learns that supermarkets are not dangerous, and one way of doing this is by exposure and staying in the situation until feeling calm once more. In hypnosis imaginal exposure can be used successfully, but the patient also needs to 'try out' the techniques in reality before true resolution is achieved.

Someone who is terrified that they will stop breathing or their heart will stop in a panic attack could, in a controlled environment, hyperventilate or develop an exercise tachycardia (fast heart rate) in order to experientially learn that this will not happen.

Panic attacks start with a burst of adrenalin usually triggered by something out of conscious awareness. This then builds into the vicious spiral described previously.

Teaching calmness anchors that the patient can use at the start of a panic attack can be useful, and a quick and effective way to interrupt the spiral is to begin to sing a familiar nursery rhyme internally. The words and the melody use different processes in the brain and also act as a distraction technique.

Noticing and then disrupting the first catastrophizing thought at the beginning of a panic attack can be useful so that instead of the patient thinking, *"Oh God, not again!"* which stimulates adrenalin, the patient deliberately says to themselves something like *"My body is sending me a message – I need to get hold of some calmness* (from their special place or from an anchor)!"

Patients who suffer from panic disorder are often 'phobic' about adrenalin, and supporting them to accept and 'be' with their feelings rather than catastrophizing and building them up is paramount, so reframing usual levels of adrenalin as excitement or anticipation can be helpful. This is important when, having worked with an anxious patient, they are ready to try out the avoided situations but are very likely to have a degree of apprehension as to the outcome. If this is framed as excitement or anticipation, they are less likely to have difficulty.

When working with anxiety

- Find the pattern – make a change.
- Teach self hypnosis.
- Ego strengthen.
- Disrupt negative internal dialogue.
- Use calmness anchors.
- Positive mental rehearsal.

Case study: Melinda – six fortnightly sessions of 30 minutes

Session 1

History

Melinda was a 22 year old clerical worker who came in requesting help with her anxiety. She had a friend at work who had suggested that she get some help as she was finding that her nervousness was stopping her going out with her work colleagues and also making her feel ill. *It is always useful to explore why someone has decided to come for help at that particular time.*

She had always been anxious and her mother had also suffered from anxiety. She was an only child and had had an uneventful childhood, although her father had worked away a lot. *Anxiety is quite often a learned response from significant others in a person's past rather than always developed in response to past traumatic and dysfunctional family backgrounds.*

At the first session the physical symptoms that could arise due to anxiety, the fight and flight reaction, and the ways she could reduce her stress levels generally were discussed.

Often people fear the physical symptoms of raised adrenalin, and spending time in education is worthwhile.

At this point Melinda was asked to fill in a questionnaire to assess how she had been feeling in the past few weeks. *Questionnaires tend to be problem oriented so it seems sensible to introduce them here before focusing the rest of the session on solutions and goals.*

Resource elicitation

She got on well with her parents and still lived at home. She had few interests but enjoyed embroidery and knitting. *An important question is to elicit resources; in this case her interests pointed to a conscientious and patient type of person rather than someone who enjoyed a lot of physical or social pursuits.*

Goals

Melinda wanted to feel more confident in herself and to feel calmer. *These goals need to be explored for specifics. The scaling question may be helpful* (see page 163).

Explanation of hypnosis

Her expectations of hypnosis were discussed: that she would continue to hear the sounds from outside the office but that they would recede into the background just as if she were lost in a good book. *Melinda had been given written information on hypnosis beforehand, but it is well worth taking time to talk about what patients expect from hypnosis and dispelling any misconceptions. Everyday trance states can be used as examples of the hypnotic state – people often expect the hypnotic state to involve being totally spaced out and in a somnambulistic torpor.*

It was also mentioned that as she became more deeply relaxed she might find that half an hour had gone by when she thought it had only been ten minutes, and it would be a good idea to always tell herself how long she was going to relax for before starting her self hypnosis. These techniques could be used to help her go to sleep but if she was very tired and did not want to fall asleep she should make sure she set an alarm to wake herself up. *Time distortion is very common during hypnosis and should be mentioned so that an intention to alert after a set time can be set before doing self hypnosis.*

Re-vivification

When Melinda was asked whether there was any physical activity she enjoyed, she said she used to enjoy swimming but had not done so for a couple of years as she had felt too anxious to go on her own since her best friend had moved away. It was suggested that she could close her eyes and imagine a time when she was swimming very fast (see page 117). She was asked to really be there, seeing, hearing and feeling the water against her skin; she could use her imagination to make it absolutely perfect rather than historically accurate. In her own time she could begin to slow her stroke down until she was gliding easily and effortlessly through the water. She could then perhaps turn over and enjoy floating on her back, completely supported by the water. After a few moments Melinda was asked to open her eyes and to report on how she had felt.

Revivification of some activity previously enjoyed is a useful way to introduce the self hypnotic state as it is non-threatening and someone who has 'never been relaxed' will find it easier to do as the relaxed state may feel very strange at first. By slowing the activity down gradually and at her own pace she will access the relaxed state more gradually, and by not making relaxation the overt aim of the exercise it is more easily achieved. Framing the exercises as experiments means that there is no sense of failure if Melinda finds difficulty . . . it is merely information that will help us both in the future.

She reported that she felt a lot more relaxed than when she first came in, and it was explained how using her imagination in this way facilitated right brain processing and the relaxation response.

It is useful to capitalize on a positive response and link this to future practice. Suggestions can be given such as "That's great – just think how much easier it will be to do sitting in your comfortable chair in the quiet of your own home rather than here in this noisy surgery!"

Self hypnosis

How and when Melinda would practice her self hypnosis and how practice would enable her to access relaxation more easily were discussed. *It is important to schedule her self hypnosis practice and to explore any practical difficulties in order to maximize the likelihood of her doing it regularly. Mind wandering is usual especially in the early stages, and it is worth pre-empting this and reassuring the patient that it does not mean they 'can't do it' but to congratulate themselves that they have noticed and just re-focus their attention.*

Special place imagery

It was suggested that Melinda could allow her mind to find a safe, special place (real or imaginary) that would be somewhere that she could find calmness and peace and that she could imagine herself going there when she did her self hypnosis. *The idea of a special place was introduced prior to induction to seed the idea and encouraged her to let her conscious mind just wonder what would come up at the appropriate time. Developing such a place that Melinda goes to when she does her self hypnosis will mean that her internalized image of the place will act as a calmness anchor when she brings it to mind. It is important to realise that not everyone is good at visual imagery and to remind people to use all their senses to connect with the place they have chosen.*

As Melinda's special place was on a beach, it was then suggested that she go back into hypnosis using her swimming and enjoy her beach for a couple of minutes. *Repetition is useful and helps build the patient's confidence that they can do it for themselves.* The suggestion was also given that, as with any new skill, it becomes easier and easier to do with practice. *This is a useful suggestion to give during the first hypnosis session.*

It was then suggested that if anything untoward were to happen whilst she was treating herself in this way she would wake, immediately but she would normally find it more comfortable to come back to the here and now more gradually by counting down from five to one so that by the time she reached one, she was fully alert, bringing back the feelings of calmness with her. *It is preferable to encourage the patient to alert themselves as people vary in the length of time they need to come back to conscious reality. It is important not to suggest everything returning to normal (as one would with altered sensation from glove anaesthesia or arm levitation) if the patient's normal state is one of high anxiety!*

Session 2

Feedback

At the next visit Melinda said that she had been practicing doing the revivification of swimming and had been feeling a bit calmer generally. *It is always important to obtain feedback and to assess whether there have been any difficulties.*

Exploring the pattern

Once Melinda discovers her pattern, she can more easily disrupt it. She was asked to consider how she generated her anxiety, and she determined that it started with a sinking feeling in her stomach accompanied by some thought such as 'I can't do this' which then spiralled until she had a full blown anxiety attack. She realized that she used her imagination to invent negative scenarios which she then ruminated on.

Pattern interrupts

Ways that Melinda could break into these patterns by heliumizing her internal dialogue (see page 176) and using imagery were discussed. *Changing the tonality of internal dialogue makes it less believable. First she needs to become aware of what she is doing internally, and then she can begin to change it.*

Ego strengthening

She was then taught ways of using imagery to focus her energy and intention on her goals such as the mirror exercise and seeing and feeling her desired end result of therapy. *Melinda can become more solution oriented by using the mirror exercise (page 160) and positive mental rehearsal (page 45) which will also help her motivation for change.*

Use of imagery

Melinda was then taught progressive muscular relaxation (see page 114) and she set a goal of going swimming at the local baths one lunchtime. During the hypnosis session she was also taught ways of using imagery to throw away negatives and to give herself positive suggestion. She liked the idea of having a bonfire and of picking up coloured crystals from around her lake of resources (see page 143). She did a mental rehearsal of going to the swimming baths feeling confident and enjoying her swimming, and she imagined telling her friends in the office how good it had been. *Teaching some alternative ways of entering self hypnosis can be useful, and it is important to teach basic uses of imagery for ego strengthening and goal setting early on in therapy so that the patient has some tools to go away and use. Imagination is a key factor in anxiety, and this can be capitalized upon as Melinda learns other ways to use her imagination.*

Session 3

Feedback

On Melinda's third visit she reported that she had been out at lunchtime swimming twice with friends from the office. Once she had said that she was going, a couple of them had decided to join her. She had been feeling hopeful that she was going to be able to feel calmer, although she had had a couple of days when she had felt very anxious.

Positive anchor

Melinda needed some way of accessing a good confident feeling quickly whenever she felt she was starting to be anxious, so setting up a good feeling anchor was discussed and the difference between association and dissociation was explained. *It is important that the patient understands this distinction* (see page 43).

She was asked to take herself into hypnosis and give a nod when she was ready to proceed. *Encouraging the patient to demonstrate their self hypnotic skills is ego strengthening and decreases any dependence on the therapist.* Melinda re-accessed some memories of when she had been happy on holiday swimming and when she had felt really pleased when she had passed the interview for her job, and one time she remembered having a really good laugh with her best friend. *It is useful to encourage one memory with joyful laughter attached – it is hard to feel anxious if you access joy!* While she was re-experiencing each event from start to finish and really enjoying it, physically and emotionally, Melinda was instructed to press the thumb and index finger of her dominant hand together as it peaked and really capture those good feelings.

Melinda checked that she had learnt this anchor by pressing her thumb and finger together and allowing herself to experience the memory or feelings of confidence that were generated. *Sometimes the memory of the event comes to mind, sometimes just the positive feelings.* Melinda also imagined the colour pink flowing over her (*she could also have had an auditory link*). It was suggested that she use her visual image of her special place as a calmness anchor and that she should practice using her anchors as often as possible because rather like a muscle, the more it is used the stronger it becomes.

Session 4

Resolving past triggers

This session was used to look at where Melinda had learnt her anxiety response. She could not recall any single incident but remembered being shy and anxious at primary school. It was suggested that anxiety (fear) is a protective emotion but that she had learnt anxiety too well so that her oversensitive alarm system fired up when the toast was burning rather than when the kitchen was on fire. She needed to reset her alarm more appropriately. *It is important to acknowledge the positive aspect of anxiety; protection. Melinda will not 'never be anxious' but hopefully will have a more appropriate level of anxiety in the future.*

Memory was discussed as well how the unconscious will produce a version of events that may be symbolic rather than historic truth. *Mentioning memory in some simple way and disabusing people that we have a video camera in our brains help prevent false memory claims* (see page 396).

Time road metaphor

A time road metaphor (see page 401) was utilized for Melinda to float up and look down on the very first time she ever felt anxious. *This should be left as an open question rather than directing to a consciously known specific incident as Melinda's unconscious mind knows where it needs to go.* She was warned that she might not have visual images but once she felt intuitively that she was over the right time she should stop, look down and allow her unconscious mind to learn whatever it needed to allow the feeling to go. *Progress can be monitored by asking the patient to nod.*

She could float down within an aura of protection and calmness to help reassure and comfort that younger her; knowing that however she was feeling then, she could know at her deepest level that she had survived and no longer needed to hang onto that feeling of anxiety. She was asked to give a nod when she had done whatever she felt was necessary or to report if she got stuck. *Taking control, giving resources and understanding at an emotional level rather than merely cognitively that she survived and no longer needed to hold onto the anxiety of her younger self for protection lead to resolution of triggers from the past.*

Once Melinda had nodded she was asked to float back up unless she was already there and to look down again on the event to see if there was anything else that needed to be done there just now. *A second chance to check out the event sometimes leads to further work that needs to be done.*

Melinda shook her head so she was asked to return to above the present, dealing with any related events between then and now that her mind directed her attention to, in the way she now knew how, and comforting and helping that younger part of herself as appropriate. *Sometimes there are particular events that the unconscious brings up into awareness that are related to the earliest event in that anxiety was the predominant emotion, and these need to be resolved in a similar fashion.*

Future age progression

Once above the present Melinda was asked to float a little way into the future and look down to see how she was now, in a situation where she would have felt those old feelings of anxiety. *Here, check again that resolution has been successful – if negative feelings are still apparent, then further work may need to be done.*

If it appeared okay, she could float down into that calmer her and enjoy how it felt. Having done this she was asked to return to the present once she had *"made whatever internal adjustments were necessary to make this her reality."* *Accessing the desired state of feeling calm reinforces Melinda's goals and is ego strengthening.*

Melinda returned to her lake of resources to find a crystal to represent the work she had just done which she added to her lake once she had bathed in its colour (green). *Again a reinforcement of work done and ego strengthening.*

Session 5

Feedback

At the next session Melinda reported that she was worried about attending a forthcoming family party, especially meeting one particular aunt who had always 'made fun of her'. *This is good news – a real chance for Melinda to practice her newly found skills. It is always useful to determine some specific instance where the patient can test out their new tools.*

Perceptual positions

We looked at the pattern of interaction between Melinda and her aunt. *Perceptual positions is a useful semi-hypnotic technique if someone is having difficulties with a particular person and often gives rise to helpful insights and perspectives.* Melinda was asked to close her eyes and imagine being her aunt and to begin to feel things from her perspective. She suddenly realized that actually her aunt probably felt a bit intimidated by being with all the family and her way of coping was to poke fun at people and try to make everything a joke.

Experiment

Framing this as an experiment means that Melinda, rather than focusing on a particular outcome, is curious to see what happens.

Melinda decided to experiment with doing something other than her usual response of looking away and trying to become invisible. She decided she would first simply smile at her aunt and whatever her aunt said she would step back from, look at and understand that her aunt's intention was not to hurt her but probably to cover up her own lack of confidence. A positive mental rehearsal of the forthcoming get together was undertaken in hypnosis.

Re-inforcement of positive anchor

The strength of feeling generated by Melinda's positive anchor needs to be eight or nine out of ten. If it is lower than this, it needs reinforcing.

Melinda's good feeling anchor was reinforced by Melinda standing up, imagining someone who had the feelings that she wanted in front of her and 'stepping into them' to pick up the feelings, as she put in her link.

Session 6

Feedback

At Melinda's final session, she reported with great glee that she had done really well at the family get together and had also arranged to go out on a work's do which she was actually looking forward to. *Melinda needs congratulating*!

She was doing her self hypnosis fairly regularly and had become much more aware of what she was feeling and thinking. She was practicing stepping back from things and evaluating them rather than plunging straight into the feeling. *Stepping back from thoughts and feelings will Melinda more choices in how she responds.*

Melinda, like many shy, somewhat introverted people, tended to disregard praise and take criticism very much to heart.

Praise and criticism were discussed, and it was stressed that criticism is feedback on actions rather than on the identity of the person. Melinda was asked in trance to imagine a set of five shelves where the top shelf (1) was where she stored the most important things that mattered most and the bottom (5) the least important. She was asked to imagine where she placed criticism and praise on these shelves, and praise was on shelf (4) and criticism on shelf (1). It was then suggested that she might like to rearrange what was on her shelves so that praise was nearer the top and criticism nearer the bottom. She did this with a smile.

The metaphor of praise as a gift helps to reinforce the point.

How one would receive a beautifully wrapped gift from someone was discussed; we certainly would not throw it in the giver's face! But this is what happens if we do not accept praise or compliments. We all are more encouraged by praise than criticism, and Melinda was taught compassionate friend imagery (see page 161) and it was suggested she review her day each evening for a while until her response became more automatic than her usual self criticism. *Compassionate friend imagery is a good way to encourage self compassion.*

Melinda reported by email some months later reporting that she was doing really well and had got a promotion.

References

Alonso, J., Angermeyer, M. C., Bernert, S., Bruffaerts, R., Brugha, T. S., Bryson, H. G., de Girolamo, R. D. G., Demyttenaere, K., Gasquet, I., Haro, J. M., Katz, S. J., Kessler, R. C., Kovess, V., Lépine, J.P., Ormel, J., Polidori, G., Russo, L. J., Vilagut, G., Almansa, J., Arbabzadeh-Bouchez, S., Autonell, J., Bernal, M., Buist-Bouwman, M. A., Codony, M., Domingo-Salvany, A., Ferrer, M., Joo, S. S., Martínez-Alonso, M., Matschinger, H., Mazzi, F., Morgan, Z., Morosini, P., Palacín, C., Romera, B., Taub, N. W. & Vollebergh, W. A. M. (2004), Prevalence of mental disorders in Europe: results from the European Study of the Epidemiology of Mental Disorders (ESEMeD) project. *Acta Psychiatrica Scandinavica*, 109 (420), 21–7.

American Psychiatric Association. (2000), *Diagnostic and statistical manual of mental disorders (DSM IV-TR)*. Washington, DC, APA Press.

Ashton, C., Whitworth, G. C. & Al, J. A. S. E. (1997), Self-hypnosis reduces anxiety following coronary artery bypass surgery: a prospective, randomized trial. *Journal of Cardiovascular Surgery*, 38 (1), 69–75.

Bányai, E. L. & Hilgard, E. R. (1976), A comparison of active-alert hypnotic induction with traditional relaxation induction. *Journal of Abnormal Psychology*, 85 (2), 218–24.

Brann, L., Mackrodt, K., & Joslin, M. (2010), Outcome audit, Chelmsford Medical Hypnotherapy Unit. Paper presented at BSCAH Conference, Birmingham, UK.

Chrousos, G. P. (1995), The HPA axis and immune mediated inflammation. *New England Journal of Medicine*, 332, 1351–63.

Dads, M. R., Bovberg, D. H., Redd, W. H. & Cutmore, T. R. H. (1997), Imagery in human classical conditioning. *Psychological Bulletin*, 122, 89–103.

Dannlowski, U., Ohrmann, P., Bauer, J., Kugel, H., Arolt, V., Heindel, W., Kersting, A., Baune, B. T. & Suslow, T. (2007), Amygdala reactivity to masked negative faces is associated with automatic judgmental bias in major depression: a 3 T fMRI study. *Journal of Psychiatry Neuroscience*, 32, 423–9.

Delgado, M. R., Nearing, K. I., Ledoux, J. & Phelps, E.A. (2008), Neural circuitry: the regulation of conditioned fear and its relation to extinction. *Neuron*, 59, 29–38.

Eisenberger, N. I. & Lieberman, M. D. (2004), Why rejection hurts: a common neural alarm system for physical and social pain. *Trends in Cognitive Psychology*, 8, 264–300.

Glisky, M. L., Tataryn, D. J., Tobias, B. A., Kihlstrom, J. F. & McConkey, K. M. (1991), Absorption, openness to experience, and hypnotisability. *Journal of Personality and Social Psychology*, 60, 263–72.

Goldin, P. R., McRae, K., Ramel, W. & Gross, J. J. (2008), The neural bases of emotion regulation: reappraisal and suppression of negative emotion. *Biological Psychiatry*, 63 (6), 577–86.

Grant, J. A., Courtemanche, J., Duerden, E. G., Duncan, G. H. & Rainville, P. (2010), Cortical thickness and pain sensitivity in zen meditators. *Emotion*, 10 (1), 43–53.

Gruzelier, J. (1998), A working model of the neurophysiology of hypnosis: a review of the evidence. *Contemporary Hypnosis*, 15, 3–21.

Hammond, D. C. (2010), Hypnosis in the treatment of anxiety- and stress-related disorders. *Expert Review of Neurotherapeutics*, 10 (2), 263–73.

Hofmann, S. G., Sawyer, A. T., Witt, A. A. & Oh, D. (2010), The effect of mindfulness-based therapy on anxiety and depression: a meta-analytic review. *Journal of Consulting and Clinical Psychology*, 78 (2), 169–83.

Houghton, D. M. (1996), Autogenic training: a self-hypnosis technique to achieve physiological change in a stress management programme. *Contemporary Hypnosis*, 13 (1), 39–44.

Huizink, C., Medina, P. R. D., Mulder, E., Visser, G. & Buitelaar, J. (2003), Stress during pregnancy is associated with developmental outcome in infancy. *Journal of Child Psychology and Psychiatry*, 44 (6), 810–18.

Iglesias, A. (2005), Awake-alert hypnosis in the treatment of panic disorder: a case report. *American Journal of Clinical Hypnosis*, 47 (4), 249–57.

Kirsch, I., Montgomery, G. & Sapirstein, G. (1995), Hypnosis as an adjunct to cognitive-behavioural psychotherapy: a meta-analysis. *Journal of Consulting and Clinical Psychology*, 63, 214–20.

Lazar, S., Kerr, C., Wasserman, R., Gray, J., Greve, D., Treadway, M., McGarvey, M., Quinn, B., Dusek, J., Benson, H., Rauch, S., Moore, C. & Fisch, B. (2005), Meditation experience is associated with increased cortical thickness. *Neuroreport*, 16, 1893–7.

Ledoux, J. (1996). *The emotional brain: the mysterious underpinnings of emotional life*. New York, Simon & Schuster.

Ledoux, J., Iwata, J., Cicchetti, P. & Reis, D. (1988), Different projections of the central amygdaloid nucleus mediate autonomic and behavioural correlates of conditioned fear. *Journal of Neuroscience*, 8, 2517–29.

Ledoux, J., Sakaguchi, A., Iwata, J. & Reis, D. J. (1986). Interruption of projections of the medial geniculate body to an archineostriatal field disrupts the classical conditioning of emotional responses to acoustic stimuli in the rat. *Neuroscience*, 17, 615–27.

McCarthy, P. (2005), Workshop given at the joint meeting of BSCAH, RSM and BSMDH, Edinburgh, Scotland, May.

O'Neill, L. M., Barnier, A. J. & McConkey, K. M. (1999), Treating anxiety with self-hypnosis and relaxation. *Contemporary Hypnosis*, 16 (2), 68–81.

Quirk, G. J. & Gehlert, D. R. (2003), Inhibition of the amygdala: key to pathological states. *Annals of the New York Academy of Sciences*, 985, 263–72.

Ranganath, C. (2006), Working memory for visual objects: complementary roles of inferior temporal, medial temporal, and prefrontal cortex. *Neuroscience*, 139 (1), 277–89.

Schoenburger, N. E. (2000), Research on hypnosis as an adjunct to cognitive-behavioral psycho-therapy. *International Journal of Clinical & Experimental Hypnosis*, 48 (2), 154–69.

Shih, M., Pittinsky, T. & Ambady, L. (2002), Stereotype susceptibility: identity salience and shifts in quantitative performance. *Psychological Science*, 10, 80–3.

Smith, W. H. (1990), Hypnosis in the treatment of anxiety. *Bulletin of the Menninger Clinic*, 54 (2), 209–16.

Office for National Statistics. (2000), Psychiatric morbidity among adults living in private house-holds. http://www.statistics.gov.uk/statbase/Product.asp?vlnk=8258

Wark, D. M. (2006), Alert hypnosis: a review and case report. *American Journal of Clinical Hypnosis*, 48 (4), 291–300.

Whalen, P., Rauch, S., Etcoff, N., Mcinerney, S., Lee, M. & Jenike, M. (1998), Masked presentations of emotional facial expressions modulate amygdala activity without explicit knowl-edge. *Journal of Neuroscience*, 18, 411–18.

Yu, C. K-C. (2005), Application of cognitive-behavioural hypnotic treatment for anxiety manage-ment in the Chinese. *Contemporary Hypnosis*, 22 (2), 104–15.

Zigmond, A. & Snaith, R. (1983), The hospital anxiety and depression scale. *Acta Psychiatrica Scandinavica*, 67, 361–70.

16

Depression

Dr Alastair Dobbin

with contributions from Dr Ann Williamson, Dr Les Brann and Dr Geoff Ibbotson

Introduction

Depression is one of the most common causes of disability and disease worldwide. World Health Organization (WHO) projections indicate that depression will be the highest ranked cause of disease burden in developed countries by the year 2020 (Murray & Lopez, 1997). The Office for National Statistics Psychiatric Morbidity Report stated that mixed anxiety and depression is the most common mental disorder in Britain, with almost 9% of people meeting criteria for diagnosis at any one time and 8–12% of the population experiencing depression in any one year (Singleton et al., 2001).

Prevalence rates have consistently been found to be 1.5–2.5 times higher in women than in men, but this could be because men present with less obvious symptomatology and culturally are more reluctant to seek help (National Statistics, 2003). Waraich et al., (2004) found that dysthymia (sub-threshold depressive symptoms persisting for more than two years) increases with age and estimated that 2.5–5.0% of people will experience dysthymia during their lifetime.

Depression arises from a complex interaction of biological, psychological and social factors and may present as an acute episode. However it often presents as a chronic relapsing condition, and the more episodes a patient suffers the more likely they are to become depressed again (Shea et al., 1992). Although depression is usually regarded as a separate entity, it is one author's opinion (AW) that it always co-exists with some degree of anxiety (see also page 170) and varies across a spectrum from mild to severe. Loss of self-confidence, social stigma, anxiety symptoms and substance misuse may cause further longer term impairment in social functioning and contribute to its chronic nature (Sartorius, 2001).

Depression does not only affect the individual but everyone around them; it may result in marital break-up, child neglect and family problems (Ramchandani & Stein, 2003). Depression is often co-morbid with other chronic conditions. Moussavi *et al.*, (2007) reported a worldwide prevalence of depression of 23% in people with two or more chronic physical disorders, whereas depression was reported in only 3.2% of healthy controls. Depression thus has a huge impact on people's lives, and this is reflected in employment statistics and in the use of health services.

Treatment Guidelines

It is strongly advised not to treat a depressed person if you have no experience with mental health; but any GP or appropriately experienced nurse (such as a community psychiatric nurse) or counsellor should not shy away from treating depression. The same rules apply for treating depressed patients in a practice with hypnosis as for treating with anti-depressant drugs. In both cases there is a strong influence of suggestion. If you have, in your practice, treated patients with support from a mental health team or a senior colleague, continue to do so, but just add in the hypnosis.

There is a four times higher risk of suicide in depressed people compared with the general population which rises with severity of the depression. Mortality from suicide is reported to be as high as 15% in people with depression severe enough for hospitalization (Bostwick & Pankratz, 2000). If your patient has suicidal ideation, the therapist needs to be cautious. There should be no hesitation in asking the question, *"Do you feel like taking your own life?"* If the answer is 'Yes', it is necessary to ask, *"Can you see yourself doing it? How will you do it?"* If the answer is a categorical *"I am going to go home to take all my tablets," "I am going to drive off a cliff," "I am going to sit in the garage with the engine running"* or the like, then a psychiatrist or psychiatric team should immediately be contacted for assessment and possible admission, possibly even with compulsory detention.

If however the answer is *"Well sometimes I feel that I can't go on," "I wish it would all end"* or even *"I felt like it last month,"* then it is probable that watchful waiting would be appropriate. Suitable local supports should be arranged, such as making sure they have the Samaritans' number or whatever else might be available locally. Another early appointment should be organized and instructions given to seek help if they do not improve. In the 1980s it was a given that you should not use hypnosis in treating depression. There was an urban myth which seemed very powerful at the time, that if you used hypnosis with depressed people they might get enough ego strength to commit suicide. As access to research has improved, it has become clear that there is no evidence to support that myth: hypnosis can be used to treat depression, it does not increase suicide risk and, as will be seen, it can be very effective through changing our relationship with our thoughts.

It is helpful to use an assessment tool, such as the Hospital Anxiety and Depression scale (HADs; Zigmond & Snaith, 1983) or PHQ-9 (Kroenke & Spitzer, 2002), to assess the level of depression. If the patient has moderate to severe depression, medication might be considered, particularly if it has been used successfully before.

Anti-depressants do work, but the difference between taking an anti-depressant and a placebo is small (Moncrieff *et al.*, 2002). Whilst the effects of anti-depressants might be small this does not detract from the fact that some people do improve, whether from chemical or placebo effect or a mixture of the two, and both drug and placebo responders do better than those with no treatment at all (Kirsch & Sapirstein, 1999). If the patient has previously improved from the use of anti-depressants, then use can be made of this often powerful association between the improvement in their depression and the medication. This will be enhanced by giving them hypnosis as well as the anti-depressant drug. Dobbin *et al.*, (2004) showed that when people were given an open choice between anti-depressants or psychological therapy, there was an over 90% choice for the latter.

There are also two categories where extra vigilance is required. Among depressed outpatients, new-onset bipolar illness has been found in up to 20% of individuals followed up for at least six years and early age is the greatest risk factor (Akiskal *et al.*, 1983). If there is a strong family history of bipolar depression one should be aware of this and have a low threshold of referral to a psychiatrist, not because there are any increased risks of using hypnosis in bipolar disorder (hypnosis is used in bipolar disorder, particularly in the United States) but because they may also need medication such as lithium. If in doubt, the opinion of a local psychiatrist should be sought and treatment suspended until the situation is clarified. Similar rules apply to psychotic disorders. However remember at all times that the therapist should be aware of the legal 'rules of engagement'; if you are called on to defend your actions you will be judged by your peers, and unless you had considerable experience in these fields it would be considered foolhardy and unnecessarily risky to be treating them without support. Despite these caveats, this author (AD) has found hypnotherapy to be a very successful and safe way of treating depression; using a self hypnosis programme (Dobbin *et al.*, 2009), over 30,000 patients in Edinburgh have been treated for depression in the past five years with no reports of harm.

Patterns in Depression

Depression has been called the 'selfish' disease because the depressed person tends to be very self focused. This self focus or personalization is one of the features of depression. When a patient is depressed they also feel that their depression is permanent and unchanging. These ideas need to be challenged at the outset when treating depression with hypnosis. This challenge begins with history taking, by emphasizing times when they were not depressed and utilizing experiential metaphor (see page 62). Reminding patients in hypnosis of the way things change such as the seasons (a truism) or their own taste in clothes and hairstyle (drawing on the patient's experience) can be used to loosen up their sense of permanency. A patient with depression tends to focus on the past rather than noticing the present or looking to the future. Accessing a future orientation in hypnosis may also be helpful especially once the patient has already started to improve. In this the patient is directed to consider a future where there *"may be places you have not seen yet that will become your favourite places, people that you have not yet met who may become good friends and things you may not yet have done that you will really enjoy. ..."* As Yapko (1994) states, one often needs a more symptom directed approach at first in order to make some change that will engender some expectation in the patient. Ideas of change and personal competence need to be seeded before addressing the underlying psycho-dynamics of the problem. As with any emotional state, making a change anywhere in the pattern of thoughts, feelings and behaviours that generate and maintain depression is a good starting point (Williamson, 2008).

Thinking styles

There are two thinking styles, ruminative and experiential. 'Rumination' means 'chewing over' thoughts associated with the same feelings and denotes thinking which is gener-alized, verbally based, de-contextualized and self evaluative. 'Experiential thinking', by contrast, denotes thinking which is contextual (relevant to task in hand), process focused and specific. Traditionally rumination has been seen generally as negative, and experi-ential thinking as positive. However summarizing extensive recent research (Wat-kins, 2008) points out that there is nothing wrong with rumination at the right time. Rumination is good when you are feeling good, if you have 'positive affect' – a good mood. Under these circumstances rumination allows one to repeatedly absorb good feelings, and Watkins suggests that rumination is our default thinking style. This only causes a problem when the person cannot swap between the two styles under pressure in a stressful situation.

Ruminative thinking is generalized and experiential is specific. This means in rumination that one focuses on abstract ideas such as *"Life is good," "I was a happy child"* or *"I wasn't good at sport,"* while in experiential thinking one focuses on specific events such as *"I can see myself enjoying meeting Tom today," "When I was a child we had a great holiday in France camping by the sea"* or *"Once I played football and no one explained I should chase the ball and pass it to others so I just stood in my position and felt stupid."* In rumination we have poor access to specific memories. This tendency with rumination to over generalize is the strongest predictor of severity, relapse and duration of depression (Hermans *et al.*, 2008). Presumably the access to specific autobiographical memories means we can remember a resolution (at the very minimum, survival) to even the most traumatic memories, which allows us access to resources which give us a sense of autonomy.

There are immediate correlations to this knowledge outside hypnosis. If you concentrate on a simple task that you are familiar with, this will establish an experiential thinking style and you will help yourself deal with challenging, potentially stressful situations. If you focus on the achievable in the short term, see what you are going to do the next day, a sense of overwhelming anxiety for an uncertain future is much relieved. One of the difficulties with depression is actually finding the internal energy to do anything at all, so the 'one small goal a day' approach may be helpful. Facilitating the patient in hypnosis to focus on how good they will feel when they have done 'x' will help motivation (see page 104). To help a depressed patient feel more positive, take them back in hypnosis to a time when things were going well and ask them to ruminate on it; absorb them in the detail and the good feelings (association) which can then be used once they come out of hypnosis.

If the patient is under stress and feeling dysphoric (low mood – negative affect) then rumination will cause them to absorb the bad feelings and they may then spiral out of control into a depressed mood. Under these circumstances the less vulnerable of us can switch into an experiential thinking style. Experiential thinking style is characterized by an external viewpoint, seeing yourself from the outside as if in a movie (dissociation). It reduces over generalization and enables greater access to specific memories, reducing self-critical and judgemental internal dialogue. This ability needs to be utilized if we are depressed, especially the tendency to be less self critical. In utilizing an experiential thinking style, our relationship to our memories change and because we can be less self critical and judgemental we are in a better position to look at any trauma memories without blaming ourselves. This may particularly help childhood memories associated with abuse (often associated with depression; see Kuyken & Brewin 1994) where patients often blame themselves as predicted by attachment theory (Phillips & Frederick, 1995, p252).

The problem depressed people have is that they are unable to switch between ruminative and experiential thinking. Therefore the depressed person needs the ability to switch into an experiential thinking style; hypnosis is the most useful tool to facilitate this, and this switch in thinking style can also be anchored during hypnosis (see page 181). The state of hypnosis is per se a state of external perspective reinforced by the 'non-volitional' nature of ideomotor phenomena.

This author (AD) believes that there is often underlying unrecognized trauma in depression, and certainly in many of the patients treated by the author (AD) an alteration in relationship with a trauma memory has been a marker for improvement. The result of this unrecognized trauma is that often others are blamed for our bad feeling; for example, a wife is 'not being nice' to us. Neurologically some aspect of the interaction with the wife is acting as a trigger to a pattern of discomfort someone else set up a long time ago. This pattern is stored in the amygdala as a conditioned fear reflex and is re-activated (see more on the neuroanatomy of trauma on page 170). Rational examination will not help to uncover the link, whereas experiential thinking may allow us better access to the event.

In depression, which could be seen as a state of learned helplessness (Abramson *et al.*, 1978), there will be over activity of the amygdala, telling us *something* is wrong – but not *what*, as we have poor access to any trauma experience which might be at the root of it. The first step in treatment should be to reduce the autonomic response to fear, as this will reduce the over activity of the amygdala and then facilitate resolution of negative traumatic events from the past. Hypnosis is one of the best ways to achieve this.

Building Resilience

The opposite of 'learned helplessness' is resilience. Resilience can be defined as that process whereby individuals respond to adversity by exhibiting positive adaptive behaviour. It denotes a combination of abilities and characteristics that interact dynamically, to allow an individual to bounce back, cope successfully, and function above the norm in spite of significant stress or adversity. External support from relatives and supportive communities facilitates adaptive behaviour, and hence resiliency is not a personal trait. Whilst an individual may be resilient in one context, they may not display this in other contexts (Luthar & Cicchetti, 2000). At different phases in life individuals may demonstrate varying resilience to stressors (Tusaie & Dyer, 2004). Resilience develops normally in early childhood as a consequence of good, consistent parenting. This allows learning of good adaptation strategies and also the formation of good physiological responses to stressors by the hypothalamic-pituitary-adrenal (HPA) axis as the child is supported and taught when they experience different challenges and stressors.

It is recognized that resilience is key in avoiding recurrent depression, and the key to resilience is the ability to access positive emotions in challenging situations. The way to access positive emotions is by accessing positive autobiographical memory. Low resilience is associated with a negative memory that is encountered in response to a challenging situation. How can this be changed? Thinking style technique tells us that we can re-experience events from the past and gain benefit from reappraising the experience. Suppressing a negative memory tends to focus the mind even more strongly on the negative feeling, leading to a vicious cycle of recurrent self criticism and low self esteem. Sometimes this may be overcome by the teaching of self hypnosis, the safe place, and positive imagery which can be used to reverse the bad feelings. Sometimes it may be overcome by using a different technique, such as collapsing anchors (see page 146), when we can overcome the negative trigger responsible for the vulnerability. This is useful if there is a sudden onset of low mood associated with specific situations.

The most widely practiced therapy for depression and generally the only available therapy recommended by NICE is cognitive-behavioural therapy (CBT) which was expounded by Aaron Beck in the 1960s, and despite the intervening 50 years has not changed in its underlying premise, that people with depression have a fixed schema of dysfunctional ideas (e.g. *"I am a failure"*). A rational examination of the logical errors – *"How do you 'know' it's true? How will you find out?"* – leads them to establish the invalidity of their assumptions which enables them to let go of the false premise. It does work: it reduces relapse. But subsequent research (Teasdale *et al.*, 2002) into 'mindfulness based' CBT (MBCT) showed that the crucial mediator of conventional CBT is the relationship to one's thoughts – such as whether thoughts were seen as part of the person or as an external phenomenon they can let go of – that causes the change, not the logical conviction that they were wrong. It is the experiential viewpoint of sitting down with an external observer and looking at the mind–body processes that brings about the change; working with a therapist is a 'mindful' (experiential) act. It is not necessary therefore to actually do the questioning logically; equally effective is to follow the long established practices of mindfulness.

Paying attention to bodily processes such as breathing and muscular tension and visualizing detailed images (the shape and form of a black umbrella, water drops running down a window pane) are enough to change the relationship with the thoughts. Thus mindfulness techniques encourage experiential thinking rather than rumination.

Published Evidence

Along with various forms of medication, CBT (Gilbert, 2000) tends to be the most commonly used form of 'talking therapy' currently available to depressed patients. Castonguay *et al.*, (1996) supports the use of cognitive therapy approaches in depression. Elkin *et al.*, (1989) found cognitive and interpersonal therapy as effective as medication, whilst De Maat *et al.*, (2006) suggest that recent estimates from controlled trials suggested that over half of patients with major depression do not remit at post-treatment, while an even higher percentage fail to maintain lasting improvements (Hollon *et al.*, 2005).

McBrien (1990) reports on the successful use of a self hypnosis programme for depression and combining cognitive therapy and hypnosis has led to improved outcomes (Alladin, 1989). Alladin and Alibhai (2007) randomly assigned 84 depressives to 16 weeks of treatment of either cognitive hypnosis (CH) or CBT alone. 'At the end of treatment, patients from both groups significantly improved compared to baseline scores. However, the CH group produced significantly larger changes in Beck Depression Inventory, Beck Anxiety Inventory, and Beck Hopelessness Scale. Effect size calculations showed that the CH group produced 6%, 5%, and 8% greater reduction in depression, anxiety, and hopelessness, respectively, over and above the CBT group. The effect size was maintained at 6-month and 12-month follow-ups' (p 147).

Dobbin *et al.*, (2009) reported a study of GP referrals who received a 12 week self hypnosis intervention by a nurse within the NHS which showed a change in the Beck Depression Inventory (BDI) from severe to minimal depression; benchmarking showed comparable outcomes to CBT and counselling studies. This programme is now in widespread use in primary care in Scotland.

One author (LB) and colleagues in the Chelmsford Medical Hypnosis Unit have routinely recorded scores from the HADs (Zigmond & Snaith, 1983) for all patients referred regardless of the nature of the problem (Brann et al 2010). Of the 323 patients seen, 84 (26%) scored 11 or more on the HADs depression scale with 54 in the moderate range and 30 in the severe range. A staggering 79 (94%) were also clinically anxious; only five of the depressed patients did not have co-morbid anxiety. Therapy was patient centred and problem orientated to each individual's need. One patient recorded a worse score but all the others improved with 73 (87%) ceasing to be clinically depressed; the other 10 patients improved but remained within the depressed range. Table 16.1 summarizes the results.

Clinically HADs seemed to underscore depression and the unit began recording BDI as well (Beck, 1961). 79 patients completed the BDI and 42 (53%) recorded scores in the moderate and severe ranges. Only 23% of those were clinically depressed according to their HADs score. Following hypnosis, 34 (84%) were no longer clinically depressed, with only

Table 16.1   Summary of Hospital Anxiety and Depression scale – Depression (HADs D) results before and after hypnotherapy

	Initial mean HADs D score (SD)	Final mean HADs D score (SD)	Change in HADs D score (confidence)	Effect size	Statistical significance t-test	Mean number of sessions
Moderate (n = 54)	12.3 (1.1)	6.0 (3.0)	6.3 (+/− 0.79)	5.7	P = 0.00 (1.8×10^{-21})	3.9
Severe (n = 30)	16.7 (1.6)	8.3 (4.7)	8.4 (+/− 1.74)	5.3	P = 0.00 (2.0×10^{-10})	4.8
Total (n = 84)	13.9 (2.5)	6.8 (3.8)	7.0 (+/− 0.82)	2.8	P = 0.00 (2.7×10^{-28})	4.2

Table 16.2   Summary of Beck Depression Inventory (BDI) scores before and after hypnotherapy

	Initial mean BDI score (SD)	Final mean BDI score (SD)	Change in BDI score (confidence)	Effect size	Statistical significance t-test	Mean number of sessions
Total n = 42	29.2 (7.7)	13.3 (7.6)	15.9 (+/− 3.0)	2.1	P = 0.00 (6.6×10^{-13})	4.1

eight patients remaining in the depressed range. Table 16.2 summarizes the results. Thus the hypnotherapy intervention yielded good outcomes for both depressed cohorts.

Working with Hypnosis

The essential element of an experiential thinking style is that you 'notice' or 'pay attention to' whatever is happening externally or internally rather than 'think about' it (Watkins & Teasdale, 2004). This small change of wording is the most significant factor in establishing an experiential mindset and has been shown *on its own* to alter mental health parameters. It converts the patient into an observer rather than an unfortunate victim trapped in a bad situation. This external viewpoint can be hugely reinforced by the phenomena of hypnosis, such as ideomotor movement, and hypnosis offers a way of promoting this viewpoint free from any social exclusivity and any religious overtones which are sometimes associated with mindfulness. This 'noticing' should be combined with relaxation, and a good way to establish experiential relaxation is through Jacobson relaxation (i.e. tensing and releasing muscles; Jacobson, 1938).

The first thing to establish in hypnotherapy for depression is 'safety and security'. The following is the author's (AD) approach, based on thinking style modification using trance induction (see below) with simple ego strengthening in the first instance.

Induction

As hypnosis (mindfulness) is a phenomenon of attention, it is useful to start with moving attention internally:

> *As you sit there with your eyes closed, I am sure you are aware of the size and shape of the room, where the doors and windows are, where the furniture is, the colour of the walls. And you can hear the sounds inside and outside the building, the sound of distant traffic, of doors opening and closing, of people talking in other rooms. All these things are examples of external awareness of your surroundings. In a moment we are going to focus on your internal awareness of your body, particularly the internal awareness of your muscle tension and relaxation. Focusing on your internal awareness is like playing with a magnifying glass when you were a kid. If you hold a magnifying glass at the right angle to the sun at the right distance from a piece of paper an intensely bright spot appears on the paper which then begins to smoulder, then burn. In this example you are focusing the power of the sun's rays 95 million miles away onto the sheet of paper, in the same way now you are able to focus the power of your unconscious mind wherever it is needed and we will use your conscious mind to guide you into the state called hypnosis in the same way as the kid uses the magnifying glass. And as we do so your unconscious mind will be able to come up with the resources you need to help you. ...*
> (Adapted from an induction from McCarthy, 2005.)

Note the use of the 'yes set' and the use of the words 'focus' and 'awareness', both experiential suggestions.
Then move on to relaxation:

> *Take in a deep breath and squeeze the fingers of your left hand as hard as you can, and hold it, hold that position, notice the tension in the muscles of your hand and forearm, hold it, and now relax, breathe out and allow your hand to relax, and notice the difference, notice how pleasantly heavy your arm and hand feel when you allow them to relax. Just allow that relaxation to spread through all your arm muscles so that all your arm muscles feel heavy and relaxed.*

This can then be repeated with all the muscle groups of the body; right hand, upper arms, shoulders, feet, legs, thighs, stomach muscles and buttocks, bit by bit or focusing on key areas. A key area is the face muscles. It is amazing how much tension people carry in their face muscles, and this cuts them off from effective communication with others and with the ability to access the deepest level of relaxation. Work through the face muscles:

> *Close your eyes, squeeze them tightly shut, notice the tension in all the muscles round your eyes, hold it and relax and notice the difference, now wrinkle your forehead, lift up your eyebrows up, make deep wrinkles in your forehead, notice the tension in your forehead muscles, hold it, and relax, let your forehead be calm and smooth, notice the difference, now clench your jaw, clench your teeth and*

notice the tension in your jaw muscles, and relax and notice the difference, let your lips be slightly apart and your tongue resting at the bottom of your mouth, now allow the feeling of relaxation in all your face muscles to deepen so you can feel more calm and more relaxed. Notice the relaxed feeling in all in your entire face, forehead, eyes, jaw and lips.

In this way you can go through all the body muscle groups. The constant suggestion of noticing physical tension makes people more aware of the tension in their body and makes it easier for them to let it go. By constantly placing stress on the action of noticing physical changes, you are also implicitly training people to notice the mental changes. In this way, when memories come up, the patient is already in the position of an observer, more easily able to accept what happened rather than blaming themselves for it.

Another aspect of relaxation induction that is particularly useful is the breathing induction. Of course breathing is a very useful and repetitive action that we all have to do, so it is an ideal topic for observation. The breathing induction can follow the experiential Jacobson relaxation as below:

Focus on the sensations of breathing as you breathe in and out gently. Notice the sensation of stretching as you breathe in (breathe in yourself along with the patient) *and relaxation as you breathe out* (wait for patient to breathe out) *and in* (wait again) *and out. And notice the sounds of your breathing, the sound of the air going in as you breathe in, and the sound of the air going out as you breathe out. Follow the sound of your breathing in* (wait) *and out. Just take in the relaxation that comes every time you breathe out. Notice also the way the temperature of the air changes, how the air is cool as you breathe in and warm as you breathe out. And now just continue noticing these sounds and sensations of breathing for a few moments until I speak to you again. And as you continue noticing these sounds and sensations its natural for all the other everyday sounds and sensations around you to just drift away, to fade away as if into a mist, so that you are only aware of the sound of your breathing and the sound of my voice. All the normal everyday sounds and sensations are still there but they do not come near you, it is as if your mind has tuned your senses away from these sounds and sensations like turning a dial on a radio, the sounds and sensations are still there but you mind does not pay attention to them, you can just let them go. And as you continue to listen to my voice in this way you become more and more relaxed. You are aware of any thoughts that drift into your mind and are able to let them go, there is no need to hold onto any of them, you can just let them go. And as you continue relaxing just follow your breathing, breathing in calm, breathing out relaxation, with every breath out drawing the relaxation deeper and deeper inside you, going down to a place of total safety and security where nothing can come near you and nothing can disturb you.*

Here is a quick induction which incorporates elements of mindfulness and experiential thinking.

First I would like you to say the word calm, out loud, quietly. Now say it again more softly. Now say it inside your head very softly and gently, repeating it over and over so that it is like the sound of a distant bell, calm . . . calm . . . just keep doing that for a few moments until I speak to you again. (Wait about 10 seconds.) *Now, how many marks out of ten would you give that as a means of relaxing your mind?* (Person gives a number.) *Good.*

Next I would like you to picture in your minds eye either a candle or a rose, you choose which. (Wait a few seconds.) *Which have you chosen?* (Patient says, *"Candle."*) *Okay, so now focus on the image of the candle, notice how the flame flickers slightly as it burns, just concentrate on the image of the candle for a few moments until I speak to you again.* (Wait a few seconds). *Okay, now how many marks out of ten would you give that as a means of relaxing your mind?* (Number again.) *Good.*

Now this time I would like you to focus on your breathing. Focus on the sensations of breathing as you breathe in and out gently. Notice the sensation of stretching as you breathe in (breathe in yourself along with the patient) *and out* (wait for patient to breathe out) *and in* (wait again] *and out. And notice the sounds of your breathing, the sound of the air going in as you breathe in, and the sound of the air going out as you breathe out. Just continue noticing these sounds and sensations of breathing until I speak to you again.* (Wait a few seconds.) *Okay so how many marks out of ten would you give that as a means of relaxing your mind.* (Patient picks number.) *Good.*

So now you have three scores go to the method which produced the highest score.

Okay so now just continue saying the word calm/picturing the candle/noticing the sounds and sensations of breathing, and as you continue doing this you can relax more and more deeper and deeper, as you focus on the picture/breathing sensation/sound you can let go of all the everyday sounds and sensations around you and go deeper and deeper into a place of total safety and security where nothing can touch you, nothing can disturb you, where you have access to solutions and inner strength that you normally donot have access to.

Not only does this induction contain many aspects of mindfulness, but also it contains a series of 'double binds'. In the author's (AD) experience, nobody in ten years of using this induction, when asked, *"How many marks out of ten would you give that as a means of relaxing your* mind?" has ever said, *"But it is not relaxing my mind!"* or *"Zero!"* So the patient is drawn into accepting the implicit premise that they are becoming more relaxed.

This can be followed with ego strengthening and a self hypnosis trigger.

Just before you leave this state of deep relaxation, I am going to give you a trigger so that you can get back into this special safe, calm, relaxed state whenever you need to. Just squeeze your left hand hard, take in a deep breath; hold your breath and now breathe out and relax your hand. Whenever you do this you will slip easily and naturally into this calm relaxed state and you will have access to all the resources and inner strength you need. You can safely stay in this state aware of all common dangers and bring yourself out at the correct time. You may do this without even realizing it but it will be equally effective.

Then after you have brought them out of hypnosis try out the trigger, suggesting, "When you have reached the state of relaxation again, just stay there for a few moments, then allow your unconscious mind to bring you out when you are ready." As they are very close to the trance state, they will be able to go back rapidly which will boost their confidence.

The self-hypnosis trigger can then be used to access a trance state very quickly, by using a conditioned reflex, like using a shortcut on a computer desktop.

Table 16.3   Results of patient questionnaires

Patient questionnaire questions	Yes	No	Ambivalent	n
Has the hypnosis solved your problem?	44	37	19	125
Has your life improved in other ways for the better?	62	35	3	123
Are you still using your self hypnosis?	77	23		123

Source: Dobbin (2004).

The importance of self hypnosis cannot be underestimated, and Dobbin *et al.*, (2004) reported the following responses to a patient questionnaire, given six weeks after a course of hypnosis delivered in an NHS clinic. (See Table 16.3.)

This shows the rather strange result that, although 44% had the problem they came with solved, and 62% felt a general improvement (so 18% more of people felt a general sense of wellbeing), 77% were still using the self hypnosis. This means that a very large proportion of patients who attended for treatment were using the tool of self hypnosis.

Stabilization is essential in the early treatment stages of depression, and it is useful to develop 'safe place' imagery. If the patient is in a state of physical relaxation they will have switched off their sympathetic 'fight or flight' response. In this state, whatever they think of will be connected to their relaxed state, so will be suitable.

> As you continue relaxing in this way, recognize that you have reached a place that is very special to you, that really feels good to you. This special place could be somewhere inside or outside, it could be a room or place in the country that you have been to before where you really enjoyed being, or it could be a place that you create for yourself. Take a little time to make this place exactly how you would like it for yourself, put in somewhere to sit down and relax. From now on we will call this your special place. Whenever you come here you can recharge and revitalize yourself and work on things in different ways. Put things in this space so that you can feel really relaxed here, so you can feel safe and comfortable, so that you can find your way back whenever you want to. (Pause here.)
>
> Put in somewhere to keep yourself warm, a fireplace or a seat in the sun, so that you can warm yourself, feeling the warmth filling your body with energy and inner strength. Sit or stand near the warmth for a while and feel the energy revitalizing and recharging your body. Enjoy this pleasant energizing feeling for a while until I speak to you again. (Pause again.)
>
> Also (optional) put in somewhere that you can write things down, words or phrases that are important to you, things that you would like to work on. This could be a board, a whiteboard or blackboard, a flip chart or a sandy area. You will be able to write how you want to feel when you wake up and then carry that feeling around with you or words that you feel you want to hold on to. Words like strong, happy, safe, secure. Whenever you go to your special place, you can change the words or not as you see fit.
>
> In a few moments I am going to suggest that you leave your special place and I want you to think of words that you can write down. You can return to your special place whenever you want

to, just close your eyes, take some deep breaths and you can be there. Or use your self hypnosis trigger and take yourself there. You can spend as long as you want there safely aware of all common dangers. You can rest and regenerate and change the words on your writing area and work on any challenges you need to. So now just relax and enjoy the good positive feelings in this place. When you want to wake up take in a few deep breaths and before you wake up, just stretch out for a few moments, and when you do wake up, you will feel relaxed refreshed and good in every way, happy that you can come back to this place whenever you need to.

Resolving Past Trauma

It is possible that you might, after stabilization, wish to look back at past trauma; sometimes the act of stabilization gives the patient enough ego strength to begin looking at memories which will spontaneously come up in *or out* of hypnosis. If trauma memories occur in hypnosis, any of the techniques discussed in the relevant chapters can be used to resolve them. If they happen out of hypnosis while reviewing progress, open discussion is fine. If a patient starts to cry when in hypnosis, this is a feeling that should be worked with (see the affect bridge on page 127). Having set up ideomotor signalling:

THERAPIST: *"These feelings that you are experiencing at the moment, would it be okay for your unconscious mind to review unconscious memories related to this problem?"*

Wait for response – if 'Yes':

T: *"Allow your mind to drift back in time to the earliest experience your unconscious mind remembers related to this current problem, and when you have found it give me a signal."*

Wait for response:

T: *"Would it be all right for your unconscious mind to review this experience in detail at an unconscious level and let me know when that is complete."* (Wait for signal.)
T: *"When did this experience occur? Was it before you were ten – before you were five?"* (By a series of questions, you can narrow it down to when it occurred.)
T: *"Would it be all right to bring this event into consciousness, knowing that you are safe in the here and now?"*

If the patient refuses, then suggest that the patient reviews the event at an unconscious level three or four times giving reassurance as needed and repeat the question. If there is still a 'No' response then suggest that the patient can continue to work on this so that it can be resolved, maybe in dreams, but without any conscious distress until the next session.

Remember when progress is reviewed at the next session to ask if the patient has been aware of having any memories or dreams.

If 'Yes' then ask the patient to look at the event, maybe using one of the dissociative techniques described in chapter 26 and suggesting that the patient (within an aura of protection) can go and help the younger self.

T.   *"Would it be okay for you to talk to me about this experience?"* (Often it is not. If 'Yes', then continue with the following.) *"In a moment you will find that you can speak but can remain in a deeply relaxed state."* (Then ask the following.) *"Where are you? Who is with you? What is happening?"*

T: *"I would like you X lying here on the couch back to help the younger X. I want you to go into this situation and go to a place where you can be with young X, and when you are there let me know* (wait for signal) *now I would like you to talk to young X and reassure him that everything is going to be okay, you know this because you come from his future, he will never need to go through this situation on his own again because you will always be with him. So just keep talking to him and watch his face. And when you can see by his face that he is reassured by what you are saying, let me know."*

T: *"Now that young X is freed from this fear, he will have a lot of extra energy. Over the last few years you have been burning up energy dealing with this fear. So now I want you to think of some where you can put this extra energy, into some new pleasant or useful outlet. And when you have chosen such an outlet let me know."* (Wait for a smile and end with the following.) *"As you come back and wake up, you can accept that the past is the past. . . ."*

Depending on the severity of the depression, a variable length of time will need to be spent stabilizing the patient using ego strengthening, anchors and self hypnosis. Sometimes change may be rapid, but is more often a stepwise, up and down process. It is important that the patient does not get discouraged and metaphors such describing the process of learning to walk, when a child falls down after every few steps but eventually walks all the time can be useful. Another useful metaphor is to liken the depression 'pattern' to an icon on a computer screen which is there but only operates if 'double clicked', and can then be minimized again.

Teaching the depressed patient self hypnosis, the use of imagery and an observer position (experiential thinking style), enabling and encouraging the patient to start to help themselves by taking small achievable steps and upsetting their perceptions that depression is permanent and unchanging are the mainstays of their early treatment. Cognitive restructuring, both in and out of hypnosis, and building up the patient's self esteem, resolving any past traumatic memories and building resilience will ensure that they have the tools to help themselves. In the authors' (AD and AW) experience, any subsequent episodes of depression, if they do occur, are less severe and shorter lasting as the patient already has the tools they need and may merely need reminding to utilize them.

References

Abramson, L. Y., Seligman, M. E. P. & Teasdale, J. D. (1978), Learned helplessness in humans: critique and reformulation. *Journal of Abnormal Psychology*, 87, 49–74.

Akiskal, H. S., Walker, P., Puzantian, V. R., King, D., Rosenthal, T. L. & Dranon, M. (1983), Bipolar outcome in the course of depressive illness: phenomenologic, familial and pharmacologic predictors. *Journal of Affective Disorders*, 5, 115–28.

Alladin, A. (1989). Cognitive hypnotherapy in depression. In *Hypnosis: the Fourth European Congress*. Oxford, Whurr.

Alladin, A. & Alibhai, A. (2007), Cognitive hypnotherapy for depression: an empirical investigation. *The International Journal of Clinical and Experimental Hypnosis*, 55 (2), 147–66.

Beck, A. T., Ward, C. H., Mendelson, M., Mock, J. & Erbaugh, J. (1961), An inventory for measuring depression. *Arch Gen Psychiatry*, 4, 561–71.

Bostwick, J. M. & Pankratz, V. S. (2000), Affective disorders and suicide risk: a reexamination. *American Journal of Psychiatry*, 157 (12), 1925–32.

Brann, L. Mackrodt, K. & Joslin, M. (2010). Outcome audit, Chelmsford Medical HypnotherapyUnit. Paper presented at BSCAH Conference. Birmingham, UK.

Castonguay, L. G., Goldfried, M. R., Wiser, S., Raue, P. & Hayes, A. M. (1996), Predicting the effect of cognitive therapy for depression: a study of unique and common factors. *Journal of Consulting and Clinical Psychology*, 64, 497–504.

De Maat, S., Dekker, J., Schoevers, R. & De Jonghe, F. (2006), Relative efficacy of psychotherapy and pharmacotherapy in the treatment of depression: a meta-analysis. *Psychotherapy Research*, 16, 562–72.

Dobbin, A., Faulkner, S., Heaney, D., Selvaraj, S. & Gruzelier, J. (2004), Impact on health status of a hypnosis clinic in general practice. *Contemporary Hypnosis*, 21, 153–60.

Dobbin, A., Maxwell, M. & Elton, R. (2009), A benchmarked feasibility study of a self-hypnosis treatment for depression in primary care. *International Journal of Clinical and Experimental Hypnosis*, 57, 293–318.

Elkin, I., Shea, T., Watkins, J. T., Imber, S. D., Sotsky, S. M., Collins, J. F., Glass, D. R., Pilkonis, P. A., Leber, W. R., Docherty, J. P., Fiester, S. J. & Parloff, M. B. (1989), National Institute of Mental Health Treatment of Depression Collaborative Research Programme: general effectiveness of treatments. *Archives of General Psychiatry*, 46, 971–82.

Gilbert, P. (2000). *Overcoming depression*. London, Robinson.

Hermans, D., Vandromme, H., Debeer, E., Raes, F., Demyttenaere, k., Brunfaut, E. et al. (2008), Overgeneral autobiographical memory predicts diagnostic status in depression. *Behaviour Research and Therapy*, 46, 668–77.

Hollon, S. D., Derubeis, R. J., Shelton, R. C., Amsterdam, J. D., Salomon, R. M., O'reardon, J.P. et al. (2005). Prevention of relapse following cognitive therapy vs medications in moderate to severe depression. *Archives of Gneral Psychiatry*, 62, 417–22.

Jacobson, E. (1938), *Progressive relaxation. Chicago*, University of Chicago Press.

Kirsch, I. & Sapirstein, G. (1999), Listening to Prozac but hearing placebo: a meta-analysis of antidepressant medications, in I. Kirsch (Ed.) *How expectancies shape experience*. Washington, DC, American Psychological Association. p 303–20.

Kroenke, K. & Spitzer, R. L. (2002), The PHQ-9: a new depression diagnostic and severity measure. *Psychiatric Annals*, 32 (9).

Kuyken, W. & Brewin, C.R. (1994), Intrusive memories of childhood abuse during depressive episodes. *Behaviour Research and Therapy*, 32, 525–28.

Luthar, S. S. & Cicchetti, D. (2000), The construct of resilience: implications for interventions and social policies. *Development and Psychopathology*, 12, 857–85.

McBrien, R. J. (1990), A self-hypnosis program for depression management. *Individual Psychology: Journal of Adlerian Theory, Research and Practice, Special Issue: Hypnosis*, 46 (4), 481–9.

McCarthy, P. (2005). Workshop given at the joint meeting of BSCAH, RSM and BSMDH, Edinburgh, Scotland, May.

Moncrieff, J., Wessely, S. & Hardy, R. (2002), Active placebo versus antidepressants for depression. Cochrane review. *Cochrane Library*, 3, 1.

Moussavi, S., Chatterji, S., Verdes, E. et al. (2007), Depression, chronic diseases, and decrements in health: results from the World Health Surveys. *Lancet*, 370 (9590), 851–58.

Murray, C. & Lopez, A. (1997), Alternative projections of mortality and disability by cause 1990-2020: Global Burden of Disease Study. *The Lancet*, 349 (9064), 1498–1504.

National Statistics. (2003). Better or worse: a longitudinal study of the mental health of adults in Great Britain. London, National Statistics.

Phillips, M. & Frederick, C. (1995). *Healing the divided self: clinical and ericksonian hypnotherapy for post-traumatic and dissociative conditions*. New York, W.W. Norton.

Ramchandani, P. & Stein, A. (2003), The impact of parental psychiatric disorder on children. *British Medical Journal*, 327 (7409), 242–3.

Sartorius, N. (2001), The economic and social burden of depression. *Journal of Clinical Psychiatry*, 62 (15), 8–11.

Shea, M., Elkin, I., Imber, S., Sotsky, S., Watkins, J., Collins, J., Pilkonis, P., Beckham, R., Glass, D., Dolan, C. & Parloff, M. (1992), Course of depressive symptoms over follow-up: findings from the National Institute of Mental Health Treatment of Depression Collaborative Research Programme. *Archives of General Psychiatry*, 49, 782–7.

Singleton, N., Bumpstead, R., O'brien, M. et al. (2001). *Psychiatric morbidity among adults living in private households, 2000*. London, Office for National Statistics.

Teasdale, J., Moore, R., Hayhurst, H., Pope, M., Williams, S. & Segal, Z. (2002), Metacognitive awareness and prevention of relapse in depression: empirical evidence. *Journal of Consulting and Clinical Psychology*, 70, 275–87.

Tusaie, K. & Dyer, J. (2004), Resilience: a historical review of the construct. *Holistic Nursing Practice*, 18 (1), 3–10.

Waraich, P., Goldner, E. M., Somers, J. M. & Hsu, L. (2004), Prevalence and incidence studies of mood disorders: a systematic review of the literature. *Canadian Journal of Psychiatry*, 49 (2), 124–38.

Watkins, E. (2008), Constructive and unconstructive repetitive thought. *Psychological Bulletin*, 134, 163–206.

Watkins, E. & Teasdale, J. (2004), Adaptive and maladaptive self-focus in depression. *Journal of Affective Disorders*, 82, 1–8.

Williamson, A. (2008), *Brief psychological interventions in practice*, Chichester, John Wiley & Sons, Ltd.

Yapko, M. D. (1994). *When living hurts: Directives for treating depression*. New York, Brunner/Mazel.

Zigmond, A. S. & Snaith, R. P. (1983), The hospital anxiety and depression scale. *Acta Psychiatrica Scandinavia*, 67 (6), 361–70.

17

Phobias

Dr Les Brann

With contributions from Mrs Jacky Owens and Dr Ann Williamson

Introduction

A simple phobia is defined as an irrational fear of a specific object, activity or situation. It is important to note that it is irrational, and this implies the subject of the phobia is not normally associated with a threat or damage to the person's wellbeing. The person concerned is fully aware of the irrationality of the fear, but logic alone has been unable to resolve the problem.

Some phobias, however, are more complex and may have more than one trigger and a complex response. Social phobias and agoraphobia are included in this category.

Judging by the plethora of advertisements in the press and on the internet, lay hypnotherapists perceive phobias as being easy to treat. Despite this there are no large scale studies comparing the use of hypnosis with other treatment methods, and although in clinical hypnotherapy circles case reports abound, the novice therapist is strongly reminded to 'Beware the simple phobia'.

Evidence for the Use of Hypnosis

Hypnosis has been traditionally used to treat phobias, and although the published evidence is now quite old it remains valid (Marks *et al.*, 1968; McGuinness, 1984). As hypnosis has become an established modality for treatment, there are many case studies available

The Handbook of Contemporary Clinical Hypnosis: Theory and Practice, First Edition.
Edited by Les Brann, Jacky Owens and Ann Williamson.
© 2012 John Wiley & Sons, Ltd. Published 2015 by John Wiley & Sons, Ltd.

although many refer to patients with needle or dental phobia (Milne, 1988; Rustvold, 1994).

One possibility for the lack of recent studies may be the contextual nature of phobia in that it may not impact greatly on mental health services. The importance of some phobias may not become apparent until some life event supervenes such as a needle phobic needing chemotherapy.

The rationale for using hypnosis for phobias is based on:

- The observation that imaginal exposure to the feared object during hypnosis is able to reproduce the fear.
- Therefore it is not necessary for the feared object/situation to be present for therapy.
- Therapy is aimed at resolving the hypnotically produced fear which can then be translated into exposure to the real object (Dads *et al.*, 1997).

The use of imagery in hypnosis to re-create the feared object and the integration of hypnosis into desensitization approaches have been described frequently in the literature (Deiker & Pollock, 1975; Hecker, 1990; Kroger & Fezler, 1976).

Many phobias, however, appear to follow some previous traumatic event and so can be treated as in chapter 26 on PTSD. Evidence supporting the use of hypnosis in resolving traumatic memory is detailed there.

Notwithstanding the paucity of trial information for the treatment of phobias using hypnosis, it is often very rewarding to work with such patients. The following 'causative event' method is a suggested framework, and this is based on the assumption that:

- The phobia has been caused by a single unpleasant event at some time in the past.
- The fear would have been an appropriate and rational response to that situation at that time – often in childhood.
- The phobia is caused by the persistence of the (childhood) fear.
- Re-identification of the event under hypnosis allows for resolution.

It is important at the beginning of the therapy to discuss the realistic expectations from the treatment. Many patients struggle with the idea that if they get better they will have to come in contact with the feared object and (from their pre-treatment) perspective this is an uncomfortable concept. Reassurance must be given that at no time will they be forcibly exposed to the feared object by the therapist. Equally therapy is not aimed at making them a lover of the object but just aimed at enabling them to cope on a day to day basis – the bird phobic is unlikely to wish to apply to run the aviary at the zoo!

Taking a History

As well as a general history, questions relating to the start of the problem are clearly relevant, and it is common to find that many patients are aware of the causal event. This is useful to feed back to them during the explanation of hypnosis and a useful pointer for the therapist but it is important not to assume that this is the definitive cause; there may have been a preceding 'sensitizer' which has been forgotten.

It is also essential to discover the reason for the patient seeking help at this time. For many it is a realization that they cannot avoid the situation anymore – mothers with young children cannot absolve themselves of that duty of care just because they are afraid of spiders! The reason for seeking help now can be a powerful ally in helping with the resolution phases of the treatment.

Explanation of Hypnosis

It is strongly advised that, whatever explanatory model is usually given by the therapist, for phobias the hemispheric specialization model is used. Many patients have struggled with trying to understand why they have not been able to sort the problem out logically – seeing the distinct separation of logic and feelings, as exemplified in the hemispheric model, immediately gives them the answer to their dilemma. Not infrequently the therapist observes a significant relaxation as they absorb the 'Ah ha' moment. Because hypnosis accesses the right hemisphere it affords a reassuring reason as to why this therapy is likely to succeed where logical thought and cognitive based therapies have failed, thus raising expectation.

During the explanation it is also helpful to pre-empt the discovery of the causative event and draw a time line showing that experiences as a child are felt and understood as a child of that age – not as the adult they are now.

Following induction, deepening and the setting up of the 'safe place', an appropriate uncovering technique (see page 123) can be used. No one method is recommended, so the method chosen should be the one with which the patient seems most comfortable. Remember always to use dissociative phraseology to emphasize the observer status but be aware that despite this they may still abreact the event. Be careful not to imply that there MUST be a reason – sometimes nothing is found.

Resolution

Assuming the uncovering technique has found the causative event, move on towards resolution. If the exposure has caused significant distress, reassure and suggest the safe place. From this position of strength take the opportunity to explain (the cognitive interlude) that the feeling/reaction was appropriate for their age/experience in that situation. It was OK for then but not OK for now! The older wiser self technique (see page 133) is probably the method of choice at this stage for helping to resolve that original distress.

In these days of computer literacy it is helpful to present this old (childhood) memory as an old programme still running in the background. It is therefore possible with this metaphor to suggest that the old programme is archived (to their personal museum) and the programmes updated by activating their 'update now' button. Some patients may wish to delete the offending memory.

Desensitization

Following the resolution technique it is necessary to translate the progress into being able to deal with the feared object. This is best achieved using desensitization. This method was first described by Wolpe (1958) and has become a standard behavioural technique. Using this under hypnosis has several advantages.

1. The feared object is readily available (in the patient's mind).
2. The observer status helps to reduce the distress.
3. The use of imagery enables a whole range of scenarios to be utilized and modified in an instant.
4. The degree of distress reduces with repeated (mental) exposure of the feared scenario.
5. Hypnotic relaxation can be utilized as well as safe place imagery and calmness anchors.

The method involves beginning with the mental rehearsal of scenarios where the patient views the feared object from a safe distance, then with the use of relaxation techniques, safe place and relaxing anchors, works through progressively harder scenarios until they feel they could cope with ordinary day to day activities without avoidance behaviour or anxiety. So for a spider phobia the initial image might be of a tiny spider several yards away and progress stepwise to, perhaps, trapping a typical house spider under a glass to remove it from the house. This method can be expanded and complicated in many ways. For example it is possible to ask the patient to score the level of distress for each scenario and then proceed with the suggestion that *"The magic of hypnosis is that each time you work through this scenario, you will notice the level of distress will reduce."*

The number of stages varies from person to person but where the causative event has been identified as the powerful cause and has been resolved, then the number of stages might be just two or three. In these cases the mental rehearsal is often just a demonstration that the phobia has now been resolved. In addition to those direct scenarios it is often useful to consider dealing with the adjunctive behaviour that often accompanies phobias. For example, many people with spider phobias have developed the habit of scanning a room that they have just entered and have become experts in spotting a small spider lurking innocuously in some distant corner. That habitual behaviour can also be modified using this technique.

In many cases the first thing that a treated phobic notices is that they do not notice the previously feared object; the hyper-vigilance component has disappeared. For example a patient who had previously been a spider phobic reported that she failed to notice a spider in the bathroom until it was pointed out to her. Some therapists, having resolved the negative affect around the sensitizing or causative event, suggest that the patient see themselves being in the previously feared situation and see whether they are okay. If not, further work may need to be done, but if they are all right then it can be suggested that the patient fully associates with the image and enjoys feeling calm and in control (a future age progression).

Not everyone with a simple phobia finds a causative event, and in these cases it is important to use that positively by saying, *"Good! That means we don't have to do any work on the past and can get straight on to sorting out the problem."* Desensitization for this group tends to be taken slower with more stages.

Homework is essential and post-hypnotic suggestions accompany instructions to begin to confront the problem in real life as soon as possible. Follow up sessions involve mopping up issues from the previous session and reviewing progress. Desensitization images can relate to difficulties encountered or anticipated. Generally speaking a simple phobia with a discovered cause can be treated in two or three sessions and often the relevant hypnotic work is done in a single session. However, because of the very nature of some phobias actual practice is not easily available. It is easy, for example to travel on a train, but less easy to practice flying! In these cases therapy is best organized alongside a planned flight.

Perhaps the hallmark of dealing with simple phobias is the adage that the response was

Ok for then but not for now

The case studies that follow are intended to show how hypnosis can be used in these situations.

Natalie – a bird phobia

Natalie had hated birds for as long as she could remember but now at 25 years old she was beginning to find it a social difficulty, and this had culminated in an embarrassing episode where she had had an anxiety attack on a visit to Trafalgar Square when she was suddenly surrounded by pigeons. This was the stimulus to seek help. There was nothing specific in her history, and after induction, deepening and establishing her safe place (which was a bird free beach) she was asked to go into the corridors of her mind. In that corridor, in the depths of her mind, was her 'Reason' room; and in that room she would find the reason for her problem. She was asked to go into that room and when she did it would be as though she was observing herself at the origin of the problem. As she did so she visibly jumped in fright. As a young child of three or four, she was holidaying on a farm, where her job was to help collect the eggs from the chicken house. As she went in a cockerel flew at her from further down the coop and this was the frightening event that had caused her to jump.

It was explained that her fear and reaction were completely normal especially at that age and size. The sheer surprise of it happening had also added to her fear. Using the older wiser self she was able to feel better but wished to delete that memory from her 'computer'. This was followed by several stages of desensitization, and after the second session she was able to walk through the park passing the lake with numerous ducks on the bank. She had also been able to visit a friend who had a pet cockatiel – previously she had been unable to go into the room where the cage was kept.

Another bird phobia case history illustrates the need for appropriate monitoring of progress (courtesy of J. Owens).

Sarah – another bird phobia

Sarah, a young woman, consulted because a phobia of birds was impacting greatly on the quality of her life. She was unable to enjoy being out of doors at all and cowered if a bird flew near her. Sarah did not remember when it started; she remembered her grandmother taking her to see a bird's nest in the garage when she was six years old and she felt unhappy. Her mother related her being frightened as a little thing in the pram and had tried to cure her in Trafalgar Square by feeding the pigeons, but she was still very scared. Whilst watching birds of prey fly in a safari park, a buzzard flew at her from behind and got itself caught in the netting close to her back; she covered her head until it was released. Sarah had been seen previously by a lay hypnotist who had visited her home, provided one session and used a cinema technique in which Sarah began at the back of the cinema and gradually moved forward, using imagery to put Wellington boots on the birds and dressing them in 'ra ra' skirts. This had helped a little but did not resolve the issue as birds moved too quickly for her to do the imagery. No follow up had been arranged. Sarah believed that she had been easily hypnotized and had felt deeply relaxed, but the treatment had not worked and she was now experiencing even more difficulty.

Despite this worsening of the problem, she had confidence that hypnosis could provide a solution, and a personal recommendation led her to consult the author (JO). Four sessions were planned.

Session 1: A full history was taken and she was assessed for hypnotizability using the Creative Imagination Scale scoring 28/40. She was taught relaxation techniques and self hypnosis.

Session 2: Explanation of the phobic response was given. No one trigger incident was identified following a regression/uncovering technique. She was taught a confidence anchor to practice.

Sessions 3 and 4: Over the next two sessions using her confidence anchor and using 'in vitro' guided imagery, she was gradually able to tolerate birds being close to her. A personal tape was made for her to use.

Two years later she reported being comfortable outdoors and still using her anchor when necessary. She is closer to achieving one of her goals, that of appreciating the beauty and skill of birds, and finds herself looking at them now, seeing the colours and sheen of their wings, whereas before she would have closed her eyes or turned away.

Although, as in the case above, merely disrupting or changing the patient's internal imagery is rarely enough to resolve a phobia, it can be a useful addition. This can be seen in the case described on page 218 as well as the case below (courtesy of Dr A Williamson).

Peter – a spider phobia

Peter volunteered as a subject for a demonstration of a hypnotic desensitization. He had a spider phobia and was already conversant with self hypnosis, special place imagery and anchoring. A hierarchy was constructed out of hypnosis which culminated in a spider being very close (he did not at this time want to pick one up) and Peter feeling quite calm and in control.

At various stages in the hierarchy it became apparent that he was feeling anxious and as well as calming suggestions and the use of his calmness anchor it was pointed out to him the various things that he might notice, such as the fact that he was *so* much bigger and stronger than the spider and that one of the thoughts he probably had as the spider stopped suddenly in its run towards him was that the spider was about to pounce. Actually the poor little thing had really excruciating cramp. A spider cannot run much further than the distance of its web before the build up of lactic acid in its muscles causes it to stop and take a rest!

As he was imagining feeling calm as the spider ran really near to him, the author (AW) had a sudden image come into her mind (see empathic metaphor, page 60) of a spider trying very hard to play the fiddle and run or dance at the same time. This image was shared with Peter, and he immediately burst out laughing. It transpired that the image had 'hit the spot' as he was a fiddle player with a Morris-dancing team in his spare time!

Mary – a woman with dental anxiety

Mary, at 78 years old, had been to the dentist many times but at a recent visit she had required some more complex treatment and as the dentist clipped a bar (her description – the exact instrument unknown) across her, she experienced a panic attack and was unable to complete the treatment. She came to discuss the problem, confident that she knew the cause. As a teenager she had needed an extraction which was carried out under gas anaesthesia, and she had hated the mask being put over her face.

Following induction and deepening she was asked to drift back as an observer to that incident. She recounted the experience and was able to use the older wiser self technique to resolve that issue. However, attempts at desensitization were unsuccessful. This and the fact that the remembered event was in her teenage years suggested that there may have been a preceding event. Thus, further uncovering work was done, using a visit to her reason room in the depths of her mind. As she went in, she smiled and said, *"Good Lord! I remember now, my sister shut me in a drawer!"* When she was about six years old, her elder sister suddenly announced that she thought Mary would be able to fit into a drawer of a chest of drawers and she was duly instructed to climb in. This she did amidst promises that her sister would let her out straight away. This promise was not kept and she was left in the drawer for a while, amid screams and panic! The older wiser self method again came to the rescue and the memory was archived in her personal museum. Following this she was able to mentally rehearse the forthcoming treatment at the dentist. This was subsequently completed a week later without any panic whatsoever.

Whilst all these phobias cause significant distress, some are clinically more important than others, for example a needle phobia in a patient requiring chemotherapy.

Pamela – a woman with needle phobia

At the age of 62 Pamela developed a persistent cough. She had been a smoker since her teens. A chest X-ray revealed a middle lobe carcinoma which was inoperable and hence she required chemotherapy. Indeed blood tests as part of her original investigations were a major ordeal. She agreed to hypnosis and following explanation, induction, deepening and establishing her safe place, she was asked to search in the depths of her mind for the beginning of her problem.

She regressed to a time when she was at boarding school around the age of nine. The dormitories were large rooms with about 20 beds, and older girls shared the room with the younger ones. The dormitory was ruled by one of the older girls who had a strange sadistic nature. This older girl would come to her bed most nights and stick sewing needles into her arm. If she resisted she was held down by the girl's friends. There were, of course, threats not to tell.

Her time at boarding school was clearly unhappy, and the 'dead tree' silent abreaction (see page 399) was used to offload this and all the other baggage that she had collected during this horrid time. This was followed by the older wiser self technique, helping to resolve her difficulties. Graded desensitization was used and was accompanied by glove anaesthetic techniques to numb the area ready for phlebotomy. Graded exposure to actually seeing and handling the hypodermic needles was performed during hypnosis. It was suggested that now she had dealt with the underlying problem, she could open her eyes when asked and she would be able to look at a needle six feet away on the desk without any anxiety or fear. This she easily achieved and was able to progress to holding the needle herself.

After four sessions she was able to attend for blood tests and have her chemotherapy without a major ordeal. She never 'liked' having it done – but then, who does?

Catherine – a woman with severe needle phobia
(courtesy of Dr A Williamson)

Catherine was a 24 year old woman with a very severe needle phobia. She had no other history of note. She was about ten weeks pregnant and as she was Rhesus negative, she needed to have blood tests the thought of which terrified her. She was unable to even look at a picture of a needle without feeling faint. Having learned self hypnosis and special place imagery as well as a calmness anchor, she was asked whether it was okay to work on whatever was driving her fear of needles. Having received an affirmative in hypnosis she was asked to float back above any relevant event using the time road metaphor for dissociation (see page 401) and she started to have a vasovagal attack. Luckily some positives were able to be salvaged from this as she was able to calm herself much more quickly than usual, using her anchor and special place but we then had the problem of how to work with someone who fainted at even beginning to imagine the problem! At the next session it was decided to treat her vasovagal response as a habit of 'body behaviour', and having set up ideomotor signalling Catherine was taken through a standard reframe to generate alternatives (see page 442). This appeared to be effective, and work could then progress on the sensitizing events to resolve them. Following a positive mental rehearsal it is good to report that she continued with her pregnancy and had several blood tests without anything more than usual anxiety.

But

Beware the simple phobia!

So far the causal event has been a normal reaction to an unpleasant event, but all too frequently the event turns out to be part of a wider, more complex problem.

Jayne – a woman with worm phobia

Jayne, a 23 year old woman, had just moved into a new house with her husband. She had a phobia of snakes and worms, and this was such that she was unable to spend any time out in her new garden. She was able to sit on the patio but unable to do any gardening for fear of seeing a worm (or snake – although these are incredibly rare in the suburban garden).

Apart from this phobia she had no other problems nor had any significant medical history. Her parents were middle class health professionals and she had been educated at private Catholic convent school.

She was a good hypnotic subject and entered a deep trance following a standard relaxing induction and deepening. As she was highly computer literate she was asked to wander into her control room and ask her mind's 'sat nav' to guide her into the relevant parts of the depths of her mind. Outside her 'reason room' she stopped and refused to go in. *"I know it's my father in there; I know he did something awful, but I don't want to remember the details."* She went on to describe how she always felt uncomfortable being alone with her father and avoided it like the plague. She had noticed that he often seemed to have an erection when he was talking to her.

For her, worms and snakes were Freudian symbols of the phallus and this had led her to the phobic response, even though, until the therapy, she had not been aware of the connection. So, far from being simple, this turned out to be a very complex case. This abuse had led to relationship difficulties, and she had, as often happens in such cases, gone through a fairly promiscuous phase but had gained very little sexual satisfaction. This spell of promiscuity had stirred up her 'Catholic guilt' and led to feelings of unworthiness and poor self esteem. Although now happily married, her libido was low and she was anorgasmic. All these issues needed to be worked through. Yet despite that 'work in progress' she was able to begin to spend more time in the garden.

A case of claustrophobia and spider phobia follows, demonstrating that sometimes the source of the phobia is not what the patient thought it was initially. Phobias are common associates of childhood abuse, and even if the abuse is known the phobias still need to be treated.

Helen – a woman with claustrophobia

Helen had been the victim of severe sexual, physical and psychological abuse as were three of her sisters. In her late teens Helen had revealed the abuse and their father had been imprisoned. As part of investigations for another matter, Helen required an MRI scan and the confined space of the scanner stirred up the memories of being shut in an old chest, a shed and cupboards as punishment for trying to resist or escape from the abuse. Sometimes she would be left in these filthy places for several hours. Dealing with the abuse is part of on-going therapy, but in order to help the immediate problem of being in the confined space she was taught a modified magic bubble technique (after Alden, 1995). In this she was asked to imagine she was inside a bubble which protected her from unpleasant feelings, whereas happy, positive feelings could flow inside. Similarly, horrible thoughts from the inside could flow out and could not get back in. For the purposes of the MRI scan she was taught how to relax herself and take herself to her relaxing place. This she would do as she got into the scanner and, as she did so, to use the magic bubble which would protect her. Interestingly, initially, the thought of being inside the confined space of the bubble was equally disturbing but she soon realized that the bubble could be as big as she liked. With this image she was able to undergo the scan without any problems.

For Helen spiders were also a problem. She put this down to her brother having given her a 'present' which was actually a box containing several spiders! As she was working through the abuse, she became aware that it was the spiders in the chest and shed which had been the real source of the problem.

Thus the novice therapist must be aware of this and work closely within their field of competence, referring on to a more experienced colleague or working closely with their clinical supervisor.

Travel phobias are also sometimes more complex than they might at first appear, although there are many case studies in the literature where hypnosis has been used

(Deyoub & Epstein, 1977; Kraft & Kraft, 2004; McIntosh, 2007; Williamson, 2004). It is important to determine exactly what the fear is triggered by (in the same way as dental phobia could be of the smell of disinfectant, the needle or the cottonwool swabs) as this may not be just the flight. For example a travel phobia could contain elements of separation anxiety, claustrophobia, agoraphobia or catastrophization.

Sometimes it can be appropriate to use a technique called retrograde desensitization as in the following case study.

Jane – a woman with flight phobia (courtesy of Dr A Williamson)

Jane was a 38 year old housewife who presented with anxiety symptoms prior to going abroad on holiday. She had flown two years previously and had taken tranquilizers (Diazepam, 5 mg) to help control her feelings of panic, but she had not enjoyed her holiday as she had continually worried about the flight home. She described herself as a fairly nervous individual, but this had not caused any particular problems until now. She had very little in the way of any relevant past history, reporting that she had had a reasonably happy childhood and was happily married with two children.

Having induced hypnosis she was taught a self hypnosis anchor to her special place (which was relaxing on a beautiful beach) and the calm feelings she was experiencing in hypnosis.

Having received agreement in hypnosis to work on her flight phobia, it was explained that she was going to take a flight in her imagination and that whatever she was able to achieve in her imagination, her unconscious mind would enable her to achieve in reality. She was told that she would be able to remain calm and relaxed, but any time if told to go to her perfect beach she was to stop whatever she was doing and go there immediately.

She was then taken through a flight scenario starting with a flight arriving at her destination on holiday, coming down the steps from the aircraft feeling really pleased with how she had coped and telling her husband how calm and in control she had felt. Thus armed with a strong positive feeling of success and achievement, it was suggested that she then imagine the aircraft landing at her destination keeping that feeling of calmness and control. We then progressed backwards through the flight until she was on her way to the airport from her home, and she was then taken forwards through the flight to her holiday and back home again in several stages, stopping each time for her to calm any anxiety using her calmness anchor, monitoring when it was appropriate to continue with a head nod.

It was then suggested she go back to her perfect beach for a moment or two before re-alerting.

It was the intention to have one more session before her holiday, but she was unable to do so. She reported that she was practicing her self hypnosis regularly and was feeling more relaxed than she had for years. She reported some months later that she had enjoyed her holiday and apart from a little apprehension had coped well with the flights.

Although a forward desensitization approach may be effective in flight phobias, using it in a retrograde fashion so that the patient starts from the successful outcome can be useful.

Complex Phobias

Whilst undoubtedly the above phobias are difficult enough, the term 'complex' tends to refer to conditions such as social phobias and agoraphobia. These are difficult to treat by any method and it would be inappropriate to suggest that hypnotherapy is universally successful. Notwithstanding the above, hypnotherapy can be helpful in many instances and, where 'cure' has not been possible, some benefit has usually accrued.

Social phobia can be defined as an anxiety disorder characterized by a strong and persistent fear of social or performance situations in which the patient might feel embarrassment or humiliation. Common performance situations are speaking in public, eating in public or simply coping with a crowd of people – especially where they are unknown.

This sort of phobia tends to start in adolescence or early adulthood, although features can often be observed (especially in retrospect) in childhood. Whilst the hypnotherapy approach to these problems can begin as with the simple phobias, the causal event may often seem trivial. In these cases it is important to expand the search to look at the overall psychosocial status at the time. Perhaps the difference between these and the simple phobias is that the event (and or the psychosocial status) makes the patient feel *bad about themselves* rather than leads to a simple fear of the object.

Therapy is therefore focused not only on the event but also on the poor self esteem or unrealistic expectations of themselves. It may be necessary to stabilize the situation before doing any specific therapy. Teaching and helping the patient to relax is a prerequisite before meaningful therapy can take place and is the mainstay of the ongoing therapy especially where the symptoms are of a general anxiety disorder. Once learnt the relaxed state can be anchored (see page 182) and so makes that feeling available in any number of anxiety-provoking situations.

Social phobia is highly prevalent in the general population. It increases the risk of developing major depression and has a high co-morbidity with other mental disorders (Ohayon & Schatzberg, 2010). The social phobic is very focused on self and how they appear to others. As they are so aware of their body they can usefully be taught how to keep their body relaxed, and perceptual positions in hypnosis can be utilized to give them an experiential understanding that they are not always the centre of attention.

Where the social phobia is confined to specific situations such as speaking to an audience, a threefold approach is recommended as well as a confidence anchor. Firstly, explore if there is a causal event. Secondly assess the wider psychosocial issues associated with that event, and thirdly use the desensitization method described above (see page 214).

Neil – a man with fear of public speaking

At 36, Neil was at the right age for promotion. He had a degree in physics and worked in research and development for a multinational communications company. Promotion meant that he would have to do a lot more presentations to his peers, and the thought terrified him. He had no problem communicating one to one with his fellow scientists, but standing up to address even a small group caused severe anxiety.

Exploration under hypnosis revealed an event when he was 13. At school he was required to present his homework to the rest of the class. He had not done very much work on the project and he felt himself turn bright red and he subsequently dried up not knowing what to say. He was ridiculed by the class and his teacher and dreaded having to do anything like that again. Looking deeper into the episode it occurred at a very emotional time – his parents had recently divorced in rather acrimonious circumstances, and he felt unwanted by his parents as they were arguing over with whom he should live. This was the reason he had not done much preparation for the homework.

Despite the fact that this home situation soon settled and he had a good relationship with both his parents, his self esteem remained low, seemingly from this point. His written work was good and examination results exemplary, allowing him to go onto university to read physics. He obtained an upper second degree and went on to complete a doctorate yet still felt he was under achieving. The incident at school was resolved using the 'older wiser self' and archiving to his personal museum, but he remained fearful of public speaking.

During hypnosis he was asked to imagine he was wandering in the countryside and it was suggested he would soon see a house and that this house would be a representation of his mind. Interestingly, the house from the exterior was large and impressive but once inside it was drab and utilitarian. He described the atmosphere as being neutral, neither inspiring nor depressing. As he wandered around the house it was suggested he search for the trophy room – such an impressive house would always have a trophy room! He eventually found it tucked away in the basement. Inside there were locked cupboards with nothing on show. Inside the cupboards he found his examination certificates and pictures of him receiving his degree and doctorate looking splendid in his academic gowns. Somewhat reluctantly he agreed to take these things out of the cupboards and spread them around the house so that wherever he was he would have a reminder of success. To this were added reminders of fun times he had had and pictures of his lovely wife and children. Gradually the house was transformed into a warm happy place.

Once this was completed it was possible to begin mentally rehearsing public speaking. He was taught the Calvert Stein technique (see page 146) to anchor a relaxed confident feeling and also utilized the bubble method to allow the doubts to flow out of harm's way. The mental rehearsal began with just chatting things over with a couple of his colleagues over coffee and gradually became more formal with a bigger audience. He practiced daily a relaxation programme which included listening to a Hartland's type ego-strengthening passage (see page 142). One particular fear of his was that he would be asked questions to which he did not know the answer, so scenarios were used in which he dealt with more and more complex questions, but he found the hardest thing was to be able to say, "I don't know," without any embarrassment or feeling of failure. This, he acknowledged, was still a reflection of that time at school. It was necessary, therefore, to revisit this and the dead tree; silent abreaction was used to offload that incident and all of the accompanying and consequential sequelae.

He did very well and by the fifth session had been able to present his work to his departmental colleagues. He came for one top up session several months later as he was about to present a paper at an international conference!

So, despite there being an apparent 'causative event' the therapy required a more complex approach chipping away at various aspects of the problem using a variety of techniques and the need to revisit a part of the problem which appeared to have already been solved. Thus confidence gained in one area of therapy can be utilized to help when revisiting a stubborn problem – often the problem seems less daunting from this different and more confident self image.

A common social phobia problem relates to difficulties eating in public. Patients describe feeling okay at the beginning of the meal, then very soon after starting they feel sick or have abdominal pain. Sometimes their mouth dries up and they find it difficult to swallow. All these follow a similar theme. Some, undoubtedly, began when the onset of a genuine physical illness coincidentally occurred whilst out for a meal and these frequently respond as a simple phobia. In others the background sensitization had already occurred despite having an initial event.

Hilary – a woman with social-eating phobia

Hilary was about to get married, but had problems eating in company because she frequently felt ill with stomach pains and needed to go home early. She was dreading the wedding in case she felt ill at the reception – indeed so common was this that she was *expecting* to feel ill. In all other respects she was a successful young woman. She had a degree in psychology and was working as an area manager for a large company. Her job required a lot of driving and staying away from home. She avoided eating out unless she was with very close friends.

During hypnosis she recalled the problem started in her early teenage years. Home life was difficult as her parents had separated, mother had left the family home and she and her two siblings stayed with their father. She described 'automatically' taking the lead with the household chores but was always aware of her father's support. Although the problem manifested itself as abdominal pain and a general feeling of illness, she described the inner feeling as 'uneasy'. Although her mother had not been a very caring or nurturing person, the time her mother left was a difficult one for the family.

Normally a hug from her father was sufficient to help these feelings disappear, but a hug from her mother did not help. She was asked to explore this under hypnosis by going into the depths of her mind and going to her 'reason' room. Interestingly, she could see the room but could not get to it: *"It is as though there is a conveyor belt taking me away from the door."* It was suggested she simply turn the conveyor belt off. This she did and went into the room in which she had an awful feeling of insecurity. She could understand why but was asked to look at the date on the wall which was the date this room was created. She said, *"1986."* It transpired that this was the year her sister was born. It was explained to her about sibling rivalry and how this feeling is particularly strong in firstborn children. She was comforted using the 'older wiser self' and the memory archived into her personal museum. Happy confident feelings were copied and filed into the spaces vacated by archiving the unwanted feeling. From this more secure base, the time her parents separated was revisited and her general confidence boosted.

Returning to the powerful effect of her father's hug it was suggested that it might be possible to allow other things to have the same effect and she realized there was nothing to stop her pressing the 'father's hug' switch. This work was followed by mental rehearsal of the forthcoming events, and she was encouraged to take every opportunity to eat out. Her wedding went very well and she had a lovely day.

Claustrophobia often has an earlier sensitizing event which, once the patient has been stabilized, can be resolved using one of the dissociative methods described elsewhere. As described in chapter 24 it can give rise to difficulties when scanning is needed in the treatment of cancer and other medical conditions, but patients may also have problems where lifts or public transport are involved. The common element to all these is the feeling of lack of control. All the methods described earlier are useful: stabilizing the patient by teaching self hypnosis, imagery and anchoring (giving the patient some control) can be followed by resolution of any relevant past events and positive mental rehearsal.

Agoraphobic symptoms often arise with someone who is suffering from a chronic anxiety state, especially if they have panic attacks (see page 183). Very often there are also personality difficulties and dysfunctional family backgrounds to take into account. An individual cannot be an agoraphobic without support. Someone has to support the patient by going shopping and doing anything else requiring travel, although online shopping these days may be a boon to those with such problems. Hypnosis can be usefully employed to facilitate in vivo graduated exposure (Harris, 1991) as in the case below.

Sheila – a girl with agoraphobia (courtesy of Dr A Williamson)

Sheila was a 19 year old student who had developed agoraphobia and had dropped out of sixth form college. She was a highly anxious individual who dreamed of going to university and doing an art degree. As part of her treatment she developed two anchors; a pinky, red 'aura' for confidence and a blue 'aura' for calmness. We constructed a hierarchy starting with her walking to her front gate and increasing by one lamppost every couple of days the distance she walked from home. We talked about how important it would be for her not to turn back if she felt anxious but to stay put and use her tools of imagery and anchoring until she felt calm again, before returning to the 'safety' of home.

She did a positive mental rehearsal in hypnosis each day of the distance she was going to walk that day, focusing on the successful outcome and the good feelings that this gave her. Although other work was needed, she rapidly overcame her agoraphobic feelings and did eventually go to university.

Often it can be useful to elicit help from a friend or relative to act as a 'companion' in the initial stages of the hierarchy especially if this involves travelling on public transport. The 'companion' can sit some way away for a few trips until the patient is ready to travel alone.

As part of her hierarchy Heather wanted to walk the mile and a half to her friend's house, and as an interim stage it was suggested that she ring up her friend when she was ready to set off so that her friend started out at the same time. In hypnosis Heather was asked to imagine walking calmly and confidently to her friend's house and to notice where it was that they met. It was then suggested that it might be interesting to wonder whether her imagination was correct and to see in reality where her friend met up with her. This of course changed her focus of attention from how she might be feeling to wondering where it was she would meet up with her friend.

Sometimes a booster session may be necessary.

Catherine was a severe needle phobic who had been treated with success a couple of years previously when she had been pregnant. Unfortunately she had lost the pregnancy but had now got pregnant again and had returned saying she was 'back at square one!' By chance a nurse had left on the desk a hypodermic needle that she had failed to clear away but Catherine sat down next to it without noticing. It was pointed out to Catherine that in the past she would have certainly noticed the needle and would not have sat down. She had just lost confidence in herself, and one session of reinforcement was all that was necessary.

With all phobias, whatever method is used for their resolution, it is important that the patient tests out the change in vivo as soon as possible after doing the hypnotic work. It is also important to reframe to the patient that any adrenalin response they feel will be natural apprehension as to whether it 'has worked' or excitement, rather than a reactivation of the phobic response. Very often having successfully resolved a phobia, the patient will find a ripple effect as other areas of their lives improve as they have the confidence to solve other problems.

References

Alden, P. (1995), Back to the past: introducing the 'bubble'. *Contemporary Hypnosis*, 12, 59–67.

Dads, M. R., Bovberg, D. H., Redd, W. H. & Cutmore, T. R. H. (1997), Imagery in human classical conditioning. *Psychological Bulletin*, 122, 89–103.

Deiker, T. E. & Pollock, D. H. (1975), Integration of hypnotic and systematic desensitisation techniques in the treatment of phobias. *American Journal of Clinical Hypnosis*, 17 (3), 170–4.

Deyoub, P. L. & Epstein, S. J. (1977), Short-term hypnotherapy for the treatment of flight phobia: a case report. *American Journal of Clinical Hypnosis*, 19 (4), 251–4.

Harris, G. M. (1991), Hypnotherapy for agoraphobia: a case study. *International Journal of Psychosomatics*, 38, 92–4.

Hecker, J. E. (1990), Emotional processing in the treatment of simple phobia: a comparison of imaginal and in-vivo exposure. *Behavioural Psychotherapy*, 18 (1), 21–34.

Kraft, T. & Kraft, D. (2004), Creating a virtual reality in hypnosis: a case of driving phobia. *Contemporary Hypnosis*, 21 (2), 79–85.

Kroger, W. S. & Fezler, W. D. (1976), *Hypnosis and behaviour modification: imagery conditioning*. Philadelphia, J. B. Lippincott

Marks, I. M., Gelder, M. G. & Edwards, G. (1968), Hypnosis and desensitization for phobias: a controlled prospective trial. *British Journal of Psychiatry*, 114 (515), 1263–74.

McGuinness, T. P (1984), Hypnosis in the treatment of phobias: a review of the literature. *American Journal of Clinical Hypnosis*, 26 (4), 26–72.

McIntosh, I. (2007), Brief selective hypnotherapy in the treatment of flying phobia. *Vertex*, 18 (74), 268–71.

Milne, G. (1988), Hypnosis in the treatment of single phobia and complex agoraphobia: a series of case studies. *Australian Journal of Clinical & Experimental Hypnosis*, 16 (1), 53–65.

Ohayon, M. M. & Schatzberg, A. F. (2010), Social phobia and depression: prevalence and comorbidity. *Journal of Psychosomatic Research*, 68 (3), 235–43.

Rustvold, S. R. (1994), Hypnotherapy for treatment of dental phobia in children. *General Dentistry*, 42, 346–8.

Williamson, A. (2004), A case of driving phobia treated with dissociative imagery. *Contemporary Hypnosis*, 21 (2), 86–92.

Wolpe, J. (1958), *Psychotherapy by reciprocal inhibition*. Stanford, CA, Stanford University Press.

18

Medically Unexplained Symptoms

Dr Michael EY Capek

with contributions from Dr Les Brann and Dr Ann Williamson

Introduction

"So it is all in my mind doctor?" This is a common, almost accusatory question from patients with significant physical symptoms but no underlying physical disease. The popular view is that this equates to the symptoms being imaginary. Such is the misunderstanding of the mind–body link and the disadvantages of the 'medical model' that the psychological (or, more correctly, the psychosocial) aspect of illness is often invoked as an afterthought when everything else has been excluded. The term 'medically unexplained symptoms' (MUS) is used to cover this group of conditions where persistent physical symptoms cannot be explained by physical illness or injury. Some symptom patterns are common enough to be collected under separate 'disease' headings such as irritable bowel syndrome (IBS) and fibromyalgia and are referred to as such, leaving MUS to refer to those other symptom complexes which fall outside the subdivisions.

Yet such somatization is very common; Simon *et al.* (1999) in a study on depression in primary care patients found that 69% of patients suffering with depression presented with physical symptoms. In another study 25% of patients presenting to hospital as emergencies with acute chest pain were, in reality, suffering from panic disorder (Huffman & Pollack, 2003). Indeed, one third of all consultations in primary care are believed to involve MUS (Kroenke & Mangelsdorff, 1989) and the prevalence in secondary care may be higher (Nimnuan *et al.*, 2001).

The Handbook of Contemporary Clinical Hypnosis: Theory and Practice, First Edition.
Edited by Les Brann, Jacky Owens and Ann Williamson.
© 2012 John Wiley & Sons, Ltd. Published 2015 by John Wiley & Sons, Ltd.

Not only does this cause unnecessary morbidity for the patient but also it is an enormous drain on any health economy. Barsky *et al.* (2005) calculated that 16% of total US healthcare spending was attributable to physical symptoms or disease co-existing with mental health disorders. Extrapolating this rate of expenditure to the United Kingdom, it is estimated that during 2008/9 £8,483m would have been spent on somatization.

Notwithstanding the above it is important to stress that management of these conditions from presentation is often far from easy and many problems which turn out to have a (major) psychosomatic element appear identical to those with proven physical disease aetiologies. Conversely, patients presenting with bizarre symptoms which do not seem to fit any known disease may turn out to have a significant physical illness. Thus, up to a point, investigations are necessary but so is the need to seed early the idea that emotional factors may be responsible for the symptoms. Salmon *et al.* (2004) report that the attitudes taken by doctors towards patients with medically unexplained symptoms can influence the patients' outcome, and if opportunities are taken to address psychological needs GPs might be able to avoid further unnecessary symptomatic intervention. Explaining to patients that test results were normal is insufficient to reassure patients with MUS (McDonald *et al.*, 1996). Clinical observation has shown that there is a pessimistic interpretation of information in the presence of (health) anxiety, and this anxiety increases the worry over symptoms. This is further evidenced by Lucock *et al.* (1997) who showed that patients with mild anxiety will be reassured over a normal result, whereas those with high anxiety will not.

The carrying out of investigations is often interpreted by the patient as meaning that the doctor believes that a physical cause will be found. This erroneous conclusion can be avoided if it is made clear that the investigations are being carried out to exclude a problem and done alongside an exploration of the emotional and stress related issues. The iatrogenic creation of MUS is depicted in Table 18.1.

Thus making the diagnosis of MUS is, at least initially, a diagnosis of exclusion in which all reasonable physical causes have been considered. The number of symptoms is an indicator for the presence of MUS as is a long duration of symptoms in the absence of deteriorating health (Mayou & Farmer, 2002).

Kirmayer and Robbins (1991) propose that there are three different and distinct syndromes. They are physical symptoms arising from an affective disorder (so-called presenting somatization), normal physical sensations elevated in the mind to serious illness (so-called hypochondriacal somatization) and disabling physical symptoms that cannot be accounted for by a general medical condition (so-called functional somatization). Clinical practice suggests that there is a fourth scenario commonly seen which is that of a confirmed physical illness but with symptoms out of proportion to the severity of the condition. The internet has increased the incidence of this, with patients 'acting out' the worst case scenario.

Despite this theoretical sub-grouping, the therapist tends to be presented with two types of patient: those who are happy to acknowledge a psychological basis for their illness, and those who are not! The latter group often need a lot of explanation and discussion before therapy begins.

In reality the student needs to be reminded of the huge complexity of the underlying mechanisms, and Figure 18.1 depicts this. Knowing the physiological process by

Table 18.1   The iatrogenic creation of medically unexplained symptoms (MUS)

Patient presents to a primary care physician with angina sounding chest pain. The patient's father died of a heart attack, and the patient knows that heart disease can run in families. What the doctor does not know at this stage is that the chest pain is caused through stress and anxiety

	Doctor A	Doctor B
Doctor says	*"I think the pain is coming from your heart. I need to refer you to a general physician. In the mean time, if it worsens or you are worried you can always go to casualty."*	*"My prediction is that your heart is fine. I had better refer you to a physician just in case. If it worsens or you are worried, you can always go to casualty."*
Patient thinks	*"The doctor thinks there is something wrong with my heart and he has told me to go to casualty."*	*"Hopefully it will turn out fine with my heart."*
Result	Increased anxiety makes chest pain worse.	Patient able to use the words of the doctor to control the anxiety.
General physician says	*"I think the pain is coming from your heart. I need to refer you to a cardiologist who will do some more tests. In the mean time, if it worsens or you are worried you can always go to casualty or come back."*	*"My prediction is that your heart is fine. I had better refer you to a cardiologist who will do some more tests just in case. If it worsens or you are worried, you can always go to casualty or come back."*
Patient thinks	*"OMG, two doctors think there is something wrong with my heart. I have something wrong with my heart!"*	*"Two doctors think my heart is fine. Hopefully it will turn out fine when I see the cardiologist."*
Result	Increasing anxiety makes chest pain worse, and now patient believes that there is definitely something wrong with his heart.	Patient able to use the words of both doctors to control the anxiety.
Cardiologist	*"All the tests show there is nothing wrong with your heart."*	*"All the tests show there is nothing wrong with your heart."*
Patient thinks	Two doctors think there is something wrong with my heart. So the cardiologist must be wrong	Patient is reassured, all the doctors agree and all the tests are fine.
Result	Patient has increased anxiety, does not know it, and returns for further investigation.	Patient's anxiety is resolved.

Note: The doctor does not know for sure that the pain is not cardiac. Hence some advice needs to be given in case the doctor's prediction is wrong. But this can be couched in terms to empower the patient without alarming him.

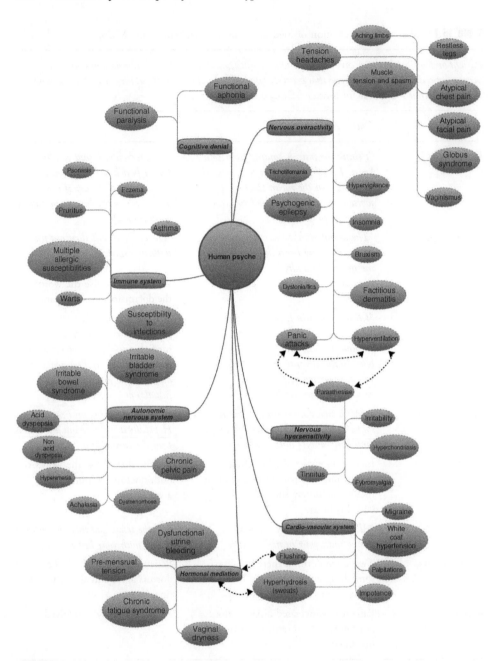

Figure 18.1   Grouping psychosomatic disorders according to the underlying pathophysiological process. © Michael E Y Capek.

which the symptom is being produced can suggest an approach for relieving the symptom. For example, those symptoms created by muscle tension or vascular over activity may be benefited by progressive muscle relaxation and vascular stabilization suggestions respectively.

Published Evidence

The clinician has observed these mind–body links from time immemorial, but progress has been slow because of the inability to identify the underlying physiological or neurophysiological mechanisms to satisfy our need for 'proof' of the clinical observations. Fortunately neuroimaging techniques have led to a much greater understanding of the links between the mind and bodily dysfunction. For example, asymmetric midbrain activity (right dominance) during emotional challenge leads to lateralization of sympathetic outflow to the heart and thus leads to a pro-arrhythmic state (Taggart *et al.*, 2005).

An explanatory model must be tailored to the specific symptoms of the patient but all follow the generic pattern of having a symptom switch, a number of switch activators and the symptom complex – the symptoms then leading to changes in behaviour. Whilst treatment can be aimed at any part of this model, the most common regimes are directed towards symptom removal; for example analgesics are given for headaches and anti-spasmodics for irritable bowel. While these have a definite role and may be all that is necessary in mild or very intermittent cases, such regimes do nothing to identify or help the underlying cause. It is true that some medicaments do attempt to reduce the activity of the switch – so-called prophylactic treatments such as *b* blockers, or pizotifen for migraine and amitriptyline for IBS – but these again have left the causal trigger unexplored and unresolved.

Hypnotherapy has the advantage in that it can have a role to play at all points in the above model: it can help moderate the physical symptom, and is a very useful tool to help explore and resolve the causal activators. Because of the heterogeneous nature of MUS and the person specific nature of hypnotherapy there are inherent problems in conducting randomized trials. Despite this there is much published evidence for the use of hypnosis in this difficult area. Some of the evidence is presented here.

Jones *et al.* (2006) studied 28 patients with angina sounding non-cardiac chest pain, in whom coronary angiography was normal and acid reflux had been excluded. In this highly selected group hypnosis was significantly superior to supportive therapy plus placebo.

In an open trial (Maudoux *et al.*, 2007), 35 out of 49 patients with tinnitus completed five to ten sessions of Ericksonian hypnosis. The collective improvement was statistically highly significant, and the authors felt that hypnosis was 'very promising'. Similar benefit, including health related quality of life, was obtained in 393 patients treated in a 28 day in-patient setting with a multi-modal treatment concept of which hypnosis was part (Ross *et al.*, 2007).

In a patient only blinded study of 41 patients with persistent idiopathic oral pain Abrahamsen *et al.* (2008) concluded that although hypnosis helped the pain, teaching stress-coping skills and addressing unresolved psychological problems were also required for the best outcome. When 28 patients with recalcitrant temporo-mandibular joint disorders were treated, statistical analysis of this open trial suggested that the improvement of symptoms was not spontaneous, the improvement was maintained after six months and there was a reduction in further medical use (Simon & Lewis, 2000).

Vulvar vestibulitis is a condition associated with coital and non-coital vulval pain. Hypnotherapy was found to be effective in a reported case (Kandyba & Binik, 2003) of a 26 year old woman with a three year history who was pain free 12 months later. A preliminary study of hypnosis into eight patents with vulvar vestibulitis was undertaken (Pukall *et al.*, 2007). It was concluded that hypnosis was 'promising' in the management of this condition and that carrying out a large control trial was recommended.

Other somatic conditions for which it is worth giving hypnosis consideration include alopecia areata (Willemsen *et al.*, 2006), chronic inflammatory bowel disease (Miller & Whorwell, 2009; Mawdsley *et al.*, 2008), acne excoriée (due to picking at the acne spots; Shenefelt, 2004), pruritus vulvae or ani (Rucklidge & Saunders, 2002), psychogenic dental pain (Golan, 1997) and functional infertility (Gravitz, 1995).

Within all of these trials are individuals. Whilst the trials aim to demonstrate an overall benefit, single case studies can be as enlightening as observational analysis. They can inform the direction of further quantitative research. But individual case studies can be instructive in their own right. When a longstanding problem suddenly resolves following an intervention, then it is likely that it was the intervention that generated the change. Patients often intuitively feel that this is the case. We contend that the single case report following a proper format is probably the best method of discovering the evidence base in complex issues.

Thus single case reports of which there are plenty should not be dismissed. The conditions include interstitial cystitis (Sidman, 2009), chronic widespread pain (Grondahl & Rosvold, 2008), dyspepsia (Zimmerman, 2001) and chronic fatigue syndrome (CFS; Hammond, 2001).

The monitoring of patients before, during, after and at interval follow up by questionnaires such as the Clinical Outcome Routine Evaluation (CORE; Evans *et al.*, 2002) and Hospital Anxiety and Depression scale (HADs; Zigmond & Snaith, 1983) confirm a reduction of symptoms, an improvement in function and an improved sense of well-being that is maintained beyond the conclusion of therapy (see Chapter 40). High levels of medication and frequent general practice and out-patient attendance can be reduced.

An ethical clinical hypnosis practitioner will endeavour to train the patient in self-hypnosis thus allowing the skill to be practiced in between therapy sessions, and making the sessions themselves move more quickly. The skills can be transferred to other situations, and the patient gains more benefit than merely the resolution of the presenting issue.

Utilizing Hypnosis

Somatic disorders, because they are physical conditions, may be managed by physical and psychological means. In MUS in the absence of a recognized medical condition it becomes clear, if not to the patient then at least to the physician, that there are psychological processes at work. Resolution will only be achieved when the patient understands what is underlying the symptom.

Referring clinicians can all help to promote the patient's well-being prior to active therapy. The initial consultations need to have the balance between ensuring there is no physical ailment and ill advised investigation reinforcing an attitude of *"These symptoms are terrible and there must be something physically very wrong with me."* The patient needs to be 'moved' to an attitude of *"My mind is telling me something about myself."* Bakal *et al.* (2006) describes this concept as an experiential mind–body approach. Hypnotherapy takes this concept further and deeper.

By the time patients arrive at therapy, they (and their families) may be quite desperate for a cure, and hopefully are well motivated. It is important to acknowledge that the symptoms are real and not imagined. These symptoms need to be validated and understood. If a period of time has elapsed, it becomes easier to utilize the arguments that a serious physical condition is unlikely. Most patients would understand that physical health in other respects, such as strength, appetite and weight, would have clearly deteriorated as a result of a major physical condition. The patient only needs to accept the possibility of the underlying psychological significance for a hypno-psychological approach to be taken. This can be further supported during the explanation of hypnosis using the hemisphere model (see page 98). Most patients will acknowledge that their symptoms are worse when they are stressed or anxious.

One way of conveying this information could be by drawing two triangles as shown in Figure 18.2, explaining to the patient that if they fell down and broke their leg, for a few split seconds it might be 100% physical, but very soon thoughts such as 'This hurts' and 'How am I going to get help?' begin and feelings of anxiety and pain commence. There is nothing that is 100% emotional as all our emotions are mediated by chemicals and hormones that have an effect on our body. So it can be demonstrated that everything has a psyche and a soma component and falls somewhere in the middle of the diagram with varying amounts of psyche and soma.

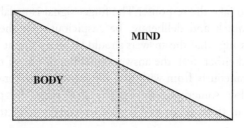

Figure 18.2   Mind–body triangles.

If not already established, the therapist would at some stage be well advised to reframe the symptoms from 'a problem' to 'a message'. Patients may well accept the notion that symptoms are messages from the mind that may not only reflect the possibility of physical illness but also can represent other features. In patients with multiple somatic symptoms, different symptoms may reflect different underlying psychological messages. An approach that could be tried within the hypnotic trance or outside it is to establish what feeling would arise if the symptom were to be removed. This may provide a clue to the underlying issue.

Ultimately it is likely to be necessary to seek out the root cause of the issue, and seven underlying causes of psychosomatic symptoms are traditionally listed (Ewin & Eimer, 2006). Williamson (2008) argues that the symptoms have a positive intent behind them and the mind–body behaviour evolved in an attempt to achieve an emotional and physical homeostasis of the person concerned.

The mnemonic 'BIG ITCH' acts a useful aide memoire:

Body language
Imprint
Guilt

Identity
Trauma
Conflict
Hysteria

All these areas can be explored outside of hypnosis, but very often this is less productive than doing so using hypnosis. It is further recommended that ideomotor signalling (IMS) (see page 24) is used to access the unconscious response. The author's (MC) approach is to enquire about each of the somatization mechanisms in turn. In order to do this, finger signalling is established. It is not uncommon for there to be more than one 'Yes' response. Further inquiry will elucidate what the issues are, and each of these can be managed appropriately.

In utilizing this approach it is necessary to be aware of possible barriers to success. A complete set of 'No' responses implies the questions need to be rephrased. Maybe the psychological and physical natures of the symptoms have not been sufficiently teased apart. It is important that the responses are truly those of the sub-conscious although, of course, it is possible to fake the response. The finger signal is usually slow and flickery, and if it seems too quick and deliberate, be suspicious that the conscious mind is intruding and anticipating what the answers should be. A tip might be to ask the patient to blank the mind and either 'feel' the answer twitching in one of the fingers or for the answer to come spontaneously from within to the mind. A deliberate answer, however, is not necessarily false; sometimes this is the first time the patient has had an opportunity to think in these terms and is able to identify with their known stressors or life events.

Each of these areas is explained below with examples of the questions used to elicit the various responses. Whilst these questions can be used verbatim the student is encouraged to develop their own phraseology, but remember that when using IMS clear unambiguous phrases must be used.

Body language (also known as organ language) occurs when the sub-conscious mind generates a metaphor and portrays that message through the physical symptom. *"Thinking about it makes my blood boil"* is a bodily description of anger. When doctors talk about certain patients being 'heart sink', the doctors are using a bodily metaphor to describe the way they are feeling.

QUESTION: *"Whether you know the message or not, by using symptom x is your subconscious mind trying to tell you about something yourself?"*
RESOLUTION: By acknowledging, validating and utilizing the insight.

Cheryl was a high flying, 22 year old business executive who presented with persistent neck pain and headaches. She acknowledged that they were worse when she was stressed. Cheryl was taught self hypnosis and calmness anchors, and upon entering her 'reason' room found it full of files and papers and spontaneously remarked, "These papers are a real pain in the neck!" The session was directed to developing her realization that her body was giving her a message and ways that she could use to help herself reduce her stress levels.

Imprint: Hetero- or auto-suggestion accepted virtually unchallenged. This is often a significant message said in a heightened state, so it is worth looking for the predisposing incident. A sensitive teenager told that she is fat and ugly may develop anorexia as a consequence.

QUESTION: *"Does symptom x relate to something that someone has said to you?"*
RESOLUTION: Resolve the incident and make the learning that what was said was an opinion rather than the 'Truth'.

Melanie was about to have in vitro fertilization (IVF) for infertility although no physical reasons for her infertility had been found. She came for help with her high levels of anxiety, and one of the questions asked using ideomotor signalling in hypnosis was *"Is there any psychological block to your becoming pregnant?"*

Having obtained a 'Yes' signal, this was explored further and she remembered her mother telling her, when she was upset as a teenager over her boyfriend of the time, that there was no way she could have a career and a baby too. She had unconsciously accepted this as her truth (this tends to happen when the recipient is in what might be called a negative trance state when upset and distressed), and as she was a high flyer in her chosen profession she had unconscious reservations about being pregnant that needed resolution.

Guilt (also known as self punishment) occurs when the person acts below their own perceived standards. The person feels that an alternative action should have been taken, and it is often recognized when the patient says *"If only . . ."* The guilt can be any form, rational or irrational, justifiable or not, or survivor guilt. Real or imagined guilt is treated exactly the same. The symptom is a form of self punishment.

QUESTION: *"Is symptom x some sort of punishment?"*
RESOLUTION: Treatment involves working towards self forgiveness. A useful question is *"What needs to happen so that you can begin to forgive yourself?"*

Alternatively, a 'compassionate mind' approach (see page 161) can be used. Whatever they did, they did within the context of what happened and their resources at the time. Looking back with hindsight we often forget how it actually was when we made a decision. A useful question might be *"Did you intend harm at the time?"* Where appropriate it may be useful to work with the patient's spirituality by exploring whether they believe in a 'forgiving' God or higher authority. If they do, then are they saying that although God forgives them they cannot, so are their standards greater than their God's?

The room of forgiveness is another technique helpful in this type of case and is a variant on the special place of bliss. The patient imagines they have gone into the corridors in the depths of their mind and along one such corridor is a room labelled 'The Room of Forgiveness'. The patient is asked to go inside and see who it is that either needs to forgive or needs to be forgiven. In this case it will be themselves and this forgiveness can take place in that room.

Hilary suffered from aphonia and was unable to speak above a whisper. After investigation it was decided that this was hysterical aphonia and she was referred for therapy. Upon ideomotor investigation Hilary brought into consciousness that she was punishing herself for being on holiday when her mother had died when she had been unable to say goodbye. Hilary's voice returned to normal once she had worked on her unresolved grief for her mother (see chapter 25) and said goodbye in hypnosis and allowed both herself and her mother to forgive her for not being there at the time.

Identity involves a strong empathic relationship with a person (often deceased). The symptom often represents a strong feature that the deceased person had, and the symptom reflects the person not letting go of the deceased.

QUESTION: *"Is there, or has there been, someone close to you who had symptom x or something similar?"*
RESOLUTION: Acknowledge the identification and use grief resolution techniques (see chapter 25). The patient needs to find an alternative means of remembering the deceased that does not require the symptom.

Adam was a brittle asthmatic and had been admitted to intensive care for ventilation on several occasions. He was often on large doses of steroids. Adam attended a group session in order to learn some stress management techniques. During one such group session, an induction was used of going back to a time when they were happily moving backwards and forwards on a swing. Adam started to abreact and become upset. The therapist reassured him and instructed him to continue with the good work he was doing and that he would resolve something important and feel very much better. The rest of the group continued with what they were doing, and after everyone had left Adam reported that he felt fine and that he now knew why he had asthma. He had accessed a time as a child when his uncle (to whom he was very close) used to play with him on the swing in his garden. Adam realized that when his uncle died in an asthma attack, he had 'taken on' his asthma in order to keep his uncle close to him in some way. Now he had made the link he felt he would not suffer with asthma anymore and could stop taking his medications. He was strongly advised to continue with these and reduce slowly, which he subsequently did. Following this session, Adam's peak flows (a measurement of asthma control) remained normal for four or five years follow up.

It is worth noting here that we do not class asthma as a 'psychosomatic' illness, since science can now explain the mechanism of asthma allowing for the development of appropriate and effective drug treatment. Whilst hypnosis should not substitute effective available medicines yet as with any condition, psychological difficulties may be a contributing factor and hypnosis may well be pertinent in such instances but only by those qualified to treat asthma in its entirety.

Trauma: An emotionally charged event can give rise to symptoms. The onset may occur immediately after the traumatic event, or be delayed, if the trauma acts as a sensitizing incident activated by later events. It is quite common for a psychologically traumatic physical injury to result in a somatic pain long after the physical injury has healed.

> QUESTION: *"What happened immediately before you developed symptom x? Without necessarily knowing the detail of what happened, is symptom x related in some way to a previous event?"*
> RESOLUTION: Use a dissociative imagery technique (see chapter 26).

Tracey suffered with severe and chronic headaches for which no 'medical' reason had been found. Her problem was explored in hypnosis using an affect bridge and the time road metaphor. Upon asking Tracey to float back above whatever was relevant to the development of her headaches, she realized that they had developed following a road traffic accident. Tracey had escaped virtually uninjured, but her car was a write off. She recalled people at the scene telling her she was lucky to be alive and she herself thought as the accident happened that she was going to die. Upon further ideomotor exploration, Tracey realized that her headache told her she was alive and that she did not need it anymore as her present self went down to comfort and reassure her younger self in the crash and let that younger part of her truly realize that she had indeed survived. After a little further work in a couple of sessions, Tracey no longer had her headaches and had stopped all her analgesic medication.

In the author's (LB) experience, trauma is the most common cause for a MUS, and a history of childhood or adult abuse in some form or another is frequently uncovered. The chapters on pain, PTSD and psychosomatic disorders are relevant here.

Conflict is the internal situation where the mind is trapped between two alternatives and not making a decision between them. This often involves conflicts between such actions as pleasing self or others, benefiting self or hurting others or agreeing to do something that you really do not wish to do.

QUESTION: *"Is there part of you that is saying that you ought to do one thing and another wanting to do exactly the opposite?"*
RESOLUTION: Identify the conflict, then work towards a decision.

Mary was suffering from panic disorder and wanted to go to college but felt she did not have the confidence and was very scared that her anxieties would prevent her. During one session, what her anxiety was doing for her was explored in a positive manner. She was asked (in hypnosis) to imagine that part of her that was the panic and anxiety to be in one hand and to appreciate what it was trying to do to help. She eventually said that her anxiety was there to stop her failing by making her too panicky to try. The positive feeling generated by this was relief and safety, leading eventually to happiness. On the other hand she imagined that part of her that wanted to go to college and appreciated what that part was trying to do for her. This part wanted her to succeed and led also to a feeling of happiness. Mary was asked to begin to realize that these two parts were both trying to help her to be happy, although the conflict was causing her problems. It was explained how the anxiety was being protective but that perhaps these two parts of her could communicate and begin to work towards achieving a balance: that the fearful part could be reassured that she would not be over confident and that the confident part could help the fearful part so that instead of being in conflict they could work together to help Mary achieve her goals. Mary's unconscious mind was asked to consider these things and as these two parts of her began their communication suggested that she might find her two hands moving together, all by themselves, to monitor her unconscious working. Slowly Mary's hands came together, and the session was ended with ego strengthening and a positive mental rehearsal.

Hysteria in its classical meaning is a symptom that serves a purpose and produces a *secondary gain*. The teenager with a migraine headache which prevents them from going to school, thus avoiding being bullied, is a secondary gain at a simple level. Compensation neurosis settles once the payment has been made because there is no further gain to be made by the symptom persisting.

QUESTION: *"I am sure you do not want symptom x, but is there at least one aspect of your life that benefits because you have symptom x? If the symptom disappeared, would there be something else you would lose?"*

RESOLUTION: Negotiate with the subconscious how to achieve the secondary gain without the symptom.

Sarah came for help with her back pain. She had had this for a considerable time, and it made walking difficult for her. She had been fully investigated, and no obvious cause had been found. Out of hypnosis Sarah said that she was looking forward to marrying her boyfriend but that she wanted her wedding day to be perfect and she was not going to get married until she had got rid of her back pain. She insisted on her fiancé being present throughout the session.

Upon ideomotor questioning in hypnosis Sarah revealed that this back pain was serving a purpose, although it would not be appropriate to bring this into conscious awareness, and that she was not prepared to let go of her pain. A post-hypnotic suggestion was given that, if appropriate, her unconscious could 'turn down' her pain and a further general suggestion given that her unconscious would help Sarah resolve in the future any difficulties that might be underpinning her back pain.

It might be felt that work on Sarah's possible misgivings about her relationship with her fiancé was probably indicated, but it was important that these perceptions were not shared with Sarah but that the direction of further therapeutic work should be guided by her. Maybe her unconscious mind had already taken a step towards resolution by having the boyfriend hear what transpired during the session.

The above comprehensive approach will stand the novice therapist in good stead, but the following will also be found useful with these complex patients. A very valuable method of accessing unconscious resources was modified by the author (AW) from that described by Stanton, modified from Rossi's ideodynamic methods of healing (Rossi & Cheek, 1988). In this an intention is set and ideomotor movement of the hands used to monitor the unconscious processing. This is a general technique applicable to a whole variety of problems such as irritable bowel cramps, dysmenorrhoea or headaches, to boost immune function or for anything else where it is appropriate to engage unconscious resources in order to help.

1   The patient is asked to hold their hands four to five inches apart, and they are instructed to ask their unconscious mind if it is prepared to work on 'the symptom' now.
   a. *"If 'Yes', then your hands will gradually come together as your unconscious mind reviews the problem and what it is all about."*
   b. *"If 'No', then your hands will move apart. Respect this and maybe try again later."*
2   *"Allow one hand to drift down to your lap as your unconscious mind mobilizes the resources it needs to deal with the problem."*
3   *"Allow the other hand to move down to your lap as your unconscious mind starts to use these resources to help you with the problem."*

Exploring alternatives using reframing (see page 442) can be very effective with psycho-somatic symptoms. The positive intent is acknowledged even though it may not be brought into conscious awareness and the unconscious may be engaged in generating alternative ways of responding to achieve the same outcome that the symptom is trying to achieve.

Resolution of underpinning emotional events can be done using a time road metaphor (see page 401), and if age progression is utilized with the suggestion *"Go forward to float above a time when you have resolved 'x' and if it is okay, float down into that you and feel how good it feels,"* a useful double bind that can be used is *"Return to the here and now when you know you have the resources to make this your reality."*

The time road metaphor can also be used to create a pre-state anchor by asking the patient to access a time before the symptom arose and anchoring it. This is useful in both migraine and asthma as it can be utilized at the start of an attack. (It is important to remember that peak flows should still be monitored in the asthmatic.)

Patient generated imagery is one of the mainstays of treating many psychosomatic disorders. Imagery may be not only visual but also auditory and kinaesthetic. Therapy follows the maxim:

If you change what you see, you change what you feel.

There are various classic images that are commonly used such as the river or canal image for IBS (see page 252) or the snowy forest and cool and comfortable mantra for eczema (see page 286). But images are limited only by the patient's imagination. It is useful to be able to suggest some images to help patients on their way, but it is important to point out that it is the imagery that comes from their own unconscious mind which is most important.

These corrective imagery techniques are used to give symptomatic relief and should be used in conjunction with the uncovering processes already discussed. The patient is asked to focus their attention on the problem and notice what it looks, sounds and feels like. If they could alter that in some way that would be helpful, what would they do?

Emma suffered from vulvodynia with no discernable medical cause. In hypnosis Emma went down into her vagina to explore the problem. The image that came into her mind was that of a purple spiral or coil that was spinning very fast in a clockwise direction. She felt that what she needed to do was change the colour so it became paler and slow the spin down. She later decided that she needed to reverse the direction of the spin, which she did. She continued to work with her imagery each day during her self hypnosis time, and over time her vulvodynia improved markedly.

The way the patient relates to their symptom has a significant part to play in their problem. Often the patient views their symptoms with hostility and anger and sees the symptom as an enemy that they have to fight or try to avoid. Some patients may relate to their symptoms with forbearance and view their symptoms as just punishment for their wrongdoings. The patient may have little insight into this, and utilizing ways to externalize the problem facilitates change.

It is well known that thoughts and feelings, like a young child trying to get a busy mother's attention, will clamour louder and louder if they are ignored. Thus the emotional reaction of the patient to their symptoms may well exacerbate their problems.

Patient generated imagery can again be useful to both explore and improve the patient's relationship to their problem. For example, in hypnosis patients are asked to imagine that if the symptom were an animal, what would its habitat look like (Mende, 2009)?

They are then asked to go there and wait to see what happens; to see if the animal appears, when the patient simply observes it. The patient is asked to describe what they are seeing and as they rest there, feeling calm and relaxed, to notice how their calmness is affecting the animal. The patient is encouraged to eventually make friends with, feed or otherwise relate in a calm way to the animal (their symptom). This can often have quite a dramatic effect of the symptom complex even without any other exploration.

Margaret – a woman with tinnitus

Margaret suffered with tinnitus and vertigo that had been thoroughly investigated from the medical standpoint without any improvement in her symptoms. When asked in hypnosis what animal came to mind when she focused on her problem, she replied that it was a small, terrier type dog. As she sat relaxing in the wood and fields that she had imagined as the dog's habitat, she described the dog as terrified and agitated. Margaret was asked just to observe and see what happened as the dog noticed her and saw that she was very calm and relaxed and not posing any threat to it. She related that the dog began to calm down and approach her. She gradually made friends with the dog, and it stopped shaking and settled down with her. It was then suggested that she meet up with her dog when she did her self-hypnosis and continue to make friends with it. Her symptoms started to improve and although other work was done as well, this was certainly the start of her improvement.

Graham – a man with post-herpetic neuralgia

Graham had suffered with post-herpetic neuralgia for three years and during one session while in hypnosis described his symptom imagery as a black octopus clamped to his side. It was suggested that he might want to go inside and ask the octopus what it needed or wanted. As Graham did this, his physiology obviously changed as he did some internal processing. He then said in a surprised tone of voice that the octopus had changed to pale blue cottonwool! After some further work Graham was no longer troubled by his neuralgia and disengaged from therapy.

Managing patients with MUS well tends to elevate the therapist's esteem with one's colleagues. They will continue to view these patients as 'heart sinks', whereas the practitioner who is able to take them on and successfully alleviate the symptoms will find it highly rewarding to succeed where others have failed.

The next two chapters look at some specific conditions, but the above general approaches will apply to all types of psychosomatic illness and, indeed, the emotional aspects of any illness.

References

Abrahamsen, R., Baad-Hansen, L. & Svensson, P. (2008), Hypnosis in the management of persistent idiopathic orofacial pain – clinical and psychosocial findings. *Pain*, 136, 44–52.

Bakal, D., Steiert, M., Coll, P. & Schaefer, J. (2006), An experiential mind-body approach to the management of medically unexplained symptoms. *Medical Hypotheses*, 67, 1443–7.

Barsky, A. J., Orav, E. J. & Bates, D. W. (2005), Somatization increases medical utilization and costs independent of psychiatric and medical comorbidity. *Archives of General Psychiatry*, 62, 903–10.

Evans, C., Connell, J., Barkham, M., Margison, F., McGrath, G., Mellor-Clark, J. & Audin, K. (2002), Towards a standardised brief outcome measure: psychometric properties and utility of the CORE—OM. *The British Journal of Psychiatry*, 180, 51–60.

Ewin, D. & Eimer, B. (2006), *Ideomotor signals for rapid hypnoanalysis: a how-to manual*. Springfield, IL, Charles C. Thomas.

Golan, H. (1997), The use of hypnosis in the treatment of psychogenic oral pain. *American Journal of Clinical Hypnosis*, 40, 89–96.

Gravitz, M. (1995), Hypnosis in the treatment of functional infertility. *American Journal of Clinical Hypnosis*, 38, 22–6.

Grondahl, J. & Rosvold, E. (2008), Hypnosis as a treatment of chronic widespread pain in general practice: a randomized controlled pilot trial. *BMC Musculoskeletal Disorders*, 9, 124.

Hammond, D. (2001), Treatment of chronic fatigue with neurofeedback and self-hypnosis. *NeuroRehabilitation*, 16, 295–300.

Huffman, J. C. & Pollack, M. H. (2003), Predicting panic disorder among patients with chest pain: an analysis of the literature. *Psychosomatics*, 44, 222–36.

Jones, H., Cooper, P., Miller, V., Brooks, N. & Whorwell, P. J. (2006), Treatment of non-cardiac chest pain: a controlled trial of hypnotherapy. *Gut*, 55, 1403–8.

Kandyba, K. & Binik, Y. M. (2003), Hypnotherapy as a treatment for vulvar vestibulitis syndrome: a case report. *Journal of Sex & Marital Therapy*, 29, 237–42.

Kirmayer, L. J. & Robbins, J. M. (1991), Three forms of somatization in primary care: prevalence, co-occurrence, and sociodemographic characteristics. *The Journal of Nervous and Mental Disease*, 179, 647–55.

Kroenke, K. & Mangelsdorff, A. (1989), Common symptoms in ambulatory care: incidence, evaluation, therapy, and outcome. *American Journal of Medicine*, 86, 262–6.

Lucock, M. P., Morley, S., White, C. & Peake, M. D. (1997), Responses of consecutive patients to reassurance after gastroscopy: results of self administered questionnaire survey. *British Medical Journal*, 315, 572–5.

Maudoux, A., Bonnet, S., Lhonneux-Ledoux, F. & Lefebvre, P. (2007), Ericksonian hypnosis in tinnitus therapy. *B-ENT*, 3 (7), 75–7.

Mawdsley, J., Jenkins, D., Macey, M., Langmead, L. & Rampton, D. (2008), The effect of hypnosis on systemic and rectal mucosal measures of inflammation in ulcerative colitis. *American Journal of Gastroenterology*, 103, 1460–9.

Mayou, R. & Farmer, A. (2002), Functional somatic symptoms and syndromes. *British Medical Journal*, 325, 265–8.

McDonald, I. G., Daly, J., Jelinek, V. M., Panetta, F. & Gutman, J. M. (1996), Opening Pandora's box: the unpredictability of reassurance by a normal test result. *British Medical Journal*, 313, 329–32.

Mende, M. (2009), Hypnotic communication in psychosomatics and somatoform disorders: the interplay of nurturing and confrontation. Workshop given at the joint meeting of BSCAH, RSM and BSMDH, London, June.

Miller, V. & Whorwell, P. J. (2009), Hypnotherapy for functional gastrointestinal disorders: a review. *International Journal of Clinical and Experimental Hypnosis*, 57, 279–92.

Nimnuan, C., Hotopf, M. & Wessely, S. (2001), Medically unexplained symptoms: an epidemiological study in seven specialities. *Journal of Psychosomatic Research*, 51, 361–7.

Pukall, C., Kandyba, K., Amsel, R., Khalifé, S. & Binik, Y. (2007), Effectiveness of hypnosis for the treatment of vulvar vestibulitis syndrome: a preliminary investigation. *Journal of Sexual Medicine*, 4, 417–25.

Ross, U., Lange, O., Unterrainer, J. & Laszig, R. (2007), Ericksonian hypnosis in tinnitus therapy: effects of a 28-day inpatient multimodal treatment concept measured by Tinnitus-Questionnaire and Health Survey SF-36. *European Archives of Oto-Rhino-Laryngology*, 264, 483–8.

Rossi, E. L. & Cheek, D. B. (1988), *Mind-body therapy*, New York, W. W. Norton.

Rucklidge, J. J. & Saunders, D. (2002), The efficacy of hypnosis in the treatment of pruritus in people with HIV/AIDS: a time-series analysis. *International Journal of Clinical and Experimental Hypnosis*, 50, 149–69.

Salmon, P., Dowrick, C. F., Ring, A. & Humphris, G. M. (2004), Voiced but unheard agendas: qualitative analysis of the psychosocial cues that patients with unexplained symptoms present to general practitioners. *British Journal of General Practice*, 54 (500), 171–6.

Shenefelt, P. (2004), Using hypnosis to facilitate resolution of psychogenic excoriations in acne excoriée. *American Journal of Clinical Hypnosis*, 46, 239–45.

Sidman, J., Lechtman, M. & Lyster, E. (2009), A unique hypnotherapeutic approach to interstitial cystitis: a case report. *Journal of Reproductive Medicine*, 54, 523–4.

Simon, E. & Lewis, D. (2000), Medical hypnosis for temporomandibular disorders: treatment efficacy and medical utilization outcome. *Oral surgery, oral medicine, oral pathology, oral radiology, and endodontics*, 90 (1), 54–63.

Simon, G., Von korff, M., Piccinelli, M., Fullerton, C. & Ornel, J. (1999), An international study of the relation between somatic symptoms and depression. *New England Journal of Medicine*, 341, 1329–33.

Taggart, P., Sutton, P., Redfern, C., Batchvarov, V. N., Hnatkova, K., Malik, M., James, U. & Joseph, A. (2005), The effect of mental stress on the non-dipolar components of the T wave: modulation by hypnosis. *Psychosomatic Medicine*, 67, 376–83.

Willemsen, R., Vanderlinden, J., Deconinck, A. & Roseeuw, D. (2006), Hypnotherapeutic management of alopecia areata. *Journal of the American Academy of Dermatology*, 55, 233–7.

Williamson, A. (2008), *Brief psychological interventions in practice*. Chichester, John Wiley & Sons, Ltd.

Zigmond, A. & Snaith, R. (1983), The hospital anxiety and depression scale. *Acta Psychiatrica Scandinavia*, 67, 361–70.

Zimmerman, J. (2001), Dyspepsia as a somatic expression of guilt: a case report. *American Journal of Clinical Hypnosis*, 44, 57–61.

19

Specific Psychosomatic Disorders

Dr Les Brann

with contributions from Mrs Karen Mackrodt and Dr Ann Williamson

Irritable Bowel Syndrome

Irritable bowel syndrome (IBS) is a very common condition and estimates of its prevalence suggest that between 10% and 20% of the population suffer from the symptoms. The initial presentation to the health service is most commonly in the age group 20 to 30 years, but it is a life-long, chronic, relapsing condition. Women are twice as likely to suffer from IBS as men although it is probable that different thresholds for consultation may account for some of this apparent difference. It accounts for more than 50% of first appointments in gastroenterology out-patient departments, and this leads to considerable over investigation at significant cost to the health economy.

IBS is characterized by the presence of the following symptoms:

- Abdominal pain or discomfort, relieved or altered by defaecation
- A change in bowel habit, either diarrhoea or constipation or both
- A sensation of or actual abdominal distension (bloating)

Longstreth *et al.* (2006) suggest that symptoms have to have been present for a minimum of six months in order to fulfil the diagnostic criteria agreed at the Rome convention on functional bowel disease. Whilst, for diagnosis, IBS does not require any sophisticated tests, it is recommended that a full blood count (to check for anaemia), erythrocyte sedimentation rate (ESR) or C reactive protein (CRP) (to exclude inflammatory bowel disease) tests and a

The Handbook of Contemporary Clinical Hypnosis: Theory and Practice, First Edition.
Edited by Les Brann, Jacky Owens and Ann Williamson.
© 2012 John Wiley & Sons, Ltd. Published 2015 by John Wiley & Sons, Ltd.

blood test for coeliac disease (e.g. transglutaminase) are also carried out – these must be normal in order to permit a diagnosis of IBS to be made. It must be said that IBS can be co-morbid with other bowel conditions such as ulcerative colitis, and treatment for both may be required.

Whilst not consistently present or essential for diagnosis it is recognized that other, non-colonic symptoms are common accompaniments of IBS. It should be noted, however, that such symptoms can have specific causes and should not be assumed to be part of the wider IBS picture without due consideration.

Non-colonic symptoms include (Whorwell *et al.*, 1986):

- Nausea
- Early satiety
- Heartburn
- Excess wind – belching or flatus
- Headaches
- Backache
- Lethargy
- Bodily aches and pains
- Thigh pain
- Urinary urgency
- Gynaecological symptoms

In addition to the above, Whitehead *et al.* (2002) noted common associations between IBS and other conditions such as chronic fatigue syndrome and fibromyalgia.

The high incidence of the condition and the diversity of the wider symptomatology have inevitably led to this having a high socio-economic cost, and Weber and McCallum (1992) reported that IBS was the second most common cause of absenteeism from work after the common cold. Consequently it is also a drain on healthcare resources.

Causes

This is not the forum for a detailed discussion on the causes of IBS, but suffice it to say that it is multi-factorial and the major contributors are summarized in Table 19.1.

Spiller (2003) reports that between 6% and 17% of IBS cases seemed to have a post-GI infection aetiology, but it is interesting to note that the major risk factor in developing such post-infective symptoms is the presence of adverse life events. What constitutes a significant life event can be debated at length, but it is clear there is a higher prevalence of sexual, physical and emotional abuse in IBS patients. Indeed, Delvaux *et al.* (1997) reported that 31.6% of IBS patients had a history of sexual abuse compared with 7.6% of healthy controls. The proportion with a history of abuse (all types) increases to nearly 50% in patients with severe symptoms visiting specialist centres (Drossman *et al.*, 1990). From a population perspective, it seems that those with childhood and adult abuse are three times more likely to have IBS (Talley *et al.*, 1998).

Table 19.1 Aetiology of IBS

Physical	*Psychological*
Gastrointestinal infection	Stress
Following antibiotic medication	Past or present life events, e.g. trauma or abuse
Surgery	Anxiety and depression
	Somatization
Specific food intolerances	Personality factors, e.g. perfectionism

Anxiety and depression are common psychiatric conditions associated with IBS. In a large outcome audit of 250 patients, Gonsalkorale *et al.* (2002) found that 59% and 20.7% had Hospital Anxiety and Depression scale (HADs) score >9 for anxiety and depression respectively. Creed *et al.* (2005) notes that in addition to anxiety and depression, there is also a higher incidence of panic disorder.

Interestingly, Whorwell *et al.* (1992) has shown increased colonic motility in IBS patients with hypnotically induced emotions, and many patients are aware that emotions make the symptoms worse. Such patients often see this response to emotions as an effect of IBS rather than the emotions being complicit in the aetiology. Lea *et al.* (2003) have shown that hypnotherapy normalizes rectal sensitivity suggesting that this sensitivity is a result of the IBS rather than the cause of it. Any or all of these symptoms can result in behavioural changes. For example, a patient with diarrhoea predominant IBS may avoid socializing or feel the need to plan an outing via a series of toilets.

Thus the symptom model for IBS could be represented as in Figure 19.1. Looking at the well documented hypnotic phenomena (see Chapter 2), it can be seen that hypnotherapy has a role to play in helping many of the symptoms of IBS such as spasm, pain and anxiety.

Published evidence

There is a considerable body of published evidence on the use of hypnotherapy with IBS to the point that in the United Kingdom the National Institute for Clinical Excellence (NICE; 2008) has recommended hypnotherapy as an 'approved' therapy for resistant IBS. NICE, however, have very rigid rules on the type of evidence that they will consider – the randomized controlled trial being the adopted format. This approach considerably under-values the hypnotherapeutic intervention in psychosomatic conditions but will be considered here to balance the individualized approach which is favoured by most clinical hypnotherapists.

Whorwell (1984) published the results of a randomized controlled trial of 30 patients with severe, treatment resistant IBS. The patients were randomly assigned to receive seven sessions of one to one hypnotherapy or seven sessions of psychotherapy plus placebo pills. The hypnotherapy was 'gut directed' using a standard script which was the same for all

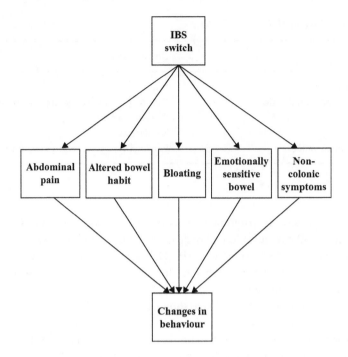

Figure 19.1   A symptom model for IBS.

participants and delivered after an arm levitation induction technique and a combination of standard deepening techniques. 'Hypnotherapy was solely directed at general relaxation and control of intestinal motility and no attempt was made at hypnoanalysis.' A sense of warmth was generated by asking the patient to place their hand on the abdomen and by stating that this sense of warmth related to asserting control over the gut motility. The control group received seven 30 minute sessions of supportive psychotherapy including a discussion of symptoms and contributory emotional problems. They also received placebo pills.

Improvements in abdominal pain, bowel habit, abdominal distension and general wellbeing were significantly greater in the hypnosis group compared with the controls ($p < 0.0001$). The control group did show a modest ($p < 0.05$) improvement in some of the symptoms but not in bowel frequency.

Whorwell *et al.* (1987) expanded on the earlier study and reported the results of a bigger group of 50 patients. They showed that patients with atypical symptoms and higher scores on the General Health Questionnaire (GHQ) did less well than those in the classical group. Patients over 50 years also did less well, although numbers in this group were small (eight). No details were given as to the duration of symptoms prior to treatment.

The poorer response by patients with a high (>5) GHQ score was also reported by Harvey *et al.* (1989). They too used a gut directed approach but also introduced a metaphor of a river scene and related the calm flow of the river to the smooth action of their gut. They confirmed the benefit of hypnotherapy in their uncomplicated patients and also felt able to conclude that group sessions were as effective as individual therapy.

In addition to Whorwell *et al.* (1984) and Harvey *et al.* (1989), NICE reviewed four other randomized controlled trials of hypnotherapy for IBS: Galovski *et al.* (1998), Forbes *et al.* (2000), Palsson *et al.* (2002) and Roberts *et al.* (2006). All had used a bowel directed approach with one to one therapy and all had shown similar benefits to Whorwell's original work enabling NICE to conclude that hypnotherapy was an appropriate therapy for IBS.

Prior *et al.* (1990) studying a group of 15 patients with IBS found that rectal sensitivity improved following a course of hypnotherapy and during hypnotherapy. This was most marked in the diarrhoea predominant group, but the trend was also noted in the constipation predominant group.

Whorwell *et al.* (1992) studied the effect of hypnotically induced emotions on colonic activity in 18 IBS patients. The hypnotic induction significantly reduced colonic activity from the baseline level. Anger and excitement both significantly increased activity, whereas happiness reduced it but not significantly from the hypnotic baseline.

Houghton *et al.* (1996) showed that not only did hypnotherapy improve the bowel symptoms of IBS but also it significantly improved the non-colonic symptoms. They also studied the effects of IBS on absenteeism from work and visits to the GP. 79% of the control group took time off from work with their IBS symptoms compared to 32% of the hypnotherapy group. Only 21% of the hypnotherapy group visited their GP compared with 58% of the controls. Thus they concluded that hypnotherapy has beneficial effects on the economic costs of IBS.

Use of hypnosis

An example of a gut directed script is presented below.

> *In a few moments time I am going to count up to three and ask you to place a hand on your tummy. . . . So ready . . . one . . . two . . . three . . . hand on your tummy.*
>
> *As your hand rests on your tummy, you will begin to feel a sense of warmth and comfort spreading around the muscles and tissues of this area. . . . This feeling will become warmer . . . warmer . . . and warmer as you channel the energies of your mind into your tummy. . . . Yes warmer . . . warmer . . . and warmer . . . a lovely feeling soothing your gut. . . . Going right inside your tummy . . . right through to every nook and cranny of your tummy . . . every muscle and fibre of your bowel is becoming warm . . . soothed . . . and comfortable. Yes warmer . . . and warmer . . . a lovely feeling soothing your gut.*
>
> *And on a count of three I would like you to put your other hand on top of the hand on your tummy and reinforce that feeling. . . . So ready . . . one, two, three . . . hand on your tummy. Now make that feeling really strong . . . warmer . . . warmer . . . and warmer . . . a lovely feeling soothing your gut. Yes warmer . . . and warmer . . . a special feeling you can identify with . . . going right inside your tummy, and with each breath that you take and with each word that I speak, this feeling of warmth and comfort will steadily increase. Yes warmer . . . and warmer . . . a comforting glow, soothing your gut.*

Yes, this feeling is a healing glow indicating that your unconscious mind is directing all the inner resources of your own mind and body to the areas where the need is the greatest. . . . You know how your feelings and thoughts affect the muscles of your gut. . . . We have discussed this previously . . . and so it follows that you (name) can control your own gut muscles. . . . You can remove pain . . . remove bloating . . . remove discomfort . . . and normalize your bowel habit to your own satisfaction.

Yes, all this is happening to you as a result of your relaxing so well at this moment . . . a result of the treatments you have had . . . but most of all as a result of your own efforts . . . your own determination to get your gut under control . . . so feel the strength of your mind . . . feel that determination growing stronger and stronger . . . feel you're going to win.

You will find you can continue to control the muscles of your gut by placing your hands in this same position whenever you feel the need. . . . If at any time you place your hands in this position . . . you will feel the same sense of warmth and comfort. This will be a signal to your unconscious mind for you to take control of the muscles of your gut . . . to remove pain . . . remove bloating . . . remove discomfort . . . and normalize your bowel habit to your own satisfaction.

Now I would like you to picture a river in your mind . . . flowing through beautiful countryside . . . picture the clean, clear water . . . and the steady . . . calm . . . peaceful . . . tranquil . . . rhythmic . . . orderly flow of the water. No rushing . . . no hurry . . . no delays . . . no hold ups . . . just a steady . . . calm . . . peaceful . . . rhythmic . . . tranquil . . . orderly flow of the water. Now I would like you to picture your gut in the same way . . . just like the river . . . a steady . . . rhythmic . . . calm . . . peaceful . . . tranquil . . . orderly . . . normal movement through your bowel. No rushing . . . no hurry . . . no delays . . . no hold ups . . . just a steady . . . calm . . . rhythmic . . . peaceful . . . orderly . . . normal movement through your gut.

As you sink deeper and deeper into this image, feel the strength of your mind . . . because the stronger your mind becomes the more and more control you will acquire . . . and consequently your tummy will feel better . . . and better . . . and better. No pain . . . no bloating . . . no discomfort . . . and a normal, regular, bowel habit. Soon you will hardly be aware that you have a tummy . . . it is working so well . . . so normally. . . . You can achieve this . . . you can and you will. . . . So feel you are going to win . . . feel a sense of control . . . feel the strength of your mind.

Let me draw your attention once more to the hands on your tummy . . . feel another surge of warmth and comfort beneath your hands and think of that healing glow . . . indicating that you are in control of your gut . . . rather than your gut . . . in control of you.

Thus the gut directed approach has proved to be very successful in the treatment of IBS symptoms. This approach, however, does nothing to specifically address the underlying psychological causes. Despite this published evidence, many experienced medical hypnotherapists do not solely use this approach in their day to day practice.

Indeed all members of BSCAH Council (Brann, 2009) who treat patients with IBS use, primarily, a patient centred, problem orientated approach aimed at identifying and treating the underlying stressors. Such an approach often obviates the need for specific bowel directed symptom removal as many patients' symptoms spontaneously subside once the root cause of the problem has been treated as in the case below. Such an approach is, of course, entirely compatible with bowel directed techniques, and these can be added if needed at any stage of the therapy.

Annette – a woman with IBS

This 63 year old lady was referred for hypnotherapy by the local gastroenterologist. Her diarrhoea predominant IBS had got so bad that she was avoiding going out or if she had to she would plan the trip around visits to the toilet – a typical visit to the local town centre for her would normally involve having to go to the toilet on five occasions. Such outings were accompanied by much anxiety. Indeed her HADs anxiety score at presentation was 19 (severe, max 21). Even with her restricted and avoidant lifestyle she reported her background symptom score at 51% which soared towards 100% on days when she was unable to keep to her protected housebound activities. Annette also had ulcerative colitis, and although this had been quiescent for several years she always found it difficult to differentiate between the IBS symptoms and an exacerbation of the colitis adding further to the anxiety.

Following the explanation of hypnosis using the hemispheric specialization model and the computer metaphor, hypnosis was induced using the method scripted on page 118. Annette used the beach as a relaxing place (interestingly the beach she imagined had no easily accessible toilet facilities!). She was asked to imagine that she had shrunk herself down and could go inside her control room in her mind and search on the cause of her problem. It had all started at the time she realized her husband was having an affair and was about to break up the marriage. Annette was devastated but was acutely aware that her own behaviour had pushed him away despite his warnings and attempts to discuss the difficulties he was having. This was a torrid time for her, but she managed to salvage her marriage and this was now stronger than it had ever been. Whilst the anxieties over her relationship gradually subsided, the bowels symptoms continued to get worse and culminated in the diagnosis of the ulcerative colitis. This was soon brought under control with medication, but the IBS persisted and her avoidant behaviour pattern became established.

Resolution was achieved using the 'older wiser self' technique following an acknowledgement that the symptoms were an appropriate response to the awful situation she found herself in so that the response was 'okay for then' but not 'okay for now'. We also used the 'Room of Forgiveness' allowing Annette to forgive herself for allowing the relationship to reach breaking point and also to forgive her husband.

Annette did remarkably well, and after the second session she had managed to go shopping in town without visiting the toilet at all. She really did not need the third session, but this was used for general relaxation and ego strengthening. For this we used the metaphorical stroll through the enchanted garden with the wise old lady giving her the cleansing water from the spring. She said afterwards, *"That old lady was my mother. She was so helpful when my marriage was at rock bottom – she was my support and guide."* Her HADs anxiety had dropped to ten (mild), and her symptom score had decreased to the normal range (18%). Annette telephoned a few weeks later to say thank you: *"Hypnosis has given me my life back!"* At no time did we mention the bowel specifically nor do any bowel directed therapy.

The case example following shows how complex the underlying issues can be, and clinical experience would seem to suggest that this is often the case when bloating is the predominant symptom.

Catherine – a woman with bloating predominant IBS

Catherine was a 42 year old divorced woman with one son aged 19. She had been referred by the gastroenterologist with a main IBS symptom of bloating. This had not responded to medication. She had also completed a lay hypnotherapy training course and was aware of its use with IBS.

Not only was the bloating uncomfortable but also it had led to some social withdrawal with a reluctance to socialize and, despite needing some new clothes, she had not felt able to go out clothes shopping for months. Notwithstanding her reluctance to socialize she was in a new relationship and was engaged to be married. Her first husband had walked out on her when her son was four months old.

Despite her hypnotherapy training the full explanation was given using the hemispheric model and computer metaphor. She used the beach as her relaxing place. The search of the problem revealed that it had started after a particularly nasty tummy bug. This had necessitated time off sick from work, but her boss had accused her of lying about the illness and had been particularly unpleasant. At the same time her boyfriend (now her fiancé) had walked out on her.

Catherine's symptoms had not improved after the first session – in truth there had been very little time for therapy – so the onset of the symptoms was revisited at the next session. The aggressive response of her boss had triggered memories of a serious sexual assault that had taken place many years before. Catherine indicated that she felt she needed to review this assault, and this was done using a dissociated video room technique. Having reviewed what she needed to, with the safety of the dissociation, the video was 'scrambled' and the cassette burnt.

Catherine confirmed, using an ideomotor signal, that the association of the assault with the bowel had been coincidental (via the boss's behaviour) and not causal, and so she was able to disconnect the inadvertent links with her bowel symptoms.

She was then asked to look specifically at the bloating and felt that the associated affect was that of a fear of rejection. This had been fuelled by her husband walking out (at a very emotional time of her life) and her boyfriend leaving too. As she was now back with her fiancé this affect was updated using the 'was okay for then but not okay for now' approach.

By the third session Catherine had begun to improve, the bloating was less and she had lost some weight. Having explained during the introductory session the model of the 'IBS switch' we explored this under hypnosis and she identified that all her anxieties seemed to focus on this switch. It was suggested that instead of triggering the IBS these anxieties could be directed to an 'anxiety filing room' where her anxieties could be held and dealt with in due course without having any impact on her bowel or other physical symptoms. She felt able to set up this room with the agreement of her subconscious mind (using ideomotor signals) if she promised to regularly check the contents of the room. This meant that she was in control of her anxieties rather than the anxieties controlling her.

By the fourth session Catherine was very much better, her bloating score had reduced from 9/10 to 4/10 and she had been out clothes shopping. The time was used to 'mop up' any other baggage that had built up over the years together with a metaphorical 'cleansing' which is always so useful in cases of sexual assault. Only then did we work through the IBS canal metaphor and modify the bloated bowel images.

These two case histories exemplify the need to expand the IBS model to include the activators (see Figure 19.2) and for therapy to focus on the activators rather than the symptoms. Both Whorwell *et al.* (1987) and Harvey *et al.* (1989) had noted that patients with a GHQ score >5 did less well with the bowel directed approach, so in such patients there is a need to find a more effective approach. It is also probable that the patient centred, problem focused approach is also superior for those with low GHQ (or equivalent) scores.

Table 19.2 compares the outcome results from the bowel directed approach of Gonsalkorale *et al.* (2002) with the patient centred, problem orientated approach of Brann (2009). The proportion of patients with clinical anxiety (HADs A > 9) was remarkably similar in both audits but following hypnosis over a third of the bowel directed hypnotherapy (BDH) group still had clinical anxiety as opposed to under a fifth of the person centred problem oriented (PCPO) group. Such a difference suggests that the BDH method was less useful with the higher levels of anxiety.

The mean HADs D scores in both audits before hypnosis were in the normal range. but the BDH group had a higher percentage in the clinical case range (36.1% versus 25%). Following treatment 14.6% of the BDH group were still clinically depressed whereas all depressed patients in the PCPO group had improved such that their scores were now in the non-depressed range.

The symptoms were scored using different methods but to aid comparison the scores have been represented as percentages of the maximum. Both methods reduced the reported symptoms scores by about 50% from the pre-treatment level. 78% of the BDH group improved with 9% showing a slight deterioration, whereas 96% improved in the PCPO group.

Thus both approaches show benefit but the major difference between the two is the BDH group required an average of 11.8 sessions each whereas the PCPO group was completed in 3.6 sessions. Whilst the PCPO method requires a higher level of hypnotherapy and psychological training than the BDH method, there are clear advantages in terms of time and cost. Whilst it has been shown that the benefits of BDH on IBS symptoms are lasting there is always the concern that symptom removal for psychosomatic problems simply leads to a change in symptoms rather than resolution. The PCPO approach is capable of preventing this symptom shift.

Notwithstanding the above, some attention to the bowel is often required especially initially in the therapy to enable the patient to identify the link between, say, stress and

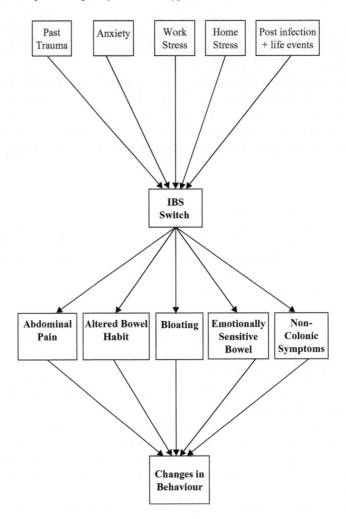

Figure 19.2   Expansion of the IBS model to include activators.

the symptoms. There are many ways in which this can be done, but one method is to ask the patient to imagine they had shrunk themselves down and were able to be inside their bowel when the symptoms were bad. The description is often along the lines of *"It is red hot, tight, active."* They are then asked to put this image to one side of their mind and then look at what is happening in their 'stress centre' when the bowel is bad. Although, deep down, most people acknowledge that symptoms are worse when stressed, some have a sense of failure at the thought that stress can cause such physical problems. Seeing the images often helps them to take ownership of this mechanism.

Sometimes it is necessary to ask them to be an observer of the two images and to watch what happens as they move into a more stressful (actual or anticipatory) situation. Once

Table 19.2   Comparison of outcome results from the bowel directed approach of Gonsalkorale *et al.*
(2002) with the patient centred, problem orientated approach of Brann *et al.* (2009)

Brann et al. (2009)	Before hypnosis	After hypnosis	Significance: t-test
Mean Hospital Anxiety and Depression scale (HADs) – Anxiety (% > 9)	12.3 (68.8%)	7.1 (18.8)	$P = 0.00$ (3.6×10^{-9})
Mean HADs – Depression (% > 9)	5.8 (25%)	3.1 (0%)	$P = 0.00$ (2.9×10^{-5})
Mean symptom score as a % of maximum	56	23	$P = 0.00$ (2.4×10^{-7})

Gonsalkorale et al. (2002)	Before hypnosis	After hypnosis	Significance
Mean HADs – Anxiety (% > 9)	11.1 (69.3%)	7.1 (34.3%)	$P < 0.001$
Mean HADs – Depression (% > 9)	7.2 (36.1%)	4.1 (14.6%)	$P < 0.001$
Mean symptom score as a % of maximum	68	32	$P < 0.001$

this link has been identified, the rest of the therapy can then be targeted at the stress rather than the bowel. Frequently, however, there is a vicious circle where the stress triggers the bowel symptoms and this then further increases the anxiety – in these cases some work on the bowel is needed. Corrective imagery work can then be carried out on both arms of the problem. The red, tight painful active image can be changed to the image of the bowel when there are no untoward symptoms, and, further, this is noted to be accompanied by a reduction in the excess anxiety.

Whatever approach is used, progress is made when the patient realizes that the symptoms are not random, uncontrollable actions as a result of some underlying disease but ordinary physiological responses over which a degree of control is possible. Mental rehearsal of them succeeding in taking control of the problem is important and to this can be added various supportive anchors (see Chapter 12) such as the Calvert Stein method or more bowel specific actions such as the warmth of the hand on the abdomen.

NICE guidelines recommend that hypnotherapy (or cognitive-behavioural therapy [CBT]) be offered where IBS symptoms have lasted for a year and have been resistant to medication. Whilst only guidelines, many health service commissioners treat such documents as absolute and commission accordingly. To be fair, the prevalence of IBS is such that it would be impossible to offer hypnotherapy to everyone – so who would benefit the most? It is likely that as the evidence from more outcome studies accumulates, the answer to that question will become clearer. For now, it would seem that for the BDH the under 50 age group with low co-morbidity would be the most suitable subset, but for the PCPO hypnotherapy those with moderate or high co-morbidity would benefit most. As databases grow, it will be possible to identify whether any particular IBS symptom complex responds better than others to a whole range of approaches. For the hypnotherapy student uncomplicated IBS is a useful problem with which to gain experience as some benefit can ensue with basic relaxation and bowel directed scripts but then more analytical techniques can be perfected on increasingly complicated cases.

Migraine and Tension Headaches

Headaches in all their guises are very common conditions for which patients seek help. The average GP with 2,000 patients will see five new cases of migraine each year and have a total of 40 consultations with their migraine sufferers (MeReC, 1997). Of course many patients with migraine do not consult their doctor, but it is estimated that the one year prevalence of migraine is 6–15% of adult men but as high as 14–35% for adult women (Stovner *et al.*, 2006). The gender difference is not seen in children or older adults, so it would seem that the hormonal profile in the reproductive years has some effect on the aetiology. As with IBS, there is a significant cost in terms of lost working days. Gerth *et al.* (2001) estimate this to be about 20 working days for each patient with migraine.

The commonest form of this condition is diagnosed if there have been at least five attacks of:

- Headache attacks lasting four to 72 hours
- Two of the following characteristics:
  - Unilateral
  - Pulsating
  - Moderate or severe pain intensity
  - Aggravated by normal physical activity (such as walking)
- Headache accompanied by at least one of the following:
  - Nausea and/or vomiting
  - Photophobia or phonophobia
- Headache not attributable to another cause

About 30% of patients with migraine also suffer an aura. These can be visual symptoms with flashing lights or with a missing part of the visual field, or sensory sensations. Again the sensory symptoms can be positive, such as giving pins and needles, or negative, for example numbness. Speech disturbance is also recognized and this is easily confused with a stroke especially if this is accompanied by unilateral weakness – the so called hemiplegic migraine. There are more detailed classifications of migraine which are not relevant for this book but the interested reader is referred to the specialist literature.

Although much research has been carried out in migraine, no clear pathophysiology has been identified. Changes in blood flow, with initial vasoconstriction followed by reflex vasodilatation, has been traditionally implicated, but a recent review (Goadsby, 2005) points to possible abnormalities in the trigeminovascular system together with altered functioning of the central pain-modulating system. Despite these research findings, what is clear to the clinician is that there are many triggers for these headaches including foods, alcohol, stress, anxiety and so on.

Tension-type headache (TTH)

In contrast to migraine, the diagnostic criteria for TTH is a bilateral headache with a pressing or tightening quality. They can last anything up to seven days and tend to be mild to moderate in intensity without aggravation by normal physical activity. Nausea or vomiting is not a usual accompaniment, and although a proportion of sufferers report photophobia or phonophobia it is rarely severe and it is unlikely that both sensory symptoms ever occur together.

Russell (2005) in a retrospective study of 4,000 people aged 40 found the prevalence of the infrequent episodic TTH to be as high as 48%. 34% suffered the frequent episodic type but only 2–3% suffered the chronic form. There does not seem to be any significant gender difference. There is no obvious pathophysiology for TTH, but Fumal and Schoenen (2008) have shown that sufferers are known to have tender myofascial trigger points and some abnormalities in central pain processing. This latter seems to be increased sensitization in the episodic types and reduced endogenous pain control in the chronic type. They also comment on the difficulties of preventative treatments and recommend relaxation based therapies.

It is worth mentioning one other type of headache which frequently presents to the hypnotherapists, namely, cluster headaches. These have significant features in common with migraine.

Cluster headaches (International Headache Society, 2005).

- Pain lasts between fifteen minutes and three hours and is associated with intense restlessness and agitation.
- Episodes occur with a frequency between once every other day and eight times daily. Headache commonly wakes the person from sleep within two hours of going to sleep, and may also occur at other times.
- At least five episodes of pain have occurred.
- It is associated with at least one autonomic feature occurring on the same side as the pain, including:
  - Conjunctival injection and/or lacrimation
  - Eyelid oedema
  - Miosis and/or ptosis
  - Nasal congestion and/or rhinorrhoea
  - Forehead and facial sweating
- In some people, attacks may be associated with migrainous features such as photophobia, phonophobia, nausea and vomiting. Up to 20% of people experience an aura as part of their cluster headache, and some people may experience persistent mild background pain between attacks.

According to Fischera *et al.* (2008) the lifetime prevalence is 1:1000 whilst 1:2000 have had an episode in the last year. This condition is four times more common in men than women. The cause is unknown but may involve the hypothalamus and some reflex autonomic vasodilatation of the ophthalmic, anterior and middle cerebral arteries (May, 2005; Waldenlind & Goadsby, 2006).

Whilst these diverse types of headache may have different pathways from symptom trigger to symptom, the hypnotherapist need not be overly concerned with these differences. However, the mechanism, or perceived mechanism, of the symptom production has been used to inform the content of the suggested visualizations. For example, Anderson *et al.* (1975) utilized the theory that the symptoms of migraine are caused by vasodilatation of the cerebral arteries and were told to visualize them as being swollen and throbbing and then to change the image to the arteries becoming smaller and comfortable. In that trial of 47 patients (23 utilizing hypnotherapy versus 24 utilizing medication) relaxation and Hartland's ego strengthening were used in addition to the visualization in each of the six sessions (Heap & Aravind, 2002). This approach resulted in a significant reduction of both the monthly number of migraines ($p < 0.005$) and the number of 'blinding' headaches ($p < 0.005$). At one year 43.5% of the hypnotherapy group had been migraine free for the previous three months compared to only 12.5% of the medication group.

A more elaborate visualization was suggested by Emmerson and Trexler (1999). This was based again on the concept of the symptoms being a result of dilated vessels and the sensation of heat that the dilated vessels produce. Their visualization was to ask the patients to imagine that their head was inside a helmet which had freezer coils fitted and that they could feel the cooling effects which reduced the pounding blood flow. This study showed a reduction in frequency ($p < 0.0001$), duration ($p < 0.0005$) and severity ($p < 0.0005$) compared with pre-treatment measures. The use of medication in this group was reduced by 49% ($p < 0.0005$).

Alladin (1988) suggested hand warming to his patients on the basis that this increased peripheral flow would lead to a reduction in cerebral flow and thus reduce the symptoms. This hand-warming suggestion was superior to glove anaesthesia induced by imagined immersion in cold water. Coolness, a sympathetic response, seemed to reduce the benefit of the relaxation which was deemed to be the main therapeutic effect. Whilst such imagery may lead to actual peripheral temperature change, Friedman and Taub (1985) found no correlation between temperature change and therapeutic outcome.

In a larger study of 136 mixed chronic headache patients (migraine, tension headaches or both), Spanos *et al.* (1993) compared an imagery based hypnotic treatment, a subliminal reconditioning group and a no treatment group. The subliminal reconditioning programme was considered to be placebo. Both the hypnotic group and the placebo group resulted in a significantly reduced frequency and severity ($p < 0.05$) compared to the no treatment group.

Using a single blind, waiting list control design, Melis *et al.* (1991) found a significant reduction in frequency, duration and severity of the headaches ($p < 0.05$) with hypnosis. These patients had been attending a headache clinic. The four session hypnosis treatment incorporated relaxation and a 'corrective imagery' type approach where an image of the headache changed as symptoms settled. Transformation of the headache to a less problematic pain (e.g. little finger ache) was also suggested.

Several studies have been conducted comparing hypnosis (future orientated pain free imagery) with autogenic training (Spinhoven *et al.*1992; ter Kuile *et al.*, 1994; Van Dyck *et al.*1991; Zitman *et al.*1992). All studies showed post-treatment benefits for both methods, but Zitman *et al.* (1992) felt able to conclude that hypnotherapy whilst not producing greater post-treatment effects did result in longer lasting effects. It seemed that labelling the method hypnotic imagery was superior to imagery alone.

Thus there is a wealth of evidence showing the effectiveness of hypnotherapy in the treatment of migraines and tension headaches. Indeed, in a review article Hammond (2007) was able to conclude that it (hypnosis) 'meets the clinical psychology research criteria for being a well established and efficacious treatment and is virtually free of side effects, risk of adverse reactions and ongoing expense associated with medication treatments' (p. 207).

The frustrating thing about this evidence is that, as with IBS, none of the studies attempted to identify and treat underlying causes yet the following case history highlights the need for this approach.

Helen – a woman with chronic headache

Helen was a married 38 year old mother of two children aged six and eight. She had a long history of headaches which would fall into the category of chronic tension type with headaches lasting for weeks at a time. She also had the occasional unilateral headache with migraine characteristics. She had been treated with a variety of analgesics without a great deal of benefit. There was no evidence of any physical cause. She had also had some counselling which she described as a *"waste of time."* Hypnosis was explained using the hemispheric model and was induced using a progressive relaxation induction with visual imagery of a beach which was her chosen 'relaxing place'.

The first session was simply used for relaxation, but in the second session she was asked to wander inside her head and see what the pain looked like. Helen said it was as though there was a hand compressing her head. The obvious next question was *"Whose hand?"* As often happens when patients get the 'Ah ha' moment, there was a few seconds' pause before she said, *"My husband's!"*

Following this, lots of emotion tumbled out and it transpired that her marriage had been a disappointment. Although her husband worked hard and financially provided for the family, she always felt under pressure and there was very little love and affection. He was fairly demanding sexually, but she had little sexual satisfaction and was anorgasmic.

Helen felt a lot better having poured all this out, and for a while her headaches were much improved. She became much more assertive and began developing her own interests. As so often happens, Helen found a new relationship which helped her confidence both sexually and as a person. She eventually found the strength to divorce her husband, although this was far from amicable, with her husband continuing to try to control her even after the divorce. He, somehow, managed to get a log of her phone calls and would turn up at the house and question her as to who she had been talking to.

Court orders were obtained, but he broke these on many occasions. Needless to say, her headaches returned at this time and she was once again referred for hypnosis.

Despite having been immensely strong during this acrimonious time, she still felt bad about herself. Where resolution of such problems has not occurred, it is often a clue that there were earlier events that were responsible for the poor self esteem developing in the first place. Using the computer technique and searching back on the feeling, it became clear that she had felt like this right through her childhood. She had an older brother who had never married and stayed living at home. She got on fine with her brother, but her parents doted on him and always made her feel she was second best.

Such entrenched feelings are never easy to resolve and in this case we used the 'older wiser self' technique, not only to give support to herself but also to see that much of her feelings were a representation of her parents' problem. She was asked to symbolically hand back the problem to them. We also used the resource room and were able to let her see that the room was full of lots of strength and courage evidenced by her ability not to crumple during the worst parts of the acrimonious divorce. Soon after these sessions, she met a new partner and has been able to settle down again.

Thus, such case histories show that using hypnosis simply for symptom removal is likely to be ineffective. That is not to say, however, that symptom removal techniques are never appropriate, but they should be used alongside or after the exploratory techniques. Where these are required, it is important to utilize the patient's own understanding of the mechanism. So, for example, with migraines, if the patient had read that migraines were caused by constriction of blood flow in the brain, then the corrective imagery appropriate for that patient would involve opening up the blood vessels to increase the blood flow. Teaching patients some symptom removal methods has the effect of empowerment and helps the patient to feel back in control so that if symptoms are experienced they can be challenged at an early stage. Whilst not all headaches are due to stressful situations and (with migraine for example) may simply be due to dietary or alcohol indiscretion, the ability to use some self hypnosis techniques to assist symptoms is obviously a bonus. For example, techniques such as Stanton's hands (page 241) or firing a pre-state anchor (page 242) can be effective in aborting a migraine headache at the aura stage and can also be useful in resolving tension headaches.

Regardless of the technique, it is always necessary to consider the consequences of symptom removal. The following non-hypnosis case history acts as a useful reminder of the psychosocial consequences of symptoms.

Mrs Smith – a woman with migraine

Mrs Smith was a 38 year old mother of two boys aged ten and 13. She attended the GP for a review of her migraine medication which consisted of analgesia and anti-nausea tablets. During the consultation it transpired that every month, around period time, she developed a bad head and needed to spend most of two days in bed. This always seemed to happen at a weekend. The GP, horrified that the migraine was causing so much trouble, suggested trying a prophylactic treatment. This seemed to work and on review three months later she had not needed to spend time in bed.

A few months after that, it was noted that the husband and both sons had started to consult with comparatively trivial problems. At one such consultation the GP made a passing enquiry as to the health of the mother and got the reply, *"She has been awful ever since she started on those headache tablets!"*

It transpired that Mother did everything for the men in the family; she cleaned, shopped, cooked, ironed, packed their bags and did all the chores. This she managed happily but when the 'migraines' came on this gave her a valid reason to have a break and as Mum was ill the boys did the day to day chores. Thus, when the 'migraines' were stopped, the time honoured family dynamics had been completely disrupted. Mum was getting more and more stressed and angry, which was putting pressure on the 'boys' who were beginning to develop 'time out' symptoms of their own. As she had been migraine free for many months, it was suggested that Mum stopped these tablets and strangely she was very happy to comply with this suggestion!

Because of the relatively short term nature of headaches, secondary gain is often relatively easy to notice from the therapist's perspective but it requires the patient to take ownership of the concept before much progress can be made. All of us are aware of the use of symptoms to avoid events and situations exemplified by the time honoured *"Not tonight, Darling – I've got a headache!"* Such things often then lead to genuine anticipatory triggers of the 'undesired' symptom. One often hears phrases such as *"I so wanted to go to the party but I got a wretched migraine, I was so disappointed"* or *"We're so excited about going, I just hope I don't get a headache and spoil it all for everyone."*

The therapist must be aware that, without adequate explanation, the idea of secondary gain can equate to malingering and imaginary symptoms. The use of the illness model helps in this regard and such a model for migraines, as shown in Figure 19.3, might be discussed.

If, as the model is explained, it is stressed that the symptoms are the same regardless of which trigger switches the symptoms on, the patient can begin to identify with some of these situations which might cause their headaches to begin. Remember that history taking is also part of the therapy, and the skilled history taker can begin to elicit links with certain facets of behaviour that the patient has yet to appreciate, with questions along the lines of *"If you didn't have this problem, what difference would it make to your day to day life?"* or *"Would all of those differences be helpful?"* Sometimes these sorts of questions are best done under hypnosis and can be coupled with therapeutic contracts such as *"Is your subconscious mind ready to work with me to help sort out this problem?"*

It should be said, however, that long established secondary gain behaviour is one of the most difficult problems to break through. This is particularly so with patients who are in

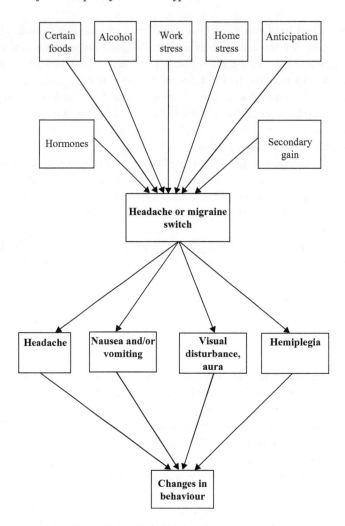

Figure 19.3   A model for the aetiology of migraine.

receipt of social benefits where their symptom is the very reason for their supporting income. In those situations the therapist is advised to give a guarded prognosis.

The therapist can make use of some symptoms especially where they are linked to stress. In these situations the symptom can be used as a signal to the patient that they are 'under attack' from their lifestyle. Thus the signal can be used as a warning that they need to slow down, reduce their hours or give up some of the jobs that they have taken on. Once the symptom is seen in a different light and has a positive use, it is often possible for the patient to modify the symptom to one which is less unpleasant as a symptom but still effective as a warning signal. The important thing with this approach is for the patient to obtain an agreement with their subconscious mind that once the stressor has been identified this is acknowledged and only then will the subconscious allow a modification of the symptom.

Methods to achieve this vary according to the patient's particular situation such as in the next case example.

John – a man with chronic headache

John was in his early 50s and worked as an IT trouble shooter for a large organization. He had a reputation for sorting out particularly difficult problems and so was always in demand. Whilst he enjoyed his job, the effect of the pressure and the long hours was taking its toll and he was getting more and more headaches and taking more and more analgesia with less and less effect. Under hypnosis he acknowledged the link between the stress and the headaches but wanted the hypnosis to help cope with the stress so he could continue with the same workload. He was afraid that if he slowed down, his job might be vulnerable; he knew there were redundancies being planned by the company and he did not want to be one of those selected.

The therapist always has an overall duty of care for their patients, and it was clearly inappropriate to let John plod on towards burnout. Following an explanation that performance drops off once stress levels reach a critical point, he agreed to use the headaches as a warning. Having discussed various options, whilst doing hypnosis he was asked to imagine he had gone into his control room and programmed his computer according to his plan. He had decided to turn up the sensitivity switch to the headaches to the point where he would become aware of the very first signs of the headache and, hence, the need to modify his activity at an early stage.

Once aware of the need and having made a plan he then was able to turn the headache down pending the carrying out of his plan. In reality much of his problem was that he would work long hours without eating or drinking. His plan, generally, was to stop working within half an hour of his headache coming on and have a tea or meal break. If he failed to do this, his headache would come back as bad as ever. He found that this helped not only his headaches but also his performance, which instead of declining actually improved.

Thus, the therapist needs to learn to work with the patient's symptoms rather than thinking of them as something that must be removed. It is always very helpful to get the patient to work out what they wish to do rather than trying to impose on them your own ideas. This rather sophisticated example is not intended as a blueprint to follow but simply to show the possibilities.

In cases where headaches seem to be triggered by specific situations, for example, where a patient always gets a headache the morning of a board meeting of if they have to give a presentation, it is important to focus on that as the problem rather than the headache. So the approach to the headache is via the trigger. As these problems are patient specific there is no such thing as a general therapy script for headaches. However general rules apply, and teaching relaxation and using ego strengthening, use of imagery and mental rehearsal are likely to be important components of most treatments.

Fibromyalgia

This interesting condition affects about 2% of the population (White & Harth, 2001) and is characterized by muscle pain and tenderness along with other associated symptoms. Women are nine times more likely to suffer from the syndrome compared to men and it is predominantly seen in the 20 to 50 year age group with a peak at around 35 years. It is sometimes seen in childhood. Whilst no genetic markers have been located there is a greater likelihood of family members being affected and the absence of biological markers has inevitably raised the question as to whether some of these symptoms and behaviours have been 'learnt'.

For a formal diagnosis to be made, pain has to have been present for at least three months and to have been present in all four quadrants of the body (i.e. above and below the waist and left and right sides). 18 trigger points have been designated, and 11 of these have to be tender at any one time in order to fulfil the criteria. Such rigid diagnostic criteria are largely unhelpful for the clinician who still has to deal with patients who have all the overall features of the disease but have, say, only eight tender points! Indeed, Wolfe (2003), an author of the original diagnostic criteria, now counsels strongly against its use.

In addition to the pain, weakness and fatigue (especially as seen in chronic fatigue type syndromes) are often reported and depression, anxiety, functional bowel disorders, interstitial cystitis and PTSD are all frequent co-morbidities. Indeed, Buskila and Cohen (2007) report that depression and anxiety are co-morbid in up to 80% and 63.5% of cases respectively. In common with those co-morbidities fibromyalgia patients are likely to have a significant burden of psychosocial 'life events' which may be wholly or partially responsible for the symptom complex and will certainly be important factors in the maintenance of the symptomatology. This is evidenced by Bennett *et al.* (2007) who conducted an internet based survey of 2,596 fibromyalgia patients. Virtually 80% reported some triggering event and of those 73% reported emotional trauma or chronic stress as being associated with the start of their symptoms. Emotional or physical abuse as a child was the trauma/stress for 20.6% (9% sexual abuse) with a further 15% reporting abuse as an adult as the onset event(s).

The same survey reported on factors which exacerbated their symptoms: emotional distress (83%), weather changes (80%), sleeping problems (79%), strenuous activity (70%), mental stress (68%), worrying (60%), car travel (57%), family conflicts (52%), physical injuries (50%) and physical inactivity (50%) were the most commonly reported.

Laboratory tests tend to be normal, fuelling the frustrations of the sufferers who are clearly experiencing genuine problems. Wood *et al.* (2007) using positron emission tomography (PET) techniques showed that fibromyalgic patients reported greater discomfort to a standardized painful stimulus compared with normal control subjects and failed to show any release of dopamine in the basal ganglia in response to that pain. In the controls dopamine release correlated with the reported level of pain.

Whilst this gives evidence of abnormal dopamine processing it remains unclear whether this is cause or effect. Indeed, Derbyshire *et al.* (2004) using fMRI techniques show that the pain 'neuromatrix' is activated as a result of the fibromyalgic pain experience and, further, that these activations can be modified (increased or decreased) following suggestion. These activations were greater when preceded by a hypnotic induction. It would be intriguing to know what happens to the dopamine release following these suggestions! Other neuro-imaging studies confirm differences in pain matrix activation or sensitivity in fibromyalgic patients (e.g. Gracely *et al.*, 2004), and whilst this may be the mechanism by which these patients experience the troublesome pain it does not help in the aetiology of the abnormal pain processing in the first place.

Given that most fibromyalgic patients can pinpoint a beginning to their symptoms it must be assumed that this abnormal processing occurred as a result of some triggering event or events. One interesting area of research would be to establish if 'cured' fibromyalgic patients retained their abnormal processing of pain or whether this abnormality resolved as their symptoms disappeared.

A model can be produced for fibromyalgia and is presented in Figure 19.4. Although, as with the other psychosomatic conditions discussed, treatments can be aimed at pure symptom relief, emphasis on both the causal and exacerbating factors is likely to result in better outcomes.

As with other psychosomatic conditions, hypnotherapy is well placed to help at many of the points in the model shown in Figure 19.4. Derbyshire *et al.* (2009) have shown that suggestions for pain reduction are more effective if given following a hypnotic induction, and provide evidence for its use at the analgesia level. Castel *et al.* (2007) had shown that hypnosis plus analgesic suggestions was better than hypnosis plus relaxation or relaxation alone in a randomly controlled trial of 45 patients with fibromyalgia. Haanen *et al.* (1991) compared hypnotherapy with physical therapy in 40 randomly allocated fibromyalgic patients. The hypnotherapy group showed a significant better outcome not only with respect to their pain experience but also on fatigue on awakening, sleep pattern and global assessment. This improvement was maintained at the three month follow up.

With such complex symptomatology and every patient having co-morbidities of varying types and severity, treatment sessions need to be based on the needs of the individual rather than any pre-planned regime. It is important for the therapist to bear in mind that with such a high proportion of reported abuse and trauma in this cohort it is essential to have skills in this area before starting therapy. Having said that, there are times when even the most experienced therapist comes across situations in therapy which they have not met before. In that situation there is no need to panic; it is always possible (under hypnosis) to explain to the patient that you will need to seek advice on dealing with that aspect of their problem and ask permission from their subconscious mind to park that problem on the back burner for attention at a later date. Equally, there may be times when discussion with your clinical supervisor will not be sufficient to provide you with the necessary skills, and in those situations it is necessary to refer on to another therapist who has the necessary expertise.

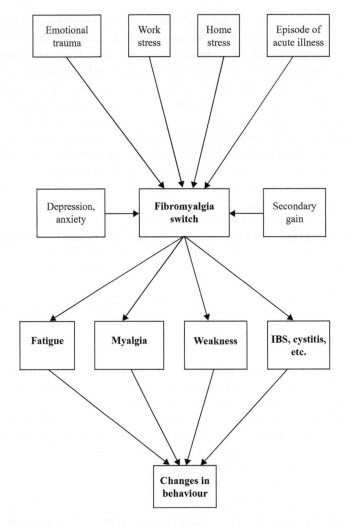

Figure 19.4   A model for the aetiology of fibromyalgia.

A complex case needs to be dealt with in stages, and the order in which the various symptoms are tackled must be left up to the patient. Audit tools such as Measure Yourself Medical Outcome Profile (MYMOP; see page 586) can give an idea as to the relative severity of the symptoms, but this may not necessarily be the order in which the patient wishes to deal with it. Frequently the patient needs a few sessions in which to feel comfortable with the therapist before they are prepared to even begin to look at some of the more horrific events that may have befallen them. Establishing rapport and showing empathy are clearly paramount, but patients do not want to be pitied. This is especially so in cases of childhood (sexual) abuse where patients have often developed a sense of being different, and being pitied just accentuates that feeling. They do not want to be treated differently once they have shared the information.

When explaining hypnosis, particularly to patients with this type of complex problem, it is important to make sure that they have understood that they do not lose control and do not just blurt out everything that is in their mind. They need to be reassured that they will only share the information when they are ready to. So, once hypnosis has been induced ask the patient to wander into their subconscious or control room or whatever metaphorical model you have used and get them to ask their mind where they wish to start. Sometimes there is simply too much and the enormity of their problem seems overwhelming; in such cases, encourage them to start explaining the situation at the time of the onset of the symptoms as this helps to break the ice and gets the therapeutic rapport on track.

Not all cases of fibromyalgia have an abusive past, and it is important not to go on searching as this can lead to the development of false memories. It sometimes seems as if fibromyalgia symptoms allow a patient not to 'feel' emotions and, as in the case below, therapy is directed primarily towards facilitating emotional release and resolution. Often the pain does not need to be specifically targeted. Dealing with the emotion allows the pain to settle of its own accord. Of course, if this has not been the case any of the specific pain-relieving techniques described in Chapter 21 could have been used.

Jennifer – a woman with fibromyalgia (courtesy of Dr A Williamson)

Jennifer was a woman of 56 who was 'known' as a heart sink or fat file patient. She recognized that her fibromyalgia worsened when she was stressed and so she presented for anxiety management. Upon taking a history it transpired that she had come from an unhappy home and married at 18 to escape. Over some years her husband had become an alcoholic and when her two daughters were teenagers she plucked up the courage to leave him. One girl was very angry with her and blamed her mother for the marital breakup. She refused to have anything to do with her mother and took every opportunity to embarrass and taunt her. When this daughter eventually had a child herself she would not allow Jennifer to see her grandchild. Around this time, unsurprisingly, Jennifer had started to have many different physical symptoms and an increasingly fat folder. She told her story without emotion and on being asked whether she felt angry she replied, *"My mother always told me that nice girls don't get angry."* Her fibromyalgia had started around two years before she came to see me and upon being questioned as to what was happening in her life around that time she replied that her other daughter had emigrated to Australia.

Therapy over six sessions consisted of various ways to facilitate Jennifer allowing herself to feel and express her negative emotions of anger, loss and rejection. Ego strengthening and imagery were used to help Jennifer come to terms with the traumas in her life. As she currently had a good supportive partner she worked well and improved very quickly. As she learnt to work with her emotions rather than suppressing them, her fibromyalgia also improved. Only part of one session of the six was utilized to teach Jennifer some ways she could help with her pain, and she made the decision to save up and visit her daughter the following year in Australia.

As a postscript, Jennifer came to see me two years after we had worked together complaining of backache. She quickly re-assured me that it was not a return of her fibromyalgia; she had been laying some flagstones in her back garden and had a bit of back strain!

A more detailed case study demonstrating the hypnotic treatment and resolution of fibromyalgia is described below.

Sharon – a fibromyalgia case study (courtesy of Mrs Karen Mackrodt)

Sharon was a 43 year old woman who had been diagnosed with fibromyalgia. She had been referred to the pain clinic because of escalating pain despite high doses of morphine. The history revealed that she was involved in litigation against a previous partner who had physically abused her. That abuse had triggered memories of abuse as a child, and she had become increasingly depressed and anxious. She also had symptoms of IBS, and her sleep pattern was very poor as she was constantly waking up at the slightest sounds. She was referred from the pain clinic for hypnotherapy.

She lived alone with her mother until the age of four. Then two children, a boy (12 years) and a girl (seven years), came to live with them. Until then she had believed she was an only child but soon learnt that these two children were her (half) brother and sister from her mother's previous relationship. Her mother began to ignore her and she remembers feeling lost, and this feeling was exacerbated because her brother began to sexually abuse her. The abuse was a regular occurrence which she endured until the age of 12 when she ran away from home and lived on the street. She had a number of relationships, married young, and had two children of her own. She later brought these up alone as she had left her alcoholic husband after he started physically abusing her. Following the marriage, she drifted in and out of relationships.

Following the explanation of the right and left hemispheres, she felt that all her life she had been pessimistic and right hemisphere reactions definitely ruled her world. She went into a deep hypnotic trance very quickly and found herself on a beach – she was able to see, smell, hear and taste the sea. She was allowed time to absorb the good feelings in her safe place before moving herself away to work on uncovering what was feeding her pain. The metaphor of the corridors in her mind was used and it was suggested she would find a storeroom where she had left something very precious. The door was locked, and she became agitated that she did not have the key. She found the key in her pocket after it had been suggested that it had been there all the time. Inside the room there was a bright light with someone behind it who she couldn't see. As she went further into the room she became frightened and could feel the fear of the person behind the light. As she got closer she saw it was a little girl of about five years old. She was asked to bring the little girl out of the room so she would be less frightened. She cuddled her and reassured her that things were going to be all right. She was asked where she wanted to take the little girl, and she offered to take her to the carnival. She began to smile and said the little girl was happy. After the hypnosis, she realized that the little girl was her and that she must have put her away to keep her safe but forgot to bring her back out and so had left her there. She felt a warm feeling and for the first time felt more connected.

She was seen again a week later and she said that she had felt happy for the first time in years. There had been lots of tears during the week, but they did not make her feel sad but were more a letting go of so many unshed tears during the years. She said that she had noticed her breathing had been better during the week and the tightness in her chest had gone. She had also been pain free for four days following the session. When asked how her sleep had been she said she had slept for longer periods than before.

Her special place this week was a field with trees bordering it. She was asked to spend time within the openness and then, when ready, to go towards the trees where she would find a gate. When she went through the gate she was surprised to see the little girl there. She described the little girl as happy and frivolous, skipping along beside her. She was asked to go towards the river but not so close as to frighten the little girl. Beside the river was an enormous boulder. The silent abreaction technique was used to enable her and the little girl to put things on that had never been said, pain, anger and frustration of years of fear. By allowing both the adult and the child to put things on she was able to remove thoughts and feelings specific to both ages. After this she was able to destroy the boulder with a huge sledge hammer. She then put the remains of the boulder in the river. After this exertion she and the little girl were asked to go to a huge tree where they could rest and sleep in peace. On wakening after a short time she was able to describe a place where the boulder had been as full of fragrant flowers. On returning to full wakefulness she was smiling and said she had felt really strong and powerful when smashing the boulder and felt more connected than ever to the little girl.

She was seen again two weeks later; she had had to cancel the previous week's session as her IBS had really been painful and debilitating. She was very positive about this - she felt that the day on the toilet was her body's way of getting rid of the toxins she had held in for so many years. Even though the previous two sessions had been difficult and tiring she had felt much happier and had noticed she was laughing at things she hadn't laughed at for a very long time. She was sleeping much better and had been able to reduce her morphine intake. She was more active and going for walks with her dog – something she had found difficult to do due to the pain. During this session we concentrated on helping her resolve more of her childhood hurts and she found a box containing many old photographs. She could only find one of herself as a child happy as all the others had been cut up by her sister. She removed all the unhappy and cut photos. With the cut photos she was able to magically glue them together and placed what she wanted to in frames and put them on the wall to see. On wakening she felt happy and rested.

Session 4 was more uncovering and connecting sessions. She found herself in a cave with a treasure chest deep within one of them. She was unable to open it as she had something heavy and breathing on her back. She became very animated and fearful, hyperventilating when describing this as if it was truly happening to her. Surrounding the chest were crystals, and she was able to pick one up and open the chest to find a beautiful blue object within. She was able to use this to remove the thing off her back. She took the object out of the cave with her and when she was in sunlight saw it was a ring. It was suggested that this ring represented her internal strength as it had overpowered the person on her back. She felt very happy until she saw 'him' on the beach and began to cry shouting for him to leave her alone. It was suggested she use the ring and her strength to banish him forever. After he had gone she noticed other people on the beach coming towards her. These were people who had once loved her and had made her feel special but who had been driven away or died. She felt more complete on wakening.

Session 5 was a lighter session where she made magic biscuits of all the good things she now possessed. She felt more alive and optimistic about getting through the trauma. She had noticed that her confidence levels had improved and she was meeting people and going to places which would otherwise have caused her dread. She had reduced her morphine to a lower level and felt good that she could reduce the strength and only take it when needed rather than all the time.

Her presenting problem had been pain and although this was never specifically discussed during the sessions, her pain levels improved each week. Her chest pain resolved as she was breathing more deeply rather than breath holding. By dealing with her emotional pain and feelings of inadequacy she felt more alive than she had ever remembered. She was happy for the first time in years and looking forwards, rather than always over her shoulder. As she had released her younger self from the protection/prison, she did not have to stay alert anymore and was sleeping through the night.

Psychogenic Arthralgia

This label is often used to describe joint pain when there is no discernable physical disease process. As each case is different there are no specific diagnostic criteria and it is used more as a description of a sub-group within the 'medically unexplained symptoms' category. Whilst there are no published trials of using hypnosis with such patients, there are case histories which show that this group is often very rewarding to work with.

Rachel – a woman with knee pain

During the early hours one morning the GP was called by Rachel's husband as she had severe knee pain. She was 27 years old and had been married for about 18 months. The GP had visited and found Rachel in bed complaining of pain in her left knee which was preventing her from sleeping. The pain had not responded to ordinary analgesics and a previous GP had been required to give her pethidine to settle the pain. She had been seen by a rheumatologist, and all tests were negative and a label of palindromic rheumatism given. Finding nothing on physical examination to account for the pain the GP explained that sometimes stressful or emotional things could cause such problems and offered to see her to discuss this aspect of her illness and the possible use of hypnotherapy to help the problem.

Following induction of hypnosis she was asked to imagine she had shrunk herself down so small that she was able to go inside her knee to see what the pain looked and felt like from inside. She said, *"It feels really tight and I feel trapped, I can't get out."* Exploring this further it transpired that she also felt trapped in her marriage and was very unhappy. She had met her husband a few years previously when they were working on a government project. The project was such that they had to live-in for most of the time and so they became friends and started going out together. As the project came to a close rather than let the relationship 'close' as well they drifted into marriage as *"It seemed the natural thing to do."* Her parents had been kind enough to assist them financially so they were able to buy a house of their own at the time of getting married and she felt indebted to her parents for this.

Unfortunately, the marriage had not been successful, and her husband seemed to have changed and no longer showed her any affection; indeed they had not had any sexual relationship since coming back from their honeymoon. She did not know what to do. She felt unable to end the marriage as her parents had been so kind to support them, and to do so, she felt, would be letting them down.

Under hypnosis an ideomotor signal was set up (see page 24) using the index finger of the right hand for 'Yes' and that of the left hand as 'No'. She was asked if this 'emotion' was the cause of her pain. She gave an unequivocal 'Yes' answer. She was then asked, *"As we now know the cause and the problem is there any need for the pain to continue?"* She replied, *"No."*

Her pain resolved and she felt able to discuss the situation with her parents, and, of course, they were supportive and she separated from her husband (amicably). Apart from a few occasional twinges she remained pain free until about two years later when her divorce absolute was about to go through. She booked another hypnosis appointment and we explored the onset of the pain and it followed her (ex) husband contacting her out of the blue asking if she was certain she wanted to go through with the divorce! This not only came as a complete surprise but also brought back the old memories and the pain. Once again the pain settled on the recognition of the stress.

She has been a patient for over 20 years and is now happily married with one son. She had one other flare-up which needed hypnotherapy and that was when she felt 'trapped' in an unhappy job; she had been made redundant from a post she loved but was rather forced to accept an alternative as she could not afford to be out of work. This time she recognized the trigger and had one session to help clear things from her mind.

This is yet another example of the unwanted symptom subsequently being used as an early warning of stress and used to the advantage of the patient.

This next case exemplifies the need to introduce emotional factors as a possible cause at an early stage in the management of the problem and how important it is to follow patients through to ensure any progress is maintained.

Katy – a girl with knee pain

At the age of 12, Katy developed a pain in her knee. She presented to the Accident and Emergency Department. Nothing significant was found on examination but she was referred on to see a rheumatologist who thought she may have an inflammatory monoarthritis although investigations could not confirm this. Her symptoms gradually deteriorated and by the time she was 14 she was using crutches and was admitted to hospital. No abnormality was found on clinical examination but she was further investigated with arthroscopy and MRI scan. These and other investigations were again essentially normal.

Each time the GP tried to introduce the idea that emotional factors might be involved, the specialists were arranging another investigation 'at the same time trying to reassure her'! Eventually, when she was nearly 16, she and her mother agreed to have some hypnosis. Having decided this was the correct course of action they felt they could not wait the four weeks for the routine NHS appointment and went to see a non-clinically qualified hypnotist.

She made a dramatic improvement and it was discovered that the 'cause' was related to her fear of cancer. A few years before a close family friend aged 17 had died with an osteosarcoma. This had started with a pain in the knee and initially it had not been possible to make the diagnosis. By the time the diagnosis was made, the cancer was beyond cure and her friend died. Understandably, Katy needed the reassurances given by each and every investigation.

Unfortunately, this improvement was only short lived and further hypnotherapy was arranged through her GP. During hypnosis she felt that her main problems were related to the death of her grandfather a few years before and a serious road traffic accident (RTA) that the family had had. Her grandfather had been a great friend and support and had helped to divert her from the ongoing hassle in the family following the RTA. In that accident her brother had received a serious head injury and had been unconscious for two days – the family had been told to expect the worse, but fortunately he made pretty well a complete recovery although the were some significant behavioural problems for a while afterwards.

She was asked to make a 'memorial room' in her mind for her grandfather somewhere she could picture herself and still enjoy the happy memories she had. For the RTA she used the older wiser self to update the emotions, and the memory was filed in her personal museum.

Apart from a few twinges, her knee pain had been much better after this first hypnosis session. In the second session she explored not only the origin of the knee pain but also the reasons why it had persisted. Home had been very difficult with her brother being very aggressive and bullying her mother and she had discovered that if her knee was bad the family focus was turned towards her and not the arguments and aggression. In order for the bullying to stop the knee pain needed to continue and so became a 'fixture' in her and the family's life. It was confirmed under hypnosis that there was no longer any need for the pain to continue and so she corrected her image of the painful knee by 'cleaning' it away. She has remained pain free following that and has become, much to her mother's chagrin, a normal stroppy teenager going out to clubs.

This case highlights the need to check whether all the factors involved in any symptom complex have been resolved. It is always very tempting when a significant cause has been identified to assume that the job is done! Indeed in most cases the job will have been done but it is important to check that there are not any other areas of fear or emotional baggage that need to be cleared before resolution is complete.

Chronic Fatigue Syndrome (CFS) or Myalgic Encephalitis (ME)

This is a condition that occurs predominantly in people who have not had a good work life balance and who tend to be over conscientious and driven and are often high achievers. As with most problems, it has a multi-factorial aetiology. Possible physical causes include genetic make-up and viral infections. These interplay with psychological factors such as anxiety, resilience and contextual factors such as the work environment and relationships (Afari & Buchwald, 2002).

20–70% of patients with fibromyalgia also meet the criteria for chronic fatigue syndrome (White *et al.*, 2000). Compared to a prevalence of 0.03% for somatization disorder in the community, the prevalence in chronic fatigue syndrome is high, with rates up to 28% (Johnson *et al.*, 1996). Levels of anxiety disorder and depression are also higher within this group of patients compared to the general population (Fischler *et al.*, 1997; Hudson *et al.*, 1992).

CFS or ME is characterized by profound fatigue and lengthy recovery times following exertion. Clumsiness, memory problems and poor concentration are also commonly found. Onset is usually fairly sudden, often following some viral infection. Beliefs that their illness has a purely physical causation are commonly found among sufferers and may exacerbate the illness and lead to greater disability (Butler *et al.*, 2001). Sometimes elements of hypochondriasis may be present and need to be recognized (Manu *et al.*, 1996).

Many of these patients are poor at pacing themselves, and as soon as they have a better day they over exercise and then feel much worse for several days afterwards. A large number of patients with chronic fatigue use maladaptive strategies such as avoidance

(Ray *et al.*, 1997), and graded exercise programs and cognitive-behavioural therapy have both shown promise in improving the outcome of chronic fatigue syndrome (Deale *et al.*, 2001). It has already been demonstrated that hypnosis facilitates good outcomes when combined with CBT (Kirsch *et al.*, 1995). The evidence base for the use of hypnosis in the treatment of anxiety and depression can be found in the relevant chapters, and there is good case study evidence that hypnosis can be a useful tool in the treatment of CFS (Hammond, 2001).

As with all illness hypnosis can help, not only with any underlying psychological factors but also with the physical symptoms. In this author's (AW) experience, regular self hypnosis together with suggestions of energy are often helpful.

Elizabeth – a teacher with ME (Courtesy of Dr A Williamson)

Elizabeth was a teacher who had suffered from ME for several years but was keen to see if hypnosis could help her. She was highly hypnotizable and quickly found that she was able to boost her energy levels by using imagery in hypnosis. She used 'the control centre' in her brain to set appropriate levels of energy, and also imagined surfing, gathering up the energy of the waves as she did so. Each day she 'connected with healing energy' when doing her self-hypnosis which she imagined as golden light flowing down, in and around her body. Over several sessions she resolved various issues that had arisen from her childhood, the major one of which was the feeling that her father did not think she was 'good enough'. She was encouraged to set realistic goals and rehearse them in hypnosis to check that they seemed intuitively right for her. She improved greatly over the following six months.

Thus hypnosis may be helpful for all psychosomatic disorders through its ability to relieve symptoms as well as identifying and resolving issues that underpin the symptoms. Hypnosis may also help in improving the patient's self esteem and coping abilities thereby increasing their sense of control and competency.

References

Afari, N. & Buchwald, D. (2003), Chronic fatigue syndrome: a review. *American Journal of Psychiatry*, 160, 221–36.

Alladin, A. (1988), Hypnosis in the treatment of severe chronic migraine, in Heap, M. (Ed.) *Hypnosis: current clinical, experimental and forensic practices*. London, Croom Helm.

Anderson, J. A. D., Basker, M. A. & Dalton, R. (1975), Migraine and hypnotherapy. *International Journal of Clinical and Experimental Hypnosis*, 23, 48–58.

Bennett, R., Jones, J., Turk, D., Russell, I. J. & Matallana, L. (2007), An internet survey of 2,596 people with fibromyalgia. *BMC Musculoskeletal Disorders*, 8, 27.

Brann, L. (2009), personal communication.

Buskila, D. & Cohen, H. (2007), Comorbidity of fibromyalgia and psychiatric disorders. *Current Pain and Headache Reports*, 11, 333–8.

Butler, J. A., Chalder, T. & Wessely, S. (2001), Causal attributions for somatic sensations in patients with chronic fatigue syndrome and their partners. *Psychological Medicine*, 31, 97–105.

Castel, A., Pérez, M., Sala, J., Padrol, A. & Rull, M. (2007), Effect of hypnotic suggestion on fibromyalgic pain: comparison between hypnosis and relaxation. *European Journal of Pain*, 11, 463–8.

Creed, F., Ratcliffe, J. O. Y., Fernandes, L., Palmer, S., Rigby, C., Tomenson, B., Guthrie, E., Read, N., Thompson, D. G. & North of England I.B.S. Research Group. (2005), Outcome in severe irritable bowel syndrome with and without accompanying depressive, panic and neurasthenic disorders. *The British Journal of Psychiatry*, 186, 507–15.

Deale, A., Husain, K., Chalder, T. & Wessely, S. (2001), Long-term outcome of cognitive behavior therapy versus relaxation therapy for chronic fatigue syndrome: a 5-year follow-up study. *American Journal of Psychiatry*, 158, 2038–42.

Delvaux, M., Denis, P. & Allemand, H. (1997), Sexual abuse is more frequently reported by IBS patients than by patients with organic digestive diseases or controls: Results of a multicentre inquiry. *European Journal of Gastroenterology & Hepatology*, 9, 327–30.

Derbyshire, S. W. G., Whalley, M. G., Stenger, V. A. & Oakley, D. A. (2004), Cerebral activation during hypnotically induced and imagined pain. *NeuroImage*, 23, 392–401.

Derbyshire, S. W., Whalley, M. G. & Oakley, D. A. (2009), Fibromyalgia pain and its modulation by hypnotic and non-hypnotic suggestion: an fMRI analysis. *European Journal of Pain*, 13, 542–50.

Drossman, D. A., Leserman, J., Nachman, G., Li, Z., Gluck, H., Toomey, T. C. & Mitchell, C. M. (1990), Sexual and physical abuse in women with functional or organic gastrointestinal disorders. *Annals of Internal Medicine*, 113, 828–33.

Emmerson, G. & Trexler, G. (1999), A hypnotic intervention for migraine control. *Australian Journal of Clinical and Experimental Hypnosis*, 27, 54–61.

Fischera, M., Marziniak, M., Gralow, I. & Evers, S. (2008), The incidence and prevalence of cluster headache: a meta-analysis of population-based studies. *Cephalalgia*, 28, 614–18.

Fischler, B., Cluydts, R., Degucht, V., Kaufman, L. & Demeirleir, K. (1997), Generalized anxiety disorder in chronic fatigue syndrome. *Acta Psychiatrica Scandinaviva*, 95, 405–13.

Forbes, A., Macauley, S. & Chiotakakou-Faliakou, E. (2000), Hypnotherapy and therapeutic audiotape: effective in previously unsuccessfully treated irritable bowel syndrome? *International Journal of Colorectal Disease*, 15, 328–34.

Friedman, H. & Taub, H. (1985), Extended follow-up study of the effects of brief psychological procedures in migraine therapy. *American Journal of Clinical Hypnosis*, 28, 27–33.

Fumal, A. & Schoenen, J. (2008), Tension-type headache: current research and clinical management. *The Lancet Neurology*, 7, 70–83.

Galovski, T. E. & Blanchard, E. B. (1998), The treatment of irritable bowel syndrome with hypnotherapy. *Applied Psychophysiology and Biofeedback*, 23, 219–32.

Gerth, W. C., Carides, G. W., Dasbach, E. J., Visser, W. H. & Santanello, N. C. (2001), The multinational impact of migraine symptoms on healthcare utilisation and work loss. *Pharmaco Economics*, 19, 197–206.

Goadsby, P. J. (2005), Migraine pathophysiology. *Headache: The Journal of Head and Face Pain*, 45, S14–S24.

Gonsalkorale, W. M., Houghton, L. A. & Whorwell, P. J. (2002), Hypnotherapy in irritable bowel syndrome: a large-scale audit of a clinical service with examination of factors influencing responsiveness. *The American Journal of Gastroenterology*, 97, 954–61.

Gracely, R. H., Geisser, M. E., Giesecke, T., Grant, M. A. B., Petzke, F., Williams, D. A. & Clauw, D. J. (2004), Pain catastrophizing and neural responses to pain among persons with fibromyalgia. *Brain*, 127, 835–43.

Haanen, H., Hoenderdos, H., Van Romunde, L., Hop, W., Mallee, C., Terwiel, J. & Hekster, G. (1991), Controlled trial of hypnotherapy in the treatment of refractory fibromyalgia. *Journal of rheumatology*, 18, 72–75.

Hammond, D. C. (2001), Treatment of chronic fatigue with neurofeedback and self-hypnosis. *Neurorehabilitation*, 16 (4), 295–300.

Hammond, D. C. (2007), Review of the efficacy of clinical hypnosis with headaches and migraines. *International Journal of Clinical and Experimental Hypnosis*, 55, 207–19.

Harvey, R., Hinton, R., Gunary, R. & Barry, R. (1989), Individual and group hypnotherapy in treatment of refractory irritable bowel syndrome. *The Lancet*, 333 (8635), 424–5.

Heap, M. & Aravind, K. (2002), *Hartland's medical and dental hypnosis*. Hong Kong, Churchill Livingstone.

Houghton, L. A., Heyman, D. J. & Whorwell, P. J. (1996), Symptomatology, quality of life and economic features of irritable bowel syndrome – the effect of hypnotherapy. *Alimentary Pharmacology & Therapeutics*, 10, 91–5.

Hudson, J. I., Goldenberg, D. L., Pope, H. G., Keck, P. E. & Schlesinger, L. (1992), Comorbidity of fibromyalgia with medical and psychiatric disorders. *American Journal of Medicine*. 92, 363–7.

International Headache Society. (2005), *The international classification of headache disorders (ICHD-II)*. London, International Headache Society.

Johnson, S. K., Deluca, J. & Natelson, B. H. (1996), Assessing somatization disorder in the chronic fatigue syndrome. *Psychosomatic Medicine*, 58, 50–7.

Kirsch, I., Montgomery, G. & Sapirstein, G. (1995), Hypnosis as an adjunct to cognitive behavioral psychotherapy: a meta-analysis. *Journal of Consulting and Clinical Psychology*, 63, 214–20.

Lea, R., Houghton, L. A., Calvert, E. L., Larder, S., Gonsalkorale, W. M., Whelan, V., Randles, J., Cooper, P., Cruickshanks, P., Miller, V. & Whorwell, P. J. (2003), Gut-focused hypnotherapy normalizes disordered rectal sensitivity in patients with irritable bowel syndrome. *Alimentary Pharmacology & Therapeutics*, 17, 635–42.

Longstreth, G. F., Thompson, W. G., Chey, W. D., Houghton, L. A., Mearin, F. & Spiller, R. C. (2006), Functional Bowel Disorders. *Gastroenterology*, 130, 1480–91.

Manu, P., Affleck, G., Tennen, H., Morse, P. A., Escobar, J. I. (1996), Hypochondriasis influences quality-of-life outcomes in patients with chronic fatigue syndrome. *Psychotherapy and Psychosomatics*, 65, 76–81.

May, A. (2005), Cluster headache: pathogenesis, diagnosis, and management. *The Lancet*, 366, 843–55.

Melis, P. M., Rooimans, W., Spierings, E. L. & Hoogduin, C. A. (1991), Treatment of chronic tension-type headache with hypnotherapy: a single-blind time controlled study. *Headache: The Journal of Head and Face Pain*, 31, 686–9.

MeReC. (1997), The management of migraine. *MeReC Bulletin*, 13 (2), 5–8.

National Institute for Clinical Excellence. (2008), CG61 Irritable bowel syndrome in adults: Diagnosis and management of irritable bowel syndrome in primary care.

Palsson, O., Turner, M., Johnson, D., Burnett, C. & Whitehead, W. (2002), Hypnosis treatment for severe irritable bowel syndrome: investigation of mechanism and effects on symptoms. *Digestive Diseases and Sciences*, 47, 2605–14.

Prior, A., Colgan, S. M. & Whorwell, P. J. (1990), Changes in rectal sensitivity after hypnotherapy in patients with irritable bowel syndrome. *Gut*, 31, 896–8.

Ray, C., Jeffries, S. & Weir, W. R. (1997), Coping and other predictors of outcome in chronic fatigue syndrome: a 1-year follow-up. *Journal of Psychosomatic Medicine*, 43, 405–15.

Roberts, L., Wilson, S., Singh, S., Roalfe, A. & Greenfield, S. (2006), Gut-directed hypnotherapy for irritable bowel syndrome: piloting a primary care-based randomized controlled trial. *British Journal of General Practice*, 6, 115–21.

Russell, M. (2005), Tension–type headache in 40–year-olds: a Danish population–based sample of 4000. *The Journal of Headache and Pain*, 6, 441–7.

Spanos, N. P., Liddy, S. J., Scott, H., Garrard, C., Sine, J., Tirabasso, A. & Hayward, A. (1993), Hypnotic suggestion and placebo for the treatment of chronic headache in a university volunteer sample. *Cognitive Therapy and Research*, 17, 191–205.

Spiller, R. C. (2003), Postinfectious irritable bowel syndrome. *Gastroenterology*, 124, 1662–71.

Spinhoven, P., Linssen, A. C. G., Van Dyck, R. & Zitman, F. G. (1992), Autogenic training and self-hypnosis in the control of tension headache. *General Hospital Psychiatry*, 14, 408–15.

Stovner, L. J., Zwart, J. A., Hagen, K., Terwindt, G. M. & Pascual, J. (2006), Epidemiology of headache in Europe. *European Journal of Neurology*, 13, 333–45.

Talley, N. J., Boyce, P. M. & Jones, M. (1998), Is the association between irritable bowel syndrome and abuse explained by neuroticism? A population based study. *Gut*, 42, 47–53.

ter Kuile, M. M., Spinhoven, P., Linssen, A. C. G., Zitman, F. G., Van Dyck, R. & Rooijmans, H. G. M. (1994), Autogenic training and cognitive self-hypnosis for the treatment of recurrent headaches in three different subject groups. *Pain*, 58, 331–40.

Waldenlind, E. & Goadsby, P. J. (2006), Synthesis of cluster headache pathophysiology, in Olsesen, J., Goadsby, P. J., Tfelt-Hansen, P. & Welch, K. (Eds.) *The headaches*. Philadelphia, Lippincott Williams and Wilkins.

Weber, F. & McCallum, R. (1992), Clinical approaches to irritable bowel syndrome. *The Lancet*, 340, 1447–52.

White, K. & Harth, M. (2001), Classification, epidemiology, and natural history of fibromyalgia. *Current Pain and Headache Reports*, 5, 320–9.

White, K. P., Speechley, M., Harth, M. & Ostbye, T. (2000), Co-existence of chronic fatigue syndrome with fibromyalgia syndrome in the general population – a controlled study. *Scandinavian Journal of Rheumatology*, 29, 44–51.

Whitehead, W. E., Palsson, O. & Jones, K. R. (2002), Systematic review of the comorbidity of irritable bowel syndrome with other disorders: What are the causes and implications? *Gastroenterology*, 122, 1140–56.

Wolfe, F. (2003), Stop using the American College of Rheumatology criteria in the clinic. *The Journal of Rheumatology*, 30, 1671–2.

Whorwell, P. J., McCallum, M., Creed, F. H. & Roberts, C. T. (1986), Non-colonic features of irritable bowel syndrome. *Gut*, 27, 37–40.

Whorwell, P. J., Houghton, L. A., Taylor, E. E. & Maxton, D. G. (1992), Physiological effects of emotion: assessment via hypnosis. *The Lancet*, 340, 69–72.

Whorwell P. J., Prior, A., & Faragher, E. B. (1984), Controlled trial of hypnotherapy in the treatment of severe refractory irritable bowel syndrome. *The Lancet*, 324, 1232–4.

Whorwell, P., Prior, A. & Colgan, S. (1987), Hypnotherapy in severe irritable bowel syndrome: further experience. *Gut*, 28, 423–5.

Wood, P. B., Schweinhardt, P., Jaeger, E., Dagher, A., Hakyemez, H., Rabiner, E. A., Bushnell, M. C. & Chizh, B. A. (2007), Fibromyalgia patients show an abnormal dopamine response to pain. *European Journal of Neuroscience*, 25, 3576–82.

Van Dyck, R., Zitman, F. G., Corry, A., Linssen, G. & Spinhoven, P. (1991), Autogenic training and future oriented hypnotic imagery in the treatment of tension headache: outcome and process. *International Journal of Clinical and Experimental Hypnosis*, 39, 6–23.

Zitman, F. G., Van Dyck, R., Spinhoven, P. & Linssen, A. C. G. (1992), Hypnosis and autogenic training in the treatment of tension headaches: a two-phase constructive design study with follow-up. *Journal of Psychosomatic Research*, 36, 219–28.

20

Dermatology

Dr Mhairi McKenna

with contributions by Dr Ann Williamson

Introduction

Skin problems are the ultimate in psychosomatic disease, as can be pointed out to any patient, for we know the brain and the skin have developed from the same cells in the embryo, the primitive ectoderm. The brain has many cell types in common with the skin such as melanocytes. This fact can be used to great effect when you are introducing hypnosis to your patient, demonstrating that emotions can have an effect on the skin; embarrassment can cause your skin to flush and an MRI scan of the brain done at the same time can show it, too, to be 'blushing'! Or the emotions of fear can cause pallor, or excitement can cause a flush. Add to this our knowledge that hypnosis can regulate blood flow and other autonomic functions which are not normally considered to be under voluntary control and that it has been shown that hypnosis can manipulate the immunological parameters of the body via the hypothalamus and limbic system (Rossi, 1993).

Published Evidence

There are a variety of reports in the research papers which indicate we can have some control over our immunoglobulins: Jasnoski and Kugler (1987) noted a decrease in salivary secretion of immunoglobulin A (IgA) with increased stress, and Olness *et al.* (1989)

The Handbook of Contemporary Clinical Hypnosis: Theory and Practice, First Edition.
Edited by Les Brann, Jacky Owens and Ann Williamson.
© 2012 John Wiley & Sons, Ltd. Published 2015 by John Wiley & Sons, Ltd.

worked with children showing they can be trained to manipulate the levels of IgA in their saliva.

Over the years there have been many papers which indicate that hypnosis is of use for skin patients even if only utilized for stress management.

Hypnosis has been used in several reported studies to reduce hypersensitivity reactions (Laidlaw *et al.*, 1994; Zachariae & Bjerring, 1993). Shertzer and Lookingbill (1987) reported on 15 patients with chronic urticaria of 7.8 years' average duration. By 14 months, six patients had resolved and another eight improved, with decreased medication requirements reported by 80% of patients.

Although the published evidence is mainly case study based, there are many reports of hypnosis being successfully used in ichthyosiform erythroderma, neurodermatitis, verrucae and warts (Felt *et al.*, 1998; Goldstein, 2005; Lehman, 1978; Schneck, 1954). Ewin (1992) describes the successful use of hypnosis in 33 out of 41 consecutive cases of warts.

Hollander (1959) reported success in controlling acne excoriée in two patients by using post-hypnotic suggestion. Under hypnosis, the patient was instructed to remember the word 'scar' whenever she wanted to pick her face and to refrain from picking by saying 'scar' instead. The excoriations resolved, although the underlying acne remained. Shenefelt (2004) also reports on using hypnosis for this condition.

Hypnosis has also been used effectively in the treatment of eczema (Mantle, 2001). Stewart and Thomas (1995) reported on 18 adults with extensive atopic dermatitis, resistant to conventional treatment, who were treated by hypnotherapy, with statistically significant benefit ($p < 0.01\%$) measured both subjectively and objectively, which was maintained at a two year follow up. Twenty children with severe, resistant atopic dermatitis were also treated with hypnosis. All but one showed immediate improvement. In 12 children, replies to a questionnaire at up to 18 months after treatment showed that ten had maintained improvement in itching and scratching, nine in sleep disturbance, and seven in mood. As well as suggestions for relaxation and stress management, direct and post-hypnotic suggestion for comfort and coolness, ego strengthening and self hypnosis was taught.

As well as case reports, Tausk and Whitmore (1999) conducted a small, randomized double-blind controlled trial using hypnosis as adjunctive therapy in psoriasis, which showed significant improvement in the more highly hypnotizable patients. Hypnotherapy has also been used, not only to lower stress levels but also to resolve underlying psychological difficulties in psoriatic patients (Kantor, 1990; Zachariae *et al.*, 1996). Often as well as direct suggestions of soothing and cooling, therapy needs to include hypnoanalysis including ideomotor questioning and reframing (Iglesias, 2005).

The attitude that hypnosis is a last resort has led to hypnotherapy being one of the least used therapies in dermatological practice, as was confirmed by a review of *Hypnosis in Dermatology* by Philip D Shenefelt (2000). The author also states in this article that 'in selected skin diseases, in appropriately selected patients, it can decrease or eliminate symptoms and, in some cases, induce lasting remissions or cures. . . . With proper selection of disease process, patient and provider, hypnosis can decrease suffering and morbidity from skin disorders with minimal adverse effects' (Shenefelt, 2003 p15).

It would seem very logical to use hypnosis with dermatological problems if it is remembered that atopic dermatitis and eczema are associated with an increase in immunoglobin E (IgE) and of cytokines in the skin. IgE increases with stress so if hypnosis is taught together with relaxation imagery or with specific instructions to reduce the IgE, the cytokines are reduced and the eczema improves.

Patients in dermatology out-patients tend to have more psychological disturbance than in many of the other out-patient clinics. In fact the first consultant dermatologist for whom this author (MK) worked was married to a consultant psychiatrist, and they agreed that there was more psychological morbidity in his 'skin out-patients' than in her psychiatric out-patients.

Society judges people by their looks, and foremost in that is our skin. In recent times society has put greater and greater emphasis on young, unlined, unblemished skin, which is basically a pre-pubertal skin. If you doubt this, just watch the advertisements on the television or in the magazines. It used to be only females who were inundated with such messages, but now it is also males who are meant to have smooth, hairless and odourless skin. For most of us this is a mythical skin; many of us have a problem, being less than happy with lines, black bags under our eyes, and the occasional pimple. Is it any wonder that patients (and maybe also their parents), who have dermatological problems such as eczema, psoriasis, warts, birthmarks, vitiligo, alopecia areata and acne, have psychological problems, maybe even a 'leper complex'?

Counselling can help, but how many patients have access to this? They are more likely to be told, *"It's only a rash, it won't kill you,"* or worse, *"You will have to learn to live with it."* This is cold comfort, especially as the latter is sub-consciously indicating it will not get better unless they die. In fact one of the most generous gestures anyone can make is to touch the patient, and show acceptance of them as they are, before starting to work with them. This can be as simple as shaking someone's hand and making eye contact.

Alternatively consider the situation of new parents, whose child inherits an atopic skin; instead of a smooth skinned baby who can be settled, they have an irritable baby who cries incessantly and tears their itchy skin to bits. The child may be helped by offering emollients to grease the skin and a variety of chemicals (often messy!) to help the dry eczematous skin; but it can be very useful to teach non-verbal hypnoidal techniques to the parents to use with their off-spring. It can be especially helpful to offer hypnotic ego strengthening and stress management to the parents, to counteract the feeling of failure and helplessness. Applying emollients can cause itching, especially if 'rubbed in well' as so often advised; maybe a gentle smoothing applies the emollient just as effectively, and is a suitable non-verbal cue to calm the child and the skin.

Once the child is older the use of hypnosis can be offered in the form of bedtime stories, or favourite television shows with the child taking part. Again ego strengthening is of great importance as the child is often excluded by their peers when they realize they are different, and 'messy activities' such playing with Playdoh, painting or even going swimming can lead to deterioration in the condition of their skin.

Psoriasis is often present in childhood, developing as the Guttate variation after a viral infection of the throat; fortunately this is often easily treated with ultraviolet B (UVB) radiation, but there is the problem of avoiding the leper complex in the child and the feeling of blame in the parents, as there is usually a strong family history (not to mention the fear of parents exposing their children to the UVB). Stress plays an important role in this scenario and as the patient grows and develops, all the problems of adolescence are exacerbated by the skin complaint; but hypnosis can be used to give better control over their skin and disease.

Blemishes, especially in babies, are always a trauma to their parents and hypnoidal work with the parents of a child with a strawberry naevus during the time it takes to resolve, often over several years, can save a great deal of anguish to all involved. In the case of a child with a port-wine birth-mark, such work with the parents can buy you time so that any laser therapy can be done when the child is older under hypnotic analgesia rather than a general anaesthetic with its attendant risks.

However, quite a few patients with skin problems are referred from colleagues, having been labelled difficult cases and where hypnosis appears at the bottom of a list. This often includes dapsone, systemic steroids, ultraviolet (UV) light with varying chemicals taken or applied to increase the effect of the UVA or UVB, and thalidomide, all with many side effects, some lethal. This can be something that has to be reframed, so that it will not hinder any therapy. A useful ploy is to tell the patient that they are a special case and we are going to give them more control over their symptoms.

Most dermatology patients fall into the category of basically normal people, responding to an organic illness. This is very obvious in the presenting symptomatology that leads to withdrawal behaviour, depression and in some cases self damage or even suicide. However there is also a very different group, body dysmorphic disorder sufferers, those with delusional beliefs about their body image, where small inconspicuous lesions are magnified in their imagination into being grotesque and disfiguring. Cotterill (1981) first called this 'dermatological non-disease' in that no skin abnormality can be found, but even so the distress felt by the patient can lead to great anxiety, depression, and sometimes to so much anger that murder or suicide occurs (Cotterill & Cunliffe, 1997). Usually these patients will not believe that nothing is wrong; it is because of the doctor's lack of skill that nothing can be found. In some cases they are suffering from a mono-symptomatic hypochondrial psychosis such as delusions of parasites. Unless the health professional has great experience in psychiatry and hypnosis, it is not advisable to attempt to treat these patients.

However, there is another group of patients within this group, who have no obvious skin disease, and who can often be helped by hypnosis, if they can be persuaded to use it. Those are individuals who complain of pain, itching or burning of their anal area, vulva or mouth or face, exacerbated by stress, and often these individuals and their families are being greatly inconvenienced by their symptoms. It is important to take a full history, as this may be the first time anyone has shown an interest. Examine them, touch them and listen to them, especially when the answer does not seem to be appropriate to the question, it may be literal and give an indication of some underlying unconscious difficulty. When you hear organ language, asking questions such as *"Who is the pain in the ass?"* *"Who or what has got under your skin?"* *"What can you not face?"* or *"Who or what is irritating you?"* will often give you an answer that is the lever you need to start therapy (see chapter 20).

Then it is a good idea to check whether there are likely to be any secondary gains which could hinder the resolution of the symptoms: *"What does this prevent you from doing?"* and *"What would you do if you had not got it?"* A couple more questions which have always been of great use are "*Would you accept an improvement?*" and *"Will you work with me?"* These give you a good idea of your patient's expectations. Other techniques which can also help are to ascertain what was happening just before the symptoms started, and also to give them a posthypnotic anchor for comfort.

Another group of patients who present with horrendous lesions, dermatitis artefacta, which heal under occlusive dressings because the lesions are being caused by the patient themselves, can often be helped by therapy which includes hypnosis. Again there is the problem that the patients deny causing the damage and direct confrontation has little benefit, so hypnosis has to be introduced as a therapy to help in the healing. Some of the sufferers have relatively superficial psychological problems and respond very well, but here is a wide spectrum and some of the artefacts can be part of a long psychiatric illness.

Some patients have benefited markedly from hypnosis, and are often willing to use it, as they have 'insight' to the fact that they are making things much worse even if not admitting to causing the problem. Often the person who attends with neurotic excoriations is a woman, and the area under attack is the nape of her neck, or shoulders and arms. By giving options and control, maybe turning down the itch, or exploring whether something or someone is getting under their skin, then using ego strengthening so that they can face up to the problem and deal with it, rather than attacking their skin, can be very helpful.

Adolescents with acne tend to squeeze and pick the individual lesions making them much more obvious and more likely to scar. Ego strengthening gives increased awareness of their behaviour and a choice of refraining from picking or finding another less damaging behaviour. The question *"Who is getting under your skin?"* asked under hypnosis gives them permission to mention the unmentionable. Recent research has shown these patients with acne excoriée tend to have an atopic tendency, and any technique that can reduce the sensitivity of the skin helps.

It should be remembered that when people are stressed they slip into a trance, such as when attending an out-patient appointment, or even going to see their GP. So, if they are in a hypnotic state, why not utilize it effectively?

Our aims are:

1 *Relaxation*: Sometimes using progressive relaxation as part of the induction can help calm patients with irritability (eczema) and with fear (coming for biopsy of a lesion), and especially with the latter, careful use of words can work miracles.

2 *Ease in communication*:

   a Between doctor and patient
   b Interpretation of ideas and re-education with a review of problems and cognitive restructuring at a conscious and subconscious level

   Patients may need help to view their difficulties as 'challenges rather than threats', to convert symptom meaning into a signal and then maybe to use reframing (see page 442). The patient may have already noticed a change in the intensity of the rash either when more relaxed or after a hypnosis session so this can be utilized.

3 *Reduction/cessation in symptoms*: This can be done with ego strengthening. Hartland observed that there were two groups of psychological reaction to illness:

a   The consequence of the illness

b   That arising from a defect in personality, such as lack of confidence; Hartland used ego strengthening with direct symptom removal where success bred success (Waxman, 1989).

Other methods of ego strengthening could also be used such as Stein's clenched fist (Stein, 1963) (see page 146), and 'power at your fingertips' (anchoring see page 147). Another method is to ask the patient to generate their own imagery of a scrap book filled with pictures that gives them a feeling of confidence, comfort and strength. They then step into the pictures and feel the comfort and maybe coolness associated with the image (Graham, 1987).

4   *Patient generated imagery*: The patient is asked to imagine going into their skin and then beginning to change what they see and feel in a way that seems intuitively right for them in order to ease their symptoms.

5   *As an adjunct to conventional therapy*: This can be done by direct suggestions:
   * Coolness, warmth, ease, time distortion
   * Increased effectiveness of a therapy
   * Positive future pacing — such as imagining looking into a crystal ball (O'Hanlon & Heum, 1990), age progression such as meeting the healed future self and looking back towards the present (Napier, 1996)
   * Visualization and treatment such as going through the screen into the computer to re-wire and adjust all the sensitivities; bathing in a magic pool of the 3 Cs (cool, calm and comfort) and seeing a film of cool, calm and comfort on their skin which can remain until the next time they enter their pool; using a magic healing ointment and going into a control room and adjusting the control for inflammation or immune response
   * Using metaphors such as the thin skinned dinosaur who had a family very similar to the child's own, the story involving sorting out the chaotic home life by telling the story with the family in the room (Stewart and Thomas, 1995)

6   *Reduction in procedural anxiety*: Obtained by using hypnosis to achieve fear control and stress management; routine procedures are easier and patients empowered to help themselves. This is done with many of the interventions mentioned; experiencing more control, altering perceptions, taking time out and other methods for help with procedural anxiety as described in chapter 22.

7   *Analytical investigation*: A useful way is to explore the seven classical causes of psychosomatic disorder (Ewin & Eimer, 2006) (see page 236) which often underpin dermatological conditions. Reframing can sometimes be done (see page 442) and maybe negotiating to keep a small patch of (for example) psoriasis somewhere out of sight rather than having 100% resolution.

8   *Self-hypnosis and education*: ALL hypnosis is self-hypnosis, a natural condition we can utilize. Some use biofeedback monitors that have the benefits that it may take less therapist time if it is available, there is less risk of transference and, best of all, the patient is given an increased awareness of their autonomy. The patient can also be taught a trigger word, symbol or scene to access the hypnotic state at will. The advantages are:

a   Decrease in dependence
b   Increase in mastery and independence
c   Increase in responsibility for their own therapy
d   Increase in the therapeutic dose between sessions
e   Decrease in transference
f   Can be keyed into specific situations
   The disadvantage is that it needs motivation on the part of the patient.

9   *Post-hypnotic suggestion*: A suggestion given at the time with the intent that it will be acted upon later or with a cue such as with anchoring. This may be used to facilitate the patient's own use of hypnosis.

At their next appointment a very potent indicator as to whether all the secondary gains have been addressed is whether they have found time for practice. If not, this needs to be explored; if they have, they are part way to being healed and empowered.

Working with Children

Let us start with children... because they are such lovely hypnotic subjects and hopefully self damaging habits can be broken before they become engrained into their behaviour. Often it does not matter whether it is an inherited tendency such as with eczema or psoriasis, or a habit such as trichotillomania; they all worsen if the child is stressed.

The child needs to be given a method to regain control; this varies according to age. A favourite technique is to use their fairy tale/cartoon hero to protect them, befriend them or teach them new ways of responding.

An example:

A little boy of five (Paul) had extensive eczema over all his limbs and his torso and most of the time he had to use occlusive dressings. On this particular day, as his body was being dressed by the nurses, we started discussing the Batman movie. He was asked if he would like to spend some time with the movie to help pass the time needed to finish the dressings. Batman was called in, and Paul was to be the stand-in for Robin. His suit had splendid healing qualities and could be worn all the time as it was invisible to all except himself and Batman, but he would feel the benefit.

This obviously gave the post-hypnotic suggestion that the healing would continue when he was away from the therapist and the hospital. He was seen weekly to have the occlusive dressings changed. Even in the first week his skin had greatly improved so that the dressings could be left off after the second week and the steroids reduced and emollients increased. At each weekly visit the opportunity to boost the hypnosis was taken and to check that Batman was continuing to need him and he was still in Robin's suit. After a month his appointments were reduced to monthly, and he was maintained on emollients and Robin's suit!

A. C. Stewart's paper, a study of hypnosis in atopic patients, described a delightful technique where the children were given an individual story on a tape to be played each night and the tape faded into *their* magic music, with the suggestion that they could sleep and wake refreshed, with their skin intact (Stewart & Thomas, 1995).

Warts have always been known to be susceptible to 'magic and psychological treatments' and to hypnosis. There are many papers from the 1930s (e.g. Wolf, 1934) to the present day (e.g. Spanos *et al.*, 1988).

A little girl, K (three years old), was excluded from nursery because of the warts on her hands. She was very fond of the Noddy stories so we wove a story of her going to Toyland with him to see his friend, who was the sister at the hospital. (To check whether she was with me, she was asked what the sister looked like and the answer was *"tall with dark hair like you"*). This sister had special lotions to paint on the warts, which would cause them to shrivel up and drop off, so she took K by the hand and they went into her ward where this could be done. Afterwards we all waved good-bye to Noddy and his friends, and the session was finished. Later the same evening K's mother rang up to say K wanted to go back to Toyland. should she allow it? We agreed with K that she would go and visit her new friends for five minutes as she went to bed before going to sleep. I reviewed K in a fortnight and her hands were clear, and were still clear many years later.

With older children and adults it is useful to describe the immune system and how the white cells can be thought of as warriors fighting the wart viruses. Do make sure what you are asking makes sense. For example if you are asking the patients to allow the immune system to do battle, increase the blood supply. If you are suggesting depriving the wart of its blood supply, so that it drops off, do not ask for the white cells to do battle—they will not get through!

Working with Adults

When you are working with adults with longstanding skin problems it is helpful to check whether they can remember a time when their skin was clear. This can be used in a number of ways. Suggest they go back to this time, when their skin was clear, and go inside to find what is different within themselves; can they make the necessary alterations to be like this again? What do they need, if anything, to help them? Check whether there were any problems in their lives around the time when the problems with their skin started. Maybe it was an inappropriate response to a stress. Whatever the cause, are there any better ways for them to react, now that they are more mature? Are there any echoes of situations which have caused the present out-break?

Often you will find that they do not remember having a clear skin but they can recall a time when it was better such as when they were on holiday, when they were taken into hospital, or when they were hot or cold. Your hypnotic intervention will obviously incorporate these. It is a potent 'ego strengthening' to realize that they can start to have some beneficial effect on their skin rather than depend on doctors, nurses and ointments.

A young man who had a severe exacerbation of his eczema attended out-patients and commented his skin was never as good as it had been when he lived in South Africa. He was asked what was different about his situation then, other than his health. He replied that he had had a very good job and lifestyle. He had enjoyed a swim each evening on his way home from work, and the sun had seemed to nourish his skin. As he was talking about the above he was obviously going into trance. He was asked if he knew about trance states and hypnosis, and it was discovered that he practiced meditation, so the breathing technique he had learned as part of his meditation was used to enable him to enter a trance. The images he had used when he had described South Africa were then enhanced, and the suggestion given that his skin would return to the state it had been in then. His skin improved over several weeks.

He asked to use hypnosis at least once a day, but if he felt he wanted or needed to use it more often, it would be fine to do so. When reviewed a fortnight later, his skin was 50% better and he had reduced his steroid cream to alternate days. He was sleeping better, and the sheets were no longer covered in blood from excoriations of his skin. He has since become a father, and his skin has remained in good condition in spite of sleep deprivation. He has used hypnosis with his son, who has an atopic tendency, and he has been maintained on this and emollients.

It is good practice to teach patients to use self hypnosis. Occasionally this is with the help of a tape, but it is preferable for them to learn to induce hypnosis whilst they are with you and to use it several times whilst they are there. This utilizes fractionation, and the implied suggestion that it will become easier each time they use it.

The patient should be asked to practice daily so that they can feed back on any problems that they are having or any secondary gains which may need to be addressed. In doing this it is ego strengthening for they are doing it for themselves, and can get a degree of independence from the doctors who may have been a part of their life for so long; some obviously need the aid of a tape.

Occasionally you find a patient who has a 'very angry skin' which does not respond to the usual topical therapy (steroid ointments, emollients, occlusive dressings or hospitalization). They have often been treated with oral steroids, cytotoxic drugs and so on, still with no benefit.

Such a patient was a young butcher (Tom) whose skin was 'in ribbons'. Tom had been admitted to the ward and was referred for hypnosis. He was a very angry young man and *"Nobody was going to control his mind."* Once convinced that what we wanted was to get *his mind* to help rather than damage *his body*, with the therapist as the teacher or coach, Tom turned out to be a very able pupil of hypnosis! Tom could not find any time when he had no problems with his skin (he was 23 years old), but he remembered one holiday when he had gone away with a friend, when it had been better. He needed a safe place and so

Tom was asked what he enjoyed. He replied walking his dogs. This was utilized by suggesting that he enjoy the fact the dogs were such splendid animals and so protective towards him. As Tom used hypnosis his red and angry skin visibly paled and felt cooler, and he smiled for the first time. He was asked to practice using the holiday as a destination and the protection his dogs gave him, allowing his skin to feel cool and comfortable. For the time he was on the ward he was able and willing to use hypnosis very effectively. When Tom went home he was teased by 'friends' about his use of hypnosis, and this peer pressure was too much, so he did not continue. Recently Tom re-appeared requesting hypnosis as he was due to be married, so maybe this time he will continue!

Another useful way of benefiting patients with the use of hypnosis is to suggest a treatment maybe even more effective than it usually is, thereby enhancing what you are doing.

An example of this was with a patient who was in her early twenties and had Crohn's disease of her lower lip but nowhere else in her alimentary tract. Diagnosis was made by incision biopsy of the indurated lesion of the lip. It was treated by intra-lesional triamcinolone, a procedure which involved injections into her lower lip every three months. When first seen, she was asked what she did normally whilst the injection was being done. *"Cry"* was the answer! But she agreed that she would like to make it easier. The imagery used was that of a holiday she had in Rio whilst her lip was being injected. At one point she laughed (apparently she was enjoying walking along the beach and viewing all the lovely boys' backsides!). It was suggested that as she felt the pressure in her lip she would be aware of how effective the substance was and maybe she could allow it to be effective for longer than in the past. She could also limit the bleeding to that which was necessary for healing.

At the time she commented how much more comfortable the whole procedure had been, and 'normally' she would have had to press hard to stop the bleeding. When she was reviewed three months later, there was no sign of lesion in her lip. She informed us that she had used the same technique when she had visited her dentist, and the experience had been much less traumatic. She is now being maintained on biannual injections and maybe they could be spaced out still further with further hypnosis.

Sometimes it may be appropriate to explore with hypnoanalysis the underpinning psychological factors of the dermatological disease (Shenefelt, 2007).

A middle-aged lady requested hypnosis for treatment of longstanding acne rosacea, which she was keeping under control with oxytetracycline, but she was unhappy with taking long term antibiotics. Simple techniques helped, but she was never clear. An affect bridge (see page 127) was used to go back to the first episode. What we discovered there led to therapy to allow her to come to terms with the relationship with her mother, at the end of which her skin was clear and has remained so for 14 years.

Although eczema often clears once stress levels have reduced, in one author's (AW) experience it is likely that unresolved loss or anger underpins psoriasis so that exploring this is an important factor in the treatment of this condition.

In conclusion hypnosis can be of great help to your dermatological patients, helping them to cope with the disease process, reduce many of the symptoms and indeed facilitate healing (Shenefelt, 2003). The patient has some areas of 'normal' skin so the premise is that their body 'knows' how to make 'normal' skin and hypnosis can utilize goal directed imagery towards this end.

References

Cotterill, J. A. (1981), Dermatological non-disease: a common and potentially fatal disturbance of cutaneous body image. *British Journal of Dermatology*, 104 (6), 611–19.

Cotterill, J. A. & Cunliffe, W. J. (1997), Suicide in dermatological patients. *British Journal of Dermatology*, 137 (2), 246–50.

Ewin, D. M. (1992), Hypnotherapy for warts (verruca vulgaris). *American Journal of Clinical Hypnosis*, 35, 1–10.

Ewin, D. M. & Eimer, B. N. (2006), *Ideomotor signals for rapid hypnoanalysis: a how-to manual*. Springfield, IL, Charles C. Thomas.

Felt, B. T., Hall, H., Olness, K., et al. (1998), Wart regression in children: comparison of relaxation-imagery to topical treatment and equal time interventions. *American Journal of Clinical Hypnosis*, 41, 130–8.

Goldstein, R. H. (2005), Successful repeated hypnotic treatment of warts in the same individual. *American Journal of Clinical Hypnosis*, 47 (4), 259–64.

Graham, G. (1987), *It's a bit of a mouthful*. Newcastle, Real Options Press. p 159.

Hollander, M. B. (1959), Excoriated acne controlled by post-hypnotic suggestion. *American Journal of Clinical Hypnosis*, 1, 122–3.

Iglesias, A. (2005), Three failures of direct suggestion in psychogenic dermatitis followed by successful intervention. *American Journal of Clinical Hypnosis*, 47, 191–8.

Jasnoski, M. L. & Kugler, J. (1987). Relaxation, imagery and neuroimmunomodulation. *Annals of the New York Academy of Sciences*, 496, 730–72.

Kantor, S. D. (1990), Stress and psoriasis. *Cutis*, 46, 321–2.

Laidlaw, T. M., Richardson, D. H., Booth, R. J. & Large, R. G. (1994), Immediate-type hypersensitivity reactions and hypnosis: problems in methodology. *Journal of Psychosomatic Research*, 38, 569–80.

Lehman, R. E. (1978), Brief hypnotherapy of neurodermatitis: a case with four-year follow-up. *American Journal of Clinical Hypnosis*, 21, 48–51.

Mantle, F. (2001), Hypnosis in the management of eczema in children. *Nursing Standard*, 15 (51), 41–4.

Napier, N. J. (1996), *Recreating your self: building self-esteem through imaging and self-hypnosis*. New York, W.W. Norton.

O'Hanlon, W. H. & Heum, A.L. (1990), *An Uncommon Casebook*. New York, W. W. Norton. p. 233.

Olness, K. N., Culbert, T. & Uden, D. (1989), Self-regulation of salivary immunoglobulin A by children. *Pediatrics*, 83 (1), 66–71.

Rossi, E. (1993), *The psychobiology of mind-body healing*, rev. ed. New York, W. W. Norton.

Schneck, J. M. (1954), Ichthyosis treated with hypnosis. *Diseases of the Nervous System*, 15, 211–4.

Shenefelt, P. D. (2000), Hypnosis in dermatology. *Archives of Dermatology*, 136, 393–9.

Shenefelt, P. D. (2003), Applying hypnosis in dermatology. *Dermatology Nursing*, 15, 513–7.

Shenefelt, P. D. (2004), Using hypnosis to facilitate resolution of psychogenic excorations in acne excoriée. *American Journal of Clinical Hypnosis*, 46 (3), 239–45.

Shenefelt, P. D. (2007), Psychocutaneous hypnoanalysis: detection and deactivation of emotional and mental root factors in psychosomatic skin disorders. *American Journal of Clinical Hypnosis*, 50 (2), 131–6.

Shenefelt, P. D. (2009), Hypnosis in dermatology. *Archives of Dermatology*, 136, 393–9.

Shertzer, C. L. & Lookingbill, D. P. (1987), Effects of relaxation therapy and hypnotizability in chronic urticaria. *Archives of Dermatology*, 123, 913–6.

Spanos, N. P., Stenstrom, R. J. & Johnston, J. C. (1988), Hypnosis, placebo, and suggestion in the treatment of warts. *Psychosomatic Medicine*, 50 (3), 245–60.

Stein, C. (1963), The clenched fist technique as a hypnotic procedure in clinical psychotherapy. *American Journal of Clinical Hypnosis*, 6, 113–9.

Stewart, A. C. & Thomas, S. E. (1995), Hypnotherapy as a treatment for atopic dermatitis in adults and children. *British Journal of Dermatology*, 132, 778–83.

Tausk, F. & Whitmore, S. E. (1999), A pilot study of hypnosis in the treatment of patients with psoriasis *Psychotherapy and Psychosomatics*, 495, 1–9.

Waxman, D. (1989), *Hartland's medical & dental hypnosis*, 3rd ed. London, Bailliere Tindall. p. 217–28.

Wolf, S. A. (1934), The treatment of warts by suggestion. *Medical Record*, 140, 552–6.

Zachariae, R. & Bjerring, P. (1993), Increase and decrease of delayed cutaneous reactions obtained by hypnotic suggestions during sensitization. *Allergy*, 48, 6–11.

Zachariae, R., Oster, H., Bjerring, P. & Kragballe, K. (1996), Effects of psychologic intervention on psoriasis: a preliminary report. *Journal of the American Academy of Dermatology*, 34, 1008–15.

21

Pain

Dr Les Brann

With contributions from Mrs Jacky Owens, Dr Ann Williamson and
Dr Caron Moores

Introduction

According to the International Association for the Study of Pain (IASP), pain is defined as:

> An unpleasant sensory and emotional experience associated with actual or potential tissue
> damage, or described in terms of such damage.(Merskey *et al.*, 1994, p. 209–14)

The definition is expanded as below:

> Pain is always subjective. . . . It is unquestionably a sensation in a part or parts of the body, but
> it is also always unpleasant and therefore also an emotional experience.(Merskey *et al.*, 1994, p.
> 209–14)

Pain is often experienced in the absence of pathology or damage for psychological or
emotional reasons, and it is impossible to distinguish this from pain due to tissue damage.

As McCaffrey and Beebe (1989) say, 'Pain is what the patient says it is' (p. 7), and notice
the IASP definition avoids linking pain to the stimulus that produced it. 'Activity induced in
the nociceptor and nociceptive pathways by a noxious stimulus is not pain, which is always a
psychological state, even though we may well appreciate that pain most often has a
proximate physical cause' (Merskey *et al.*, 1994, p. 209–14).

The Handbook of Contemporary Clinical Hypnosis: Theory and Practice, First Edition.
Edited by Les Brann, Jacky Owens and Ann Williamson.
© 2012 John Wiley & Sons, Ltd. Published 2015 by John Wiley & Sons, Ltd.

Thus much progress has been made since the simple concepts of stimulus and response and has continued to develop via the 'Gate Theory' (Melzack & Wall, 1965) and its various expansions (Wall, 1989), to a pain 'neuromatrix' (Melzack, 2001). This neuromatrix anatomically consists of a widespread network of neurones linking cortex, thalamus and limbic system and has sensory, affective and cognitive components. Figure 21.1 shows diagrammatically the various inputs and outputs related to the functioning of the neuromatrix.

Neuroimaging techniques have now made it possible identify which areas of the brain are active when responding to painful stimuli and thus form the basis of the pain neuromatrix. These areas include the anterior cingulate cortex, insula, prefrontal regions and both primary and secondary somatosensory cortices (Apkarian *et al.*, 2005; Derbyshire, 2000, 2003; Treede *et al.*, 1999). Such studies have also shown that pain can be experienced independently of injury (Lane *et al.*, 2009) and, as such, pain can be considered a disorder in its own right. The definition of pain, therefore, now needs to include these neuroimaging findings and could be as simple as: pain is the subjective experience which accompanies the activation of the pain neuromatrix. Whilst circular in its formulation, it, like the IASP definition, is devoid of the need for the identification of the stimulus.

Other important discoveries in the understanding of pain include the inhibitory descending pathways. Such pathways inhibit the signals from the painful area and damp down the pain. Much interest has been directed at an inhibitory pathway known as the diffuse noxious inhibitory controls (DNIC). These descending activations are not confined to the area of the original stimulus and are relatively long lasting. Thus the natural tendency of the body is to restore the body to a non-painful state as soon as possible after the original noxious stimulus.

It is also worth making a distinction between acute and chronic pain. Chronic pain is defined as such if the pain has lasted for more than three months. It is argued that chronic pain is associated with changes in pain processing; the detailed physiology is beyond the scope of this book, but for example Apkarian *et al.* (2004) suggests that there is a significant loss of grey matter in the dorsolateral prefrontal cortex and right thalamus. There is also a high incidence of psychological co-morbidity with chronic pain.

Such definitions and observations tie in with other medical models and Engel's (1977) biopsychosocial model identifies the involvement of these wider factors in the experience of pain. This is amply demonstrated in the case below.

Mary, a 63 year old lady with advanced ovarian cancer, was plagued with intractable abdominal pain. She went easily into trance, and the therapist suggested that they look at her pain. She responded with "What pain?" Exploration of this revealed several issues; predominant among these was the fact that she would be leaving behind an adult paralysed son and she was concerned as to how he would be cared for. She described herself as 'a lapsed Catholic' and also needed to find peace within herself regarding her religious beliefs. Pain was never again an issue for this lady.

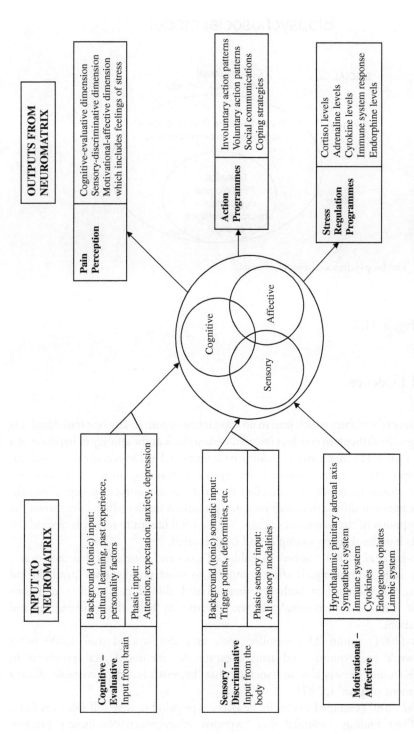

Figure 21.1 The pain neuromatrix comprises cognitive, affective and sensory neuromodalities. The diagram shows the factors which input into the matrix, and the output reflects the complex aspects of pain perception, behavioural responses and appropriate homeostatic adjustments.

Source: Re-drawn after Melzack (2001).

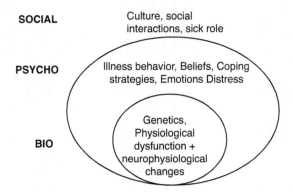

Biopsychosocial model

Figure 21.2   The biopsychosocial model of pain.

See also Figure 21.2.

Published Evidence

Given the array of variables which lead to an experience of pain in any one individual it is always going to be difficult to conduct research trials to look at the efficacy of hypnosis as a treatment for pain. The much loved randomized control trial is always going to struggle for credibility especially when the major underlying problem may only surface as a result of the therapy and cannot therefore be controlled for in the non-treatment group. Notwithstanding the inherent difficulties there are many published studies which have shown the benefit of hypnosis in the treatment of pain. Whilst a full literature review is beyond the scope of this handbook a few examples will be presented.

Montgomery *et al.* (2000) studied 18 published trials and concluded that there was a moderate to large hypnoanalgesic effect compared to other non-hypnotic psychological interventions. They looked at both experimental and clinical pain studies, and they were able to show that hypnoanalgesia was effective in both the experimental and clinical situations.

Hawkins (2001) found 23 controlled trials and also studied over 1,000 other published work on hypnosis and pain. Despite the methodological problems in many of the studies he was able to conclude that 'hypnosis has demonstrable efficacy in the treatment of pain' (p. 47).

Elkins *et al.* (2007) excluded studies for headache type pain but were still able to evaluate 13 trials. Their findings indicated that 'hypnosis interventions consistently produce significant decreases in pain associated with a variety of chronic-pain problems. Also, hypnosis was generally found to be more effective than non-hypnotic interventions such as attention, physical therapy, and education' (p. 275).

It is pleasing that there is much trial evidence to support the use of hypnosis for pain but as the hypnotherapy in these instances was directed towards symptom removal, using a standardized programme for each patient, the results are very likely to underestimate the benefit of hypnotherapy. This is at variance with the clinical situation where the therapy is tailored to the specific needs of the individual patient. As we have seen those needs are not related just to the pain but to the psychosocial elements too. Thus the question hypnotherapists need answering is, does hypnotherapy help with the pain and the associated, perhaps even causal, problems of the patients that are referred? Clinicians are unable to select their patients and most do not conveniently fall into a specific category as per the clinical trial. The most useful evidence, therefore, is that derived from outcome audits where pre- and post-treatment data have been collated.

Brann *et al.* (2008) reported outcome data on 61 consecutive chronic pain patients who had been referred from the hospital pain clinic and had completed therapy. A further 17 patients had been referred, but two were unsuitable for hypnosis because of a previous history of psychosis, eight patients decided not to take up the offer of hypnotherapy and seven others failed to complete the course of treatment. The hypnotic interventions were individualized to the patients' specific needs. The measures used were a symptom score which was a composite questionnaire looking at pain, functioning, quality of life and sleep. Anxiety and depression were measured using the Hospital Anxiety and Depression scale (HADs; Zigmond & Snaith, 1983). (See Table 21.1.)

The group carried a high psychiatric burden with 28 of the patients already being known to the mental health services. This is confirmed by the very high proportion of the group having HADs scores in the clinically significant range. The hypnotic intervention shows highly significant improvement for all three outcome measures. The therapy revealed a high proportion of past trauma with 36% having suffered some form of child abuse,

Table 21.1 Outcome data on 61 consecutive chronic pain patients

Chronic pain patients (n = 61)	Mean score before hypnosis (% severe + moderate)	Mean score after hypnosis (% severe + moderate)	t-test significance
Symptom score (max. 100)	62.2 (77%)	37.0 (16%)	$P = 0.00\ (1.79 \times 10^{-19})$
Hospital Anxiety and Depression scale (HADs) – Anxiety	12.3 (71%)	7.6 (26%)	$P = 0.00\ (1.8 \times 10^{-13})$
HADs – Depression	10.2 (46%)	5.9 (10%)	$P = 0.00\ (7.8 \times 10^{-12})$

domestic violence, rape, sexual assault and other events likely to be responsible for PTSD type symptoms. These outcomes were obtained in an average of 4.3 (one hour) sessions per patient. Interestingly the authors report that very little work was carried out using pain-relieving techniques and that symptoms improved markedly once the underlying psychological problems were treated. These findings support the view that continued activation of the pain neuromatrix is multifactorial and that the peripheral physical input may not be a major component.

Mechanism of Hypnoanalgesia

The mechanism of hypnoanalgesia is not clear and several studies have compared hypnosis with acupuncture. Others have examined whether the hypnoanalgesic effect could be blocked by naloxone to establish whether the effect was via the endorphin route.

Using electrical stimulation of the supraorbital nerve, Li *et al.* (1975) showed a significant increase in pain threshold in the hypnosis group compared with no hypnosis or with acupuncture at real or sham points in a cohort of 14 male subjects. This difference with acupuncture was also shown by Stern *et al.* (1977) using a cold pressor pain stimulus on 20 male volunteers. Thus the mechanism seems to be different and more effective than that of acupuncture.

Also using a cold pressor test, Moret *et al.* (1991) again showed a significant increase in pain threshold with hypnosis (and acupuncture, but less than with hypnosis), and this was demonstrable with or without the administration of naloxone. Spiegel and Albert (1983) and Goldstein and Hilgard (1975) have also shown that naloxone failed to prevent the hypnotic response in the clinical as well as the experimental setting.

Sandrini *et al.* (2000) examined the effect of hypnosis on the DNIC. Using the nociceptic flexor reflex of the biceps femoris and a cold pressor test they were able to show that hypnotic suggestion was able to impair the reflex and seemed to block the DNIC. They were able to postulate that hypnosis and DNIC used the same pathway. These findings were only seen in the high hypnotizable group.

Whilst neuroimaging studies demonstrate changes in activation of the pain neuromatrix with hypnosis (e.g. Derbyshire *et al.*, 2004), the mechanism through which this occurs is unknown. So despite being able to demonstrate its efficacy in pain relief our understanding remains incomplete. It is important not to allow this lack of understanding to hinder its use.

Techniques for Pain Relief

There are many documented methods of using hypnosis directly for pain relief without any attempt at looking at the underlying issues. These have a wide range of applications in the clinical field (e.g. in acute pain management, preparation for medical or dental procedures, chronic pain and childbirth).

Relaxation

This is mentioned here first as it underpins all the other methods. Relaxation per se reduces the pain experience. No one method of relaxation is better than any other for pain relief and the therapist must work with the patient's own preferences. It is suggested that even with good hypnotic subjects who can use quick induction methods it is advised to spend time with a relaxing induction and deepening to maximize the benefits of any subsequent technique. Relaxation also forms the bulk of any self hypnosis regime and is therefore useful for patients to use themselves.

Glove anaesthesia

Perhaps the most well known is that of glove anaesthesia which as its name implies follows no anatomical distribution. In this technique the patient is asked to make their hand numb or anaesthetized as a precursor to transferring this numbness to the painful area. There is no 'right' script for this, and it is suggested that the therapist adapts and modifies according to their preference and especially that of their patients. It may be worth suggesting a 'comfortable' numbness as some patients equate 'numbness' with unpleasantness.

Following induction and deepening, a suggested script might be:

> *Imagine you are out walking in the snow through a wood. The snow is lovely and soft and lying on the branches of the trees . . . the soft snow is so inviting that as you pass each tree you take a handful of snow in one of your hands and . . . feel it crunch in your hand . . . as only fresh snow can crunch . . . as you pass tree after tree . . . you notice that your hand is feeling numb . . . and gets more and more numb with each tree you pass . . . until it is so numb you can hardly feel your hand at all . . . take your time enjoying that walk . . . but let me know by lifting a finger or nodding when that hand is numb. . . .*
>
> *Good . . . now that hand is numb the magic of hypnosis is that you can transfer that numbness to whichever part of your body you wish . . . see . . . just move your numb hand across to your other hand and feel the numbness being transferred . . . that is good, really good. . . .*

Not every patient is able to do this, and the therapist should not be disappointed if significant numbness does not ensue. Sometimes it is helpful (having warned the patient beforehand that you are going to do it) to touch the back of the numb hand and the normal hand so that the patient is aware of a difference. This positive feedback can help to accentuate the difference. It is also useful to use each transfer as an enhancing technique: "*. . . not only will you notice the numbness in your other hand . . . but the numbness gets more and more with each transfer. . . .*"

Traditionally this technique has been tested by passing a sterile hypodermic needle through the skin on the back of the numb hand and whilst this can be a very powerful reinforcement it is really unnecessary and therapists are advised against its routine use. Sometimes one can ask the patient to give an ideomotor signal on the opposite hand once sufficient numbness has occurred.

The experienced therapist builds up a whole variety of scenarios for this technique, and an alternative image might be: "... *Imagine you are out in a boat, on a lake on a lovely sunny afternoon... as you are being rowed slowly around... you let one hand dip into the water... the coolness is welcome on such a warm day... as your hand drifts through the water... it begins to feel numb. ...*"

In all cases it is essential that the scenario you use does not produce any problems for the patient – the above suggestions would not be used if the patient did not like the snow or the water.

There are other variations on this theme of creating glove anaesthesia. One method is to ask the patient to imagine they are applying an anaesthetic or magic cream or putting on a magic glove – this latter is very good for children who get totally absorbed in the idea of magic things. It can be suggested that the glove is so thick that *"no unnecessary sensation can be felt."* Another method is to explain that the sensation in the hand is carried to the brain along nerves which are like tiny wires. These wires travel up into the brain and are plugged into the central processor rather like the wires of an old fashioned telephone exchange. The patient is then asked to unplug the wires which connect to the hand and so make it numb. Some can just set the intent for numbness and ask for their subconscious to give an ideomotor signal when it has been done.

It is well worth giving the patient several options, and the options can be used in a sort of a bind: *"Do you want to make your hand numb ... (this way or that way)?"*

Once the hand is numb, by whatever method, the numbness can be transferred to the painful area by placing the numb hand on that pain. Patients who are able to do this are taught to do it themselves during self-hypnosis, and they soon realize that the initial use of the glove anaesthesia is unnecessary and they learn to make the painful area numb directly. This seems to be easier if they have used the telephone wire image or the anaesthetic cream. This technique is useful as preparation for painful clinical procedures as well as part of the overall management of chronic pain.

The pain dial

This technique is delightful for its simplicity and also has the kudos of having been shown to effect changes in activation of the pain neuromatrix in fMRI studies (Derbyshire *et al.*, 2004). During hypnosis patients are asked to picture a dial which measures the level of pain they are experiencing. The actual type of dial is irrelevant the image can be whatever the patient wishes, but they are asked to have it graduated from zero (no pain) to ten (as bad as it could get). To effect pain relief they are simply asked to turn the dial down!

Some authorities (e.g. Heap & Aravind, 2002) indicate that paradoxical injunction can be useful for pain patients and in this, instead of asking the patient to turn the pain down, they are instructed to turn it up. The pain dial affords a very good method of achieving this but should always be used with an ego-strengthening and enlightening observation that if they are able to turn it up they have a level of control over their pain that they never realized and can, of course, turn it down. The value of doing this clinically, especially if the patient has already been able to turn the dial down, seems to be limited and is not usually recommended. However experience has shown that some patients, especially sickle cell patients in crisis, find it easier to turn the pain up first before being able to turn it down.

The pain dial can have other applications particularly if the patient is not able to turn the dial down. In such cases, it can become a tool for helping to uncover other problems.

Diane – a woman with chronic back pain

This 42 year old woman suffered from chronic back pain and was referred for hypnotherapy from the hospital pain clinic. Diane was one of the few patients whose symptoms were such that she needed to lie down for the therapy as it was too painful to sit in the armchair. During hypnosis she was asked to imagine she had shrunk herself down so she was able to go inside her control centre in her mind. She was then asked to look at her pain dial and report her level of pain. This was hovering between seven and eight out of ten. When asked to turn it down, Diane said, *"It won't go! . . . I can't move it at all."* During the history taking and at a previous session it had been established that her pain did vary and there were times when it was better, so it was pertinent to say, *"That is odd! We know your pain does fluctuate so we know the dial must be able to move. Have a closer look to see who or what is stopping it moving."*

Observation showed her eyes were moving as she was 'looking' and after a silence of about a minute she said, *"My mother!"* It transpired that her mother was an unkind, dominant woman and Diane's back pain had been an (unconscious) saviour as she had a bona-fide reason not to go to visit her or if she did struggle to see her she was unable to do the running around which she was always expected to do. We agreed to work on various strategies to help her deal with the problem of her mother, but was it okay for her back to be better *". . . most of the time?"* Using an ideomotor response she answered, *"Yes."* Returning to the pain dial she was then able to turn it down to four!

Another similar application of this technique is to ask the patient what other 'control dials' influence the pain. Sometimes the therapist needs to give some guidance: *"You said you tend to be a worrier; I wonder what happens to your pain dial when the worry dial is up high?"* This sort of approach can help both the therapist and the patient to build up a picture of the pertinent psychosocial issues which may be involved. It is possible then to 'tweak' a series of dials to affect improvement in the symptoms while the causes are being sorted. Do not be afraid to revisit the dials after some work on a cause, so *"If you have been able to turn down your worry dial and your work stress dial, and your relaxation dial has gone up – can you now turn down the pain dial a bit more?"*

The endorphin reservoir

Most people have heard of endorphins as the body's own strong pain killers but it is always useful to give a little preamble explaining that they work in the same way as morphine and are, therefore, very powerful. Not only are they powerful painkillers but they give a lovely feeling of euphoria too. This technique can be used in a wide variety of situations but is particularly useful in preparation for painful procedures or anticipatory pain such as childbirth. After induction and deepening:

> *Imagine you have shrunk yourself down so small you have been able to wander into your arm (or wherever the pain or procedure is to take place) . . . there you will see your endorphin reservoir . . . full and ready for use . . . there is a tap at the outlet with a hose that you can move to which ever part needs the endorphin. I want you to gently open the tap and let the endorphin flood over the arm (or painful area) . . . as it does . . . you feel the soothing effect . . . letting the area become numb so that nothing will bother you . . . and at the same time you will feel that overwhelming sense of wellbeing . . . you can repeat this whenever you need to. . . .*

Using this in childbirth it is possible to set up automatic release: *". . . the muscles of the womb are linked to the endorphin reservoir . . . so that the very signal that sets off another contraction . . . automatically . . . opens the tap . . . and you feel the glow of the soothing fluid flowing over your womb . . . and the wonderful wellbeing. . . ."*

In reality it is probably best to teach all of the above techniques to your patients when preparing them for painful procedures, and they will choose which combination is best for them. Some patients find that it is difficult to anticipate the pain but can quickly adapt to use any method once they are aware of the sensation they need to modify.

This technique can be used with chronic pain patients but may not be straightforward. The tank may be empty or the tap stuck or any variety of 'blocks' may be encountered. So, as with other techniques, the description becomes a metaphorical representation of their problem and can be explored. Sometimes resolution can be simple *". . . perhaps the tap just needs a bit of oil."* The therapist must move into intuitive, trance logic mode (see page 22) and not get bogged down with reality; the statement *"Perhaps the tap just needs a bit of oil"* is said in a matter of fact tone as if you always have a can of oil with you!

Resolution, however, is not always simple and try as you might the tank remains empty or the tap will not be opened. Never let these situations cause unnecessary anxiety as in reality the patient is no worse than before therapy began and at least you have a starting point from which to work. One method would be to ask when the reservoir was last working and get some idea when and what was happening at the time. Sometimes it is necessary to move away from this to another image with the tacit agreement that this problem will be revisited once other work has been done.

Chris – another case of back pain

This 50 year old man had been referred from the pain clinic. He had a ten year history of back pain which had got worse following surgery and fell into the category of 'failed back surgery syndrome'. He described the endorphin reservoir as empty and all suggestions to get the system working again proved unhelpful. Everything was treated in a very negative way. His BDI score had been 47 which is in the extreme depression range. He described his depression like a black hole that just sucks everything in and

"*... that's why it* (the reservoir) *is empty ...*" So attention was then shifted to the black hole. This began when he was 11 and he revealed sexual abuse by a friend of the family which had gone on between the ages of 11 and 14. He had tried once to tell his parents, but they did not seem to believe him. He had never told anybody else about it. His pain was such that, initially, he was not able to sit in the comfortable armchair but sat, perched uncomfortably in a lopsided way on an ordinary chair, but by the session following the revelation he was sitting upright and his analgesic requirements had been less. Having worked on the abuse problem, he volunteered that "*... the reservoir is beginning to fill up!*"

Distraction

Most people have observed that if they are concentrating on something it seems as though the pain is less troublesome. This experience is utilized in the hypnotic context by asking the patient to focus on something other than the pain. This can be a task such as *"Start counting backwards from 300"* or an experience such as *"Imagine you are lazing on the beach feeling the warmth of the sun."* Whilst this can be done simply with mental imagery its use for procedural pain is probably best when it involves the patient actually talking as well as experiencing the image. So, for instance, asking the patient to describe in detail their 'relaxing place' and how it makes them feel is a good method to adopt while the patient is having the procedure carried out. But some others, conversely, prefer to be left to immerse themselves in their imagery and find verbalization lightens the trance state. This ability to take themselves somewhere pleasant in their imagination "*... whilst what we are doing here need not bother you at all ...*" requires more cognitive processing and concentration, so it may not be as useful in certain situations where the patient needs to communicate with the medical staff alongside producing analgesia such as in childbirth.

Dissociation

Whilst doing hypnosis some patients are able to dissociate from the part of the body experiencing the pain. Suggestions can be given so that the part of the body with the pain is somehow separated so that the pain is happening elsewhere. These techniques tend to require patients to be very highly hypnotizable. Some patients report a type of 'out of body' experience as though they are observing what is happening to them from a distance. Those patients that can do it find it easy so a direct suggestion for dissociation is all that is necessary following induction and deepening. A variation of this is sometimes called displacement (Heap & Aravind, 2002) in which the pain is shifted to another part of the body where it can be more easily tolerated. This variation may be more useful to stress generated pains so that a headache may be displaced to a little finger enabling the sufferer to continue with day to day activities.

Time distortion

This is not really a separate method but this hypnotic phenomenon can be utilized in many of the techniques especially those used for procedural pain (see chapter 22). The majority of patients doing hypnosis significantly underestimate real time so the procedure seems to be completed much quicker and consequently with less discomfort.

Corrective imagery

This method is one of the best for use with chronic pain patients. Patients are asked to describe what their pain looks like and then change the image to one which feels more comfortable. The imagery can sometimes be very simple, and a change of colour can often effect a reduction in pain.

Peter – a man with testicular pain

This 47 year old man had been troubled by testicular pain for many years. He had been investigated thoroughly and no cause had been found. He was never without the pain and reported it at six out of ten at the beginning of the hypnosis session. After induction and deepening he was asked to see what colour the pain was and he described one side of his scrotum and contents as being a vivid, intense dark blue. He was asked to change it to a colour that was not so painful. This he did and he reported his pain had gone. This was not simply a within hypnosis experience as he had no pain on awakening.

The imagery can be much more complex and is often a representation of the patient's interpretation of the doctor's explanation. For example one of the common descriptions given for degenerative conditions of the spine is that it is 'crumbling'. When patients are attending the doctor for results of investigations they are invariably anxious and this tends to lead to a negative interpretation of the information and to 'fix' the image in their mind. When working with such images the 'cognitive interlude' is important so that the inaccuracies in the image are understood. Listening to the descriptions of the painful area gives a timely reminder to health professionals to be careful with the words used to describe disease processes. It hardly needs to be emphasized that if a patient believes that their spine is 'crumbling' (actively and continuously) they will be convinced that their pain can never be improved. This belief then feeds into the pain neuromatrix and enhances its activation. The term 'slipped disc' is another greatly misunderstood term.

Debbie – a woman with a 'slipped disc'

During the history taking, it became apparent that Debbie believed that her 'slipped disc' was going to be with her forever. She had made no progress since the onset of the pain three and a half years ago. During hypnosis she was asked to shrink herself down and go inside her back to where the pain was. She said it was very red and the disc was hard like metal and sticking into the nerves. *"I saw it on the scan."* She was asked to change the image but she could not alter the disc: *"... Well it's out now so it can't change."* She was then asked to imagine a fruit pastel which had been left in the sun and to describe what it would feel like. She said, *"... Well it would be sort of crusty on the outside but squidgy in the middle, quite soft."* It was explained to her that the disc was not hard but just like the soft pastel and that the body tries to heal itself so that the squidgy bit of the disc would have shrunk as it healed. Enlightened by this she changed the image and mentally rehearsed becoming gradually more and more active. Within six weeks, she was able to stop all the strong analgesics and only needed the occasional paracetamol tablet.

Another good example of imagery incorporating information gleaned from health professionals is that of a 55 year old man with failed back surgery syndrome.

Post-operatively the surgeon had told him that the nerves had been damaged so he was bound still to have pain. The image created as a result was of thick cables where some of them had been severed and in others the insulation had been torn off so that there were lots of sparks coming from the bare wires. So it can be seen how important it is to investigate whilst doing hypnosis the patient's own ideas and images of the problem.

Not all images are a result of other people's words; many are simply the patient's own interpretation of the feelings and ideas as to what sort of problem must be giving rise to the symptoms. One man described his back as having been fractured: *"... it has got to have been broken to give a pain like that!"* Whatever the underlying components of the image, the management is largely the same and follows the principle 'Changing the image changes the feeling'. It is important to let the patient decide on the change but for some the therapist may need to give an example such as *"What would it feel like if it was pink instead of red or warm instead of hot?"* but once the patient gets the hang of it then take a step back.

When using hypnosis for pain management it is useful be able to use composite programmes which incorporate several different methods described above. There is nothing wrong in using, for example, corrective imagery, the pain dial and the endorphin reservoir all at the same time. When practicing at home the patient will choose the method that works best for them.

So hypnotic techniques may be used to get chronic pain under control and to teach self-hypnosis to give patients another way of managing acute-on-chronic episodes or the pain associated with an operation. The next case study highlights all three of these.

David – self hypnosis for pain management

A 14 year old boy, David, got his left arm caught in the rigging of a trawler whilst on work experience and sustained an avulsion injury to his brachial plexus; two days later he developed compartment syndrome of the lower arm, requiring fasciotomy. At the end of the first week he had no motor function but an extremely painful arm. The pain was there most of the time, but with acute exacerbations lasting up to an hour at a time which were excruciating. He was seen by one of the author's (CM) anaesthetic colleagues during one of these attacks; his appearance was described as the closest thing to *The Scream* by Edvard Munch he had ever seen – his face was contorted with pain but he was making no noise. He was on fentanyl and ketamine by PCA, and he was admitted to the intensive care unit for administration of intravenous lignocaine to control the pain in the short term, but this was obviously not a long term option.

When the author (CM) was asked to see David one month after the initial accident he had a 'useless' but painful arm and there had been some discussion about amputation. He was due for an exploratory operation to assess the damage prior to making a decision about future management. He was still on opiates and ketamine intravenously by patient controlled intravenous analgesia (PCA) and he had been started on amitriptylene. The author (CM) was asked to help with both the acute and chronic elements of his pain and with post-operative analgesia.

David was open to any treatment options by this stage, and he proved to have a great imagination that was used to good effect with client generated imagery. The surgeon had described the injury to his brachial plexus to him. David knew the nerves at the top of his arm had been damaged (and possibly snapped) by the stretching injury. He knew that the nerves had to grow back to bridge the gap. He had two mental pictures of the pain. The background pain he imagined as being caused by a bowling ball being bowled down inside his arm towards his hand; the further down the ball got the worse the pain got because the ball was too big to fit. For the acute pain he imagined a jack-in-a-box; the raw ends of the nerves were stuffed into the box, and when the lid was opened the nerves waved about in the breeze causing the acute episodes of pain.

Under hypnosis he was able to reduce the size of the ball being rolled down his arm to the size of a golf ball, and practice putting the nerves back into the box and shutting the lid. The author (CM) did not want to stop the ball going down his arm all together because it was felt that it represented the fact that nerve impulses were able to cross the injured brachial plexus and this is what needed to happen to make his arm 'useful' again. He was taught self-hypnosis and was able to use it to good effect pre-operatively, so much so that he was able to come off all his intravenous analgesia, which allowed him to go out of the hospital for an afternoon's shopping prior to his operation.

Post-operatively he developed all of the same kinds of pain that he had suffered following the initial injury, but the time scale was very much shortened and he was discharged to his local hospital on oral medications only after one week.

Phantom limb pain

This troublesome condition presents a challenge to both the theorists and the clinician. Indeed it was this, amongst other problems, which led Melzack (2001) to develop the neuromatrix theory of pain, for in order to explain why patients' experience of phantom sensations is so real it was necessary to construct a theory in which peripheral stimuli were not necessary for the production of the sensation.

There are approximately 5,000 new amputees each year in the United Kingdom with over 40,000 (in England and Scotland) regularly visiting prosthetic centres. Jensen *et al.* (1985) reported that 72% experienced phantom pain eight days post-surgery, and this fell to 65% at six months. Longer term follow up showed that a staggering 60% were still experiencing pain seven years later. Extrapolation of these data would suggest that there are over 24,000 amputees remaining in pain in the United Kingdom.

Original theories of phantom limb pain rested on the idea that the cut nerves from that limb continued to send signals. However it would seem that with greater understanding of the dynamic nature of the nervous system this approach was far too simplistic.

Feedback loops 'report back' activity following commands from the motor cortex. The 'instruction' from the motor cortex is copied to a wide range of areas of the brain but especially the cerebellum and parietal lobes (which seem to store the body image). Feedback from vision, proprioception and other senses to these areas is compared to the original instruction to assess whether the intended activity has occurred and subsequent fine tuning of the activity can take place to achieve the intended goal.

With amputees, however, the feedback information is incomplete and it is argued that the system 'hangs' as it is waiting for further data which cannot now arrive. The system simply continues to report the last message which is the (painful) sensations of the limb just prior to amputation. This 'last message' model would help to explain why some, particularly post-trauma amputees, report their phantom limb to be disfigured – presumably a proprioceptive record of its last position before the nerves were severed. This lack of feedback has been shown to alter the actual cortical structure with areas of the somatosensory cortex representing the absent limb dying back and being overtaken by areas on either side (Ramachandran & Blakelee, 1999). Equally, Willoch *et al.* (2000) have shown using positron emission tomography (PET) that the phantom limb sensations produce activations in the same brain areas as in an intact limb.

In order to restore feedback into these loops, Ramachandran (Ramachandran & Blakelee, 1999) developed the use of a mirror box in which the patient viewed the reflection of their normal limb as though it was in the position of the absent limb. Movement of this image was then perceived by the brain as coming from the phantom limb. This perceived movement enabled reactivation of the areas in the somatosensory cortex. This was accompanied by a reduction in phantom sensations and eventually to a telescoping of the phantom limb.

Oakley *et al.* (2002) reviewed the literature on the use of hypnotherapy for phantom limb pain and found only single case studies. They report on 12 cases including two of their own and show two main methods. One which they call an ipsative imagery method is where the patient modifies their own imagined representation of the pain to effect relief. The other method – a movement/imagery approach – is where the patient, during hypnosis, is encouraged to move the phantom limb and, hence, take control of it. Both methods resulted in improvements, but it was not possible to conclude which method was the better approach.

Jamie – a man with sickle cell disease and phantom limb pain

Jamie, a 29 year old with sickle cell disease, used hypnosis during a prolonged hospitalization. On admission his sickling pains were in his left shoulder, and over the course of his stay he learned differing ways to manage. Trance was always achieved using a progressive relaxation, a staircase to deepen and a magic carpet to transport him to his safe haven, which invariably was a park. The first technique he used was the changing numbers imagery (see page 46) and he could reduce his pain down from eight to a manageable level of three or four. It was apparent that all was not well with his right foot, and scans revealed the presence of a tumour, the reason for his need to use crutches for walking. Visual in his imagery, he also chose to work with colours and shapes seeing his pain in trance as a red oblong shape. He found it very 'powerful' to change the shape to a round one taking off the hard edges and letting the colour fade away to a creamy white, bringing comfort into his body. Throughout a series of investigations and drug treatment that eventually led to a below knee amputation, he regularly used his hypnosis either on his own or with the therapist and reduced his dependence on analgesia. Phantom limb pain began shortly after surgery and he would cry with pain in his now non-existent right ankle. None of the skills he had learned helped. Discussion in supervision led to the suggestion of moving this ankle. In trance Jamie was asked to look at his amputated ankle and see what position it was in. He said it twisted up underneath him and his body weight was crushing it. On instruction he could place it where it should be resting in front of him, feeling at ease and 'comfortable'. He was not bothered again by phantom pains.

Bamford (2006) reports the results of using a four component method for a series of 25 patients with phantom limb pain. The components were:

- *Hypnotic analgesia using a dissociative technique*: In this the patients were taken through guided imagery to a healing pool. In this pool they were asked to imagine the limb in an ice plaster cast and to transfer each component of the pain into the ice. Having completed this task they were asked to imagine warm healing water flowing over the ice and *"as the ice gets smaller the pain gets smaller."* Once the ice had melted it had carried away the pain leaving them with a warm comfort where the pain used to be.
- *Visualization and movement of an imaginary limb*: This was again carried out in the water and they were asked to visualize a normal limb and as they 'watch' the limb they see the whole range of movements of that limb. They were then asked to swim, with the emphasis being on the use of all four limbs.
- *Psychological therapies*: For many the phantom pain was associated with psychological co-morbidities, depression, anger, anxiety, symptoms of PTSD etc. These were addressed using re-framing techniques, silent abreaction and other methods appropriate to that patient's needs. Ego strengthening was also a fundamental part.
- *Self hypnosis*: Patients were asked to practice three times a day.

Six weekly sessions of hypnosis were used and her results showed a highly significant ($p = 0.001$) reduction in pain comparing pre-treatment to post-treatment and a six month follow up. She also reported that after each session the phantom limb became more mobile and in most cases telescoping of the image of the phantom limb occurred as the pain reduced. Interestingly, prior to treatment, four patients reported that they perceived themselves walking on their phantom limb rather than the prosthesis. Following hypnosis all reported telescoping of the phantom limb and began, for the first time, to experience walking on the prosthetic limb.

Bamford's impressive results serve as a reminder that composite individualized methods are likely to be the most effective in all areas of therapy. A 'one size fits all' approach is unlikely to maximize the full potential of such a complex problem, and the novice therapist is reminded that there is not one technique for each problem.

Albert – An above knee amputee

This 70 year old man had required his above knee amputation following failed total knee replacements. The replacement had been required for osteoarthritis but the first replacement became infected so he required a second operation. This too failed and the poor condition of the bones meant that there was no possibility of any further replacements with amputation being the only option. He had phantom pain ever since the operation and described two pains, one coming from his knee which was like the pain he had been experiencing and one from his ankle. The ankle pain was also a result of osteoarthritis, but the phantom pain was more like a burning sensation. He was on analgesics and gabapentin. He had also tried the mirror box therapy.

Following explanation and induction he was asked to recount his story from the time of the first operation. So complex and vivid was his story that it needed about two and a half sessions to complete. Of particular note was his recollection of the attitude of the staff and being made to feel he was making a fuss and being left without adequate pain relief. There was a lot of anger, but he found being able to tell his story was cathartic and he was able to move these memories into his personal museum. During what was left of the third session, he was asked to use the pain dial to turn down the pain and to try to dissociate from it. He reported, *"I do feel better – but I can't explain how."*

At the fourth session, he was asked to look at the circuitry in his mind to see why he was still getting signals from his leg. During a 'cognitive interlude', he was given the explanation that the brain was waiting for response from his phantom limb. He was encouraged to move it. Not only did he begin moving the phantom limb but also he imagined rewiring the circuits. When he returned for his fifth session, he was amazed at the improvement and did some further imagery work on some of the old pains from his ankle. At his sixth session, he was pain free – the first time for 13 years! He reported that he was able to move the phantom limb as normal. He said, *"If I wasn't experiencing this I wouldn't have believed it was possible!"*

It is impossible to say whether the same result would have been obtained if the therapy had been carried out in a different order but experience would suggest that dealing with the psychological burden at the beginning gives the best results. The importance of getting the patient to move the limb is obvious, but do not underestimate the need to explain why such an action would be beneficial.

Conclusion

The interpretation of pain depends on the patient's past experience and future anticipation of their pain; together with their cognitions and emotional state at the time, set within their cultural background. It may be useful to frame pain as a sensation or discomfort when talking to the patient but it is also important to be accepting of their experience. A pain is a pain whatever its physical or psychological underpinnings.

Hypnosis can act to reduce the intensity or the bothersomeness of any pain and can often help both so that it may be useful to score these concepts separately. Any pain which has no variation in intensity will have psychogenic origins which will need exploration. In acute pain there are usually high levels of anxiety which means that the patient is often already in trance, especially if they are in shock with an injury. Everything said or implied in these situations may act as a hypnotic suggestion, whether this is intended or not. Direct suggestions of comfort, cooling, healing and so on can therefore be used with good effect. Negative suggestions given unwittingly at this time may well underpin future problems.

When working with chronic pain, the mindset of expectancy can be generated by using stories and metaphors in hypnosis such as remembering how it felt as a child to receive a present, how it feels to wonder what is around the next corner or what view one might see from the top of a hill one is climbing. The patient may need reminding that their unconscious mind is a vast storehouse of resources, that their conscious mind is like a torch beam only illuminating a small part of it at any one time. Stories of how people find great strength in a crisis such as lifting a car off a small child trapped underneath can be useful. Experiential learning is always effective so helping the patient experience an alteration of any sensation such as weight or temperature can be useful (see page 24). The implication of course is that if they can alter one type of sensation, they can alter another (i.e. their pain).

That we delete a huge amount of sensory information from our conscious experience can be pointed out in hypnosis to the pain patient. It can be helpful to share stories about how after a while we stop hearing ticking clocks and traffic noise, and how we are unaware of parts of our body until we direct our attention to them. Distraction is also a useful tool, and stories about how people are able to ignore injuries in battle, or simple cuts and bruises when busy, can be related. Until we focus our attention on the injury we may not even be aware of it. Glove anaesthesia can be produced using suggestions of ice-cold water, snow, a thick glove, or the feeling of local anaesthetic. Classic imagery such as a turning down a dimmer switch, re-wiring a computer, rubbing out an image on a blackboard or connecting to some wellspring of healing can be used. But as has been said before, client generated imagery is one of the most powerful ways of producing change.

Any improvement in trance should be assessed and the post-hypnotic suggestion given that this may continue out of trance. Although feelings such as heaviness or lightness need to be reversed it is of course important to maximize any feelings of comfort accessed during the hypnosis session. Sometimes the patient reports being pain free for some while after trance reversal. In this case the suggestion could be given that they cue themselves to enter a mini-trance for a few moments on a regular basis and that the period of comfort will get longer over time. Because pain is at some level a message, a useful suggestion to give is that a pain need not clamour at a level of eight or nine if the patient pays necessary attention when it changes (for example) from two to three. The metaphor of a child clamouring for attention from its busy mother may be useful here as may talking about how a mother is so alert to the sound of her child crying that it wakes her even when much louder noises do not.

The use of an anchor to the state of comfort accessed in hypnosis may be very useful with those patients who find that they are pain free for a short post-hypnosis period. By firing the anchor and accessing a 'mini-trance' for a few moments they may find that their pain free period lengthens over time. Some patients (especially those who are bedridden) may find it useful to bring their head 'out of trance' so that they can communicate easily, whilst keeping the rest of their body in the comfort of the hypnotic state.

In chronic pain all these ideas can be seeded earlier with the patient out of hypnosis and reiterated during the hypnotic session.

References

Apkarian, A. V., Bushnell, M. C., Treede, R. D. & Zubieta, J. K. (2005), Human brain mechanisms of pain perception and regulation in health and disease. *European Journal of Pain*, 9, 463–84.

Apkarian, A. V., Sosa, Y., Sonty, S., Levy, R. M., Harden, R. N., Parrish, T. B. & Gitelman, D. R. (2004), Chronic back pain is associated with decreased prefrontal and thalamic gray matter density. *Journal of Neuroscience*, 24, 10410–15.

Bamford, C. (2006), A multifaceted approach to the treatment of phantom limb pain using hypnosis. *Contemporary Hypnosis*, 23 (3), 115–26.

Brann, L., Mackrodt, K. & Joslyn, M. (2008), Hypnosis for chronic pain. Paper presented at the European Society of Hypnosis Conference, Gozo, Malta, September.

Derbyshire, S. (2000), Exploring the pain "neuromatrix. *Current Pain and Headache Reports*, 4, 467–77.

Derbyshire, S. W. G. (2003), A systematic review of neuroimaging data during visceral stimulation. *American Journal of Gastroenterology*, 98, 12–20.

Derbyshire, S. W. G., Whalley, M. G., Stenger, V. A. & Oakley, D. A. (2004), Cerbral activation during hypnotically induced and imagined pain. *Neuroimage*, 23, 10.

Elkins, G., Jensen, M. P. & Patterson, D. R. (2007), Hypnotherapy for the management of chronic pain. *International Journal of Clinical and Experimental Hypnosis*, 55, 275–87.

Engel, G. (1977), The need of a new medical model: a challenge for biomedicine. *Science*, 196, 129–36.

Goldstein, A. & Hilgard, E. R. (1975) Failure of the opiate antagonist naloxone to modify hypnotic analgesia. *Proceedings of the National Academy of Science*, 72, 2041–3.

Hawkins, R. M. F. (2001), A systematic meta-review of hypnosis as an empirically supported treatment for pain. *Pain Reviews*, 8, 47–73.

Heap, M. & Aravind, K. K. (Eds.) (2002). *Hartland's medical and dental hypnosis*. Edinburgh, Churchill Livingstone.

Jensen, T. S., Krebs, B., Nielsen, J. & Rasmussen, P. (1985), Immediate and long-term phantom limb pain in amputees: Incidence, clinical characteristics and relationship to pre-amputation limb pain. *Pain*, 21, 267–78.

Lane, R. D., Waldstein, S. R., Critchley, H. D., Derbyshire, S. W., Drossman, D. A., Wager, T. D., Schneiderman, N., Chesney, M. A., Jennings, R., Lovallo, W. R., Rose, R. M., Thayer, J. F. & Cameron, O. G. (2009), The rebirth of neuroscience in psychosomatic medicine, part 2: clinical applications and implications for research. *Psychosomatic Medicine*, 71, 135–51.

Li, C. L., Ahlberg, D., Lansdell, H., Gravitz, M. A., Chen, T. C., Ting, C. Y., Bak, A. F. & Blessing, D. (1975), Acupuncture and hypnosis: effects on induced pain. *Experimental Neurology*, 49, 272–80.

McCaffrey, M. & Beebe, A. (1989), *Pain: clinical manual for nursing practice*. St. Louis, MO, Mosby.

Melzack, R. (2001), Pain and the neuromatrix in the brain. *Journal of Dental Education*, 65, 1378–82.

Melzack, R. & Wall, P. D. (1965), Pain mechanisms: a new theory. *Science*, 150, 971–9.

Merskey, H., Bogduk, N. & International Association for The Study of Pain. (1994), *Classification of chronic pain: descriptions of chronic pain syndromes and definitions of pain terms*. Seattle, IASP Press.

Montgomery, G. H., Duhamel, K. N. & Redd, W. H. (2000), A meta-analysis of hypnotically induced analgesia: how effective is hypnosis? *International Journal of Clinical and Experimental Hypnosis*, 48, 138–53.

Moret, V., forster, A., laverrière, M. C., lambert, H., gaillard, R. C., Bourgeois, P., Haynal, A., Gemperle, M. & Buchser, E. (1991), Mechanism of analgesia induced by hypnosis and acupuncture: is there a difference? *Pain*, 45, 135–40.

Oakley, D. A., whitman, L. G. & Halligan, P. W. (2002), Hypnotic imagery as a treatment for phantom limb pain: two case reports and a review. *Clinical Rehabilitation*, 16, 368–77.

Ramachandran, V. S. & Blakeslee, S. (1999). *Phantoms in the brain*. London: Fourth Estate.

Sandrini, G., Milanov, I., Malaguti, S., Nigrelli, M. P., Moglia, A. & Nappi, G. (2000), Effects of hypnosis on diffuse noxious inhibitory controls. *Physiology & Behavior*, 69, 295–300.

Spiegel, D. & Albert, L. H. (1983), Naloxone fails to reverse hypnotic alleviation of chronic pain. *Psychopharmacology*, 81, 140–3.

Stern, J. A., Brown, M., Ulett, G. A. & Sletten, I. (1977). A comparison of hypnosis, acupuncture, morphine, valium, aspirin, and placebo in the management of experimentally induced pain. *Annals of the New York Academy of Sciences*, 296, 175–93.

Treede, R.-D., Kenshalo, D. R., Gracely, R. H. & Jones, A. K. P. (1999), The cortical representation of pain. *Pain*, 79, 105–11.

Wall, P. (1989), Introduction, in Wall, P. & Melzack, R. (Eds.) *Text book of pain*, 2nd ed. Edinburgh, Churchill Livingstone.

Willoch, F., Rosen, G., Tolle, T. R., Ove, I., Wester, H. J., Berner, N., Schwaiger, M. & Bartenstein, P. (2000), Phantom limb pain in the human brain: unraveling neural circuitries of phantom limb sensations using positron emission tomography. *Annals of Neurology*, 48 (6), 842–9.

Zigmond, A. & Snaith, R. (1983), The hospital anxiety and depression scale. *Acta Psychiatrica Scandinavica*, 67, 361–70.

22

Anaesthesia, Surgery and Invasive Procedures

Dr David Rogerson, Mrs Jacky Owens and Dr Les Brann

Introduction

In the early 1970s, as a student, one author (DR) recalls one evening sitting in the lecture theatre of the Victoria University of Manchester Medical school. The Medical Society had invited a local general practitioner to talk about his clinical uses of hypnosis. The memory that endures is of a demonstration of a willing volunteer, seemingly immune to any discomfort, when a large bore serum needle was inserted through the skin of his hand. Not the sort of demonstration that would perhaps be recommended today, but it was impressive!

Interestingly, it took the lecturer no time at all to induce a sufficiently deep level of surgical anaesthesia for the volunteer to comfortably undergo the procedure. This is in stark contrast to the mesmeric techniques reported by Dr Esdaile, whilst working for the Dutch East India Company in the latter part of the nineteenth century. As part of his technique, his assistants (perhaps the forerunners of modern anaesthetic nurses) would pass the wand up and down the subject's body for many hours, until a deep trance had been induced. Following this the surgery could take place, and of note were the profound analgesia and lack of post-operative shock that were often prevalent without mesmeric anaesthesia. Hammond (2008) quotes extensively from historical examples of hypnosis as sole anaesthesia for major surgery in the 1800s.

In the example of the medical society lecture above, a selection process had taken place to ensure that the volunteer was an individual who was highly susceptible to hypnosis. However, with Esdaile's patients, a selection process was not reported, so it is unlikely that

The Handbook of Contemporary Clinical Hypnosis: Theory and Practice, First Edition.
Edited by Les Brann, Jacky Owens and Ann Williamson.
© 2012 John Wiley & Sons, Ltd. Published 2015 by John Wiley & Sons, Ltd.

more than 5–10% of them ever entered a sufficiently deep level of trance for the painless surgery to proceed, and the use of traditional techniques such as strong armed assistants to restrain the patient, alcohol, opiates or freezing or the anaesthesia from tightly applied tourniquet techniques would have been used.

It was about this time that modern chemical anaesthesia was in its infancy, and the benefit of an assured level of anaesthesia, without the requirement of being born a highly hypnotically susceptible subject and which could be administered by anybody, was very attractive. These comments make no regard as to the safety of these new anaesthetic agents. Thankfully, modern, balanced anaesthetic techniques are safely administered to millions of patients worldwide by highly trained professionals.

In the general population, if only 5% were able to achieve surgical levels of anaesthesia then in my own hospital where we administer about 40,000 anaesthetics per annum, at least 2,000 patients would be spared the side effects of modern anaesthesia.

Pre-operative Uses

Anxiety

It is often difficult to separate out procedural anxiety and pain since the two are inevitable linked in patients' minds and the anxiety is due in a large measure to the belief that the procedure will be painful. On the other hand some patients become very anxious because their condition is painful and requires an intervention to resolve it.

As an anaesthetist (DR), part of the pre-operative assessment of patients is to decide whether they needed any anti-anxiety premedication before their operation. Being a patient and worrying about what is going to happen when you relinquish control and put yourself in the hands of the operating theatre staff is normal. Generally, with adequate explanation and the opportunity to ask questions, most patients will be content. However, a small group of patients are 'life's worriers'. No matter how thorough the explanation, written and/or verbal, they will find something to be anxious about. In this group, even if premedication drugs were used, they will often arrive in the anaesthetic room hypertensive and with a tachycardia. Having a high level of endogenous catecholamines circulating is not necessarily the best way to start an anaesthetic!

Simple hypnotic techniques were used by the author (DR) with pre-operative patients. During a brief session of hypnosis (five to ten minutes), patients were taught a simple relaxation exercise and this relaxation was 'anchored' with a finger anchor technique. They could use this relaxation on the wards before the operation to feel more comfortable and in control at otherwise worrying times such as when the porters arrived to take them to theatre, whilst travelling along corridors on their back looking at the ceiling lights, when they passed through the theatre doors aware of the different noises and smells. The impression was that they appeared calmer and many said they felt more in control. Interestingly, the ward nurses became aware of the benefits to some of their patients and would point out individuals: *"Can you see Mrs. X and see if you can calm her down?"*

These observational benefits are supported by published trials. Pre-operative anxiety reduction was assessed in a group of gynaecology patients using a brief hypnotic intervention by Goldmann *et al.* (1988). 52 female patients who underwent gynaecological operations as day cases received either a short pre-operative hypnotic induction or a brief discussion of equal duration. Hypnotized patients who underwent vaginal termination of pregnancy required significantly less methohexitone for induction of anaesthesia. They were also significantly more relaxed as judged by their visual analogue scores for anxiety. Less than half of the patients were satisfied with their knowledge about the operative procedure even after discussions with the surgeon and anaesthetist. A significant correlation was found between anxiety and perceived knowledge of procedures. The results suggest that pre-operative hypnosis can provide a quick and effective way to reduce pre-operative patient anxiety and anaesthetic requirements for gynaecological day case surgery.

Several researchers have found hypnosis to be of benefit in reducing anxiety associated with surgery both pre- and post-operatively (Saadat *et al.*, 2006; Schnur *et al.*, 2008). Blankfield (1991) in his review of clinical trials concludes that hypnosis, suggestion and relaxation are under-used techniques which can promote physical recovery, help emotional and psychological responses and shorten post-operative hospital time. Genuis (1995) carried out a review of the systematic studies pertaining to the use of hypnosis generally since 1980, and Montgomery *et al.* (2002) conducted a meta-analysis of the effectiveness of adjunctive hypnosis with surgical patients. Mendoza and Capafons (2009) also summarize the current empirical evidence for the efficacy of clinical hypnosis.

Post-operative Nausea and Vomiting

Many confounding variables affect whether a patient suffers nausea or vomiting post-operatively such as whether they are male or female, undergoing a major or minor procedure, the operative site, duration of surgery, hydration, cigarette consumption and so on. There are no published RCTs assessing the effectiveness of hypnosis and allowing for all the possible confounding factors in this area.

However, some of the published literature attempts to address these issues, although whether the suggestions are considered 'hypnotic' is debatable (Williams *et al.*, 1994). In this study, women undergoing total abdominal hysterectomy were randomized to a control or treatment group. 19 patients in the treatment group listened intra-operatively (i.e. whilst anaesthetized) via special headphones to a 12 minute recording of suggestions repeated three times on each side of the tape.

The first nine minutes of the tape gave information on the normal post-operative procedures with advice on how best to cope with them; for example, *"How quickly you recover from your operation depends on you – the more you relax, the more comfortable you will be."* Then two minutes of direct suggestion: *"You will not feel sick; you will not have any pain."* Finally, one minute of third person suggestions, *"The operation is going well and the patient is fine."* The control group listened to a blank tape.

The results showed that the mean stay for the suggestion group was 1.3 (16%) days less than the control group. Similarly the suggestion group had 1.8 (45%) fewer half days of pyrexia and a significant reduction in gastrointestinal problems than the control group. The primary outcome of the study demonstrated no difference in the incidence of post-operative nausea and vomiting, pain and anxiety scores. Nevertheless, the nursing staff rated the suggestion group as having better recoveries than the control group, who behaved as normally expected. None of the patients recalled intra-operative events or conversations. Interestingly, all but one in the suggestion group guessed correctly that they had listened to the tape. In the control group, the guesses as to which tape they had listened to were randomly distributed. If using taped suggestions during anaesthesia, then the aspects of informed consent need to be addressed.

Ewin (1990) reports on intra-operative recall of information (possibly underpinning psychosomatic symptoms) and describes a hypnotic technique for recovering memories of sounds heard under general anaesthesia. 'The things that are recallable are: 1) Salient, 2) Said (usually) by the surgeon or anaesthetist, and 3) Said at an appropriate time during the procedure'.

Children

Lambert (1996) describes 52 children, who were due to have operations who were randomly assigned to be taught guided imagery or hypnosis, which included suggestions for a favourable post-operative course, or assigned to a control group. Significantly lower post-operative pain ratings and shorter hospital stays occurred for children in the experimental group. State anxiety was decreased for the guided imagery group and increased post-operatively for the control group. The study demonstrated the positive effects of hypnosis and guided imagery for the paediatric surgical patient.

Calipel *et al.* (2005) studied hypnosis versus midazolam for pre-medication in children. 50 patients were randomized into two groups. One group received hypnosis and the other midazolam pre-operatively. They found, 'Hypnosis seems effective as premedication for children scheduled for surgery. It alleviates preoperative anxiety, especially during induction of anaesthesia and reduces behavioural disorders during the first postoperative week' (p. 275).

Procedures where Anaesthesia Drugs would Normally be Used for Invasive Medical Procedures

Goldie (1956) reports using hypnosis in a London casualty department across an age range of three and a half to 57 years, specifically to deal with reducing fractures and dislocations, suturing lacerations and dental extractions.

Meurisse (1999) reports that having used hypnosis routinely in more than 1,400 procedures in plastic surgery they decided to see if hypnosis could be used adjunctively with conscious intravenous sedation for endocrine surgery, instead of general anaesthesia. The technique termed 'hypnosedation' was used in 296 cases of thyroidectomy and 33 cases of cervical explorations for hyperparathyroidism. Conversion to general anaesthesia was necessary in only three cases and all patients reported a pleasant experience. In the thyroid study Meurisse states, 'The post-operative convalescence was significantly improved after HS [hypnosedation] and full return to social or professional activity was significantly shortened' (p. 150).

Ewin (1999) also advocates the use of hypnosis in the accident and emergency setting especially with regard to burns injuries. Using the suggestion 'cool and comfortable' within the first two hours post-burn is said to reduce the inflammatory response to the burn which is often responsible for much of the later problems.

Burns dressings often need anaesthesia and Wright and Drummond (2000) studied the effect of rapid induction analgesia (RIA) on the resting and procedural pain, anticipatory anxiety, relaxation levels and medication consumption in 30 hospitalized burn patients. RIA was conducted in 15 patients, and the other 15 control patients had their dressings changed as usual. Self reported ratings of the affective and sensory components of pain decreased significantly during and after RIA, particularly in patients who became readily absorbed and relaxation increased during burn care. Anticipatory anxiety decreased before dressing changes in the RIA group, and analgesic intake decreased between treatment sessions. RIA appears to be a viable adjunct to narcotic treatment for pain control during burn care.

Frenay (2001) reported a study in which two psychological support interventions are compared for controlling peri-dressing change pain and anxiety in severely burned patients over a 14 day period. Patients received either hypnosis or stress-reducing strategies adjunctively to routine intramuscular pre-dressing change analgesia and anxiolytic drugs. Visual analogue scale (VAS) scores for anxiety, pain, pain control and satisfaction were recorded at two day intervals throughout the 14 day study period, before, during and after dressing changes. Anxiety VAS scores were significantly decreased before and during dressing changes when the hypnotic technique was used instead of SRS, and although no difference was observed for pain, pain control and satisfaction, the VAS scores for anxiety were always better in the hypnosis group.

As with almost all significant trauma, burn patients often necessitate frequent regular physiotherapy to regain and maintain mobility of the affected area. Anxiety and pain often affect the patients' ability to co-operate fully with physiotherapy demands resulting in less than optimum outcomes. In Harandi and Esfandani's (2004) randomized controlled trial, 44 female patients in a burn unit were entered into either the intervention or control group; the former had four hypnosis sessions, whereas the control group did not. When evaluated using a Visual Analogue Scale (VAS), it was found that the degree of pain and anxiety caused by physiotherapy had decreased significantly in the intervention group as compared to the control group.

A further randomized trial looking at adjunctive non-pharmacological analgesia for invasive medical procedures was reported by Lang *et al.* (2000*a*). She randomized 241 patients to receive standard intra-operative care, structured attention or self hypnotic relaxation. All had access to patient controlled intravenous analgesia with fentanyl and midazolam. Pain score remained flat in the hypnosis group but increased linearly with time in the attention and control groups. Drug use was significantly higher in the attention group than the other two. Procedure times were significantly shorter in the hypnosis group. Anxiety decreased over time in all three groups. Structured attention and self hypnotic relaxation proved beneficial during invasive medical procedures with hypnosis having more pronounced effects on pain and anxiety reduction and was superior in that it also improved haemodynamic stability.

Wobst (2007) reviewed literature on pre- and peri-operative suggestions for a wide range of surgical procedures along with a historical time line for hypnosis in his article 'Hypnosis and Surgery: Past, Present and Future'. He states that 'Contemporary clinical investigators claim that the combination of analgesia and hypnosis is superior to conventional pharmacologic anaesthesia for minor surgical cases with patients and surgeons responding favourably' (p. 1199). Another review of contemporary literature and controlled research on the use of hypnosis in relation to surgery and prior to medical procedures is reported by Hammond (2008).

A further study by Lang *et al.* (2008) to determine how hypnosis and empathic attention during percutaneous tumour treatments affect pain, anxiety, drug use and adverse events found, 'Procedural hypnosis including empathic attention reduces pain, anxiety and medication use with patient controlled fentanyl and midazolam. Conversely, empathic approaches without hypnosis that provide an external focus of attention and do not enhance patients' self-coping can result in more adverse events' (p. 897). Adverse events are defined as occurrences requiring extra medical attention, including systolic blood pressure fluctuations, vasovagal episodes, cardiac events and respiratory impairment.

Procedures associated with either the diagnosis or treatment of cancer carry enormous anxiety in that the patient has to deal with not only the procedure itself but also the uncertainty over the results that follow. Lang (2000b) reported that 236 women referred for large core needle breast biopsy were randomized to receive standard care, structured empathic attention, or self-hypnotic relaxation during the procedure. Women's anxiety increased significantly in the standard group, did not change in the empathy group and decreased significantly in the hypnosis group. The researchers conclude that while both structured empathy and hypnosis decrease procedural pain and anxiety, hypnosis provides more powerful anxiety relief.

Children, perhaps because of their easy ability to use hypnosis, have featured in many articles looking to mitigate anxiety and associated pain with medical and surgical procedures. Zeltzer and LeBaron (1982) reports comparing hypnosis with non-hypnotic behavioural techniques in a group of 27 children and adolescents prior to and during bone marrow aspiration. Pain was reduced to a large extent by hypnosis and to a smaller but significant extent by non-hypnotic techniques, and anxiety was significantly reduced by hypnosis alone. In the same study the comparison was again made with 22 children and adolescents during a lumbar puncture procedure, where it was found that only hypnosis significantly reduced pain; anxiety was reduced to a large degree by hypnosis and to a smaller degree by non-hypnotic techniques.

In another study using hypnosis with adolescents undergoing bone marrow aspirations, chemotherapy injections and lumbar puncture procedures, Kellerman *et al.* (1983) found that reductions in pain and anxiety were significant at levels ranging from $p < 0.02$ to $p < 0.002$ (two-tailed t-tests) for 16 out of the 18 participants. Two participants rejected hypnosis, and they were found to have had unusually higher levels of pre-treatment anxiety.

Clinical psychologist Dr Leora Kuttner in 1985 made a groundbreaking video of herself working with eight children in BC Childrens Hospital Vancouver. Mind–body techniques including hypnosis enabled them to undergo cancer related procedures. The video, entitled *No Fears, No Tears*, was followed 13 years later with another one entitled *No Fears, No Tears 13 Years Later*, in which the same eight children relate the long term benefits of the techniques they had learnt whilst undergoing the cancer treatments.

Liossi and Hatira (2003) conducted a prospective controlled trial in which she investigated hypnosis as a means of helping youngsters aged six to 16 years undergo regular lumbar punctures. Patients were randomly assigned to one of four arms; direct hypnosis with standard medical treatment, indirect hypnosis with standard medical treatment, attention control with standard medical treatment and standard medical treatment alone. Those in the hypnosis groups reported less pain and anxiety, there being no discernable difference in direct and indirect hypnotic suggestions. Liossi and Hatira also report that therapeutic benefit degraded when patients used self hypnosis, thus success may depend upon the therapist being present. Clinically it has been found that reinforcement is often necessary, as such youngsters in hospital rarely practice.

In a later study, Liossi *et al.* (2006) worked with 45 paediatric patients to relieve the pain and anxiety associated with lumbar puncture procedure. Patients were assigned to either analgesic cream (EMLA) or EMLA plus hypnosis or EMLA plus attention. Those in the EMLA plus hypnosis group reported less anticipatory anxiety and less procedure-related pain and anxiety. She reports an association between the level of hypnotizability and the magnitude of benefit gained. In addition the patients could be taught to use hypnosis independently and in so doing maintained this benefit.

Colonoscopy is an uncomfortable procedure requiring sedation, and Elkins *et al.* (2006) recorded levels of anxiety in six patients before and after a hypnotic induction using Visual Analogue Scales (VAS). VAS were used to assess anxiety and pain during colonoscopy, perceived effectiveness of hypnosis, and patient satisfaction with medical care. Ten consecutive patients who received standard care were monitored for vasovagal occurrences. The authors conclude that hypnosis is a reasonable method to manage anxiety and pain associated with colonoscopy and that it also reduces the need for sedation. It may also impact on the incidence of vasovagal attacks and recovery time.

Some types of surgery lead to specific complications – for example post-operative atrial fibrillation (AF) following coronary artery bypass surgery. Such complications require further medical intervention. Novoa and Hammonds (2008) showed that those ($n = 50$) who received hypnosis had significantly ($p = 0.003$) fewer episodes of AF compared to case matched controls. Although it fell short of statistical significance, they also showed a trend towards lower narcotic use, shorter lengths of stay and lower total hospital charges in the hypnosis group.

A reduction in health care cost has also been reported by Montgomery *et al.* (2007). 200 patients undergoing breast biopsy or lumpectomy were randomly assigned to receive either hypnosis or non-directive empathic listening. The brief hypnosis (15 minutes) was delivered pre-operatively. The hypnosis group had not only less pain intensity, pain unpleasantness, nausea, fatigue, discomfort and emotional upset but also a 9% cost saving compared to the control group.

Whilst the value of published trial data cannot be overestimated, the importance of case reports for patient specific problems must be highlighted and the following two examples are cases in point.

Case study 1

A 52 year old lady presented for the operation of rhinoplasty and appeared on pre-operative assessment to have a grade 3 Mallampati airway score and despite 10 mg each of temazepam and metoclopramide was virtually unable to extend her neck and was plainly presenting as a difficult airway management problem. Two and a half years previously she had suffered facial injuries and underwent an uneventful nasal septoplasty operation. The week after this operation she complained of left sided, soon becoming bilateral, neck pain. Rheumatology investigation found muscle spasm and no bony abnormality. As the patient usually found it difficult to swallow tablets, she requested physiotherapy, which seemed to make her symptoms worse and exacerbated the headaches she was then experiencing. Further rheumatology review, two years after her accident, noted persistent stiff neck movements, particularly on rotation to the right, and a previous history of migrainous headaches was elicited.

Further to discussing airway management techniques with the patient, hypnosis was suggested as a way of inducing profound muscle relaxation in order to further assess neck movement. She readily agreed to this. Following preliminary explanations and reassurance, hypnosis was induced with a hand levitation technique. There was rapid jerky and uncoordinated elevation of her hand towards her face. The trance was deepened with suggestions of hand heaviness by asking her to hold her arm horizontally in front of her at shoulder height and palm facing upwards. She was then to imagine very heavy dictionaries being sequentially placed upon her hand, which would cause it to fall back onto her lap. Liberal suggestions of deepening and relaxation were interspersed. Further deepening was achieved by thinking of a safe place, known only to her, where she could imagine being free of all tension and completely relaxed. Suggestions of progressive muscular relaxation were then given, commencing with her feet and ascending through her body, ending with strong suggestions of deep relaxation in her head, neck, facial and shoulder muscles. By this stage she appeared to be in a deep trance and on request was able to demonstrate a full and free range of neck movements and mouth opening.

The patient was given post-hypnotic suggestions of general wellbeing and persistent relaxation and then alerted to the present by counting from one to five, five being the cue to return to the present. Following this procedure, reassurance was obtained that this lady's airway would be safely secured and she subsequently underwent a routine general anaesthetic and no problems were encountered with the endotracheal intubation in this now 'Grade 1' (normal) airway patient.

Following discharge, the patient was subsequently interviewed and the author found some of the improvements had been maintained and took the opportunity to assess hypnotic susceptibility using Barber's Creative Imagination Scale. She scored 37 out of a maximum of 40. Similarly, having noted the rapid response to hand levitation, she would have scored highly on the Stanford Hypnotic Arm Levitation Induction Test (SHALIT). Additionally, unlike a previously unsuccessful visit to a lay therapist for smoking cessation, she commented on the close rapport with the current therapist for the airway problem, which seems to be one of the many features needed for the induction of hypnosis. Hypnosis on this occasion was helpful in gaining information about the patient's airway in the relaxed state without the need for her to endure unnecessarily uncomfortable, orthodox anaesthetic techniques. Furthermore, it is a non-invasive way of assessing the airway as an alternative to using local anaesthesia as described by Heard *et al.* (2009).

Case study 2

A patient in her late forties was due to have a total abdominal hysterectomy operation. She was anaesthetized by a colleague but due to difficulties passing an oral endotracheal tube, the procedure was abandoned and scheduled for another day. She suffered from severe ankylosing spodylitis and as such had very limited mouth opening with markedly reduced neck flexion and extension. The operation was rescheduled for a few weeks later when a flexible intubating laryngoscope would be available (this was some years ago when such equipment was not routinely available). Involvement with this patient was originally because of experience with the specialized equipment rather than hypnosis expertise.

The patient was visited pre-operatively and found to be a delightful, stoical lady who understood the reasons for deferring the operation. However, she was a little apprehensive when it was explained that the intubation would be carried out under local anaesthesia, with her awake, albeit with a moderate amount of sedation. She happily accepted the invitation to learn some self hypnosis relaxation skills. This was done during a brief session with her on the ward. The suggestion was given that a finger anchor could be used to access the relaxation in the future without the need for a formal hypnotic induction. Interspersed were some post-hypnosis suggestions that she would recover from the operation just as quickly and appropriately as was right for her, without the need for any side effects from the operation or anaesthetic that she may have experienced in the past. It was suggested that the relaxation achieved during the session could be accessed any time, in the appropriate circumstances, as profoundly as was appropriate by using her finger anchor.

The fibre optic intubation, anaesthesia and operation went uneventfully. When she was visited on the ward 24 hours later, surprisingly she was walking about the ward, attending to other patients' needs, and certainly did not appear to have just undergone a major operation! She had not needed any anti-emetics, major analgesia or any other medication. She was just keen to get on with living her life. She made an uneventful recovery and was so pleased with her care that she subsequently fundraised enough money to buy the hospital a new fibre optic intubating laryngoscope.

This patient was not given authoritarian, specific suggestions such as *"No pain, no sickness, mobilize early,"* but rather permissive suggestions that were in keeping with her life and that she could accept or reject as she chose. There does not appear to be any evidence to say which type of suggestion is best but from experience when bringing up children, when they are told authoritatively to do something, the expected response is not always forthcoming!

Whilst the use of hypnosis as the sole anaesthetic agent is well reported (see Hammond 2008 for a review), Coveney (2009) reports the use of hypnosis plus local anaesthetic (LA) in situations where patients are unfit for general anaesthesia in the two cases below:

Thus, published evidence and case reports verify the use of hypnosis in anaesthesia, in

A 63 year old woman was admitted as an emergency with a strangulated femoral hernia. She was unfit for general anaesthesia because of severe emphysema and alcoholic liver disease. She underwent a hypnosis susceptibility test and was found to be a good subject. Hypnosis was induced and she was asked to take herself to her special place. She was given suggestions for comfort and to ignore any other sensations. She was given posthypnotic suggestions for analgesia. Lignocaine (10 ml) was used for the skin incision, and the infarcted small bowel was resected without any further anaesthesia. She made an uneventful recovery and did not require any post-operative analgesia for 48 hours.

An unfit 83 year old lady with locally advanced breast cancer elected to have a mastectomy done under hypnosis and local anaesthetic, susceptibility tests having confirmed her suitability. She had a relaxing induction and took herself to her special place. Glove anaesthesia was induced and the numbness transferred to her breast. The mastectomy was carried out with just 45 ml of LA. She did not have any sedation.

surgery and for invasive procedures. Techniques involve the teaching of self hypnosis as well as general positive suggestions and anchoring (see page 145). Also useful is positive mental rehearsal whereby the patient associates with the visualization of the desired outcome of having the procedure feeling calm and comfortable (see page 45). Using revivification (see page 116) or special place imagery can enable the patient to dissociate from the procedure. Giving the suggestion that *"You can leave your leg* (or whatever part of the body that is required for the procedure) *here for us to help whilst you can take yourself away to that very special place and really enjoy being there, so that whatever we do here need not bother you at all"* can be very effective.

Anticipatory anxiety often arises many days before the procedure and as well as teaching the patient all the tools detailed above, the use of metaphor such as that shown below can be added to good effect.

The Time Capsule (courtesy of Mr D Simons)

For many people an injection (maybe in dentistry) or the venepuncture and intravenous delivery of chemotherapy is incredibly anxiety provoking. This crescendo of anxiety will inevitably affect their response to the trauma, thus prejudicing their next episode of treatment or chemotherapy. So the sequence tends to be weeks of growing anxiety, a few minutes of trauma, followed by weeks of distressful thinking about it.

The following visualization was devised to address this, in its way almost a cognitive approach to the amounts of time involved in the sequence.

> *I wonder if you can imagine a really stretched out length of cotton or string... really long... really stretched out... maybe it has a colour... maybe you can see that colour in your mind... and that string or cotton is all about time... it is about 28 days long.... I wonder if you can imagine it with 28 little marks so that each day is just so long on the cotton... but each of those days is 24 hours so there are hundreds of tiny markers... and each of those hours is 60 minutes... thousands of minutes .... and each of those minutes is 60 seconds... and do you know that that length of thread measures well... millions of seconds on that thread... and right in the middle is the bit that used to bother you... and I know it use to bother you a lot... but it was actually for a short time... maybe used to last about half a minute... so it's a really tiny mark... and on that long thread it is almost impossible to see... and it stands alone... so there is no need for the huge length of thread before it and the huge length after it to have anything to do with it.... I wonder if you can see that mark maybe as an absolutely tiny droplet hanging onto the thread... really tiny... maybe that tiny droplet itself has a colour... or maybe not... maybe it is shining as the light reflects on it... maybe not... and I wonder if you can imagine that droplet like a tiny droplet of paint, or glue, or nail varnish... and you know that if you leave that out it will develop a shell around itself... and imagine that droplet on the cord developing a shell so that it does not exist outside the shell... and you realize somewhere in your mind that for all those seconds and minutes and hours and days before the (chemo, blood test, procedure) it is as though that capsule does not exist... it is just in its shell... and for all those seconds and minutes and hours and days afterwards it does not exist... as though it is in its own time capsule... and in the middle... for that so brief moment... you will break through the shell and into the capsule... feeling so good... so strong... so confident... so comfortable... and afterwards close up the capsule again... and as that happens you will be aware of the instant of time involved... and feel so comfortable and good that you will hardly notice it happening. ...*

Note the use of past tense "*... used... to bother you.*" This is always valuable, particularly in dealing with recurrent or ongoing pain or anxiety.

Hypnosis is also used widely in dental surgery. Moore and Abrahamsen (2002) all show hypnosis is effective in dealing with dental anxiety, and this is supported by Mendoza and Capafons (2009). Gow (2007) highlights the use of hypnotic suggestion to control post-extraction bleeding, and Lucas (1975) was helping haemophiliac patients with severe dental anxiety many years ago and reports that extraction and post-extraction bleeding can be controlled using hypnotic suggestion.

A detailed discussion of hypnosis in dentistry is beyond the scope of this book, but the interested reader is referred to existing texts such as *Hypnosis and Communication in Dentistry* (Simons *et al.*, 2007) for a comprehensive account of its application and uses. However it would be inappropriate not to exemplify the use of hypnosis as a very powerful tool in this field and the following case history by courtesy of Dr Mike Gow illustrates its use as the sole anaesthetic agent in dental surgery. The detail included in the case report evidences the need for painstaking preparation for such cases. Such cases also require the support of colleagues skilled in working with patients during hypnosis. Whilst detailed, the summary presented here omits the expert commentary on the rationale behind the chosen techniques, and interested readers are advised to consult the original papers.

Hypnosis as the sole anaesthetic agent in dental surgery

A 43 year old woman required implants to her central incisors, a procedure normally carried out with local anaesthetic and sometimes sedation. The patient had enquired about having it carried out under hypnosis rather than having the usual local anaesthetic.

A full discussion about hypnosis took place during the first (hypnosis) appointment, and this included the details of the procedure of placing the implant so she was well aware of what was required. The second appointment allowed the patient to have a brief, basic hypnotic experience lasting approximately 40 minutes.

At the next session, hypnotic pain control techniques were introduced. The technique of 'glove anaesthesia' was introduced. The patient was also asked to create an image of a 'comfort dial'. The 'comfort dial' is a dial or gauge of the patient's choice, which the patient imagines with numbers zero to ten. It is important that the imagery of the dial is created by the patient. The patient in this case chose that her dial would have a black dial in middle, with white numbers. The patient stated that the maximum score which she would be prepared to tolerate during the procedure on her dial would be a score of eight. It was agreed with the patient that should she report a score of eight or higher, then local anaesthetics would be delivered immediately.

'Future rehearsal' allowed the patient to positively rehearse the procedure in her mind, seeing the final, successful outcome and culminating in her smiling with her new teeth. During this session the patient was also taught an anchoring technique. Upon giving herself the 'signal to herself, from herself' of touching the tip of her thumb and index finger on her left hand, it was suggested that she would be able to instantly access positive emotions, such as confidence, calmness, control and relaxation.

At a further visit, the techniques that had been previously taught were rehearsed. When the patient was comfortable and 'glove anaesthesia' had been successfully achieved, the patient was taught how to transfer the altered sensations to the tissues surrounding the upper central incisors. This area was then tested for anaesthesia. This test was performed using a sharp dental probe, which was introduced to the periodontal ligament of the teeth with enough force to satisfy the clinicians that the patient was indeed experiencing satisfactory anaesthesia.

A final preparatory session was arranged for the day before the surgery was to be performed. This gave the patient a chance to rehearse the techniques she had learned as some time had elapsed since her last visit. It also allowed the further use of relaxation techniques and 'future rehearsal' to ensure that her motivation and expectations for the following day were high.

On the day of the surgery, the patient was prepared following pre-operative consent, antibiotics and mouth rinsing with chlorhexidine gluconate 0.2%. The patient was reminded of her anchor signal. It was discussed that the chair was likely to be adjusted during the procedure, but the suggestion was given that any time it was moved she could feel even more relaxed.

A pulse oximeter was used to monitor the patient's pulse as a measure of the patient's comfort and supported the clinician's observations. The patient's resting pulse rate had been recorded as 70 bpm at the previous visit. At start of this session, the pulse was 86 bpm. A rapid induction technique using arm movement and eye closure quickly induced trance. Following eye closure it was suggested that if she 'tried' to open her eyes she would notice how heavy they had become. Care was taken to give suggestions on the patient's outward breath. It was suggested that she could *"Allow mind and body to separate, allowing her mind to drift away to a special place in the imagination."* The patient chose her 'special place' to be 'on the beach, watching and listening to the waves'. She was asked to *"see* (sea) *and hear the waves of relaxation which can tumble through the body from head to toe. With each wave tumbling onto the beach, the body feels more and more relaxed . . . sinking deeper into the chair . . . using all the senses to elaborate this special place . . . any noises in the room can drift away to the back of the mind."*

Suggestions continued that *"as you notice the weather you can wonder whether the weather will stay the same or become even more comfortable, even more pleasant."* Simple breathing techniques were introduced. The patient visualized 'dark grey colours in her tummy', which she was able to breathe out. These negative feelings were then 'evaporated by the sun'. The patient was then able to increase her relaxation by breathing in her chosen relaxing colour, a 'nice, blue colour'. It was suggested that the 'blue could wash away any remaining dark grey' while she continued to enjoy focusing on her breathing, becoming even more relaxed. An ego-strengthening technique involving a mantra of 'calm, control, confident and comfort' written around a triangle drawn by the patient in the sand was employed. The patient was able to use her 'anchoring' signal of touching her thumb and index finger together to strengthen these positive feelings. It was suggested that *"each wave of relaxation makes the body feel heavier and more relaxed."*

After 23 minutes, while further ego-strengthening and relaxation techniques were used, standard surgical scrub and drapes were employed. It was suggested that as she was 'tucked in' she would feel 'safe and entirely comfortable'. Continued suggestions were given to elaborate her 'special place' at the beach. Suggestions were given that *"Your conscious may be wondering how these techniques work, but the unconscious is powerful and already knows how to do this naturally. You have the resources within you to allow this procedure to be entirely comfortable. This procedure will improve the health and function of your teeth and mouth, so it is reasonable that it should be allowed to happen comfortably. The unconscious can access the areas in the brain which receive signals from any part of the body. In the same way as you could operate an old telephone exchange, the unconscious can disconnect the appropriate cables and connections for as long as is necessary for the procedure to be carried out comfortably."*

The patient was reminded about her 'comfort dial', which she described as having a black dial with white numbers, with zero on the left. A confusional statement followed by a positive suggestion was given that *"as you zero in on the dial, you can turn it down. With the zero on the left, it's right that zero can be left, as you turn the dial right down, zero is all that's left. And that's your right because it is right that the procedure can be carried out comfortably."* With the 'comfort dial' set at zero, the pulse was recorded at 74 bpm.

Ordinarily, it would be prudent to avoid asking the patient to record their 'comfort dial' score too often as although it gives an indication of comfort, asking someone to focus on the dial may have the detriment that it focuses their attention back onto any discomfort they may be experiencing. Regular scores were taken, however, for the purpose of this case study as it had been pre-determined that the maximum the patient would be prepared to tolerate on her dial would be a score of eight, and that local anaesthetics would be delivered if her score reached this level.

Some 28 minutes into the session, 'glove anaesthesia' was induced and transferred to the tissues around the central incisors. The patient was given the suggestion that she should *"take all the time needed in the next few moments to transfer all the sensations."* It was also suggested that *"the unconscious can remember what it feels like to have had local anaesthetic at the front of the mouth. As you transfer the numbness from the fingers to the teeth, it can recreate this numb sensation which it remembers."* Using ideomotor signalling, it was suggested that *"the unconscious mind will signal that it is ready for this good work to begin by allowing the hand to leave the mouth and drift down to the lap."*

The patient was given a pad of paper and a pen to write down her 'comfort dial scores' some 35 minutes into the session. Her first, baseline, score of zero, indicating complete comfort, was recorded and her pulse was recorded at 70 bpm. Suggestions continued that *"as you write any numbers, it is right for you to turn the dial left"* and that she could *"zero in on the comfort of these sensations, writing down a wee number."* At 36 minutes, analgesia was tested around the central incisors using a probe. The 'comfort dial score' remained at zero during this testing and the pulse at about 70 bpm, indicating that the patient was comfortable.

The upper central incisor teeth were carefully loosened using periotomes 39 minutes into the session. It was emphasized that all the patient would feel was 'pressure, movement and perhaps the sensation of the sand under her feet' as she walked along the beach of her 'special place'. The pulse was recorded as between 65 and 70 bpm, and the 'comfort dial scores' varied between zero and one over the next three minutes.

After 41 minutes, forceps were used to lift away the UL1. Bleeding control was achieved with suction and by asking the patient to visualize a flowing tap which she was able to turn down. It was suggested that the suction tip could also suck away any remaining 'normal' sensations, leaving the area even number. At 43 minutes, forceps were used to lift away the UR1 at which time a 'comfort dial score' of two was recorded. It was suggested she refocus on her 'comfort dial' and 'zero' in on it.

51 minutes into the session, the first implant was inserted with a 'comfort dial score' of zero and pulse of 65 bpm recorded. At 56 minutes the implant drill prepared the second

socket. At 58 minutes a 'comfort dial score' of two was recorded with the pulse elevated to 74 bpm, and one minute later this had raised again to a 'comfort dial score' of three, with pulse of 71 bpm. At this stage, further 'deepening' and 'hypnoanaesthesia' suggestions were given. At 60 minutes, the 'comfort dial score' had reduced to one, and it was suggested that *"a comfortable one is right because it is right for one to feel comfortable."* At 63 minutes the second implant was inserted in the socket at the 11 region and further bleeding control suggestions were successfully employed. Bone, harvested earlier in the procedure, was packed into the space between the implants and the buccal plate.

Standard post-operative protocols were followed. Post-hypnotic suggestions are important in any hypnosis case, and in this case were used to ensure the continuing comfort of the patient and rapid healing. Suggestions were given that *"you will be surprised by how easily and quickly the area heals. You may be aware of comfortable, healing sensations in the following hours and days."* Suggestions were given that any altered sensations would return to normal when appropriate, in the same way as the effects of local anaesthetics wear off gradually. Standard hypnotic safeguards and ethical blocks were given to ensure the patient's safety during future experiences with hypnosis and trance was reversed. Interestingly the pulse when the patient was alerted was 86 bpm, considerably higher than it was at any time during the surgery. The patient stated at the conclusion of the procedure that she was surprised that her highest 'comfort dial score' was 'only a three'. She said that she recalled the whole procedure and was surprised by how easy she found it. The patient returned to work as normal the following day.

This case featured on BBC 2's *Alternative Therapies'* three-part documentary series presented by Professor Kathy Sykes, Professor of Science and Society at Bristol University, which began on Monday 17 March 2008.

In Conclusion

Hypnosis is capable of being used in medicine as a means of managing pain and anxiety. There is also a reduced amount of analgesia and chemical sedation needed to help patients complete various medical and surgical procedures. Treatment costs and a reduced length of hospital stay are both repeatedly reported in the literature. There is very little written to suggest that hypnosis has any significant side effects. It appears capable of reducing pain and distress amongst patients, and it results in increased patient satisfaction. Milling (2008) concedes that hypnosis may be more effective in patients with high hypnotic susceptibility, and a few rare cases of hypnosis as the sole anaesthetic for major surgery, in highly hypnotically susceptible individuals, will continue to be occasionally reported. However, the main use will be in balanced anaesthesia.

Thus the literature supports the contention that there is a reduction in anxiety, pain, adverse events and analgesic and sedative drug dosage, when hypnosis is added to the management plan.

References

Blankfield, R. P. (1991), Suggestion, relaxation, and hypnosis as adjuncts in the care of surgery patients: a review of the literature. *The American Journal of Clinical Hypnosis*, 33 (3), 172–86.

Calipel, S., Lucas-Polomeni, M. M., Wodey, E. & Ecoffey, C. (2005), Premedication in children: hypnosis versus midazolam. *Paediatric Anaesthesia*, 15 (4), 275–81.

Coveney, E. (2009), Presentation to BSCAH Eastern Counties Branch, Norwich, autumn.

Elkins, G. W. J., Patel, P., Marcus, J., Perfect, M. M. & Montgomery, G. H. (2006), Hypnosis to manage anxiety and pain associated with colonoscopy for colorectal cancer screening: case studies and possible benefits. *International Journal of Clinical and Experimental Hypnosis*, 54 (4), 416–31.

Ewin, D. (1990), Hypnotic Technique for recall of sounds heard under general anaesthesia, in Benno, B., Fitch, W. & Millar, K. (Eds.) *Memory and awareness in anaesthesia*. Amsterdam, Swets & Zeitlinger.

Ewin, D. (1999), Hypnosis in the emergency room, in Temes, R. (Ed.) *Medical hypnosis: an introduction and clinical guide*. London, Churchill Livingstone.

Frenay, M. (2001), Psychological approaches during dressing changes of burned patients: a prospective randomised study comparing hypnosis against stress reducing strategy. *Burns*, 27 (8), 793–9.

Genuis, M. L. (1995), The use of hypnosis in helping cancer patients control anxiety, pain, and emesis: a review of recent empirical studies. *American Journal of Clinical Hypnosis*, 4, 316–25.

Goldie, L. (1956), Hypnosis in the casualty department. *British Medical Journal*, 3, 1140–2.

Goldmann, L., Ogg, T. W. & Levey, A. B. (1988), Hypnosis and day case anaesthesia: a study to reduce pre-operative anxiety and intra-operative anaesthetic requirements. *Anaesthesia*, 43 (6), 466–9.

Gow, M. A. (2007), Dental hypnosis and suggestion in post-extraction bleeding control. *Scottish Dentist*, 86, 33–4.

Hammond, D. C. (2008), Hypnosis as sole anesthesia for major surgeries: historical and contemporary perspectives. *American Journal of Clinical Hypnosis*, 51 (2), 101–21.

Harandi, A. A. & Esfandani, A. (2004), The effect of hypnotherapy on procedural pain and state anxiety related to physiotherapy in women hospitalized in a burn unit. *Contemporary Hypnosis*, 21 (1), 28–34.

Heard, A. M. B., Green, R. J., Lacquiere, D. A. & Sillifant, P. (2009), The use of mandibular nerve block to predict safe anaesthetic induction in patients with acute trismus. *Anaesthesia*, 64, 1196–8.

Kellerman, J., Zeltzer, L., Ellenberg, L. & Dash, J. (1983), Adolescents with cancer: hypnosis for the reduction of acute pain and anxiety associated with medical procedures. *Journal of Adolescent Health Care*, 4, 85–90.

Lambert, S. A. (1996), The effects of hypnosis/guided imagery on the postoperative course of children. *Journal of Development and Behavioural Pediatrics*, 17 (5), 307–10.

Lang, E. V., Benotsch, E. G., Fick, L. J., Lutgendorf, S., Berbaum, K. S., Logan, H. & Spiegel, D. (2000a), Adjunctive nonpharmacologic analgesia for invasive medical procedures: a randomized trial. *Lancet*, 355, 1486–90.

Lang, E. V., Faintuch, S., Hatsiopoulou, O., Halsey, N., Li, X., Berbaum, M., Laser, E. & Baum, M. (2000b), Adjunctive self-hypnotic relaxation for outpatient medical procedures: a prospective randomized trial with women undergoing large core breast biopsy. *Pain*, 126 (1), 10.

Lang, E. V., Berbaum, K. S., Pauker, S. G., Faintuch, S., Salazar, G. M., Lutgendorf, S., Laser, E., Logan, H. & Spiegel, D. (2008), The beneficial effects of empathic attention during percutaneous tumour treatment: when being nice does not suffice. *Journal of Vascular and Interventional Radiology*, 19 (6), 897–905.

Liossi, C. & Hatira, P. (2003), Clinical hypnosis in the alleviation of procedure related pain in pediatric oncology patients. *The International Journal of Clinical and Experimental Hypnosis*, 51 (1), 4–28.

Liossi, C. W., White, P. & Hatira, P. (2006), Randomized clinical trial of local anesthetic versus a combination of local anesthetic with self-hypnosis in the management of pediatric procedure-related pain. *Health Psychology*, 25 (3), 307–15.

Lucas, O. N. (1975). The use of hypnosis in hemophilia dental care. *Annals of the New York Academy of Sciences*, 240 (4), 263–6.

Mendoza, M. E. & Capafons, A. (2009), Efficacy of clinical hypnosis: a summary of its empirical evidence. *Papeles del Psicólogo*, 30 (2), 98–116.

Meurisse, M. (1999), Thyroid and parathyroid surgery under hypnosis: from fiction to clinical application. *Bulletin et Memoires de l Academie Royale de Medecine de Belgique (Brussels)*, 154, 142–50.

Milling, L. S. (2008), Is high hypnotic suggestibility necessary for successful hypnotic pain intervention? *Current Pain and Headache Reports*, 12 (2), 98–102.

Montgomery, G. H., Bovbjerg, D. H., Schnur, J. B., David, D., Goldfarb, A., Weltz, C. R., Schechter, C., Graff-Zivin, J., Tatrow, K., Price, D. D. & Silverstein, J. H. (2007), A randomised clinical trial of a brief hypnosis intervention to control side effects in breast surgery patients. *Journal of the National Cancer Institute*, 99, 1304–12.

Montgomery, G. H., David, D., Winkle, G., Silverstein, J. & Bovbjerg, D. (2002), The effectiveness of adjunctive hypnosis with surgical patients: a meta-analysis. *Anesthesia and Analgesia*, 94, 1639–45.

Moore, R. & Abrahamsen, R. (2002), A 3-year comparison of dental anxiety treatment outcomes: hypnosis, group therapy and individual desensitization vs. no specialist treatment. *European Journal of Oral Sciences*, 110 (4), 287–95.

Novoa, R, & Hammonds, T. (2008), Clinical hypnosis for reduction of atrial fibrillation after coronary artery bypass graft surgery. *Cleveland Clinical Journal of Medicine*, 75 (2), 44–7.

Saadat, H., Drummond-Lewis, J., Maranets, I., Kaplan, D., Saadat, A., Wang, S. M. & Kain, Z. N. (2006), Hypnosis reduces preoperative anxiety in adult patients. *Anesthesia and Analgesia*, 102, 1394–6.

Schnur, J. B., Kafer, I., Marcus, C. & Montgomery, G. H. (2008), Hypnosis to manage distress related to medical procedures: a meta-analysis. *Contemporary Hypnosis*, 25, 114–28.

Simons, D., Potter, C. & Temple, G. (2007), *Hypnosis and communication in dental practice*. New Malden, Quintessence.

Williams, A. R., Hind, M., Sweeney, B. P. & Fisher, R. (1994), The incidence and severity of postoperative nausea and vomiting in patients exposed to positive intra-operative suggestions. *Anaesthesia*, 49 (4), 340–2.

Wobst, A. H. K. (2007), Hypnosis and surgery: past, present, and future. *Anaesthesia and Analgesia*, 104, 1199–1208.

Wright, B. R. & Drummond, P. D. (2000), Rapid induction analgesia for the alleviation of procedural pain during burn care. *Burns*, 26 (3), 275–82.

Zeltzer, L. & Lebaron, S. (1982), Hypnosis and non-hypnotic techniques for reduction of pain and anxiety during painful procedures in children and adolescents with cancer. *Journal of Pediatrics*, 101 (6), 1032–5.

23

Oncology

Mrs Jacky Owens and Dr Leslie Walker

with contributions from Mrs Phyllis Alden

Introduction

Since the early 1980s, there has been growing interest in what is now generally referred to as 'psycho-social oncology'. There is a wealth of empirical literature addressing key issues, including the prevalence of distress, the prevention of distress and adaptation to cancer, the assessment and amelioration of cancer-related concerns, psychosocial interventions for treatment side effects, psychosocial aspects of screening and the relationship between psychosocial factors and cancer outcomes.

For many years, it has been recognized that cancer treatment should address not only the medical needs of patients, but also their psychological, social and spiritual needs. This was originally acknowledged in the Calman-Hine Report (Calman & Hine, 1995), and it has been emphasized more recently in Improving Supportive and Palliative Care for Adults with Cancer (National Institute for Clinical Excellence, 2004).

Because it is possible to improve significantly patients' psychological wellbeing and quality of life, working with cancer patients can be immensely rewarding. Hopefully, the techniques described below will enable clinicians to work more effectively with cancer patients. Some of the techniques are supported by robust evidence from randomized controlled trials, whereas others have not been adequately evaluated: the latter are included here in the hope that others will develop and evaluate them. We have tried to make the strength of the evidence for each intervention clear in the text. We wish to emphasize that,

The Handbook of Contemporary Clinical Hypnosis: Theory and Practice, First Edition.
Edited by Les Brann, Jacky Owens and Ann Williamson.
© 2012 John Wiley & Sons, Ltd. Published 2015 by John Wiley & Sons, Ltd.

for ethical reasons, and to avoid mutual disappointment, it is important that therapists do not make claims for their interventions which are not supported by appropriate evidence.

Finally, we suggest that clinicians unfamiliar with medical and surgical treatments for cancer, and their specific side effects, should obtain relevant background information from an up to date, reputable textbook of clinical oncology.

Hypnotherapy for Cancer-Related Problems

Whilst the focus on this section of this chapter is on cancer-related problems, it is worth emphasizing that some patients cope very well with the diagnosis and treatment. Indeed, some people experience post-traumatic growth, as witnessed by a number of research studies (Mols *et al.*, 2009) as well as many autobiographies.

For patients who have significant problems that can be helped with hypnotherapy, it is important first of all to evaluate the biological, psychological, social and spiritual aspects of the presenting problem. A good history should be taken to obtain information about the person's background, coping style, family circumstances, past experience of illness (including cancer) and beliefs about cancer.

Problems associated with the diagnosis

In an attempt to diagnose cancers as early as possible, screening has been used increasingly in the last 25 years. In the United Kingdom, there are national programmes for breast, cervical and colorectal cancer, and it is likely that screening tests for other types of cancer will be introduced nationally in the future. Waiting for a screening result can be stressful, although in the case of breast screening the largest study to date showed that, for the majority of women, breast screening in the context of the UK national programme does not increase anticipatory anxiety or depression (Walker *et al.*, 1994). However, being recalled for further evaluation following false positive screening does increase anxiety, particularly in women with a family history of breast cancer (Gilbert *et al.*, 1998). If women present with significant anxiety whilst waiting for the result of screening, it can be helpful to give them the opportunity to discuss their concerns and fears, whilst being careful to avoid giving false reassurance. If need be, relaxation training or a stress control hypnotic routine can be used. For women with persistent anxiety following a false positive recall, in addition to discussion of their concerns and fears, and a relaxation-based intervention, helping them to distinguish between constructive and destructive worrying may be very beneficial.

Patients who are claustrophobic may be unable to undergo certain diagnostic investigations, for example magnetic resonance imaging (MRI). In addition, up to 10% of patients experience significant MRI-related distress, although modern scanners are less claustrophobic than older models (Anderson & Walker, 2002). We have found in practice that teaching patients cue-controlled relaxation or self hypnosis, setting up hypnotic anchors and encouraging the use of time distortion during scans can all be beneficial.

Hypnotherapy can also help with painful diagnostic or staging investigations. For example, Lang (2000) carried out a randomized controlled trial with women undergoing large core breast biopsy. Although pain rating in all groups increased, those in the hypnosis arm increased the least and these patients also experienced less anxiety.

When cancer is diagnosed, the value of appropriate information and support should not be underestimated. Patients may blame themselves for what they perceive to be an undue delay in diagnosis, or alternatively they may blame others, for example their general practitioner. Pre-conceived beliefs and concerns about the diagnosis, for example that it is already 'too late', should be assessed and some patients may require help in changing dysfunctional beliefs (Geffen, 2006). Experience suggests that recently diagnosed patients may abreact when introduced to a safe place in hypnosis; on exploration of the abreaction, these patients usually express a sense of peace or relief.

Studies evaluating the prevalence of psychological and psychiatric morbidity in cancer patients have shown that up to 50% of patients have at least a moderate level of anxiety or depression (Burgess *et al.*, 2005), and other studies have found that the level of morbidity in partners can be at least as high (Brennan, 2004). However, more recent research has demonstrated that much can be done to prevent morbidity. For example, Walker *et al.* (2009a) reported very low levels of clinically significant anxiety and depression in patients receiving their cancer treatment within the context of a fully integrated psychosocial support service. After 18 weeks of neo-adjuvant chemotherapy for locally advanced breast cancer, only 4% of the women had clinically significant anxiety or depression, and 24 weeks after the diagnoses of early breast cancer only 2% were clinically anxious or depressed using internationally agreed criteria.

Although true post-traumatic stress disorder (PTSD) associated with the diagnosis of cancer is relatively uncommon, post-traumatic symptoms occur frequently (Mehnert & Koch, 2007).

Problems associated with treatment

Surgery.   Hypnosis can be valuable to the surgical patient in a number of ways.

• Peri-surgical distress

A number of randomized controlled trials have demonstrated the value of hypnotherapy in reducing pre-surgical anxiety. Flory *et al.* (2007) randomized 76 patients to hypnotherapy, attention control or standard care. They concluded that hypnosis dramatically reduced the anxiety of patients undergoing ambulatory surgery. Schnur *et al.* (2008) randomized 90 patients waiting for breast biopsy to receive either a 15 minute pre-surgery session of hypnotherapy or a 15 minute session to control for the effects of attention. The results showed that, compared to those in the control arm, those who received hypnotherapy were significantly less emotionally upset, less depressed, less anxious and more relaxed going into surgery. In a randomized attention controlled trial, Saadat *et al.* (2006) also showed that patients in the hypnosis arm had less anxiety than those in the control group, both on entering the operating room and on post treatment. These studies demonstrate that even brief hypnotherapeutic interventions can be beneficial to the pre-surgical patient.

In the author's (LW) Behavioural Oncology Unit, a relaxation induction technique is used to ameliorate pre-surgical distress, followed by suggestions for deep relaxation, a comfortable experience of surgery and decreased distress, nausea and pain. Training in self-hypnosis may engender a beneficial sense of control.

Enquist *et al.* (1997) studied the role of hypnotherapy in reducing post-surgical distress. He found in patients undergoing breast surgery that preoperative hypnosis reduced the incidence of post-operative nausea and vomiting, as well as reducing the need for post-operative analgesia. Meurisse (1999) also reports that analgesic use was significantly reduced post-surgically in the hypnosis group.

In conclusion, there is evidence that hypnotherapy before surgery can reduce anxiety and minimize post-surgical sequelae.

Recovery from surgery.   It has been suggested that hypnotherapy can enhance post-surgical recovery. A meta-analysis of 22 studies found that hypnotherapy had beneficial effects on negative affect, amount of pain, quantity of pain medication, physiological indicators, recovery time and treatment time (Montgomery *et al.*, 2002). However, it should be emphasized that the largest studies which were included in the analysis were of plastic surgery and endocrine surgery, and the extent to which the results can be generalized to patients with cancer remains uncertain.

Body image problems.   Some types of surgery, for example mastectomy, vulvectomy, block dissections of the neck and colonic stoma formation, can cause significant distress in terms of how patients feel about their appearance, and this in turn can lead to social and sexual problems.

The opportunity to express concerns and feelings about body image can be helpful in identifying dysfunctional thoughts which can be addressed using cognitive therapy methods. Sometimes the role-reversal technique can also be helpful: the patient is asked how he or she would think and feel about another (unknown) person who had the same disfigurement. Cue-controlled relaxation or auto-hypnotherapy can also be beneficial.

Procedural distress.   A range of medical procedures can cause significant distress and behavioural avoidance, for example biopsies, bone marrow aspirate, lumbar puncture, venepuncture and cannulation. Not only can these cause considerable distress, but also they can result in patients receiving sub-optimal chemotherapy, and it is important therefore to identify and treat these problems when they occur.

In the case of needle phobia, we recommend careful assessment of the exact nature of the fear as this can vary considerably. For example, the patient may fear the sight of blood, pain or 'losing control', or the problem may reflect an underlying ambivalence about having chemotherapy in the first place.

Chemotherapy. Despite attempts by the pharmaceutical industry to develop effective cytotoxic compounds with as few side effects as possible, and despite improvements in medications to ameliorate side effects, there are a number of common chemotherapy associated problems, some of which can be helped by hypnotherapy.

* Gastro-intestinal side effects

Despite the optimal use of anti-emetic medication, some patients will experience nausea and vomiting as a result of the pharmacological action of the chemotherapy on the brain and gastro-intestinal tract. Unfortunately, if left uncontrolled, patients may find that the side effects become worse with each cycle, and indeed they may find that they feel nauseous and may even vomit in anticipation of their next cycle. This phenomenon is best understood as a classically conditioned response to the pharmacological side effects (Walker *et al.*, 1988b).

A range of interventions including distraction, relaxation, desensitization and hypnotherapy have been shown to have some benefit, especially for anticipatory nausea, vomiting and anxiety (Walker, 1992). In clinical practice, we have found that a package comprising training in cue controlled relaxation, direct suggestion and 'nausea management training' (NMT) is very effective (see Walker *et al.*, 1988a for further procedural details and clinical outcomes). NMT involves helping patients to experience nausea by means of appropriate stimuli; then, whilst hypnotized, using direct suggestion and a substitute response signal (gentle abdominal self massage), patients are given practice in eliminating the nausea. Exploration of how the patients construe chemotherapy can be very helpful in eliciting ambivalence and dysfunctional beliefs, for example that chemo is 'bad'. If patients can be encouraged to see chemotherapy in a positive light, for example as a 'friend' that will help them to have the best possible health in the future, this in itself can be beneficial.

Some patients experience constipation and/or diarrhoea which can be caused by chemotherapy (as well as pelvic-abdominal irradiation and opiate medication). Some help may be afforded using a modified version of Whorwell's technique for irritable bowel syndrome (Whorwell *et al.*, 1984). This gut directed hypnosis aims to achieve normal bowel activity, sensation and pace and features river imagery (see also page 251).

Distressing weight change can occur during chemotherapy. Weight gain is often associated with steroid treatment and may cause distress because of associated body image changes. In cases such as these, anxiety management may be helpful as well as advice about healthy eating and exercise. Hypnotic techniques involving visualization of appearance after weight loss may be beneficial for some patients.

Mucositis refers to the painful inflammation and ulceration of the mucous membranes which line the digestive tract. Some types of chemotherapy, for example 5-fluorouracil, and bone marrow transplantation have a high incidence of oral mucositis. Mucositis also occurs in patients who are having radiotherapy to the head and neck, pelvis or abdomen.

Whilst hypnotherapy does not affect the severity of mucositis, hypnotherapeutic pain control methods can be helpful. For example, Syrala *et al.* (1995) showed that hypnosis consisting of relaxation and imagery mitigated oral mucositis pain.

- Fatigue

Chemotherapy induced fatigue is an unremitting and overwhelming tiredness that is unrelieved by sleep. It has long been described as the commonest symptom of cancer and of many cancer treatments, especially chemotherapy and radiotherapy (Curt, 2001; McAuley *et al.*, 2010). Fatigue can last long after treatment ends, even when the cancer has been cured (Kuhnt *et al.*, 2009).

The aetiology of fatigue may be multifactorial, and Dy *et al.* (2008) has argued that there are causal links with depression, pain and poor sleep patterns. McAuley *et al.* (2010) suggest that fatigue may be an outcome of depression rather than the cause of it. In their systematic review, Brown and Kroenke (2009) concluded that, in addition to depression, anxiety was a correlate of cancer-related fatigue. Other factors include anaemia, metabolic disturbances, nausea, vomiting, poor nutritional intake due to anorexia and psychological factors for example anxiety and depression. It should be clear therefore that a careful assessment should be made before attempting any therapeutic intervention.

Early studies suggested that patients should be advised to conserve energy (Markes *et al.*, 2006), whereas more recent publications recommend graded exercise to reduce cancer fatigue (Cramp & Daniel, 2008; McCauley, 2010). Because of this finding, therapists may consider using an active alert induction when treating fatigue using hypnosis; Wark (2006) provides a review.

Hypnotic interventions having a positive outcome on fatigue are reported by Montgomery *et al.* (2009) in a study designed to treat radiotherapy-related fatigue using cognitive-behavioural therapy with hypnosis (CBTH) or standard care. Measuring fatigue on a weekly basis using the fatigue subscale of the Functional Assessment of Chronic Illness Therapy (FACIT) and daily using visual analogue scales, he was able to show that CBTH participants' fatigue did not increase over the course of treatment, whereas control group participants' fatigue increased linearly, and the conclusion states, 'The results suggest that CBTH is an effective means for controlling and potentially preventing fatigue in breast cancer radiotherapy patients' (p317).

Collingwood and Elliott (2010) report a trial using hypnosis to improve quality of life in which cancer patients received six sessions of hypnosis and were given a hypnosis CD to listen to once a day. This study used the EORTC QOL-QC 30 core questionnaire to assess changes in perceived quality of life. Statistical analysis using paired t-test analysis showing statistically significant improvements with fatigue ($p < 0.0044$).

It is advised that suggestions include the ability to recognize personal indicators of fatigue, employ strategies to maximize energy levels, utilize energies well yet respect energy limitations and emphasize good sleep hygiene (day time cat-napping will interfere with the ability to sleep at night).

• Alopecia

Several cytotoxic chemotherapies, especially in high doses, will cause hair loss. Whilst this includes all bodily hair, it is usually alopecia of the scalp which causes most distress. In some cancers, hair preservation techniques are offered with limited success and patients are advised to wear short styles. Commercial hypnotherapy tapes are available, but there is no good evidence that hypnosis can either prevent chemically induced hair loss or promote growth following loss. The role of hypnotherapy is to enable patients to value themselves and to face the world with confidence until such time as the chemotherapy treatment has been completed and hair growth is re-established naturally. Also the techniques described above to address body image problems following surgery can also be employed.

Radiotherapy.   New innovations in radiotherapy techniques are resulting in more efficient targeted approaches reducing side effects and allowing previously difficult tumours to be treated; for example, the use of the cyber or gamma knife for cancer in areas such as the liver, brain and prostate. for patients undergoing simulation for thoracic radiotherapy and thoracic radiotherapy itself, unpredictable breathing and chest wall movement can be a significant cause of having to irradiate surrounding healthy tissue. an ongoing clinical trial in kingston upon hull, uk, is currently comparing the effects of standard preparation for radiotherapy with a combination of relaxation training, hypnotic suggestion and exposure in imagination and in vivo prior to thoracic radiotherapy in an attempt to help patients breathe shallowly and predictably.

Head and neck cancers present a particular problem as radiation is often the treatment of choice. These patients will be required to wear a head mask which is fixed to the table to ensure minimum movement ensuring safe targeting. Patients with claustrophobia may be unable to tolerate simulation or radiotherapy itself. Ideally, the difficulty should be identified in advance so that patients can be trained in cue-controlled relaxation or self-hypnosis and allowed to spend as much time as they need in order to feel comfortable in the simulation environment. However, it is not uncommon for the problem to be identified only when the patient attends to have the mask made. In these cases, hypnotizing the patient on the table before the mask is fixed and continuing to give suggestions of relaxation and control until the procedure has been completed can be highly effective.

Radiotherapy can cause debilitating side effects such as decreased salivary flow and difficulty swallowing food (see section on mucositis above) (Macmillan, 2009a). Radiotherapy directed to the pelvic area for prostate, vaginal or rectal cancers may cause distress particularly with intimacy or sex with partners (Macmillan, 2009b). Anal cancer treated with radiotherapy can cause embarrassment: difficulties such as diarrhoea, skin infection and skin soreness may make sitting very uncomfortable. A similar approach to body image problems discussed above may be used.

Loss, or distortion, of taste can occur as a result of radiotherapy or chemotherapy. Kraft reported a single case of a patient who lost all taste sensation after radiotherapy. The hypnotic treatment involved powerful imagery of the preparation and eating of various food dishes. Though there were no explicit instructions as regards vasodilatation or increased warmth, he believed that this could be a crucial factor in the accelerated healing of taste sensation (Kraft, 1996).

As already noted, fatigue is one of the most commonly reported side effects of radiotherapy (see the above section on chemotherapy for interventions).

Hormone therapy.   Hormone therapy is widely used in prostate cancer, endometrial therapy and breast cancer. In breast cancer, anti-oestrogens may cause a wide range of side effects, including hot flashes, vaginal itching or dryness, decreased sex drive, impotence, difficulty having an orgasm, depressed mood, weakness, weight loss, nausea, headache, dizziness and thinning of hair. Side effects of hormone therapy for prostate cancer include hot flushes and sweating, erection difficulties and loss of sexual desire, nausea, vomiting, anorexia or weight gain and fatigue.

There is evidence from clinical trials that a range of psychosocial and complementary interventions, including relaxation therapies, meditation, yoga and tai-chi breath, are helpful in alleviating vasomotor and other menopausal symptoms also (Mols *et al.*, 2009). Clinically, we have found that some patients derive some benefit from CBT and relaxation training. There is also an established role for anti-depressants such as venlafaxine and sertraline (Adelson *et al.*, 2005).

Sexual difficulties, including reduced libido, can be treated using traditional methods derived from those of Masters and Johnson (Kleinplatz, 2001), and gels can be used for vaginal dryness (Biglia *et al.*, 2010).

Problems associated with prognosis

Following the diagnosis, many patients become pre-occupied with the future and suffer from what has been called the syndrome of Damocles. This involves unproductive and destructive ruminations about what the future may hold in terms of treatment efficacy, relapse and recurrence. Techniques to help patients to distinguish constructive from destructive worrying can be very helpful. Constructive worrying occurs when worrying leads to a solution (for example, arranging an appointment with an oncologist to examine a new lump), whereas destructive worrying involves worrying about a situation which cannot altered (for example, worrying whether cancer will recur after clear scans).

Remission does not always afford the expected relief and lead to the ability to get on with living 'normally' (Baker *et al.*, 2001). The majority of patients will enter a 'watch, wait and see policy' group; further treatment being offered only if and when either symptoms or testing indicates a need. Many patients describe this period as a feeling of being abandoned by their cancer team or as being in a black hole cut off from the previously frequent hospital visits. Some become hyper-vigilant, living constantly with the fear of relapse (Hodges & Humphris, 2009; Mehnert *et al.*, 2009). Affording psychological support to these patients may greatly improve quality of life for them (DeMarinis *et al.*, 2009).

Recurrence may cause even more distress than the initial diagnosis (Brennan, 2004). Therapy should address the presenting symptoms such as anxiety or depression. Ego strengthening, confidence building and generation of realistic hope and ensuring the patient is holding helpful health beliefs may be helpful.

The issues facing the cancer patient as approaching death becomes inevitable often have to do with the ability to accept what is happening to them. During this time, which may be lengthy, a whole gamut of emotional responses may be experienced. Helping patients to see and achieve their realistic goals and to be at peace when death comes is perhaps the greatest challenge that therapists face.

Other Issues Regarding Hypnotherapy and Cancer

So far, this chapter has addressed the role of hypnotherapy in helping patients at various stages of their cancer journey, and it has addressed problems associated with the different anti-cancer treatment modalities. This final section addresses other issues relevant to the practice of hypnotherapy with people who have cancer.

Survival

One of the questions that patients often ask is whether or not psychosocial interventions, including hypnotherapy, can prolong survival. We therefore review the evidence base here so that clinicians can give an informed response.

In addition to our own reviews (Anderson & Walker, 2003; Walker *et al.*, 2005), other reviews include Butow *et al.* (2000), Garssen (2004), Petticrew *et al.* (2002), Ross *et al.* (2002) and Kissane (2009). Most of these reviews are critical of existing studies for a range of reasons such as diagnostic heterogeneity, lack of adjustment for potential confounding factors, publication bias and failure to study the interaction between psychosocial and biomedical risk factors. However, some of the reviews, themselves, can be criticized for not distinguishing between factors that might 'cause' cancer and factors that might be relevant to disease progression. Also, some fail to recognize that what is true for one type of cancer may well not hold true for others.

Patients not uncommonly ask the question *"Do psychological interventions prolong survival?"* and the answer to this question must be *"It depends."* For example, some patients refuse chemotherapy because of conditioned nausea and/or vomiting, and others, particularly those with head or neck cancers, may refuse radiotherapy because of claustrophobia. As indicated elsewhere in this chapter, hypnotherapeutic interventions may enable such patients to have chemotherapy and radiotherapy. To the extent to which chemotherapy and radiotherapy will prolong survival for them, then obviously for them hypnotherapy will enhance survival.

A number of factors, therefore, are relevant to the question, such as patient variables (such as claustrophobia), the effectiveness of the psychosocial intervention in alleviating barriers to effective medical and surgical treatment, disease factors (type and stage of disease) and concomitant treatments (radiotherapy, chemotherapy or surgery).

Also, whether a psychosocial intervention prolongs survival may depend on the nature of the 'control' condition, particularly how much information and support are offered. It is interesting that earlier studies tended to report positive effects on survival, whereas more recent studies do not; one possible explanation may be that 'control' patients nowadays receive a higher standard of care which may make it more difficult to show an intervention effect (Walker *et al.*, 2009b).

Some of the complexities of this issue are well illustrated in one of our early studies of 62 patients with lymphoma who participated in a randomized controlled trial of relaxation with, or without, hypnotherapy to minimize chemotherapy side effects (Walker, 2004). When these patients were followed up on average 13 years following diagnosis, patients who had received relaxation with or without hypnotherapy had lived significantly longer than control patients. However, survival was also independently predicted by stage of disease at diagnosis, depression scores on the Hospital Anxiety and Depression scores at diagnosis, and L scores on the Eysenck Personality Inventory (Cox proportional hazards analysis) (Ratcliffe *et al.*, 1995). When the data were analysed further, it emerged that it was only patients with high L scores who appeared to benefit from the intervention in terms of survival. This study was not designed or powered as a survival study, and the results therefore need to be viewed as preliminary. However, the results do suggest that recruiting a consecutive cohort of newly diagnosed patients and randomizing them to standard care or to hypnotherapy may not be an appropriate strategy, a point made some time ago by Cunningham and Edmonds (2005) with reference to group interventions.

In conclusion, there are situations where hypnotherapy can result in behaviour change that will be life prolonging. However, we should not claim that, in unselected patients, there is robust evidence that hypnotherapy prolongs survival.

Quality of life

Quality of life is an elusive concept that has been variously defined. Whilst it is related to the health of the patient ('health-related quality of life'), it is also influenced by economic, political, cultural and spiritual factors (Wilson & Cleary, 1995). Many years ago, Ferrans (1990) defined quality of life as 'a sense of well-being that arises from satisfaction with areas of life that are important' (the 'feel good' factor). This definition rightly emphasizes the fact that quality of life is essentially a subjective phenomenon, in that people have different values and priorities. In practice, however, most people would agree that some types of experience such as depression and chronic pain are incompatible with a good quality of life.

Generic measures of health-related quality of life typically assess a number of domains, including physical wellbeing, functional abilities, emotional wellbeing and social satisfaction (e.g. Fallowfield, 2009; Sharma *et al.*, 2007).

In the context of cancer therapy, quality of life is a key 'patient-reported outcome'. Especially in the context of palliative care, an intervention which is not life-prolonging may still be of benefit in terms of improving quality of life, and this is recognized by health economists in calculations of quality adjusted life years (QALYs).

Interestingly, a number of studies have shown in patients with cancer that quality of life has significant prognostic value in terms of survival (such as Sharma *et al.*, 2007). In particular, depression has been shown to have adverse biological effects. For example, Walker *et al.* (1999a) found that depression scores predicted both clinical and pathological responses in women undergoing neo-adjuvant chemotherapy for locally advanced breast cancer, and Ratcliffe *et al.* (1995) reported that depression scores were significant independent predictors of survival in patients with haematological cancers.

Interventions to improve quality of life

In this section, interventions that have been found to improve generic health-related quality of life are reported. The reader should consult other sections in this chapter and the next for specific cancer-related problems adversely impacting quality of life, for example nausea, depression and treatment-related anxiety.

A number of studies have found that relaxation with or without guided imagery is effective in improving various aspects of quality of life as assessed by standardized measures (Baider *et al.*, 2001; Cheung *et al.*, 2002). Walker *et al.* (1999b) showed in 96 women with newly diagnosed locally advanced breast cancer that, during the 18 weeks they were receiving chemotherapy, the women randomized to relaxation therapy and visualization had improved mood, coping and overall quality of life. In this study, relaxation and imagery were taught using live training sessions and audio recordings. They were given a portfolio of colour cartoons to help them to visualize their host defences destroying cancer cells or in some other way improving their health.

Many other studies have found benefit when relaxation with or without guided imagery has been combined with other interventions such as psycho-educational group therapy (Fawzy *et al.*, 1993). Similarly, benefits have been found when training in auto-hypnosis has been combined with other interventions such as supportive-expressive therapy (Spiegel *et al.*, 1981).

Some Unresolved Issues and Practical Considerations

Relaxation therapy and guided imagery are often used together, and their relative individual effects have received scant attention. A recent randomized controlled trial of 151 patients with colorectal cancer did not find that relaxation or guided imagery, alone or in combination, improved quality of life. This could have been due to the fact that the quality of life of the control group (who also had access to the Oncology Health Service) was extremely good (Walker *et al.*, 2009b).

Another factor that may have contributed to this negative finding could be that patients were taught relaxation and guided imagery using audio-recordings alone. The relative effectiveness, and cost effectiveness, of 'live' training sessions versus training by means of audio recordings has not been established in patients with cancer. An ongoing study in

Kingston-upon-Hull, United Kingdom, is currently addressing this issue by comparing the effects on quality of life of audio recordings alone with audio recordings plus 'live' training delivered by behavioural oncology nurses.

Although the author (LW) has generally recommended that patients practice relaxation and imagery on average once daily, there is no robust evidence on which to base this recommendation. It has been shown that, in terms of psycho-neuroimmunological effects, there is a relationship between the frequency of practice and the number of CD4+ (T helper) cells, the CD4+ : 8+ (helper:cytotoxic) ratio and IL1beta levels (Eremin *et al.*, 2009). However, whether the frequency of practice and the effects on quality of life are correlated in this way is not known. Clinically, our experience is that whilst it is important to emphasize the need for regular practice, it is essential to ensure that patients do not feel that they are obliged to practice frequently, or indeed to use these techniques in the first place (Walker *et al.*, 2007).

Hypnosis and the Neuro-Endocrine and Immune Systems

Many patients with cancer turn to complementary and alternative medicine (CAM). In 1998, a systematic review of the use of CAM in cancer patients reported an average use across 13 countries of 31%, although the range was wide (7–64%) (Ernst & Cassileth, 1998). Estimates of the use of CAM by cancer patients in the United Kingdom have ranged from 32% in patients undergoing radiotherapy (Maher *et al.*, 1994) to 16% in unselected oncology patients (Downer *et al.*, 1994). Not infrequently, patients use CAM because of concern that conventional treatments such as surgery, chemotherapy and radiotherapy may have an adverse effect on the ability of their 'natural defences' to fight cancer and they turn to complementary therapy, including hypnotherapy, in an attempt to 'boost' their immune system. In this section, we review the effects of hypnosis on the neuro-endocrine and immune systems to help clinicians to have an evidence-based discussion with patients when appropriate.

Psycho-neuroimmunology can be defined as the study of the multidirectional interaction of the brain and the endocrine and immune systems (Irwin & Vedhara, 2005). A number of pathways have been identified whereby psychosocial stimuli can alter the endocrine and immunological systems. Sometimes overlooked is the fact that the pathways are multidirectional; the endocrine and immunological systems can alter brain functioning and psychological processes (Walker *et al.*, 2005).

A number of studies of the effects of hypnosis on normal subjects have been reported, and it is clear that hypnotherapeutic suggestions can alter immune functioning (Walker *et al.*, 1993). The clinical significance of these changes in cancer populations, however, is far from clear.

For example, Fawzy *et al.* (1990) randomized 68 patients with newly malignant melanoma to a group psycho-educational programme (including relaxation training) or routine care. Patients in the intervention group had an increased percentage of large granular lymphocytes and NK cells, as well as an increase in NK cell activity and a decrease in the percentage of CD4+ cells. However, the changes induced by the intervention did not appear to affect survival.

In a large randomized controlled trial with 227 women with Stage 2 or Stage 3 breast cancer, a group intervention consisting of progressive muscular relaxation training, problem solving, education and lifestyle advice (27 therapy hours over four months) produced a number of beneficial psychological and behavioural changes, as well as a number of immunological changes (Andersen *et al.*, 2004). Lymphocyte proliferation was higher in the intervention group, although the authors did not measure Th1/Th2 balance, and the effect on disease free survival was not studied.

Lekander *et al.* (1997) also studied the effects of relaxation training; 22 women undergoing chemotherapy for ovarian cancer participated. The relaxation group showed higher lymphocyte counts, but not NK cell activity or proliferative response to non-specific mitogens.

The effects of group relaxation, health education and coping skills training in 24 women with early breast cancer were reported by Schledowski *et al.* (1994). They found an increased number of lymphocytes after the intervention which appeared unrelated to changes in cortisol.

Most recently, Eremin *et al.* (2009) reported a randomized controlled trial of the effects of relaxation therapy and guided imagery in 80 women with newly diagnosed locally advanced breast cancer. Women randomized to relaxation therapy and guided imagery had more activated T cells (CD25+), and more lymphokine activated killer cells (CD56+), and the number of mature T cells (CD3+) and lymphokine activated killer cell activity was significantly higher following chemotherapy and radiotherapy.

Carlson *et al.* (2003) randomized 49 patients with early breast cancer and ten patients with prostate cancer to a 'mindfulness stress reduction programme' or control condition. In the intervention group, cell production of IL-4 increased and IFN-gamma decreased, whereas NK cell production of IL-10 decreased.

To summarize, a number of studies have demonstrated that hypnotic interventions can produce measurable neuroendocrine and immunological changes in patients with different types of cancer. However, not a single study has demonstrated that these changes have translated into enhanced survival. Whilst we can say to patients that there is evidence that hypnotherapy and related interventions can alter neuroendocrine and immunological functioning, it is important not to imply that there is evidence that these changes will translate into an improved clinical outcome.

Conclusions

Hypnotherapy and related interventions can play an important part in improving the quality of life of patients at various stages of the cancer journey. They can also be effective in treating a wide range of problems related to the diagnosis and treatment of malignant disease. Because cancer-related problems usually have biological, psychological and social ramifications, it is our view that the needs of patients are best served when hypnotherapy is carried out within a service which is fully integrated physically and functionally with other parts of the cancer services (Sharp *et al.*, 2009).

References

Adelson, K., Loprinzi, C. & Hershman, D. (2005), Treatment of hot flushes in breast and prostate cancer. *Expert Opinion on Pharmacotherapy*, 6, 1095–1106.

Andersen, B. L., Farrar, W. B., Golden-Kreutz, D. M., Glaser, R., Emery, C. F., Crespin, T. R. & Shapiro, C. L. (2004), Psychological, behavioral, and immune changes after a psychological intervention: a clinical trial. *Journal of Clinical Oncology*, 22, 3570–80.

Anderson, J. & Walker, L. G. (2002), Psychological aspects of MRI breast screening in women at high risk of breast cancer. In Warren, R.& Coultard, A. (Eds.) *Breast MRI in practice*. London, Martin Dunit.

Anderson, J. & Walker, L. G. (2003), Psychological factors and cancer progression: involvement of behavioural pathways. In Lewis, C. E., O'Sullivan, C., Barraclough, J. (Eds.) *The psychoimmunology of cancer*, 2nd ed. Oxford, Oxford University Press.

Baider, L., Peretz, T., Hadani, P. E. & Koch, U. (2001), Psychological intervention in cancer patients: a randomized study. *General Hospital Psychiatry*, 23, 272–7.

Baker, F., Zabora, J., Polland, A. & Wingard, J. (2001), Reintegration after bone marrow transplantation. *Cancer Practice*, 7, 190–7.

Biglia, N., Peano, E., Sgandurra, P., Moggio, G., Panuccio, E., Migliardi, M., Ravarino, N., Ponzone, R. & Sismondi, P. (2010), Low-dose vaginal estrogens or vaginal moisturizer in breast cancer survivors with urogenital atrophy: a preliminary study. *Gynaecological Endocrinology*, 26, 404–12.

Brennan, J. (Ed.) (2004), *Cancer in context: a practical guide to supportive care*. New York, John Wiley & Sons.

Brown, L. F. & Kroenke, K. (2009), Cancer-related fatigue and its associations with depression and anxiety: a systematic review. *Psychosomatics*, 50, 440–8.

Burgess, C., Ramirez, A. & Cornelius, V. (2005), Depression and anxiety in women with early breast cancer: five year observational cohort study. *British Medical Journal*, 330 (7493).

Butow, P. N., Hiller, J. E., Price, M. A., Thackway, S. V., Kricker, A. & Tennant, C. C. (2000), Epidemiological evidence for a relationship between life events, coping style, and personality factors in the development of breast cancer. *Journal of Psychosomatic Research*, 49, 169–81.

Calman, K. & Hine, D. (1995), A policy framework for commissioning cancer services. Report by the Expert Advisory Group on Cancer to the Chief Medical Officers of England And Wales. London, Department of Health.

Carlson, L. E., Speca, M., Patel, K. D. & Goodey, E. (2003), Mindfulness-based stress reduction in relation to quality of life, mood, symptoms of stress, and immune parameters in breast and prostate cancer outpatients. *Psychosomatic Medicine*, 65, 571–81.

Cheung, Y., Molassiotis, A. & Chang, A. M. (2002), The effect of progressive muscular relaxation training in anxiety and quality of life after stoma surgery in colorectal cancer patients. *Psycho-Oncology*, 12, 254–6.

Collingwood, B. R. & Elliott, N. J. (2010), Clinical hypnosis cancer trial. http://hypnosisforcancer.net/Hypnosis%20Cancer%20Trial%20-%20Clinical%20Report

Cramp, F. & Daniel, J. (2008), Exercise for the management of cancer-related fatigue in adults. *Cochrane Database of Systematic Reviews.* DOI: 10.1002/14651858.CD006145.pub2

Cunningham, A. & Edmonds, C. (2005), Possible effects of psychological therapy on survival duration in cancer patients. *Journal of Clinical Oncology,* 23, 5263.

Curt, G. A. (2001), Fatigue in cancer. *British Medical Journal,* 322 (1560).

DeMarinis, V., Barsky, A., Antin, J. & Chang, G. (2009), Health psychology and distress after haematopoietic stem cell transplantation. *European Journal of Cancer Care,* 18, 57–63.

Downer, S. M., Cody, M. M., McCluskey, P., Wilson, P. D., Arnott, S. J., Lister, T. A. & Slevin, M. L. (1994), Pursuit and practice of complementary therapies by cancer patients receiving conventional treatment. *British Medical Journal,* 309, 86–88.

Dy, S. M., Lorenz, K. A., Naeim, A., Sanati, H., Walling, A. & Asch, S. M. (2008), Evidence based recommendations for cancer fatigue, anorexia, depression, and dyspnea. *Journal of Clinical Oncology,* 26, 3886–96.

Enquist, B., Bjorklund, C., Engman, M. & Jakobsson, J. (1997), Preoperative hypnosis surgery of the breasts: a prospective, randomized and reduces postoperative vomiting after blinded study. *Acta Anaesthesiologica Scandinavica,* 41, 1028–32.

Eremin, O., Walker, M. B., Simpson, E., Heys, S. D., Ah-See, A. K., Hutcheon, A. W., Ogston, K. N., Sarkar, T. K., Segar, A. & Walker, L. G. (2009), Immuno-modulatory effects of relaxation training and guided imagery in women with locally advanced breast carcinoma undergoing multimodality treatment: a randomised controlled trial. *The Breast,* 18, 17–25.

Ernst, E. & Cassileth, B. R. (1998), The prevalence of complementary/alternative medicine in cancer: a systematic review. *Cancer Practice,* 83, 777–82.

Fallowfield, L. (2009), What is quality of life? http://www.medicine.ox.ac.uk/bandolier/painres/download/whatis/WhatisQOL.pdf

Fawzy, F. I., Fawzy, H. W. & Hyun, C. S. (1993), Malignant melanoma: effects of an early structured psychiatric intervention, coping and effective state on recurrence and survival 5 years later. *Archives of General Psychiatry,* 50, 621–89.

Fawzy, F. I., Kemeny, M. E., Fawzy, N. W., Elashoff, R., Morton, D., Cousins, N. & Fahey, J. L. (1990), A structured psychiatric intervention for cancer patients. II. Changes over time in immunological measures. *Archives of General Psychiatry,* 47, 729–35.

Ferrans, C. (1990), Quality of life: conceptual issues. *Seminars in Oncology Nursing,* 4, 248–52.

Flory, N., Salazara, G. M. M. & Lang, E. V. (2007), Hypnosis for acute distress management during medical procedures. *International Journal of Clinical and Experimental Hypnosis,* 55, 303–17.

Garssen, B. (2004), Psychological factors and cancer development: evidence after 30 years of research. *Clinical Psychology Review,* 24, 315–38.

Geffen, J. (2006). *The journey through cancer healing and transforming the whole person.* New York, Three Rivers Press.

Gilbert, F. J., Cordiner, C. M., Affleck, I. R., Hood, D. B., Mathieson, D. & Walker, L. G. (1998), *Breast screening: the psychological costs of false positive recall in women with and without a history of breast cancer European Journal of Cancer,* 1998, 2010–14.

Hodges, L. J. & Humphris, G. M. (2009), Fear of recurrence and psychological distress in head and neck cancer patients and their carers. *Psycho-Oncology,* 18, 841–8.

Irwin, M. & Vedhara, K. (2005), *Human Psychoneuroimmunology.* Oxford, Oxford University Press 18.

Kissane, D. (2009), Beyond the psychotherapy and survival debate: the challenge of social disparity, depression and treatment adherence in psychosocial cancer care. *Psycho-Oncology,* 18, 1–5.

Kleinplatz, P. J. (Ed.) (2001), *New directions in sex therapy: innovations and alternatives*. New York, Taylor and Francis.

Kraft, T. (1996), Using hypnosis to aid recovery of taste sensation after a course of radiotherapy: a case study. *Contemporary Hypnosis*, 13, 115–19.

Kuhnt, S., Ernst, J., Singer, S., Ruffer, J., Kortmann, R., Stolzenburg, J. & Schwarz, R. (2009), Fatigue in cancer survivors: prevalence and correlates *Onkologie*, 32, 312–7.

Lang, E. V., Benotsch, E. G., Fick, L. J., Lutgendorf, S., Berbaum, M. L., Berbaum, K. S., Logan, H. & Spiegel, D. (2000), Adjunctive non-pharmacological analgesia for invasive medical procedures: a randomised trial. *Lancet*, 355, 1486–90.

Lekander, M., Furst, C. J., Rotstein, S., Hursti, T. J. & Fredrikson, M. (1997) Immune effects of relaxation during chemotherapy for ovarian cancer. *Psychotherapy and Psychosomatics*, 66, 185–91.

Macmillan, C. S. (2009a) Radiotherapy to the head and neck. http://www.macmillan.org.uk/Cancerinformation/Cancertreatment/Treatmenttypes/Radiotherapy/Sideeffects/Specificareas.aspx

Macmillan, C. S. (2009b) Effects of radiotherapy on sexuality. http://www.macmillan.org.uk/Cancerinformation/Cancertreatment/Treatmenttypes/Radiotherapy/Sideeffects/Sexuality.aspx

Maher, E. J., Young, T. & Feigel, I. (1994), Complementary therapies used by cancer patients. *British Medical Journal*, 309, 671–2.

Markes, M., Brockow, T. & Resch, K. L. (2006), Exercise for women receiving adjuvant therapy for breast cancer. *Cochrane Database of Systematic Reviews*, (4) art. CD005001. DOI: 10.1002/14651858.CD005001.pub2

McAuley, E., White, S. M., Rogers, L. Q., Motl, R. W. & Courneya, K. S. (2010), Physical activity and fatigue in breast cancer and multiple sclerosis: psychological mechanisms. *Psychosomatic Medicine*, 72, 88–96.

Mehnert, A., Berg, P., Henrich, G. & Herschbach, P. (2009), Fear of cancer progression and cancer-related intrusive cognitions in breast cancer survivors. *Psycho-Oncology*, 18, 1273–80.

Mehnert, A. & Koch, U. (2007), Prevalence of acute and post-traumatic stress disorder and comorbid mental disorders in breast cancer patients during primary cancer care: a prospective study. *Psycho-Oncology*, 16, 181–8.

Meurisse, M. (1999), Thyroid and parathyroid surgery under hypnosis: from fiction to clinical application. *Bulletin et Memoires de l Academie Royale de Medecine de Belgique (Brussels)*, 154, 142–50.

Mols, F., Vingerhoets, A. J., Coebergh, J. W. & Van De Poll-Franse, L. V. (2009), Well-being, posttraumatic growth and benefit finding in long-term breast cancer survivors. *Psychology & Health*, 5, 583–95.

Montgomery, G. H., David, D., Winkel, G., Silverstein, J. H. & Bovbjerg, D. H. (2002), The effectiveness of adjunctive hypnosis with surgical patients: a meta-analysis. *Anesthesia & Analgesia*, 94, 1639–45.

Montgomery, G. H., Kangas, M., David, D., Hallquist, M. N., Green, S. & Bovbjerg, D. H. B. (2009), Fatigue during breast cancer radiotherapy: an initial randomized study of cognitive-behavioral therapy plus hypnosis. *Health Psychology*, 28, 317–23.

National Institute for Clinical Excellence. (2004), *Improving supportive and palliative care for adults with cancer*. London, National Institute for Clinical Excellence.

Petticrew, M., Bell, R. & Hunter, D. (2002), Influence of psychological coping on survival and recurrence in people with cancer: systematic review. *British Medical Journal*, 325, 1066–75.

Ratcliffe, M. A., Dawson, A. A. & Walker, L. G. (1995), Eysenck Personality Inventory L-scores in patients with Hodgkin's disease and non-Hodgkin's lymphoma. *Psycho-Oncology*, 4, 39–45.

Ross, L., Boesen, E. H., Dalton, S. O. & Johansen, C. (2002), Mind and cancer: does psychosocial intervention improve survival and psychological well-being? *European Journal of Cancer*, 38, 1447–57.

Saadat, H., Drummond-Lewis, J., Maranets, I., Kaplan, D., Saadat, A., Wang, S. M. & Kain, Z. N. (2006), Hypnosis reduces preoperative anxiety in adult patients. *Anesthesia & Analgesia* 102, 1394–6.

Schledowski, M., Tewes, U. & Schmoll, H. J. (1994), The effects of psychological intervention on cortisol levels and leukocyte numbers in the peripheral blood of breast cancer patients. In Lewis, C. E., O'Sullivan, C., & Barraclough, J. (Eds.) *The psychoimmunology of cancer*. Oxford, Oxford University Press.

Schnur, J. B., Bovbjerg, D. H., David, D., Tatrow, K., Goldfarb, A. B., Silverstein, J. H., Weltz, C. R. & Montgomery, G. H. (2008), Hypnosis decreases presurgical distress in excisional breast biopsy patients. *Anesthesia & Analgesia*, 106, 440–5.

Sharma, A., Walker, A. A., Sharp, D. M., Monson, J. R. T. & Walker, L. G. (2007), Psychosocial factors and quality of life in colorectal cancer. *The Surgeon*, 5, 344–54.

Sharp, D., Walker, M., Bateman, J., Braid, F., Hebblewhite, C., Hope, T., Lines, M., Walker, A. & Walker, L. (2009), Demographic characteristics of patients using a fully integrated psychosocial support service for cancer patients. *BMC Research Notes*, 2, 253 [Epub ahead of print].

Spiegel, D., Bloom, J. R. & Yalom, I. (1981), Group support for patients with metastatic cancer. A randomized outcome study. *Archives of General Psychiatry*, 527–33.

Syrala, K. L., Donaldson, G., Davis, M. W., Kippes, M. E. & Carr, J. E. (1995), Relaxation and imagery and cognitive-behavioural training reduce pain during cancer treatment: a controlled clinical trial. *Pain*, 63, 189–99.

Walker L. G. (1992), Hypnosis and cancer. *American Journal of Preventive Psychiatry and Neurology*, 3, 42–9.

Walker, L. G. (2004), Hypnotherapeutic insights and interventions: A cancer odyssey. *Contemporary Hypnosis*, 21, 35–45.

Walker, L. G., Cordiner, C. M., Gilbert, F. J., Needham, G., Deans, H. E., Affleck, I. R., Hood, D. B., Mathieson, D., Ah-See, A. K. & Eremin, O. (1994), How distressing is attendance for routine breast screening? *Psycho-Oncology*, 3, 299–304.

Walker, L. G., Dawson, A. A., Pollet, S. M., Ratcliffe, M. A. & Hamilton, L. (1988a) Hypnotherapy for chemotherapy side effects. *British Journal of Experimental and Clinical Hypnosis* 5, 79–82.

Walker, L. G., Dawson, A. A., Ratcliffe, M. A. & Lolley, J. (1988b) Sick to death of it: psychological aspects of cytotoxic chemotherapy side effects. *Aberdeen Postgraduate Medical Bulletin*, 22, 11–17.

Walker, L. G., Green, V. L., Greenman, J., Walker, A. A. & Sharp, D. M. (2005), Psychoneuroimmunology and chronic malignant disease: cancer. In Irwin, M.& Vedhara, V. E. (Eds.) *Human psychoneuroimmunology (PNI)*. Oxford, Oxford University Press.

Walker, L. G., Heys, S. D. & Eremin, O. (1999a) , Surviving cancer: does the fighting spirit help? *Journal of Psychosomatic Research*, 47, 497–503.

Walker, L. G., Johnson, V. C. & Eremin, O. (1993), Modulation of the immune response to stress by hypnosis and relaxation training in normals: a critical review. *Contemporary Hypnosis*, 10, 19–27.

Walker, L. G., Walker, M. B., Heys, S. D., Ogston, K., Miller, I., Hutcheon, A. W., Sarkar, T. K. & Eremin, O. (1999b) , The psychological, clinical and pathological effects of relaxation training and imagery during primary chemotherapy. *British Journal of Cancer*, 80, 262–8.

Walker, L. G., Walker, A. A., Walker, M. B., Bateman, J. S., Braid, F., Ellwood, K., Hebblewhite, C., Hope, T., Lines, M., Mack, P., Macfie, J., Monson, J. R. T., Russell, D., Russell, I. M.

& Sharp, D. M. (2009b) , The effects of relaxation and guided imagery, alone and in combination, on mood and quality of life in men and women with colorectal cancer: a randomised controlled trial. *Psycho-Oncology*, 18, S57–S58.

Walker, L. G., Walker, A. A., Walker, M. B. & Sharp, D. M. (2007), Relaxation, visualisation, and hypnosis. In Barraclough, J. (Ed.) *Enhancing cancer care: complementary, expressive and supportive therapies in oncology.* Oxford, Oxford University Press.

Walker, M. B., Bateman, J. S., Braid, F., Hebblewhite, C., Hope, T., Jackson, J., Lines, M., Lewis, E., Walker, A. A., Sharp, D. M. & Walker, L. G. (2009a) Preventing psychiatric morbidity in people with cancer. *Psycho-Oncology*, 18, S238.

Wark, D. M. (2006), Alert hypnosis: A review and case report. *American Journal of Clinical Hypnosis*, 48, 291–3.

Whorwell, P. J., Prior, A. & Faragher, E. B. (1984), Controlled trial of hypnotherapy in the treatment of severe refractory irritable bowel syndrome. *The Lancet*, 324, 1232–4.

Wilson, I. B. & Cleary, P. D. (1995), Linking clinical variables with health-related quality of life: A conceptual model of patient outcomes. *JAMA*, 273, 59–65.

24

Cancer Care

Mrs Phyllis Alden and Mrs Jacky Owens

Introduction

The previous chapter has reported on the evidence from published trials and forms an important basis on which to commission care for cancer patients. The results of trials, however, relate only to the study population and not to individuals; overall results may mask significant benefits to subsets or individuals within that study population. The experienced clinician observes these benefits and tries to adapt an approach according to the specific needs of the individual. This chapter, therefore, outlines some suggested methods for utilizing hypnosis for the individual patient. Accordingly the opinions and beliefs are those of the author (JO) and contributor (PA) whose approach is based on years of experience and clinical observation in caring for cancer patients. There is no intention to imply that this approach is *the* right way, but it is here as a guide for students and practitioners who find themselves working with this patient group. It is strongly advised that they should work within their own areas of competence and closely audit their outcomes.

However, before embarking on this chapter it is imperative that the practitioner understands the importance of being clear about the intention of therapy and its possible achievements. Indeed, Walker *et al.* (2005) counsels strongly,

> Although the psychoneuroimmunology of cancer is an exciting area of research, journalists and others often make claims that cannot be substantiated from existing findings. Not only could this unfairly discredit this field of research, but false promises can undoubtedly have adverse effects on patients and their families. As responsible clinicians, it is important that we promise only that which we can deliver. (p144–5)

The Handbook of Contemporary Clinical Hypnosis: Theory and Practice, First Edition.
Edited by Les Brann, Jacky Owens and Ann Williamson.
© 2012 John Wiley & Sons, Ltd. Published 2015 by John Wiley & Sons, Ltd.

This point cannot be stressed too highly. It may be that future research results will allow us to be more definite about just what can and cannot be achieved using hypnosis based on psycho-neuroimmunological principles. However the current position is that many patients and therapists *believe* that there is therapeutic benefit to be had from engaging in the techniques described below. Belief cannot and should not be construed as fact. It is important therefore to exercise caution when explaining to patients who are new to this type of therapy exactly what the aim of the therapeutic technique is without creating false hope of what it is that most patients are wanting, cure and longevity, or introducing a sense of guilt.

Guilt is an emotion that many cancer patients have to deal with, and the therapist should have a care not to add to the difficulties such patients experience because of diagnosis and treatments. Spiegel and Moore (1997) allude to this in their article when they point out that imagery techniques, whilst appearing to be harmless, can create a sense of guilt when disease progresses. We also have to consider those patients for whom hypnosis is not an option, either because they are not hypnotizable or are unwilling, for whatever reason, to engage with it. This group of patients can very easily be made to feel guilty that they cannot do what others can.

> *Suggestion does not consist in making an individual believe what is not true. Suggestion consists in making something come true by making a person believe in its possibility.*
> J. D. Hadfield (qtd in Jacobs, 1991)

General Approach

Although the techniques described are generalized to a particular problem, such as nausea, each intervention should be tailored to the specific patient's need. Some suggestions are aimed specifically at the goal of the intervention and are termed 'key suggestions'; these are specific to the problem and should be repeated as post-hypnotic suggestions.

Health Beliefs

Much is written about the need for cancer patients to be positive and develop a fighting spirit, but it is advised to shy away from the term 'positive'. Invoking a positive implies the existence of a negative, and, further, being positive is not always realistic. Thus, the aim is for healthy, realistic thinking:

Unhealthy thinking: I will be dead within two years regardless of what I do.
Positive thinking: I will be alive and healthy two years from now.
Healthy thinking: I may or may not be alive two years from now, but what I do can make a significant difference to how I am within that time.
Unhealthy thinking: This cancer will continue to consume me regardless of what I do.

Positive thinking: I can beat this cancer.

Healthy thinking: The cancer may or may not go entirely from my body, but what I do can make a significant difference to how I am.

All our patients are looking for health and help to get that health. How they think colours how they feel, and holding unhelpful health beliefs is detrimental to wellbeing. Often the beliefs that individuals hold about their cancer, and their emotional response to it, increase their morbidity (Simonton, 1986). Such beliefs may be changed through education, and new ones instigated. Hypnosis is a powerful tool to help cement the new and helpful beliefs.

Engendering Healthy and Helpful Beliefs

The questionnaire (see below) devised for the Simontons by Malzby (Simonton, 1986) is useful in helping patients to identify their health beliefs and then acts as a tool to re-pattern their underlying belief system towards a more helpful one. The questions are listed below.

* Does this belief help me protect my life and health?
* Does it help me achieve my short-term and long-term goals?
* Does it help me resolve or avoid my most undesirable conflicts (whether those conflicts are within myself or with other people)?
* Does it help me feel the way I want to feel?

And when appropriate, also ask:

* Is the belief based on facts?

Getting clients to articulate their belief systems and then helping them re-pattern it in a helpful way is possibly the most important first step in cancer care. Imagery is an essential component to internalizing the new beliefs (Achterberg, 1985; Wells & Hackman, 1993) in order to move the client forward. It is revealing how imagery changes when one is holding a helpful health belief system as opposed to an unhelpful one.

Patients are asked to articulate their overriding emotion and link that to their disease; it is interesting to note that patients often give fragmented and incomplete sentences (see Table 24.1 for examples) when telling their story. Five or more such statements are elicited, and it is useful to tabulate them on the left hand side of the page. These statements/ beliefs are then evaluated against the five above criteria, and if necessary the therapist helps to re-pattern them and the re-patterned belief is then entered on the right hand side of the table. This session is often an emotional one for the patient and should not be rushed.

For example feeling scared is a common overriding emotion experienced by many cancer patients. The therapist would ask such a patient to share some views on that, and five or more statements are entered into the table.

Table 24.1   Re-patterning beliefs

The emotion(s) causing distress: **Scared**	Re-patterned beliefs are said as affirmations. *(Italics refer to suggestions accompanying the affirmation.)*
Very frightened when first diagnosed that I was going to die. . . . After treatment feel better about it. . . . Scared of dying, suddenly not being.	Daily there are many pleasures for me to enjoy. *Let one of the many pleasures come into your mind and play with it.*
Unfair, lots of things I want to do that others can do.	I have lots of goals still to achieve. *Bring a goal into your mind and work with it – what do you need to do to achieve it? How will you do it? How will you feel when you have achieved it?*
Don't normally cry very easily, but I'm feeling quite vulnerable.	I have many strengths: organizing, encouraging others, presenting myself. *See yourself utilizing one of those strengths right now.*
Hardest not to see my granddaughters grow up.	Tony, Jonathan and Michael support and sustain me. I feel loved. *Let one or more of them come into your mind now. How do they look? How do they sound? What are they wearing? Smile at them now.*
One of the things I struggle with is 'What is there after death?' – Jewish culture and religion – started to think about a sort of energy – "Shechinah.	Exploring my spiritual beliefs may lead to greater comfort. *Let some relevant appropriate imagery come into your mind, and hold it for 20 to 30 seconds.*

a Shechina or Shekinah (Hebrew) n. Judaism. 1. the radiance in which God's immanent presence in the midst of his people, especially in the Temple, is visibly manifested. 2. the divine presence itself as contrasted with the divine transcendence.

Affirmations should be framed in the present tense; do not deny the unhelpful belief but concentrate on the uplifting aspect directed by it. If you have reframed this then you need to check out that the words you have used sound and feel right to the patient.

Key suggestions:

- *"(Name). . . As you practice finding this deeply relaxed state, you will find that your confidence in your ability to cope in any situation strengthens and grows."*
- *"(Name). . . In saying your healthy and helpful beliefs aloud, you will find that your confidence in your ability to cope in any situation strengthens and grows."*
- State their new beliefs.

Post-hypnotic suggestion

> *These affirmations repeated . . . aloud, daily . . . engender hope, optimism, and courage to follow that path which is right for you . . . a path that leads you in the direction of joy and fulfilment.*

When helpful and healthy beliefs are held patients are more likely to be self aware. Having established the statements that are to form their new health beliefs it is suggested the patients are taken into hypnosis, into their safe haven, and the statements reiterated together with the key suggestions.

Whilst any induction technique can be used, the following has been found useful as it helps to build confidence, can raise self-esteem and can be used as a protection measure.

A modified use of the 'Star Induction' is given here (Gindes, 1953). The subject is requested to close their eyes. After giving suggestions for comfort and easy breathing the therapist opens with:

> *With your eyes closed, allow your mind to become dark and blank . . . in one corner of your mind's eye, however you imagine it, just be aware of a small pin prick of light. . . . Concentrate on the light . . . and as you concentrate on the light notice how it becomes just a little bigger and a little brighter . . . keep concentrating on the light . . . breathing easily and gently . . . the light becoming bigger and brighter . . . the light is emanating from the star . . . a star in the northern hemisphere whose light has special properties . . . feel yourself getting nearer and nearer to the light . . . and as you do really become aware of the light . . . as the light grows in size you feel yourself drawn towards it . . . as you get nearer to the star perhaps you can see all the myriad colours in the light . . . a star is a sun and just like our sun the light is warming . . . feel the warmth of the light . . . feel its brightness . . . breathing deeply, easily now . . . feel the light all around your body and through your body warming you . . . comforting you . . . bathed in this light you feel safe and secure . . . calm and confident. This light allows you to hold out all that you need to hold out and hold in all that you need to need to hold in . . . breathe deeply now and bask in the warm, comforting starlight. . . .*

Continue until the patients is fully relaxed and judged to be in trance. Insert therapy suggestions at this point if required.

> *Shortly you will leave the starlight and return to the here and now . . . but know this . . . you can find the starlight whenever you want to or need to . . . today you were drawn into it but . . . you may like to find it by simply stepping into it rather like stepping into sunlight from a darkened room . . . you may like to snuggle down under it like a duvet . . . or wrap it around you like a blanket or a towel . . . may even find a special door and go through it into the starlight. . . . However you find the starlight is fine.*

The two key suggestions are *"Bathed in this light you are safe and secure, feeling sure and confident"* and *"This light allows you to hold out all that you need to hold out and hold in tight all that you need to hold in."*

The author (JO) has found this metaphor a useful tool for the following problems as well as with cancer patients at the beginning of treatment:

- An opera singer who was suffering stage fright; the stage light became her starlight.
- A patient who experienced allergic reaction to local anaesthetic; she pulled the starlight down over her head inside a golden helmet and provided her own pain management in the dentist chair.
- As a measure where one has to leave a charged emotional room and go quickly into a different but yet still charged environment; this has proved to be a useful technique to teach nurses.
- It is useful in relationship difficulties to have the patient stand inside the starlight and dialogue with the other partner, who is outside the starlight, gradually working to have them both inside and both experiencing the protective measures of the light.

Ego strengthening should be used at every opportunity. The following mnemonic KUFALE has been found useful:

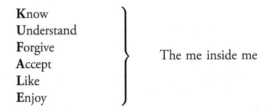

Know
Understand
Forgive   The me inside me
Accept
Like
Enjoy

Useful topics to explore are:

- When you look in a mirror you should see your best friend looking back.
- How do we make a best friend?
- We spend time with them and get to *know* them little by little.
- We *understand* them.
- They are not carbon copies of us, so we *forgive* those times when they hurt, irritate or annoy us.
- We *accept* them as they are and do not try to change them.
- We *like* them for who and what they are.
- We *enjoy* them – their company, their friendship.
- Not many of us spend very much time on developing this best friend inside of us – the 'me' inside 'me'.
- We go to school where day dreaming and self exploration are frowned upon.
- We grow up and enter higher education or the work force and join in the business of life.
- Homes, families and mortgages keep us locked into this business with even less time to develop our own best friend.
- A life event of some sort brings us up short, and we find we need that best friend.

These are then anchored to a personal image arising in hypnosis. In trance invite the patient to imagine, as you speak, something that represents these concepts. Examples have been a boat, a leafy glade, flowers (many different ones, especially roses), perfume, a mirror, a pet, a piece of music and a painting.

Building confidence

ACE.   Begin in their place of safety and ask the client to tell you the first image that comes into their mind when you say the word 'ace'. examples patients have found are a suit of playing cards, an aeroplane, a sport and a racing car.

Ask the patient to fill their ACE with the letters.

> *Be aware that A represents acceptance . . . C is for confidence . . . and E is to remind you to place the emphasis on all that is helpful and healthy in your life . . . make these letters brighter and richer in colour . . . begin to slowly rotate the your ace seeing all the colours in three dimensions . . . now begin to spin the ace even faster and you will find that a channel opens up between it and you, so that you can draw down into yourself all of these concepts and qualities . . . acceptance . . . confidence . . . emphasis. Allow this feeling to spread out through your body so that every cell in every part of your body is aware of how it is when you feel when you are accepting of yourself, confident in yourself and your abilities and resolved to place the emphasis on all that is healthy and helpful in your life. These feelings will stay with you for as long as you need them to or want them to, enabling you deal confidently with any situation you find yourself in. Whenever you feel your confidence levels are low, you can take yourself down into trance and use your ace to replenish your store of confidence. When you are ready to leave this visualization and return to the here and now, you will wake feeling confident and relaxed.*

Framing suggestions

Suggesting that some cancers can and do spontaneously enter into remission or that undergoing chemotherapy can be relatively free of unpleasant side effects are examples of perfectly sound suggestions. Suggesting that your particular patient *will* experience either of the above is both unethical and cruel. The semantics you use when framing your suggestions is crucial. Unless therapists are fully conversant with the cancer process, treatment options and the ramifications of both, they cannot safely guide this very vulnerable and often emotionally fragile group of people, nor will they be able to frame suggestions appropriately.

Tools for formulating imagery

Cancer patients want information about their disease (Chelf *et al.*, 2001; Drew & Fawcett, 2002) and the National Institute for Clinical Excellence in their *Guidance on Cancer Care* (2004) directed that information should span the cancer continuum and be tailored to the individual. Written materials reinforce discussion points. It is helpful to provide patients with both written explanations and, for some techniques, charts in order to help them to develop imagery that has relevance and personal meaning.

Incongruence

Imagery held in conscious awareness is often not the same as that described when the imagination is freed in a hypnotic state. Discovering the difference can be very revealing and useful. Working with the patient's personal imagery is most useful.

Safe haven

A most important aspect of this work is to find a place of safety for the client, however, for someone locked in fear this may take several image processes before reaching the one most helpful place that they can always find at will. Patients often find themselves in their safe haven imagery but have aspects that signify that there are not settled such as a dark sky, rain or fog. Usually when the planned intervention has been carried out these aspects will have changed but they should be checked before re-alerting the patient.

When patients are working with imagery in hypnosis, it is preferable to remain silent or feed in key suggestions and have them work for about one minute. It can be quite taxing, especially for those who are already debilitated or feeling unwell, and not all cancer patients are able to work at this intense level.

Some patients do not enjoy practicing (Kaempfer, 1982; Redd *et al.*, 1983). Sims (1987) found that many patients with cancer believed the mental, physical and time demands of relaxation training exceeded their resources and were unable to practice regularly. At times, families may have more interest and need for relaxation training than the patient. Furthermore, nurses and patients may have unrealistic expectations, contributing to a sense of failure (Spiegel & Moore, 1997). A risk also exists of masking undiagnosed illnesses or withholding other treatments (Van Fleet, 2000; Zahourek, 1988).

Specific Interventions: Chemotherapy

Whilst chemotherapeutic agents can be delivered by many routes, this technique is intended for use with intravenous administration. Chemotherapy regimens may entail a single dose given at regular intervals over a period of time or in divided doses with a rest recovery period. Chemotherapy cannot tell the difference between healthy cells and cancer cells. It affects them all by interfering in some way with their ability to reproduce. Healthy cells, not in the process of dividing, are difficult to kill, whereas cancer cells are weak disorganized cells and are easy to kill. Each course of chemotherapy will result in a weakened immune defence necessitating a recovery rest period before another course of chemotherapy is given. The low point is called a 'nadir', and for some patients this can necessitate a dose reduction or delay in treatment and some regimens require hospitalization during nadirs.

The simple graph in Figure 24.1 illustrates the point and forms a basis for a more detailed explanation of the chemotherapy drugs and their associated particular side effects.

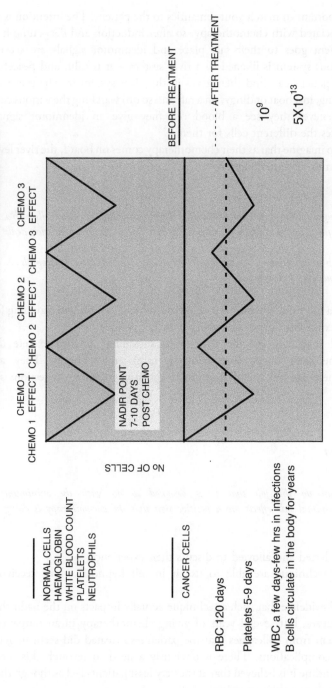

Figure 24.1 Effect of chemotherapy on normal and cancer cells. © Jacky Owens.

Hypnotic intervention

Remember that it is important to match your semantics to the patient. The intention is to minimize the nadir associated with chemotherapy, so after induction and deepening it is suggested that the patient goes to their safe place and ideomotor signals are set up (see page 24). The venous system is likened to a river system – it is calm and peaceful. It is suggested that the patient can find themselves in this river system in whatever way feels right to them (wading, in a boat or dingy, on a raft and so on) watching the various cells travelling around. Whenever they see a blood cell they give an ideomotor signal. The therapist enumerates the different cells for them.

They are then asked to imagine that as their chemotherapy comes on board, the river level rises and the river becomes more turbulent.

Key suggestions:

> *The chemotherapy is doing the job that it is designed to do, killing (destroying) the cancer cells with a minimum of unwanted side effects and any unwanted side effects that do occur can be safely dealt with.*
> *Now . . . your job . . . is to hang onto . . . in whatever way you want . . . all those neutrophils . . . and as many white blood cells . . . as you can.*

Ask them to do this for a full minute whilst repeating the key suggestions and watching for the IMR, which often comes in flurries of activity with lull periods.

It is then suggested that they see the river levels subsiding, as they excrete the chemotherapy, and the river once more becomes calm and tranquil. They are then taken back into their safe place, and appropriate ego-strengthening suggestions are given.

Post-hypnotic suggestion

> *Your chemotherapy can do the job that it is designed to do with the minimum of side effects. Those minimal side effects are a positive sign that the chemotherapy is doing its job.*

The patient is then re-alerted and allowed to discuss their experience.

Patients taught this technique are able to use it in self hypnosis whilst receiving their chemotherapy.

There is no empirical evidence that such a technique actually impacts on the nadir that cancer chemotherapy causes, but several years of giving chemotherapy in an outpatient setting did draw comment from colleagues that the patients so treated did seem to get a better ride with fewer complications. There is obviously a need to research this more scientifically. In the meantime it is believed that at the very least patients feel as though they have a measure of control over their situation.

Nausea

It is explained to the patient that there are two trigger mechanisms for nausea; one is located in the upper part of the small intestine and the other in the limbic system/higher centre. The suggested technique below allows the patient to focus on both.

Hypnotic intervention

In hypnosis, ask the patient to envision their body as a series of rooms connected by a corridor and encourage them to explore each of these rooms to look for a nausea switch. Give as little explanation as possible and let the patient's own creative powers work; it is the patient's imagery and not the therapist's that matters. Patients are looking for a switch and when they find it they will know what it is. When they find one let them tell you which room it resides in and how it appears to them. Often they will describe the heart room or lounge. Ask if the switch is on or off and how they feel in terms of nausea. Now encourage them to go on patrolling the corridors looking into the rooms until they have explored their entire body. They may or may not find another switch. If they do, let them tell you again which room it resides in and how it appears to them. They will know which one is the master switch (not all patients relate the higher centre one as being the master), but they need to work with the master switch last. Now you can begin to work with these switches: on-off, up-down, using whatever switch method is preferred. Use the imagery they give you to take the nausea in and out several times. Images for switches have been as diverse as a lever, a round knob, a gun, a gold arrow, a ladder, a button, a key, a electrical switch and even a lever high up on an almost impossible to climb wall.

Key suggestion – as they switch the nausea out: *"You will find that you bring a calm, settled feeling into your tummy, a clear cool head and a pleasant taste in your mouth."* This is combined with lots of ego strengthening and a post-hypnotic suggestion for mastery followed by re-alerting the patient and allowing some time for debriefing.

One patient had a set of stone steps carved into a wall and his switch was a large clock hand (lever) just out of reach but he clawed up the wall to reach this lever and successfully turned his nausea off. Another patient's switch appeared as a rifle with which he fired the nausea out and then said, *"That's better – she needs cleaning now."* The commonest imagery for switches are the old brown Bakelite ones which is quite incredible since many of the patients are far too young to personally have seen such switches.

It is interesting to note that this technique was so successful in one unit that some doctors took note of where patients located their trigger when prescribing anti-emetic medication.

Cancer Attack Programme

A simplified chart to give some understanding of the complexity of the normal functioning immune system is helpful. (See Figure 24.2.) It will depend on what aspect of immune

Haematopoiesis is the differentiation process for blood cells and is based on need: most of these cells have a shelf life

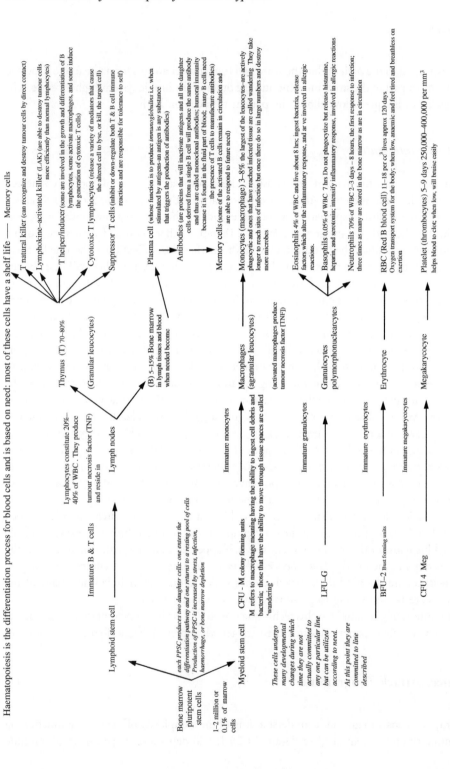

Figure 24.2   Haematopoiesis chart. © Jacky Owens.

function your patient needs to work with as to how you can help them use their imagery, starting and ending in their safe haven.

For patients who are in treatment for cancer, it is suggested working in trance, with the following.

Hypnotic intervention

What image comes up when they concentrate on their immune system?
What do the cancer cells look like and feel like?
What do the white blood cells (WBC) look like and feel like?
Discover how the WBC wants to get rid of the cancer cell.
What does that process look like and feel like?
Then, when the area is clear, what does it look like and feel like?

The variety of images presented by patients over the years is amazing, and it is these images with their personal meaning that are so powerful. No matter how knowledgeable or creative a therapist becomes, they cannot come up with images that hold the same potential for change.

Having developed the imagery, patients are asked to keep running the loop of imagery for about one minute whilst feeding back to them the information they have given.

Key suggestions in this scenario would be along the lines of:

> *Your immune system can* (important: not 'will') *function properly for your wellbeing. As you imagine your cancer being killed/smashed/eaten* (as appropriate for their image) *be aware that your body can become just as healthy and strong as it can be. The human body has a great capacity to play host to, and deal with, all manner of unwanted cells, bacteria, viruses, mutating cells, cancer cells and cells which have reached the end of their natural life span. Our bodies regularly destroy and get rid of all of these using the apoptosis system and your body can function properly in this very natural way. Your immune system can function normally and properly for your wellbeing.*
>
> *Become aware of your immune function. Observe it in action, marvel at its ability to protect you. Thank it for working so robustly on your behalf.*

And so on.

Imagery in this circumstance has been as diverse as red daggers that melted into yummy food for the WBCs, jagged, black, heavy rocks that turned brilliant white, smooth and light when ingested by a WBC, or a bunch of black grapes that the white cells nibbled on and one patient who imagined his throat cancer as jagged mountains and polished it with a soft cloth until smooth; he used this both as a cancer attack programme and successfully as pain relief.

Post-hypnotic suggestions for mastery are then given.

Cancer Patrol Programme for Patients in Remission

Because of the watch, wait and see policy governing much of cancer care, many patients are fearful of a recurrence of their cancer despite no evidence of activity.

It is necessary to explain the normal mechanism of immune surveillance, and the example given below has been found useful:

> When a normal cell transforms into a cancer cell, it may display cell surface components called tumour antigens. These are molecules that are rarely, if ever, displayed on the surface of normal cells. If the immune system can recognize tumour antigens as non-self, it can destroy the cancer cells carrying them. Such an immune response is called immunologic surveillance and is carried out by cytotoxic T cells, macrophages, and natural killer cells. It appears to be most effective in eliminating tumour cells that arise due to a cancer-causing virus. (Tortora, 1994, p337)

Following such an explanation, many patients are keen to utilize the 'cancer patrol programme'.

There is no set script for this programme, although for all we start and terminate each hypnosis session in their safe place. The content depends entirely on the particular patient that you are working with such as in the examples below.

Hypnotic intervention

· Patients who have had surgery may wish to patrol the surgical area and utilize the cancer attack programme if they find any cancer cells. It is important that these patients are enabled to put this sort of work into perspective and encouraged to get on with their daily living.
· Some patients will concentrate on the thymus gland releasing mature T lymphocytes to seek out possible lurking cancer cells.
· More commonly patients will follow through the immune process in imagery thus:
  ○ From a safe place, ask the patient to shrink down into their bone marrow and describe it.
  ○ Ask them to describe the activity within the bone marrow and discover the different cells.
  ○ Allow the body to send these cells off on whichever pathway it wants (i.e. myeloid or lymphoid), following a normal developmental and maturation process. Even when the problematic line is known, do not give direction but suggest that the unconscious mind knows which pathway a particular stem cell needs to be on. (There is no premise for this other than the fact that the unconscious processes have been sending stem cells down pathways without interference previously.)
  ○ Ask the patient to find themselves travelling around the river system of their blood and see these cells fully mature and functioning in their designated role.
  ○ Get the patient to remove, in whatever way feels right to them, cells which do not appear or feel to be complete whole robust cells, but reminding them that stem cells should be circulating as well and that these should be allowed to continue circulating.
  ○ Switch them back and forth between the bone marrow and the blood, asking them to work for a minute whilst continuing to give key suggestions. Experience shows that it is useful for patients to witness the stem cells being produced, making the daughter

cells and one being sent off on either the myeloid or lymphoid pathway, but then also to travel around the circulatory system checking out the various cells as being strong, robust, healthy, fully functioning cells and getting rid of ones that are not.

Key suggestions:

"Your bone marrow is able to produce healthy stem cells."

The stem cells that ought to can travel on the appropriate pathway developing and maturing in the right sequence and at the right time they can form fully functioning robust healthy cells carrying out their designated role.

"Your immune system functioned properly before the cancer overwhelmed it and now that the cancer has been . . . removed/treated (insert appropriately) *it can once more carry out its designated work."*

Post-hypnotic suggestion is then given for mastery and for trust in their immune system. Examples of imagery obtained with this technique:

- One lady imaged her immune system as a field of daisies which she patrolled, weeding and replanting bare patches as necessary.
- A man saw his immune system as coral, blackened by an oil spill; that lots of little creatures cleaned up, until the coral was pink and cream and alive with a myriad of brightly coloured fishes.
- One young boy saw his immune system as a team of footballers kitted out in white playing the blue team (he did not like the colour blue). He played football in self-hypnosis daily.

Dealing with Recurrence

This is often a very challenging and a more frightening time for patients than the original diagnosis. Alongside the natural fear of premature death is the recalled memory of the first line treatment which may possibly have been difficult for them. Where possible start with their health belief system, and help patients re-pattern it as necessary. It is useful to help them discover what they learned from the first experience that can help now and what they might do differently. Great care is needed not to introduce a sense of guilt here.

Hypnotic intervention

This is whatever the patient deems to be most useful; sometimes they will choose the cancer attack programme, sometimes the cancer patrol programme. This group of patients are often firmly held in a grip of fear and would find the specific cancer programmes frightening, so begin with lots of ego strengthening. You can build on their past experience, reframing it, if it was a difficult journey for them, and include lots of suggestions around 'trust'. Trust in their treatments and in their health care teams' expertise. Trust in their bodies to withstand the treatments. Trust that having done it all once, they can do it again. It is helpful in this context to remind the patient in trance of the normal natural functioning of the immune system generally and key cells in particular.

Key suggestions:

"You have recovered from cancer in the past and you can do so again" (only make this suggestion if you believe it is a realistic possibility).

Repeat healthy beliefs if done previously.

Post-Hypnotic suggestion

"Resolve to carry out those behaviours that are helpful to you." Then name these behaviours.

Haematological Cancers

Hypnotic intervention

In trance and safe place imagery the cancer patrol bone marrow imagery can be used, watching the production of stem cells. Explaining the process to the patient can be facilitated by the use of Figure 24.2. As they travel the pathways they can go through their developmental processes in the correct order and at the correct time maturing to become fully functioning robust healthy cells. Whereabouts in the pathway we concentrate the most depends on the exact diagnosis. They will have been given their precise diagnosis and know which cells and at which point those cells are malforming. Thus for myeloma patients we could work with the mature B cells as uncontrolled growth of plasma cells characterizes this, as yet, incurable disease. We may work with the abnormal immunoglobulins that these plasma cells produce or the possible platelet dysfunction. Equally we may use the cancer attack programme to work on the plasma tumour masses that occur when the plasma cells invade bone marrow. This work is not prescriptive in the sense that a formulated and prepared script could be used for all myeloma patients or all leukaemias. To work at the cellular level it is necessary to have an understanding of the specific disease process in each individual case and to formulate a hypnotic intervention that targets both their special anomaly and their presenting symptoms.

Key suggestions:

Cells develop and mature along designated pathways into fully functioning cells.
Each stage of cell development occurs in the right sequence and at the right time.

Post-hypnotic suggestion

Repeat key suggestions plus anything that is of particular relevance to the patient you are working with.

Many haematological cancers and increasingly some solid tumours are being treated with either bone marrow or stem cell transplants. This treatment involves obliterating the immune system with either radiotherapy and/or chemotherapy followed by a rescue of either previously harvested (their own or donated) bone marrow or stem cells. The rescue cells need to find their way into the bone marrow, and before the immune system can begin to rebuild thus there is a period of time in which the patient is without immune protection. This waiting period can last up to three weeks and whilst the patient is immunosupressed, working in the ways previously described will, in the author's (JO) opinion, be counter-productive although other hypnotic interventions described below can be used. The appearance of neutrophils in the daily sampling signals that chymarism has occurred (i. e. the graft has taken).

Pre-chymarism

During this waiting period (i.e. after obliteration of the bone marrow and before chymarism occurs), it is possible to work with these patients to prepare for the new immune system.

Hypnotic intervention

In safe place imagery talk to the patient about the ways in which they may make their home so welcoming that friends do not want to leave. This is their home and their ways, so give little guidance but ask for lots of details from them. Perhaps suggest some spring cleaning, preparing food or playing music to encourage them to begin creatively preparing to receive and welcome their friends.

Ask them to image their bone marrow and really explore it. Suggest they make their bone marrow as welcoming and as friendly as they can and to simply patiently watch for their friends arriving and see what the stem cells look like.

Key suggestion:

Patiently wait.

Carry out all the prescribed necessary instructions such as mouth care, HL care, daily hygiene, watch nutritional intake etcetera. (HL refers to Hickman line which is a plastic catheter inserted into a vein and tunnelled underneath the skin to prevent infection and through which intravenous therapy is delivered.)

Post-hypnotic suggestion

> *Your stem cells will find their way into your bone marrow in good time. During the waiting period, you can feel calm, relaxed and confident carrying out all those behaviours necessary for your wellbeing.*

When working in the hospital with patients undergoing bone marrow or stem cell transplants whilst waiting for chymarism to take place (the graft to take) and counts are non-existent, encourage patients to imagine their bone marrow and work with the imagery to encourage chymarism. Some examples of imagery patients described are:

- Old war time brown suitcases out of which, when opened, poured white liquid full of stem cells
- Men in white coats in a factory making small white bits to fit (precision made) into a machine
- Bone marrow as a sponge, stem cells rather like sea-horses settling into the deep recesses, feeling at home there
- Tiny white specks floating into large rooms, attaching themselves to the walls and growing

Post-chymarism

Hypnotic intervention

Whilst in their safe place introduce the analogy of a factory. For any factory to be productive it needs to be well managed. The boss needs to have the welfare of his workers in hand. A happy workforce is more productive. The factory will employ checkers who get rid of imperfect goods. Factories may be closed for annual holiday during which time overall cleaning, servicing and repair work can be done; or perhaps if orders are short then part-time working operates, or there is full-time working for normal orders, or the factory may even be on overtime if rush orders come in. This is their factory; they are the boss and can put the factory on overtime.

The stem cells can now follow the normal pathways. Some will form a resting pool in the circulating blood to be drawn on in times of need, some will follow the myeloid pathway and others will follow the lymphoid pathway. They are to nurture their new and emerging immune system by following all the medical and nursing advice.

Key suggestions:

Will be dependent upon daily blood results.

Post-Hypnotic suggestion

To nurture their emerging new immune system.

Working with Tumour Markers

Some cancer cells exhibit proteins known as tumour markers, for example prostate specific antigen (PSA) for prostate cancer, and cancer antigen (CA) 125 for ovarian cancer. These serum markers are used in screening programmes, but importantly they are used to indicate response to cancer treatment regimens and their presence is an indication in the watch, wait and see policy that treatment should resume, even when patients are asymptomatic.

It is paramount to use these techniques as an adjunct to normal treatment and not instead of it. Therapists are reminded to work only within their field of competence and in conjunction with other members of the oncology team. It is possible therefore to devise hypnotic interventions to help patients deal with elevated markers.

One patient who, in hypnosis, visualized he was excreting PSA via every excretory route possible and reduced his levels from nine to two in one week and to zero the following week. There is no way of knowing if this work together brought about the change, but he certainly believed that it did and it was of immense help to him psychologically.

Similar visualizations can be done with other tumour markers.

It should now be possible to see how one might work at this level for all sorts of diagnostic and treatment procedures. For example one might create a scenario for bone marrow aspirate or stem cell harvest seeing the life-saving stem cells in abundance, or develop imagery to use whilst having radiotherapy, both for the treatment and for cool, calm skin afterwards.

Finally

The three 'C's' of Healthcare

It is of paramount importance that patients have trust and confidence in the health care team. The following suggestions given early in therapy can be helpful.

Teachers speak of the three 'R's' but in healthcare we talk of the three 'C's':

- *Each member of your health care team is well trained, competent and experienced.*
- *They work confidently, for competence breeds confidence and people who work confidently do so calmly and professionally.*
- *You will find that your team works in a caring manner, seeking to optimize your health and wellbeing.*

The above approach utilized hypnosis for treating problems as they arose during cancer treatment. Alden's view is that hypnosis should be used in a pre-emptive manner and taught early in the cancer journey so that skills can be used to help any type of problem the patient may face on a day to day basis. In her clinical experience, patients who learn to use self-hypnosis early do appear to maintain higher self-esteem and self-efficacy. They also appear to cope better with treatments, remain more relaxed and optimistic and feel more in control.

This view is supported by Peynovska *et al.* (2005), who in a study of patients concluded that 'hypnosis is best offered early, at diagnosis, rather than later in the cancer journey so that patients can develop coping skills, which may prevent the development of severe anxiety, depression and panic attacks' (p6). Bejenke (2000) also notes benefits in instigating supportive therapy early in the cancer patient's journey.

Simple self hypnosis, including 'safe place' imagery, ego strengthening and 'healing imagery', plus appropriate anxiety management and symptom control techniques as required, are easily taught and help patients cope with the numerous hurdles that they have to 'leap over' with the various cancer treatments. From this baseline, modifications of imagery or other techniques can be utilized at any hurdle.

The following suggestions (after Bejenke, 2007), when incorporated into ego strengthening, can be very helpful in preparation for treatment. These are only a guide, as suggestions should always be developed according to the language and needs of the patient.

Pre-surgery

And you might be very surprised to discover that you can feel so much better than you might have expected in so many ways.

You might be surprised to find that the night before your surgery you can be so much more calm and relaxed than you might have expected.

After all, you can so look forward to looking back over this time and seeing yourself coping, being surprised at how comfortable you can feel; how quickly you recover.

And on the day, enjoying such a sense of calm relaxation all the way to your surgery. Looking forward to looking back. Finding yourself seeing yourself well and recovered.

And after you awaken, feeling so much more comfortable than you might have expected, finding yourself comfortable, calm and feeling a great sense of achievement, you've done it! Finding yourself ready to eat and enjoying the taste of food.

Pre-chemotherapy

And I would like to talk to you about your chemotherapy. I wonder if you have considered just how important a role you have in your treatment team. Yes, they might tell you when to turn up, what to do, and they give you those very powerful drugs that can so powerfully kill cancer cells, but you have a very important job to do. Your job is to take care of you while they take care of you. They cannot treat you without you.

And your body can surprise you by really helping those powerful drugs to work in all kinds of ways.

And you know you might really be very surprised to find yourself feeling so much more relaxed and comfortable that you might have believed possible, knowing that you are having powerful treatment and that you can enjoy playing your part in helping yourself here.

And enjoying being surprised, feeling so much more calm and relaxed and comfortable as you go through treatment, being able to use your self-hypnosis during and after treatment in the ways that you have learned.

And I wonder just how much you might find yourself feeling surprised at just how much better you can feel after treatment. How much more comfortable and relaxed. And how much better food tastes and finding yourself enjoying new tastes. Looking forward to eating and enjoying all kinds of foods. . . .

Pain Control

Cancer pain can be highly responsive to hypnotic interventions. As with all pain interventions, the importance of a thorough assessment cannot be overemphasized. As this book contains a chapter on pain, the reader should find that the principles can be applied to cancer-related pain. However there are a few points that should be borne in mind.

Cancer pain is usually an indication of disease, or disease progression, and it can be exacerbated by an emotional component.

We advise that this should always be explored fully before attempting any intervention; for example, issues of control, and fears related to death and dying, are commonly associated with increasing pain levels. The following examples illustrate these points.

> A man with advanced disease who was suffering from severe pain was referred for hypnotic pain control. When asked what went through his mind when he experienced pain he said, *"Well I know I'm not going to die tomorrow."* Exploration of this resulted in an immediate reduction of pain which was then enhanced hypnotically.

> A woman with advanced bowel cancer whose pain became unresponsive to medication was concerned about loss of control over her life and death. She had seen her father die of the same disease. Discussion of control issues resulted in rapid response to analgesic medication and hypnosis.

It is always worth using ideomotor signalling (IMS) to ensure that a pain control intervention is acceptable. Patients may fear that if they allow hypnotic pain control, something significant disease-wise could be missed. This applies not only to pain but also to symptoms such as nausea as seen in the following example.

> A woman with metastatic breast cancer had developed intractable nausea and vomiting for which there was no apparent physical cause. She had previously experienced hypnosis for needle phobia and through the use of IMR disclosed that her symptoms were functioning as an anxiety management technique. She was afraid that if she did not keep the oncologist's attention on her symptoms, something important would be missed.

Radiotherapy

For many patients undergoing radiotherapy, having to lie still, on their own, whilst a 'big machine' hovers over them can generate anxiety about coping, and for the claustrophobic patient it may be terrifying. Patients with head and neck cancers, or brain tumours, are particularly vulnerable given the masks they have to wear.

There are some studies demonstrating the efficacy of CBT with hypnosis (CBTH) (Schnur *et al.*, 2009; Stalpers *et al.*, 2005).

Dissociative distraction imagery, for example being in a safe relaxing place (safe haven), can be enough to enhance coping. It is important to ensure the patient experiences as vivid imagery as possible, for example by enhancing as many sensory experiences within their imagery as possible.

Once established, suggestions such as the following can be included:

> *You can be so comfortable that nothing need bother you, nothing need disturb you, nothing need trouble you. In fact you can be so calm, relaxed and comfortable that there need be no other feelings but your relaxation and comfort . . . and you can be aware of sounds, sensations and you can allow everything you notice to be part of your experience helping you to be more and more comfortable. And you can really enjoy that comfort.*

Imagery approaches can also including 'floating away to a beautiful place in a safe protective bubble'.

Cancer-Related Anxiety

As an enhancement to CBT, the following metaphor included in a hypnotic intervention may be helpful:

> *Have you ever looked out of the window on a misty morning and noticed just how little you can see? How everything looks vague and even familiar buildings across the street can look unreal . . . strange . . . different. Sometimes the mist can be so thick you cannot really see anything at all. Yet if you try to hold mist in your hand, it might feel cool and damp . . . but it is insubstantial. Just mist. But it can really cloud your view. Then when the sun burns through, it clears and you can see everything clearly again. . . . Bright and clear.*
>
> *Thoughts are just like mist. They have no substance . . . just like mist you cannot hold them in your hand. They are not evidence . . . they are only thoughts. But they can really cloud your view. . . . They are not reality. Just because you think it does not make it true. And just like mist, when they clear. . . . You can once again see things clearly.*
>
> *But unlike the mist which will clear when it is ready, you can clear the mist of thoughts. You can challenge them and watch them melt away . . . just like mist. And sometimes when an unwanted or discomforting thought comes into your mind, you can perhaps find yourself saying to yourself, it is just mist . . . and let it go . . . float away like a wisp of mist. . . .*

Furthermore, some patients find themselves gripped with immobilizing fear on being diagnosed with cancer. Hypnosis is a means whereby such patients can release their fear and be helped to address whatever issues the diagnosis brings up for them. Experience shows that this group of patients may well abreact when introduced to a safe place in hypnosis; yet on exploration of the abreaction, these patients usually express a sense of peace or relief.

Conclusions

Hypnotherapy and related interventions can play an important part in improving the quality of life of patients at various stages of the cancer journey. They can also be effective in treating a wide range of problems related to the diagnosis and treatment of malignant disease. Because cancer-related problems usually have biological, psychological and social ramifications, it is the authors' view that the needs of patients are best served when hypnotherapy is carried out within a service which is fully integrated physically and functionally with other parts of the cancer and wider health services (Sharp *et al.*, 2009) as the cancer may be only one of a number of health problems for any particular individual.

References

Achterberg, J. (Ed.) (1985), *Imagery in healing shamanism and modern medicine*. Boston, Shambhala.

Bejenke, C. (2000), Benefits of early interventions with cancer patients. *Hypnos*, 26.

Bejenke C. (2007), Workshop given at the joint meeting of BSCAH, RSM and BSMDH, Edinburgh, Scotland, May.

Drew, A. & Fawcett, T. N. (2002), Responding to the information needs of patients with cancer. *Professional Nurse*, 17, 443–6.

Gindes, B. C. (1953), *New concepts of hypnosis: as an adjunct to psychotherapy and medicine*. London, George Allen and Unwin.

Chelf, J. H., Agre, P., Axelrod, A., Cheney, L., Cole, D. D., Conrad, K., Hooper, S., Liu, I., Mercurio, A., Stepan, K., Villejo, L. & Weaver, C. (2001), Cancer-related patient education: an overview of the last decade of evaluation and research. *Oncology Nursing Forum*, 28, 1139–47.

Jacobs, D. T. (1991) *Patient communication for first responders and EMS personnel – the first hour of trauma*. Englewood Cliffs, NJ, Brady.

Kaempfer, S. (1982), Relaxation training reconsidered. *Oncology Nursing Forum*, 9, 15–18.

National Institute for Clinical Excellence. (2004), Improving supportive and palliative care for adults with cancer. London, National Institute for Clinical Excellence.

Peynovska, R., Fisher, J. & Mathew, V. (2005), Efficacy of hypnotherapy as a supplement therapy in cancer intervention. *European Journal of Clinical Hypnosis*, 6, 6.

Redd, W., Rosenberger, P. & Hendler, C. (1983), Controlling chemotherapy side effects. *American Journal of Clinical Hypnosis*, 25, 161–72.

Schnur, J. B., David, D., Kangas, M., Green, S., Bovbjerg, D. H. & Montgomery, G. H. (2009), A randomized trial of a cognitive-behavioral therapy and hypnosis intervention on positive and negative affect during breast cancer radiotherapy. *Journal of Clinical Psychology*, 65, 443–55.

Sharp, D., Walker, M., Bateman, J., Braid, F., Hebblewhite, C., Hope, T., Lines, M., Walker, A. & Walker, L. (2009), Demographic characteristics of patients using a fully integrated psychosocial support service for cancer patients. *BMC Research Notes*, 2, 253. (Epub ahead of print).

Simonton, O. C. (Ed.) (1986), *Getting well again*. London, Bantam.

Sims, S. E. R. (1987), Relaxation training as a technique for helping patients cope with the experience of cancer: a selective review of the literature. *Journal of Advanced Nursing*, 12, 583–91.

Spiegel, D. & Moore, R. (1997), Imagery and hypnosis in the treatment of cancer patients. *Oncology*, 11, 1179–96.

Stalpers, L., Da Costa, H., Merbis, M., Fortuin, A., Muller, M. & Van Dam, F. (2005), Hypnotherapy in radiotherapy patients: a randomized trial. *International Journal of Radiation Oncology · Biology · Physics*, 61, 499–506.

Tortora, G. J. (1994), *Introduction to the human body: the essentials of anatomy and physiology*. New York, Harper Collins College Publishers. p 337.

Van Fleet, S. (2000), Relaxation and imagery for symptom management: improving patient assessment and individualizing treatment. *Oncology Nursing Forum*, 27, 501–10.

Walker, L. G., Green, V. L., Greenman, J., Walker, A. A. & Sharp, D. M. (2005), Psychoneuroimmunology and chronic malignant disease: cancer, in Irwin, M. & Vedhara, V. E. (Eds.) *Human psychoneuroimmunology (PNI)*. Oxford, Oxford University Press. p 154–5.

Wells, A. & Hackmann, A. (1993), Imagery and core beliefs in health anxiety: content and origins. *Behavioural and Cognitive Psychotherapy*, 21, 265–73.

Zahourek, R. (1985), *Clinical hypnosis and therapeutic suggestion in nursing*. New York, Grune & Stratton.

25

Death, Dying and Loss

Dr Kottiyattil K Aravind, Mrs Jacky Owens and Dr Ann Williamson

Introduction

Grief is the spontaneous response that accompanies the realization of loss. Grief may manifest as simple grief or as dysfunctional psycho-social behaviours. Grief is not confined to bereavement but can occur with any loss of job, position or relationship, and such adjustment disorders are covered elsewhere. For the purposes of this chapter, we will look at death and bereavement in more detail.

Helping the Terminally Ill Patient

For many years, six coping mechanisms in the stages of dying identified by Kübler-Ross (1969, 1986) have served as a model guiding clinicians to help their patients achieve an accepting hopeful state despite disease progression. According to the Kübler-Ross model there are five stages that a dying person goes through when they are told that they have a terminal illness, and a sixth coping mechanism (i.e. 'hope') is relevant to all stages. The five stages go in progression through denial, anger, bargaining, depression and acceptance, and whilst many feel that this linear progression is too rigid it is still accepted that the terminally ill experience many, if not all, of the model's stages.

The Handbook of Contemporary Clinical Hypnosis: Theory and Practice, First Edition.
Edited by Les Brann, Jacky Owens and Ann Williamson.
© 2012 John Wiley & Sons, Ltd. Published 2015 by John Wiley & Sons, Ltd.

Denial

For some, denial is a coping strategy, and caution should be used when patients are using it. To remove a coping strategy without replacing it will lead to more distress. not less, yet it is important not to collude with the denial. Hypnoanalysis can be very useful in helping these people move to acceptance, for when locked in denial it is not possible to consider desired goals, let alone achieve any.

Anger

Anger is common amongst those who feel cheated out of an expected life span. Helping patients work through their anger is often the most useful approach and can safely be done in hypnosis such that energies are productive and not destructive.

Bargaining

Many terminally ill patients engage in bargaining. They bargain with their God, their medical team and their families. Hypnosis is a means whereby personal insights can be gained, and bound up in self-awareness is the ability to set realistic goals. When patients can set realistic goals, bargaining tends to cease.

Depression

Some believe that the extent and commonality of depression to be found in those who know they are dying are problems not properly addressed in modern medicine (Macleod, 2007).

In an article that addressed using the hypnotherapeutic relationship to help terminally ill patients, Frederick, (1998) concluded,

> Current psychiatric practice does not offer much to the terminally ill patient beyond support and compassion... symptom control, and supportive care (whilst laudable) '... ignores the very active and dynamic work that many terminally ill patients need – may require before they can die peacefully. (p149)

Techniques described throughout this book to deal with depression can be used with this patient group.

Acceptance

When a patient is a state whereby they are neither fearful of dying nor angry that it is imminent and feel that they have achieved their important goals they are more likely to be accepting of what is to be. Whilst this is so for the majority of patients it does not pertain to all and some patients will die fighting to the bitter end to survive: this should not be a source of guilt for the therapist.

Hope

Kübler-Ross acknowledged hope to be a fairly constant coping strategy for many of the patients she interviewed. It is a quality (concept) that all therapy should encourage.

Guiding patients to a dignified and peaceful death using hypnosis is now considered.

Terminal restlessness afflicts many in the final days of life, and the use of imagery may be extremely helpful in giving insights, helping the patient to find quiet acceptance of what is to be, rather than the often fearful and anxious state that so many find themselves in.

A young Greek woman came to casualty one Saturday afternoon complaining of abdominal pain. She had put this down to constipation due to pre-wedding nerves, but was diagnosed with an advanced lymphoma. She worked with the hypnotherapist often throughout her illness managing her pain, nausea and the emotional issues surrounding the non-event of her wedding. Safe place imagery for her was always either the balcony of her student flat or that of her grandmother's house in Greece.

Safe place (haven) was reached via a magic carpet in hypnosis; this allows deeply held images to surface which can then be assessed for safety and are often more powerful than those determined in the waking state. On what was judged to be her final admission and with her family surrounding her she became very restless, tossing and turning and constantly crying out. The therapist asked her in trance to find the magic carpet to transport her to her safe haven. With surprise in her voice she said she didn't have her carpet, she had a coffin that was being carried by big black ravens. She said that black was not really black but had lots of beautiful colours in it. The coffin was empty and she did not know who ought to be in it. She did not know where it was going but she thought perhaps her grandmother's house. None of this imagery alarmed her either in trance or afterwards; she was more curious than anything. This was possibly her first insight of what was to be for her. She died a few days later with her sister lying on the bed beside her, but from that session onwards she had become calm and still.

Geffen, (2006) describes using a metaphor of taking off a pair of tight fitting shoes with a lady fearful of dying. It is a metaphor the author (JO) has used successfully on occasions with patients in the final stages of dying who are anxious or afraid. She simply weaves a story around the metaphor and makes it last, or repeats it, until the patient quietens.

Fear and Loss

Liossi and White, (2001) in a study involving cancer patients were able to show that the use of hypnosis can reduce death anxiety. Ego strengthening was a core component of the hypnosis intervention used, as indeed it is in most hypnotherapeutic approaches.

An individual may keenly feel the loss of a loved one (e.g. parent, sibling or friend), but we need to remember that the dying person is losing everyone in their lives at one time. At one time paternalistic medicine and the church between them provided support to the dying and their families. Modern medicine demands that patients take responsibility for themselves and their healthcare (indeed many patients expect this, no longer agreeing to passively submit to medical dicta). At the same time faith in orthodox religions has declined (Greely, 2004), and many people feel as though they are floundering in a void when death is approaching. Voids are frightening places to be in.

Although many patients fear the mode of death rather than death itself (Spiegel, 1993) there are some for whom 'not being' is the more frightening. Bernie Siegel, founder of e-cap (exceptional cancer patients, a global support group accessible via the net), suggested the concept of using a white room for those patients who hold fear and anxiety around loss of life (personal communication). A development of this concept has proved to be extremely useful in helping people come to terms with their situation.

White room metaphor

In this intervention, after induction and deepening, it is suggested to the patient that they find themselves in a plain white, empty room. They are asked to sit in this room and describe how they are feeling. Rarely will those who are fearful report feeling calm and settled. Some therapists may choose to use hypno-analysis at this point, but asking the patient to dialogue with their feelings to facilitate understanding and calmness is often sufficient.

The therapist provides a door and invites the patient to go and sit or stand beside it and listen. The therapist then talks to them about a party that is taking place beyond the door and suggests that whilst they have no idea who is attending the party the people there are relevant to the patient. It may be that previously departed loved ones are there; famous historical figures or simply strangers may make up the party. The patient is instructed to listen at the door whilst the therapist talks to them about parties in general, how they are fun to attend, that often you meet up with friends and acquaintances that you have not seen in a while and it is a time to relax and enjoy the company. If appropriate the patient may be invited to join the party for a little while and if they so wish they are allowed to open the door and go inside. They are asked to give as much detail about the party as possible to the therapist before being brought back into the white room. Here, based on the description of the party, the therapist can give more helpful suggestions before terminating the session.

For those people who have a religious faith it may be suggested that the door leads into whatever religious building is appropriate and they are allowed time to dialogue with their God, the therapist responding to them only as and when seems necessary. Post-hypnotic suggestion for these patients will always include considering making contact with their local religious minister.

People do not die in isolation; family dynamics and relationships can present complex difficulties. Flemons, (2002) discusses handling family dynamics where a family member is dying in his book *Of One Mind*. Since it is a particularly sensitive time for families and therapists need to be able to help all of those involved, not just the patient, it is recommended that those who want to work with this patient group undertake some appropriate training first.

Bereavement

Normal or 'harmless' grief

Similar to those described above, there are various suggested stages of normal grief which are initially shock, denial, numbness and disbelief, changing into anger, bargaining and compromise leading to depression; progressing through a period of mourning, expressing emotional, physical and social sufferings and a period of emotional reckoning to acceptance, and eventually the re-establishment of the world of normality (Kübler-Ross, 1969). This is not necessarily a linear sequence; some may not experience all these stages and a variable time is needed to re-establish their lives.

Abnormal or 'harmful' grief

Grief that falls outside the 'normal' has many labels such as pathological, abnormal, atypical, morbid, chronic, delayed or somatized (Jacobs and Kim, 1990). Such unresolved grief may underlie various emotional and psychosomatic symptoms that are presented to the health professional.

It is beyond the scope of this short chapter to go into detailed exploration of all the symptomatology, theories and possible interventions for grief but for further reading *Handbook of Bereavement; Theory, Research and Intervention* (Strobe *et al.*,1993) and *Grief Counselling and Grief Therapy* (Worden, 2005) are recommended.

Historically, therapy serves to help the bereaved cope with the pain and associated problems of grief. This may vary between simple supportive counselling and a psychoanalytic, psychodynamic or some other psychotherapeutic approach (Hart *et al.*,1990; Hodgkinson, 1980).

Allowing expression of negative emotions can be very helpful in facilitating their resolution. Using imagery and metaphor within a hypnotic context can be useful, such as silent abreaction (see page 136) to resolve anger towards the deceased or God/the Universe (Cerny & Buskirk, 1991) or having conversations and saying farewell with the deceased in their special place (or somewhere appropriate) in their imagination (Hart, 1988). Writing poems or a letter to the deceased can sometimes allow release of feelings (see page 65).

In some respects grief can be treated as a form of PTSD (Spiegel, 1981), and use of imagery as below can assist with flashbacks (Gravitz, 2001; Williamson, 2008).

> Alison kept having flashbacks to the sight and smell of her sister's body in the chapel of rest which distressed her very much as the body had not been kept as well as it might, so that the flesh looked purplish and there was an unpleasant smell. She changed her internal image so that the body looked merely sleeping (as she had found her sister originally) and filled the chapel of rest with her sister's favourite flowers, strongly scented roses.
>
> Having worked to resolve the various negative emotions associated with her sister's death, Alison was asked to imagine she was holding in her hand something to represent *the value* of the relationship between them such as light or golden stardust and to throw this into her future so that as she looked towards her future she could see it there twinkling and know that it would always be there for her.

Apart from those cited already there is little in the literature in the way of evidence base for the use of hypnosis in the treatment of grief but several case studies have been published (Grosklags, 2006; Hart *et al.*, 1990; Hodgkinson, 1980). There is also, of course, the weight of evidence referred to in other chapters when dealing with the concomitant feelings of anxiety, depression and loss of control. Self hypnosis is a useful tool in any emotional distress (Fromm & Eisen, 1982). Patients often have difficulty in accepting that there are some things over which they have no control, and metaphors such as the boat metaphor (below) may be found useful. It is obvious that, to keep rapport, the therapist has to work within the patient's spiritual beliefs and it is important to be sensitively aware of these when helping someone to resolve grief.

'Question and answer' model

Growing up and working as a medical practitioner in rural communities of Kerala, South India, this author (KKA) was taken aback with the remarkable lack of 'abnormal' grief in his native community compared with the abundance of mental and physical health problems following bereavement in his UK practice population despite their better 'quality of life'. The cultural expressions of grief in Kerala included wailing dialogue where the mourners asked questions and others replied. These included any perceived wrongdoings on both sides for which forgiveness was requested and received. Such catharsis seemed to prevent the generation of resentment, anger or guilt. Children were included in the mourning process rather than excluded as is often the case in the United Kingdom. The funeral itself and the rituals immediately afterwards were heavily weighted with gestures of goodbye to the departed followed some time later by a feast to celebrate the life of the loved one, underpinning the end of mourning and time to get back to normality.

In the United Kingdom, similar questions pass through the minds of the bereaved all the time but they are rarely admitted or talked about. Once good rapport has been achieved, many patients will talk about these inner thoughts and feelings regarding their loss and find great release in so doing. Often these thoughts may have been held for many years and are associated with feelings of guilt and shame. By helping the patient find answers to such questions, often using metaphors, it was noted that they were often more able to move forward from their loss.

Faced with death or any tragic event, all human beings try to analyse what happened, to try and determine whether something should or could have prevented the tragedy altogether, or maybe delayed the inevitable, as in cases of terminal illness. The only way to do this is by asking questions. From an evolutionary perspective, survival depends on the answers that are given.

All the bereaved ask questions. Some will produce answers using their intelligence and lifetime learning, or may get answers from listening to other people. Whatever source the answers may come from, as long as they are accepted satisfactorily by the bereaved in terms that everything has been done that could have been done, the grief will remain 'harmless'. These need no therapeutic interventions.

The story is different in many others when faced with the loss of a loved one. Most of their questions may be irrational. Some of them can be based on ill understood medical details, or about things that have happened, such as perceived misconduct from professionals and other persons. The weight of sadness paralyses their ability to be logical. On the one hand they wish to be left alone, doing nothing at all, to be swallowed up in their sadness but at the same time they have to deal with the funeral and any business affairs of the deceased. They may feel that they have to please their visitors, often agreeing with other people's advice, suggestions or demands, which they may later regret. These delayed regrets can raise questions later about their own integrity as they may have gone against their own or the perceived wishes of the deceased. This may generate feelings of guilt and inadequacy, turning a 'harmless' grief into a 'harmful' one. They may look for someone to blame and feel anger towards them as an easier option than blaming themselves or 'fate'. Cultural, social and religious dogmas and family values influence the nature of some of the questions, but the compelling force is always the immense sorrow for the loss of the loved one.

Thus it can be seen that grief becomes 'harmful' when the chain reactions of questions-answers-judgments-verdicts generate negative emotions. Guilt or anger towards oneself can easily be understood as self-punishment, while if there is anger, resentment and hatred towards another party, the patient may not recognize this as punishing themselves indirectly. Harbouring and processing such emotions will, of course, have negative effects on the person carrying them.

The bereaved may believe that forgiving or forgetting wrongdoings will be disrespectful to the deceased or the love they bear them. They may also have no idea that their grief is the prime cause for their somatic illness, which seemingly fails to respond to all conventional treatments. Some fear that they will 'forget' the bereaved if they let go of their grief.

Importance of Rapport

As in any therapeutic situation, the therapist has to accept whatever views the patient brings, in their totality. Clichés such as *"Time is a great healer,"* and *"X* (the dead person) *would not want you to . . . "* should usually be avoided.

One can often suspect that unresolved grief may influence the presenting illness especially when, on taking a history, their body language changes when they talk about a loss. If someone is unable to talk about the deceased without becoming upset, then it is useful to offer an early appointment as talking about it has stirred up the emotions.

The patient should be invited to talk freely about the deceased and the details of the circumstances in which they died.

The Boat Metaphor for Life

This metaphor is introduced by the author (KKA) telling the patient that he would like to compare life to this metaphor which has helped many people afflicted by the death and loss of their loved one.

> *Imagine we are put in a boat at the precise moment when our life begins, when we start our life in our mother's womb* (rather than when we are born). *During the time in the mother's womb, we make all the preparations necessary to come and sail out in the wide world. One day we decide to come out of our mother's womb, and with the help of our mother we are born.*
>
> *Imagine the world as a large ocean. All the people on the earth are moving forward in a line across it. Whether we are sleeping or rushing about, all of us would be travelling at the same speed and cover the same distance. We all have the same 24 hours in a day. No one can have one second more or one second less, and also cannot go any faster or slower. You have been sailing your boat by yourself from the start of your life and only you can take it to your port.*
>
> *We may shout at each other in anger or we can express our love or sail in flotilla, still no one else can sail your boat. Each person has a specifically designated port. When we reach that port we have to stop sailing, and whether we like it or not we have to leave our boat. We have to say goodbye to the others, who will continue to sail until they find their own designated port. Nobody can know where their specific port is. You will know it is yours and your boat will stop. There is nothing you can do apart from saying goodbye to the rest of the people and then leave your boat, to travel on some other way. Even if your boat is damaged or broken you still have to take the boat to your port.*

Until death happens the person is alive; a person is either alive or dead, with only a thin line separating the two. So someone with a terminal illness or a poor prognosis is not yet dead but living, admittedly with serious problems. We all know patients with cancer who continue to live for many years whilst other patients, who are apparently healthy, die suddenly. Many people believe that death comes at a predetermined time and that if it is not 'our time' then we survive even against all the odds. This may not be provable truth, but many people believe it and find it useful and helpful to do so.

So let us accept for argument's sake that it is the time-for-death that determines when we die and not what has happened before death. If it was not that particular event, something else would have happened, so that the death occurs anyway. Philosophically speaking the question of *"What caused the death?"* even in homicide or suicide, can be again questioned as *"What caused the cause?"* and so on until we end up with birth, meaning if we had not been born we would not die. Most people have no problem in accepting this philosophy. Moreover a lot of questions related to the cause and timing of death that may have been troubling them may disappear instantly.

It is basic human nature to ask a lot of questions, as an essential part of our survival strategy. These are mainly aimed at finding a cause for a death which could have been avoided. The other group of questions would be about what different people, including the bereaved, could have done differently in relation to the loss. A third group of questions would be thoughts about any wrong done to the dead person. This could be from a long time in the past; maybe something that seemed trivial at the time. However these feelings of guilt can become very hurtful and 'stuck' after the death as an apology cannot be made to the dead person. The commonest guilt is not loving or showing enough love or being unkind to the deceased in the past.

Discussion is necessary to resolve all the questions that come to the mind of the bereaved. This may be at a practical level as to what happened during the final illness and death or be at a more philosophical level, and the therapist needs to be comfortable in facilitating this enquiry. This questioning stage is complete when the grieving person feels that they are no longer carrying any guilt, anger or hatred towards anyone, including themselves.

The way the author (KKA) facilitates resolution of grief within one session is best demonstrated by a case study which shows how to work using imagery and metaphor.

John – grieving the death of his father

Having discussed and resolved to John's satisfaction any questions that he had, he was in quite a deep level of hypnosis, relaxed and peaceful but with his eyes open.

> *"What we are going to do now will set you free to become that person you wish to be, without any restriction or reservation. When we finish, you will know that you will never have the feeling in you that you miss your father because he will always be with you in the healthy, happy future which you really deserve. Before we do this part, I must ask you again, is there any issue or question, however trivial or irrelevant it may seems to you, anything at all, please bring it out and discuss it, because if one little issue remains untouched, this process will not work a hundred percent."*
>
> After a few moments John answered, *"No."*
>
> *"Okay John, I want you to sit back. May I have your dominant hand* (in this example, his right hand)?*"*

The dominant hand was lifted to a horizontal position with the palm facing upwards and the elbow bent at a right angle and resting on the arm of the chair. This is useful as they will be holding it up for a few minutes.

"John, I want you to hold the hand as still as you can and keep looking at it. I want you to create a complete image of your father, but not to include any period of his last illness. I repeat, not to include anything that happened during his final illness and death. You will have to include everything you remember about your father, not only just the good times that you had; but also the bad times like arguments and fall-outs as well. Then only will it be a complete image and do justice to him. You can take as long as you need, and do not take any short cuts or omissions. You could do it by making a sculpture, or just have an awareness, that your father is in your hand, while you describe the details which will complete the memory. Do not make any attempt to wipe away the tears. They are beautiful, in honour of your father and you can let them flow down as freely as they come, and feel proud of it. Let me know by nodding your head when you are as satisfied as you can be with the making of the image."

Wait for the nod, which usually takes five minutes or less. John nodded.

"Now I want you to turn you head this way and look at your left hand."

At the same time, John's left hand was lifted up and held gently, palm uppermost.

"Do not move or let your right hand fall down, until I ask you to. In a moment you will know what this is all about. I want you to focus entirely on your left hand and as you are concentrating on this hand (holding out the left hand), *just imagine that you are sitting by the side of your father's bed, even if you were not there at the time of actual death. I am asking you to pretend, but put all your heart into that imagining, that you are watching the last minutes of your father's life. He is looking at you now, again, John, simply pretend that he is, and talking to you, in spite of what has happened. Your father is saying that it is time for him to go, he has reached his port and he has to say goodbye to you. He cannot stay any longer and it is not fair on him, when he has reached the end of his journey.*

"We have to say goodbye properly and I will guide to do that properly. Your father has something to give you, which will be the greatest treasure you will ever have. He is looking at you and waiting for you to say everything that you want him to know. It is important that you do tell him everything because it will be the treasure which he is going to keep in his heart. You can say it out loud if you wish or silently in your mind. It does not matter, as long you say everything, I mean everything, and finally make him very happy. Please do not leave anything out so there can be no misunderstandings."

The therapist will then take the role of the deceased and make the replies on behalf of the deceased. This allows the patient and the deceased to express regrets or any wrongdoing and make their apologies. More importantly they will have a chance to let each other know how much they loved, in spite of all the shortcomings in the past. Indirectly, this will help tremendously where the patient always felt that the departed never loved them enough.

He understands exactly what you are saying and there is no need to apologize as you are his dearest son and he loved you very much; even though he could not properly express his love to you. Despite nothing being said, your father knew all along, that you loved him in your heart. Now he can carry your love in his heart and take it with him wherever he is going. Not only can you keep his love in your heart, but he also is leaving the greatest treasure, just for you, which you will find in a moment. He has been waiting all this time (duration from the time of death till the time of treatment), *unable to leave his port without saying a proper goodbye. He is ready now and he is saying goodbye, he has loved you always and he is very proud of you. Now it your turn to say goodbye to your father and it is all right to repeat how much you loved him. You can see his face smiling, looking contented and happy.*

While John said goodbye, the author (KKA) also said goodbye as if he was John's father speaking, and lowered the left hand down as far as possible, turning the palm upside down, symbolically dropping all the troubles and sadness associated with the death or loss, as well as anything to do with the last illness, which was usually very hurtful. The right hand, which had been held with the palm turned up containing the complete image of his father, was then placed on John's heart, saying, *"This is the treasure your father had left for you to keep. You can carry it in your boat; no one can touch it, or take it away from you, or do anything at all to it. This treasure will stay with you forever and wherever you go. You have no cause or need to look back as everything you need will accompany you. From now on, you can row your boat looking ahead to the future."*

The author (KKA) will summarize the session by telling the patient that they have learned a lot of things in a very short time. They have a lot to absorb. Not only will they have a lot to think about during the coming few days, but also everything touching their life will be changed. Another appointment in two or three weeks' time is given for them to return and raise any other issues.

Often they will phone the author (KKA) to let him know how much better they are or to boast about all the new things that they have started to do. Sometimes they want to enter into a new relationship but are not sure whether it would be all right to love another person; would it be unfair to their late partner, whom they loved so much?

The following three metaphors may help in this situation, which can arise even in cases of harmless grief.

The Honey Pot Metaphor

It is not uncommon for people to believe that there is only one piece of love in one life and it cannot be shared without halving that love. They therefore feel guilty for taking away part or whole of the love which they once gave to the deceased. The author (KKA) tells his patients that love is like pots of honey, and rather than having just one pot of honey that we have to share out, we actually have many pots. Each pot that we give is always filled to the brim. We can produce more and fresh pots of love, without throwing away, emptying or refilling any of the pots we already have, because all we need to do is just to think in terms of taking a new pot for every new relationship. Most of us know that the love we give to others, such as our children, grandchildren or other family members and friends, is just as full as the love we give to the deceased.

Another useful metaphor is that if one shares a cake one has less for oneself, if information is shared the amount of information remains the same but if love is shared it increases to give even more.

The Bomb Blast Metaphor

When a very dear person dies, the surviving person may feel as if a bomb has exploded shattering their pot of life; with pieces strewn everywhere, deafening all emotions and normal feelings. Given time, the living person will start picking their way up, gathering as many pieces as possible, but never all of them. Then they start sticking the pieces together to recreate the pot of life, but it is never anything like the original. They will find the pot is turning into a new shape and colour, having new usage and fresh purpose. Fresh pieces have to be used to stabilize the pot, to make it stronger and to become full and useful once again. So it is perfectly right to take a new relationship as one of the new pieces which will make life useful and full again while we are continuing with our own journey.

The Forest Fire Metaphor

When people lose someone very close to their heart, it may feel like a forest fire that burns everything into ashes. The trees are no longer visible, nor do they provide shelter or shade to the animals. But the fact remains that the roots and the stumps of the tree are alive. Some day the rain will fall, the ashes will be washed down into the soil and the tree will start putting out fresh branches. This time the tree has the freedom to put its branches in any direction it wishes, to catch more sun, giving it a new shape. The new branches take up new directions which they could not do before, and this time it can grow and cover fresh areas likely to provide better shelter and shade for the animals. There is nothing wrong with having new branches.

People easily pick the message in these metaphors, and this can help them enter into new loving relationships.

Post Script

The boat metaphor can be used to prevent 'harmful' grief, if used when death is imminent in serious illnesses like cancers and other terminal diseases. Also the relatives may be introduced to the model of how normal grief can be turned into harmful grief and can be encouraged to ask questions during the terminal illness processes.

References

Cerny, M. S. & Buskirk, J. R. (1991), Anger: the hidden part of grief. *Bulletin of the Menninger Clinic*, 55 (2), 228–37.

Flemons, D. (2002), *Of one mind: the logic of hypnosis the practice of therapy.* New York, W. W. Norton.

Frederick, C. (1998), The hypnotherapeutic relationship with the terminally ill patient: an overview. *Hypnos*, 25 (3), 145–52.

Fromm, E. & Eisen, M. (1982), Self-hypnosis as a therapeutic aid in the mourning process. *American Journal of Clinical Hypnosis*, 25 (1), 3–14.

Geffen, J. (2006), *The journey through cancer healing and transforming the whole person.* New York, Three Rivers Press.

Gravitz, M. A. (2001), Perceptual reconstruction in the treatment of inordinate grief. *American Journal of Clinical Hypnosis*, 44 (1), 51–5.

Greely, A. M. (2004), *Religion in Europe at the end of the second millennium: a sociological profile.* New Brunswick, NJ, Transaction.

Grosklags, K. (2006), Healing from loss: using clinical hypnosis to help navigate the way. *Minnesota Medicine*, 89 (10), 46–8.

Hart, O. V. D. (1988), An imaginary leave-taking ritual in mourning therapy: a brief communication. *International Journal of Clinical and Experimental Hypnosis*, 36 (2), 63–9.

Hart, O. V. D., Brown, P. & Turco, R. N. (1990), Hypnotherapy for traumatic grief: Janetian and modern approaches integrated. *American Journal of Clinical Hypnosis*, 32 (4), 263–71.

Hodgkinson, P. E. (1980), Treating abnormal grief in the bereaved. *Nursing Times,* January 17.

Jacobs, S. & Kim, K. (1990), Psychiatric complications of bereavement. *Psychiatric Annals*, 20, 314–17.

Kübler-Ross, E. (1969), *On death and dying.* New York, MacMillan.

Kübler-Ross, E. (1986), *Death: the final stage of growth.* New York, Simon and Schuster.

Liossi, C. & White, P. (2001), Efficacy of clinical hypnosis in the enhancement of quality of life of terminally ill cancer patients. *Contemporary Hypnosis*, 18 (3), 145–60.

Macleod, S. (2007), *The psychiatry of palliative medicine: the dying mind.* Milton Keynes, Radcliffe.

Spiegel, D. (1981), Vietnam grief work using hypnosis. *American Journal of Clinical Hypnosis*, 24 (1), 33–40.

Spiegel, D. (1993), Psychosocial intervention in cancer. *Journal of the National Cancer Institute*, 85 (15), 1198–1205.

Strobe, M. S., Strobe, W. & Hansson, R. O. (Eds.) (1993), *Handbook of bereavement; theory, research and intervention.* Cambridge, Cambridge University Press.

Williamson, A. (2008), *Brief psychological interventions in practice.* Chichester, John Wiley & Sons, Ltd.

Worden, J. W. (2005), *Grief counselling and grief therapy: a handbook for the mental health practitioner.* London, Routledge.

26

Post-traumatic Stress Disorder (PTSD)

Dr Geoff Ibbotson
with contributions from Mrs Phyllis Alden and Dr Ann Williamson

Introduction

Post-traumatic stress disorder (PTSD) is a collection of symptoms first described by Pierre Janet – a colleague of Sigmund Freud, the forefather of psychoanalysis. He recorded the use of hypnosis with women believed to be displaying dissociative responses to emotional, sexual or physical abuse and trauma (Phillips & Frederick, 1995). Kardiner and Spiegel (1947) also report of hypnosis being used in the two world wars to help soldiers address combat related trauma. In WW I, it was called shell shock but was grossly under-diagnosed as many soldiers who were clearly suffering from PTSD were executed for 'cowardice in the face of the enemy'. During the Second World War the label 'combat fatigue' was attached and then after that 'post-Vietnam syndrome'. The label PTSD was first used in 1980 when the *Diagnostic and Statistical Manual of Mental Disorders*, third edition (DSM-III), was published (American Psychiatric Association, 1980).

PTSD is a condition that can occur after experiencing or witnessing traumatic events such as in military combat, during natural disasters or following serious accidents, terrorist attacks and violent deaths. It can also follow personal assaults such as rape and other situations in which the person felt extreme fear, horror or helplessness. Police, fire brigade or ambulance workers are more likely to have such experiences as they often have to deal with horrifying scenes.

The Handbook of Contemporary Clinical Hypnosis: Theory and Practice, First Edition.
Edited by Les Brann, Jacky Owens and Ann Williamson.
© 2012 John Wiley & Sons, Ltd. Published 2015 by John Wiley & Sons, Ltd.

In addition to the life-threatening (real or perceived) event, three main types of symptoms are required to allow a diagnosis of PTSD to be made:

- Recurrent re-experiencing the event as nightmares, flashbacks and intrusive thoughts, images or perceptions together with intense psychological distress at exposure to internal or external cues that symbolize or resemble an aspect of the traumatic event. In young children, repetitive play may occur in which themes or aspects of the trauma are expressed, or they may have frightening dreams without recognizable content.
- Avoidance and emotional numbing including efforts to avoid thoughts, feelings, conversations, places, people or activities associated with the trauma; maybe an inability to recall an important aspect of the trauma; a general withdrawal from people and activities and a sense of a fore-shortened future where the patient feels they will not have a career, relationships or a normal life span.
- Hyperarousal symptoms including difficulty falling or staying asleep, irritability or outbursts of anger, difficulty concentrating and hypervigilance with an exaggerated startle response (American Psychiatric Association, 2000).

Acute PTSD is where such symptoms have lasted between one and three months after the trauma, whilst the condition is said to be chronic if it endures for more than three months.

Acute Stress Disorder

People have emotional symptoms immediately following a traumatic event ranging from acute shock and disorientation often followed by high levels of anxiety, disordered sleep pattern and rumination on the event itself. The diagnostic category of acute stress disorder (ASD) was first described in 1994 to address concerns that diagnosing post-traumatic stress disorder could incorrectly pathologize transient stress reactions (American Psychiatric Association, 1994). ASD occurs between two days and four weeks after the trauma, and for diagnosis the victim needs to display three dissociative type reactions such as numbing, detachment, depersonalization, derealization or disso-ciative amnesia. Wilson *et al.* (2004) describe the symptomatology as often comprising high levels of anxiety, withdrawal, narrowing of attention, apparent disorientation, anger, verbal aggression, despair, hopelessness, over-activity or excessive grief. Koren *et al.* (1999) reported that the development of PTSD at a year can be predicted as early as one week after the trauma on the basis of the existence and severity of early PTSD-related symptoms, and McFarlane and Papay (1992) found that co-morbidity of depression, panic disorder and anxiety states appeared to be an important predictor of chronic PTSD. The distinction between ASD and adjustment disorder lies more in the perceived severity of the trauma than the emotional sequelae and the distinction could be seen as academic in the clinical context where therapy is directed to the individual's emotional state and symptoms.

Resilience is an important factor in determining a person's reaction to trauma (see page 200). A significant number of people presenting with acute reactions or established PTSD can be expected to recover within a relatively short space of time (Bryant, 2003). The rate of remission is higher for those with milder symptoms. Where symptoms are mild and have been present for less than a month after the trauma, watchful waiting, as a way of managing the difficulties presented by individual patients, should be considered by healthcare professionals with a follow-up appointment for re-assessment within four weeks. For a more detailed exposition, see National Institute for Clinical Excellence (2005).

PTSD is unique as a psychiatric diagnosis because great importance is placed on the aetiology rather than the clinical presentation. It is not possible to meet the official criteria unless the patient has experienced a very traumatic stressful event. The clinical course is complex – not everyone who experiences such traumatic events develops PTSD. Similarly there are some who make a spontaneous recovery, whilst others have enduring and disabling symptoms (Friedman, 2007).

Often patients are seen where the symptoms are all or part of those as set out above, but the traumatic event does not meet all the diagnostic criteria as set out in DSM-IV (American Psychiatric Association, 1994). In these cases it is possible to use PTSD as a 'working diagnosis' and to treat them accordingly. In such circumstances it is perhaps prudent to refer to 'symptoms of PTSD' to show that these patients do not meet the full criteria. This distinction is only important from a medico-legal perspective.

Associated Problems

There are often associated problems such as major depression (Kilpatrick *et al.*, 2003), other anxiety disorders, alcohol and substance abuse (Brown *et al.*, 1995; McFarlane, 1998), violence or criminal behaviour (Resnick *et al.*, 2006; Sareen *et al.*, 2004) and somatization disorder (Beckham *et al.*, 1998).

Such patients can be treated using dissociated imagery but it is necessary to spend more time ensuring stability and also to move at a slower pace.

Researchers found that following trauma young adults suffering from PTSD had a 2.7-fold excess risk for suicide. Those who experienced similar events but did not develop PTSD had no increased suicide risk. The reasons for this are not known, but depression and impulsivity may be factors (Wilcox *et al.*, 2008).

Prevalence of PTSD

One important finding, which was not apparent when PTSD was proposed as a diagnosis in 1980, is that it is relatively common. PTSD affects around 5% of American men and 10% of American women at some point in their life (Kessler *et al.*, 2005). Within the emergency services and the armed forces, the incidence of PTSD can be as high as 15% (Kinchin, 2004). Approximately 30% of men and women who have spent time in a war zone experience PTSD (Johnson & Thompson, 2008).

Holeva *et al.* (2001) reported that, in the United Kingdom, the incidence of PTSD at four to six months after a road traffic accident was 23%. Scragg *et al.* (2001) found that the incidence of PTSD was 27.5% in a study of patients who underwent treatment in intensive care units compared with a prevalence of PTSD in the general population of 2.7%.

The incidence of PTSD in asylum seekers can be as high as 85%. However caution is needed when the concept is applied to asylum seekers in the West. Experience as a psychiatrist in Nicaragua and work with the Medical Foundation for the Care of Victims of Torture have led Summerfield (1997) to suggest that social and cultural dimensions need to be taken into consideration. The social context determines the outcome after severe trauma such as wartime, loss and suffering. Solely applying the medical model ignores the fact that first it is necessary to rebuild social worlds.

Asylum seekers need support and help with medical and social issues, and they need solidarity in their struggle against hostility and racism. Victims of violence may need time to talk about what has happened to them. We must resist the fashionable tendency to use the medical model and simply frame this distress in terms of PTSD.

Meichenbaum (2009) reports that there have been 67 suicides and 31 suspected suicides in the last six years committed by those American military personnel who have returned from Iraq and Afghanistan. However it is necessary to be cautious in the interpretation of such figures. Suicides in the US military are actually higher in those who have never been to war as many such soldiers already have dysfunctional backgrounds. More veterans of the Falklands and first Gulf War are believed to have committed suicide than died in action, and added to this 20,000 ex-servicemen are in jail or on probation.

> *After living in hell you can't expect people to be angels.*
>
> Unknown origin

Neurophysiology

Neuroimaging has led to more understanding of the mechanisms of PTSD. Three brain regions have been identified that may be involved in the pathophysiology of PTSD: the amygdala, the medial pre-frontal cortex and the hippocampus (Shin & Rauch, 2006). (See Figure 26.1.)

Input from our sense organs travel to the thalamus from which they travel via two pathways. The fast pathway passes directly to the amygdala and is not cortical or conscious, and the other pathway, which takes at least twice as long, travels to the cortex where the threat is identified consciously. The sensory cortex evaluates the input and then passes impulses back down to the amygdala to modulate the response, but these fibres transmit at a slower rate than those that run between the thalamus and the amygdala. Hence the

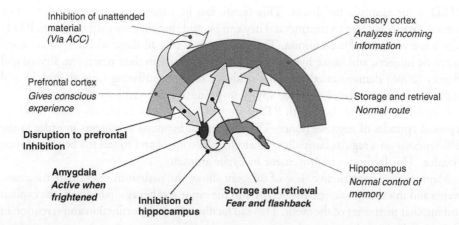

Figure 26.1   Schematic diagram showing normal and traumatic memory mechanisms. © Peter Naish.

Changes in PTSD: Activity of the amygdala disrupts both the normal memory processes and the controlling influence of the prefrontal cortex. The amygdala now dictates what appears in memory – the flashback.

emotion has already been experienced before the evaluation takes place. The amygdala exerts a greater effect on the cortex than vice versa. Also once an emotion has been turned on it is difficult for the cortex to turn it off (Muller, 1997). In PTSD it has been reported that there is excessive activation of the amygdala and decreased volumes and diminished responsivity of the medial prefrontal cortex (Nutt & Malizia, 2004).

For traumatic memory, two memory systems are functioning – explicit (conscious) memory and implicit (unconscious) memory. Explicit memory comprises details of the circumstances such as who was there, the context and other details of the experience. This is mediated by the hippocampus and other components of the temporal lobe. Implicit memory is re-vivifying of the physiological response to the event – such as changes in respiration, pulse and blood pressure. This part of the memory is mediated by the amygdala and its neural connections. Both systems operate in parallel in order to produce the full memory and its associated physiology and emotions.

In PTSD it has been found that there is a reduction in the volume of the hippocampus or reduction of chemical transmitter levels (Shin & Rauch, 2006).

Hypnotizability and PTSD

It is thought that those suffering from PTSD have higher hypnotizability (Bryant *et al.*, 2001; Spiegel *et al.*, 1988). However all the studies looked at patients after the trauma and hence it is not clear whether hypnotizability causes susceptibility to PTSD or is a consequence of it (Yard *et al.*, 2008). Certainly hypnotic phenomena are factors in

PTSD – for example flashbacks. This factor can be used to boost expectation when assessing patients prior to treatment. They can be told that they are suffering from PTSD which is a very treatable condition. The good news is that all those with PTSD are good hypnotic subjects, and hence hypnosis can be very effective in their treatment. Bryant and Harvey (2006) demonstrated that the incidence of those suffering from flashbacks and nightmares was correlated with the ability to produce more vivid visual imagery.

It could be said that those with PTSD are suffering from a condition where there are repeated episodes of negative trance. The teaching of hypnosis to patients in order to use self-hypnosis on a regular basis allows them to take control and to feel the benefit of such practice. This facilitates improvement in hyper-arousal.

Memory is re-constructive. Use of imagery allows the patient to re-evaluate traumatic events and insert more acceptable details into the event and hence change both the explicit and implicit memories of the event. This can facilitate both the extinction and retention of fear conditioning.

Evidence Base for the Use of Hypnosis in PTSD

The recent evidence base for the use of hypnosis in PTSD is reviewed in a paper by Mendoza and Capafons (2009).

Brom *et al.* (1989) compared the effects of hypnotherapy, systematic desensitization and psychodynamic psychotherapy in the treatment of post-traumatic stress. All three of these interventions proved to be more effective than a waiting list control group both at the end of treatment and at a three month follow up, but none of them was superior to the others. However, the hypnotherapy group required fewer sessions of treatment than the other groups, and hypnosis along with desensitization were more effective than psychodynamic therapy in treating intrusion symptoms.

More recently, a study on the treatment of ASD (Bryant *et al.*, 2005) compared hypnosis as an adjunct to cognitive-behavioural therapy (CBT) with CBT alone and with supportive counselling. At the end of treatment, the best of the three interventions for re-experiencing symptoms was the one including hypnosis, although at six month and three year follow ups it was shown to be equivalent to the CBT alone. Both interventions were better than supportive counselling at all three testing times regarding symptoms of post-traumatic stress and depression.

There have been many studies of the efficacy of imagery techniques in PTSD showing reduction or cessation of nightmares and flashbacks (Forbes *et al.*, 2003; Long & Quevillon, 2009; Smucker *et al.*, 1995) as well as individual case reports (Degun-Mather, 2006; Grigsby, 1987). Often case studies report the use of hypnosis combined with cognitive and behavioural approaches (Kwan, 2007; Poon, 2007).

Krakow *et al.* (2001) reported on a randomized controlled trial (RCT) conducted in New Mexico over a four year period of 168 women. 95% had moderate to severe PTSD, 97% had experienced rape or other sexual assault, 77% reported life-threatening sexual assault, and 58% reported repeated exposure to sexual abuse in childhood or adolescence.

Participants were randomized to receive treatment (88) or to the waiting list control group (80). The treatment group received three sessions of 'imagery rehearsal', which consisted of changing the internal visual imagery of the event, and rehearsed this daily. There was a significant decrease in chronic nightmares, an improvement in sleep quality and a decrease in PTSD symptom severity such as intrusive thoughts and emotional arousal in the treatment group at both three and six month follow up.

There is therefore much evidence that hypnotic imagery techniques are effective, not only in reducing the flashbacks and nightmares associated with PTSD but also for associated symptoms of depression and anxiety.

Computer Metaphor

A useful metaphorical analogy can be found in the functioning of a computer. When a programme is running, the window can be minimized and relegated to a small symbol at the bottom of the screen yet the programme continues to function fully in the background. An icon is displayed on the taskbar, and as soon as that is clicked the programme shows on the screen but has been functional whilst not displayed. Patients with PTSD could be regarded as having the sensitizing event running in the background. Sights, sounds, smells or bodily sensations may trigger this background programme to come to the fore causing flashbacks.

Educational Model

Many patients suffering from PTSD feel they are going mad because of the flashbacks and hypervigilance they experience. A useful metaphor to deal with this is to reframe PTSD as a modified phobia. Most patients accept the concept of phobias and would find it acceptable to feel they suffered from one. The objects or contexts that trigger flashbacks can be ascertained. It could be explained that these trigger marked anxiety symptoms just as a phobic object would. These feelings of fear and anxiety accompany the internal imagery of the flashback.

Past Trauma Model

In this model (see page 128) unresolved negative emotion from past events is 'trapped' under successive memories that are laid down like layers in an onion. An event in the present can link back to related events, with similar affect, in the past so that the person experiences not just the affect from the present but also that from the past (see the affect bridge on page 127). This explains why certain external stimuli trigger flashbacks.

Memories

It is *absolutely essential* when working with past trauma that the therapist is aware of the concept of false memories. The therapist must also have discussed this openly with the patient. Both must understand that material 'recovered' using hypnosis is the 'working memory' of an event (i.e. what they think happened). It may bear very little resemblance to the historic truth. However since it is what they feel had happened, it is that which is used for the purposes of therapy to achieve resolution of their emotional problems. False memories can occur with any talking therapy or the use of leading questions (Conway *et al.,* 1996; Loftus, 2005). How often do you find that two people who were at the same event have a totally different recollection of what was said or done?

A useful reference on memory is *Guidelines on Memory and the Law*, produced by the Research Board of the British Psychological Society. It suggests that the term 'imagination inflation' is used as this avoids the emotional overtones generated by the term 'false memory' (British Psychological Society, 2010).

Treatment of PTSD

The first stage of treatment is the assessment of the patient. It may be that the patient does not fall within the strict criteria for PTSD but experiences certain of the symptoms. In this case a 'working diagnosis' can be made and they can then be treated using the same approaches as for PTSD.

History taking needs to be done with care in those suffering from PTSD. It is not necessary to have great detail of the trauma; in fact it can be detrimental for the patient to give such details as they tend to re-experience and re-live the trauma and become re-traumatized.

An assessment of the pre-morbid personality needs to be made from the history. Those with a stable life in terms of education, relationships and work prior to the traumatic event are often suitable for rapid treatment such as three one hour long treatment sessions, whereas those who do not have this stable background need to be treated much more slowly. For such patients it may be necessary to use supportive social interventions to facilitate their day to day functioning and deal with social isolation.

Illicit drug use and heavy alcohol consumption may mitigate against improvement, and hence these issues may need to be addressed prior to embarking on therapy for the traumatic event. However some patients with PTSD who are very troubled by nightmares may consume large quantities of alcohol simply in order to get themselves to sleep. In these circumstances the appropriate approach may be to use imagery to address the PTSD and break the cycle. This is a clinical judgment call that requires experience of working in the field in order to make the appropriate decision.

When working with those suffering from PTSD, teaching self hypnosis helps achieve stabilization prior to doing specific work on the traumatic episode. If an imagery technique is utilized for trance induction in those suffering from frequent and troublesome flashbacks, care is needed as they may abreact and suffer a flashback as they enter a 'negative trance'. In order to avoid this situation, it may be better to use a progressive muscular relaxation (see page 114).

If addressing the trauma is to be delayed, then approaches for self hypnosis, ego strengthening (see page 141) and changing internal dialogue (see page 175) may be appropriately taught as below.

Imagery for Self Hypnosis and Ego Strengthening

The section written in bold is the trance induction; the section in bold and italics is the use of metaphor to get rid of negatives and then ego strengthen. The section in italics only is the teaching of self hypnosis, and the last part in bold is the reorientation.

Remember that the words are there to stimulate the patient to generate *their own* imagery:

When you are comfortable and ready... just let your eyes close... now take three slow deep breaths... and each time as you breathe out... just let it go... that is fine... after the third breath then just breathe naturally... just the right amount for you... and now just let your imagination take you into a wood... it can be a wood that you know... or an imaginary wood... or a mixture of both... just see what you can see... perhaps all the different greens... is it not interesting... all the different greens in a wood... perhaps you will notice the patterns of light and dark... or see something else... notice the sounds that are there... perhaps you will hear birds or animals... perhaps the wind in the trees... or maybe you are rustling through leaves... maybe a twig cracks... notice the smells... perhaps the smell of pine... wild flowers... wild garlic... and now notice the temperature... whether it is warm or cold... sunny or frosty... whether there is snow on the ground... but above all notice the feelings... this is your wood... nothing goes on in this wood that you cannot control... you can feel comfortable and secure. ...

...And there is a place in the wood where there is a little stream... with a small bridge over it.... I would like you to find that stream and when you are standing on the bridge, facing downstream... then give me a nod...* (wait for nod) *...and now I would like you to decide on something that you want to get rid of... perhaps a feeling... a memory... or a behaviour... and to have some leaves in your hand... and when you are ready to get rid of that thing... just let the leaf go... and watch it fall down through the air... and land in the stream... and then be carried right away downstream... and as it is carried away... you can feel good and pleased to be rid of that thing... that has perhaps bothered you for some time... and now I would like you to take the time to drop in as many leaves as you want... take as long as you want... and when you are ready to move on... then give me a nod* (wait for nod). ...

And now... I would like you to go up the side of the stream... until you find a pool... a beautiful, still pool of clear water... as you gaze at the water, enjoying the sound of silence... or whatever sounds you experience... you can notice that on the bottom of the pool there are various stones and pebbles... in some way... through your

mind's eye . . . in the back of your mind . . . you may see that these stones could represent resources that you have . . . a resource may be a skill you have . . . a memory you have . . . or perhaps a person that you know . . . you may be aware of resources that you had forgotten you had . . . and just think how good it will be to tap into those resources again . . . or you may be aware of resources that you did not realize you had . . . and just think how great it will be to use all those resources . . . but if there is a resource that you feel you need . . . and you feel that it is not there or you would like more of it . . . then walk around near the pool . . . your pool of resources . . . and find the right stone . . . you will know which one it is . . . pick up that stone . . . and drop it gently into your pool, watching it drift down through the clear water to settle safely and securely on the bottom . . . along with all your other resources . . . and when you have got all those resources just right for you . . . let me know with a nod . . . (wait for nod) *. . . and now . . . when you are ready to make connection with all your resources . . . do it in whatever way feels right for you . . . perhaps you would like to swim in your pool . . . float on the pool . . . perhaps dabble your hands or feet in the pool . . . or whatever feels just right for you . . . and enjoy soaking up all those resources* (wait for a few moments). . . .

    And as you are soaking up those resources . . . I want to remind you . . . how easy it is to get into this state of focused attention . . . all you need to do is to find an appropriate place . . . let your eyes close . . . take three slow deep breaths . . . and then use all your senses to see, hear, feel and smell the place where you want be . . . and as you do this . . . each day . . . you will find that you get more and more focused each time . . . until you have just the right amount of focus for you . . . and then you will be able to get just the right amount of focus each time . . . and as you do this every day you will find that you are able to get things more in perspective . . . and feel how you want to feel . . . behave how you want to behave . . . believe what you want to believe . . . you will only use this when it is appropriate and safe to do so . . . and if any emergency should arise you will come out of trance immediately and behave appropriately . . . and you will never do this for entertainment but only for your own self. . . .

    . . . And now I would like you to find somewhere especially peaceful in the wood . . . perhaps you would like to sit or lie down . . . and take in all the peace and calm . . . and if an animal approaches you . . . then perhaps you would like to stroke it . . . or even feed it . . . and enjoy the communication between the two of you . . . and then when you are ready. . . . I would like you to come back to the here and now . . . in your own time . . . perhaps by counting backwards from five to one . . . coming back gradually . . . at your own pace . . . so that when you get to one . . . you will be wide awake . . . feeling good . . . and then open your eyes.

The word 'resources' was used above. In some cases it may be more appropriate to refer to 'strengths' or 'abilities'. Once this process has been successfully completed, it is not necessary to do further trance inductions afterwards. All that is necessary is to ask the patient to close their eyes, go to the place that they have chosen and give a nod when they are ready for you to proceed with the hypnotic intervention. The patient should be asked to do regular self-hypnosis on a daily basis.

    It is important to ascertain from the patient how they interpret their symptoms. Many interpret the flashbacks as a demonstration that they are going mad. Most find the symptoms extremely distressing. Sometimes quick techniques as described below can cause symptom relief, and these build rapport and expectation as well as make the patient more comfortable.

Dealing with Internal Anger

A strong feeling of anger is frequently present in those suffering from PTSD, and it is wise to deal with this using the author's (GI) modified silent abreaction (see page 399) prior to addressing the trauma. The technique as described here would be used with a patient who is using imagery of a wood for self hypnosis. If the patient is uncomfortable with that situation, then the technique will need to be modified appropriately, or another approach used to vent the anger. In patients with anger from past events, it is most important to use silent abreaction to vent the anger prior to working on the traumatic event. An analogy is that prior to working on a dam wall, one would lower the level of water behind the dam in order to make the work safer.

Prior to commencement, the idea is seeded about what happens when a dead tree is felled; at first the movement is slow but then it gains momentum and the tree hits the ground with great force and smashes into hundreds of pieces.

The patient is then asked to settle down in trance in 'their wood'. They give a nod when they are settled and ready to proceed. They are asked to find a dead tree that is standing in the middle of a clearing and give you a nod when they are there (i.e. associated). They then attach to the tree all the unwanted anger. This can be done by carving the tree, painting on the tree, nailing things to the tree, hanging things from the tree or doing whatever seems right for them.

During the process of attachment of anger to the tree it can be seen from observation of the patient's body language that they experience physiological changes of anger. They should be asked to proceed quickly at this stage and to give a nod when they have got all the anger they want to be rid of attached to the tree.

The patient is then asked to look around and see what is available to fell the tree. There may be an axe, a chainsaw, a JCB tractor or perhaps something else. They are asked to let the therapist know, with a nod, when the tree is felled and been smashed into many pieces.

They then decide what they want to do with the wood on the ground. They may like to have a bonfire, turn it into wood chippings or perhaps something else. They give the therapist a nod when they have done that and then decide whether they need to do something further with the ashes if they have had a bonfire.

The patient is then asked to go to a calm place in the wood, sit or lie down and soak up all the calmness and peace. Perhaps an animal approaches. If so, they may like to feed or stroke it. They may want to look into its eyes and communicate with it, or learn from it whatever they need to learn right now.

When they feel calm and at peace, they are invited to come back to the here and now in their own way, at their own pace.

(The essence of this process is facilitation, with suggestions and structure but allowing them to develop and use their own imagery at their own pace.)

Internal Dialogue

The vast majority of people are aware of internal dialogue, and it is through this that they are aware of their thoughts and evaluations of situations and events. When talking about this dialogue, it is important to reassure patients that this is a normal process and not a sign of impending schizophrenia. Such internal dialogue in patients with emotional difficulties tends to be weighted towards the negative and often drives the anxiety response and poor self esteem. Changes can be made in the voice tone to lessen the believability of the negative self talk as described on page 175.

Quick Techniques Using Imagery

Imagery can be used when patients feel fear or anger towards an individual. The patient is asked to see the individual in question and report the location of the image; often it is right in their face. In this case they are asked to move the image back slightly and make a change to the face; maybe putting on a clown's nose, a silly hat or whatever they wish. This alone often has a marked effect on the patient as they see the absurdity and enjoy taking control over the image. They are then able to shrink down the image and may wish to attach strings and see it as a puppet.

Regression

Historically, although regression and abreaction have been used extensively it has classically been used in an associated way so that the patient actually regresses back into the past experience and relives it. If this is done with the patient fully in touch with their current resources and supported by the therapist, then this can be very effective. It is, however, distressing to the patient and the therapist now that we have dissociative techniques available. As a general rule never associate anyone with a negative state. Having said this it is common to find that the patient slips into an emotional state even when dissociated imagery is utilized, and this needs to be acknowledged and worked with in a sensitive and supportive manner.

Other Approaches

Other approaches such as narrative therapy, eye movement desensitization and reprocessing (EMDR) and emotional freedom therapy (EFT) can also be used but are beyond the scope of this book. In the opinion of the author (GI), imagery techniques along with hypnosis have proved sufficient to resolve PTSD in very many of his patients.

One hypnotic method that does not involve dissociation (which may be useful in cases where the patient is functioning in a dissociated manner and has difficulty associating) is the 'Once upon a time' technique (Alden, 2005). In life it could be said that we bring the past into the present and in therapy we bring the present into the past.

This method involves paying attention to and noting more detail during the history taking so that it can be woven into a story. Attention is also paid to identifying the achievements the patient has made in their life to date. A story is then told to the patient, *"Once upon a time there was..."* reflecting the event in detail while emphasizing the 'littleness' and 'young-ness' of the younger self. The emotions associated with the event such as fear and helplessness are reflected back to the patient and all the things they 'couldn't do at the time' emphasized.

The therapist then moves to the present to emphasize, *"You are no longer that little boy and you can do so many things he cannot ..."* such as drive a car, work or be married. A positive set of emotions, *"Things he would have been so frightened of but you do with so much confidence,"* are reflected upon. The therapist then adds, *"And I wonder if you can let him know that as he is no longer the little boy, he does not need to be frightened anymore."* The therapist then gets confirmation to the statement: *"That's true, isn't it?"*

The patient is asked to describe everything that their younger self is feeling as the therapist comments sympathetically. The patient is then encouraged to comfort and to let the younger self know that he is from the future and come to let him know how he is going to grow up, do so many things without fear and not need to fear any more. Once the patient is reoriented to the present, they are asked to rehearse in trance what they could not do before and review how they feel. They then need to test this in reality as soon as possible to ratify the therapeutic change.

Permission

Before embarking on work on past trauma, it is vital that one has permission from the patient. They must answer *"Yes"* to the question *"Is it all right to work on this now?"* Then the question should be repeated when the patient is in trance. Hence one has agreement at both conscious and unconscious levels.

Dissociation

Using a dissociative approach to treatment means that the event can be dealt with, any necessary learning or understanding made and the negative emotion released, without the patient having to experience the full impact of the emotion. Despite the therapist's best efforts the patient may still become associated with the traumatic event and will need compassion and support. This is also a reason why a good safety anchor is essential.

There are several ways of doing this, but they all involve dissociating the patient from the event that is being dealt with. These include:

- Imagine watching the event on a cinema screen, video or TV (see case example 1).
- Imagine looking down from a hot air balloon or magic carpet onto a time road or life line (see page 162).

- Imagine being in a protective bubble (or a space ship) through which you can see and hear but not feel negative emotion (Alden, 1995).
- Seeing it through a camera lens as if you were the photographer.
- Or simply *"...see it over there, whilst you remain feeling comfortable here."*

Safety Anchor

This is essential before embarking on any trauma work. It may be a kinaesthetic anchor as described on page 145, a visual safety anchor as described below or as in the cinema technique.

Dealing with the Traumatic Event

- Identify resources from adult experiences, or from the unconscious, which would help the younger self – even if the event was only a few weeks ago, this can still be an appropriate way to work.
- Find a resourceful 'you' or contact with your 'higher self' that can comfort and heal.
- Give advice and resources to the younger you and maybe significant others in the event.
- Replay the event differently by changing the imagery.
- Payback if appropriate.

Getting the older you to go down into the action and help the younger you

At the time of the trauma the patient did not have sufficient resources in order to deal fully with the trauma. The 'older you' can be a resource in order to go into the action and help the 'younger you'. Before using such an approach, it is important to ascertain that the patient feels that it is safe for the 'older you' to do this and suggest that the 'older you' will be protected from the trauma (maybe in a protective aura or bubble) but will be able to intervene and support the 'younger you' or to speak with others involved in the episode. It is seen that the use of this approach adds another layer of dissociation.

Also this can be very useful where the 'younger you' thought they were going to die. Clearly the presence of an 'older you' is confirmation that this did not happen. It may be that the 'older you' can speak to others in the event and explain to them the error of their ways.

Payback

After a traumatic episode, there may be issues with unresolved anger or injustice. It is as if the fact that this remains unresolved keeps the issue active and without closure. Imagery can be used in order to allow the patient to use, *in imagination*, whatever payback they may feel is appropriate. This payback will be appropriate to the age at which the sensitizing event occurred. It is important that the therapist sets the scene and the opportunity for payback but that it is the patient who decides what payback is appropriate (see case example 1).

Humour and the sense of the absurd

Humour is a very powerful intervention in that if the patient can start to laugh at part of an event, they are no longer afraid of the event (Stanton, 1993) (see case example 3). Clearly rapport is vital when utilizing such approaches, but one must never attempt to work on past trauma before an appropriate level of rapport has been established.

> ### Case example 1: Peter, a young assault victim (courtesy of Dr A Williamson)
>
> Peter was a seven year old boy who had been the victim of a failed assault in the local park. He had had his videotaped interview with the police but he had become very clingy since the incidence, and was refusing to go to school or sleep on his own as he had been doing previously. His father had brought him along to see if anything could be done to help. The use of imagination (hypnosis was not mentioned) was discussed, and it was ascertained that Peter enjoyed playing football. Peter was asked to imagine a TV 'over there' which he did and then it was suggested that he watch a film of him playing football. Once it was established that he could do this, Peter was asked to go into the action and really enjoy scoring lots of goals; after all it was his imagination and he could make it as good as he wanted. This was Peter's safety anchor. Peter was then asked if it would be all right to look at the incident in the park. Having got agreement Peter was asked to see himself in the park just before the event and play it like a film but very fast until the end when he had been taken back home. He was asked what he could do to help that little boy in the film. After some discussion he decided to climb up a nearby tree and when the perpetrator came on the scene to empty a large container of bright orange gloop over him. He then climbed down and comforted the little boy, and they ran off to play football. This simple intervention, which took approximately 20 minutes, sufficed to allow Peter to take control, face his fears and change the internal image that he carried around of the man who had tried to harm him. He very quickly became again the happy little boy he had been before.

The Cinema Technique

Once stabilization has been achieved, the author (GI) uses dissociated imagery in a technique that he has developed and calls the cinema technique. This technique is a developed form of V-K dissociation (Ibbotson, 2006). The V-K dissociation technique was reported by Fromm, (1965) who described the procedure as separating or dissociating the observing ego from the experiencing ego. Although the technique uses rewinding it is not the same as the rewind technique first described by Dr David Muss (1991), as it involves a range of other interventions during the imagery.

This technique is extremely effective in resolution of past trauma. Even extremely distressing past events can be resolved and handled in a comfortable and sensitive way. One important factor is that the therapist directs the process rather than getting involved with the content.

Sometimes there is difficulty achieving resolution, and in this case the therapist needs to elicit more detail of what is happening and what appears to be preventing them from helping the younger part of themselves. Often therapeutic work on a traumatic event can be almost content free. According to Van de Kolk (2009), the first time a patient describes the full detail of a trauma should be after resolution, and the very fact that they are able to do this proves that they have dealt with the event.

The structure of the technique builds in dissociation in a way that allows flexibility of approach. Many different therapeutic approaches can be used as appropriate to the needs and processing style of the patient.

Cinema

No formal induction need be undertaken. The patient is asked to close their eyes and imagine. Once imagery is in progress, they should be asked to confirm that they are prepared to work using imagery to resolve a previous event.

> *I would like you to let your eyes close . . . take three long deep breaths . . . now breathe naturally, just as it feels right for you . . . and then I would like you to go into a cinema . . . it can be one that you know . . . or an imaginary one . . . or a mixture of the two . . . you are the only person in the cinema . . . and you feel really comfortable . . . you go and sit on the second row . . . and look up at the blank screen . . . what colour are the seats?* (If they cannot tell you the colour, then they do not have enough visual imagery to proceed with the technique.) *That's right . . . are there any curtains at the side of the screen? . . . that's right . . . and now I would like you to allow yourself to float right up to the back of the cinema . . . and go into the projection room . . . you are quite safe in here . . . you can lock the door if you wish . . . and you can see through the glass window through which the film is projected . . . you can see the back of your head . . . as you sit on the second row . . . watching the blank screen.* (This gives double dissociation.)

Setting the safety anchor

It is necessary to have a safety anchor in case they get too distressed and become re-associated into negative events. This can be done using a kinaesthetic anchor (see page 145). However the author (GI) chooses not to touch patients who are in trance and so uses a 'film' of a happy event that the patient previously experienced. A special 'button' is created and when the patient presses that, the happy film comes on and they are associated into the action.

> *You are the projectionist and can operate all the equipment . . . I would like you to put on a film about a happy event in your life when you felt safe . . . play that film over a few minutes . . . give me a nod when you have finished . . .* (wait for nod) *. . . now float down into the action as you play it again . . . enjoy the experience . . .* (watch for change in body language as patient gets involved in the happy experience and acknowledge verbally) *. . . float back up to the projection room . . . now make a button that switches on the happy film and floats you down into the action . . . what colour is the button? . . . Test it out by pressing the button now . . .* (that's right) *. . . If I ask you to press the button I want you to do so . . . if you feel you need to go to your happy place I want you to press the button . . . but if you do so please tell me so that I know where you are. . . .*

Permission

"I would like to check that it is okay to work on the problem that we discussed . . . please give me a nod if that is okay." If a nod is not forthcoming, then this needs to be explored with further questioning as to what needs to be done before the event can be resolved.

Target event. The patient is asked to allow a still image to form on the screen just before the event they are wishing to resolve. The image is controlled by the patient and can be black and white, sepia, in or out of focus and whatever size seems appropriate to the patient. They then start the action and play the film quickly to the end. After this they are asked to score the distress of watching the film on a zero to ten scale; the higher the number, the worse the distress.

> *I would now ask you to place a still image on the screen . . . of the event that you need to review in order to work on this event . . . it can be just as you wish to show it . . . in or out of focus, black and white or colour . . . grainy or sharp . . . as large as you want . . . give me a nod when you have formed that image . . .* (wait for nod) *. . . good, that's fine . . . now I would like you to play it as a film over about two minutes . . . remember you are the projectionist in the projection room . . . just playing the film . . . give me a nod when you have finished . . . I would like you to score watching the film on a scale of one to ten, with one being not bothersome at all and ten being the worst imaginable. . . .* (Wait for score.)

Rewind

It is then desirable to disrupt the image, and this is done by rewinding the film, with the suggestion that this gives it a bizarre, surreal feeling. They are then asked to play the film forwards and backwards three times and give a nod when they have finished. They are then asked to what number the score has reduced. Commonly the reduction may be from eight or nine to five or six.

> *In a few moments I would like you to rewind the film . . . it will take on a different character . . . speech will go backwards . . . those who have said things will have to eat their words . . . people will walk*

backwards...what went up will go down...it may look quite funny and strange...please do that...now...I would like you now to play the film backwards and forwards...three times...in your own time...and give me a nod when you have done that...(wait for nod)...Okay–I would like you to give me the score the last time you played it forwards...(Wait for score.)

Payback

Now perhaps there are people in that event who need to be taught a lesson...perhaps you can change things so that happens...so they make a learning...maybe an older, wiser you from the future could go down and tell the relevant people what needs to be said...give me a nod when you have done that....(Wait for change in body language indicating resolution.)

Humour

Sometimes it can be useful to access humour, although this is not always appropriate. *"I would like you to look at that event now...using your sense of the absurd...and see something that you have not seen before...* (wait for change in body language indicating resolution) *...that's right."*

Other interventions

They are the director of the film and can stop it at any time to use various psychotherapeutic interventions. These include letting the 'younger you' know that however unpleasant the event was, they survived through it; allowing the older wiser self to help the 'younger you' in the event; talking to people in the film or changing the imagery in some way.

They can cut the film to have a lower censor rating so long as the film remains recognizable as the target event. One patient changed the imagery so that the guns used in an armed hold up were bananas.

The therapist uses their own intuition as to which intervention is suggested and keeps getting further re-scores to ascertain the effectiveness of the interventions. The patient is their own best therapist and knows what is needed to help the younger part of themselves feel better and resolve the event.

Would it be okay for the older you to go down into the film...protected from the event...but able to comfort the younger you...the older you controls the action...and can stop or start the film whenever he wants...and say to the people who are there...whatever needs to be said....

Re-score

A useful technique is to enquire about the present score and then ask what would be an acceptable score. If they are still above the appropriate score, then they are told that they have already reduced the score, told to allow themselves to let their unconscious mind continue the process and asked to give a nod when the score is down to the appropriate level. They are unlikely to have a score of zero on a very traumatic event, but two might be acceptable.

> *I would like you to re-score the film now* ... (wait for score) ... *is that score okay?* ... (if yes, then finish off; if not, then continue) ... *now you are doing well* ... *you have got the score down from** *to** ... *what number do you feel it should be got down to?* ... (wait for answer) ... *well, you are your own best therapist* ... *you, better than anyone else, knows what that younger you needed to feel better.* ... *I want you to continue working on it in the way that is just right for you* ... *and when you have got it down to**, *then let me know with a nod.* ... (Wait for nod.)

Stuck

Sometimes the score does not reduce. In this situation there may be an earlier event that needs resolution, maybe again using the cinema technique. Once this event has been successfully resolved, it is possible to continue with successful resolution of the sensitizing event.

After resolution

After successful resolution it may seem appropriate to ask the patient what they want to do with the final film. Where and how do they want to store it? It may need to be archived in their personal museum.

> *What do you want to do with the new film?* ... *Maybe store it in a box?* ... (Wait for reply and, if a box, then let them choose box, decide on label etc.)

The patient is then asked to leave the projection room and re-associate with that 'part' of themselves in the auditorium of the cinema, coming back to the here and now in their own time and opening their eyes when they are ready.

> *I would now like you to float back inside yourself on the second row* ... *leaving behind what you want to leave behind* ... *bringing back what you want to bring back* ... *all parts working together* ... *and when you are ready* ... *come back to the here and now* ... *in your own way* ... *in your own time* ... *and when you are ready* ... *open your eyes feeling comfortable and pleased with the work you have just done.*

The important features are always to be guided by the body language of the patient, but if you do not know what is happening with them – ask. Interventions are added or removed according to the progress. If the score does not go down in a satisfactory way, then put that film in a box and ask them to go back to an earlier event that is relevant and use the process to resolve that event. Then return to the event in the box, and satisfactory resolution should be possible.

Examples of the Use of the Cinema Technique

Case example 2: a man with fear of water

A gentleman presented with fear of the water. He was not even able to let water splash over his face in a shower. At his first session he stated that he had booked into a hotel ten days later. He had enrolled on an intensive swimming course and was determined to succeed as the fear of water interfered with holiday activities with his young children. Hence there was a very strict time scale for the therapy. It was ascertained that he could be seen for his second session one week later; hence before the swimming training. The strong determination of the patient enabled a rapid and successful treatment.

The history was that when he was eight, he was taken by his mother to the swimming baths for the first time. He wanted to go in the male changing room on his own and was instructed to come out of the changing room and wait at the pool side for his mother. He did so. Unfortunately the male changing room exit was at the deep end. He was waiting there when two youths ran from behind him and grabbed him by the upper arms and dived with him, head first, into the pool. He inhaled water and was lying unconscious on the bottom of the deep end. He was rescued by the lifeguards, who dragged him out and successfully resuscitated him. Subsequently he was taken by ambulance to hospital where he was observed for 24 hours and discharged fully recovered.

It was explained to him that the cinema technique was going to be used and he would find this extremely helpful. The rewinding of the film would make it a surreal event. He would be lying comfortably in a hospital bed, wheeled backwards to Accident and Emergency and then picked up by an ambulance team that would wheel him backwards to the ambulance and then reverse to the swimming pool. They would pull him backwards to the poolside and walk away backwards. Here two lifeguards would do cardiac massage and mouth to mouth, drag him to the bottom of the deep end and swim away backwards. Then two youths who he did not know would grab him by the shoulders and suddenly and miraculously jump backwards out of the pool. He then walked backwards, got dressed and was driven backwards home by his mother.

His body language indicated that he was already visualizing this, and it is probable that resolution took place at this stage. However the cinema technique was performed, but after only one re-wind the score was zero and he burst out laughing.

He returned one week later and stated that he was already fine in the shower and had tried putting his face under the water and holding his breath. He was taught self-hypnosis at this session and asked to send a postcard or phone up to report his progress. He sent a card from the hotel and reported that at the end of the week, he had managed to swim a length of the pool.

Case example 3: a soldier with PTSD

A patient presented with PTSD. He was suffering from difficulty in getting off to sleep and nightmares. Each night he would consume very large amounts of alcohol in order to get off to sleep.

He had served in the army and was overseas in a 'peace-keeping' situation. He had been in an armoured personnel carrier that had been blown up. His best friend was sitting next to him and was blown to pieces. The patient and other persons in the vehicle were physically unhurt. A short time after, he was in another personnel carrier and this was again blown up but no one was injured. During the cinema technique, he was working on the second event and was asked to *"see something that he had not seen before"* in that event. After a few moments his whole body language changed and he had a very broad grin on his face and clearly the event was resolved.

After completion of the process he asked if he should explain to the therapist the nature of this new information. In view of the dramatic resolution the therapist was clearly very keen to understand how he could start to grin and resolve such a traumatic episode that had links back to the death of his best friend.

He said that the personnel were leaving the vehicle very rapidly. The soldier at the back was first to leave and dived out. The exit is tall and slim, and his rifle was trapped horizontally across the exit and he dived back in. He shouted, *"My flippin' arm's stuck."* He repeated the process and the same thing happened, but this time the language was more colourful. When he made the third attempt, my patient calmly rotated the rifle through ninety degrees and his colleague fell in a heap outside and all the others were able to leave the vehicle without significant injury.

Was this a false memory that was initiated by the phrase *"See something that he had not seen before"*? Possibly this could have been the case, but we will never know. Perhaps his unconscious had made a change to the story in order to lighten the process. It is also possible that this did in fact happen. The description of the dimensions of the exit and the size of a rifle makes it a very plausible explanation. The important fact is that this came out of a process and that he resolved his difficulties around that episode. The patient dramatically reduced his drinking, slept better and functioned better. He was discharged after treatment lasting three sessions.

From all the above it can be seen that the use of imagery in hypnosis combined with re-nurturing and comforting the younger self and ego strengthening can be an effective way of dealing with PTSD and past traumatic memory generally. Outcome audit has demonstrated good results in the author's (GI) psychology department where he worked with this approach (Ibbotson & Williamson, 2010). An audit of 28 patients showed marked improvement in both their emotional state and the impact of the traumatic event in an average of less than five one hour sessions using trauma focused hypnosis as described above. The 'facts' of the patient's life history cannot be changed, but the emotional impact can be resolved by such interventions whereby they gain 'control' and work through the negative emotions attached to the memory.

References

Alden, P. (1995), Back to the past: introducing the 'bubble'. *Contemporary Hypnosis*, 12, (2), 59–64.

Alden, P. (2005), Once upon a time: a one session treatment for treatment anxiety – outcomes on 20 cases. Paper presented at the Joint Conference of the British Society of Experimental and Clinical Hypnosis (BSECH), the British Society of Medical and Dental Hypnosis (BSMDH), the Royal Society of Medicine and BSMDH Scotland, Glasgow, Scotland, April.

American Psychiatric Association. (1980), *Diagnostic and statistical manual of mental disorders*, 3rd ed. Washington, DC, American Psychiatric Association.

American Psychiatric Association. (1994), *Diagnostic and statistical manual of mental disorders*, 4th ed. Washington DC, American Psychiatric Association.

American Psychiatric Association. (2000), *Diagnostic and statistical manual of mental disorders*, 4th ed., text rev. Washington DC, American Psychiatric Association.

Beckham, J. C., Moore, S. D. & Feldman, M. E. (1998), Health status, somatization, and severity of posttraumatic stress disorder in Vietnam combat veterans with posttraumatic stress disorder. *American Journal of Psychiatry*, 155, 1565–9.

British Psychological, Society. (2010), *Guidelines on memory and the law*. London, British Psychological Society.

Brom, D., Kleber, R. J. & Defare, P. B. (1989), Brief psychotherapy for post-traumatic stress disorder. *Journal of Consulting and Clinical Psychology*, 87, 607–12.

Brown, P. J., Recupera, P. R. & Stout, R. (1995), PTSD Substance abuse comorbidity and treatment utilization. *Addictive Behaviours*, 20 (2), 251–4.

Bryant, R. A. (2003), Early predictors of posttraumatic stress disorder. *Biological Psychiatry*, 53, 789–95.

Bryant, R. A., Guthrie, R. M. & Moulds, M. L. (2001), Hypnotizability in acute stress disorder. *American Journal of Psychiatry*, 158, 600–4.

Bryant, R. A. & Harvey, A. G. (2006), Visual imagery in posttraumatic stress disorder. *Journal of Traumatic Stress*, 9 (3), 613–19.

Bryant, R. A., Moulds, M. L., Nixon, R. D., Mastrodomenico, J., Felmingham, K. & Hopwood, S. (2005), Hypnotherapy and cognitive behaviour therapy of acute stress disorder: a 3-year follow-up. *Behavioral and Research and Therapy*, 44, 1331–5.

Conway, M. A., Collins, A. F., Gathercole, S. E. & Anderson, S. J. (1996), Recollections of true and false autobiographical memories. *Journal of Experimental Psychology: General*, 125 (1), 69–95.

Degun-Mather, M. (2006), The value of hypnosis in the treatment of chronic PTSD with dissociative fugues in a war veteran. *Contemporary Hypnosis*, 18 (1), 4–13.

Forbes, D., Phelps, A. J., Mchugh, A. F., Debenham, P., Hopwood, M. & Creamer, M. (2003), Imagery rehearsal in the treatment of posttraumatic nightmares in Australian veterans with chronic combat-related PTSD: 12-month follow-up data. *Journal of Traumatic Stress*, 16 (5), 509–13.

Friedman, M. J. (2007), www.ptsd.va.gov/professional/pages/ptsd-overview.asp

Fromm, E. (1965), Hypnoanalysis: theory and two case excerpts. *Psychotherapy: Theory, Research and Practice*, 2 (3), 127–33.

Grigsby, J. P. (1987), The use of imagery in the treatment of posttraumatic stress disorder. *Journal of Nervous and Mental Disease*, 175 (1), 55–59.

Holeva, V., Tarrier, N. & Wells, A. (2001), Prevalence and predictors of acute stress disorder and PTSD following road traffic accidents: thought control strategies and social support. *Behavior Therapy*, 32, 65–83.

Ibbotson, G. P. (2006), in Degun-Mather, M. *Hypnosis, dissociation and survivors of sexual abuse.* Chichester, John Wiley & Sons, Ltd.

Ibbotson, G. P. & Williamson, A. (2010), Treatment of post-traumatic stress disorder (PTSD) using trauma-focused hypnosis. *Contemporary Hypnosis*, 27 (1), 257–68.

Johnson, H. & Thompson, A. (2008), The development and maintenance of post-traumatic stress disorder (PTSD) in civilian adult survivors of war trauma and torture: a review. *Clinical Psychology Review*, 28 (1), 36–47.

Kardiner, A. & Spiegel, H. (1947), *War stress and neurotic illness.* New York, Hoeber.

Kessler, R., Berglund, P., Demler, O., Jin, R., Merikangas, K. R. & Walters, E. E. (2005), Lifetime prevalence and age-of-onset distributions of DSM-IV disorders in the National Comorbidity Survey Replication. *Archives of General Psychiatry*, 62, 593–700.

Kinchin, D. (2004), *Post traumatic stress disorder: the invisible injury.* Oxford, Success Unlimited.

Kolk, B. V. D. (2009), Workshop given at the Evolution of Psychotherapy Conference, Anaheim, CA, December.

Koren, D., Arnon, I. & Klein, E. (1999), Acute stress response and posttraumatic stress disorder in traffic accident victims: a one-year prospective, follow-up study. *American Journal of Psychiatry*, 156, 367–73.

Krakow, B., Hollifield, M., Johnston, L., Koss, M., Schrader, R., Warner, T. D., Tandberg, D., Lauriello, J., Mcbride, L., Cutchen, L., Cheng, D., Emmons, S., Germain, A., Melendrez, D., Sandoval, D. & Prince, H. (2001), Imagery rehearsal therapy for chronic nightmares in sexual assault survivors with posttraumatic stress disorder. *Journal of the American Medical Association*, 286, 537–45.

Kwan, P. S. K. (2007), Hypnosis in complex trauma and breast cancer pain: a single case study. *Contemporary Hypnosis*, 24 (2), 86–96.

Loftus, E. F. (2005), Planting misinformation in the human mind: a 30-year investigation of the malleability of memory. *Learning & Memory*, 12, 361–6.

Long, M. E. & Quevillon, R. (2009), Imagery rescripting in the treatment of posttraumatic stress disorder. *Journal of Cognitive Psychotherapy*, 23 (1), 67–76.

McFarlane, A. C. (1998), Epidemiological evidence about the relationship between PTSD and alcohol: the nature of the association. *Addictive Behaviors*, 23 (6), 813–25.

McFarlane, A. C. & Papay, P. (1992), Multiple diagnoses in posttraumatic stress disorder in the victims of a natural disaster. 180 (8), 498–504.

Meichenbaum, D. (2009), Workshop given at the Evolution of Psychotherapy Conference, Anaheim, CA, December.

Mendoza, M. E. & Capafons, A. (2009), Efficacy of clinical hypnosis: a summary of its empirical evidence. *Papeles del Psicólogo*, 30 (2), 98–116.

Muller, J. (1997), Functional inactivation of the lateral and basal nuclei of the amygdala by muscimol infusion prevents fear conditioning to an explicit conditioned stimulus and to contextual stimuli. *Behavioral Neuroscience*, 111 (4), 683–91.

Muss, D. C. (1991), A new technique for treating post-traumatic stress disorder. *British Journal of Clinical Psychology*, 30, 91–2.

National Institute For Clinical Excellence., (2005), The management of PTSD in adults and children in primary and secondary care. National Clinical Practice Guideline no. 26. London, Gaskell and the British Psychological Society.

Nutt, D. J. & Malizia, A. L. (2004), Structural and functional brain changes in posttraumatic stress disorder. *Journal of Clinical Psychiatry*, 65 (1), 11–17.

Phillips, M. & Frederick, C. (1995), *Healing the divided self: clinical and Ericksonian hypnotherapy with posttraumatic and dissociative conditions*. New York, W. W. Norton.

Poon, M. W. (2007), The value of using hypnosis in helping an adult survivor of childhood sexual abuse. *Contemporary Hypnosis*, 24 (1), 30–7.

Resnick, H. S., Foy, D. W., Donahoe, C. P. & Miller, E. N. (2006), Antisocial behavior and post-traumatic stress disorder in Vienam veterans. *Journal of Clinical Psychology*, 45 (6), 860–6.

Sareen, J., Stein, M. B., Cox, B. J. & Hassard, S. T. (2004), Understanding comorbidity of anxiety disorders with antisocial behavior: findings from two large community surveys. *The Journal of Nervous and Mental Disease*, 192 (3), 178–86.

Scragg, P., Jones, A. & Fauvel, N. (2001), Psychological problems following ICU treatment. *Anaesthesia*, 56 (1), 9–14.

Shin, L. M. & Rauch, S. L. (2006). Amygdala, medical prefontal cortex and hippocampal function in PTSD. *Annals of the New York Academy of Sciences*, 1071, 67–79.

Smucker, M. R., Dancu, C., Foa, E. & Niederee, J. (1995), Imagery rescripting: a new treatment for survivors of childhood sexual abuse suffering from posttraumatic stress. *Journal of Cognitive Psychotherapy*, 9 (1), 3–17.

Spiegel, D., Hunt, T. & Dondershine, H. E. (1988), Dissociation and hypnotizability in posttraumatic stress disorder. *American Journal of Psychiatry*, 145, 301–5.

Stanton, H. (1993), Submodalities II: theatre technique in the treatment of post-traumatic stress disorder. *International Journal of Psychosomatics*, 40 (1–4), 90–1.

Summerfield, D. (Ed.) (1997), *Psychological trauma: a developmental approach*. London, Gaskell and the Royal College of Psychiatrists.

Wilcox, H. C., Storr, C. L. & Breslau, N. (2008), Posttraumatic stress disorder and suicide attempts in a community sample of urban American young adults. *Archives of General Psychiatry*, 66 (3), 305–11.

Yard, S. S., Duhamel, K. N. & Galynker, I. I. (2008), Hypnotizability as a potential risk factor for posttraumatic stress: a review of quantitative studies. *International Journal of Clinical and Experimental Hypnosis*, 56 (3), 334–56.

27

Adjustment Disorders

Peter J Hawkins

Introduction

In the *Diagnostic and Statistical Manual of Mental Disorders*, fourth edition (DSM-IV; American Psychiatric Association, 1994), adjustment disorder is defined as 'a stress-related phenomenon in which the stressor has resulted in maladaptation and symptoms that are time-limited until the stressor is removed or a new state of adaptation has occurred' (Strain *et al.*, 1994 p671). It can occur with

- Depressed mood (e.g. tearfulness or hopelessness)
- Anxiety (e.g. worry or nervousness)
- Disturbance of conduct (e.g. truancy or vandalism)
- Or a mixture of any of the above

   The diagnostic criteria include:

- The development of emotional or behavioural symptoms in response to an identifiable stressor occurring within three months of the onset of the stressor.
- Marked distress in excess of what is to be expected from exposure to the stressor.
- Significant impairment in social, occupational or academic functioning.
- The symptoms do not represent bereavement.
- Once the stressor (or its consequences) has terminated, the symptoms do not persist for more than an additional six months.

The Handbook of Contemporary Clinical Hypnosis: Theory and Practice, First Edition.
Edited by Les Brann, Jacky Owens and Ann Williamson.
© 2012 John Wiley & Sons, Ltd. Published 2015 by John Wiley & Sons, Ltd.

In adolescents many major psychiatric illnesses eventually occur, and adjustment disorder differs from PTSD because the stressor is usually less severe and within the range of common experience, and some symptoms characteristic of PTSD, such as flashbacks, are absent.

Adjustment disorder is found in all cultures and in all age groups. The presence of a causal stressor is essential before a diagnosis of adjustment disorder can be made, while the symptoms vary and include those that are found in other common psychiatric disorders. However, despite the relative frequency with which the diagnosis of adjustment disorder is made, there is a very limited research literature regarding its cause, epidemiology and treatment (Laugharne *et al.*, 2009).

There are many stressors which can affect the individual; some are current whereas others may be related to experiences earlier in an individual's life. Current stressors (e.g. financial, interpersonal or health) are commonplace in most individuals' lives and are related to life experiences, as well as to physical and environmental situations (Moos & Swindle, 1990).

It is clearly demonstrated in the case study later in this chapter that the inter-relationship between mind and body, and the influence of social and economic factors, is important in the development of an integrated treatment strategy.

Individuals can usually cope with a degree of stress by utilizing a range of strategies some of which may be ineffective and stress enhancing, such as diet (Conner *et al.*, 1999; Michaud *et al.*, 1990), smoking (Carey *et al.*, 1993) and alcohol (Cappell & Greeley, 1987). Continuous and intense stress can lead to serious psychosomatic problems such as cardiovascular morbidity, along with possible life-style consequences and a diminution of quality of life. A number of recent studies have also shown that 'stress' can compromise the immune system, which makes it more vulnerable to opportunistic infections (Dhabhar *et al.*, 2000; Kiecolt-Glaser *et al.*, 2001), and can lead to a prolongation of any problems and further psychosomatic symptomatology (Gruzelier, 2002; Kiecolt-Glaser *et al.*, 2001).

Conversely hypnosis can effectively modulate immune system functioning by altering hypothalamic activity (Kiecolt-Glaser & Glaser, 1992; Rossi, 2003; Solloway, 2004).

Many dysfunctions are often associated with or exacerbated by psychosocial stress. There are many psychosocial situations that might give rise to acute anxiety, such as surgical and dental interventions, gynaecological examinations as well as adverse family and work situations.

There is increasing evidence that hypnosis can be useful in the treatment of a wide range of stress related problems including, for example, anxiety (Barnier *et al.*, 1999; Hammond, 2010), psychosomatic disorders (Flammer & Alladin, 2007; Younger *et al.*, 2007), dermatological problems (Hawkins *et al.*, 2009; Shenefelt, 2007) and bruxism (Hawkins & Almeida-Melikian, 2009).

Integrative Hypnotherapy and Problems of Adjustment

The ultimate goals of treatment are to mobilize the patient's stress-coping mechanisms and to prevent the 'disorders of adjustment' from developing into another, more chronic condition, such as generalized anxiety disorder.

The evolution of integrative psychotherapy has gained considerable momentum in the past decade (Hawkins & Nestoros, 1998; O'Leary & Murphy, 2006). Integrative hypnotherapy applies similar guidelines to the analysis of integration although this is often more pragmatically oriented (Hawkins, 2006*b*). Clinical interventions with respect to stress-related problems, including those utilizing hypnosis, can be made at any of the levels described below:

- Assisting the patient to realistically appraise daily hassles
- Helping the patient recognize and enhance positive experiences and create new ones
- Dealing directly with the 'stress response' by using general therapeutic techniques such as relaxation, ego strengthening, reframing or cognitive restructuring
- Accessing unconscious healing resources for psychosomatic healing and reframing (i.e. Rossi's hypnotherapeutic work)
- Dealing with the ineffective coping strategies that are often associated with stress (e.g., smoking, problem drinking and food-related behaviours such as over-eating)
- Dealing with the longer term effects of chronic stress (e.g. psychosomatic problems, alcoholism, obesity and diminished quality of life)
- Identifying the stressors (current or historical), and dealing with them therapeutically ('working through', catharsis, reframing, restructuring, relationship counselling, family therapy and so on)
- Assisting the patient in identifying and changing mediating factors such as social support, exercise and coping styles
- Helping the patient identify and change the way they appraise potential stressors
- Helping the patient to become more assertive so that they may engage in appropriate personal, social and political action

A useful summary of hypnosis approaches in dealing with stress related problems is provided by Gravitz and Page (2002) and Hawkins (2006a).

Case study

The client was a volunteer for a demonstration at a hypnosis workshop for psychologists and psychotherapists. It transpired that her problems started from the time when she was made redundant from her post as a counsellor in a local drop-in centre. Throughout this presentation a number of short extracts from the clinical intervention will be provided to give the reader an indication of the clinical approach.

Session 1 (group demonstration)

The session began by addressing the class in the following way:

For most of us, hypnosis is really about healing . . . is it not? So I would like to ask if there is anyone in the group today who is in a state of distress. Someone who feels that they can do some effective work this morning? So this is not merely a demonstration – this is the real thing!

This introduction is adapted from Rossi's 2002 book *The Psychobiology of Gene Expression*. It begins with a positive statement/question, *"hypnosis is about healing . . . is it not?"* Erickson regarded this type of question that ends with *". . . is it not?"* as a mild therapeutic double-bind that disarms potential resistance by stating the negative as well as the positive, so that the subject does not have to waste any effort in negation and denial. Asking for a volunteer who really can do effective work today and stating that it is the *"real thing"* increase psychological arousal and heightened expectations. The casual and permissive attitude of these questions facilitates a positive, receptive mental attitude, a kind of 'yes set'.

The volunteer, Cristine, was 38 years old, and the initial interview revealed that she was suffering from a number of symptoms, which started or were exacerbated from the time she was made unemployed six months previously. These included:

- Difficulties in sleeping combined with bruxism
- Fatigue
- Irritability
- Anxiety
- Low self esteem and lack of confidence
- Feelings of pessimism and lack of hope for the future
- Deterioration of relationship with her partner including lack of sexual desire
- Increase in her psoriasis condition
- Waking up every morning with temporo-mandibular headaches

Although only a brief clinical interview was made, sufficient evidence suggested that she was not coping well with her loss of job resulting in behavioural, emotional and somatic symptoms. The patient also provided a narrative as to how she came to manifest her symptoms thus allowing a practice formulation to be derived.

Cristine's beliefs about hypnosis were carefully explored. It was explained to her that hypnosis is a natural 'healing' state that people enter every 90 to 120 minutes for approximately 20 minutes, the 'common everyday trance' (Rossi *et al.*, 1995).

Erickson and Rossi consider that the 'hypnotic trance' can be healing in its own right, and further that everyone is capable of developing appropriate levels of trance. In hypnotherapeutic work, Rossi induces a permissive state of therapeutic hypnosis which 'allows' clients to identify the sources and history of any emotional problem or symptom with consequent psychosomatic reframing. He argued that, in their efforts to explain their problems, clients review the state-dependent memories associated with their origin and their psychosomatic symptoms. This internal review often leads to a spontaneous cathartic reaction, where stress hormones are released, which re-evoke and release state-bound memories associated with the original trauma and stress. Hypnotherapeutic work, facilitated by the ideodynamic use of language and mind-body signalling, provides a way to access and facilitate psychobiological healing and creativity in stress management (Rossi, 2002).

You may be wondering whether you have already been in this healing trance state earlier today or perhaps even now as you listen to my voice, but I imagine that you will go into an even deeper trance before you leave this room.

The 'treatment' was then explained to Cristine with an emphasis on the following:

- She had the personal internal (unconscious) healing resources to make positive psychosomatic changes in the way she functioned.
- In order to facilitate the healing process, it was essential that she collaborate fully in the therapeutic endeavour (attending sessions, carrying out homework assignments and so on).

Cristine's hypnotic capacity was assessed by using an adaptation of Spiegel's Hypnotic Induction Profile (Spiegel & Spiegel, 1978/2004). This indicated that she could produce good ideodynamic finger movements and arm levitation; it also taught her a method of self-hypnosis (i.e. by looking at her hand), which could be used in future sessions as well as for her homework assignments.

An initial ego-strengthening and relaxation technique was used in order to help with stress-related issues and to improve Cristine's self-esteem and levels of confidence. During the session Cristine showed signs of entering a profound trance state. The good feelings of control and confidence were anchored by putting the thumb and forefinger together so that she could have immediate access to them on future occasions.

A further 'de-stressing' exercise was carried out which demonstrated to Cristine that she could access remembered positive experiences psychosomatically. These positive regressions allow the patient to experience feelings of control, hope and expectation with important consequent healing ramifications for the treatment. In this exercise Cristine 'floated' to her favourite place and accessed all of her sensory modalities.

It was suggested to Cristine that she use self hypnosis (by looking at her hand and allowing it to float) and then explore her favourite place on a daily basis, and that it might help if she "... *took my voice with her.*"

At the end of the demonstration, Cristine was invited to continue with the hypnotherapy on a weekly basis. She later made contact to accept this invitation for six sessions.

Session 2

Cristine said that she had practiced the self hypnosis every day and although she was feeling a little better she was still waking very tired after a disturbed sleep with facial pains.

A brief intervention was given to enable Cristine to sleep better.

Close your eyes and go inside your mind and find all those psychosomatic memories of sleeping well in the past ... allowing those resources to flow around your body and mind ... relaxing every part of your body and mind ... and when you really know that you can utilize these natural healing resources to engage in a peaceful, restorative sleep, will your finger lift? ... That's good! ... as you drift into a peaceful restorative sleep ... so relaxed that even the muscles of your face are deeply asleep ... calm and comfortable ... and will there be times when you dream healing experiences? ... Waking in the morning with every part of your mind and body feeling relaxed and refreshed and ready to deal with issues in your life that need attending to. I don't know whether you will experience a good restorative sleep tonight or will it be tomorrow night or the night after but before the weekend? ... And when your unconscious mind knows that this healing process is continuing and that your inner mind has learned something useful to help you find comfort and healing when you lay down to rest will your eyes open?

Cristine was requested to repeat this exercise every day prior to sleeping and to preface it with the following affirmation, *"I can sleep well and wake up feeling relaxed and peaceful."* A general outline of the exercise was written on a card to help her remember the various elements.

The session ended by telling Cristine a story about climbing a mountain to help her develop greater self-esteem (Hammond, 1990). It was also suggested that at the summit she might meet a significant person in her life or a friendly animal who might provide an answer to an important personal issue (Jaffe & Bresler, 1980). It was also suggested that she might find further answers in a dream later that night.

Session 3

Cristine reported that she was sleeping better and waking with lessened facial pain and headaches. Generally, she felt better during the day and found the anchoring procedure very effective. She also commented that she had had some strange dreams which she understood as having some relevance to her problems. After discussion it was agreed to focus the session around the pain aspects of her bruxism such as the temporo-mandibular pain and headaches. Before doing so the following was presented without any comment or discussion.

> *Have you ever thought about transformation? For example, when a block of ice starts to get warmer then the temperature gradually changes, but it stays as a solid until it reaches zero degrees centigrade when it changes into water. As the temperature continues to rise the water becomes hotter and hotter but remains as water until one hundred degrees is reached when it changes into vapour. Each new state appears as a leap, suddenly interrupting and checking the gradual succession of temperature changes at each transition point. It is also interesting to contemplate that as the temperature increases so the invisible particles in the ice and water move faster and faster.*

Cristine commented that she was currently experiencing some facial pain. The intervention for helping her control pain used transformations (i.e. changing shape, colour, temperature and size), relaxation (autogenics and a healing ball of light), guided imagery (a healing place), future age progression and goal setting. Throughout the session the following were used: utilization, implied directives, analogies, double binds, direct and indirect suggestions and ideodynamic signalling.

After the session Cristine reported that she felt considerably more relaxed including her facial muscles, and that her headache had disappeared. It was stressed that she had done this herself and had the internal healing resources to do this in the future. In the intervention above, the following should be noted:

• The process of anchoring positive feelings and sensations was reinforced.
• The development of a positive future orientation through goal setting (i.e. hypnotic age progression; such suggestions contain a strong psychological implication that the desired response will take place).

- The continuation of a general cognitive reframing of Cristine's problems so that she creates a new interpretation of her discomforting symptoms and a more positive perspective concerning her future functioning.
- The establishment of a positive ideodynamic response (i.e., arm levitation) which can be utilized in a future session.
- The continuation of unconscious search processes for finding solutions to her problems.

Before Cristine left she was asked to describe how she would travel home to ensure that she was fully re-orientated and what she was looking forward to doing during the coming week. She was also reminded to continue with the homework assignment.

Session 4

Initially Cristine's progress was discussed. She commented that she was sleeping better and that in the morning she felt calm and relaxed. Her temporo-mandibular pain and headaches had virtually disappeared, and daytime jaw clenching only occurred when she was under considerable stress. Her partner had also informed her that night-time grinding had seemingly decreased, and this had had some positive effect on their relationship.

However, she was still feeling very anxious and felt self conscious when with other people. It was then explained to her that psychosomatic pathologies can often be understood as a product of underlying unresolved emotions, and that hypnoanalysis could allow the uncovering of the repressed dynamics with consequent insight into the aetiological events as experienced at physiological, affective and cognitive levels (Hawkins, 2006a). Cristine concurred with this view and said that it seemed sensible to utilize the session to explore the origins of her feelings of inadequacy. Although she attributed these feelings to her unemployment and failure in finding a new job, she stated that she had experienced similar feelings at school.

During this session dissociation was managed by asking Cristine to project an image of herself onto a television screen. The level of emotion could be further decreased by suggesting to her that the picture projected on the screen could be black and white or even 'blurred', or by adjusting the sound. Ideodynamic arm levitation signals (i.e. 'Yes' and 'No') were established followed by 'pinpointing, access, and review' (see recursive ideodynamic finger questioning; Rossi & Cheek, 1988).

As Cristine reviewed the relevant underlying event to her feelings of inadequacy that had occurred when she was seven, she showed some signs of distress and a few tears. She was encouraged to stay with this and, staying in touch with her knowledge and experience of the present, various techniques were integrated into the procedure acknowledging the fear that her seven year old self had felt by using the present tense *"I am feeling afraid,"* using Gestalt 'empty chair' dialogues with relevant people, focusing on the feeling and use of an affect bridge (see page 127), using mindfulness, observing her feelings without judgement, putting a sound to a movement, putting a movement to a sound and using a dreaming arm procedure: I *I wonder if as your arm rises up, all by itself . . . you can have a dream that will be really helpful to you . . . it can be your dreaming arm . . . and as you finish the dream your arm can gently return to your lap.* " The use of these approaches both facilitated and maintained an appropriate level of catharsis leading to an increase in insight and intentionality. Further suggestions were then given for post-hypnotic work.

> *And I wonder whether you will find interesting learnings and solutions from this important experience in order that you may go into the future without the problem . . . perhaps you will continue to find relevant experiences and memories as your unconscious mind continues with this process of exploration and discovery even though you do not know that this is happening . . . even whilst you are asleep . . . with no conscious distress. . . . And when your unconscious mind knows that it can utilize the learnings from this experience or to understand yourself differently, will you find your body becoming more alert so that your eyes open? . . . It will be interesting and exciting to see how things are different . . . what changes you might notice.*

For homework Cristine was asked to use the imagery exercise related to 'her favourite place', which she had experienced in Session 2. An outline was again provided on a card.

In this session Cristine had explored an early experience that was ostensibly linked generically to her feelings of anxiety. It is important to note that she expressed and resolved considerable emotion, which was encouraged by the therapist using a variety of therapeutic techniques (emotional focusing, literal description and older and younger self). Expectations and hope for positive change in the future were created.

Session 5

Cristine reported that she was sleeping well and had given up the night-time splint. In the morning she felt relaxed without any mandibular pain or headache. If she felt stressed during the day, she would make use of her anchor (i.e. putting her thumb and forefinger together). She also felt less anxious and more confident with an increased self-esteem and improved body image. However, there was little diminution in her dermatological problem so the session focused on this aspect.

Cristine was asked to indicate, using arm levitation, the current intensity of her skin condition (an example of a visual analogue scale, or VAS). She was also asked to experience a time in her life when the symptoms were worse. This provides the therapist with a useful device to monitor the progress of the therapy during the session or over the course of treatment. It also heightens the patient's sensitivity to their symptoms, so that they can better appreciate those periods throughout the day when symptoms threaten to get worse as well as just noticeable therapeutic improvements that can motivate and reinforce their progress. It may also be valuable to have the patient produce the symptom (i.e. symptom prescription) as this helps the patient 'learn how to make the symptom better' by accessing the state dependent encoding of mind–body problems.

As well as ego strengthening (healing place) a therapeutic story or metaphor was given:

> *There is a story about a beautiful young woman who was invited by the king to accompany him when he went out to give alms to the poor in spite of the fact that she had a severe skin problem.*

However, the young woman notices that the falling snow cools and soothes the skin eruptions on her face and, at the king's suggestion, she applies the snow to her arms and legs. As she does she feels the benefit of its cooling effect and the skin ceases to itch. On her return to the castle, she finds that whenever she feels like scratching her skin she thinks about the snow and immediately the skin is soothed and the irritation goes. Because of this she becomes much more relaxed and does not mind going to class and meeting with other young people . . . she feels more confident and enjoys joining in with their activities. In addition she also finds that she sleeps better at night and is, therefore, better able to engage in her studies the next day. (Adapted from Mantle, 2001)

Session 6

Two weeks later there was some diminution in Cristine's skin problem (self-report). She also commented that she was sleeping much better and had more confidence and less anxiety. After discussion it was decided to use this session to review progress and to terminate the treatment.

Follow-Up

During the following six months, progress was maintained. Cristine reported that she felt very positive and confident about herself, was sleeping well, had significant improvement in her skin condition and had a satisfying sexual relationship with her partner. She was still unemployed but engaged in voluntary work, which she found very satisfying. She was optimistic about the future and in eventually finding permanent work. She continued to use self-hypnosis on a daily basis.

Summary

The major clinical approaches used in the treatment of Cristine's problem included ego strengthening and relaxation, stress management, pain control and the psychodynamic uncovering of formative experiences. The session was essentially Ericksonian in that utilization and implication were the basis of the interventions, with the patient engaged in inner mind–body healing. The author (PH) used a range of approaches: direct suggestion, Ericksonian psychotherapy (languages of implication), psychodrama, Gestalt therapy, cognitive behavioural therapy (CBT) and mindfulness. These were drawn from behavioural, cognitive, psychodynamic and humanistic-phenomenological perspectives, and stressed the significant relationship between mind and body. Importantly too, she was taught self-hypnosis which she used regularly throughout the treatment and continued to do.

Other factors, which probably played a part in the apparent successful treatment, include her positive and collaborative relationship with the author (PH), the significant emotional catharsis that occurred, her high motivation and the expectation and hope for a successful outcome (i.e. curative factors).

This case study demonstrates that many patients present a wide range of symptoms, which are exacerbated by stressful situations. It promulgates a philosophy of the uniqueness and healing qualities of each patient and an individually tailored and creative intervention, rather than adopting a formal diagnosis and treatment of adjustment disorder based on published research. However, this in no way mitigates against the importance of evidence-based approaches in diagnosis and treatment but is to encourage creativity and flexibility in working with patients. Adjustment disorders often follow a change in life circumstances and may present with somatization as in the example below.

Nicola – a woman with fibromyalgia (courtesy of Dr Les Brann)

Nicola was referred for hypnotherapy by the local consultant in pain management. She had recently had a diagnosis of fibromyalgia made by a rheumatologist, but she was not responding to analgesics or pregabalin. The pain specialist was concerned about her emotional state and had explained that it was unlikely the pain would respond to medication until she had sorted out the emotional problem.

She was married with two children, one teenager and one aged ten. She cried through most of the first session which was used as an introduction to hypnosis and for relaxation. During the second session she was asked to explore the time when the pains all started. Crying pretty well through most of the hypnosis, she recounted how things had been happy until her husband's business had taken a dip, and this resulted in a change of direction in that regard and had led to a move of house from a fairly idyllic country village to a much more ordinary suburban situation. During this time it transpired that her husband had been getting a lot of emotional support from a close female friend of Nicola's; there was no infidelity, but Nicola felt undermined and betrayed. As a consequence, her relationship with her husband became distant and she also lost her close friend.

Although these events had taken place a few years previously, she was still experiencing the emotion as though it had only just happened. Intellectually she had come to terms with the situation, but the emotion was still very raw. The 'older wiser self' technique was used to help her realize that she had come through the ordeal, and the event was moved to her 'personal museum'.

Whilst still very tearful she had begun to improve. During the next hypnosis session she explored the other areas of loss that had ensued. The pains had prevented her from playing her sport. Not only did she miss the physical activity but also she missed her friends. This also had meant that she had spent a lot more of the time at home and as her husband worked from home, there was a constant reminder of the tension between them. No special hypnotic techniques were needed, just the cathartic effect of her letting go of all the emotion.

She did not cry at all during the fourth session. Her pains were much improved to the point where she was going to explore playing some sport. The issues of the lack of emotional support and the sexual side of her marriage were still issues but were no longer all consuming, and she was able to put it much more in perspective.

The art of healing requires that the clinician pay particular attention to meeting the psychological needs of patients, a process which requires compassion and sensitivity, as well as to the social aspects of the patient's life (e.g. social support, financial status and interpersonal and familial relationships). In hypnotherapy particular attention is paid to the quality of the therapeutic relationship as well as to the active involvement of the patient. Above all the therapist demonstrates through their interventions that they really care for the patient. This is the sine qua non of psychotherapy. For this to happen, a high degree of personal awareness is necessary and a capacity for the clinician to trust in their own inner resources.

References

American Psychiatric Association (1994), *Diagnostic and statistical manual of mental disorders*, 4th ed. Washington DC, American Psychiatric Association.

Barnier, A. J., Mcconkey, K. & O'neill, L. M. (1999), Treating anxiety with self-hypnosis and relaxation. *Contemporary Hypnosis*, 16, 68–80.

Cappell, H. & Greeley, J. (1987), Alcohol and tension reduction: an update on research and theory, in Blane, H. T.& Leonard, K. E. (Eds.) *Psychological theories of drinking and alcoholism* (pp. 15-54) New York: Guilford Press.

Carey, M. P., Kalra, D. L., Carey, K. B., Halperin, S. & Richard, C. S. (1993), Stress and unaided smoking cessation: a prospective investigation. *Journal of Consulting & Clinical Psychology*, 61, 831–8.

Conner, M., Fitter, M. & Fletcher, W. (1999), Stress and snacking: a diary study of daily hassles and between-meal snacking. *Psychology and Health*, 14, 51–63.

Dhabhar, F., Satoskar, A., Bluethmann, H., David, J. & McEwen, B. (2000), Stress-induced enhancement of skin immune function: a role for gamma interferon. *Proceedings of the National Academy of Sciences*, 96, 1059–64.

Flammer, E. & Alladin, A (2007), The efficacy of hypnotherapy in the treatment of psychosomatic disorders. *International Journal of Clinical & Experimental Hypnosis*, 55 (3), 251–74.

Gravitz, M. A. & Page, R. A. (2002), Hypnosis in the management of stress reactions, in Everly, G. S. & Lating, J. M. (Eds.) *A clinical guide to the treatment of the human stress response*. New York, Kluwer/Plenum. p 241–52.

Gruzelier, J. (2002), A review of the impact of hypnosis, relaxation, guided imagery and individual differences on aspects of immunity and health. *Stress*, 5, 147–63.

Hammond, D. C. (Ed.) (1990), *Handbook of hypnotic suggestions and metaphors*. London, W. W. Norton.

Hammond, D. C. (2010), Hypnosis in the treatment of anxiety- and stress-related disorders. *Expert Review of Neurotherapeutics*, 10 (2), 263–73.

Hawkins, P. J. (2006a), *Hypnosis and stress: a guide for clinicians*. Chichester, John Wiley & Sons, Ltd. p 90–122.

Hawkins, P. J. (2006b) Hypnoanalysis: an integration of hypnosis and psychodynamic approaches. In O'Leary, E. & Murphy, M. (Eds.) *New approaches to integration in psychotherapy*. New York, Brunner-Routledge.

Hawkins, P. J. & Almeida-Melikian, A. (2009), Hipnose no tratamento do bruxismo. In Maciel, R. N.& Gil, A. R. (Eds.) *Bruxism*. São Paulo, Editora Artes Médicas.

Hawkins, P. J. & Nestoros, J. (1998), Beyond the dogmas of conventional psychotherapy: the integration movement, in Hawkins, P. J. & Nestoros, J. (Eds.) *Psychotherapy: new perspectives on theory, practice and research*. Athens, Ellinika Grammata.

Hawkins, P J., Vargha, J-L. & Szabó, K-G. (2009), One-session demonstration treatment of psoriasis. *European Journal of Clinical Hypnosis*, 9 (1), 19–26.

Jaffe, D. T. & Bresler, D. E. (1980), The use of guided imagery as an adjunct to medical diagnosis and treatment. *Journal of Humanistic Psychology*, 20 (4), 45–59.

Kiecolt-Glaser, J. K. & Glaser, R. (1992), Psychoneuroimmunology: can psychological interventions modulate immunity? *Journal of Consulting & Clinical Psychology*, 60, 569–75.

Kiecolt-Glaser, J. K., Marucha, P., Atkinson, C. & Glaser, R. (2001), Hypnosis as a modulator of cellular immune dysregulation during acute stress. *Journal of Consulting & Clinical Psychology*, 69, 674–82.

Laugharne, J., Van der Watt, G. & Janca, A. (2009), It is too early for adjusting the adjustment disorder category. *Current Opinion in Psychiatry*, 22 (1), 50–54.

Mantle, F. (2001), Hypnosis in the management of eczema in children. *Nursing Standard*, 15 (51), 41–4.

Michaud, C., Kahn, J. P. & Musse, N. (1990), Relationships between a critical life event and eating behaviour in high school students. *Stress Medicine*, 6, 57–64.

Moos, R. H. & Swindle, R. W. (1990), Stressful life circumstances: concepts and measures. *Stress Medicine*, 6, 171–8.

O'Leary, E. & Murphy, M. (Eds.) (2006), *New approaches to integration in psychotherapy*. New York, Brunner-Routledge.

Rossi, E. L. (2002), *The psychobiology of gene expression*. New York, W. W. Norton.

Rossi, E. (2003), Gene expression, neurogenesis, and healing: psychosocial genomics of therapeutic hypnosis. *American Journal of Clinical Hypnosis*, 45 (3), 197–216.

Rossi, E. & Cheek, D. B. (1988), *Mind-body therapy*. New York, W. W. Norton.

Rossi, E., Lippencott, B. & Bessette, A. (1995), The chronobiology of mind-body healing: ultradian dynamics in hypnotherapy, part 2. *European Journal of Clinical Hypnosis*, 2 (2), 6–14.

Shenefelt, P. D. (2007), Hypnosis: applications in dermatology and dermatologic surgery. www.emedicine.com

Solloway, K. (2004), Can clinical hypnosis prevent stress-related immune deficiency? *European Journal of Clinical Hypnosis*, 5 (5), 44–56.

Spiegel, H., & Spiegel, D. (1978/2004), *Trance and treatment: clinical uses of hypnosis*. Washington, DC, APA Press.

Strain, J. J., Newcorn, J., Wolf, D. & Fulop, G. (1994), Adjustment disorder, in Hales, R. E., Yudofsky, S. C. & Talbott, J. A. (Eds.) *Textbook of psychiatry*, 2nd ed. Washington, DC, APA Press.

Younger, J. W., Rossetti, G. C., Borckardt, J. J., Smith, A. R., Tasso, A. F. & Nash, M. R. (2007), Hypnotizability and somatic complaints: a gender-specific phenomenon. *International Journal Clinical & Experimental Hypnosis*, 55 (1), 1–13.

28

Eating Disorders

Dr David Kraft and Dr Peter J Hawkins

with contributions from Dr Duncan Shrewsbury, Dr Adrian Hamill and
Dr Lucy Coffin

Introduction

Eating disorders in DSM-IV (American Psychiatric Association, 1994) are divided into
bulimia nervosa (BN) and anorexia nervosa (AN) as well as the category 'Eating Disorders
not Otherwise Specified' (EDNOS) which is reserved for those patients who do not meet all
the necessary criteria for the diagnosis of anorexia nervosa or bulimia nervosa.

AN is a condition of compulsive restriction of intake and weight loss, whereas BN is
characterized by episodes of uncontrollable binge eating interspersed with tightly controlled
and restricted intake. Both are also characterized by a dysmorphic sense of appearance and a
desire to lose weight.

It is thought that females are more often affected than males. However, whilst this may be
true, the extent to which males are affected may be severely underestimated. Diagnostic
criteria for AN and BN are strict, thus many patients with even moderately severe eating
problems do not fulfil criteria for treatment in the National Health Service and therefore
cannot access help and services.

The Handbook of Contemporary Clinical Hypnosis: Theory and Practice, First Edition.
Edited by Les Brann, Jacky Owens and Ann Williamson.
© 2012 John Wiley & Sons, Ltd. Published 2015 by John Wiley & Sons, Ltd.

Anorexia Nervosa

The lifetime prevalence of AN among adult women has been reported as 0.5% to 0.6% in two large population based surveys in the United States (Walters & Kendler, 1995) and Canada (Garfinkel *et al.*, 1996).

An epidemiological study in 2007 showed an incidence of 0.9% in women and 0.3% in men. This later population based study was based on a house-to-house survey on a national level, carried out by the Harvard Medical School ($n = 9,282$). The results of this study showed that there has been an increase in the number of men suffering from this condition or, alternatively, that the diagnostic tools have developed to the extent to where more men fit the criteria for AN (Hudson *et al.*, 2007).

Most often diagnosed in females (up to 90%), anorexia is characterized by failure to maintain body weight of at least 85% of what is expected, fear of losing control over their weight and fear of becoming 'fat.'

Much research has been completed on this disorder, and results indicate a strong familial undercurrent. Many individuals with anorexia come from over-controlling families where nurturance is lacking. Studies suggest that sexual abuse survivors are more prone to the disorder, as are fraternal twins and first degree relatives of those who have anorexia, the latter suggesting a biological component as well (Walters & Kendler, 1995). A frequent finding in anorexic patients is that they are often caught up in a highly complex, emotionally charged and disturbed family environment. Anorexics are often high achievers, obsessional and perfectionist. In many cases, anorexics have internal hostilities that present themselves in the form of starvation: these feelings of hostility are directed towards parental figures, usually the mother.

Individuals with anorexia want to lose weight despite their actions compromising their health, and are often already seriously underweight. This irrational desire may start from the current cultural belief that glamorizes thinness so that dieting starts to become a way of life. There is typically a distorted body image, where the individual sees themselves as overweight despite overwhelming evidence to the contrary. Often the anorexic will rationalize why they are not eating; maybe they do not like the food, feel ill or have already eaten elsewhere. They may obsessively read food labels and know exactly how much sugar and fat is in their food. When they do eat they may induce vomiting, which over time leads to dental problems; over-exercise compulsively; or take laxatives to excess. The anorexic takes control over the only activity they perceive that they can – their dietary intake. It must be remembered that this is often at an unconscious rather than conscious level of awareness.

Fundamentally, eating disorders can be considered a serious form of self-harm. Sufferers tend to have experienced a history of domestic violence, mental illness or catastrophe. The destructive behaviour can be triggered, or exacerbated, by psychological stressors and is directly related to a sense of fear and control. The fear is related to perceived inadequacy of their physical form or appearance, and the sense of control is often related to an underlying need for the individual to establish and (secretly) maintain control over a specific aspect of their lives. Sufferers tend to have low confidence and a very low belief in their own worth and abilities, which can significantly affect treatment.

It is in the nature of sufferers to keep the disorder hidden, and therefore they develop many strategies to hide, cope and mask both the physical and psychological aspects of the condition. The most significant is the denial that there is a problem, which is also the greatest barrier to recovery. Whilst eating disorders can occur on a spectrum of severity, it is important to be aware of the cues to involve more specialist help. All severe cases of established anorexia and bulimia nervosa should be under the care of a psychiatrist, and their treatment should be approached from a multi-disciplinary angle.

Anxiety states and other emotional problems are often found alongside the AN (O'Brien & Vincent, 2003). AN is treatable, especially if caught early, but often the anorexic denies that there is a problem, sometimes until their weight is such that they become seriously ill and end up in hospital.

Treatment has to start with gaining rapport, and this can be difficult if someone else has insisted that the patient come for therapy. Interim goals need to be agreed, and creative ways of helping the patient start to achieve better health and self esteem generated. Their cognitive distortions need addressing, but experiential learning is much more effective than just being told, so experiments may need to be devised to help the patient address these.

There is little or no randomized controlled trial evidence for the use of hypnosis in anorexia but numerous case studies indicate that hypnosis can be a useful therapeutic tool in resolving underlying issues and giving the anorexic self hypnotic tools that can give them feelings of greater control (Gross, 1984; Nash & Baker, 1993; Vanderlinden & Vandereycken, 2006; Yapko, 1986).

Treatment of a case of anorexia (outlined below courtesy of Dr D Shrewsbury)

Helen was under the care of a team, which included a consultant psychiatrist and a senior clinical psychologist. She had acknowledged her problem and had begun to engage in the treatment. Of significance, it was the thought of getting better, and not retaining the level of control over her eating that triggered anxiety.

She had a background of family violence with a very controlling mother who actively encouraged her to lose weight (even though her BMI was less than 15 by the time she was seen in clinic) on the premise that thin women were more successful in life. Helen had originally been able to ignore such comments and influences, but as the family situation deteriorated and the divorce of her parents approached, her psychological wellbeing deteriorated, culminating in a sense of being out of control. In order to cope with this, she had developed a habit of fastidiously controlling the number of calories that she consumed each day, and exercised in excess of two hours a day.

Having liaised with the psychiatrist and psychologist, the girl was seen for an hour and a half session, during which time a good level of rapport and trust was established. The main aim of the treatment was to build her confidence and the belief that she was worthy of a long, good-quality life; capable of controlling many aspects of her life, and of accepting that everyone is unable to control all aspects of their lives; strong and capable of successfully taking control of her life and not allowing her condition and perceived control to dictate her health and wellbeing.

Treatment was divided into three elements, which could be considered as questions aimed at the condition.

The first question was regarding what learnings, beliefs or events from Helen's past underpinned her choice of behaviour. Using trance and guided imagery her 'safe place' was enhanced and ego strengthening was employed to prepare her to explore this. The psychologist had previously alluded to much of what was revealed in trance; however, it was important for Helen to recognize the underlying factors for herself and come to her own conclusions. Once a root cause was established, it was possible to go back along her timeline to help resolve her negative perceptions and emotions regarding these events.

Secondly enquiry was made concerning how choosing this behaviour related to the way she was feeling and the way she wanted to feel; what did it gain for her? In this step, it is important to identify and manage specific fears in a sensitive manner. Helen experienced fear of losing control; becoming unacceptable and being rejected. These fears were so severe that it was, and often is, sensible to treat them as phobias. Treatment consisted of a combination of guided imagery and ego strengthening, establishing an anchor for her safe place and generating a strong feeling of safety, comfort and confidence (note that the exact combination of feelings are unique to the individual and can be tailored to fit what they feel they need most).

At this stage it is wise to confront, and provide a means of dealing with, triggers. By far the simplest, and probably most effective, way of doing this is stacking anchors (see page 147) and using a Swish pattern technique (Bandler, 1985) to change the behavioural responses to the trigger situations using visualization (see pages 138, 453).

Finally it was important to connect Helen with her desired future by asking her what her future would be like if she was able to choose different behaviours. It is important to approach this situation last as the 'future pacing' of the individual, and the success of the whole process, is influenced by the altered perception of their triggers.

Bulimia Nervosa

The lifetime prevalence of bulimia nervosa in adult women has been estimated as 1.1–2.8% in three large population based surveys in New Zealand (Bushnell *et al.*, 1990), the United States (Kendler *et al.*, 1991), and Canada (Garfinkel *et al.*, 1995). The incidence of BN for women in the 2007 Harvard study was 1.5% for women and 0.5% for men (Hudson *et al.*, 2007).

BN refers to a condition in which the patient has a combination of binge eating and purging; again, patients have an obsession with body weight and size. To make the diagnosis, the purging and bingeing cycle must occur at least twice a week for at least three months.

The features of bulimia include episodic eating patterns involving rapid consumption of large quantities of food in a discrete period of time, usually less than two hours; awareness that this eating pattern is abnormal; fear of being unable to stop eating voluntarily; and depressed mood and self-deprecating thoughts following the eating binges. The eating binges usually happen in private, and are often followed by purging (elimination of the food through artificial means such as forced vomiting, excessive use of laxatives, periods of fasting or excessive exercise) (American Psychiatric Association, 1994).

Bulimics often have a history of unresolved early trauma: a common feature is that patients feel that it is someone else who is binge eating and purging, and that they are out of control (Covino *et al.*, 1994). It has also been shown that patients with bulimia are more highly hypnotizable than the norm (Barabasz, 1990; Pettinati *et al.*, 1985), although a study done in 1995 failed to demonstrate any association between hypnotizablity and outcome (Griffiths *et al.*, 1995).

The average bulimic can be characterized as a white, single, college educated woman from an upper- or middle-class family (Fairburn & Cooper, 1982). The age of onset is usually in the late teens, with a duration of about four to five years before the woman first seeks treatment (Fairburn & Cooper, 1982; Johnson *et al.*, 1982). In almost every case the women are struggling to obtain a below normal ideal weight (Katzman & Wolchik, 1984). The frequency of binge-eating episodes varies widely across studies; however approximately 50% of the bulimic women in treatment report binge eating at least daily, whilst some women only binge twice a month or even less often (Johnson *et al.*, 1982).

There seems to be a number of factors which may precipitate an eating binge in a susceptible person. Most women say that before a binge they are unduly tense, and that loneliness or boredom precipitates a binge (Leon *et al.*, 1985). Constant thoughts of foods and a craving to eat, which they are eventually unable to control, are also factors. Bulimics are constantly concerned about their body image and usually perceive themselves as fat and ugly.

The disturbed eating pattern of a bulimic can have serious effects on their physical health as well as their social relationships. Treatment has included hospitalization, pharmacological approaches using anticonvulsants or depressants, behaviour therapy, cognitive-behavioural treatment, group therapy and family therapy. Weiss *et al.*, (1985) have developed a treatment programme for bulimia based on research findings that bulimic women suffer from depression, low self-esteem, poor body image, perfectionist tendencies, a high need for approval as well as difficulties in handling negative emotional states such as anger and anxiety, and in the setting of unrealistic goals for thinness. They also suggest that bulimic women need to refine their existing coping styles and to develop competencies.

Barabasz, (2007) reviewed the evidence base for hypnosis and reported that many of the studies available provide insufficient information regarding the specifics of the hypnotic intervention to facilitate replication and clinical implementation. Therefore, only studies with replicable methodological descriptions were included (Coman, 1992; Griffiths *et al.*, 1998). This need for standardization to eliminate variables is not applicable to the clinical context, where the interventions are tailored to the individual. As has been stated elsewhere in this book, this is very likely to undervalue hypnotic intervention.

Further studies can be found in Degun-Mather, (1995), Griffiths (1995a, 1995b) and Kraft and Kraft, (2009).

It may often be helpful to disrupt the patterns around the binging, as in the case example from Dr A Williamson below.

Sue – a case of Bulimia

Sue, a single woman of 23 years who lived alone in her own flat, presented with binge eating often followed by self induced vomiting. At the first session the pattern of her binging was established as she would start feeling 'fed up', and then begin to think about food. After a little while Sue would go down to the kitchen and stand in front of the refrigerator eating whatever she could find. It was suggested to her that she might find it useful to disrupt the pattern in some way and she decided that she would, instead of standing up eating in the kitchen, go and lay a place setting on the dining room table and take the food out from the refrigerator and eat at the table. Work was done in later sessions to devise ways she could interrupt and maybe resolve the 'fed up' feeling and stop using food as a way of self soothing when distressed and feeling lonely. By teaching her various hypnotic tools such as self hypnosis, ways of discarding negative feelings and replacing them with positive ones, anchoring and goal setting she began to feel more in control and more confident. This led to increasing social activity which in turn boosted her self esteem. After four sessions (in one of which we used the time road metaphor to improve her feelings of self esteem; see page 162) she decided that she had improved to the point when she stopped therapy, and follow up six months later showed continuing improvement.

Bulimia may vary along a continuum of severity with many patients not reaching the diagnostic criteria as such but suffering intermittent symptoms depending on their circumstances at the time.

The case history that follows demonstrates an integrative hypnotic treatment approach embracing psychodynamic, behaviourist and phenomenological paradigms; where hypnosis (both 'formal' and 'naturalistic') is used to enhance the therapeutic process. The approaches used include ego strengthening, dealing with negative emotions, assertiveness training, relaxation, reframing, hypno-analysis, goal setting, action planning and stress management.

Case study of a woman with Bulimia

Katherine was a 16 year old female who was referred to the author (PH) by a local general practitioner. She was asked to provide an autobiographical account of her eating problems prior to the first therapy session. The account written by Katherine illustrated many of the behavioural and psychological conditions of bulimia. These included preoccupation with weight and thinking 'thin', excessive exercise, depression, tiredness, attempts at concealment from the family, vomiting, poor self-image and distorted body-image, feelings of guilt and shame following a 'binge' and suicidal thoughts.

Statements made by Katherine included the following:

I had always admired skinny people, and at 13 I still disliked myself because I felt fat. So I ate less and less because I wanted to be skinny because to me that meant beautiful, and I wanted people to look at me and be jealous because I had the best figure. ... I did one and a half hours exercise in the morning and the evening. Purposefully forgot to bring things from upstairs just so I could run up and down again to stay thin. ... I was happy with my body when I was anorexic. I was somewhere between five and five and a half stone. ... I started to miss school a bit because I was so depressed and tired but I liked myself because I was thin. ... I was still obsessed about exercising and my weight; even when brushing my teeth I would be doing some kind of exercise to help burn off the calories. ... One night after eating too much chocolate and feeling guilty because I was still trying to get a flat stomach, I tried to be sick but could not manage to do it.

The only enjoyable thing left seemed to be eating and vomiting afterwards; about twice every two weeks ... The thought of dieting bored me. I hated my size but I had lost control and tried to commit suicide. ... I concealed what I was doing for weeks and told Mum I was improving, until she found evidence in the bathroom, and buckets under my bed.

I couldn't sleep some nights if the following day I had a binge planned because it excited me so much. ... I took no pride in my appearance and made no friends.

My wages were spent on food, and all the money saved in the building society was withdrawn to buy more food. ... If my mum was out for the evening that was wonderful for me, but if she was in I would pretend that I was working, but I was eating and being sick in my bedroom, playing the radio to disguise the noise.

Session 1: Preliminary interview

Katherine attended this first session with her mother. Confidentiality was briefly discussed and agreed. A brief history of Katherine's problem was obtained, including when the problem began, the course of the problem, any treatment received or ongoing, the current position and related problems. A brief description of the therapy approach was provided, and it was agreed that Katherine would come for five one hour sessions. The General Health Questionnaire (Goldberg & Williams, 1988), and the Eating Disorders Inventory (Garner & Olmsted, 1987) were administered to provide additional information. Katherine was given an ego-strengthening tape and asked to listen to it at least once a day. It was explained that this was to help her relax in order to 'de-stress' her mind and body to counteract anxiety and depression, and to increase her confidence in herself and her ability to control her own destiny.

Session 2: Ego strengthening and self hypnosis for eating

Katherine was asked to share anything that was good about her life over the past week. She described a new job that she had just started.

Katherine was then taught self-hypnosis by Spiegel's eye roll followed by arm levitation (Spiegel & Spiegel, 1978). In hypnosis she was asked to repeat three phrases, *"For my body nourishment is essential,"* "*I need my body to live,"* and "*I owe my body this respect and attention,"* and to repeat this exercise at least ten times a day over the next week.

Katherine was asked to imagine that she had a photograph album on her knee. She was asked to experience 'good' events from her past, and to 'carry' the good feelings into a future experience (goal setting). This also was to be repeated daily.

Session 3: developing alternative coping strategies

As Katherine acknowledged that she used to binge when she was anxious and upset, this session was devoted to helping her 'construct' alternative coping strategies for the management of anxiety. The mirror exercise (see page 160) was used to help Katherine connect with her desired state, and various metaphors for change were used (Graham, 1988).

Katherine was invited to consider alternative ways in which she could 'treat' or nourish herself apart from food. In the context of relaxation she came up with the following: taking a bath, playing her clarinet, making a cup of coffee, buying a magazine and reading it, telephoning a friend, relaxing and watching television. She was asked to imagine herself doing these things and feeling good and positive about doing so. Katherine was asked to write these down, and whenever she felt depressed or anxious to choose one of them instead of eating. She was also asked to continue with the ego-strengthening tape and the exercises.

Considerable emphasis was put on the use of such homework assignments, not only for the intrinsic value of the exercises themselves, but also for building up Katherine's autonomy and mastery of her own life.

Session 4: hypnoanalysis

It was explained that it would be valuable to examine some of the causes of her problem. It was proposed to use a hypnotic technique called ego-state therapy (Karle & Boys, 1987). In this session Katherine used the self-hypnosis technique that she had learnt earlier. In trance she was asked to 'go inside her mind and find that part that thinks thin'. This procedure was carried out using ideodynamic finger responses, and Gestalt techniques, in particular the 'negotiation of parts', were employed to work through various conflicts.

Afterwards Katherine reported that 'the part of her mind that thinks thin' would help her by 'stopping her from being fat'. She said that the 'thin' part had agreed to be active only when she reached a weight of more than seven and a half stones. In other words she could use this 'negative programme' as a resource (or friend) to manage her eating behaviour. It was also established during this session that the negative programme had developed when she was about ten years old and for a number of reasons: family relationships, self-concept and messages about 'thinness' from family, television and advertisements.

Further work was done using ideodynamic finger signalling. This essentially followed the approach described in Rossi & Cheek, (1994) as the 'retrospective approach to ideodynamic signalling', but with the addition of future pacing.

Session 5: anger and assertiveness

It has already been indicated that eating is often precipitated by a difficulty in handling negative emotional states such as anger and anxiety (the latter has already been examined with respect to treatment strategies.) Many bulimic women appear to have difficulty expressing their emotions directly or assertively.

In this session it was explained that anger is a normal and healthy emotion, and that repressing it is unhealthy and can lead to a number of psychosomatic problems, including anorexia and bulimia. Katherine was invited to participate in an exercise which would involve her experiencing any angry feelings she had at the time when her problems commenced. During trance she was asked to participate in a guided imagery sequence which involved the evocation of anger. She was encouraged to ventilate her feelings somatically. Research has demonstrated that a somatic-emotional discharge of feelings is of greater therapeutic benefit than cognitive-emotional catharsis (Hawkins, 1986).

Katherine was then asked whether there was anything in her current life that made her angry. She said that her boss did, although it would be inappropriate to express it. She was encouraged to express her anger towards him using the Gestalt empty chair technique. Afterwards she said that she felt a lot more relaxed and confident.

This session helped Katherine express her anger that had been 'bottled up'. In this way it was hoped that the repressed dynamic underlying her problems could be dissolved, and that she could become more assertive and in control of her current life. It was therefore an ego-strengthening technique as well as one aimed at dynamic resolution.

Session 6: inner guide

In this session Katherine was asked to close her eyes and imagine that she was in her favourite outdoor place. A guided imagery approach was used and she was asked to meet a 'friendly animal' with whom she could share her problems and who could give her advice (Jaffe & Bresler, 1980). Katherine imagined a dog that she had as a pet when she was a child. The dog (whose name was Fudge) advised her to look after herself and to respect her body. Katherine later said that this exercise was the most significant of the treatment sessions.

She was also encouraged to examine aspects of her body image, using the body mirror exercise described in Weiss *et al.* (1985). This concentrates on helping the individual experience themselves more positively. Katherine experienced no problems in doing this.

This was the final contracted session and considerable progress had been made over the three months. Katherine was feeling more positive about herself with respect to her body, her sexuality and her life. She no longer had problems concerning food, relationships had improved, she had menstruated for the first time and she was generally enjoying life. One year later there had been no remission of the symptoms.

Conclusions

The therapeutic style adopted reflects a balance between directive and non-directive approaches, and was clearly patient centred. The non-directive aspect was essentially implicit, in that it was not part of a formally adopted model. Respect, empathy, unconditional positive regard and genuineness were important core conditions of the approach. Katherine was invited to participate in a way which allowed her to assume responsibility for herself.

Obesity

Obesity and overweight are becoming huge problems both in the United States and increasingly in the United Kingdom. Many people know that they should eat healthily and take more exercise but because of perceived time or financial constraints fail to do so. Large numbers of patients ask for help in losing weight, and the media bombards people with 'get thin quick' diets and pills.

Many people suffering from stress and anxiety resort to 'comfort eating', with a preference for sweet foods such as cakes, biscuits, chocolate and junk food rather than healthy options such as vegetables and fruit. This may become a habitual pattern, and the resulting weight gain leads in turn to other health problems such as diabetes and high blood pressure.

Outcomes have been shown to be greatly improved when hypnosis is combined with a cognitive-behavioural therapy (CBT) weight loss programme compared with CBT alone (Kirsch, 1996) in 78% of patients and this actually increased over time. Hypnosis and imagery have been shown to be effective in improving the self regulation of eating behaviour in a study of 80 students (Hutchinson-Phillips *et al.*, 2005). For a more comprehensive look at weight management and the role of hypnosis, see Evans *et al.* (1997).

Hypnosis can help with connecting the patient to their desired goals, but it may be useful to have the patient consider re-directing their goal to the positive one of being healthy rather than to a somewhat negative one of weight loss. Cravings for various foods or for sweet things at various times can be treated with re-framing (see page 442). Occasionally a negative anchor can be used as in the example below.

Paula was somewhat overweight at 12 stone and stated that she could not pass the biscuits, cakes and sweets shelves in the local supermarket without buying a considerable quantity which she would consume later leading to an unpleasant feeling of bloating and sluggishness. One intervention that she found effective was to anchor this uncomfortable feeling to pressing her left finger and thumb together and to fire this anchor when she approached the tempting foodstuffs. This she found helped her not to feel compelled to buy them.

Often, including in the example above, work needs to be done on improving self esteem (see page 162), dealing with past underlying events (see page 123) and goal setting (see page 104). Exploration of the 'meaning' of food to the overweight patient can lead to the discovery and subsequent resolution of imprints, fears and emotional difficulties. Work with the obese patient, in the author's (AW) opinion, needs to be directed to both the present behaviours and the future goals, whilst taking note and helping to resolve past emotional events that may have contributed to the current problem.

There follows a case study courtesy of Dr A Hamill which demonstrates how the presenting problem (overweight) may be resolved by tackling the underpinning emotional difficulties (grief, in this case).

Sheila – a case of overweight

Sheila was a music teacher who attended the author's (AH) practice (who was known to use hypnosis) and asked the nurse if he could help her with weight loss as she had put on three stone since her husband, Paul, had died two years previously.

The author (AH) already knew a lot of her background and her medical and social history, so at the first session hypnosis was explained. It was stressed that she would always be in control, and that this light trance would allow her creative, emotional side to help her at what was a very emotional time.

Sheila was asked to say in her own words how she saw the problem. She immediately stated that 15 months before her husband died (some five months before Paul's diagnosis), her stepson had committed suicide.

Paul had left his first wife and young son to marry her, and although he had kept in touch and supported his first family financially and emotionally, there was always guilt associated with this. The son had never really accepted the situation, which had been made worse when their own child was born. Paul and Sheila had given the stepson lots of support, but he always had issues. Paul had helped him financially with a deposit to run a pub, but this had failed and alcohol became a problem. When his son committed suicide, Paul found him. They had never really discussed all this because, just when things were starting to settle, Paul was diagnosed with cancer and died eight months later.

They had had one big argument six weeks before he had died over pain control when he wanted to downplay it and she felt very guilty about this. She then added that she had not felt a moment of calm or peace since Paul had died, even though her GP had prescribed anti-depressants. She had not continued taking them as she did not like taking pills.

It was suggested that with all this turmoil, grief and emotional storm ongoing it was no wonder she had turned to eating as her comfort; "Exactly" was her reply. She now felt fat and knew her health was at risk, at over 15 stone and five foot two inches tall.

It was decided to firstly assess her hypnotizability, to teach her self-hypnosis and to give her a sense of peace and refuge from the 'storm' in her own special safe place.

The author (AH) uses the 'Is it possible?' technique (Margolin *et al.*, 1992) to introduce the patient to hypnosis and to enable tailoring of any further induction to their answers.

Sheila was then taught a simple self hypnotic exercise and this was repeated (fractionating).

She achieved peace and serenity, and whilst in that state the author (AH) gave her a metaphor about grief, the cycles of time and the seasons, and where Sheila's responsibilities lay with decisions regarding how Paul experienced his last days. The boat metaphor and Aravind's hand technique for grief were then employed (see page 383).

On re-alerting, she reported that this was the first time that she had felt calm since Paul's death. A suggestion was given that she would continue to improve on this feeling each time she practiced her self-hypnosis. This immediate post-hypnotic phase is a great

436

time to make suggestions as it bridges and cements conscious and unconscious communications in place.

On the second session she reported feeling improved and it was decided that we deal with her remaining feelings of guilt. We talked about responsibility: how we all need to be responsible for our own thoughts and feelings, and not to blame others or to accept blame from others.

Sheila then stated that she had felt guilty about being alive when Paul was dead. She now hardly did anything that she and Paul had previously done together as she felt disloyal. This was reframed by suggesting she could keep Paul's memory more alive if she did some of the things they had shared as a celebration of their love and good times together. She really liked that idea!

Having induced hypnosis it was suggested that she had a rucksack on and was walking across to a hot air balloon tethered in a field. She was asked to empty her rucksack, looking at each object as she pulled it out. Each object represented a problem or an unresolved grief or guilt. As she looked at them again in a new light she was to ask herself if she still needed to carry them around all the time or had she learnt all she needed from them. If she had no more need for them, she was to place them in the balloon. If she was not sure or still felt more work was needed on them, she was to put them back in the sack.

When this was accomplished, she was to untie the balloon and watch it soar away; and as it soared away it could take any associated pain with it, far away until it disappeared.

It was then suggested that she continue to walk until she came to a stream. A metaphor was used describing how a stream meets obstacles in its path but uses many ways to get around them, under them or over them! As she walked up the stream she would come to a rock pool which she could bath in, a refreshing pool of new or old resources re-found, re-energized. It was suggested that she might like to incorporate this pool into her special place and find new or different ways of meeting her problems. Before returning to the here and now, she was asked if there were any other issues concerning her now that she needed to look at. Sheila shook her head and said she felt confident and good.

It was then suggested that we could finish now as she already knew all about how to diet. She said she certainly did. She was asked to contact the author (AH) if she needed any more help and to let him know how she was getting on. Ten weeks later the author received a thank you note, saying she still missed Paul but she was getting there, and had lost just over two stone.

Emma – a woman with PCOS (courtesy of Dr Lucy Coffin)

Emma was a 29 year old with no significant past medical history apart from polycystic ovarian syndrome (PCOS). She had been trying to conceive for four years and was obese with a BMI of 30. She also had anovulatory cycles, excess body and facial hair and acne.

Emma reported that she never ate breakfast; she had a late morning snack, lunch, snacks and then supper. She ate a lot of processed foods, caffeine and junk food and usually had ready-meals in the evenings.

A long discussion prior to induction indicated she would like to stop craving these foods and instead wanted to make more healthy choices. We also talked about the benefits of regulating blood sugar levels and raising metabolism by eating regularly, particularly including breakfast. Emma wanted to change the way she saw junk food so that it would lose its appeal. Our treatment plan consisted of using hypnotic relaxation to help induce homeostasis; to help lose weight by changing her eating behaviour and focus for exercise and to use dynamic imagery to assist Emma's body into more regular menstrual cycles and to reduce her symptoms.

Emma was initially very nervous about hypnotherapy and required a lot of reassurance together with in depth explanations of how the process could work. A permissive approach suited her well as she was invited to gently relax and be in control. She established, with guidance, a 'safe place' where she could always return in order to feel comfortable and secure. She also developed a 'waste disposal' system so she could get rid of any unwanted beliefs or baggage she came across.

She wanted to tackle the weight issue first. Emma was asked how she sees the food at the moment and she described how it smelt amazing and tasted great, licking her lips and laughing as she thought the image of eating chocolate and crisps felt so real in imagery. She was then asked how the food is broken down and what benefit it gives to her body. She replied by stating that she likes the taste of it but that was all, as it only caused a build up of fat in her body. We explored what she would gain by losing weight, things she could not do whilst continuing to over-indulge on junk food. She was then asked which was more important to her, the achievement of her goals or the experience of tasting the food. She picked the former.

She was gently facilitated into thinking about how she could detach herself from wanting these foods so badly, and she went on to decide she would like to start to see the food differently. With that she began to talk about how the food breaks down into fat in her body. Emma was asked if she would like to really not fancy the food she had formerly loved, and she expressed a wish to be almost repulsed by it and to crave healthy foods to bring nutrition to her body. We agreed it should be a positive outcome if she had the confidence and self esteem to recognize that she deserved to have the best thing in her body to be as healthy as she could. We also added in the motivation of preparing her body for pregnancy.

She started to see the items of food as lumps of gelatine which she did not want to eat. She imagined various scenarios, including a trip around the supermarket, where she easily saw herself moving past the junk food aisles and opting instead to fill her basket with fresh fruit and vegetables. Emma was asked if she would like to accept a suggestion that she would no longer feel drawn to these junk foods and would automatically think of the gelatine and the negative impact on her body. She readily agreed, and this direct suggestion was given.

Emma also did imagery work on her metabolism which she saw as a slow sausage with the sluggish contents stuck in places. Once empowered, she was able to locate a switch to get it moving and a lever to speed it up. We checked in on this in subsequent sessions, and it was gradually getting faster. Emma had also learnt self hypnosis and was able to check in on this at home too.

The result has been a steady weight loss around one pound per week, and she genuinely does not want to eat junk food and is almost nauseous at the prospect. She is really happy with this and is now creating a new lifestyle of eating regularly and putting nutritious healthy foods into her body which she feels really positive about.

We went on in subsequent sessions to use dynamic imagery to help her body reach homeostasis, and she has found that her menstrual cycles are greatly improved with obvious signs of ovulation.

Thus it can be seen that hypnosis can facilitate treatment with obesity and eating disorders by connecting the patient with their inner resources, helping to resolve underlying emotional difficulties and encouraging them to focus on desired behaviours and goals.

References

American Psychiatric Association. (1994), *Diagnostic and statistical manual of mental disorders*, 4th ed. Washington, DC, American Psychiatric Association.

Bandler, R. (1985), *Using your brain – for a change*. Moab, UT, Real People Press. p 131–52.

Barabasz, M. (1990), Treatment of bulimia with hypnosis involving awareness and control in clients with high dissociative capacity. *International Journal of Psychosomatics*, 37, 53–56.

Barabasz, M. (2007), Efficacy of hypnotherapy in the treatment of eating disorders. *International Journal of Clinical and Experimental Hypnosis*, 55 (3), 318–35.

Bushnell, J. A., Wells, J. E., Hornblow, A. R., Oakley-Browne, M. A. & Joyce, P. (1990), Prevalence of three bulimia syndromes in the general population. *Psychological Medicine*, 20, 671–80.

Coman, G. J. (1992), Hypnosis in the treatment of bulimia: a review of the literature. *Australian Journal of Clinical and Experimental Hypnosis*, 20, 89–104.

Covino, N. A., Jimerson, D. C., Wolfe, B. E., Franko, D. L. & Frankel, F. H. (1994), Hypnotizability, dissociation, and bulimia nervosa. *Journal of Abnormal Psychology*, 103 (3), 455–9.

Degun-Mather, M. (1995), Group therapy and hypnosis for the treatment of bulimia nervosa. *Contemporary Hypnosis*, 12, 69–73.

Evans, B. J., Coman, G. J. & Burrows, G. D. (Eds.) (1997), *Hypnosis for weight management and eating disorders: a clinical handbook*. Victoria, Australian Journal of Clinical and Experimental Hypnosis.

Fairburn, C. & Cooper, P. J. (1982), Self-induced vomiting and bulimia nervosa: an undetected problem. *British Medical Journal*, 284, 1153–5.

Garfinkel, P. E., Lin, E., Goering, P., Spegg, C., Goldbloom, D. S., Kennedy, S. & Al, E. (1995), Bulimia nervosa in a Canadian community sample: prevalence and comparison subgroups. *American Journal of Psychiatry*, 152, 1052–8.

Garfinkel, P. E., Lin, E., Goering, P., Spegg, C., Goldbloom, D., Kennedy, S., Kaplan, A. S. & Woodside, D. B. (1996), Should amenorrhoea be necessary for the diagnosis of anorexia nervosa? *Evidence from a Canadian community sample. British Journal of Psychiatry*, 168 (4), 500–6.

Garner, D. M. & Olmsted, M. P. (1987), *Eating Disorders Inventory*. Berkshire, NFER-Nelson.

Goldberg, D. & Williams, P. (1988), *A user's guide to the General Health Questionnaire*. Berkshire, NFER-Nelson.

Graham, G. (1988), *The happy neurotic*. Newcastle, Real Options Press.

Griffiths, R. (1995a), Hypnobehavioural treatment for bulimia nervosa: a treatment manual. *Australian Journal of Clinical and Experimental Hypnosis*, 21, 25–40.

Griffiths, R. A. (1995b), Two-year follow-up findings of hypnobehavioural treatment for bulimia nervosa. *Australian Journal of Clinical and Experimental Hypnosis*, 23, 135–44.

Griffiths, R. A., Channon-Little, L. & Hadzi-Pavlovic, D. (1995), Hypnotizability and outcome in the treatment of bulimia nervosa. *Contemporary Hypnosis*, 12 (3), 165–72.

Griffiths, R. A., Hadzi-Pavlovic, D. & Channon-Little, L. (1998), The short-term follow-up effects of hypnobehavioural and cognitive behavioural treatment for bulimia nervosa. *European Eating Disorders Review*, 4 (1), 12–31.

Gross, M. (1984), Hypnosis in the therapy of anorexia nervosa. *American Journal of Clinical Hypnosis*, 26 (3), 175–81.

Hawkins, P. J. (1986). *Catharsis and psychotherapy*. Durham, University of Durham.

Hudson, J. I., Hiripi, E., Jr, H. G. P. & Kessler, R. C. (2007), The prevalence and correlates of eating disorders in the National Comorbidity Survey Replication. *Biological Psychiatry*, 61 (3), 348–58.

Hutchinson-Phillips, S., Jamieson, G. A. & Gow, K. (2005), Differing roles of imagination and hypnosis in self regulation of eating behaviour. *Contemporary Hypnosis*, 22 (4), 171–83.

Jaffe, D. T. & Bresler, D. E. (1980), The use of guided imagery as an adjunct to medical diagnosis and treatment. *Journal of Humanistic Psychology*, 20 (4), 45–59.

Johnson, C. L., Stuckey, M., Lewis, L. D. & Schwartz, D. M. (1982), Bulimia: a descriptive study of 316 cases. *International Journal of Eating Disorders*, 2, 3–16.

Karle, H. & Boys, J. H. (1987), *Hypnotherapy*. London, Free Association.

Katzman, M. A. & Wolchik, S. A. (1984), Bulimia and binge eating in college women: a comparison of personality and behavioural characteristics. *Journal of Consulting and Clinical Psychology*, 52, 423–8.

Kendler, K. S., Maclean, C., Neale, M., Kessler, R., Heath, A. & Eaves, L. (1991), The genetic epidemiology of bulimia nervosa. *American Journal of Psychiatry*, 148, 1627–37.

Kirsch, I. (1996) Hypnotic enhancement of cognitive-behavioral weight loss treatments – another meta-reanalysis. *Journal of Consulting and Clinical Psychology*, 64 (3), 517–19.

Kraft, T. & Kraft, D. (2009), The place of hypnosis in psychiatry, part 3: the application to the treatment of eating disorders. *Australian Journal of Clinical and Experimental Hypnosis*, 37 (1), 1–20.

Leon, G. R., Carroll, K., Shrank, B. & Finn, S. (1985), Binge eating and associated habit patterns within college student and identified bulimic populations. *International Journal of Eating Disorders*, 4, 43–7.

Margolin, C., Byrne, B. & Holst-Goltra, P. (1992), The 'is it possible' protocol. Paper presented at the 12th International Congress of Hypnosis, Jerusalem, Israel, July.

Nash, M. R. & Baker, E. L. (1993), Hypnosis in the treatment of anorexia nervosa, in Rhue, J. W., Lynn, S. J.& Kirsch, I. (Eds.) *Handbook of clinical hypnosis*. Washington, DC, American Psychological Association.

O'Brien, K. M. & Vincent, N. K. (2003) Psychiatric comorbidity in anorexia and bulimia nervosa: nature, prevalence, and causal relationships *Clinical Psychology Review*, 23 (1), 57–74.

Pettinati, H. M., Horne, R. L. & Staat, J. M. (1985), Hypnotizability in patients with anorexia nervosa and bulimia. *Archives of General Psychiatry*, 42, 1014–17.

Rossi, E. L. & Cheek, D. B. (1994), *Mind-body therapy; methods of ideodynamic healing in hypnosis.* New York, W. W. Norton.

Spiegel, H. & Spiegel, D. (1978), *Trance and treatment.* Washington, DC, APA Press.

Vanderlinden, J. & Vandereycken, W. (2006), The use of hypnotherapy in the treatment of eating disorders. *International Journal of Eating Disorders*, 7 (5), 673–9.

Walters, E. E. & Kendler, K. S. (1995), Anorexia nervosa and anorexic-like syndromes in a population-based female twin sample. *American Journal of Psychiatry*, 152 (1), 64–71.

Weiss, L., Katzman, M. & Wolchik, M. (1985), *Treating bulimia.* New York, Pergamon Press.

Yapko, M. D. (1986), Hypnotic and strategic interventions in the treatment of anorexia nervosa. *American Journal of Clinical Hypnosis*, 28, 224–32.

29

Habit Disorder and Addiction

Dr David Medd and Dr Ann Williamson

with contributions from Dr Geoff Ibbotson and Mr Duncan Shrewsbury

Habit Disorders

Habit disorders (stereotypic movement disorder in DSM-IV; American Psychiatric Association, 1994) consist of repetitive, non-functional motor behaviours that interfere with normal activities in a relatively benign way or that can result in bodily injury.

Common habits that often arise in childhood include thumb sucking, nail biting, nose picking and breath holding. In many cases these habits are outgrown but may sometimes persist for a variety of reasons into adulthood as a habit disorder. Many may be stress related such as bruxism (teeth grinding), head banging or rocking movements, and increasing anxiety almost invariably causes any habit to increase. Habit disorders may range from relatively benign (nail biting) to causing harm (bruxism or smoking).

Repetitive or habitual behaviours may be associated with an underlying condition, such as a sensory impairment or developmental disorder, an unrecognized medical or neurological condition, the side effect of a medication or a psychiatric disorder. For example, body rocking occurs in most infants, but most commonly persists in children with developmental disabilities or sensory impairments. Certain genetic syndromes are associated with repetitive behaviours (e.g. skin picking in Prader-Willi syndrome, hand flapping and wringing in Rett syndrome and hand flapping in fragile X syndrome).

For the purposes of this chapter, trichotillomania (hair pulling) can be regarded as a habit although its DSM-IV classification is as an impulse control disorder alongside such problems as gambling (see page 449).

The Handbook of Contemporary Clinical Hypnosis: Theory and Practice, First Edition.
Edited by Les Brann, Jacky Owens and Ann Williamson.
© 2012 John Wiley & Sons, Ltd. Published 2015 by John Wiley & Sons, Ltd.

A habit could be defined as a recurrent, usually unconsciously driven behaviour that is reinforced through frequent repetition. As with anything else we do, a habit comprises thought, feeling and behaviour patterns that have 'collapsed down' so that it appears to occur automatically.

Evidence for the use of hypnosis in habit disorders

There is plenty of case study evidence for the use of hypnosis in certain habits such as nail biting (Bornstein *et al.*, 1980; Luca & Holborn, 1984) and impulse disorders such as trichotillomania (Barabasz, 1987). Often cognitive-behavioural approaches are combined with relaxation training (Galski, 1981; O'Connor *et al.*, 2001). Relaxation training can be construed as a form of self hypnosis. Hypnotic interventions may be useful at various stages. Teaching self hypnosis, special place imagery and calmness and confidence anchoring will act to reduce concomitant anxiety. Underlying problems may need to be addressed (Tanaka *et al.*, 2008), and hypnosis can be an effective way of facilitating this, as well as addressing and resolving underlying issues of low self esteem and insecurity (Rowen, 1981).

Sometimes a habit has arisen to give comfort at a time of trauma, and this may be revealed using ideomotor questioning (see page 236) or imagery of the 'reason room' (see page 126) or control centre screen (see page 126). In this situation some form of dissociative imagery such as the time road may be used to obtain resolution of the event by the patient comforting and reassuring their younger self (see page 401).

Anchoring a good feeling, maybe with a clenched fist and giving a post-hypnotic suggestion that such an anchor is activated when the habitual behaviour is triggered, can work well especially when, as in habit reversal, such an action is incompatible with the habit being treated. For example: clenching the fist as soon as the hand approaches the mouth in nail biting or relaxing the jaw as the teeth touch in bruxism.

Other hypnotic interventions may consist of substituting a different response to the trigger that activates the habit; this is often termed a 're-frame'.

Re-framing

The technique of a re-frame is useful for any behavioural response that a person wishes to change. It can also be used for psychosomatic symptoms such as headache or eczema but really comes into its own when dealing with habit disorders or addictions such as smoking, bruxism or nail biting. It consists of five steps or stages and involves a model whereby the mind can be seen to have different 'parts' that can work together to help the patient achieve the outcome they desire.

One important point is to accept that any 'bad' habit has arisen for a reason; that at the time it was the best way the patient's mind and body coped or responded in some situation or context. The habit may have outlived its usefulness but may still be helping the person in some way. This needs to be acknowledged, and alternative ways found of satisfying that need in a more acceptable way.

First ideomotor finger signalling for 'Yes' and 'No' is set up, and permission to work on the specific behaviour (X) that the patient wishes to change is obtained. If a 'No' is obtained at this stage, then this must be respected and obeyed. Any such 'block' may need to be explored and resolved therapeutically. Sometimes it can be suggested that maybe the patient can continue to work at an unconscious level "... *in their dreams without any conscious distress"* so that they will feel able to work to change 'X' in the future.

The part that knows all about 'X' is then thanked for doing its best to help the person because at the time that behaviour 'X' was set up, it achieved something or was the best way of dealing with something, so that it had a positive intention even if now circumstances have changed and 'X' is causing a problem.

The creative part of the mind, *"That part that knows all about new behaviours and new ideas,"* is then asked if it would be willing to help and to give a 'Yes' signal if it would.

The patient is then asked if the part of their mind that knows all about 'X' and the creative part of their mind *"can get together and generate some new ways of responding or some different strategies that would satisfy the need that 'X' does, as well if not better than 'X' and to give a 'yes' finger signal each time that it comes up with one and to give a 'no' finger signal when it has finished."*

It is very important to then check into the future: *"I would like you now to see yourself in the future practicing these new ways of being and responding and to just check whether they are alright for you as a whole person and to give a 'Yes' or 'No' signal accordingly."* If someone has, for example, generated an alternative of drinking a bottle of whisky each day instead of smoking, this would obviously not be good for the whole person and would be rejected at this stage. If a 'No' is obtained, then they need to discard the alternative that is harmful, backtrack, generate some more alternatives and continue.

If the response is affirmative then the patient needs to commit to trying out the alternatives generated. *"Will your unconscious mind undertake to use these alternatives?"* If the response is a 'Yes', then it is fine to congratulate the patient and reorient them. If a 'No' is obtained at this stage, then it is possible to ask if they will try them out some time into the future "... *next week or even sooner."* It may be necessary to ask if it would be possible for the reason for the hesitation to come into conscious awareness so that it can be explored and resolved.

There are many variations on the above but they all involve ideomotor movement of a finger or arm, the appreciation of the reason (conscious or unconscious) why the habit came into being, the generation of alternative ways of responding, a check that these changes are ecologically right for the whole person and the context in which they live and a commitment to implement the changes in behaviour.

It is worth both being aware and also informing the patient that the alternatives generated may often remain at an unconscious level. They "... *might be pleasantly surprised to find that they are doing something in a different way!"*

Metaphor can be usefully employed to guard against feelings of failure if a momentary relapse occurs (compare to the process of learning to walk) or if there is some feeling of 'strangeness' with the new behaviours (compare with first wearing a new pair of shoes).

A case study follows that demonstrates using a re-frame with a woman who bit her nails.

Rose – a woman who bit her nails

Rose at 37 bit her nails and had done so since childhood. She had come from a family where there had been a lot of conflict, but she was holding down a good managerial job and was happily married with two children. She had decided she wanted to stop biting her nails because she was ashamed of how they looked and she felt she could not remonstrate one of her children who had also started the habit if she was continuing to bite her own nails. A couple of sessions were used to work on issues surrounding her childhood, and she was taught self hypnosis together with calmness and confidence anchors. She noticed that she was not biting her nails as much as previously, so on session 3 a re-frame was performed on her nail-biting habit.

Ideomotor finger signalling

Ideomotor finger signalling for 'Yes' and 'No' was set up (see page 236).

Permission

It was confirmed with a 'Yes' finger signal that it was all right (at an unconscious level) for Rose to work on her nail biting. She was then asked to thank *"... that part that knows all about your nail biting for doing its best to help you, because when you started to bite your nails it achieved something or was the best way of dealing with something, so it was trying to help you even if now circumstances have changed and it is causing a problem. Ask inside if it would be willing to work with you and to give a 'Yes' finger signal if it would."*

Generating alternatives

Having received a 'Yes' signal, Rose was asked if the creative part of the mind, *"... that part that knows all about new behaviours, new ideas and new ways of doing things, would be willing to help and to give a 'Yes' signal if it would."* Following a 'Yes' signal, she was asked *"... if it would generate some new ways of responding or some different strategies that would satisfy the need that your nail biting does, as well if not better than your nail biting, and to give a 'Yes' finger signal each time that it comes up with one and a 'No' finger signal when it has finished."* Rose came up with four alternatives.

Ecology check

It was then suggested that *"I would like you to see yourself in the future practicing these new ways of being and responding and to just check whether they are all right for you as a whole person and to give a 'Yes' or 'No' signal accordingly."* Rose responded with a 'Yes' so she was then asked the next question.

Commitment to change

"Will your unconscious mind undertake to try out and use these alternatives now?"

Rose replied with a 'Yes' signal, so it was then suggested that she see herself in the future behaving, thinking and feeling the way she wanted to behave, think and feel, and if it was okay then for her to go into that future her and really experience it. It was further suggested when her unconscious mind had gathered up all that she needed to make this future her reality, she would gradually reorient, feeling calm and pleased with herself.

Two years later Rose no longer bit her nails and reported that she found her self hypnosis very useful to 'recharge her batteries' and her calmness anchor helped whenever she started to feel anxious.

Nervous tics

Many people suffer from transitory nervous tics which may be motor, such as a twitch of an eyelid, or vocal such as continually clearing the throat. Sometimes these problems can become chronic and last for years. These may all be treated as psychosomatic problems and dealt with accordingly (see chapter 18). Tourette's is a more severe form of vocal tic. We will look now at how hypnosis may be used in some other movement disorders.

Movement disorders

The umbrella term 'movement disorders' denotes a large number of neurological conditions marked by involuntary movements. Several have their causes in the basal ganglia, with or without added involvement of the cerebral cortex, and many are aggravated by stressors.

Butler and Duffy (1996) reported that dystonia is socially very visible, as it often affects the head, neck and face. It starts typically in the sixth decade, and affects more women than men. Touching the troubled muscles may trigger spasm, so physiotherapy is problematic. Many patients, however, do receive help from botulinum toxin being injected directly into the offending muscles every 10 to 14 weeks. More than 80% of patients experience partial or total reduction of pain and a similar reduction in muscle spasms. Anxiety about injections interferes physiologically with their success.

Hypnotherapy has been used with a number of different movement disorders with varying degrees of success (Medd, 1999a). Its use by this author (DM) has not been free of complications. In a woman with sleep-onset epilepsy, long controlled by medication, a hypnotic induction was followed by a petit mal seizure. Her epilepsy and dystonia had begun after brain surgery for a stroke. In another case, a patient with generalized dystonia moved once during hypnosis, experiencing a wave of spasms which ascended from the lower abdomen and shocked him badly (Medd, 1999b). Undiscouraged he later amazed himself and hospital staff by using self hypnosis to cope successfully with deep-brain surgery for implanting electrodes to control the disorder. The surgeon's prior description of this operation had left him 'terrified'. Repeated relaxation and the use of an affect bridge (see page 127) to the post-operative state led through self hypnosis to easy preparation and a good recovery.

The hypnotic state alone (Benson, 1989) usually confers several benefits and in that sense may be considered a therapy in its own right. Some generalizations are reported here from work in a movement disorder clinic with variants of chorea, dyskinesia, tics and myoclonus, but predominantly dystonia, followed by a case study of the latter.

In more than 90% of cases, the involuntary movements ceased during hypnosis. Typically a patient might say, *"That's the first time in years that I have managed to be completely still."* In several disorders, movements may be absent for a while after leaving sleep, which may be replicated somewhat by hypnosis (see use of the mini-trance page 311).

During the hypnotic state, most patients reported that the pain also eased. Patients who did not take botulinum injections or who were little helped by them appreciated this relief. Repeated self hypnosis with its systemic relaxation probably allowed some healing of painful tissues, and this reduced pain and movement were highly valuable in social situations.

For patients who avoided people for fear of being stared at, these initial benefits stimulated their desire to practice anxiety management, beginning perhaps with standing on the front doorstep in daylight, and ending up back at work or waiting calmly in the supermarket check-out queue (see mental rehearsal on page 45).

How the patient construes the meaning of the disease may add to the distress and will invite reframing. Frequently the disorder was understood only as caused by, rather than exacerbated by, stress. If there is a genetic factor, anxiety about 'passing it on' to one's children might add guilt. Medical explanations of facts alone are rarely enough to dispel the personal sense of responsibility. This is where hypnosis and use of imagery can be helpful in enhancing emotional understanding and acceptance rather than this merely happening at a cognitive level.

Exploring these attributions and feelings usefully precedes hypnosis work on the movement disorder itself and how the patient views themselves and their symptoms. Reframing these perceptions of 'facts' sometimes radically improved the patient's ability to coexist more constructively with the condition.

Even where botulinum toxin injections achieved their maximum benefit, the patient is not always liberated from future threat. In the hypnotic state with its initial physical relief, the patient can at least use 'safe place' imagery and allow for the logical possibility of feeling slightly differently about tomorrow. During hypnotherapy a frequent use is made of anchoring (see page 145), a desired emotional or physical state to an action cue such as clenching a fist or pressing the finger and thumb together. A good number of dystonia patients when asked what they would like to use as an anchor for relaxation or physical comfort suggested the peace and comfort of the hypnosis session itself.

For some people, whose chief identity is as a successful worker, hypnotherapy has worked if they get back to work. For almost everyone, being able to go shopping is a victory. Similarly, managing the torticollis enough to be 'a bit more normal' enables attendance at a family wedding and other social events without using extra alcohol or tranquillizers. Some patients are very happy to announce that they had visited a town centre in comfort and then spent some time in a coffee shop.

Last, but not least, there are the benefits from decreased use of anti-depressants, benzodiazepines and analgesics, several of which may either cause or aggravate movement disorders.

It is the author's (DM) wish to encourage a greater use of hypnotherapy with modest expectations for the wider group of movement disorder patients, which may implicate as many as one in 500 of the general population. Unusually, therefore, a case has been selected which is statistically most representative rather than one which shows the therapeutic methods in a model presentation.

Case study – Nicola

Nicola was a married woman in her late fifties and still worked full-time. She had left-side spasmodic torticollis with effects down to the shoulder. She noticed the first signs in her early fifties, and fortunately was diagnosed within one year. She saw the author (DM) for six counselling sessions, four including hypnotherapy, at a botulinum treatment clinic where she declined injections.

The torticollis was worst when she was at work performing as a staff trainer, but sometimes in front of senior managers. She was worried also by her financial state and the future of her husband's job, by deadlines at work and by shopping in public. The dystonia was least bothersome for the first 30 minutes after waking, and then while travelling to work.

Regarding the discomfort, she said that life was "... *physically hard going*," her neck and shoulder permanently hurt and, atypically, there was no ease on sleeping, although alcohol did ease it a little. Work, however, also brought a sense of challenge, and seeing trainees make progress was rewarding. At home, she was most peaceful when gardening or in a warm bath. She said of herself, *"I don't relax,"* and in front of a mirror, *"I feel deformed"* (see changing internal dialogue, page 176). She felt her left shoulder was pulled up high. She also had a slight smoker's cough.

In the second session, Nicola declared herself sceptical about relaxation. She agreed to an experiment with only a hypnotic induction, consisting of a sensory focus on her own breathing and on the therapist's voice, with suggestions of peace and quiet, and a shield around her. Once started, she very quickly entered the hypnotic state. After alerting, she produced a short cough and announced, *"I never thought I could do it. I was so relaxed. I felt I was more in control. . . . I felt I didn't have to hold my hand against my head."*

Session 3 included the first agreed hypnosis work. Since the last session, she had been trying to relax and found it very difficult! People at work, however, had said she looked different and her head did not look so bad. She still had limited sleep and energy, however.

The hypnosis plan made with her was built around her feelings of general comfort and safety in the garden. No attention was given to the specific troubled muscle. Regarding the remote superiors at work, a re-framing was suggested that they were *". . . not really interested in you personally, only in the job."* Similarly, when with strangers, people's minds were really on their own affairs and not on her. The closing suggestion was that her current thoughts and feelings of relaxation, comfort and security would stay with her.

At the fourth session, the second with hypnosis, she reported she had been a bit more relaxed and had had some holiday time off work. Now, on a day off, she lived *". . . in low gear."* She was doing more jobs for herself too, and was able to put things off till she had time.

The hypnosis procedure repeated the suggestion for general relaxation, adding the mental image of her superiors being wrapped up in their own thoughts. A post-hypnotic suggestion was given that she could attend to breathing easily and deeply at work, as at the clinic, and be more relaxed.

As the session outcome, she felt that the troubled muscle was more relaxed and was not 'pulling'. It was now *"as if it wanted to go straight."*

At session 5, she reported that the low back ache had returned when at home in the evening. She was all right standing and walking. The employers were seeking volunteers for early redundancy, which triggered conversation about the pleasures of having a job.

During hypnotherapy, a suggestion was made for regular comfort for the lower back when standing, sitting and lying. The author's (DM) single mention of the word 'work' triggered slight coughing. (This could be explored further if appropriate.)

On alerting the head was aligned normally, and the lower back felt warm and free of pain. As Nicola left the room, she pulled the door open without pain in her shoulder or neck, and the head remained straight.

The sixth and last session included hypnotherapy. The lower back was *". . . quite a lot better"* without medication. The ache at night was now rated at about 30% of its previous level. She was now inducing relaxation at night by focusing on her breathing (the post-hypnotic suggestion, or PHS). In giving her Friday 'pep talk' to staff at work, she was fine and relaxed before and during it. Away from work she now felt 100% better. Now, even on leaving work, she felt more relaxed. She was also now able to talk to her husband about how she was feeling, which she had not done in the past.

The hypnotherapy plan repeated work for the lower back. The suggestion embodied the concept that *"the relaxed muscles allow better alignment."* Her successes in self hypnosis were reinforced. To increase her sense of self efficacy, the easy part of 'getting off the world' in visualization was alternated with 'getting back onto the world' calmly and confidently. For work, more suggestion was given about remaining calm and in control when faced with deadlines. A logical notion was given that *"being relaxed helps you to get things done more easily, which conserves your energy and therefore helps you to get more done."*

Because this patient seemed to be so very hypnotizable, a post-hypnotic suggestion was offered and accepted that she would be subconsciously protected against being accidentally hypnotized, and that hypnosis would be reserved for professional therapeutic purposes.

The session left her with head aligned normally and the lower back feeling all right.

Addiction

Substance abuse causes huge individual and social problems and consists mainly of problems around using illicit drugs and alcohol, although of course other substances such as glue may also be implicated. Dependency may then arise which gives rise to another whole set of problems both for the individual and for the society in which they live.

DSM-IV states, 'When an individual persists in use of alcohol or other drugs despite problems related to use of the substance, substance dependence may be diagnosed. Compulsive and repetitive use may result in tolerance to the effect of the drug and withdrawal symptoms when use is reduced or stopped' (American Psychiatric Association, 1994).

Addictions, however, do not always have a physical dependency component, and those such as gambling, trichotillomania (hair pulling) and kleptomania are classified as impulse control disorders.

The key feature of these disorders can be thought of as seeking a small, short term gain at the expense of a large, long term loss. Those with these disorders repeatedly demonstrate failure to resist their behavioral impulsiveness. This runs alongside the physical dependency in substance dependence such as alcoholism.

The addictive cycle

All human behaviours could be seen in terms of movement towards pleasure and away from pain. This is the underlying basis for the addictive cycle.

Immediate gratification in time gives rise to negative consequences which in turn trigger further need for gratification. Gambling gives excitement but then may give rise to money worries, which in turn lead the gambler to try and address this. Not only does the gambler feel that he might win this time, but also gambling changes his focus of attention from his anxieties and difficulties, and he enters a gambling trance where he is no longer thinking anxious thoughts or feeling anxious. A cocaine addict will take drugs to try to feel better, maybe to 'blank out' past trauma or deal with anxieties. After the initial high comes the low, which in itself will tend to trigger further drug use, again in an effort to avoid painful feelings or anxieties.

All addicts, whether they gamble or misuse drugs, will suffer both physically and emotionally because of their behaviour. Their addictive behaviour will eventually impinge on their work, family and friends, and this needs to be taken into account when working with such patients.

Evidence for the use of hypnosis in addictions

Hypnosis can be a very useful adjunct in the treatment of addictions (Katz, 1980; Manganiello, 1984; Potter, 2004), smoking (Ahijevych et al., 2000; Barber, 2001; Carmody et al., 2008) and alcoholism (Wadden & Penrod, 1981).

As with psychosomatic disorders, there are often underlying emotional difficulties that the patient will need to resolve before resolution of the addiction, and ideomotor questioning may facilitate this (see page 236). Patients may suffer from the so-called addictive personality, but it has been amply demonstrated that stress and anxiety (Coman et al., 1998) and past traumatic and emotional difficulties (Raylu & Oei, 2002) underpin much addiction, and this is borne out by clinical experience.

Since negative affective states lead to relapse (Eckhardt & Deffenbacher, 1995; Marlatt & Gordon, 1985), using hypnosis to help resolve anxiety, anger and other negative emotions may be useful in reducing potential triggers to relapse, and if patients can learn to engage calmness and positive emotional states when in high stress situations, they may develop the skills necessary to prevent the vicious cycle back to drug and alcohol abuse (Sarafino, 2001).

Thus work with the person to improve self esteem and resolve emotional difficulties is an important part of working with any addicts, including alcoholics or drug addicts (Pekala et al., 2004), and needs to be done alongside or before work on the addiction itself.

Drug addicts and alcoholics are notoriously famous for being unreliable when it comes to keeping appointments, and a very clear firm contract needs to be arranged where there is agreement on number and frequency of sessions and agreed penalties for non-attendance. There has to be some motivation therefore on behalf of the patient; a family member or institution insisting on treatment will not lead to a successful outcome unless the patient themselves are agreed on the treatment goals and methods (see page 104).

Self hypnosis, ego strengthening, anchoring and goal setting are basic components in the initial stages of treatment, followed by resolution of any underlying problems. These may be extremely complex, and such therapeutic work may take a long time depending on the patient. Alongside working on the psychological components of the addiction, other techniques may be employed such as reframing.

Tom – a case study of a gambler (courtesy of Dr G Ibbotson)

Tom was a 36 year old bank employee who earned a good salary but was courting financial disaster through gambling. If the bank found out about his habit he would be dismissed, and this added even more of 'a buzz' to what was an already risky pursuit. Tom had decided to come for help as his fiancée had given him an ultimatum; either he stopped gambling or she would leave him.

On taking a history Tom described how he had formerly played football with the local team but had given this up to please his fiancée who had felt neglected when he was 'out with the boys'. Although he did not really want to change, he did want to please his fiancée and felt he could stop gambling if he decided to. He was asked to refrain from gambling for ten days before his next appointment and explore how that felt.

Upon questioning about this he said he had managed but had really 'missed it'. Time was spent determining in great detail what exactly it was that he 'missed'. It was the excitement, even if he knew he had little chance of winning it was the 'being on the edge' that he loved. He said that prior to his gambling habit, which was now fruit machines and going to the book makers, he used to have bets on his football games and that this and playing football itself had previously provided the excitement that he craved.

This feeling of excitement was anchored (see page 145), and he was taught self hypnosis and goal setting. Tom's ability to choose and take control while he was in the grip of gambling was discussed. He decided that he would have himself barred from the local book makers and by doing this, he was taking control.

A future age progression was suggested for Tom to imagine how his life would be if he failed to take control and continued to gamble. Tom was then asked to imagine a future that he would prefer and saw himself playing football and feeling really good. We used perceptual positions for Tom to appreciate how his different behaviours 'felt' to his fiancée, and he realized that he needed to negotiate with her to spend time doing the things she enjoyed as well as sometimes taking time for himself to play football.

A mixture of behavioural and hypnotic approaches combined enabled Tom to stop gambling and negotiate a change with his fiancée so that he is now enjoying football on a regular basis but no longer going to the book makers or playing fruit machines.

Sometimes an aversion anchor can be effective, whereby negative feelings (maybe of nausea and a bad hangover) can be linked to a cue (such as a clenched fist) which is fired when the patient has a craving for a drink in much the same way as Antabuse used to be used medically.

More effective, in the author's (AW) view, is the anchoring of the good feeling generated by the drug which can then be accessed harmlessly when needed without the need for the actual substance.

It could be said that by abusing various substances the addict is trying to attain an altered state of consciousness (McPeake *et al.*, 1991) and that by teaching self hypnosis the therapist is showing the addict how to access this without the substance misuse.

Alcoholism

Alcoholism can disrupt and destroy family relationships and someone's professional and personal life. Sufferers are often in denial of the fact either that they have a problem or that the problem is as serious as the consequences would indicate. It is important to avoid taking a judgemental and chastising stance, as this will impede the development of trust and rapport with the individual. Alcoholics can be, roughly, divided into three groups: those who wish to change, those who know that they have a problem but do not (or do not fully) want to change, and those who do not acknowledge that they have a problem. It is important to get the individual to a place where they accept that they are suffering from an affliction that requires help to recover from, and that recovery is necessary and possible. It is important to stress that they are more than their habit, their alcoholic behaviour, and even if they have a so-called addictive personality, they can still be temperate and enjoy life.

Once they have agreed to accept responsibility for and work towards their recovery, they are asked to keep a diary. This diary should contain detailed information pertaining to their intake of alcohol as well as what triggered the perceived need, and what they were feeling before, during and after consumption of the drink. This kind of reflection and subsequent explorative analysis uses principles of cognitive-behavioural therapy, of which there is a large body of evidence and theory. Simple techniques like this are key to establishing how someone maintains their habit and therefore how to help them break the pattern.

Peter – a case of alcoholism, courtesy of Dr D Shrewsbury

Peter was a middle-aged gentleman who was desperate to recover. He acknowledged his condition and genuinely recognized the need to get better. Furthermore, he had strong motivation for recovery. Fortunately, his employers had given him compassionate dispensation to seek treatment on extended sick leave (fortunately, because it is often the case that alcoholics lose their jobs, which can serve as either a stimulus to seek help or the start of a slippery slope into deterioration).

Peter's father, who had also been an alcoholic, had been rather abusive towards him as a child and his mother. Peter had some anger management issues, and his mother had chastised him for "... *behaving exactly like your father*" towards his own wife and children. This, combined with tensions and disquiet within his immediate family, led him to attempt a concerted effort at recovery.

A process of guided imagery was used within his 'safe place' to run through a movie of what happened both externally and within himself when something happened to trigger the habit. This in itself allowed him to realize what contributed to this harmful behaviour. After this the Swish technique (Bandler, 1985) was adapted, whereby the image of the desirable response would overlay (and eventually overcome) the image of the present triggers and responses (see pages 138, 453). Peter had a strong preference to the auditory modality, so the experience was enriched with sensory information by instructing Peter to remember the sounds associated with what he wanted to change and replace them with sounds he could associate with the sense of achievement and conquering (it was, ironically, his father's voice cheering him on).

This technique, alone, would be insufficient to overcome a deep-seated and long-standing addiction. Teaching self hypnosis and providing patients with a recorded guide for further self directed sessions is very important. With Peter, as his preference was for the auditory modality, a recording was provided; but he was also given a script so that he could make his own recording. This process can be used to reinforce and 'top-up' post-hypnotic suggestions. Such suggestions play a highly significant role in empowering these individuals in their recovery, and should be specifically tailored to the triggers, the sensory modality preferred by them and their goals.

Smoking cessation

With smoking cessation one has three factors to deal with; the physical addiction, the habit and the psychological factors are all important. This is why hypnosis alone (using aversion therapy and goal setting or affirmation) is often not very effective for smoking cessation but when combined with behavioural approaches can be most successful. Some people do respond dramatically, but equally some people just decide to stop smoking and do so with no intervention at all. More often a more graded approach is needed.

Often it may be necessary to bring the habit into conscious awareness so that using the 'wrong' hand to smoke and using various behavioural ploys such as placing cigarettes and a lighter somewhere where a little effort is required to go and fetch them can be useful. There are many ways that the patient can disrupt the habit and make it more difficult (Williamson & Ibbotson, 1998).

Cutting down the physical addiction can be done (once the patient has reduced generally to about 20 cigarettes a day) by suggesting that they smoke less of each cigarette and gradually reduce the amount smoked until they are only taking two or three puffs before discarding it. This also helps motivation as it is such an obvious waste and the psychological need is satisfied by lighting up and the first few puffs. Often using nicotine replacement may give rise to addiction (for instance an addiction to the nicotine chewing gum), and as the patient has often not been taught tools to help themselves with day to day anxieties and insecurities the relapse rate may be high.

Once the patient is ready to declare the day that they are going to become a non-smoker, the author (AW) makes them two appointments. During the first appointment any positive aspects of smoking are acknowledged and explored together with the pattern and links between the smoking behaviour and the patient's day to day activities so as to determine what scenarios pose most risk of relapse. It is also useful to suggest that the patient disrupts the patterns around smoking, sitting in a different chair, washing up immediately after a meal when in the past they would have had a cigarette and so on. Any method of connecting the patient strongly to their desired goal may be used to enhance motivation.

Self hypnosis and anchoring are taught, as is an adaptation of the mirror exercise to enhance motivation and act as a goal set *"Imagine behind you a full length mirror with an image of you as a smoker, with several cigarettes sticking out of your mouth, coughing and wheezing, and smelling like a stale ashtray. then imagine in front of you a mirror with an image of you as you would like to be, breathing easily, feeling healthy, smelling fresh and saying to someone* (maybe with a tiny bit of pleased smugness) *'No, I don't smoke any more!'"* As they step forward (one hopes) into the image in front with a feeling of triumph, they can say to themselves something along the lines of *"I'm really pleased that I can do this."*

At the second session, from which they emerge as a non-smoker, a re-frame is done (see page 442) to generate any alternative responses needed, followed by the use of ideomotor response. This latter is used to accentuate the decision already taken to be a non-smoker. On one hand they are asked to 'image' their conscious mind and its desire to be a non-smoker, and on the other their unconscious mind and its previous desire to smoke. One then talks about how when the conscious and unconscious parts of our mind are working together we feel really good (such as athletes being in the zone), and in these cases we are unstoppable and able to achieve our goals. As their unconscious mind has already agreed to alternative ways of satisfying the need that smoking formerly did, they can allow communication between these different parts of their mind so that as their hands move together 'all by themselves' any remaining hesitations can be resolved, and when their hands touch they can feel the power of the decision to be a non-smoker, that all parts of them have agreed and are working for, as they step into an image of themselves the way they want to be.

Mental rehearsal of the scenarios that the patient has already identified as being the most difficult such as when offered a cigarette when drinking in the pub or immediately after eating dinner can be enacted in hypnosis utilizing the patient's desired response. It can also be suggested that if the patient does find they start to crave a cigarette, then they should physically move and then sit and do the mirror exercise as described above to reinforce their motivation and the suggestion given that by doing this the desire to smoke will disappear.

Another useful suggestion to give is that they *"might be surprised to find how good and easy it is to be a non-smoker and that the longer the time it is from that last cigarette the easier it is for you to remain a non-smoker. You will become so deeply interested in whatever you are doing and whoever you are with* (from Hartland's ego strengthening) *that it will hardly cross your mind and if it does it will be only to give you a feeling of great satisfaction that you are now a non-smoker."*

Thus it can be seen that hypnosis can be used generally with addictive problems to ego strengthen and enhance motivation. Anchoring may be helpful both to access positive affect and to help interrupt the addictive cycle. Hypnosis may also facilitate resolution of underlying problems that drive the addictive behaviour. In any habitual behaviour hypnosis may be effectively used to interrupt the pattern and to facilitate the generation and implementation of alternative behaviours.

References

Ahijevych, K., Yerardi, R. & Nedilsky, N. (2000), Descriptive outcomes of the American Lung Association of Ohio Hypnotherapy Smoking Cessation Program. *International Journal of Clinical and Experimental Hypnosis*, 48 (4), 374–87.

American Psychiatric Association. (1994), *Diagnostic and statistical manual of mental disorders*, 4th ed. Washington, DC, American Psychiatric Association.

Bandler, R. (1985), *Using your brain – for a change*. Moab, UT, Real People Press. pp. 131–52.

Barabasz, M. (1987), Trichotillomania: a new treatment. *International Journal of Clinical and Experimental Hypnosis*, 35, 146–54.

Barber, J. (2001), Freedom from smoking: integrating hypnotic methods and rapid smoking to facilitate smoking cessation. *International Journal of Clinical and Experimental Hypnosis*, 49 (3), 257–66.

Benson, H. (1989), Hypnosis and the relaxation response. *Gastroenterology*, 96, 1609–11.

Bornstein, P. H., Rychtarik, R. G., Mcfall, M. E., Winegardner, J., Winnett, L. R. & Paris, D. A. (1980), Hypnobehavioral treatment of chronic nailbiting: a multiple baseline analysis. *International Journal of Clinical and Experimental Hypnosis*, 28 (3), 208–17.

Butler, A. G. & Duffey, P. O. F. (1996), The epidemiological survey of dystonia in the North-East of England. *European Journal of Neurology*, 3, 28.

Carmody, T. P., Duncan, C., Simon, J. A., Solkowitz, S., Huggins, J., Lee, S. & Delucchi, K. (2008), Hypnosis for smoking cessation: a randomized trial. *Nicotine & Tobacco Research*, 10 (5), 811–18.

Coman, G. J., Burrows, G. D. & Evans, B. J. (1998), Stress and anxiety as factors in the onset of problem gambling: implications for treatment. *Stress and Health*, 13 (4), 235–44.

Eckhardt, C. & Deffenbacher, J. (1995), Diagnosis of anger disorders, in Kassinove, H. (Ed.) *Anger disorders: definition, diagnosis, and treatment*. Washington, DC, Taylor & Francis.

Galski, T. J. (1981), The adjunctive use of hypnosis in the treatment of trichotillomania: a case report. *American Journal of Clinical Hypnosis*, 23, 198–201.

Katz, N. W. (1980), Hypnosis and the addictions: a critical review. *Addictive Behaviors*, 5 (1), 41–7.

Luca, R. V. D. & Holborn, S. W. (1984), A comparison of relaxation training and competing response training to eliminate hair pulling and nail biting. *Journal of Behavior Therapy & Experimental Psychiatry*, 15 (1), 67–70.

Manganiello, A. J. (1984), A comparative study of hypnotherapy and psychotherapy in the treatment of methadone addicts. *American Journal of Clinical Hypnosis*, 26 (4), 273–9.

Marlatt, G. A. & Gordon, J. R. (Eds.) (1985), *Relapse prevention: maintenance strategies in the treatment of addictive behaviors*. New York, Guilford Press.

McPeake, J. D., Kennedy, B. P. & Gordon, S. M. (1991), Altered states of consciousness therapy: a missing component in alcohol and drug rehabilitation treatment. *Journal of Substance Abuse Treatment*, 8 (1–2), 75–82.

Medd, D. (1999a), Hypnosis with selected movement disorders. *Contemporary Hypnosis*, 16 (2), 81–6.

Medd, D. (1999b), A single-case study of generalised dystonia and hypnosis, with unexpected immobility and an untoward effect. *Contemporary Hypnosis*, 16 (1), 45–8.

O'Connor, K. P., Brault, M., Robillard, S., Loiselle, J., Borgeat, F. & Stip, E. (2001), Evaluation of a cognitive-behavioural program for the management of chronic tic and habit disorders. *Behaviour Research & Therapy*, 39 (6), 667–81.

Pekala, R. J., Maurer, R., Kumar, V. K., Elliott, N. C., Masten, E., Moon, E. & Salinger, M. (2004), Self-hypnosis relapse prevention training with chronic drug/alcohol users: effects on self-esteem, affect, and relapse. *American Journal of Clinical Hypnosis*, 46 (4), 281–97.

Potter, G. (2004), Intensive therapy: utilizing hypnosis in the treatment of substance abuse disorders. *American Journal of Clinical Hypnosis*, 47 (1), 21–8.

Raylu, N. & Oei, T. P. S. (2002), Pathological gambling: a comprehensive review. *Clinical Psychology Review*, 22 (7), 1009–61.

Rowen, R. (1981), Hypnotic age regression in the treatment of a self-destructive habit: trichotillomania. *American Journal of Clinical Hypnosis*, 23, 195–7.

Sarafino, E. P. (2001), *Behavior modification: principles of behavior change*. Mountain View, CA, Mayfield.

Tanaka, O. M., Vitral, R. W., Tanaka, G. Y., Guerrero, A. P. & Camargo, E. S. (2008), Nailbiting, or onychophagia: a special habit. *American Journal of Orthodontics & Dentofacial Orthopedics*, 134 (2), 305–8.

Wadden, T. A. & Penrod, J. H. (1981), Hypnosis in the treatment of alcoholism: a review and appraisal. *American Journal of Clinical Hypnosis*, 24 (1), 41–7.

Williamson, A. & Ibbotson, G. (1998), *Smoke free – no buts*. London, Crown House.

30

Obsessive Compulsive Disorder

Mrs Phyllis Alden and Dr Ann Williamson

Introduction

As the name suggests, obsessive thoughts and/or compulsive behaviours are the two main components of obsessive compulsive disorder (OCD). Intrusive obsessional thoughts generate extreme anxiety which the patient then attempts to reduce by some repetitive behaviour. These behaviours may include repetitive hand-washing, repeated checking that taps and switches have been turned off, opening and closing doors before passing through or walking backwards and forwards taking certain numbers of steps at a time. There is often an irrational belief that if these behaviours are not completed, then something terrible will happen. There may be an excessive focus or avoidance of certain numbers, and sometimes the patient may have intrusive thoughts that they might do something awful such as harm their child. These thoughts and behaviours obviously cause severe emotional distress and are often very disruptive of normal life both at work and at home.

OCD sufferers generally recognize their intrusive thoughts and obsessive behaviour as irrational, and they may become further distressed by this realization. It may be useful to talk about OCD being on a continuum from complete unconcern, through over-conscientiousness to mild, and then more severe OCD. Many people have mildly obsessive traits and ritual behaviours such as having to straighten pictures hung crookedly or always having to do things in a certain order but the anxiety generated if they are prevented from carrying out the behaviour is less extreme and is more manageable. Many sufferers from OCD are also perfectionists (Frost & Steketee, 1997).

The Handbook of Contemporary Clinical Hypnosis: Theory and Practice, First Edition.
Edited by Les Brann, Jacky Owens and Ann Williamson.
© 2012 John Wiley & Sons, Ltd. Published 2015 by John Wiley & Sons, Ltd.

OCD is the fourth most common mental disorder in the United States; a household survey of more than 30,000 people estimated that the lifetime prevalence rate for OCD was around 2–3% (Karno *et al.*, 1988) with similar prevalence in five other countries (Canada, Germany, Korea, New Zealand and Puerto Rico) (Weissman *et al.*, 1994). Some literatures report an equal sex distribution of OCD (Rasmussen & Eisen, 1990).

Comorbidity with other psychiatric disorders such as panic disorder, social phobia, eating disorders and Tourette's is common, with a lifetime history of major depression present in two thirds of OCD patients (Rasmussen & Eisen, 1994).

The main treatment approaches have been behavioural, such as response prevention, or cognitive-behavioural therapy (CBT) which adds the exploration of thoughts and beliefs and the techniques of challenging them. Common cognitive distortions include equating thinking with action, thinking that they have the power to either prevent or create catastrophes happening and often feeling over-responsibility for the well being of others.

More recently there has been research looking at the 'narratives' that sufferers create around their obsessions; creating a scenario whereby totally unrelated events can become linked as a rationale for the obsession. For example, a pregnant woman noticed a condom lying in the gutter and made a link between that condom and her pregnancy, that in some way semen on that condom had somehow impregnated her, and she developed an obsessional ritual.

Use of Hypnosis

Flooding and response prevention have been used with hypnosis (Scrignar, 1981), but hypnosis has not generally been considered a useful medium for the treatment of OCD because OCD has seemed to be associated with low hypnotizability (Hoogduin, 1988). This may be because the older more traditional approaches were more authoritarian and less flexible than in recent years. It is important that the patient begins to understand that they are capable of more than being just their problem, that they have within resources and strengths that they can draw upon, that they have achieved things despite their difficulties and that they did not always have OCD or that there have been times when their OCD was less troublesome. Exploring these times and discovering what was happening to the patient when their OCD developed may be productive. Hypnosis can provide a useful tool to connect patients with their inner resources.

As in so much psychological disturbance, there is a tendency to take on the label at identity level whereas if the patient understands that it is something they do (patterns of both thought and behaviour) for some underlying reason, then it can give them hope that they can change. Also most sufferers from OCD realize that their intrusive thoughts and obsessional behaviours are worse when they are stressed and anxious, so hypnotic techniques can at least help reduce their base line of anxiety.

Another reason that hypnosis has previously not been thought to be successful is that patients with OCD may not display autonomic arousal as the condition is mainly cognitively based (Eysenck, 1997) and so 'relaxation based' inductions may not be appropriate.

However, hypnosis can be effective in cases where one has a well-motivated patient who has the capacity to engage in hypnosis and when it is used in conjunction with behavioural and cognitive-behavioural approaches.

Pattern Interrupts

One author (AW) has found pattern interrupts a useful tool to begin to 'loosen up' the behaviours in OCD. The patient is asked to change one pattern a day that is unrelated to their OCD behaviours. This may be how they brush their teeth, the order in which they get dressed, or which seat they sit in, but it should be done light-heartedly and for fun.

Response Prevention

When using response prevention sometimes a hierarchy is more appropriate, starting with the least anxiety-provoking behaviour if the patient has several. It is important that the patient stays with the feeling of anxiety, generated by not performing the behaviour, until it subsides.

A 20 year old university student had developed moderate OCD which centred on rituals around bedtime. She had to check the alignment of every object in her bedroom several times, which could result in at least one extra hour of activity before she could go to sleep. Her belief was that if she did not do all this, something would happen to her boyfriend. The behaviours were not present at other times. She used response prevention to reduce her checking, learning that her anxiety would subside. Once it had reduced she used self-hypnosis as a consolidation technique but she did not initially use it to reduce anxiety, as part of the therapy was for her to learn that she could challenge her behaviour and that the anxiety thus triggered would reduce on its own.

For the same reason it is important that the patient confronts their thoughts rather than avoiding them or using thought stopping. Self hypnosis and calmness anchoring can then be useful as the patient builds up their confidence in doing things differently. Sometimes it is more useful to delay rather than prohibit the behaviour as in the case example below.

Helen was an obsessive cleaner and some days spent hours cleaning her skirting boards with a toothbrush. One intervention was for Helen to go and make herself a cup of tea when she knew she had an irrational urge to clean. Once she had done this, she would allow herself to do some cleaning if she still wanted to. Her cleaning certainly decreased with this intervention, although other therapeutic work was also done.

Intrusive thoughts can be dealt with in much the same way as negative internal dialogue; so that rather than stopping the thought, it is changed in some way. This may be by a change of voice tone, or singing the thought out loud so that it sounds ridiculous and generates laughter rather than anxiety. Writing down the thought and changing one word can also disrupt it. Often there is some past event or imprint that needs resolution before the irrational belief accompanying the intrusive thought can be changed.

Response prevention does not always work, and sometimes other techniques such as re-framing or hypnotic dreaming are more successful.

Re-framing and hypnotic dreaming

An obsessional house cleaner

An obsessional house cleaner could not identify any rationale for her behaviour, except that she worried if she did not constantly clean. Her anxiety would become intolerable if she tried to leave things such as the ironing while she watched a favourite TV programme. She described how she could see the basket of ironing becoming 'bigger and bigger' or a room becoming increasingly dirty by the minute. Response prevention (not cleaning her children's bedroom for a day) resulted in panic attacks and night and unbearable stress.

She was happy for hypnosis to be used and the approach taken was a classical re-frame (see page 442). During the 'ecological' check, a 'part' was unsure about using 'new behaviours' but agreed to a week's trial. A week later, the patient reported an immediate improvement in her anxiety level and she had been much less obsessional; again, a 'part' was unsure but agreed to another week.

At the next session, further improvement was reported, but once again, the 'part' was unsure but willing to continue and also agreed that a solution would be acceptable. It was suggested that she would have 'a dream' during the next week which would resolve the problem.

When she returned she reported that she had indeed had a dream in which she had returned to find her house absolutely filthy. There was dust and muck everywhere, inch high mug rings on the table, rubbish everywhere. She reported that she 'came to' in her lounge beating at an armchair. At that point she heard a 'little voice' in her head saying, *"You silly cow. Your house is perfectly clean. You don't need to clean like you used to anymore."* On checking, all parts were 'happy' with her resolution and on follow up several months later she was still symptom free. Interestingly, she never did identify what had triggered and maintained the problem.

A hypnotic check

A 47 year old woman had a long history of OCD and was finding that she was avoiding going out and socializing as it took her so long to continually go back and check that light switches and appliances were switched off. She also had problems with this when going to bed at night. It was suggested to her that the problem was that she could not confirm to herself whether she had turned things off, in the way that someone without OCD did, and that she could use her self hypnotic skills to allow herself to go back in time and see that she had. She put a chair by her front door and when she was going out she would sit down and go into self hypnosis to see herself turning off the appliances and lights. This worked well and, following work on past issues that underpinned her OCD, she was eventually able to go out or go to bed without a problem.

It is often found that the OCD developed at a traumatic time in the patient's life, and here hypnosis is clearly appropriate.

A man with a history of OCD

A 64 year old man with a 44 year history of OCD, which consisted of obsessional checking of doors, taps, gas and electrical appliances, requested treatment. He also engaged in various bathroom rituals such as having to wash in a certain sequence or he would have to repeat the process. He stated that the degree of severity varied with stress. His first marriage had been destroyed by it; he used to switch off the gas and electricity when he went to work, leaving his wife without heat or power.

He identified his anxiety as a 'need to keep everyone safe' and a sense that it was his responsibility to do this. He dated this back to a very traumatic childhood. He explained that his mother had been extremely violent, describing how on one occasion, when he was aged nine, she had held his father's head down on the dining room table and threatened to behead him with the carving knife. He had wanted to protect his father but had felt terrified, helpless and powerless and that he had 'failed' to protect. He also reported that he suffered recurring nightmares in which he was driving a car very fast on a steep winding road and that he would lose control of the car and wake just before it crashed.

He was keen for hypnosis to be used and was highly responsive. Hypnosis was used to explore the dream with dream re-enactment, allowing him to change the dream by taking control of the car and driving it fast and skilfully on the twisting road. He reported finding this extremely powerful and noted after this a substantial reduction of anxiety and checking.

However, there remained the issue of 'responsibility' and his distressing memories of childhood. One of his other memories was of being in the car, again aged about nine. His parents were in the front, his mother was driving and they were arguing which made her driving extremely erratic, again terrifying him as he believed they were going to crash.

Given that his recurring dream had been of driving and the car going out of control, he was asked to 'dream' of being back in his parent's car, aged nine, seated in the backseat while he watched helpless and terrified as his parents argued. Then he was invited to take his 'adult self' into the car to sit beside him and tell him the following. *"It's okay, I'm from the future, and I'm you grown up. The car isn't going to crash; you're going to be fine. And I have to tell you something important. You can't drive your parents' car. You can't do that. It isn't your job. They have to sort this out themselves and you really can't take on that job. You are just a little boy and you can't drive your parents' car from the backseat. And you don't have to do that anymore."* He then 'comforted' his younger self acknowledging how awful this was for a little boy who should not have had to go through all this.

Following this, he was able to 'let go' of the checking. Follow up several months later showed no recurrence of symptoms.

All these cases demonstrate that hypnosis can be employed as part of the treatment of OCD. However, as can been seen from the range of approaches, the approach must be tailored to the patient. From the authors' experience, hypnosis is not suitable for all patients, nor has either author used it with any cases where the severity of the condition had resulted in an inability to function such as go to work, interact socially or engage generally in the activities of daily living.

References

Eysenck, M. W. (1997), *Anxiety and cognition: a unified theory*. Hove, Psychology Press.

Frost, R. O. & Steketee, G. (1997), Perfectionism in obsessive-compulsive disorder patients. *Behaviour Research and Therapy*, 35, (4) 291–6.

Hoogduin, K. (1988), Hypnotisability in obsessive compulsives. *Hypnos: Swedish Journal for Hypnosis in Psychotherapy and Psychosomatic Disorders*, 15, 15–19.

Karno, M., Golding, J. M., Sorenson, S. B. & Burnam, M. A. (1988), The epidemiology of obsessive-compulsive disorder in five US communities. *Archives of General Psychiatry*, 45, 1094–9.

Rasmussen, S. A. & Eisen, J. L. (1990), Epidemiology of obsessive compulsive disorder. *Journal of Clinical Psychiatry*, 51 (Suppl. 2), 10–14.

Rasmussen, S. A. & Eisen, J. L. (1994), The epidemiology and differential diagnosis of obsessive compulsive disorder. *Journal of Clinical Psychiatry*, 55 (Suppl.) 5–10.

Scrignar, C. B. (1981), Rapid treatment of contamination phobia with hand-washing compulsion by flooding with hypnosis. *American Journal of Clinical Hypnosis*, 23 (4), 252–7.

Weissman, M. M., Bland, R. C., Canino, G. J., Greenwald, S., Hwu, H. G., Lee, C. K., Newman, S. C., Oakley-Browne, M. A., Rubio-Stipec, M., Wickramaratne, P. J., Wittchen, H. U. & Yeh, E. K. (1994), The cross national epidemiology of obsessive compulsive disorder: the Cross National Collaborative Group. *Journal of Clinical Psychiatry*, 55 (Suppl. 3), 5–10.

31

Obstetrics

Mrs Diana Tibble and Dr Les Brann

Introduction

Women require a high standard of care throughout pregnancy; it is a unique situation where the wellbeing of two lives is at stake, and consequently training in midwifery and obstetrics is closely regulated. Warnings have been given throughout this book insisting that therapists work only within their area of competence, and using hypnosis in pregnancy should not be carried out by anyone who is not, first and foremost, qualified to look after the pregnant woman. The explosion of unqualified hypnotists offering to prepare women for childbirth is frightening and is to be deprecated. For those suitably qualified, however, it is a real privilege to work with pregnant women and their partners.

There are only a few maternity units where hypnosis is routinely provided, so most women have to specifically seek it out. Alexander *et al.* (2009) reported a variety of reasons for women opting for hypnosis to enhance their birth experience. Many are either frightened of hospitals or of the actual birth itself, and these anxieties are often as a result of myths that surround their families' experience or they are particularly susceptible to media coverage of birth. For some, they seek hypnosis as they found a previous birth to have been a traumatic experience. Regardless of the underlying reason for requesting hypnosis, they are positive about the belief that hypnosis will enhance their pregnancy and birth experience and, therefore, compliant with attendance and practice. This optimistic belief that hypnosis will indeed enhance their birthing experience is magnified by sharing with them research evidence of a better outcome and illustrating this with case histories.

The Handbook of Contemporary Clinical Hypnosis: Theory and Practice, First Edition.
Edited by Les Brann, Jacky Owens and Ann Williamson.
© 2012 John Wiley & Sons, Ltd. Published 2015 by John Wiley & Sons, Ltd.

Support (and referrals) from the maternity unit staff who are now recognizing the benefits of hypnosis also acts as further encouragement.

Hypnotizability is considered to be a stable trait, yet there is mounting evidence that hypnotizability increases during pregnancy. Tibia (1990), in a study of 180 pregnant women, found that the average hypnotizability score on the Harvard scale was 8.12 compared with 5.15 for the population average. This was also confirmed using the Creative Imagination Scale (CIS) obtaining scores of 25.0 and 20.7 for pregnant and non-pregnant women respectively. Scores also increased from the second to the third trimester (23 vs. 27). Alexander *et al.* (2009) studied the CIS scores on a group of 37 women during and after pregnancy. Scores were significantly ($p = 0.001$) higher during pregnancy (23.5 vs. 18.7). This is useful in that it will allow a greater proportion of women to benefit from hypnotic phenomena than would otherwise be the case. Pain relief, time distortion and dissociation (from contractions) are examples. This concurs with the finding of Cogan and Spinnato (1986), who showed a significant increase in pain threshold in late pregnancy and labour.

Hypnosis can be applied to all stages of pregnancy, and the rest of the chapter will work through the potential problems encountered during a typical pregnancy.

Nausea and Vomiting

Nausea and vomiting affect approximately 80% of pregnancies commencing as early as five weeks gestation, and for the vast majority is resolved by 12 weeks. Hormone changes and fluctuations in blood sugar seem to trigger the nausea and vomiting; for the vast majority, the symptoms are mild and adopting a 'little and often' diet is effective, and most do not require any specific treatment.

For a minority the symptoms become serious and develop into hyperemesis gravidarum (HG) which is characterized by severe vomiting, weight loss, acidosis and dehydration. These severe cases occur in about 2:1,000 pregnancies and require hospitalization, anti-emetics and intravenous fluids. Symptoms are so severe in some cases that termination of pregnancy is required. Evidence for the use of hypnosis in the treatment of HG is mainly in the form of case reports, but Fuchs (1983) presented a series of 138 women, all of whom improved (see also Cyna *et al.*, 2004a; Simon & Schwartz, 1999).

Hypnotic techniques for nausea and vomiting are focused on deep relaxation and optimism for a normal healthy pregnancy. Cyna *et al.* (2004a) advise the inclusion of the following:

- Honouring the body's adjustment to the magnificence of pregnancy
- Ego-strengthening suggestions
- Deepening to a deeply relaxed state and using the mother's imagery to warm and protect her stomach, belly and uterus
- Locating and adjusting the nausea dimmer switch within her
- Locating and adjusting the part of her mind that controls appetite and digestion

- Special place
- Knowing that the baby is growing despite altered diet
- The baby and mother looking forward to getting to know each other during pregnancy and meeting in approximately six months or how long it is to term

A useful post-hypnotic suggestion is:

At the first feelings of nausea, you will take three, automatic deep breaths . . . you will become deeply relaxed producing a feeling of optimism and become responsive to your physical and emotional needs and your appetite.

This encourages the first feelings of nausea to act as a cue (anchor) to a more positive state.

Torem (1994) reported four different hypnotic techniques for use in this area which suggests that the actual technique is not critical. Hartland (1984) counsels against simple symptom removal and reports that up to 50% of cases require some uncovering technique to locate the source of the problem. The pregnant women's feelings and belief about her pregnancy, whether planned and wanted, and existing psychological problems may need exploration.

A woman with hyperemesis gravidarum

A multiparous woman's previous two pregnancies were uneventful. Hyperemesis gravidarum was diagnosed at nine weeks gestation, after three weeks of vomiting between six and eight times a day, which had resulted in weight loss and dehydration. She had already been hospitalized twice prior to her appointment for hypnosis. During the consultation she became very tearful reporting that her mother had just been diagnosed with breast cancer. Her fear was naturally for her mother's wellbeing but with two young children, the pregnancy and subsequent newborn baby she was worried that she would be unable to give her mother the support that she might need. Her husband was self employed and very hardworking, and she was reluctant to lean too heavily on him. She was also reluctant to share her fears with him as she knew he would reassure her that he would mind the children whilst she cared for her mother if necessary. She was horrified that she was secretly wishing that she would miscarry. At this first appointment hypnosis was discussed, myths dispelled and a personalized 'special place' was created. After induction (breathing focus) and deepening by direct suggestion to relax, she was asked to imagine a very grand wooden lift that would take her down ten floors, one for each count. The lift opened out onto her special place, which was a glorious beach on a blustery spring day.

It was suggested that, following hypnosis, she would know when she would be able to share her concerns with her husband and she would do so with ease: "*. . .and I don't know whether you will want to share your worries with your husband soon . . . or in* *a short while but you will know when it feels right.*" A further suggestion was given that the feeling of the fresh sea air of the blustery beach would wash over her at the first hint of nausea, enabling her to relax and feel an easy sense of comfort, so that her body relaxed automatically. The hypnosis session was recorded, and she listened to it at home.

At follow up a week later, she reported that she and her husband had discussed the practicalities of having to care for her mother and the children. Her husband was wholly supportive and prepared to share as much of the care as required. This discussion took place the evening after the first session. She vomited in the morning for two more days, then her husband suggested that she listened to the tape whilst he got breakfast ready. Thereafter, she had no more vomiting and the only time she had any significant nausea was when she was tired in the evenings.

The hypnosis was instrumental in enabling her to resolve her anxieties and also provided the relaxation and nausea control to settle her symptoms.

A further session of hypnosis addressed her fears that she may have damaged the baby During this session she allowed herself to feel excited about the arrival of a third child which she felt would complete her family. We noted that the pregnancy would be a wonderful distraction for her mother and a reason to be positive with the treatment that she would undergo!

Not all women want to get rid of the nausea as it is a positive sign of a continuing pregnancy. This is sometimes seen after a period of infertility where the woman is so overjoyed by the pregnancy that the symptoms just reinforce that happy state. Providing the baby is growing well, treatment is aimed at minimizing the symptoms but still enough to give reassurance. Vomiting usually stops the moment foetal movements are felt!

The Anxious or Unhappy Mother

It is important in early pregnancy to identify factors which may lead to complications later in pregnancy. Anxiety and depression and other psychosocial factors including previous miscarriage, termination of pregnancy, single motherhood and low Body Mass Index have been implicated (Hedegaard *et al.*, 1996; Lobel *et al.*, 1992) in an increase in premature labour and other birth difficulties.

Hypnosis can be used specifically to treat the anxiety and depression (see chapters 15 and 16), but exploration and methods of resolution may be needed for specific problems, for example guilt over a previous termination or fear over another miscarriage. There are no specific treatment regimes as each must be tailored to the mother's needs, but relaxation and ego strengthening will be central to any approach.

Premature Labour

This is defined as labour occurring after 24 weeks and before 37 weeks gestation. It is perhaps the greatest single cause of neonatal mortality and morbidity, so any method which helps to prolong the pregnancy is of vital importance. It must be stressed that hypnotherapy is only to be used as an adjunct to conventional therapy and never in isolation and always with permission of, and in close collaboration with, the obstetrician.

The rationale for using hypnosis to help in premature labour is based on the ability of hypnosis to relax smooth muscle (see hypnotic phenomena) but given the complex aetiology of premature labour it may be that hypnosis is able to target more than one of the causal components. There are many physical causes of premature labour which include uterine or cervical abnormalities, multiple pregnancies, placental abruption and haemorrhage, placenta praevia, poly- or oligohydramnios, premature rupture of membranes, infection (especially urinary tract infection) and birth defects (see Goldenberg *et al.*, 2008 for a full review). Of more concern to the hypnotherapist however are the psychosocial factors which are clearly associated with increased risk of premature labour but for which the mechanism is unknown (see the previous section of this chapter for details and references).

Omer *et al.* (1986) showed that the addition of a comprehensive hypnosis programme to conventional treatment prolonged pregnancy by an average of 18.8% compared to conventional treatment alone ($n = 39$ for the hypnosis group). Case histories offer further support for the use of hypnosis in premature labour, and Brown and Hammond (2007) provide an excellent review of the literature.

Techniques should be tailored to the specific requirements, but the following components are suggested:

- Special place
- Honouring the body's adjustment to the magnificence of pregnancy
- Ego-strengthening suggestions
- Deepening to a deeply relaxed state and using the mother's imagery to warm and protect her stomach, belly and uterus
- Locating the labour 'dimmer switch' within her and turning it down
- Locating the control centre of her mind that controls uterine tone and turning it down
- Using the controls and imagery to keep the cervix long and closed
- The baby and mother looking forward to getting to know each other during pregnancy and meeting at 37 to 41 weeks gestation

Kim – a woman with premature labour

A young couple, Kim and Owen, in their early twenties were expecting their first child. The planned pregnancy had been obstetrically normal. At 29 weeks gestation, they moved from their family's home to a tiny second floor flat that they could ill afford on their income. She did not participate in the move as advised by the midwife. Her sister, six years previously, had an unexplained stillbirth at 42 weeks and two days gestation. The family felt that she was neglected during labour as the staff had been overstretched. As a consequence Kim decided to have a home birth believing that she would have one to one care as the midwife would remain with her until the baby was born. However at 31 weeks she went into premature labour and was admitted to the same hospital as her sister had previously been in.

Investigations were normal. She was given standard treatment and her uterus relaxed, her cervix remaining long and closed despite the contractions, and she was able to be discharged with an out-patient follow up appointment.

During our consultation she spoke about how being in her own flat left her feeling very alone and isolated and scared, preoccupied with her sister's loss and strongly identifying with her. She was concerned as to how she would manage a baby on the second floor and whether she would leave the baby in the ground floor lobby whilst she carried heavy shopping up to her flat, or should she take the baby upstairs first and leave the baby there whilst she retrieved her shopping from the lobby? She was preoccupied with the logistics of coping with a baby on her own, away from her family and on the second floor with all that that entails. Trying to get her to explore her feelings for her sister's loss was extremely difficult, and she kept returning to the minutiae of her domestic arrangements.

Hypnosis was induced and deepened, and a safe uncovering technique was used. She created a home cinema room with comfortable furniture and played a movie which also had stills that she controlled with a remote control. She was surprised and overwhelmed when she revisited her sister's loss, how desperately alone and at a loss as to how to help her sister she had felt. She was only 15 at the time and remembers feeling acutely alone and aware that she needed to make herself scarce as her mother and her sister 'huddled together'; she felt excluded. Nothing that she did was right. It was understandably a very difficult time for Kim. Kim was encouraged to have a dialogue with her mother and sister in hypnosis, about how she felt not only for her sister's loss but also for the effect that it had had on her. They 'responded,' understanding her needs, and apologized for neglecting her. It was an emotional session which we only concluded once she felt that she had bridged the gap with her family. Concluding the hypnosis, she was alerted with "*. . . bringing with you all the good feelings that you have felt and any insights that you may have gained to help you resolve your anxieties, into your ordinary waking state.*"

She was almost elated when she recounted to me that how she felt when her sister grieved and she was excluded had exactly the same quality as her anxiety when alone in her new flat. She realized that she did not need to feel that way anymore and that she did not need to have the baby early for fear of being overdue and having a stillborn herself. Unfortunately she did go post-term by five days which is 'normal', but of course she started getting highly agitated; a wonderful session to induce her was successful, and she gave birth to a plump healthy boy.

Pregnancy Induced Hypertension

Pregnancy induced hypertension (PIH) should *NOT* be treated solely with hypnosis. PIH remains, along with haemorrhage, the highest cause of maternal mortality. However hypnosis can be used effectively as an adjunct to standard PIH treatment. It is of great value where blood pressure is labile and goes up at anxious times such as clinic appointments. Self hypnosis practice is essential in these cases.

Suggested content:

- Relaxation
- Ego-strengthening techniques
- Imagery to correct their image of the high blood pressure: improving the smooth flow of blood, arteries becoming more relaxed and responsive
- Encouragement to turn down the adrenalin 'dimmer switch'

Breech and Malpresentation

In a small proportion of pregnancies (4% for breech), the baby is not lying in the normal head down position. This can lead to more difficult births, and very high proportions require an operative delivery.

Whilst it seems that malpresentation is a purely physical problem, Mehl (1994) reported a series in which hypnosis was used to encourage breech presentations to revert. 81% of the hypnosis group ($n = 100$) turned to cephalic presentation compared to 48% of the controls ($n = 100$). The following approach is suggested, and a recording of the session may be useful for the mother to listen to at home after a warm bath or shower.

Recommend the woman gets comfortable, lying on the side that the baby is facing, with her bottom propped up on several cushions to enable the baby's bottom to come out of the pelvis, allowing free movement to turn.

- Use induction and deepening.
- Many mothers worry that they are forcing their baby to turn when it does not want to, so give permission for the baby to stay in the breech position if it is appropriate.
- Focus on the tone of the abdominal and uterine muscles, and encourage them to:

... Relax, heavy ... loose and comfortable, floppy ... lax and at ease ... Find yourself at the top of a gently sloping meadow ... (fill in the scene) ... trees easily swaying in the light breeze ... wild meadow flowers ... the sound of the stream babbling ... fresh clean and bountiful ... warm sun soothing you ... light breeze just brushing the side of your face and neck ... keeping you from overheating ... just right ... sound of farm animals grazing in the next field ... enjoying just being ... maybe a bi-plane in the distance ... a tractor ... a dog barking ... all the activities of a wonderful day in the country with hours and hours to play and stay just enjoying the peaceful activity of this wonderful place ... and do you remember the excitement as a child when you did

head over heels . . . all the way down to the bottom of the slope . . . well for a moment, that can seem like a long time, let's just enjoy the fun and carefree excitement . . . as you put your head to the soft springy grass . . . ready to roll forward . . . rolling all the way down the slope . . . doing your best ever head over heels . . . all the way down to the bottom . . . feel the fun and ease as your body just follows your heads lead . . . maybe going a little bit faster . . . maybe needing to slow yourself . . . there is no hurry . . . perhaps shrieking with delight as you pick up speed . . . nearly there . . . ready to finish . . . your expert head over heels . . . so fun . . . so energizing . . . so exhilarating . . . feeling your body do what it knows how best to do . . . landing spread eagled . . . right at the bottom of the soft springing slope . . . laughing . . . excited . . . full of joy as you stop gently in a dip that feels as if it were made for your body to rest and settle. . . .

Feel your baby within you now . . . and in your own way . . . you can give it your love and encouragement . . . to enjoy its body's ability . . . to roll and turn and move just as it knows exactly how to do. . . .

Stroke your tummy now as you encourage your baby to enjoy . . . rolling head over heels . . . resting with its head . . . cradled at the brim of your pelvis . . . enabling it to engage easily and comfortably . . . and for a few moments that may seem like a long time . . . just quietly reassure your baby . . . coax . . . your baby . . . soothe and encourage your baby to allow it to follow its head's lead and turn almost as if it was a synchronized swimmer . . . that's wonderful. . . .

Itching

Itching is a common symptom, and although rarely it may be a sign of cholestasis – a more serious condition of pregnancy which needs to be excluded – it is usually just a nuisance. Hypnosis can be used with benefit, as an adjunct to topical moisturising creams, light cotton clothing and reduction in the ambient temperature.

Suggested content after induction and deepening:

- Honour the body's adjustment to the magnificence of pregnancy.
- Ask the mother to identify a special place where the itch feels easier – usually a cool place, not a hot beach! Useful examples of images are being under a beautiful cool waterfall, in a magical snowy scene or an exhilarating walk on a windy beach on a bright, spring day.
- Locate and adjust the 'itching' dimmer switch within her.
- Locate the control centre of her mind that controls liver function and adjust it to work efficiently (for cholestasis)
- Know that the baby is comfortable in the perfectly adjusted temperature of the amniotic waters.
- The baby and mother are looking forward to getting to know each other during pregnancy and meeting in approximately one month or however long it is to term.

Induction of Labour

Some women appear 'ripe' for labour, yet go beyond their expected date of delivery by more than a week. Cyna and Andrew (2004) suggest that such women may have issues that make them reluctant to 'let go' to labour with a free mind, and these benefit from an exploration, under hypnosis, of the problem. Once identified, the issues can be resolved. No trials have been published on this approach, but Tiran (2006) also supports its use.

Helping to start labour

Annette, in her early thirties, had found her previous birth a very traumatic experience – she was frightened and horrified by the power of labour with no tools to facilitate the process. Her baby had been in the occipital posterior position causing intense 'back labour'. She required two doses of pethidine and an epidural but subsequently managed a normal vaginal delivery. The experience made her reluctant to extend her family, but Annette had become pregnant again two years later.

During this pregnancy, her mother died after a long illness two months before her due date. Although Annette felt that she had been able to grieve with the support of her siblings and husband, she was fully aware that the loss of her mother might well re-surface once she had her second child. As this response was discussed Annette became aware that it was a normal, natural desire to wish that her mother would see the children grow up. She realized that there would be a deep sadness at various stages of the children's lives, but 'there was no getting away from it!'

Experiencing the joy that a new baby can bring would also be her 'story' as she realized that this birth was likely to be part of the healing process, especially as she had optimism and confidence to deliver her second child easily. It would also renew her father's grief and joy to meet his new grandchild.

The labour rehearsal script (page 478) was used to induce her with a little more emphasis on her cervix being loose and responsive to her uterine contractions. Contractions commenced during the hypnosis session and continued until she delivered her second baby smoothly and easily in four hours, feeling so happy and relieved. She reported, *"I think just acknowledging my sadness about Mum enabled me to go into labour."*

Hypnosis in Labour

Hypnosis is used in the preparation for labour because it has been shown to significantly:

- Reduce the length of labour.
- Reduce the need for analgesia.
- Reduce the need for instrumental or operative deliveries.
- Improve Apgar scores.

Reducing the duration of labour

Early reports of using hypnosis in labour (August, 1960; Freeman *et al.*, 1986; Werner *et al.*, 1982) did not show any reduction in labour length, but their hypnotic intervention did not include any instructions to shorten labour. Once suggestions for a quicker labour were given, evidence has accrued to support that claim.

Harmon *et al.* (1990) in a randomized controlled trial of 30 patients compared with 30 usual treatment controls found that the first stage of labour was 2.8 hours shorter for high hypnotic susceptibility women and 2.2 hours for low susceptibility patients compared with controls. The results were significant at the $p < 0.001$ level.

In a large study, Jenkins and Pritchard (1993) reported a mean reduction of first stage of labour of 2.9 hours for primigravida women ($n = 126$ vs. 300 normal treatment controls, $p < 0.0001$) and 0.9hrs for the parous group ($n = 136$ vs. 300 controls, $p < 0.01$).

Although not reported in terms of labour length Cyna *et al.* (2006) showed that significantly fewer ($p < 0.05$) nulliparous women using hypnosis required labour augmentation with oxytocics.

Jenkins and Pritchard (1993) and Harmon *et al.* (1990) both report a reduction in the second stage of labour with hypnosis, but this was confined to the primiparous group. The smaller effects with parous patients may simply be explained by the shorter duration of labour anyway, and larger group sizes may be required to show statistical significance. Whilst supporting the shortening of the first stage of labour, Brann and Guzvica (1987) did not find any reduction in the second stage.

Reducing the need for analgesia

Jenkins and Pritchard (1993) reported that a significantly greater proportion of the hypnosis group did not require any analgesia (33/126 primiparous and 50/136 multiparous vs. 13/300 and 33/300 controls, $p < 0.001$) or did not require pethidine (66/126 primiparous and 80/136 multiparous vs. 49/300 and 99/300 controls, $p < 0.001$). Harmon *et al.* (1990) also report a significant reduction in analgesic requirements ($p < 0.001$). Cyna *et al.* (2004b) reviewed the literature on the use of hypnosis for pain relief in labour and performed a meta-analysis on three trials. This showed that, compared with controls, hypnosis parturients required less analgesia (RR = 0.51 95% confidence intervals 0.28, 0.95). Cyna *et al.* (2006) using epidural rates as a measure of analgesic requirements showed that only 36% of the hypnosis group had an epidural compared with 53% controls (RR = 0.68, 95% confidence intervals 0.47, 0.98).

Reducing the need for operative deliveries

Data from the literature for this aspect are less easy to find, but Martin *et al.* (2001) report significantly less surgical intervention ($p < 0.0001$), fewer complicated births ($p < 0.05$) and shorter hospital stay ($p < 0.01$) in the hypnosis arm. Mehl-Madrona (2004) reports significantly fewer complicated deliveries and caesarean sections in the hypnosis group when compared to usual treatment controls and a supportive psychotherapy group.

Improving Apgar scores

Whilst the above data imply that the outcome for the baby is better, only one of the studies specifically recorded the Apgar scores. Harmon *et al.* (1990) showed the improvement to be at the $p < 0.001$ level.

Birth Preparation: the Hypnosis Programme

With hypnosis having potential benefit in so many areas of pregnancy and childbirth, it is essential to deliver a programme which enables each expectant mother to learn the skills and practice the techniques to maximize the outcome. Ideally the pregnant women and her intended birth partner would attend the course, enabling the birth companion to support the mother in an appropriate way. The following is a suggested approach, but other programmes are available (e.g. Brann, 1987). These sessions can be done in groups but are probably best done with each couple on their own.

Session 1: setting the scene

- Emphasize initially that using hypnosis to enhance their physiology and birthing experience will *not* exclude some from needing a lower uterine segment Caesarean section (LSCS) – that a needed LSCS is a life-promoting operation ... and can be wonderful!
- Examine preconceptions: pain free childbirth versus agonizing childbirth, for example. Advice is given to avoid:
  ○ Listening to other peoples' stories of awful experiences of childbirth
  ○ Watching births on television, especially when they are depicted as torturous and agonizing
- Take a family history and identify and discuss any family trends or myths. *"All the women on my mother's side have had awful labours."*
- Letters and case histories from ordinary women who have used hypnosis are discussed. These women have had a wide range of experiences in childbirth, and all had their own concerns and anxieties and were able to adopt new skills and increase confidence. These 'real' cases have been found to be very helpful to the expectant mothers and their partners.
- Give an explanation of the physiology of pregnancy and the mechanics of labour: it seems to be that knowledge is power in this instance. Only health professionals qualified to care for the pregnant woman should be running the programme and should be aware of the need to give the explanation at the level of understanding of the patient, emphasizing details where myths and misunderstandings have been highlighted in the history taking.

- Give a brief outline of the effects of anxiety and fear on the body and explain the negative effects of the adrenalin response on labour.
  - ○ Explain that the programme should help to eradicate all fear that stems from anxieties and thought processes that are not congruent with the realities of the situation. For a women to feel confident about how her body is working, knowing the normal course of events and knowing what she is feeling and why, this can allow her to embrace the situation confidently and fearlessly ... so no adrenalin and no slowing down of contractions.
  - ○ Reducing anxieties, fears and worries enables the body to work optimally allowing labour to unfold smoothly efficiently and effectively.
- At the end of the first session the CIS or similar can be performed. This can help couples to feel confident in the hypnotic process. It can also be useful in identifying the modality preferences that can be used during hypnosis.

Session 2: using hypnosis

- Review the previous session, and resolve any concerns or misunderstandings.
- Give a formal introduction to hypnosis with an explanation of what hypnosis is and is not. Dispel any myths and preconceptions, and answer any questions.
- A 'special place' is created either with the couple or collectively as a group.
- Induce and deepen hypnosis, and get them to take themselves to their special place as their first hypnotic experience.
- Explain the importance of breathing properly to maximize oxygen for the uterine muscles.
- Teach a breathing technique to use during labour. The following is an example of a suitable verbatim script:

Get comfortable and place one hand on your belly and one on your chest. Ideally breathe through your nose.... Take a breath in ... directing the breath all the way down to the bottom of your belly ... feeling your 'belly hand' rise. Perhaps, imagine that your breath is travelling into a large balloon ... and you are filling the balloon with your breath ... firstly ... right down to the bottom of the balloon ... deep into your belly and ... as the balloon fills up with your breath ... it expands and eventually fills right to the top ... at your upper chest ... where your 'chest hand' rises. This is diaphragmatic breathing.... And ... for the outward breath ... firstly release the breath from the top of the balloon ... feeling your chest hand fall ... pouring the air out from the top ... right to the bottom of your belly ... the bottom of the balloon ... and you will feel your 'belly hand' fall. Focusing on the outward breath ... being a tiny bit longer than the inward breath ... this will prevent your breathing from getting shorter and more rapid and less effective. Practice breathing six breaths prior to sleep ... six breaths on waking ... six breaths whilst standing and ... six breaths whilst sitting. So 24 breaths a day is more than adequate practice for a few weeks prior to birth ... it will then become easy to do ... whatever positions that you choose to adopt during labour. Whilst breathing deep down into your belly ... feel yourself giving your uterus ... and baby ... all the oxygen it needs to contract and perform this wonderful feat.... Holding your breath causes lack of oxygen ... cramp and pain ... your subconscious mind will remind you to start this special breathing as soon as you notice yourself holding your breath during the building contraction.

Post-hypnotic suggestions have been used in the above example, but adding the following is useful:

Whenever you find yourself rubbing your tummy, your baby, a feeling of peace and joy will wash over you, connecting you with your baby and the growing love and awe that you feel to be part of this miracle of procreation.

Session 3: letting nature take over and giving up control

- Explain that this is the most liberating area to be explored. Labour will begin and go to completion without any conscious thought. Women unconscious through illness or trauma still labour successfully. It is one of the most amazing feats of nature. Many women try to remain in control, to override nature, in the belief that this will make things easier. In reality nature has been doing this for millions of years and can do it all on its own! *"Let go of the idea of trying to control, and give yourself up to nature. Your preparation is there to assist nature, not to control it."* So, remove the inhibitors – anxiety, fear, resistance and unreal expectations – and install the enhancers – analgesia, relaxation and positivity – and yield to the wonder of nature.

- Gather information for individualising hypnosis; the following example is used as an illustration.
  - A woman explored the coping mechanisms she used to climb Kilimanjaro on her honeymoon, and these were adapted for managing the journey of labour. She walked looking at the ground, at only one step ahead and imagined that the ground was flat ... and seeing in her mind's eye and feeling the joy that she knew that she would feel when she looked out from the top of Kilimanjaro! From this she realized that the importance for her was the old saying 'One step at a time'. During her labour she remained in a birthing pool with eyes closed, and with each contraction all she could see was her goal which was her husband's face tearful and laughing with joy as he met his baby. Each contraction she felt was a gift bringing them closer to their reality of meeting their baby. Most of us have not climbed Kilimanjaro! Some may have run a marathon; some may have had the experience of doing something that was challenging that would be applicable.

- Explore and suggest imagery which can be used by women to ride each contraction.
  - Picture a sailing boat, the colours, the sails and the size, and see and feel yourself masterfully steering the boat in the direction that you choose. Experience riding the choppy waters and the spray of the ocean, the salt on your lips, and notice that just a short distance away are calm sparkling waters, calm and still with that wonderful green glass colour that you know will feel soothing and peaceful as each contraction comes to its end. (Ensure that they are comfortable with water!)
  - Surfing the waves, noting the exhilaration of rising up as the contraction gets stronger taking you to the top of the wave and again the smooth gliding as you descend from the peak of the wave, of the contraction, until you lie in the shallows bathed and warm and relaxed, floppy and smiling.

○ Some like to be on their beach watching each wave (contraction) come to shore and then recede, and then at the stage of transition (from stage 1 to 2) they start to surf the waves rather than just watching them.

○ Sitting around a perfect open fire in an isolated cottage in the most spectacular surroundings. They could be on a hill, in a meadow or in an alpine log cabin with the quiet of the snow; all that can be heard is the crackling of the log fire. *"As each contraction begins you find yourself breathing deeply, deep down into your belly and blowing at the fire enabling it to ignite and burn gloriously warming you, feeling the warmth and richness within, that you know that you will feel, when you hold your baby in your arms. If each contraction can have say five, six or seven breaths to ignite the fire, then the breaths become slower, more controlled and directed to the base of the fire, just as your breath reaches your magnificent uterus, oxygenating it, enabling it to open, easing your baby smoothly and easily into the world and your arms."*

○ For more practical women, the image of the uterus all powerful and pink is helpful: *"... engorged with life-promoting blood, enriching the enormous wonderful muscle to perform its function of contracting effectively, synchronized like synchronized swimmers, opening the pink soft and responsive cervix efficiently, enabling it to open swiftly and smoothly, bringing you your baby safely and calmly, into your arms."*

○ Ruler of relaxation: *"Sitting in a luxurious setting and chair, seeing a metre high wooden ruler wooden standing upright in front of you. Look at a number on the ruler and as the contraction builds cast your eye on the little black lines and numbers going down the ruler, feeling more relaxed and floppy as you focus on the numbers as you look down, down, down to one hundred right at the bottom to correlate with the peak of the contraction, and as the contraction reduces gaze at the numbers going back up to your original number when the contraction abates, feeling more alert, able to rest until the next contraction."*

○ For some visualizing and imagery do not come easily, and then 'mantras' are sought. For example:
   "RE" for the inward breath and *"LAX"* for the outward breath.
   "FLOPPY, FLOPPY, FLOPPY" for each breath.
   "Oxygenating my body" for the inward breath, and *"To do what it knows what to do"* for the outward breath.
   "Strong, powerful and open" for the inward breath, and *"Relaxed, at ease and calm"* for the outward breath.

Session 4: uncovering obstacles

Despite the above preparation, some women still harbour fears and concerns about their labour. Sometimes the issues have been voiced and dealt with logically, but emotionally (subconsciously?) the fears remain strong. These unresolved issues can interfere with the focus, calm and patience that are required for labour.

Having induced and deepened hypnosis, an uncovering technique can be used with built in dissociation (see page 401). For most women they are not surprised by what appears in hypnosis – perhaps outdated family myths, a previous labour that was not as they hoped or a friend's horror story – but for a few it can unearth issues that do need deeper therapeutic work.

Once the unfolding is done and the negative pictures, symbols or word or even a thought has been burnt or destroyed in a manner of their choosing – a bonfire, a shredder, feeling free and open, strong and at ease – then, *but only then*, is it possible to move on to the amazing scene of the three of them ... the moment of birth.

A woman with a traumatic memory

A primigravida in a group of four couples stayed behind at the end of the session to report her experience to me. Once she had viewed her cine film, she threw it in the fire to melt and disintegrate. But she said that this had been a wonderful experience: About 12 years ago when she was 21 years old she was in a pub chatting to a man she happened to be sitting next to. When she left to walk home, he followed her and attempted rape in a park that was her route home. Fortunately a passerby helped her and chased off the attacker. She reported that it was the first time since the incident that she had recalled his face without becoming tearful and distraught. She did receive excellent care from the police, received counselling and was informed when he was released from prison. She felt that more than ever the experience was behind her.

Having cleared away the obstacles, it is appropriate to give suggestions and imagery to enhance the 'birth scene'. The following is a suitable verbatim script:

Feel your baby on your chest all wet and warm and small, feel the baby's bottom cupped in your palm ... hold your baby against you ... against your chest ... smell your baby for the first time ... feel the joy and pride ... feel the delight and relief to meet your baby ... such a perfect body ... little ears all formed and perfect ... funny little elbows and shoulder blades ... and I don't know why babies feet always look too big for their little legs ... but they do! Maybe your baby has a mop of hair and maybe it's all downy ... maybe dark or fair ... it doesn't really matter ... see it's little pixie face all new and sweet ... maybe a boy ... maybe a girl and again it doesn't really matter ... and just for a moment notice how when it's Daddy (or name of father if an individual session) *says 'Hello little one' or whatever he says ... notice how your baby's gaze darts to greet its dad ... because of course his voice is so familiar. Your baby knows its daddy. .... Glance now in your mind's eye and see his* (name of partner) *face overwhelmed with delight, relief and amazement ... maybe laughing ... maybe crying ... maybe both at the same time ... feel yourself totally elated and proud ... feel your love and wonder.*

This is really emotional and often creates tears – even in the therapist – it is so wonderfully moving!

Continue to create positive images and suggestions – the following are examples:

"See yourselves in your bedroom ... snuggled up in bed together ... maybe with your other children ... a moment of magic to be enjoyed ... savoured ... delighted in."

"For a moment . . . allow yourself to decide what it is that you will feel in labour perhaps pressure . . . or a heaviness . . . or a tightening . . . or numbness . . . it is up to you . . . just decide."

"And you will find that time has no meaning for you . . . and should you gaze upon a clock, it will bear no relevance to you . . . because each half hour feels just like five minutes whilst birthing your baby . . . so much so that it becomes a source of amusement between you both when you recount your experiences . . . time had absolutely no meaning . . . each half hour feels as though it is only five minutes."

"Just allow the baby to let a number come into your head, that is the length of your active labour . . . not too long to be too tiring and not too short to be too quick . . . just let that happen automatically . . . now."

End the session with these positive thoughts and excitement about their forthcoming baby lingering in their mind.

Session 5: rehearsing for labour

Whilst formal training in hypnosis is not necessary for midwives looking after patients using hypnosis for childbirth, they do need to be aware of it. It is suggested that a letter is sent to the midwife explaining the hypnosis preparation and giving guidance for the staff to support the process. One of the main points for them to note is that labour seems to progress quicker than outward appearances suggest, so careful monitoring is essential.

This session is used to explore what is left to be done to set them free to labour. It may be as simple as confirming arrangements for their other children whilst they labour and birth or putting in place help to enable the first few weeks after the birth to be as smooth and stress free as possible. The main purpose of this session is to rehearse the preparation for the labour.

- Induce and deepen hypnosis and establish special place.
- Script:

And for a moment that may seem like a long time . . . see and feel yourself at night . . . in bed . . . waking and noticing a difference . . . maybe a contraction, maybe waters leaking, it is not really important which, any order is normal . . . just see and feel yourself getting up . . . maybe to go to the toilet . . . drink a large glass of water . . . and if comfortable return to bed to sleep or nap between sensations . . . should you prefer . . . just see yourself . . . perhaps taking a cover and pillows onto the sofa and quietly enjoying the peace and excitement that at last your body is doing exactly what it knows how best to do . . . just see yourself dozing and rousing as necessary to be comfortable . . . knowing that sometimes there is a lull . . . there is no hurry . . . your body can do this perfectly . . . all on its own . . . and if I were a strong man I would wear a loose sleeve to accommodate my bulging muscles . . . not tight and restrictive . . . and as you to go to the toilet . . . keeping your bladder empty to give maximum room to your contracting uterus . . . you feel confident and calm and should you be hungry just eat what you fancy . . . little and often . . . as you fuel your body to gently and efficiently perform this magnificent task . . . feel yourself quietly, slowly pottering . . . and resting . . . and just notice the change in your demeanour as you deepen your relaxation . . . powerful . . . trusting . . . and loose . . . powerful . . . trusting . . . and loose . . . your uterus eases open your cervix . . . feel the power in your body increase . . . fuelling your uterus with the oxygen it relies on . . . to perform this wonderful task . . . see and feel yourself breathing deeply into your belly . . . powerfully . . . trusting . . . body loose . . . welcoming the contraction . . . encouraging it to work . . . in just the way it knows how best to . . . see and feel yourself all floppy and at ease . . . allowing all your life-promoting blood to go to your uterus . . . no need to use it for other muscles . . . they can be passive today . . . allow your uterus . . . today . . . to take centre stage . . . and as time goes on . . . the rhythmic . . . regular . . . reliable contractions . . . become more frequent more effective . . . more efficient and as they respond to your breath . . . and as your contractions build . . . see yourself . . . and feel yourself . . . immersed . . . floppy . . . breathing deeply as you focus . . . maybe you will be in your hot air balloon going higher and higher and higher or . . . or riding the waves in a boat or on a surf board . . . maybe you can sit on the shore as the frothy waves wash over you powerful . . . cleansing and soothing . . . and as your labour progresses . . . you'll find that you . . . deeply connect with an imagery that enables you to ride your contractions . . . relaxed and confident . . . as your breath enables your uterus to contract smoothly . . . efficiently and productively opening wider and wider and wider . . . as you become more and more deeply relaxed . . . and as you feel each contraction easily stretching your cervix open . . . you notice that the sensations signal that you cervix becomes more open and wide as it knows it no longer needs to hold your baby inside . . . your baby is ready . . . your cervix is ready to continue . . . loose and responsive stretchy and open . . . and as each contraction subsides . . . feel the elation . . . that your body works . . . just the way it needs to . . . to bring you your baby . . . and you simply can't help but smile as each contraction subsides . . . so proud of your efficient body . . . so powerful . . . and relaxed and responsive . . . and as your contraction subsides feel yourself move confidently . . . powerfully with an ease in your sway to your special place where you can rest and recharge leaving the last contraction . . . forgotten . . . allowing you to be ready to greet the next contraction . . . resting gently breathing in and out . . . in and out . . . restful and calm . . . restful and calm . . . as you go deeper and deeper . . . and as your partner offers you a drink in between contractions, you enjoy the care and love that are offered enabling you to remain hydrated to allow your magnificent body to perform the muscular contractions that allow your body to work so efficiently . . . noticing the awakening of another wave of opening . . . filled with awe and a desire to participate . . . giving your uterus your powerful deep, deep, deep breaths . . . fuelling your magnificent muscle to work . . . automatically . . . as all the muscles in your body do . . . so reliably . . . you can depend on it . . . breathing deeply . . . powerfully and calmly . . . with trust . . . such a deep, deep trust . . . feeling the opening . . . feeling your baby descend . . . nearer and nearer to greeting your beautiful baby . . . and should you want to reduce the intensity of the sensations . . . just see a measuring device . . . in your mind's eye . . . perhaps a dial with numbers one to ten, or maybe a measuring jug, a tape measure . . . thermometer . . . you choose . . . and now locate the numbers . . . perhaps one to ten . . . on any measuring device that you choose or alter it, one to 12 for a clock, or one to 100 for a ruler . . . it is your measuring device . . . you choose . . . see your chosen measuring device . . . the materials that it is made from . . . the shape and colour . . . really see it in your mind's eye . . . and should you want to reduce any intensity just locate where the levels are . . . and reduce them by using your breath and watching in your mind's eye the level of intensity reduce . . . as you watch the level reduce to your chosen number on your device . . . feeling the intensity reduce becoming more numb . . . more like a pressure, perhaps a heaviness . . . or a dragging . . . reducing the intensity as you choose . . . and as you await your midwives or travel to your birth place . . . allow yourself to care for yourself by going deeper and deeper with each breath that you take . . . during your journey . . . any traffic is immaterial . . . as you descend into your inner place of peace and optimism and trust . . . so many wonderings about this moment . . . now so relaxed . . . so at ease . . . so trusting . . . and your journey or your wait for your midwife . . . at an end . . . see and feel yourself . . . getting out of the car or greeting her . . . slowly . . . easily . . . patient . . . with yourself and walking softly and gently to your place of birth maybe going up in the lift . . . maybe the stairs . . . there is no hurry . . . just walking easily . . . softly . . . and the noises and activities of your birth place enable you to relax more and more . . . feeling powerful in your 'bubble' of relaxation . . . getting settled and breathing more deeply as your labour continues . . . rhythmically . . . reliably and efficiently . . . assisting each contraction with your wonderful deep breath enhancing your uteruses action as it opens the last bit of your cervix . . . slipping gently behind the baby's wet head . . . allowing your gorgeous slippery little baby to swiftly descend just as it knows how to do . . . and should the ending . . . of your first stage of labour . . . make you breath more deeply as the ultimate opening occurs you may find that you sigh out your breath . . . make a song . . . sing a low note . . . hum . . . rejoice in your heart . . . as your uterus performs its magnificent feat . . . of opening fully and evenly and smoothly . . . and you can feel excited and delighted knowing that you will be greeting your baby shortly . . . and it is funny how you can sense the changes in the action of your uterus as it shortens and gently eases your baby to the outside world . . . just for a moment . . . now . . . honour the reliability of your body . . . move your body to a place of comfort to breathe your baby down . . . down . . . down notice how your uterus nudges your baby down and you join together with your body . . . in unison . . . to push your baby . . . gently at first . . . resisting . . . resisting deep pushing at first . . . slowly but surely . . . slowly but surely . . . as you feel your baby within . . . low, low down . . . you and your body together . . . as you listen to your midwife . . . responding to her guidance . . . easily and precisely as you . . . bear down . . . push . . . and sometimes . . . when she suggests . . . you pant . . . to avoid pushing . . . allowing your uterus to take . . . centre stage . . . to bear your baby . . . easing it down . . . down, down smoothly stretching you slowly . . . slowly so that you can stretch easily and wide . . . and maybe the midwife will suggest that you push as she watches your baby descend and maybe she will ask you to pant . . . allowing you to stretch and birth your baby . . . and each time . . . you hear your midwife's voice . . . you relax more and more as you respond . . . attentively . . . actively to her suggestions . . . and for now . . . just know deep in your heart now . . . that as your wonderful baby comes through you into your loving arms that that moment will be the best moment of your life . . . see your face now . . . change . . . from your focus on birthing . . . to an overwhelming delight as you feel your baby for the very first time all warm and wet and new . . . hold your baby against you.

- Repeat suggestions and imagery to enhance the 'birth scene'.
- Re-alert from hypnosis with strong suggestions that all this preparation will automatically take over once labour has started and the midwife has been contacted.

Potential complications: The main fear of using hypnosis in labour is that it could mask the signs of an obstructed labour. In this respect hypnosis is no different from any other form of analgesia in labour and simply confirms the need for careful monitoring by the midwife, and any failure to progress must be evaluated appropriately.

Uses of Hypnosis in the Post-Partum Period

All the skills learnt by the mother in her preparation for labour can be extended and utilized not only in the immediate post-partum period but also for the rest of her life.

Discomfort from tears or episiotomies is common, and any of the pain-relieving techniques discussed in this and other chapters are appropriate for use here. Sleep can also be a problem especially when the normal pattern is disturbed by feeding demands. The hypnotic relaxation can be used to help the mother to drift easily and quickly back to sleep but confident that she will be able to hear her baby when she needs to.

Sauer and Osler (1997) report that hypnosis helps with an easier transition into breastfeeding, and this is supported by the clinical observation that relaxation is the key to successful breastfeeding. Direct suggestions can be given that lactation will establish earlier and the body's natural response to childbirth will take over.

Postnatal 'blues' are common around day four and are simply a response to the hormonal changes and are usually transient, but some women go on to develop postnatal depression. General relaxation and ego strengthening with reliving of happy memories help to support the woman through the 'blue' days. Postnatal depression, however, needs referral to the GP, and although hypnosis can be used (see chapter 16) it is to be seen as an adjunct to standard treatment rather than instead of it. Care must be taken if the mother seems to be developing a puerperal psychosis where hypnosis (at least initially) would be contraindicated.

Thus it can be seen that hypnosis can be used at every stage of the pregnant woman's journey and is eminently adaptable to match the bio-psycho-social needs of the individual woman.

References

Alexander, B., Turnbull, D. & Cyna, A. (2009), The effect of pregnancy on hypnotisability. *American Journal of Clinical Hypnosis*, 52 (1), 13–22.

August, R. V. (1960), Obstetric hypnoanaesthesiae. *American Journal of Obstetrics & Gynaecology*, 59, 1069–74.

Brann, L. R (1987), Just close your eyes and relax. Wellingborough, Thorsons.

Brann, L. R. & Guzvica S. A. (1987), Comparison of hypnosis with conventional relaxation for antenatal and intrapartum use: a feasibility study in general practice. *The Journal of the Royal College of General Practitioners*, 37 (303), 437–40.

Brown, D. C. & Hammond, D. C. (2007), Evidence-based clinical hypnosis for obstetrics, labor and delivery, and preterm labor. *International Journal of Clinical and Experimental Hypnosis*, 55 (3), 355–71.

Cogan, R. & Spinnato, J. A. (1986), Pain and discomfort thresholds in late pregnancy. *Pain*, 27 (1), 63–8.

Cyna, A. M. & Andrew, M. (2004), Hypnotherapy as an adjunct for induction of labour. Sydney, Paediatric and Women's Anaesthesia, Government of South Australia.

Cyna, A., McAuliffe, G. & Andrew, M. I. (2004a), The effect of hypnosis on nausea and vomiting in pregnancy. Sydney, Paediatric and Women's Anaesthesia, Government of South Australia. http://www.wch.sa.gov.au/research/publications/report/research04/pdfs/anaesthesia.pdf

Cyna, A. M., McAuliffe, G. L. & Andrew, M. I. (2004b), Hypnosis for pain relief in labour and childbirth: a systematic review. *British Journal of Anaesthesia*, 93 (4), 505–11.

Cyna, A. M., Andrew, M. I. & McAuliffe, G.L (2006), Antenatal self-hypnosis for labour and childbirth: a pilot study. *Anaesthesia and Intensive Care*, (34) 464–9.

Freeman, R. M., Macaulay, A. J., Eve, L., Chamberlain, G. V. P. & Bhat, A. V. (1986), Randomised trial for self-hypnosis for analgesia in labour. *British Medical Journal*, 292, 657–8.

Fuchs, K. (1983), Treatment of hyperemesis gravidarum by hypnosis. Paper presented at the Third European Congress of European Society of Hypnosis in Psychotherapy and Psychosomatic Medicine, Haifa, Israel.

Goldenberg, R. L., Culhane, J. F., Iams, J. D. & Romero, R. (2008), Epidemiology and causes of preterm birth. *The Lancet*, 371, 75–84.

Harmon, T. M., Hynan, M. T. & Tyre, T. E. (1990), Improved obstetric outcomes using hypnotic analgesia and skill mastery combined with childbirth education. *Journal of Consulting and Clinical Psychology*, 58 (5), 525–30.

Hartland, J. (1984), *Medical and dental hypnosis.* Eastbourne, Balliere Tindall.

Hedegaard, M., Henriksen, T. B. & Secher, N. J. (1996), Do stressful life events affect duration of gestation and risk of preterm delivery? *Epidemiology*, 7 (4), 339–45.

Jenkins, M. W. & Pritchard, M. H. (1993), Hypnosis: applications and considerations in normal labour. *British Journal of Obstetrics & Gynaecology*, 100, 221–6.

Lobel, M., Dunkel-Schetter, C. & Scrimshaw, S. C. M. (1992), Prenatal maternal stress and prematurity: a prospective study of socio-economically disadvantaged women. *Health Psychology*, 11 (1), 32–40.

Martin, A. A., Schauble, P. G., Rai, S. H. & Curry, R. W. (2001), The effects of hypnosis on the labor processes and birth outcomes of pregnant adolescents. *Journal of Family Practice*, 50 (5), 441–3.

Mehl, L. E. (1994), Hypnosis and conversion of the breech to the vertex presentation. *Archives of Family Medicine*, 3 (10), 881–7.

Mehl-Madrona L.E (2004), Hypnosis to facilitate uncomplicated birth. *American Journal of Clinical Hypnosis*, 46 (4), 299–312.

Omer, H., Friedlander, D. & Palti, Z. (1986), Hypnotic relaxation in the treatment of premature labour. *Psychosomatic Medicine*, 48, 351–61.

Sauer, C. & Oster, M. I. (1997), Obstetric hypnosis: two case studies. *Australian Journal of Clinical and Experimental Hypnosis*, 25, 74–9.

Simon, E. P. & Schwartz, J. (1999), Medical hypnosis for hyperemesis gravidarum. *Birth*, 26 (4), 248–54.

Tibia, J. (1990), Clinical, research and organisational aspects of preparation for childbirth and the psychological diminution of pain during labour and delivery. *British Journal of Experimental and Clinical Hypnosis*, 7, 61–4.

Tiran, D. (2006), Late for a very important date: care must be taken when using complementary therapies for induction. *Practising Midwife*, 9 (3), 16–21.

Torem, M. S. (1994), Hynotherapeutic techniques in the treatment of hyperemesis gravidarum. *American Journal of Clinical Hypnosis*, 37, 1–11.

Werner, W. E. F., Schauble, P. G. & Knudson, M. S. (1982), An argument for the revival of hypnosis in obstetrics. *American Journal of Clinical Hypnosis*, 24, 149–71.

32

Infertility

Dr Les Brann

Introduction

The true incidence of infertility is unknown as not everyone with a problem seeks help, but the annual incidence seems to be around 1.2 couples per 1,000 as judged by referrals to a specialist centre. Many more couples consult with concerns over (perceived?) delayed conception, and it is estimated that as many as one in seven couples will seek help whilst they are trying to conceive (Wilkes *et al.*, 2009). Whilst, of course, most of those will go on to conceive either naturally or with some form of assisted conception, a proportion will remain childless. Many factors are implicated as causes of infertility such as ovulatory disorders, blocked tubes, endometriosis and male factors including oligospermia and azoospermia. A proportion, however, despite advances in reproductive endocrinology, remain in the 'unexplained' category. This group is difficult to quantify and estimates vary markedly from 8% to 30% (European Society of Human Reproduction and Embryology, 1996).

Psychological factors are frequently implicated for conditions where no physical cause can be found, and infertility is no exception to this. O'Moore *et al.* (1983), for example, deduced this because 46% of infertile patients attending a fertility clinic conceived during the course of investigations and before treatment began. This clinic placebo response had been previously noted (Harrison *et al.*, 1981; Sandler, 1968), and they surmised that this could partly be due to the 'relief of stress that occurs once the couple are sharing the problem with a third party', implying that it is the stress of the infertility that is causal to the problem.

The Handbook of Contemporary Clinical Hypnosis: Theory and Practice, First Edition.
Edited by Les Brann, Jacky Owens and Ann Williamson.
© 2012 John Wiley & Sons, Ltd. Published 2015 by John Wiley & Sons, Ltd.

Conception after adoption is another frequently quoted reason for implying a psychological cause. The supposition (Sandler, 1965) is that adoption focuses attention away from the infertility and releases the built up stress and tension. This presupposes that the stress and tension in some way, hitherto unexplained, impair the reproductive physiology and, furthermore, that the release of this tension restores the physiology to normal. Following this argument, a greater number of conceptions would be expected in couples who adopt compared with those infertile couples who do not. The evidence, however, does not support this view (Aronson & Gilienke 1963; Sandler, 1965). Arronet *et al.* (1974) found that a greater proportion of those not adopting had conceived compared with the adopting group (66% and 20% respectively). The groups were not strictly comparable; the adopting group had been known to be infertile longer than the non-adopting group, and it was not known how 'active' the adoption group had been in trying to conceive.

If psychological factors are causal or contributory in the infertility process, what could be the possible underlying mechanism(s)? Whilst it is possible to observe the effects of stress on the reproductive system, the mechanism remains unknown. For example, before the days of the contraceptive pill, it was common to see changes in menstrual patterns in young women going off to university. For infertility, two such mechanisms have been suggested (Domar & Seibel, 1990): firstly, tubal spasm and, secondly, prolactin production.

In a comprehensive review, Brann (1996) presents the details and evidence for these mechanisms, and a brief summary is presented here.

The rich autonomic innervation of all the pelvic viscera and in particular the fallopian tubes consists of both alpha and beta receptors. Alpha receptors appear to be excitatory, whilst beta receptors are inhibitory. However, the receptors are modified by the simultaneous action of several other substances such as prostaglandins, oestrogens and progestogens. Oestrogen enhances and progesterone reduces the activity of the excitatory alpha receptors, and it is possible to postulate that, at mid-cycle with high levels of oestrogen and high levels of circulating catecholamines (in the stressed subject), the circular muscle at the ampullisthmic junction acts as a sphincter and can, therefore, prevent the passage of sperm to the egg and vice versa.

Thus, the complex responses that occur in the endocrine, neuroendocrine and autonomic systems to 'psychological problems' make it feasible that, for some patients, the resultant mixture of this biochemical response does, in fact, make the fallopian tube hostile to the mechanism of fertilization. As Domar and Seibel (1990) make clear in their review article, the above mechanisms are further confounded by the continuing cycle that the infertility brings. Simply being able to identify a possible mechanism does not mean that this is the way in which psychological problems cause or compound infertility, and currently this remains a theoretical possibility.

Prolactin is secreted by the pituitary gland, and as with other hypothalamic-pituitary hormones its release is both episodic and pulsatile. The lowest levels are found at midday, and the highest levels are found shortly before the onset of deep sleep.

The main function of prolactin in humans seems to be the initiation and maintenance of lactation. It has also been found to have profound effects on immune function and increases T cell proliferation, cytotoxic T cell activity and IL-2 synthesis. Significantly raised serum prolactin (hyperprolactinaemia) usually results from a pituitary adenoma and causes symptoms such as amenorrhoea, other menstrual disturbances and galactorrhoea. Hyper-prolactinaemia accounts for some 20% of cases of secondary amenorrhoea and consequently is a major cause of infertility.

In addition to the above, prolactin is also a stress hormone increasing sometimes markedly, although variably and idiosyncratically in some people, after exposure to various physical, sexual and psychological stressors (Miyabo *et al.*, 1977; Noel *et al.*, 1972). Sobrinho *et al.* (2003) was able to demonstrate rises in prolactin to a variety of emotions, induced during hypnosis, including rage and humiliation but not, despite the known physiological correlate, during the evocation of a memory of breastfeeding. Links with prolactin and unexplained infertility patients were noted by Lenton *et al.* (1979) and Harrison *et al.*, (1981) and further supported the view that prolactin was a possible mechanism in these patients.

Given its possible role in infertility, Noel *et al.* (1972) also studied the effect of sexual intercourse on prolactin levels and found that there was no increase in levels in a sample of five men. Of the seven women who took part in this study, three, all of whom experienced orgasm, showed rises of tenfold or more. There was little or no rise in prolactin levels of the remaining four women, two of whom reported experiencing orgasm. One woman volunteered for the experiment three times and showed the massive increase in prolactin levels on the two occasions she reached orgasm but no rise at all when she did not reach orgasm. Teleologically, it seems odd that the very act which biologically is the mechanism for reproduction should lead to rises in a hormone which inhibits conception!

Notwithstanding the above, it is clear that infertility causes considerable psychosocial morbidity. Domar *et al.* (1993) compared groups of female patients with infertility, chronic pain, cancer, HIV, hypertension and cardiac disease. They used the Symptom Checklist–90 to assess the level of psychological symptoms and found that infertile women had global symptom scores equivalent to the cancer, hypertension and cardiac patients' but lower than the chronic pain and HIV positive patients'. They concluded that 'psychological symptoms associated with infertility are similar to those associated with other serious medical conditions' and suggested that infertile couples should be given the psychological support afforded to other groups of chronically ill patients.

Further to this, Domar *et al.* (1992) found significantly higher depression scores in a group of infertile women compared to fertile controls, and Connolly *et al.* (1987) found high levels of emotional distress in a large group of infertile couples. The most striking finding was the effect of male infertility. Both men and women reported increases in marital difficulty, and women saw a male cause as creating more marital distress than if the cause lay with the woman. The converse, however, does not seem to hold, and men do not report more problems with female causes of infertility. Nobody has published any, even speculative, ideas as to why male causes are associated with increased problems.

In addition to marital disharmony, sexual dysfunction is known to accompany infertility and a review paper (Keye, 1984) has summarized the psychosexual responses to infertility and went on to report the findings of a survey of nearly 500 infertile men and women and listed ten causes of sexual dysfunction in that group:

1   Dyspareunia
2   Drug induced inhibited sexual desire (particularly with progesterone and analogues)
3   Stated or perceived need for 'sex on schedule'
4   Goal orientated approach to sex
5   Unrealistic sexual demands by partner
6   Stated or perceived need to have coitus in a structured and predetermined way
7   Poor body image
8   Depression
9   Guilt
10 Ambivalence

Looking at sexual practices a common theme became apparent resulting in increased coital frequency at mid-cycle, decreased coital frequency at other times of the cycle, decreased variety of sexual expression and a change in who initiates sex. Sexual function suffered too, with increased orgasmic failure in the woman, especially at mid-cycle (often due to 'spectatoring'), and impotence or delayed ejaculation (again especially at mid-cycle and probably due to performance anxiety) for the man.

Published Evidence

Thus whatever the causal mechanisms, hypnotherapy has a role in helping all the factors mentioned above and has long been recognized as useful in infertility (August, 1961) but has not been the subject of any published trials. A review of the literature has revealed only two articles. Mackett and Madden (1989) presented a series of four women with infertility who had failed to respond to treatment. Three of the four had had previous pregnancies. They were treated individually with hypnotic relaxation and given instructions to forget about trying to get pregnant. The sessions included Hartland's (1971) ego-strengthening routine, and the patients were taught self-hypnosis. All four conceived naturally, but one, sadly, aborted. This paper was presented at a hypnosis conference and the discussion afterwards revealed that many practitioners used hypnosis with infertile patients. One common theme amongst the hypnotherapists was to utilize visual imagery as part of the hypnotic programme. The imagery could be either symbolic or realistic. Each therapist claimed the success of his technique.

The other published report (Gravitz, 1995) describes the use of hypnosis in two cases of unexplained infertility. The therapy consisted of hypnotic relaxation and imagery. The patient was told that her 'infertility was due to the tension (tightening up) within her fallopian tube musculature, consequently resulting in a narrowing of the passage so that the ovum could not be propelled down it' (p23). She was then asked to note that as she relaxed she could visualize the fallopian tube muscle relaxing to a point where the egg could pass. She conceived two months after the single session. The second case concerned a 32 year old friend of the first woman, and she was treated in exactly the same way. She too conceived in less than three months following the hypnotic intervention. The author commented on the positive mindset created for the second patient by the success of her friend.

The successful case report is a compelling way to promote the use of hypnosis, but it should be noted that practitioners tend not to report their failures. The following case histories demonstrate how useful it is to identify any psychological 'block' to fertility.

Case example: Susan

Susan was a 28 year old nurse who had been told that she was producing antibodies to her husband's sperm and that her chances of conceiving naturally were 'a million to one'. She had been hypnotized before for the infertility, but nothing was revealed. She and her husband were saving up for another cycle of IVF, the first having been unsuccessful. She presented to the GP in a very distressed state because colleagues had given her maternity leave leaflets for 'a bit of fun'. Arrangements were made for her to have another session of hypnotherapy whereupon, immediately after induction, she burst into tears and recounted how she had been raped while on holiday in Greece when she was 17. She was allowed to work through this in her own time and felt the need to be 'cleansed'. This she did by visualizing herself being scrubbed with disinfectant. She had never previously told anyone of the rape and felt relieved to have been able to share it. The following month she conceived naturally against all the odds and successfully delivered a healthy baby girl.

Case example: Jane

Jane was a 30 year old midwife who had experienced four years of infertility for which no cause had been found despite extensive investigations. Under hypnosis she was asked if her unconscious mind knew of any reason why she had not become pregnant. Jane responded with ideomotor signalling that there was a reason. An ideomotor signal indicated that it was all right to investigate the reason, and she spontaneously regressed to about 12 years old and said, *"I must not get pregnant."* It transpired that at that time an elder sister had become pregnant out of wedlock and had caused great upset in the family. Mother had sat her down and instructed her, *"And you, my girl, must not get pregnant!"* She was able to edit this instruction as being appropriate at the time but not appropriate now. That file was archived, and she indicated that she felt she could now conceive. Within a month of that session she had separated from her husband and soon began a relationship with her neighbour (now her husband), following which she had two children.

Of course, it is impossible for anybody to say that the pregnancies occurred because of the hypnosis, but both cases serve to show the value of hypnotic intervention in helping patients come to terms with their own set of circumstances.

Brann (1996) further developed the idea of using hypnosis as a tool to uncover any psychological block to pregnancy. In a series of 23 patients, 11 indicated that they had a psychological block to pregnancy. The blocks varied between family stresses, expectation, grief, work stress and an image of a 'hostile womb'. The study also utilized the concept of 'corrective imagery'. Of note is that only a quarter of the infertile women could visualize eggs in their ovaries, and it should be remembered that this group had been thoroughly investigated and all knew that they ovulated! Strangely only 40% of the fertile control group could see eggs. Using corrective imagery the reproductive system was changed to look and feel as they wished it to.

Case example: Edwina

At 25, Edwina was already a high flying financial analyst and she had found it difficult to come to terms with her inability to conceive. She had had very irregular periods since coming off the contraceptive pill eighteen months before. She was also somewhat sceptical about how emotions could affect fertility. Despite only a very light trance (self-reported three out of a ten point scale) at the first session, she did report the absence of eggs in the ovaries and was unable to visualize conception, *"There are no eggs and the sperm just sit doing nothing."* She also reported that her ovulation centre was *"closed down."*

She had found the relaxation tape unexpectedly useful and came for the second session in a completely different frame of mind. She self-reported a trance depth of 8–9 and reported at the psychological block question, *"There are no eggs, my ovaries are dormant; it's all because of the pill."* Before it was possible to 'reboot' her ovaries, it was necessary to search back to an earlier incident. Her 'computer' took her back along the corridors of her mind to the time she started the pill at age 16. Her doctor had told her that with an irregular cycle she might have problems with her periods later. She was reassured that this need not be permanent and that the ovaries could 'fire-up' at any time. She then 'rebooted' her ovaries and felt good about it. She was easily able to visualize conception and reported that her ovulation centre was 'all systems go'. She conceived naturally two months later.

This study identified not only the usefulness of identifying an underlying psychological block but also the benefit of using 'corrective imagery' in the therapy. Although the study was too small to obtain any meaningful data on pregnancy rates, the techniques used showed benefits on depression, anxiety, emotional distress and sexual satisfaction for all participants. The following approach to infertility is, therefore, recommended:

- Induce and deepen hypnosis using any relaxation method.
- Use an uncovering method (e.g. computer search, room in depths of mind and ideomotor signalling) to identify if there are any psychological blocks to pregnancy.

If an affirmative answer is received, then resolve the block using whatever method seems appropriate.

- Ask them to shrink themselves down so small they can go inside their body and look at their reproductive organs: ovaries, tubes, womb and vagina. Check as to whether there are eggs in the ovaries; if not, then ask them to correct the image until they are satisfied. Make sure the tubes are patent and the womb is comfortable, cosy and ready to receive the egg, correcting any unsatisfactory images. At this point it can be useful to get them to check their 'hormone control centre'; many women feel this is *"a mess," "chaotic"* or *"muddled,"* and correcting this is useful.
- Once the basic images are okay, ask the patient to imagine she is inside her womb just after intercourse and get her to describe what happens. This can often be quite enlightening: *"Nothing is happening – the sperm can't get through" "The sperm are just sitting there doing nothing," "My womb is hostile"* or *"The sperm are biting me!"* Whatever is described, it is important to correct the image and, if necessary, explore the reason for the problem.
- Continue with this theme asking the patient to observe an egg being released from the ovary and moving down the tube to be met by the sperm: *"The egg is too hard"* or *"The sperm are not even trying."* Once this is corrected and conception visualized, the fertilized egg is encouraged and guided to a welcoming, warm cosy womb so that the egg can nestle into the wall to obtain nourishment.
- Once the imagery of the reproductive tract and conception are satisfactory, suggest that they turn down any anxiety or depression, and turn up their relaxation and sexual satisfaction. Suggest they mentally rehearse returning to a sexual relationship unhindered by the thoughts of infertility.
- Use ego strengthening.
- Use post-hypnotic suggestion that they will feel good, relaxed and positive.
- Bring out of hypnosis.

A second session about a month after the initial one is suggested. It is important not to 'promise' a successful outcome but to reassure that they are doing all that they can and nature will be the final arbiter. One of the benefits of hypnosis is that it allows resolution of some of the sequelae of infertility, and even if conception does not occur they may feel more accepting and less distressed by the situation.

There is also a role for hypnotherapy in supporting patients through assisted conception programmes. These are incredibly stressful, and evidence suggests that outcomes are more favourable for those who use hypnosis.

Meadowcroft *et al.* (1990) conducted a prospective controlled study of the effect of hypnotherapy on stress levels and outcome of treatment in couples undergoing IVF treatment. 49 couples, who were on the waiting list for IVF as part of their investigation, were randomly assigned to a training programme in relaxation training by autohypnosis or IVF alone. One third of those offered hypnosis refused and thus became a third group.

Analysis of all couples' initial questionnaire scores showed female stress levels to be higher than those of their partners. Stress was highest where a male cause of infertility was present and increased with longer duration of infertility. Stress levels rose in all couples at the time of oocyte recovery but the rise was lowest in those using autohypnosis and greatest in those refusing the hypnotherapy treatment. Following IVF scores were lower than prior to treatment in those using autohypnosis but remained high in those who refused treatment. Although there were too few pregnancies for valid comparison, the conception rate was higher in those using autohypnosis, compared to those refusing hypnosis or undergoing IVF alone (27% vs. 17% vs. 17% respectively).

Levitas *et al.* (2006) in a controlled trial have also shown that patients using hypnosis at the time of embryo transfer in their IVF programme have a better outcome than those in the normal treatment group. Out of 98 cycles 52 (53.1%) clinical pregnancies were obtained in the hypnosis group compared to 29 from 96 cycles (30.2%) in the control group. Implantation rates were also better, 28% vs 14.4% respectively. Interestingly, they report that patients attitude to the treatment was more favourable with the hypnosis.

Relaxation and mental rehearsal are useful techniques to use with those undertaking assisted conception programmes. Each stage of the cycle is stressful, and the time awaiting the outcome of each stage seems like eternity. Time distortion is a feature of hypnosis, and suggestions that the waiting times seem to go very quickly are much appreciated by the patients. Levitas *et al.* (2006) likened the embryo transfer to the reception of long-awaited and very welcome guests. Interestingly, they discuss the role of uterine contractions in failure at the embryo transfer stage, yet their paper does not record that they give specific suggestions for uterine relaxation. Early reports of using hypnosis in pregnancy showed that labour was prolonged due to relaxing and slowing of the contractions, but when specific instructions for a quicker labour were given, labour length shortened. It is likely to be helpful to specifically suggest, and mentally rehearse, the womb relaxing at the time of embryo transfer.

It should not be forgotten that similar techniques can be used for men with oligospermia prior to collection of semen for intra-cytoplasmic sperm injection (ICSI). Time scales are important here: spermatogenesis takes about 64 days, so it is important to begin the therapy several weeks before semen collection.

References

Aronson, H. & Gilienke, J. (1963), A study of the incidence of pregnancy following adoption. *Fertility and Sterility*, 14, 547–51.

Arronet, G., Berquist, C. & Parekh, M. (1974), The influence of adoption on subsequent pregnancy in infertile marriage. *International Journal of Infertility*, 19, 159–62.

August, R. (1961), *Hypnosis in obstetrics*. New York, Blakiston.

Brann, L. (1996), Unexplained infertility: can hypnosis identify those who have a psychological block to pregnancy? Sheffield, Sheffield University, Department of Psychiatry.

Connolly, J., Edelmann, R. & Cooke, I. (1987), Distress and marital problems associated with infertility. *Journal of Reproductive and Infant Psychology*, 5, 49–57.

Domar, A. & Seibel, M. (1990), Emotional aspects of infertility, in Seibel, M. (Ed.) *Infertility: a comprehensive text*. Norwalk, CT, Appleton Lange. p 23–35.

Domar, A., Zuttermeister, P. & Friedman, R. (1993), The psychological impact of infertility: a comparison with patients with other medical conditions. *Journal of Psychosomatic Obstetrics and Gynaecology*, 14, 45–52.

Domar, A., Zuttermeister, P., Seibel, M. & Benson, H. (1992), Psychological improvement in infertile women after behavioural treatment: a replication. *Fertility and Sterility*, 58, 144–7.

European Society Of Human Reproduction and Embryology. (1996), Infertility revisited: the state of the art today and tomorrow. *Human Reproduction*, 11, 1779–1807.

Gravitz, M. A. (1995), Hypnosis in the treatment of functional infertility. *American Journal of Clinical Hypnotherapy*, 38, 22–6.

Harrison, R. F., O'Moore, A. M., O'Moore, R. R. & McSweeney, J. R. (1981), Stress profiles in normal infertile couples: pharmacological and psychological approaches to therapy, in Insler, V. & Bettendorf, G. (Eds.) *Advances in diagnosis and treatment of infertility*. Amsterdam, Elsevier. p 143–57.

Hartland, J. (1971), *Medical and dental hypnosis and its clinical applications*. London, Bailliere Tindall.

Keye, W. R. (1984), Psychosexual responses to infertility. *Clinical Obstetrics and Gynaecology*, 27, 760–6.

Lenton, E. A., Brook, L. M., Sobowale, O. & Cooke, I. D. (1979), Prolactin concentrations in normal menstrual cycles and conception cycles. *Clinical Endocrinology*, 10, 383–91.

Levitas, E., Parmet, A., Lunenfeld, E., Bentov, Y., Burstein, E., Friger, M. & Potashnik, G. (2006), Impact of hypnosis during embryo transfer on the outcome of in vitro fertilization-embryo transfer: a case-control study. *Fertility and Sterility*, 85, 1404–8.

Mackett, J. & Maden, W. (1989), Simple hypnotherapy for infertility, in Waxman, D., Pedersen, D., Wilkie, I. & Mellett, P. (Eds.) *Hypnosis: the Fourth European Conference at Oxford*. London, Whurr. p 201–5.

Meadowcroft, J., Hinton, R. A., Wardle, P. G., Pike, D. & Hull, M. G. R. (1990), unpublished report.

Miyabo, S., Asato, T. & Mizushima, N. (1977), Prolactin and growth hormone responses to psychological stress in normal and neurotic subjects. *Journal of Clinical Endocrinology and Metabolism*, 44, 947–51.

Noel, G. L., Suh, H. K., Stone, J. G. & Frantz, A. G. (1972), Human prolactin and growth hormone release during surgery and other conditions of stress. *Journal of Clinical Endocrinology*, 35, 840–51.

O'Moore, A. M., O'Moore, R. R., Harrison, R. F., Murphy, G. & Carruthers, M. E. (1983), Psychosomatic aspects in idiopathic infertility: effects of treatment with autogenic training. *Journal of Psychosomatic Research*, 27, 145–51.

Sandler, B. (1965), Conception after adoption: a comparison of conception rates. *Fertility and Sterility*, 16, 313–22.

Sandler, B. (1968), Emotional stress and infertility. *Journal of Psychosomatic Research*, 12, 51–9.

Sobrinho, L. G., Simões, M., Barbosa, L., Raposo, J. F., Pratas, S., Fernandes, P. L. & Santos, M. A. (2003), Cortisol, prolactin, growth hormone and neurovegetative responses to emotions elicited during an hypnoidal state. *Psychoneuroendocrinology*, 28, 1–17.

Wilkes, S., Chinn, D. J., Murdoch, A. & Rubin, G. (2009), Epidemiology and management of infertility: a population-based study in UK primary care. *Family Practice*, 26, 269–74.

33

Psychosexual Problems

Dr Peter J Hawkins and Dr Les Brann

Introduction

Before working with sexual problems the clinician should be familiar with the physiological, medical, psychological and cultural aspects of normal and abnormal sexual functioning. Dysfunctions occur when there are disruptions of any of the four stages of sexual response (i. e. desire, excitement, orgasmic and resolution). They may be life-long or develop after a period of normal sexual functioning. They may also be present in all sexual activities or may be situational, such as a man who has an erection during masturbation but not during sexual interaction with a partner.

Psychosexual Problems

There are a number of common psychosexual problems (Watson & Davies, 1997). They can be defined as an inability to derive pleasure and satisfaction from sexual activity and include lack of libido, aversion and avoidance of any genital contact with a partner, male erectile disorder (inability to attain or maintain an erection conducive to sexual activity) and ejaculation problems (the most common being premature ejaculation), lack of female sexual arousal or orgasm, dyspareunia and vaginismus.

It should be noted that for a diagnosis to be made, the above dysfunctions need to be persistent and recurrent. The possibility of there being an organic basis for the dysfunction

The Handbook of Contemporary Clinical Hypnosis: Theory and Practice, First Edition.
Edited by Les Brann, Jacky Owens and Ann Williamson.
© 2012 John Wiley & Sons, Ltd. Published 2015 by John Wiley & Sons, Ltd.

should be excluded before assuming a psychological causation. Kaplan (1995) argues for a multi-causal theory of sexual dysfunctions on several levels (intrapsychic, interpersonal and behavioural) and lists four factors as playing a role in the development of these disorders. These are misinformation or ignorance regarding sexual and social interaction, unconscious guilt and anxiety concerning sex, performance anxiety (the most common cause of erectile and orgasmic dysfunctions) and partners' failure to communicate with each other regarding their sexual feelings and those behaviours in which they want to engage.

One of the main barriers to successful performance and enjoyment is stress and anxiety. Worrying about performance can cause impotence or premature ejaculation, and repeated failure during intercourse leads to anxiety and frustration. In women, unconscious conflicts concerning sexual activity may be responsible for vaginismus, an involuntary reflexive spasm of the vaginal muscles and perineum that prevents penetration from taking place. Cognitions (thoughts) and moods (emotions) shape each person's experience of sexual arousal and behaviour. Attentional processes are also important: in the common experience of spectatoring, people focus on their own performance, often expecting failure, rather than on the sensuality of lovemaking. Pain, ruminations and worries also divert attention. Intense negative emotions tend to reduce sexual activity and performance, but the association is not close. In depression, sexual enjoyment is often diminished but occasionally increased; the preferred erotic behaviour may alter, often becoming more passive; and it must be borne in mind that anti-depressant drugs may also adversely affect sexual response.

One of the most common sexual problems is inhibited sexual desire, which affects more women than men. Low libido is something that one in three women experience at some point in their lives (Laumann *et al.*, 1999), often with a concomitant feeling of inadequacy and abnormality. The usual response of a sex therapist is to design a programme to restore or enhance the woman's libido, whereas a more appropriate intervention might be one of reassurance. Pertot (2005) contends that the male model of sexual appetite has duped both women and professional sex therapists. She argues that women are now beginning to challenge the male model of sexual needs, which as a result may cause considerable discord between couples. This clearly demonstrates how behaviours and consequent medical and psychotherapeutic interventions are essentially politically and culturally defined. In a similar vein it has recently been postulated that variations in female orgasmic functioning may be a result of genetic influences rather than socio-cultural ones (Dunn *et al.*, 2005). Their results showed a significant genetic influence with an estimated heritability for difficulty reaching orgasm during intercourse of 34% and 45% for orgasm during masturbation. As with most human functioning, it is multi-factorial and complex.

Philips and Frederick (1995) have suggested that sexual dysfunction may be related to interpersonal traumatic re-enactment. There is extensive evidence of impaired sexual functioning among victims of childhood sexual abuse, rape, domestic violence and combat (e.g. Becker *et al.*, 1986). Issues may include fear of sex, arousal dysfunction and decreased sexual satisfaction. Specific issues that may need to be explored by the therapist include frequency of sexual contact; degree of satisfaction; arousal level; nature of sexual interactions; thoughts, feelings and fantasies that accompany arousal and any concerns that patients may have about their sexual functioning. One of the major hypnotherapeutic methods used to deal with this type of problem is ego-state therapy, although other hypnoanalytical methods may also be utilized (Phillips & Frederick, 1995).

Good accounts of human sexual functioning can be found in standard textbooks (e.g. Kleinplatz, 2001; Leiblum & Rosen, 2000; Masters *et al.*, 1995; Wincze & Carey, 2001).

Hypnosis and Sexual Problems

Hypnosis has been used in the treatment of sexual disorders for many years. Erickson and Kubie (1941) presented the earliest known case of the successful treatment of inhibited sexual desire with hypnosis. Hypnotic interventions with sexual dysfunctions seem to hold considerable promise in sex therapy (Araoz, 2005), although the literature consists almost exclusively of case studies and outcome reports (Araoz, 1985; Bakich, 1995; Beigel, 1980; Crasilneck, 1982; Degun & Degun, 1982; Erickson & Rossi, 1953/2001; Hammond, 1984, 1985; Zilbergelt & Hammond, 1988). Sexual problems can often be dealt with by self hypnosis, which helps the individual relax. Hypnosis can also be used to assist with issues relating to poor body image, guilt, fear of sex and fear of sexual encounters.

Often, there is an overemphasis on the individual patient with the neglect of important relationship factors; and therapy should be aimed at fostering healthier interactions with partners and family. If the relationship between partners is bad, then this is not conducive to sexual desire and consequently sexual problems may be manifested. In the context of the treatment of sexual problems, it should be recognized that hypnosis is often a secondary or facilitating strategy, which increases the effectiveness of a range of adjunctive psychotherapeutic approaches, such as insight oriented psychotherapy, rational emotive cognitive restructuring, desensitization and so on.

Hammond (1990) presents some of the advantages of using hypnosis in sex therapy in that it may be used in the treatment of the individual patient without the presence of a partner (the largest and most extensive follow-up reports on the use of hypnosis with sexual dysfunction have been on individual patients with erectile dysfunction – see Crasilneck, 1982). It allows rapid exploration and identification of underlying conflicts, factors outside of conscious awareness and unresolved feelings about past events. Such events and their associated feelings can be accessed and 'worked through' at an unconscious level by using ideodynamic finger signalling. Self hypnosis may provide the patient with a sense of self control and a technique for stress management. This can provide them with a tool for anxiety reduction as well as for the arousal of sexual passion through sexual imagery prior to sexual involvement. Hypnosis can increase hope and expectation of change, together with increased feelings of confidence and self esteem. 'Trance ratification' procedures such as arm levitation can convince patients of the power of their own mind to do things without consciously trying such that they have more potential than they realized. Perhaps their mind is powerful enough to stir sexual desire, facilitate orgasm or create erections.

The use of hypnosis can facilitate the resolution of negative emotions and allow access to the patient's strengths and resources. Imagery can allow the patient to release 'bottled up' feelings such as anger (see page 136) or resentment, and ego-strengthening techniques can help build the patient's self esteem.

Hypnotic age regression may allow revivification of memories that help rekindle and recapture positive sexual feelings and affection. Hypnotic imagery and self hypnosis can help to focus attention and increase sensory awareness, thereby facilitating increased arousal and pleasure.

Various uncovering techniques can lead to the exploration of unconscious material that may underpin the problem.

Use of Hypnosis

Hypnoanalysis

The aims of hypnoanalysis in sex therapy are to uncover unconscious conflict, to release fears which inhibit sex arousal, to restructure associations and orientation to sex objects, to dispel inhibiting identifications and to be ego strengthening.

There are a number of reports of the use of hypnoanalytical approaches in dealing with sexual problems including hypnotic age regression (Wijesinghe, 1977), dream analysis (Degun & Degun, 1982), and ventilation of repressed negative feelings (Levit, 1971). Rossi and Cheek (1988) suggest that a 'combination of light hypnosis with use of unconscious, symbol movements or ideomotor responses allows rapid access to significant information and rapid, productive rehearsal with problems of sexual dysfunction in the time limitations of three office visits, comprising two hours' (p. 346).

Direct symptom removal

Several studies involving direct symptom removal have been reported, for example visualization of sexual encounters with suggestions of improved sexual performance (Schneck, 1970), hypnotic recall of previous positive sexual experiences coupled with hypnotic time distortion to prolong pleasure (Hawkins, 1996), positive imagery of having successful sexual intercourse combined with positive self statements (Cheek & LeCron, 1968) and suggestion of catalepsy (see case study, session 3).

Indirect approaches

Hammond (1990) describes a number of metaphors and guided imagery approaches which could be used as a basis for working with sexual problems, for example 'The Master Control Room Technique' (for inhibited sexual desire, ejaculatory inhibition, orgasmic dysfunction, erectile dysfunction and sexual addictions), 'Pee Shyness' (a brief metaphor illustrating the fact that sexual responses are automatic and unconscious), 'Going out for Dinner' (facilitating salivation and lubrication; moistening and lubrication could also be achieved by facilitating ideosensory responses), and 'Perspiring on a Warm Day' (useful for women who have problems with sexual arousal, and specifically in becoming lubricated). Guided imagery and erotic fantasy where the patient is engaged in spectatoring (see case study, session 4) and induced erotic dreams (see case study, session 5) have also been used.

Hypnosis as an adjunct in behaviour therapy

Specialist centres may have access to sex educational videos, but it is not recommended practice for the lone practitioner to use these due to the potential risks of abuse to both patient and therapist. However, hypnosis may facilitate relaxation and vivid imagery in order that graded hierarchies of sexual scenes and situations can be presented in the hypnotic state (systematic desensitization); this may contain elements of sexual foreplay and scenes of progressive social and physical involvement (Beigel & Johnson, 1980; Degun & Degun, 1982). Araoz (1985) described a number of approaches in systematic desensitization with hypnosis such as hypnosis with ego strengthening, watching a series of video tape scenes of normal sexual relationships whilst hypnotized, watching a graded series of slides of sexual situations whilst hypnotized and hypnotic recall where under hypnosis patients imagine past successful sexual experiences.

The conditioning process is reinforced by post-hypnotic suggestion, deep relaxation, visual imagery and the recall of past experiences. Self hypnosis is used to reinforce post-hypnotic suggestion.

Cognitive and experiential approaches

Negative self statements and sexual imagery may create and perpetuate symptoms, which happens particularly after sexual failure has been experienced. This is covert self reinforcement and acts as a turn-off. Hypnosis is used to re-create negative mood and the rehearsal of negative statements, dramatizing the adverse effects of the process. It is then employed to elicit counter-positive statements and imagery. Finally, self hypnosis is taught to reinforce cognitive restructuring (Burte & Araoz, 1994).

The case study that follows demonstrates how an integrative hypnotherapeutic approach can be used for the treatment of an erectile problem. Each session is briefly described paying attention only to the main interventions.

Case study – male erectile disorder (inability to attain or maintain an erection conducive to sexual activity)

The patient was referred for hypnotherapy by a physician at the local hospital.

Session 1

As well as asking the normal questions that would be expected in taking the case history, it is important to ask questions that are relevant to clinical hypnosis strategies in the treatment of sexual problems. As already explained the initial interview is critical in establishing rapport and building the therapeutic alliance. It is also useful to obtain information regarding the euphemistic and vernacular vocabulary that the patient uses to describe sexual organs as well as their knowledge of sexual anatomy and sexual functioning. After taking the case history (during which it was established that he had been examined by a urologist), John was taught how to increase sensory awareness by accessing the times early on in his marriage when he was able to become aroused quickly and achieve a good erection followed (appropriately) by orgasm. He was asked to:

> *Look at your hand and allow it to become lighter and lighter and float into the air . . . just allowing your mind to go back to the time when you were first married and enjoyed having sex with your wife . . . an activity that you both enjoyed . . . be aware of the sensations all over your body. You can feel the same sensations and pleasure, and function just as you did then . . . just allowing that to happen . . . knowing that you have the resources to allow that to occur when it is appropriate in the future, maybe even later today or tomorrow or sometime soon. Just allowing those sensations in your body to increase in intensity and enjoying those feelings as they flow into your penis . . . noticing how enjoyable that is. Just as it happened then so it can happen again now . . . nothing has changed. The only important things are the sensations you experience. Experience the texture, temperature, pressure and movement. Immersed in feeling and sensation . . . nothing to do but to feel and experience the pleasure.*
>
> *You can feel the same feelings, experience the same sensations and pleasure, and function just as you did then. Everything can be just as it was when you first married.*

This technique accessed the positive psychosomatic memories which John had and allowed him to become more confident, expectant and optimistic. This approach is an effective method of stress management and can be expected to lower feelings of anxiety and despair.

The level of experiencing of sensations could also be 'controlled' by the patient with an imaginary dial ('Master Control Room Technique'), so that they could turn the level of felt sensations up and down.

It was also important that John set realistic goals early on in the treatment process.

> *Now that these sensations are very strong, take them into the future . . . experiencing yourself making love with your wife . . . engaging in foreplay that is satisfying for both of you . . . achieving a good erection and inserting your penis into her vagina . . . both enjoying this and*

then reaching an orgasm. Be aware of how you are now feeling ... knowing that this can happen if you and your wife allow this to occur ... feeling more confident and exited about this prospect and wondering whether this will happen later today or tomorrow ... but knowing that this is a goal that you can aspire to and reach at some time in the future if it is appropriate for you and your partner to do that. And this is something that you can practice at home between now and the next session. All you need do is look at your right hand and as it floats then allow your eyes to close trusting in your unconscious mind to find an appropriate level of trance for accessing those early positive sexual experiences ... and experience yourself at some time in the future utilizing those sexual resources for a mutually satisfying sexual relationship with your wife.

Session 2

Ideomotor signalling is particularly useful for exploring relevant past events, and their associated distressed feelings, related to current psychological and psychosomatic problems. 'Yes' and 'No' finger signals were first established, and then John accessed prototypical experiences that were related to his sexual problem. Some conscious awareness of these events occurred, for instance an early relationship with his mother, and a later homosexual experience. These events were reviewed with minimal emotional abreaction. In this instance no interpretations were made by the therapist nor were any interventions made that actively encouraged the emotional ventilation, although this could have been a viable option.

John gave an unconscious 'Yes' signal that he was able to go into the future (sometime) without the problem. He hallucinated a date when this could happen at approximately four weeks from the date of the session. He was progressed to this date and experienced intensive positive responses. In hypnosis he was told that:

You have the resources to allow this to happen and you already know that you can change your bodily responses in an appropriate way to allow you to respond sexually when you are with your wife ... and your unconscious mind is utilizing the learnings that you have experienced here today concerning the origins of the problem to help you find solutions by the date that you have experienced or even earlier if it is appropriate for you ... and you may experience these pleasant sensations and experiences when you are dreaming later tonight ... and wake to find that you have a strong erection ... and you may be wondering when and whether this can really happen ... maybe tonight or will it be some other time ... although part of you knows that it really can.

Session 3

In this session, arm rigidity was suggested in order to demonstrate the control that John had over his own somatic functioning, and that he had the (unconscious) resources to allow his arm to become rigid and hard without doing anything to make that happen.

Just as you have complete control over your hand and arm, that you can make your arm go rigid, so you have the resources to control any part of your body in the same way, including your penis ... and you can keep the rigidity for as long as is appropriate for both you and your partner to enjoy a sexual relationship together. You have complete control over every part of your body including your penis. Your fears and anxieties will be less and as time progresses you may gain some understanding of your problem if this is appropriate for you.

The utilization of hypnotic phenomena in psychotherapy has recently been comprehensively discussed by Edgette and Edgette (1995).

Session 4

It is useful to encourage the impotent patient to talk about their innermost sexual fantasies and to replay them in trance. Whilst knowing the finer details of their fantasy is not necessary, it is essential to learn if these fantasies involve harm to another person or such things as paedophilia. If such things are revealed or suspected, rehearsal in trance must be avoided, and therapy specifically related to this will almost certainly be necessary. If you find yourself straying outside your area of competence, stop and refer on appropriately. It might be useful to engage the partner in these sessions. Patients can also take themselves on a guided sexual fantasy:

Allow yourself to imagine an exciting sexual fantasy, watching as people undress and seductively explore one another, and experience the excitement flow through your own body and into your genitals . . . perhaps encouraging your own real memories of fun and pleasure . . . and I don't know whether you will be able to use these important sexual memories tonight, or tomorrow, or after the weekend . . . and you can wonder when your unconscious mind will allow you to enjoy a sexual experience with your partner . . . and when it does you may find it particularly surprising to discover how aroused you can become.

Session 5

John entered hypnosis (using a self hypnosis method taught earlier) and was given a gardening metaphor which included references to green shoots, development beneath the soil, the seasons of the year and so on. The session concluded by utilizing creative dreaming as a way of involving unconscious search processes in problem resolution:

You already know how to experience stimulating dreams. And it is perfectly natural, following the kind of work we are doing, to have some pleasurable dreams. And your unconscious mind can work to increase your sexual desire towards your wife . . . and you may find that your dreams can be very creative and enjoyable . . . and you may be already wondering what you can dream later tonight. . . . And because your goal is to increase your sexual desire, in all probability you will have an interesting experience tonight, or it may be tomorrow night or even the night after . . . and you may be surprised when it actually happens but I would be surprised if you have to wait until the week-end. And those desires will be carried with you into your day, where they will appropriately influence your thoughts and behaviour. And even though you won't remember all your erotic and sexy dreams, in the morning, you can still sense and know that something is different, even if you can't quite put your finger on precisely what it is. And even if you don't believe that this can really happen you will be even more surprised when it does, knowing that you have this resource to allow you to find solutions even whilst you are asleep.

John reported that on the night following the session, he had a very erotic dream in which he awoke and 'discovered' that he had an erection. He was extremely pleased with this 'discovery' and the fact that he still had this ability. John was requested to replay his dream in trance and to indicate ideodynamically that appropriate physiological changes occurred. In this session, emphasis was placed on further ego strengthening and goal setting.

Session 6

This was a conjoint session involving both the patient and his wife. They were both regressed to a positive sexual experience early on in their marriage. Afterwards they were encouraged to describe their experiences to each other including the sensations and feelings they experienced in their bodies. Both partners were then progressed (in hypnosis) to sometime in the future when these experiences could be actualized, "... *knowing that your unconscious minds are already searching for the solutions even though you are not aware that this is happening.*" In this session the emphasis was on the development of hope and optimism, of personal control and of positive feelings of mastery.

Follow up

A follow up six months later revealed that the couple were now functioning sexually in ways that were appropriate for both of them. They were not concerned about the struggle to have 'good sex' anymore, and consequently a major stressor in their lives had been removed.

The above format is a good baseline for treating psychosexual problems, although different emphasis is needed for each condition and the interventions have to be personalized to the specific needs of the patient.

With more and more social pressure being put on performance and despite better sex education, many adults have totally unrealistic expectations as a result of being 'internet' trained; feelings of inadequacy tend to dominate the problem list. The therapist, therefore, has to be aware of the realistic 'norms'.

Premature Ejaculation

There is a need to be mindful of normal situations where ejaculation is likely to be quicker such as in teenage years (especially where the situation is far from ideal such as in the back of the car or while parents are out), new relationships and intercourse after a period of abstention. Reassurance of normality forms the basis of therapy. Waldinger *et al.* (2005) in a multinational study of 500 volunteer couples report a range of 55 seconds to 44 minutes with a mean of 6.4 minutes. They suggest that premature ejaculation is defined as an intra-vaginal ejaculatory latency time (IELT) of less than two minutes. However, Kinsey (1953) reported that 75% men ejaculated within two minutes.

The importance of taking a good history in these cases is highlighted by the following two case histories.

Anthony aged 32 was engaged to be married. The history highlighted that much of his problem related to regular absences from his partner when he was away on business and on return the re-bonding excitement in addition to the forced abstinence resulted in premature ejaculation. Exploration under hypnosis exposed a difficult previous relationship which he felt had ended because of his premature ejaculation, and he was terrified that his fiancée would leave him for the same reason. This fear was fuelled by her remarking that previous partners had lasted an hour! Therapy consisted of 'archiving' the previous relationship and deleting the perceived 'instruction' to last an hour. Direct suggestion was given that he would relax and last longer. He used the control dial to increase the IELT. He improved markedly, and they are now married with a new baby.

Jason was in a new relationship – he had clearly been very aware of his ability to last a long time, but since his previous relationship he had required treatment for a lymphoma and felt that this had impaired his performance. Concerns over health and body image following his treatment were explored under hypnosis. He reported that he could now last only seven and three quarter minutes. He was asked how he was so sure of the time, and it transpired that he spent most of his lovemaking looking at the clock! Therapy consisted of strong suggestions that his partner would appreciate some attention and that he turn the clock around! He did not attend for any more therapy.

Vaginismus and Dyspareunia

It is important to exclude any physical cause for these conditions and highlight, once again, that therapy is best done by health professionals who are able to treat any physical component of the problem. Special attention is needed when taking a history as to whether these problems are primary or secondary. Primary is where the patient always had the problem, secondary is where the problem started after a period of normal functioning. If secondary, events occurring around the onset are particularly pertinent. Consent is essential in these cases especially where there is a male therapist, and it is strongly recommended that the session be videoed or a chaperone be present. It is advised that the patient informs their partner that they are attending for therapy, but try to avoid having the partner in during the session as all too frequently the partner is causal to the problem.

A case of vaginismus

Stephanie was referred by the practice nurse as she had been unable to have a smear due to vaginismus. The vaginismus prevented all but the most cursory of examinations, but there did not appear to be any physical cause. Intercourse, although never especially pleasurable, had been possible until about a year ago, then gradually she began to tighten up to the point where penetration was impossible and attempts painful.

Under hypnosis the time around the onset was explored, and it transpired that a few months previously she had contracted genital warts from her partner. Stephanie was horrified at this and found the experience of attending the genito-urinary clinic degrading and unpleasant. The anxiety had caused her to tense up, and the investigations were very uncomfortable. Treatment was successful, but she never felt comfortable with intercourse following this, afraid that she would contract the warts or some other disease – even though this was with her regular partner. The older wiser self technique was used to reassure that these feelings were normal for that situation. Relaxation and graded mental rehearsal were used without effect. Regression was carried out to a time when intercourse was okay, and the feelings linked to further mental rehearsal, all to no avail.

At a further session she was asked to go into the depths of her mind to her questioning room where the answers would come from her subconscious rather than her conscious mind. 'Yes/no' lights were present in that room, and she was asked to indicate which light had switched on. She was asked if her subconscious mind knew what she had to do to solve the problem. A 'Yes' answer was obtained for *"I am with the wrong partner."* She subsequently ended that relationship and is now happily married. Intercourse was fine initially, but the vaginismus returned following a bout of thrush and she had some more hypnotherapy to regain her confidence.

It is inherent with this type of problem to identify relationship difficulties, and even if the therapist suspects these it is essential that it is the patient who arrives at that conclusion without having had it suggested. Where relationships are going through a bad patch, the approach outlined in the first case history is advised: utilize the feelings from a time early in the relationship when sexual relations were good, and mentally rehearse these feelings being re-kindled at the present time.

Female Anorgasmia

Primary anorgasmia is difficult to treat as there is no previous experience to utilize. Treatment is aimed at locating and removing any blocks to sexual feelings and, commonly a rigid upbringing is found, particularly where there has been an excessive emphasis on guilt and punishment as in certain religious denominations. These feelings have often arisen in childhood, and the programme is still running in the adult. The computer technique is useful here as it enables the old programme to be archived, and pressing the 'update' button allows adult, socially accepted feelings to replace it. Hypnosis must be accompanied by actual practice with the patients asked to use graded touching of themselves so that they feel comfortable with their own body. At this stage it is helpful to involve the partner (if appropriate) which enables a Masters and Johnson sensate-focusing approach to be undertaken (Masters *et al.*, 1995). Relaxation is the key to success and permission to explore and enjoy feelings from the sensual areas.

Many women struggle with a perceived problem of not being able to orgasm with penetration and need reassurance that only about 25% have had orgasms with penetration and that for many of those it is irregular and possibly a learnt response as the years pass.

Secondary anorgasmia is usually the result of a life event, illness or change of partner, and treatment is aimed at locating and resolving the causal event, then recalling experiences before the problem to re-instigate the response that they know exists. Unsatisfactory relationships are by far the most common cause of this problem.

Working with patients who have psychosexual difficulties is an area where specialist expertise is obviously necessary and where there is much potential for harm. It should be remembered that the therapist may be at risk as much as the patient, and safeguards such as having a chaperone may be relevant.

References

Araoz, D. L. (1985), *The new hypnosis*. New York, Brunner/Mazel.

Araoz, D. L. (2005), Hypnosis in human sexuality problems. *American Journal of Clinical Hypnosis*, 47 (4), 229–42.

Bakich, I. (1995), Hypnosis in the treatment of sexual desire disorders. *Australian Journal of Clinical & Experimental Hypnosis*, 23 (1), 70–7.

Becker, J. V., Skinner, L. J. Abel, G. G. & Cichon, J. (1986), Level of postassault sexual functioning in rape and incest victims. *Archives of Sexual Behavior*, 15, 37–49.

Beigel, H. G. (1980), The hypnotherapeutic approach to male impotence, in Beigel, H. G. & Johnson, W. R. (Eds.) *Application of hypnosis in sex therapy*. Springfield, IL, Charles C. Thomas.

Beigel, H. G. & Johnson, W. R. (1980), *Applications of hypnosis in sex therapy*. Springfield, IL, Charles C. Thomas.

Burte, J. M. & Araoz, D. L. (1994), Cognitive hypnotherapy with sexual disorders. *Journal of Cognitive Psychotherapy*, 8, 1–2.

Cheek, D. B. & Lecron, L. M. (1968), *Clinical hypnotherapy*. New York: Grune & Stratton.

Crasilneck, H. B. (1982), A follow-up study in the use of hypnotherapy in the treatment of psychogenic impotency. *American Journal of Clinical Hypnosis*, 25 (1), 52–61.

Degun, M. D. & Degun, G. (1982), The use of hypnosis in the treatment of psychosexual disorders: with case illustrations of vaginismus. *Bulletin of the British Society of Experimental and Clinical Hypnosis*, 1, 27–32.

Dunn, K. M., Cherkas, L. F. & Spector, T. M. (2005), Genetic influences on variation in female orgasmic function: a twin study. *Biology Letters*, 8 June.

Edgette, J. H. & Edgette, J. S. (1995), *The handbook of hypnotic phenomena in psychotherapy*. New York, Brunner/Mazel.

Erickson, M. H. & Kubie, L. S. (1941), The successful treatment of a case of acute hysterical depression by a return under hypnosis to a critical phase of childhood. *Psychoanalytic Quarterly*, 10, 583–609.

Erickson, M. H. & Rossi, E. (1953/2001), *Impotence: facilitating unconscious reconditioning*, in Erickson, M. H., *Milton H. Erickson: complete works. CD*. Phoenix, AZ, Milton H. Erickson Foundation Press.

Hammond, D. C. (1984), Hypnosis in marital and sex therapy. In Stahmann, R. F.& Hiebert, W. J. (Eds.) *Counseling in marital and sexual problems*. Lexington, MA, Lexington Books. p. 115–30.

Hammond, D. C. (1985), Treatment of inhibited sexual desire, in Zeig, J. (Ed.), *Ericksonian psychotherapy*, vol. 2: *Clinical applications*. New York: Brunner/Mazel. p. 415–28.

Hammond, D. C. (1990), Hypnotherapy with sexual dysfunctions: the master control room technique, in Hammond, D. C. (Ed.), *Handbook of hypnotic suggestions and metaphors*. London: W. W. Norton. p. 354.

Hawkins, P. J. (1996), Hypnosis in sex therapy. *Rivista di Sessuologia Clinica*, 111 (1), 19–30.

Kaplan, H. S. (1995), *Sexual desire disorders: dysfunctional regulation of sexual motivation*. New York, Brunner/Mazel.

Kinsey, A. C., Pomeroy. W. B., Martin C. E. & Gebhard, P. H. (1953), *Sexual behaviour in the human female*. Philadelphia, Saunders.

Kleinplatz, P. (Ed.) (2001), *New directions in sex therapy: innovations and alternatives*. Florence, KY, Brunner-Routledge.

Laumann, E. O., Paik, A. & Rosen, R. C. (1999), Sexual dysfunction in the United States: prevalence and predictors. *Journal of the American Medical Association*, 281, 537–44.

Leiblum, S. R. & Rosen, G. M. (2000), *Principles and practice of sex therapy*, 3rd ed. New York: Guilford Press.

Levit, H. I. (1971), Marital crisis intervention: hypnosis in impotence-frigidity cases. *American Journal of Clinical Hypnosis*, 14 (1), 56–60.

Masters, W. H., Johnson, V. E. & Kolodny, R. C. (1995), *Human sexuality*. New York, Longman.

Pertot, S. (2005), *Perfectly normal: a woman's guide to living with low libido*. New York, Rodale.

Phillips, M. & Frederick, C. (1995), *Healing the divided self: clinical and Ericksonian hypnotherapy for post-traumatic and dissociative conditions*. New York, W. W. Norton.

Rossi, E. & Cheek, D. B. (1988), *Mind -body therapy*. New York: W. W. Norton.

Schneck, J. M. (1970), The psychotherapeutic use of hypnosis: case illustrations of direct hypnotherapy. *International Journal of Clinical and Experimental Hypnosis*, 18 (1), 15–24.

Waldinger, M. D., Quinn, P., Dilleen, M., Mundayat, R., Schweitzer, D. H. & Boolell, M. (2005), A multinational population survey of intravaginal ejaculation latency time. *The Journal of Sexual Medicine*, 2 (4), 492–7.

Watson, J. P. & Davies, T. (1997), Psychosexual problems. *British Medical Journal*, 315 (7102), 239–42.

Wijesinghe, B. A. (1977), A case of frigidity treated by short-term hypnotherapy. *International Journal of Clinical and Experimental Hypnosis*, 25, 63–7.

Wincze, J. P. & Carey, M. B. (2001), *Sexual dysfunction: a guide for assessment and treatment*. New York, Guilford Press.

34

Children

Dr David Byron and Dr Sobharani R Sungum-Paliwal

Introduction

The use of hypnosis with children has a considerable history. Several ancient civilizations (Chinese, Egyptian, Greek, Indian, Mayan and Roman) had processes akin to hypnosis with children (Olness & Kohen, 1996). Weitzenhoffer (1959) observed that the therapeutic use of hypnosis with children has been recorded as far back as 200 years.

In France, Franz Anton Mesmer (1734–1815) applied 'animal magnetism' with both children and adults in his experiments, which in essence used imagination, suggestion and touch during the hypnosis process (Bailly, 1784). John Elliotson (1791–1868) actively used mesmerism as a cerebral physiological process in the management of various childhood problems and denied that imagination played any role in the cures (Olness & Kohen, 1996). John Milne Bramwell (1852–1925) succeeded with a wide range of childhood disorders using hypnosis.

Reports from the nineteenth century of the use of hypnotherapy with children have been noted by Olness and Gardner (1988), who also acknowledge its wide use today in many paediatric institutions in the United States for treating various problem behaviours in children.

Child Development

Child development encompasses not only chronological age and language but also cognitive, emotional, behavioural, physical, social and psychological development (Wall, 1991).

The effectiveness of the therapist's use of hypnosis with children will partly be contingent upon their ability to assess and adapt to the young person's developmental level and in particular to adapt to their level of language development. It is important to avoid treating the young people simply as small adults (Olness & Kohen, 1996; Wall, 1991). This illustrates the importance of training in child development.

Referring to a developmental stage which children under six pass through when they begin to differentiate between what is and what is not real. Kuttner (1991) observed, 'They can move easily between the states of fantasy and reality' (p. 42). This could account for why use of play, imagination, storytelling and therapeutic metaphor with hypnosis may be so much more effective with a young child than the more formal approach that includes eye closure and relaxation as used with adults.

Hypnotic Susceptibility of Children

It has been observed that children may have higher hypnotizability than adults and that this peaks in the pre-adolescent years (Morgan & Hilgard, 1973). The ability of the subject to experience hypnosis is a skill of the subject (Olness & Kohen, 1996).

Published Evidence

A review of clinical evidence by Gardner (1977) concludes that infants and toddlers respond to parental repetitive soothing actions and can become entrained and entranced by soothing music or stroking of the child's body showing that these phenomena are hypnosis in a primitive form. James Braid (1795–1860) recognized psychological aspects of hypnosis including faith and confidence in the process and considers that children use power of mind over body better than adults (Olness & Kohen, 1996). Kuttner and Catchpole (2007) reported that distraction by listening to a story is better for young children than the removal of the self through their own fantasy.

Whilst some may have doubted the effectiveness of hypnosis with children, studies have concluded that compared to adults the responsiveness of children to hypnotherapy is greater (Olness & Kohen, 1996).

A review of paediatric hypnosis research views clinical hypnosis as a promising tool with the potential to manage a variety of behavioural and medical conditions, and pain (Gold *et al.*, 2007). A large longitudinal study by Kohen *et al.* (1984) studied outcomes of relaxation and mental imagery for behavioural disorders, whereas Anbar (2002) used favourite place imagery, relaxation and positive suggestions for improving medical conditions along with self hypnosis. Clinical hypnosis is an efficient and effective tool for addressing the mind–body connection for children with respiratory disorders (Anbar, 2010). Saadat and Kain (2007) recommend the use of hypnosis as an adjunct for treatment in children.

Kohen (2001) elicits six categories of clinical application for child hypnosis: habit conditions, behavioural problems, bio-behavioural disorders, pain, anxiety and chronic or terminal diseases. Erickson (1959) emphasizes that hypnosis is not an absolute answer for terminally ill patients and that it cannot replace other medical procedures. Rather, it is one of the synergistic measures that can be employed to meet the patient's needs. Kohen (2001) believes that hypnosis can become an important potential tool in both adjunctive and primary management of a wide variety of clinical issues in child health care.

The use of hypnosis with children and young people appears to offer a wide range of benefits. Improvements in self esteem, locus of control, personal targets, home life and reduction in anxiety and in hopelessness have been recorded for a group of ten young people after being taught self hypnosis (Byron, 2007). A six month follow up recorded the maintenance of these changes. Today hypnotherapeutic approaches are used with children and young people to help address a variety of wellbeing issues.

Mental Health and Emotional Wellbeing

There are claims made that this is the 'age of anxiety' and that life today is more demanding, stressful and complex (Yapko, 2003). Whilst it is unclear as to whether there are more mental health problems in children than previously or if this is due to better recognition (Hartley-Brewer, 2001), children, it appears, do experience surprisingly high levels of mental health problems (Weare, 2004).

Modern definitions of mental health are observed to overlap with definitions of emotional wellbeing. As Weare (2000) and Hartley-Brewer (2001) note,

Mental health as it is now commonly defined includes the ability to grow and develop emotionally, intellectually and spiritually; to make relationships with others, including peers and adults; to participate fully in education and other social activities; to have positive self-esteem; and to cope, adjust and be resilient in the face of difficulties. (Weare, 2004, p. 7)

It is also important to bear in mind that any mental disorder has many causative factors, not least the external circumstances of the child concerned (Green *et al.*, 2005). Studies show that children with emotional and behavioural difficulties have increased susceptibility as adolescents and adults to mental illness (Buchanan, 2000).

Use of Hypnosis

Hypnotic suggestions should focus on goals rather than symptoms using concentration following deep relaxation (Spiegel & Spiegel, 2004). It is the author's (DB) experience that involving the young person in establishing their goals in therapy can also facilitate rapport, involvement and empowerment in addition to informing beliefs and setting expectations (Byron, 2007; Kirsch, 1990; Yapko, 2003).

Hypnosis training teaches sensitivity to language, to the patient's state of awareness and to the power of our own positive expectancy and rapport that underlie what is called the 'art of medicine' (Sugarman, 1996). The use of language patterns developed by Erickson to enhance and facilitate hypnotic experiences emphasizes a patient centred approach and gives rise to a much more playful and creative use of jokes, puns, metaphors and symbols (Grinder *et al.*, 1977). Since all hypnosis is self hypnosis (Araoz, 1981), it is important that a child says, *"Now I know I can do this!"* thereby forming psychophysiological resilience (Sugarman & Wester, 2007).

Cyberphysiology refers to self regulation or self governance of physiological processes by relaxation imagery training and biofeedback in addition to hypnosis. Children are much less critical and are usually much more amenable to persuasion and suggestion (Hartland, 1971). The main focus needs to be on imagery rather than relaxation Spiegel and Spiegel (2004), Hilgard and Le Baron (1982) and Zeltzer and Le Baron (1982) show that hypnotic imagery works especially well with children because they are so highly hypnotizable and so easily absorbed in imagery.

Children understand hypnosis as the same as or analogous to pretending, daydreaming or imagining (Kohen, 1986). Elman (1964) narrates a case of a three year old girl who demonstrated to a class of doctors the successful use of auto-suggestion in using make believe play to control her itching. Children's play and their creation and enactment of stories are richly permeated with metaphors (Gardner & Harper, 1997). Wester (2007) emphasizes that the transition from a relaxation technique to a deepening technique must flow smoothly confirming that deep relaxation is a key component of hypnosis among children. Individual pain management strategies include dissociation from the environment as well as suggestion, imagery of a favourite safe place and metaphors (Wobst, 2007).

Empowerment and Self Hypnosis

Storytelling and particularly collaborative storytelling have been described by Rhue and Lynn (1993) as a useful hypnotherapeutic strategy in treating sexually abused children. They and Friedrich (1991) note the critical relevance of establishing rapport and of the therapist listening carefully and using the child's own language in hypnosis. Teaching the child self hypnosis (Alman & Lambrou, 2002) can establish a sense of mastery and control in the child, and the author (DB) has noted the value of this in working with many children. A case of a 16 year old boy suffering night terrors after prolonged exposure to domestic violence provides an example (see page 518).

Children often perceive or experience help as something done to them or for them, usually by an adult. But by using hypnotherapy, children and young people can be taught a way of mastering their problems. Learning to use self hypnosis and how to help themselves can be a most empowering experience for the young person. This provides them with independence and a feeling of competency and control enabling them to access previously unrecognized, inner strengths.

Behaviour and Rapport

Young children may become very active during hypnosis and appear restless. Even adolescents may sometimes move constantly during hypnosis (Olness & Kohen, 1996; Yapko, 2003). Some children respond better to hypnosis if they have their eyes open. The younger the child is, the less they may be able to attend for more than small periods of time. For example, one seven year old was able to manage two to three minutes at a time before taking a couple of minutes out to visit Mum on the other side of the room. Consequently, a more direct approach and shorter sessions are used with this age group.

In addition to setting expectations, hypnotherapy can help to establish the degree of commitment to change. Byron (2007), for example, confirmed the previous findings of Keisler (1971) that anxiety reduction correlated with high commitment to improve. It is strategic and helpful at the outset to establish and clarify their desired outcomes. Whilst these may not always be the same as those of the parent(s), they can be most influential, particularly on expectations (Battino, 2009), and help to engage the child in the process.

It is important that the child feels safe and secure. This can usually be facilitated by a parent being present and in some cases doing the therapy in the home. The author (DB) has found parental presence during therapy extremely helpful and informative for all concerned, making it much easier for the child and parent to discuss any aspect of the treatment with each other between the therapy sessions.

Recording Results

Whilst it is important to record results, success may be due to factors other than hypnotherapy. However, when successful outcomes are recorded consistently, the link between hypnotherapy and the success becomes extremely persuasive. This has certainly been the experience of the author (Byron, 2007), and Olness and Kohen (1996) felt able to conclude, 'We believe that when some patients are treated for some problems while in the state of hypnosis, changes occur that would not have occurred had the patients been in the usual state of awareness' (p11).

Many of the difficulties experienced by children and young people can be seen to cluster around anxiety, depression or trauma. So these areas will now be more closely examined with case studies which illustrate the remediating effects of hypnosis.

Anxiety

Anxiety disorders can be very powerful and overwhelming. Anxiety can involve irrational worry and lead to avoidance of situations on which the worry focuses (Andrews *et al.*, 2003). Anxiety has been linked to various paediatric disorders such as sleep difficulties, enuresis, tics, headaches, irritable bowel syndrome, asthma, headaches (Schultz, 1991) and school attendance issues (Byron, 2002). It would be wrong to attempt to eliminate anxiety completely as it is a normal and useful response, as in fight and flight situations. Indeed a certain amount of anxiety can help students to study and perform well (Gibson, 1998). Hypnosis, however, can facilitate appropriate responses to anxiety, which may have previously resulted in fears and phobias. Where the child is able to identify the anxiety, self hypnosis can be particularly beneficial, and by learning what and how to do it they are empowered by having a way to control it.

Group study

Byron (2007) compared the effect of progressive muscular relaxation (PMR) with self hypnosis on anxiety in 20 secondary school children, referred for anxiety related difficulties, who were randomly assigned to either of the two treatment groups with similar numbers of male and female students in each group.

Each student, accompanied by a parent, attended four sessions to learn the treatment approach. The hypnosis group were taught to utilize various strategies such as imagery and ego strengthening when doing their self hypnosis. Follow up was undertaken on three occasions over the following six months to check for maintenance of the changes.

Anxiety was reduced in both groups. There was a non-significant, consistently superior trend of anxiety reduction, as measured by participants and parents, for the self hypnosis group compared with the PMR group. Improvements were also recorded for the self hypnosis group in self esteem, locus of control, personal targets and home life together with a reduction in hopelessness. In the self hypnosis group the improvements in all parameters were maintained over the following six months.

Depression

Wolraich (1996) describes childhood depression as:

> Sadness, irritability, or a loss of interest in normally pleasurable activities is a common and normal response to disappointment, failure, or loss. Such mood changes only present a problem if they persist for more than a few days and if they represent intense distress or significantly impair the child's ability to function or relate to others at home, school or play. ... Children and adolescents may not present with sadness, but may report aches and pains, low energy, or moods such as apathy, irritability or even anxiety. (p. 153)

Several hypnosis studies (Lynch, 1999; Montgomery *et al.*, 2000) have reported a reduction in depression alongside positive outcomes in anxiety, pain and other physical and psychological conditions. There is an increasing body of empirical evidence that hypnosis, particularly by empowering the individual, improves treatment results (Yapko, 2006). It had been previously thought that as depression was linked to adult psychosocial development it could not be experienced by children. However Kohen and Murray (2006) refer to epidemiological evidence that depression is growing rapidly in prevalence in children and young people.

In developing a treatment plan it is both important and helpful to address the child's understanding of their expectations, feelings and motivations. It is also helpful to identify their resources and to incorporate them into the therapy (Kiesler, 1971; Kohen & Murray, 2006).

Case study: Helen (anxiety and depression)

Helen (15 years) had been diagnosed with anxiety and depression by her psychiatrist. Helen had not attended school regularly since the age of 11, and her mother had been taken to court. There had been numerous school meetings attended by Helen and her mother and a group conference which had included wider family members.

Helen led a very isolated existence and was described by her mother as lacking in confidence. She was over-sensitive about what others thought of her and appeared paranoid at times yet also criticized herself. Her mother said she tried to get Helen to go to school but she just said, *"I can't do it."* Eight months ago, the psychiatrist added respiridone to the amitriptyline she was already taking at night, yet despite these she still took over an hour to go to sleep. She was also receiving support from a Child and Adolescent Mental Health Services social worker.

Helen presented as withdrawn, with most of her face hidden by her hair, and what could be seen was covered with heavy make-up. She had not been placed at secondary school with anyone she knew and, at the end of her first week, her father had walked out of the family home. Helen had then begun to panic and have headaches. No school work was being sent home, and consequently Helen had fallen far behind her peers.

The plan was to address the anxiety and depression as well as build confidence, relaxation and empowerment and improve her self image and sleep.

Session 1: relaxation, habit change and confidence building

Preparation for hypnosis included both physical and mental relaxation. Calmness was induced by suggesting she imagine watching a television able to receive any programme in the world. She was invited to select a programme which she thought she would enjoy using an imaginary control held in her hand, then to get comfortable and settle down to watch it. Then she was invited to relax beginning with her eyes, by letting the little muscles that operate them 'let go'. This approach was used until every part of her body had been visited.

Deepening was achieved using a breathing technique and counting from one to ten – reaching her special place at ten. She had been told that her special place could be real or imaginary but where she could imagine being safe and secure and the most in charge and in control of how she thinks and feels and behaves. She was then invited to explore her special place with each of her senses in turn to make it as real as if she was really there.

> *When you are so relaxed like this, because you are so much closer to that part of your mind where all your habits are stored, this is a unique opportunity to change any habit that you would like to change.*

She was asked to imagine a video of all her habits and to stop the tape and signal with her finger when she saw something which she would like to change. Once the tape was taken back to the beginning, she was able to rerun it but this time changing whatever part she wished, making it the way she would like it to be.

Benson's 'Magic Biscuit' method (2002) was used for confidence building. The subject was invited to make some special biscuits to eat which contain lots of things that people need to feel cared for, wanted, loved and happy. The ingredients for the biscuits included examples of good times which she had had, good things about Helen, times when she had had fun and names of people who wanted things to turn out well for her.

She was taken through each stage of the biscuit making and cooking. Then she was invited to eat as many of the biscuits as she wished, remembering that they contained lots of things which people need to feel cared for, wanted, loved and happy. Any remaining biscuits she was to put somewhere safe so she could nibble at one any time she wished. Helen was then invited to re-alert and given an opportunity to give feedback on the session.

Session 2: ego strengthening and determination, and presenting better image

Ego strengthening and determination were based on a script by Stanton (1990) in which the subject is taken to the top of a snowy mountain and invited to make a snowball. Down in the valley all the targets for improvement are waiting, for example feeling more in control, sleeping better and so on. In between these and the top of the mountain are barriers such as tiredness, fear, avoidance and so on. The subject is invited to roll the snowball down the mountain and to watch how quickly it grows bigger and travels faster until it is so huge and powerful that it smashes through each barrier as if it was not there until it comes to a halt near the targets.

> *...And now the way is clear... there is nothing to stop you completing your journey to get as close to your targets as you wish...just decide how you wish to complete the journey... by skiing or toboggan or any other way and then give me a signal by moving your finger... good... and before you begin, remember to register how good it feels each time you go through a barrier knowing that it cannot stop you any more...so take your time and let yourself have a really enjoyable time completing your journey and give me the usual signal when you have reached as close as you feel you need to be to your targets.*
>
> *Good... now notice how good it feels to you to know you can get as close as you want to your targets...you may even like to notice where in your body you feel this... and now I want you to let the scene fade and see yourself back sitting in the comfortable chair.*

Presenting a better image

She was asked to imagine looking out over what used to be a garden but which had become a mass of enormous weeds:

> *Your task today is to begin to pull each weed up by the roots and burn it on a bonfire... as you do you may notice little plants or flowers that come into view that have been struggling so hard to grow the way they were meant to be but couldn't because of the horrible, enormous weeds... they may even seem to perk up and even smile at you as you get rid of the weeds who have been taking their water and light and nutrition...just do what you feel comfortable doing today...you may water the flowers if you think they would like that... but I want you to do a really good job to make this a garden you can be so proud of... you can rearrange the plants and flowers if you wish to make the garden the way you want it to be... just give me a signal in the usual way when you have done what you feel comfortable doing today.*

Session 3: self hypnosis

Helen was taught self hypnosis in order to help through self talk, visualization, imagination and perception (Araoz, 1995). Having listened to tapes of her previously recorded hypnosis sessions and having become familiar with the process, it is quite rare for the child to find any difficulty in self hypnosis practice. It can also enhance the child's confidence in the therapeutic relationship from the very start by their knowing that the therapist is ultimately guiding them to this independence.

She was invited to practice by repeating the process that had been used each session to reach her special place and then to count herself back from five to one, opening her eyes on two and feeling wide awake on one. Helen was encouraged to do self hypnosis practice each day after first deciding what she was going to use (e.g. the snowball script) once she reached her special place.

Session 4: post-measures and review of self hypnosis

Self hypnosis practice and experience were reviewed with positive observations, and any necessary problem solving completed.

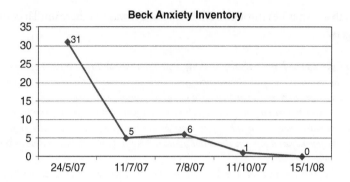

Figure 34.1   Outcome measures for Helen: Anxiety.

Pre-treatment scores were repeated after the fourth session, and the results showing progress were discussed with Helen. There were three further evaluation sessions at one, three and six months following session 4.

Results

Anxiety (measured by the Beck Anxiety Youth Inventory) reduced from 31 (24/5/07) to 5 (11/7/07) and to 0 (15/1/08). Depression (measured by the Birleson Depression Scale) reduced from 20 (24/5/07) to 2 (11/7/07) and to 0 (15/1/08). Self esteem (measured by the Butler Self-Image Profile) improved from 66 (24/5/07) to 2 (11/7/07) and to 0 (15/1/08). (See Figures 34.1, 34.2 and 34.3.)

At the final follow up session Helen was smiling and chatty, and she looked relaxed and happy. She was studying English and maths at home and determined to raise her grades so

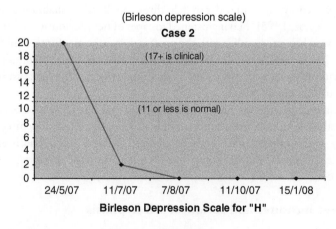

Figure 34.2   Outcome measures for Helen: Depression.

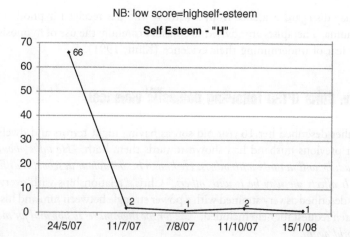

Figure 34.3 Outcome measures for Helen: Self esteem.

she could study hairdressing. Helen's mother confirmed her improved confidence (e.g. she had been to the dentist on her own for the first time following a traumatic experience when she was eight years old). Helen now talked to other people, and when they said they liked her she no longer disbelieved them.

Trauma

Schultz (1991) reports that children do experience post-traumatic stress disorder (PTSD) including flashbacks, diminished interest in activities and reduced affect.

Children and young people can become traumatized by experiences such as illness, medical treatment, abuse, accidents, domestic violence and natural disasters. The post-traumatic stress reaction can contribute to emotional and physical pain and depression. In particular, sexual abuse (Phillips, 2006) often leads to a childhood form of PTSD (Schultz, 1991).

One author (DB) has interestingly encountered examples of trauma in children caused by them overhearing adults discussing an event which took place before their birth! Trauma is a common antecedent to dissociation (Putnam, 1985) with the dissociation being an adaptation to the trauma experience (Spiegel, 1986).

In regard to the use of hypnosis with trauma related difficulties, Milton Erickson noted,

> Insight into the past may be somewhat educational. But insight into the past is not going to change the past. . . . Your patient has to live in accord with things of today. So you orient your therapy to the patient living today and tomorrow, and hopefully next week and next year. (qtd in Zeig, 1980, p. 69)

Courts may disregard evidence from a witness who has received hypnotherapy for the effects of trauma. Therapists are advised to consider carefully the use of hypnosis with such patients for fear of undermining their evidence (Kluft, 1991).

Case study: Chris (PTSD following domestic violence)

Chris's mother described her 16 year old son as having night terrors and dwelling on the violence her previous husband had shown towards them both. *"He talks about going and killing his dad; he will not mix with others. He knows his behaviour at school is different after a nightmare. It affects the way he is with others."* Chris's relationships with everyone in the family were described as very strained with a power struggle between him and his stepfather. Chris's written request for help included, *"... for the nightmares to stop and for me to like and trust the world again."*

The therapy plan was to address the PTSD, night terrors, assertiveness, relationships and confidence with family members.

Session 1: reprogramming habits and confidence building

Following induction and deepening with relaxation, the habit change script (see above) was used.

Session 2: ego strengthening and problem solving

A similar ego-strengthening method was used as above. Then the imaginary desk metaphor was used for problem solving.

Now Chris, it is about time that this desk, your life, had a really good sort out. So I would like to invite you to go through all the drawers in the desk, your life, and give them a really good sort out today. Get rid of any rubbish, any bad old memories you find in there that you don't need ... in any way which feels satisfying ... and if you are not sure whether to throw something away just wrap it up in a parcel and put it on one side until you are ready to deal with it. Now I want you to do a really good job on sorting out this desk, your life ... just do what you feel comfortable doing today ... you can always go back to do more any time you wish ... remember that you do have to practice habits to make them stick.

Session 3: age progression

He was asked to wander along a corridor in his mind. Each door had the name of a month on it, beginning with the present month.

THERAPIST: *I want you to stop when you come to the door which has the name of the month on it when you feel you will have reached where you want to be on all of your targets and then signal in the usual way by moving a finger.*

Good; now tell me the name of the month on the door.

Chris: *May.*

THERAPIST: *Okay, in a moment I shall invite you to open the May door and go inside. What you will find is an empty room with carpet and a chair and on the opposite wall a large video screen with video of yourself going about your usual activities but it will be in May. So now I would like you to open the door and see yourself entering the room and closing the door behind you . . . decide how you wish to make yourself comfortable . . . now just tell me what you can see yourself doing on the screen in May"* (sometimes it is helpful to ask either/or questions such as *"Is it day or night? . . . Are you inside or outside?"* and so on).

Information thus obtained from Chris was summarized back to him, and he was asked, *"I want you to notice any little bit of evidence that proves to you that you have reached where you feel you need to be on one of your targets."* When Chris gave this information it was again summarized back to him, and he was asked how it made him feel to know this will be how it is in May. This can be elaborated further by asking whether they would share this with anyone (parent, sibling or friend), or will they keep it to themselves? How do they think this person would respond, and how would they feel receiving this response? This was repeated a couple of times, and the suggestion given that Chris could return to the 'May room' whenever he wished.

Results

Night terrors reduced from 75% of nights before session 1 to 10% after three sessions and to zero at a follow up session one month later.

'Getting on with stepfather' improved from 30% before session 1 to 70% after three sessions and 80% at a follow up session one month later.

Assertiveness improved from 40% before session 1 to 80% after three sessions and 90% at a follow up session one month later.

Chris confirmed, *"My relationship with (Step) Dad is really improved, I can communicate a lot more clearly and don't see things as such a big deal. I have become a lot more confident."*

Mother observed, *"He is dealing calmly with things, is easier to communicate with and is more affectionate; before there was a big barrier."*

Noctunal Enuresis

Genetically many children do not achieve bladder control until seven or even later, and usually the history will highlight that one or other of their parents or close family has also been a 'late developer'. Secondary enuresis is when children begin wetting after a period of being dry and is usually a behavioural problem. However it is essential to exclude underlying physical causes such as diabetes or urinary tract infections before considering hypnosis.

Despite the later development, hypnosis can be used in primary hypnosis as some of the persistence of symptoms may be due to habit, and indeed Olness (1975) encourages this description as this helps to reduce blame, and avoids the problem becoming 'an issue' and the child feeling pressured.

Various published reports of the successful use of hypnosis in treating children with enuresis include Stanton (1979), Dowd (1996) and Banerjee *et al.* (1993). Stanton's work recorded that 15 out of 20 children in his hypnosis treatment group remained dry 12 months later.

When using hypnosis for this condition, it is important to take a history from the child and the parent in such a way as to avoid as much as possible the child's answers being influenced by the parent's. A 'brief therapy' technique can sometimes be beneficially employed by asking the child for exceptions to the difficulty (i.e. dry nights). This can then be explored and vivified with the child as evidence that there are already times that they are in control.

Where possible, and taking account of their developmental level, providing the child with education about enuresis, including a simple diagram of the process of producing, storing and releasing urine and the part played by their brain, can be most helpful (Olness & Kohen, 1996).

For secondary enuresis, however, some form of exploratory method may need to be used to link the beginning of the problem with causal life events. Using the 'room in the mind' method is good for children as is the use of a mental computer game where the hero finds how to open the secret door to expose the problem.

The use of therapeutic metaphor has proved effective in treating nocturnal enuresis. The writer (DB) has used successfully, with an 11 year old boy named Brian, a therapeutic metaphor described by Mills and Crowley (2001) about Sammy, a little elephant. In this case study Sammy is provided with similar interests and likes to those of Brian and even uses some of Brian's typical language to help the child identify with Sammy.

In the story Sammy has problems when carrying buckets of water and often spills the water. He is taught by a friendly camel how to carry the water carefully and to HOLD ON to it until he gets to exactly the RIGHT PLACE before he LETS GO. One day there is a fire in the village by the river. The other grown up elephants are away working, and Sammy is the only elephant left who can help. Everything depends upon him carrying buckets of water from the river without spilling them to help the villagers to put out the fire. By learning how to HOLD ON to the water until he gets to exactly the RIGHT PLACE to LET GO, Sammy is able to help them put out the fire. When the other elephants come back, he is seen as a hero.

Only the school and Brian's mother, but never Brian himself, had mentioned the enuresis problems to the author (DB). This may have been due to Brain's embarrassment. According to his mother he had never had more than two dry nights in a week since he was seven years old. A tape of the story of Sammy was made for his mother to play to him just before he went to sleep at night. At the next appointment with Brian's mother, her completed chart recorded Brian as having had 18 consecutive dry nights.

References

Alman, B. M. & Lambrou, P. T. (2002), *Self-hypnosis: The complete guide to better health and self-change*. London, Souvenir Press.

Andrews, G., Creamer, M., Crino, R., Hunt, C., Lampe, L. & Page, A. (2003), *The treatment of anxiety disorders: clinician guides and patient manuals*. Cambridge, Cambridge University Press.

Araoz, D. L. (1981), Negative self-hypnosis. *Journal of Contemporary Psychotherapy*, 12 (1), 45–52.

Araoz, D. L. (1995), *The new hypnosis: techniques in brief individual and family psychotherapy*. London, Jason Aronson.

Bailly, A. (1784), *Rapport des commissaires chargés par le Roi, de l'examen du magnétisme animale. Imprimé par ordre du Roi*. Paris, A Paris, de L'Imprimerie Royale.

Banerjee, S., Srivastav, A. & Palan, B. M. (1993), Hypnosis and self-hypnosis in the management of nocturnal enuresis: a comparative study with imipramine therapy. *American Journal of Clinical Hypnosis*, 36 (2), 113–19.

Battino, R. (2009), *Expectation: the very brief therapy book*. Carmarthen, Crown House.

Benson, G. (2002), Training handouts on using hypnosis with children and adolescents. In Heap, M. & Aravind, K. K. (Eds.) *Hartlands medical and dental hypnosis*, 4th ed. London, Harcourt.

Buchanan, A. (2000), Present issues and concerns, in Buchanan, A. & Hudson, B. (Eds.) *Promoting children's emotional well-being*. Oxford, Oxford University Press.

Byron, D. A. (2002), The use of hypnosis to help an anxious student with a social communication disorder to attend school. *Contemporary Hypnosis*, 19 (3), 125–32.

Byron, D. A. (2007), *Student anxiety and performance: a comparison of training in self-hypnosis with progressive muscular relaxation to enable students to increase control of their anxiety*. Unpublished doctoral thesis, University College London. p. 63.

Dowd, E. T. (1996), Hypnotherapy in the treatment of adolescent enuresis, in Lynn, S. J., Kirsch, I. & Rhue, J. W. (Eds.) *Casebook of clinical hypnosis*. Washington, DC, American Psychological Association. pp. 293–307.

Elman, D. (1964), The handshake technique, in *Hypnotherapy*, Glendale, CA, Westwood Publishing. p. 34.

Erickson, M. H. (1959), Hypnosis in painful terminal illness. *The American Journal of Clinical Hypnosis*, 1, 117–21.

Friedrich, W. N. (1991), Hypnotherapy with traumatised children. *International Journal of Clinical and Experimental Hypnosis*, 39 (2), 67–81.

Gardner, D. & Harper, P. (1997), Chapter 6: using metaphors and imagery, in Dwivedi, K. N. (Ed.) *The therapeutic use of stories*. London, Routledge.

Gardner, G. G. (1977), Hypnosis with infants and pre-school children. *The American Journal of Clinical Hypnosis*, 19, 158–62.

Gibson, H. B. (1998), Hypnotherapy and anxiety, in Heap, M. & Dryden, W. (Eds.) *Hypnotherapy: a handbook*. Buckingham, Open University Press.

Gold, J. I., Kant, A. J., Belmont, K. A. & Butler, L. D. (2007), Practitioner review: clinical applications of pediatric hypnosis. *Journal of Child Psychology and Psychiatry*, 48, (8), 744–54.

Green, H., McGinnity, A., Meltzer, H., Ford, T. & Goodman, R. (2005), *Mental health of children and young people in Great Britain*. Basingstoke, Palgrave MacMillan. p. 8.

Grinder, R., Delozier, J. & Bandler, R. (1977), *Patterns of the hypnotic techniques of Milton H. Erickson, M.D.*, vol. 2 Scott Valley, CA: Grinder and Associates.

Hartland, J. (1971), Chapter 3: general principles underlying the principles of induction. In Heap, M.& Aravind, K. K. (Eds.) *Hartlands medical and dental hypnosis*, 4th ed. London, Harcourt.

Hartley-Brewer, E. (2001), *Learning to trust and learning to learn*. London, IPPR.

Hilgard, J. R. & Le Baron, S. (1982), Relief of anxiety and pain in children and adolescents with cancer: quantitative measures and clinical observations. *International Journal of Clinical and Experimental Hypnosis*, 4, 417–42.

Kiesler, C. A. (1971), *The psychology of commitment: experiments linking behaviour to belief*. London, Academic Press.

Kirsch, I. (1990), *Changing expectations: a key to effective psychotherapy*. Pacific Grove, CA, Brooks/Cole.

Kluft, R. P. (1991), Hypnosis in childhood trauma, in Wester, W.C. & O'Grady, D. J. (Eds.) *Clinical hypnosis with children*. New York, Brunner/Mazel.

Kohen, D. P. (1986), Applications of relaxation/mental imagery (self-hypnosis) in pediatric emergencies. *International Journal of Clinical and Experimental Hypnosis*, 36 (4), 275–83.

Kohen, D. P. (2001), Application of clinical hypnosis with childrenl, in Burrows, G. D., Stanley, R. O. & Bloom, P. B. (Eds.) *International handbook of clinical hypnosis*. Chichester, John Wiley & Sons, Ltd.

Kohen, D. P. & Murray, K. (2006), Depression in children and youth: applications of hypnosis to help young people help themselves, in Yapko, M. D. (Ed.) *Hypnosis and treating depression: applications in clinical practice*. London, Routledge.

Kohen, D. P. & Olness, K. (1997), Hypnotherapy with children, in Rhue, J. W., Lynn, S. J. & Kirsch, I. (Eds.) *Handbook of clinical hypnosis*. Washington, DC, American Psychological Association.

Kohen, D. P., Olness, K., Colwell, S. & Heimel, A. (1984). The use of relaxation/mental imagery (self-hypnosis) in the managementof 505 pediatric behavioural encounters. *Journal of Developmental and Behaviour Pediatrics*, 1, 21–5.

Kuttner, L. (1991), Special considerations for using hypnosis with young children, in Wester, W. C. & O'Grady, D. J. (Eds.) *Clinical hypnosis with children*. New York, Brunner-Mazel.

Kuttner, L. & Catchpole, R. E. H. (2007), Chapter 2: developmental considerations: hypnosis with children, in Wester, W. C. & Sugarman, I. (Eds.) *Therapeutic hypnosis with children and adolescents*. Carmarthen, Crown House.

Lynch, D. (1999), Empowering the patient: hypnosis in the management of cancer, surgical disease and chronic pain. *American Journal of Clinical Hypnosis*, 42 (2), 122–31.

Mills, J. C. & Crowley, R. J. (2001), *Therapeutic metaphors for children and the child within*. Philadelphia, Brunner/Mazel.

Montgomery, G., Duhamel K. & Redd, W. (2000), A meta-analysis of hypnotically induced analgesia: how effective is hypnosis? *International Journal of Clinical and Experimental Hypnosis*, 48 (2), 134–49.

Morgan, A. H. & Hilgard, J. R. (1973), Age differences in susceptibility to hypnosis. *International Journal of Clinical and Experimental Hypnosis*, 21, 78–85.

Olness, K. (1975), The use of self-hypnosis in the treatment of childhood nocturnal enuresis: a report on forty patients. *Clinical Pediatrics*, 14 (3), 273–5.

Olness, K. & Gardner, G. G. (1978), Some guidelines for the uses of hypnotherapy in paediatrics. *Paediatrics*, 62, 228–33.

Olness, K. & Kohen, D. P. (1996), *Hypnosis and hypnotherapy with children*, 3rd ed. New York, Guilford Press.

Phillips, M. (2006), Hypnosis with depression, post traumatic stress disorder and chronic pain, in Yapko, M. D. (Ed.) *Hypnosis and treating depression: applications in clinical practice.* Abingdon, Routledge.

Putnam, F. W. (1985), Dissociation as a response to extreme trauma, in Kluft, R. P. (Ed.) *Childhood antecedents of multiple personality.* Washington, DC, APA Press. pp. 65–98.

Rhue, J. W. & Lynn, S. J. (1993), Hypnosis and storytelling in the treatment of child sexual abuse: strategies and procedures, in Rhue, J. W., Lynn, S. J.& Kirsch, I. (Eds.) *Handbook of clinical hypnosis.* Washington, DC, American Psychological Association. pp. 445–78.

Saadat, H & Kain, Z. N. (2007), Hypnosis as a therapeutic tool in paediatrics. *Pediatrics*, 120, 179–81.

Schultz, J. R. (1991), Hypnosis and anxiety in children, in Wester, W. C. & O'Grady, D. J. (Eds.) *Clinical hypnosis with children.* New York, Brunner/Mazel.

Spiegel, D. (1986), Dissociating damage. *American Journal of Clinical Hypnosis*, 29, 123–31.

Spiegel, H. & Spiegel, D. (2004), Chapter 15: pain control. In *Trance and treatment: clinical uses of hypnosis*, 2nd ed. Washington, DC, APA Press.

Stanton, H. E. (1979), Short-term treatment of enuresis. *American Journal of Clinical Hypnosis*, 22, 103–7.

Stanton, H. E. (1990), Increasing determination: the snowball. In Hammond, D. C. (Ed.) *Hypnotic suggestions and metaphors.* London, W. W. Norton.

Sugarman, L. I. (1996), Hypnosis: teaching children self-regulation. *Pediatrics in Review*, 17, 5–11.

Sugarman, L. I. & Wester, W. C., II (2007), Chapter 1: hypnosis with children and adolescents: a contextual framework, in Wester, W. C., II & Sugarman, L. I. (Eds.) *Therapeutic hypnosis with children and adolescents.* Carmarthen, Crown House.

Vandenberg, B. (2002), Hypnotic responsivity from a developmental perspective; Insights from young children. *International Journal of Clinical and Experimental Hypnosis*, 50, 3, 229–47.

Wall, V. (1991), Developmental considerations in the use of hypnosis with children, in Wester, W. C. & O'Grady, D. J. (Eds.) *Clinical hypnosis with children.* New York, Brunner-Mazel.

Weare, K. (2000), *Promoting mental, emotional and social health: a whole school approach.* London, Routledge.

Weare, K. (2004), *Developing the emotionally literate school.* London, Chapman.

Wester, W. C., II (2007), Chapter 5: induction and intensification techniques, in Wester, W. C., II & Sugarman L. I. (Eds.) *Therapeutic hypnosis with children and adolescents.* Carmarthen, Crown House.

Weitzenhoffer, A. M. (1959), A bibliography of hypnotism in paediatrics. *American Journal of Clinical Hypnosis*, 2, 92–5.

Wobst, A. H. K. (2007), Hypnosis and surgery: past, present, and future. *Anesthesia & Analgesia*, 104, 1199–1208.

Wolraich, M. (Ed.), (1996), *Diagnostic and statisical manual: primary care, pediatrics (DSM-PC)* Elk Grove Village, IL, American Academy of Paediatrics.

Yapko, M. D. (2003), *Trancework: an introduction to the practice of clinical hypnosis.* Hove, Brunner-Routledge. p. 436.

Yapko, M. D. (Ed.) (2006), *Hypnosis and treating depression: applications in clinical practice.* Abingdon, Routledge.

Zeig, J. (Ed.) (1980), *A teaching seminar with Milton H. Erickson.* New York, Brunner/Mazel.

Zeltzer, L. & Le Baron, S. (1982), Hypnotic and nonhypnotic techniques for reduction of pain and anxiety during painful procedures in children and adolescents with cancer, *Journal of Pediatrics*, 101, (6), 1032–5.

35

Learning Disability and Autistic Spectrum Disorder

Mr Cliff Robins

Learning Disability

As there is often confusion in the literature about the term it is important to define at the outset what is meant by 'learning disability'. Learning disability as used here is synonymous with 'intellectual disability' and the American term 'mental retardation'. The term is principally used to describe people with an IQ of 70 or less, who have a significant impairment of social and adaptive functioning with these problems present in the developmental period and not acquired as an adult (Department of Health, 2001). The degree of disability a person has can vary enormously. Some people never learn to talk; some need 24 hour support. On the other hand, people with mild learning disabilities can very often live independently.

Estimates of the number of people in the population with mild to moderate learning disabilities do vary, but the prevalence rate suggested is around 25 per 1,000 population, or 1.2 million people in England. For severe and profound learning disabilities the estimate is that there are about 210,000 people overall (Department of Health, 2001).

Despite advances in identifying pre-natal causes of learning disabilities, sometimes the cause remains unknown. There can be genetic syndromes such as Down's syndrome, cri du chat syndrome, or fragile X syndrome. There can also be prenatal drug and toxin exposure; foetal alcohol syndrome is a common cause. Other possibilities are exposure to chemotherapy, drugs or radiation, or exposure to lead or methylmercury.

There may be peri-natal causes such as complications related to prematurity, breech or high forceps delivery, multiple births, preeclampsia or asphyxia.

The Handbook of Contemporary Clinical Hypnosis: Theory and Practice, First Edition.
Edited by Les Brann, Jacky Owens and Ann Williamson.
© 2012 John Wiley & Sons, Ltd. Published 2015 by John Wiley & Sons, Ltd.

Post-natal causes such as malnutrition and lack of physical, emotional and cognitive support during infancy, viruses or bacteria, brain trauma, meningitis and accidents that cause severe head injuries may also occur.

With the move to deinstitutionalization and 'normalization' that came with the closure of long-stay institutions and the development of Care in the Community policies and Valuing People (Department of Health, 2001), there has been a growing interest in how people with learning disabilities manage community living. At the present time the majority of people with learning disabilities live in relatively small residential group homes in the community supported by staff who provide for their day to day needs (Robertson *et al.*, 2005). However, those who are able to live independently are encouraged to rent or buy property in the private and public housing sector. Whatever their situation, people with learning disabilities should be supported by local Health and Social Services community learning disability teams, although the eligibility criteria are becoming ever more stringent.

While the move to community living and 'normalization' is to be applauded, people with learning disabilities often experience powerlessness in everyday decisions, little self deter-mination and high levels of stress in community living (Lowe *et al.*, 1998). And although learning disabilities are not a mental illness per se, people with learning disabilities are more likely to develop mental health problems or have additional developmental disorders such as autism spectrum conditions (Department of Health, 2001).

Diagnosis

There have been advances in interventions for the mental health problems of people with learning disabilities (Bouras & Holt, 2010) with an expansion of research into this field (Cooper *et al.*, 2007; Deb *et al.*, 2001). However, the whole area of mental wellbeing in this group has received relatively little attention when compared to similar research in the general population. Psychological disorders are often overlooked in people with learning disabilities (Willner, 2005).

Deb *et al.* (2001) published diagnostic guidelines to assist with identifying mental health problems in this patient group. McGillivray and McCabe (2009) reported evidence for the diagnosis of familiar psychological problems in people with learning disabilities such as depression and anxiety, but diagnosis can be problematic; the evidence is that few people with learning disabilities and symptoms of a mental health disorder actually receive a diagnosis from their medical practitioner, or a referral to mental health services. There are specific scales that have been adapted for assessing psychological distress with these patients for example (Dagnan & Lindsay, 2004).

Published Evidence

The popular view that patients with learning disability cannot be hypnotized has been made in the absence of supporting data (Marcuse, 1950). Hypnotizability is more related to attention span, ability to respond to vivid imagery and creativity rather than to intelligence (Kroger, 2008). Garitte *et al.* (2009) found that young people up to the age of 17 with Down's syndrome could respond to suggestions in hypnosis. Hacker Hughes (2000) from his review of the literature argues that despite the limited data, 'there is without doubt, considerable evidence that people with learning disabilities are susceptible to hypnotic procedures' (p. 74–5).

Whelen (2007) reports benefit with cognitive therapy in this patient group, and as there is a significant body of evidence that hypnosis augments the effectiveness of cognitive-behavioural therapy (CBT; Gibson & Heap, 1991; Karle & Boys, 1987; Kirsch *et al.*, 1995) this would suggest that hypnosis has a role to play with these patients.

The Creative Imagination Scale (CIS; Barber & Wilson, 1978) is suitable for assessing hypnotic susceptibility, and is a simple and straightforward way of introducing hypnosis and of discovering how the individual may respond to suggestion (see page 21).

McCord (1956a, 1956b) found low levels of intelligence did not limit hypnotizability. He reported hypnosis not only improved relaxation and helped overcome sleep problems in people with learning disabilities, but also increased their attention span, improved their self concept and increased motivation and the belief they could achieve more in learning tasks. Johnson *et al.* (1981) argue that hypnosis may have a positive and constructive role in increasing self esteem, because hypnosis is essentially something done by the individual, rather than to them, and it involves the positive internal control of cognitions.

The case study with discussion and commentary below will illustrate the successful use of hypnosis and CBT.

Case Study: depression and anxiety

Angela was 25 when she was referred by her GP for problems of depression associated with anxiety and low self esteem originating in childhood. Over time she had developed negative cognitive schemata for herself. Angela said she attended a 'special needs' school because she was 'slow and stupid'. She felt that she was different from other people; she experienced a sense of hopelessness and felt she was a failure, that she 'falls short of some internalized ideal or standard' (Gilbert, 1998). She carried an awareness of what she saw as her 'differences, limitations and overall lack of power to effect change' (McGillivray & McCabe, 2009). Angela had internalized the stigma of having a learning disability, and it had become a core negative belief. She considered herself overweight, and she had experienced a long term decline in self esteem, body image and belief in her abilities which seriously affected her quality of life.

Whelan (2007) suggests that people with learning disabilities are exposed to detrimental life experiences, including repeated episodes of failure, which can influence the development of poor self esteem. Dagnan and Sandhu (1999) concluded that social comparison is associated with self esteem and depression in people with learning disability in the same way as it is for people without.

Fennell (1997) suggests negative experiences over time lead to global negative beliefs about the self. Angela certainly saw her problem as an integral part of who she was. She believed she was inadequate because of her 'learning disability', and this belief had been reinforced by belittling comments from significant people in her life. Angela lived with her partner, a man with borderline intellectual functioning whom, she said, called her 'fat, ugly and stupid'. She said she was fat, but that dieting didn't work. She felt strangers 'laughed' at her because of her size and because she was 'stupid'. Angela said that she felt alone, that she had no one to help her and that this made her feel depressed. She often felt people were 'getting at her', but didn't always understand why because she was 'too stupid'.

There is a well recognized link between depression and poor relationships and low levels of social support (Nezu *et al.,* 1995), and Angela experienced depression partly because of poor relationships and equally poor social supports. Following care proceedings by Social Services, her four year old son was in the care of Angela's parents, although she still saw him every day. She experienced the removal of her son as a rebuke; she was being 'told off' by the court as well as by everyone else; Angela felt that she had been found wanting and that the court action was more evidence of her lack of ability: evidence that she was, in her words, *". . . not good enough to be a Mum,"* showing the sort of negative persecutory thoughts often seen in people with learning disabilities (McGillivray & McCabe, 2009).

The main focus of the therapy was Angela's negative self image and low self esteem. Fennell (1998) sees low self esteem as a 'learned, negative, global judgement about the self, which influences how the person 'thinks, feels and behaves'. The problem is reinforced by negative self judgements based on 'hidden emotions' of shame and humiliation that lead the person to feel 'an object of scorn' (Gilbert, 1998).

The assessment was informed by functional diagnostic criteria (Deb *et al.,* 2001) which revealed that Angela had symptoms of depression, anxiety and poor self esteem. Angela's IQ was measured at 68 which demonstrated a mild level of learning disability (Wechsler, 1997) and indicated that she had the capacity to consent to the treatment and to benefit from the use of hypnosis in therapy (Stenfert-Kroese *et al.,* 1997). Her scores on the CIS were discussed with Angela in terms of her overall susceptibility, with positive emphasis placed on her ability in hypnosis and the modalities she scored highly on to highlight her specific aptitudes.

Angela contracted for ten sessions of cognitive-behavioural therapy with the adjunctive use of hypnosis. The approach used was a planned and integrative use of 'symptom-oriented' cognitive therapy aimed at the specific problem of low self esteem (Williams & Jones, 1997). Hypnotic suggestions were used to facilitate change in Angela's patterns of thoughts, feelings and behaviours as well as to help her gain insights into any underlying problems. The intervention included consideration of the spiral of negative thinking creating negative automatic thoughts (NATs), and how these affected her relationship to the outside world.

It was agreed that hypnosis would be used to address Angela's poor sleep pattern, and her eating, coffee drinking and weight issues. The intervention included post-hypnotic suggestions for relaxation and ego strengthening which were adapted to Angela's assessed needs.

The establishment of good rapport is always part of a successful therapy outcome (Hammond, 1990). Development of good rapport and a collaborative working relationship was considered vital, and every opportunity taken to enhance the relationship and emphasize Angela's central role in the process. It was pointed out her ability in hypnosis was not due to her being weak-willed, as she suggested, but a particular attribute she possessed.

Angela undertook the Self-Esteem Check Up (Schiraldi, 2000) which showed improvement in her self esteem over therapy. Relaxation scales also showed a marked improvement in her relaxation following hypnosis. These scales and the Zung Depression Scale (Zung, 1965) were administered sessionally to monitor progress.

Sessions 1–5

The induction was an adaptation of a simple loosening of attention (Karle & Boys, 1987) with a focus on letting everything just drift away. Once her eyes had closed, she relaxed quickly with her hands in her lap, her head and shoulders dropped and her breathing slowed. The trance was deepened using an adaptation of progressive muscular relaxation and walking down steps into a garden. Angela was then invited to imagine a special place where she felt happy and calm. In the hypnotic state Angela was then taken through the therapeutic and post-hypnotic suggestions and was able to use ideomotor signalling to indicate her readiness at all stages.

The therapy covered problems she had presented earlier in the session as problematic; the need to improve her low self esteem was considered a fundamental issue, and ego strengthening featured in all sessions (Whelen, 2007). The post-hypnotic suggestions given were that she would find it easier to sleep, control her eating, and, through understanding, not get so upset with others.

At the end of the treatment phase, Angela was brought back to her special place and through an alerting routine to normal waking. On debriefing after the first session, she said she felt very relaxed. She had found the experience strange at first, then 'easy'. It was commented that she had done really well. She had no questions, and she remembered the session in detail. She said she thought she might be able to follow the post-hypnotic suggestions, but was not sure. Her homework was to practice the suggestions when she could.

As the procedure from the first session worked well for Angela there was no reason to change it, and by session 3 Angela said she had almost 'cut out' coffee and was eating less chocolate. She said she had also been sleeping better and that she reported feeling 'less wound up' generally.

By session 4, Angela said she was now having just two small cups of coffee with only one sugar a day and a small amount of chocolate, saying, *"I am eating a lot less, and I am not eating it all the time."* She still felt frustrated because she could not understand why her partner and son got on her nerves so much. We considered the possible links between her feelings and thoughts. She said she still saw herself as being different from her partner and son. They were good, she said, and she was bad. And when we looked at how she could be 'bad', she related being bad to how she felt about herself and how she thought she appeared to others. We agreed to concentrate more on her beliefs about herself, including how she looked.

Sessions 5–8

Angela did not hold a positive image of herself and despite the fact that she hated to see herself in mirrors, she said she would try using an 'imaginary mirror' (Oakley & Halligan, 2002) to try to picture her 'ideal self', or the person she wanted to be. Ego strengthening would continue, as would work on her relationships and habits. Post-hypnotic suggestions focused on anchoring any positive image in the mirror and carrying it forward as part of ego strengthening.

In the fifth session debriefing after using a hypnotic mirror, Angela said she felt very relaxed. She said before the session she was feeling 'very uptight', but in the session she felt as if *"... a weight was taken off my shoulders."* (She mimed a weight being lifted off her.) When asked what she thought of herself in the mirror, she said, *"It was really me."* She was very positive about the experience, and she was reminded of how well she had done. The mirror was kept for the remaining sessions.

Sessions 9 and 10 were used to reinforce the work of sessions 1 to 8 and bring the therapy to an end. In the last session, Angela said she had decided she would try to go back to college *"... to do the things I didn't do before because I was worried what everyone thought about me."* Angela rated her experience of therapy and hypnosis as positive. She saw herself in more positive terms than before the therapy.

- She had reduced her intake of caffeine.
- She had cut down her intake of sugar and fats.
- Her sleeping pattern had improved.
- She was determined to go to college to improve her skills.
- She was losing weight and stated she did not feel so 'paranoid' about people watching her in public places.
- She was less self critical.

In conclusion

From the evidence the author (CR) argues that hypnosis can be extremely useful as an adjunct to psychological interventions for people with learning disabilities. In her final session, Angela said the experience of hypnosis was positive and useful. Whilst the therapy could have worked without hypnosis, the intervention was enhanced by hypnosis particularly with the 'hypnotic mirror' that allowed Angela to see a possible future she had previously been unable to see. This future was a powerful incentive for her to change the long-held image of her as 'fat, ugly and stupid', with little in the way of self esteem, to her in a long blue dress and twirling round, happy with the image she saw; she afterwards said with conviction, *"I know I can be like that."*

There was evidence from the assessments that Angela experienced an improvement in her self esteem, and that she was less depressed and less anxious. Angela said hypnosis had provided her with a depth of relaxation she had not experienced before. She developed a new positivity about herself and her future, and in the absence of any other causes the improvement is attributed to the intervention.

Angela expressed no negative views of her experience of hypnosis. Her own words at the end of the final session perhaps capture the general flavour of her experience.

Before the hypnosis sessions I felt uptight like I usually do. But when I'm in hypnosis I feel like a weight has been taken off my shoulders. It's so relaxing. The first time I was surprised. I didn't think it would be like that. I never could relax like that before. And when you said to see myself in front of the mirror in the dress, I really could see myself. The dress was swirling and blue and me all slim. It was really me. I can see myself really being like that.

The Use of Hypnosis for People with Autistic Spectrum Conditions

Autism is a pervasive condition that begins in childhood and continues throughout the life span. In autism we see problems with communication, problems with understanding social interactions and ritualistic or obsessive behaviours. Individuals with autistic spectrum conditions (ASC) experience these problems to a greater or lesser degree depending on the severity of the condition. In the wider community, many individuals who do not meet the diagnostic criteria for autism nevertheless reveal traits of autism. When considering autism, a number of issues need to be taken into account.

The term 'autism' does not describe a single problem, but covers a broad spectrum of conditions. Autism and Asperger syndrome can be seen as being on a continuum of social impairment, with varying clinical presentations depending on the nature and severity of the cognitive, language and motor skill issues present (Wing, 1991; Wing & Gould, 2003).

Furthermore, people with ASC may experience a wide range of mental health problems, a high prevalence of stress related conditions, anxiety, depression, low self esteem, low self confidence as well as other issues such as obsessive behaviours (see e.g. Bradley *et al.,* 2004; Ghaziuddin, 2005).

A major emerging approach to help these individuals is cognitive-behavioural therapy (CBT) (Anderson & Morris, 2006; Hare & Paine, 1997). Part of the argument for using CBT is that it provides a logical approach that works well for people with ASC. Hare *et al.* (1999) talked about the 'faultless logic' in ASC, and logical reasoning about issues is a fundamental part of CBT. The therapeutic focus in CBT for people with ASC can be around their reasoning and explanations about their own thoughts and actions, and their interpretation of the thoughts and actions of others, to address faulty theory of mind (Baron-Cohen *et al.*, 1985). It is at this cognitive level that the person with ASC often shows rigidity and literalness in thinking which can lead to problems in social interactions.

Experience shows that patients with ASC can be very black and white in their thinking, but this, in itself, can help them take in logical and rational explanations of psychological problems and their aetiology. When negative beliefs are presented, they can be asked for evidence for the belief and then be given alternative ways of looking at matters.

To help reduce anxiety, focus should be made on specific symptoms and problems rather than broad matters, or otherwise the patient may become anxious within the therapeutic situation. The intervention needs to be structured to help the person with ASC work with the turn-taking process. The number of sessions and length of sessions have to be made clear. Metaphors and interpretations may not be understood and generally are best avoided by the therapist as lack of understanding may increase levels of anxiety. However, some patients do present with their own metaphors and images to describe their world. Once these have been introduced by the patient, and the meanings are clarified within the sessions, they can be an additional therapeutic tool.

Depression and anxiety scores on instruments such as the Beck Depression Inventory or the Beck Anxiety Inventory can be given routinely to the patient to provide concrete evidence of positive change. Providing a written synopsis of the session also gives the patient concrete evidence of progress. This synopsis, and any work together in the sessions, can also be illustrated visually, with photographs, drawings or montages. In fact any concrete means that meets the patient's needs can be used, again providing more material points of reference to illustrate session content as well as an additional resource to refer to in between sessions.

Published evidence

As with other patient groups and psychological problems, we can then consider hypnosis as an adjunct to the therapeutic approach. However, there has been little in the way of research investigating the use of hypnosis with people with ASC. There was a successful early report of hypnosis with an adolescent from Gardner and Tarnow (1980). Although the 16 year old patient was not able to work with traditional induction methods, he was able to enter trance using a favourite piece of calming music. The patient made substantial therapeutic gains that he maintained to an 18 month follow up. Throughout the intervention the patient was actively engaged in the treatment plan and its progress; the focus of the work was on solutions to the problems rather than on the problems themselves; the patient's obsessive relationship with music was framed positively rather than as a problem and, while the patient's problem behaviours, such as self harm by biting, were framed negatively, the patient himself was given continuing positive reinforcement and ego enhancement. More recently, Austin *et al.* (2008) developed a 'virtual reality' hypnotherapeutic procedure with two 14 and 15 year old boys as an intervention for reducing anxieties and other symptoms associated with ASC. The patients reportedly appreciated the sessions and were relaxed throughout. The parents felt the technique was effective and that there was significant potential for hypnosis such as this in ASC.

The use of hypnosis and CBT in ASC will be illustrated by a case study that reflects what in the author's (CR) experience is a recurrent presenting problem.

Percy said he had not really enjoyed school because he felt 'different' and felt he was always standing on the edges of activities wondering what to do to fit in with the other children.

Case study: Percy - a young man with ASC

Percy was a 19 year old young man with Asperger syndrome and an IQ in the superior range. He presented with severe levels of anxiety and depression as measured by the Beck Anxiety Inventory and the Beck Depression Inventory, as well as low self confidence and low self esteem. Percy said he had found himself becoming more and more isolated from the people he knew at school during his developmental period as they moved on to work, university and other adult arenas, whilst he found himself at a loss as to understand what to do, or what was expected of him.

Percy said he had 'given up' on college and he had not been able to find any work that satisfied him. He had tried working at a job repairing computers but had become disillusioned as the work had not met his expectations of 'working with computers', and he felt he had been 'stuck in one place'. Percy said that he had come up against a 'brick wall' and that he was now hardly venturing out of the house (he was living with his parents).

Percy described his anxiety as his heart racing, his feeling unable to breathe properly, his stomach churning and his thoughts racing around the possibility of everything going wrong, although he was unsure what 'everything' entailed. He said over recent months he had become more and more disillusioned with life and with himself, and he had developed a sense that he was a failure in life.

Percy said he had read about hypnotherapy and CBT on the internet and he wondered if either or both interventions might be able to help him to overcome his problems. The processes involved in hypnosis and CBT in relation to depression, anxiety and self esteem were explained to Percy, and a contract for treatment was agreed. As well as the initial assessment session, he agreed to six sessions of CBT with the adjunctive use of hypnosis to address anxiety, depression and self esteem issues.

To underline the process and nature of hypnosis, Percy undertook the Creative Imagination Scale (Barber & Wilson, 1978). Having considered the possibilities for the intervention, we agreed to use hypnosis within the intervention. The induction agreed was a progressive relaxation which Percy found relatively easy to understand and engage in. A major portion of the work was around developing his self esteem and self confidence through ego-strengthening techniques. He responded well to a synthesis of Stein's clenched fist technique and Hartland's ego strengthening (Hammond, 1990).

As well as ego strengthening, the heart of the intervention was cognitive-behavioural techniques to tackle the anxiety and depression. Percy's depression reflected his belief that he was a failure in life because of his anxieties that in turn were related to his autistic traits of misunderstanding social situations and a perceived failure to make friends.

The main work of the therapy involved helping Percy to understand and reframe his autistic traits not as deficits, but as facets of himself that were neither negative nor positive. He was encouraged to recognize that everyone shows some level of autistic traits, that he was not so different from others, that he had many talents and that he could adapt to his traits to enable them to be more positive for him.

The therapeutic work was kept as concrete as possible, with no additional use of metaphors, other than his own such as his 'hitting a brick wall', which proved useful when he could construct a doorway in the wall and then create a key and so find a way through.

Percy proved an able candidate for hypnosis. He used the sessions well and took techniques, such as the clenched fist, for calming and reinforcing his sense of self esteem and mastery of a situation or problem, away with him between sessions to utilize with his homework to continue what had been learned in session.

During the review of the therapy in the final session, Percy said since commencing the therapy he had taken on voluntary work and that he was looking for a permanent position. He had gone to London to the Tate Gallery, something he had wanted to do for some time, but had never had the nerve to. He saw this foray as a concrete example of a real advance; he had the train ticket to prove he had done it, and he had a guide book to the gallery. This was a real example of him passing the 'brick wall'. His scores on the Beck Anxiety Inventory and Beck Depression Inventory had reduced to mild levels on both. He said he felt much better about himself compared to how he had felt at the start of the intervention. He felt more confident in how he engaged with other people. He was working in a charity shop and talking to people; he was going out rather than staying at home alone. Overall, he judged the intervention to be a positive one. He felt his ASC was no longer something to be feared, nor was it something that controlled him; rather he saw it as just another aspect of who he was as a person.

Although hypnosis is a relatively new introduction to therapeutic work in this field, early results are encouraging and further publications are eagerly awaited.

References

Anderson, S. & Morris, J. (2006), Cognitive behaviour therapy for people with Asperger syndrome. *Behavioural and Cognitive Psychotherapy*, 39, 293–303.

Austin, D. W., Abbott, J. M. & Carbis, C. (2008), The use of virtual reality hypnosis with two cases of autism spectrum disorder: a feasibility study. *Contemporary Hypnosis*, 25, 10–29.

Barber, T. X. & Wilson, S. C. (1978), The Barber Suggestibility Scale and the Creative Imagination Scale: experimental and clinical applications. *American Journal of Clinical Hypnosis*, 2, 84–108.

Baron-Cohen, S., Leslie, A. M. & Frith, U (1985), Does the autistic child have a 'theory of mind'? *Cognition*, 21, 37–46.

Bouras, N., & Holt, G. (Eds.) (2010), *Mental health services for adults with intellectual disability: strategies and solutions.* Maudsley series. Hove, Psychology Press.

Bradley, E. A., Summers, J. A., Wood, H. L. & Byron, S. E. (2004), Comparing rates of psychiatric and behaviour disorders in adolescents and young adults with severe intellectual disability with and without autism. *Journal of Autism and developmental Disorders*, 34, 151–61.

Cooper, S., Smiley, E., Morrison, J., Williamson, A. & Allan, L. (2007), Mental ill-health in adults with intellectual disabilities: prevalence and associated factors. *The British Journal of Psychiatry*, 190, 27–35.

Dagnan, D. & Lindsay, B. (2004). Research issues in cognitive therapy, in Emerson, E., Hatton, C., Thompson, T.& Parmente, T. R. (Eds.) *The international handbook of applied research in intellectual disabilities*. Chichester, John Wiley & Sons, Ltd.

Dagnan, D. & Sandhu, S. (1999), Social comparison, self-esteem and depression in people with intellectual disability. *Journal of Intellectual Disability Research*, 43 (5), 372–9.

Deb, S., Matthews, T., Holt, G. & Bouras, N. (2001), *Practice guidelines for the assessment and diagnosis of mental health problems in adults with intellectual disability*. Brighton, Pavilion.

Department Of Health., (2001), *Valuing people: a new strategy for learning disability for the 21st century*. London, HMSO.

Fennell, M. (1997), Low self-esteem: a cognitive perspective. *Behavioural and Cognitive Psychotherapy*, 25, 1–25.

Fennell, M. J. V. (1998), Low self-esteem, in Tarrier, N., Wells, A.& Haddock, G. (Eds.) *Treating complex cases: the cognitive behavioural therapy approach*. New York: John Wiley & Sons.

Gardner, G. G. & Tarnow, J. D. (1980), Adjunctive hypnotherapy with an autistic boy. *American Journal of Clinical Hypnosis*, 22, 173–9.

Garitte, C., Gay, M-C., Cusinier, F. & Celeste, B. (2009), Hypnotic susceptibility in children with Down's syndrome. *Contemporary Hypnosis*, 26 (2), 111–20.

Ghaziuddin, M. (2005), *Mental health aspects of autism and Asperger syndrome*. London, Jessica Kingsley.

Gibson, H. B. & Heap, M. (1991), *Hypnosis in therapy*. Hove, Lawrence Erlbaum.

Gilbert, P. (1998) Shame and humiliation in the treatment of complex cases. In Tarrier, N., Wells, A. & Haddock, G. (Eds.) *Treating complex cases: the cognitive behavioural therapy approach*. New York: John Wiley & Sons.

Hacker Hughes, J. G. H. (2000), Clinical hypnosis as an adjunct to assessment and therapy with people with learning disabilities. *Contemporary Hypnosis*, 17 (2), 71–7.

Hammond, D. C. (1990), *Handbook of hypnotic suggestions and metaphors*. New York: W.W. Norton.

Hare, D., Jones, J. & Payne, C. (1999), Approaching reality: the use of personal construct assessment in working with people with Asperger syndrome. *Autism*, 3 (2), 165–76.

Hare, D. J. & Paine, C. (1997), Developing cognitive behavioural treatment for people with Asperger's syndrome. *Clinical Psychology Forum*, 110, 5–8.

Johnson, L. S., Johnson, D. L., Olson, M. R. & Newman, J. P. (1981), The uses of hypnotherapy with learning disabled children. *Journal of Clinical Psychology*, 37 (2), 291–9.

Karle, H. & Boys, J. (1987), *Hypnotherapy: a practical handbook*. London: Free Association.

Kirsch, I., Montgomery, G. & Saperstein, G. (1995), Hypnosis as an adjunct to cognitive-behavioural psychotherapy: a meta-analysis. *Journal of Consulting and Clinical Psychology*, 63 (2), 214–20.

Kroger, W. S. (2008), *Clinical and experimental hypnosis in medicine, dentistry and psychology*, 2nd ed. Philadelphia, Lippincott Williams & Wilkins.

Lowe, K., Felce, D., Perry, J., Baxter, H. & Jones, E. (1998), The characteristics and residential situations of people with severe intellectual disability and the most challenging behaviour in Wales. *Journal of Intellectual Disability Research*, 42, 375–89.

Marcuse, F. L. (1950), *Hypnosis: fact and fiction*. Harmondsworth, Penguin.

McCord, H. (1956a), Hypnotizing the mentally retarded child. *British Journal of Medical Hypnotism*, 8, 17.

McCord, H. (1956b), The hypnotisability of the mongoloid-type child. *Journal of Clinical and Experimental Hypnosis*, 4, 21.

McGillivray, J. A. & McCabe, M. P. (2009), Detecting and treating depression in people with mild intellectual disability: the views of key stakeholders. *British Journal of Learning Disabilities*, 38 (1), 68–76.

Nezu, C. M., Nezu, A. M., Rothenberg, J. L., Dellicarpini, L. & Groag, I. (1995), Depression in adults with mild mental retardation: are cognitive variables involved? *Cognitive Therapy and Research*, 19 (2), 227–39.

Oakley, D. A. & Halligan, P. W. (2002), Hypnotic mirrors and phantom pain: a single case study. *Contemporary Hypnosis*, 19 (2), 75–84.

Robertson, J., Emerson, E., Pinkney, L. Caesar, E. Felce, D., Meek, A., Carr, D., Lowe, K., Knapp, M. & Hallam, A. (2005), Treatment and management of challenging behaviours in congregate and noncongregate community-based supported accommodation. *Journal of Intellectual Disability Research*, 49, 63–72.

Schiraldi, G. R. (2000), *The self-esteem workbook*. Oakland, CA, New Harbinger.

Stenfert-Kroese, B., Dagnan, D. & Loumides, K. (1997), *Cognitive behaviour therapy for people with learning disabilities*. London, Routledge.

Wechsler, D. (1997), *Wechsler Adult Intelligence Scale 3rd edition (UK)*. London, Pearson Assessments.

Whelen, A. (2007), Low self-esteem: group cognitive behaviour therapy. *British Journal of learning Disabilities*, 35, 125–30.

Williams, H. & Jones, R. S. P. (1997), Teaching cognitive self-regulation of independence and emotion control skills, in Stenfert-Kroese, B., Dagnan, D.& Loumides, K. (Eds.) *Cognitive behaviour therapy for people with learning disabilities*. London, Routledge.

Willner, P. (2005), The effectiveness of psychotherapeutic interventions for people with learning disabilities: a critical overview. *Journal of Intellectual Disability Research*, 49 (1), 73–85.

Wing, L. (1991), The relationship between Asperger's syndrome and Kanner's autism, in Frith, U. (Ed.) *Autism and Asperger's syndrome*. Cambridge, Cambridge University Press.

Wing, L. & Gould, J. (2003), *Diagnostic interview for social and communication disorders*, 11th ed. Bromley, National Autistic Society.

Zung, W. W. K. (1965), A self-rating depression scale. *Archives of General Psychiatry*, 12, 63–70.

36

Sleep Disorders

Dr Les Brann

Introduction

Despite being common, sleep disorders are generally poorly managed in the health service. As a backlash from the over-prescribing of sleeping tablets in the past, many hypnotic medications are licensed for short term use only for fear of creating addiction. The training of junior doctors in this regard tends to make them feel that they are bad doctors if they prescribe hypnotic medication, and they are led to rely heavily on 'sleep hygiene' methods. Such methods are indeed valuable, and avoidance of caffeinated and other stimulant drinks and the development of 'shut down' activities near bed time are sensible and helpful, but despite this many patients remain with significant sleep problems.

Busy lifestyles and stress have led to a significant proportion of the population being deprived of their natural sleep requirement with estimates of up to 20% of the adult population in the western world having insufficient sleep (Hublin *et al.*, 2001). Insufficient sleep is associated with a whole range of morbidities including hypertension, cardiovascular disease, depression and psychosocial stress as well as an increase in accidents (Hublin *et al.*, 1996). Indeed, such is the impact of impaired sleep that the total effect on mortality and morbidity is greater than the influence of cholesterol (Stanley, 2009). Despite its importance, scant attention and resources are paid to this topic.

The Handbook of Contemporary Clinical Hypnosis: Theory and Practice, First Edition.
Edited by Les Brann, Jacky Owens and Ann Williamson.
© 2012 John Wiley & Sons, Ltd. Published 2015 by John Wiley & Sons, Ltd.

Published Evidence

There are a whole range of sleep disorders, but from the hypnotherapists' viewpoint insomnia is the commonest presenting problem. Nightmares, night terrors and sleepwalking are also frequent reasons for referral. Despite the traditional use of hypnosis for these problems, there is very little empirical research in the literature. Graci and Hardie (2007) and Ng and Lee (2008) provide comprehensive reviews and highlight the need for more research. What evidence there is (e.g. Becker, 1993; Borkovec & Fowles, 1973) suggests that hypnotherapy can lead to a rapid improvement in a few sessions. Relaxation and direct suggestion form the basis of the approach. Despite the paucity of published trials, sleep disorders form a significant part of the hypnotherapist's workload, either as the primary problem or as consequences of other morbidities which affect sleep.

Insomnia

It is important here to distinguish between primary and secondary insomnia. Some people are simply naturally short sleepers and despite only getting four or five hours of sleep (or less in some cases), they feel well and function normally. Hypnotherapy has no role in trying to change these genetically determined patterns with one exception. From time to time, such patients go through spells of worrying about this relatively little sleep and it becomes an issue. These spells are often triggered by stressful situations. Because they are lying awake they have more time to ruminate on the problem and blame the lack of sleep for it. Whilst the hypnotherapy can help with the stresses, it is unlikely that their primary sleep pattern will change. The intervention helps to restore the patients to the state where their length of sleep is no longer an issue and functioning returns to normal.

Secondary insomnia, by contrast, develops from a background of a normal sleep pattern so therapy is aimed at restoring the sleep to its baseline state. This form of sleep dysfunction is often characterized by general hyperarousal and cognitive over-activity (Hammond, 1990). The therapeutic process follows the same principles as outlined in the stages of therapy.

When taking the history of the problem, it is important to note whether the patient has difficulty getting off to sleep or if it is early morning (or repeated) wakening. The latter is frequently associated with depression, whilst the former is more often associated with anxiety, but there is significant overlap with the co-morbidities. If the mental health examination or questionnaires reveal significant depression, it is important to consider if medication is being taken or required, and discussion with the GP may be necessary. If there is wakening it is useful to know how the patient feels as they awake. For example, do they always wake with specific thoughts in their mind, or feelings of panic?

Most patients can identify the reason for the onset, and although this should be noted the details can be gathered if needed during hypnosis. In these cases the hemispheric lateralization model is best used as it helps to reassure the patient that there is a good reason why their logical attempts at resolution have failed.

Following the taking of the history and the giving of the explanation, hypnosis is best induced and deepened using a relaxing method. This can subsequently be taught and used for self hypnosis to help with getting off to sleep initially or back to sleep following wakening. Recording this induction and deepening (or the use of a pre-recorded pro-gramme) assists in the self-hypnosis practice, and many patients find it a reassuring support during the night.

From this relaxed platform, examination of the causal events can be started. Whilst Hammond (1990) advises that this may only be necessary if the relaxation and self hypnosis approach has not proved successful within four or five sessions, the author (LB) strongly suggests that exploration is carried out early in the therapy. No time is then wasted if an underlying conflict is identified, but if not a transition to a simple relaxation approach is seamless.

Various uncovering methods (see page 123) may be used to reveal the issues that led to the disturbance and to explore the wider background situation at the time. Sometimes, re-exposure of the event under hypnosis is sufficient to enable the patient to resolve the issue, but often some sort of resolution technique is required.

One useful method is to use the concept of the 'sleep room'. Patients are asked to wander into the depths of their mind and through 'the corridors of their mind' and find the sleep room. They are asked to enter with either an implied or a direct suggestion that in the sleep room they will find the reason underlying their problem. Once the problem has been found and resolved, they are then in a position to re-adjust the sleep control settings to suit their needs. It is useful to remember to also reset the 'habit' control as much sleep behaviour soon becomes habitual.

Linda – panic attacks

Linda presented with panic attacks which woke her from sleep. She also had some panic attacks at other times, but it was the sleep disturbance which caused her most distress. She was 25 years old and the panic had been a feature since the age of 13. She would wake sometimes several times a night, feeling frightened, with a rapid heartbeat and hyperventilating; but she did not know what was causing that fear.

During hypnosis she was asked to go into her sleep room and search back through the files to the beginning of the problem. Although she had an older sister and brother, they did not live at home. Her parents had separated, and she lived with her mother who suffered from depression. One night (she was 13) she awoke to hear the dog barking; not a typical 'need to go out bark' but a worried bark. She lay there for a while expecting her mother to respond, but she heard nothing and so, apprehensively, she went to investigate and found the dog outside the bathroom. She could hear her mother crying and went in to find she had cut her wrists. The scene was horrific. Despite her young years, she handled the situation brilliantly and called for help. Her mother recovered but remained with episodic depression. The fear that something similar would happen again remained with Linda, and it was this fear she experienced during her sleep.

Resolution was achieved using the older wiser self method and archiving the memory. She was no longer living at home, so she did not have the responsibility for 'listening out' for her mother, and so her sleep control was re-programmed.

Although things improved, she indicated using an ideomotor response that there was further work to do. Embroiled in this panicky feeling were feelings of anger aimed at her mother for putting her through this, her father for leaving the family home and exposing her to this responsibility and the relative lack of support from her older siblings.

Silent abreaction (see page 136) was used to offload these other problems. Her night time panics never entirely disappeared but became much less frequent such that they were no longer causing her significant sleep deprivation.

Maureen – work stress

As a single mother, Maureen's life was inevitably busy, and although her teenage son was largely self caring she still had her parental responsibilities. She had a middle management post, and work pressure was the major stressor in her life such that she took work home most days and had very little social life. She reported, "I just can't get off to sleep – every time I shut my eyes, my mind is full of all the things I have got to do!"

During the history taking, it became clear that her job had been her salvation at the time of her marriage break up, giving her the financial security she needed. By keeping herself busy, it had also taken her mind off the hurt of the divorce. This, however, had escalated to the point where she had lost control.

Therapy was aimed initially at relaxation, and during the first session she was taken through several relaxation methods including progressive muscular relaxation (PMR) as well as more visual imagery techniques. The PMR is particularly useful in these cases as it is something physical to do, and this physical activity helps to override the tendency to lose concentration with imagery. These were accompanied by mental rehearsal of her using these techniques on a daily basis.

Whilst she had dutifully practiced the relaxation, she was still taking a long time to go off to sleep. At the second session she was asked to imagine a dustbin just outside the exit from work. She was asked to imagine that every night as she was leaving for home, she would dump all the day's work in the bin and feel the relief as she did so. She was asked to rehearse a relaxing evening, having a good night's sleep and returning to the office in the morning when she could pick up the problems as she went in, noting that the problems did not seem so onerous after a refreshing sleep. In addition to this she was taught a magic bubble procedure so that when the habitual intrusive thoughts were generated by her mind, they would flow out into the bubble and float away, whereas the relaxing thoughts would stay surrounding and protecting her.

She found these methods much easier and more effective than she expected and not only was sleeping better but also had been able to find time to pick up a social life again.

Thus, as with other uses of hypnosis, there is not one technique for one problem but an amalgam of methods tailored to the individual's needs and responses.

Nightmares, Night Terrors and Sleepwalking

Hypnotherapy is very effective for nightmares, night terrors and sleep walking. Hurwitz *et al.* (1991) reported that 74% of a series of 27 cases of sleepwalking and night terrors improved following hypnosis where the patients were asked to visualize themselves on a screen sleeping peacefully. Brann *et al.* (2007) presented a series of seven cases showing that resolution was obtained in one or two sessions.

Nightmares

Katy's (29 years old) nightmares were always the same; she was being disturbed by a dark figure and she was trying to get away. She also suffered from obsessive compulsive disorder (OCD), and the more frightening dreams she had, the worse her OCD became. She also awoke from these dreams exhausted and on one occasion awoke with painful ribs from the tension.

First session: Katy found two dream rooms. The good dream room was all light and cosy. The bad dream room was dark and dismal, and in this room she saw a dark foreboding figure. This did not seem to relate to any previous event. She was able to banish the figure from the room, and once she had done this she found she could change the room by decorating it and making it bright. After this she felt happy to be in the room and could see her own face in a mirror looking happy and healthy.

Second session: Katy had not experienced any further dreams which had disturbed her. She also noticed that her OCD behaviour had decreased. Katy's Hospital Anxiety and Depression scale (HADs) scores also showed a marked improvement (initial: anxiety 3, depression 17; after therapy: anxiety 4, depression 1).

Night terrors

Jo (43 years old) had a continuous feeling of being dead in her dream or on waking. She would wake up not knowing if she was alive or dead. Jo had palpitations and severe anxiety for the first few moments after waking.

First session: Jo was frightened to go into her dream room. She was unable to go through the door as she sensed a feeling of foreboding. She felt that if she removed the feeling, it would leave a void, a 'nothingness'. She felt these feelings were a part of her and could not be removed, but although she was unable to remove the feeling, she was able to put it in a box and lock it, and was then able to archive it.

Second session: Jo was still experiencing terrors but not as often. She went into her control room and noticed the anger dial on full blast. She was able to turn this down, as well as the fear dial. Once these had been turned down, she was able to increase the self esteem and confidence dials.

Third session: Jo had not had any nightmares and had not even woken up during the night. She had not realized how angry she had been, and she felt much calmer now that the anger had gone.

Nightmares and enuresis

Vanessa (19 years old) not only had bad dreams in which she was panicking and feeling she had not got enough time to do anything, but also she had started wetting the bed. Her parents had divorced when she was four years old, and she described her older sister as always behaving like a 'little princess'. Both parents had remarried and had new families, and she felt left out. This was particularly so when she went to university as her sister had taken over her room at her mother's house, so she had to live with her father.

First session: Found her good dream room which was light and airy with a big picture window. It was pink and a fun place to be. It made her feel good, like a happy little girl. Her bad dream room was small and dark with a small window. The air felt dank, and there was a feeling of desperation. She was asked to change this, and she made a bigger window which she could open to get some fresh air. She decorated the room and, as it was small, used it as a closet for her shoes. She felt really happy once she had done this. She also found another room, a kitchen with a big table around which all her family were seated happily and getting on with each other.

Second session: Vanessa had not wet the bed or had any bad dreams. The hypnosis had made her realize how lonely she was and how much she wanted both families to get on.

Recurrent intrusive dreams

Polly (26 years old) was already a successful businesswoman but for one year had been having vivid dreams about marrying a colleague who she felt was the 'man of her dreams'. So real were these dreams that she felt he must know, and she became embarrassed and tongue tied when seeing him. There was no chance of a relationship with him, but she could not clear the dreams from her mind to allow her to move on into a real relationship. She had been smoking cannabis regularly since the age of 15.

First session: Polly was allowed to talk endlessly about 'her man'. Having seemingly talked enough, she was asked to anchor a good feeling which had nothing to do with him.

Second session: Despite the very simple previous session, she had had only one dream of him. She realized that other relationships in her life, especially with her parents, had been poor, and so she felt she must have been searching for an idealized relationship. All these thoughts were muddled, and using a computer metaphor she pressed the 'sort' button and put them in order, filing them away appropriately.

Third session: Polly had not had any further troubling dreams, and she felt much calmer and was not smoking anywhere near as many cigarettes. She was asked to look inside her lungs and see what damage the smoking was doing, and she filed smoking and nail biting away. Polly mentally rehearsed being the new person she wanted to be.

Fourth session: Polly had had no more dreams and had almost stopped smoking. She now felt able to move away from the 'dream man' and look for a real relationship.

Night terrors

Martin (23 years old) had always had night terrors, but this had not been a problem until he got married, when these terrors would wake his wife. He came for help following one incident when he frightened her by putting his hand over her mouth and shaking her violently; he was totally unaware of doing this. These events tended to take place between two and three in the morning, and there seemed to be no relationship with work or alcohol.

In hypnosis the computer technique was used to look for the cause. Martin said, "The house was haunted!" This referred to the house of his childhood and he described the ghosts. One visitation was by a friendly Victorian couple in classic pose with the man standing beside his seated wife. They smiled and said, "You'll be all right," but he never knew why they needed to reassure him. There was also a ghost of a little girl from next door who had died. He was asked to go to his dream room and as he did not want to delete these dreams he archived them into his childhood file 'where they belonged'. He re-programmed his sleep control centre so as not to include these night terrors.

Second session: Martin had not had any nightmares, and his wife reported he had slept undisturbed for the first time since she had known him.

Sleepwalking

Mark (18 years old) had been a sleepwalker all his life, but it had never bothered him and his family took no notice until one night he put his hand through a glass door and lacerated a tendon. He required plastic surgery to repair it.

In hypnosis the problem was explored using the computer technique, but no cause was found. He was asked if it would be okay to stop sleepwalking, and he responded positively. In his dream room, the sleep control was re-programmed.

He did not sleepwalk again after that first session.

Sleep paralysis

Samuel was six foot four inches tall and as strong as an ox, yet for 15 months he had been having panic episodes at night where he felt as though he was awake but 'paralysed'. He was so scared of going to sleep that he had to have the door open and the light on.

In hypnosis the problem was explored using the computer technique, and he felt the problem was 'anger'. The anger was with himself for letting the family down. His parents had split when he was eight, and he was fine until his mother remarried and he rebelled against his stepfather. The older wiser self was used to help him feel better. In the dream room he re-programmed his sleep pattern.

He attended the second session only to report that he was sleeping well with the door closed and the light off and had not had any night terrors. Samuel had talked things through with his mother and stepfather and apologized. Initially his HADs anxiety score was 13 and his depression score five. Following the one session of hypnosis, the scores had dropped to one and zero respectively.

The above examples show how useful hypnotherapy can be with these types of problems. The dream room metaphor can be used as an uncovering method and for resolution. This coupled with the re-programming of the sleep control seem to be the basis of a remarkably quick and successful treatment for this troublesome problems. For children, Hall (1999) uses the concept of a 'dream catcher' metaphorically installed above the bed which triages the dreams and only allows nice dreams through.

Recurrent dreams are not always scary, yet, because of their regularity, they may cause some concern to the sufferer. It is important that the therapist leaves the analysis to the patient even if the theme seems blatantly obvious. One method of allowing the patient to consider the underlying issue is to utilize the metaphor of a dream machine. They are asked to imagine the recurrent dream is in the 'dream player' and this is played through once, then

Recurring dreams

Jean (36 years old) frequently had the same dream of her being taken to her school sports day where she would see herself getting changed and ready for the race. The dream always ended before the race began, and she never really felt disturbed by it; she was just puzzled why she should have this dream over and over again.

Having reviewed it using the analysis button, she smiled and said, "My sister." Her sister was academically bright, and Jean had always felt she needed to succeed to avoid being a disappointment to her parents. Sport was one thing at which she could out-perform her sister, hence the importance of her parents watching her at sports day. This sibling rivalry had long since gone, and she and her sister were the best of friends. Having been relieved to understand the dream, she elected to leave it in the dream room, but, interestingly, she never experienced that dream again.

immediately played again but this time the 'analysis' button is pressed on the remote control. The suggestion is that the meaning of the dream will become clear after this viewing.

Children often have nightmares about recent events and frequently after seeing scary videos. If children are prone to this, it is useful to teach them dream control.

Functional seizures

James (11 years old) had been diagnosed as having hysterical fits. He had 'collapsed' several times and was thought to be suffering from epilepsy, but he had one such episode whilst having an electroencephalogram (EEG). This showed absolutely no epileptic activity at all, so a diagnosis of psychogenic fits was made and he was referred to see the child psychiatrist. His parents, aware of our interest in hypnosis, enquired of the psychiatrist if hypnosis would be useful. She said, "Hypnosis would not be any use because we would know the cause but James would not." Confused by this and frustrated by James' lack of progress, his parents asked if he could try hypnotherapy.

During hypnosis, James was asked to observe from inside his mind what was happening when he had one of these 'fits'. He said, "They're attacking me, trying to stab me – chickens with huge beaks." Exploring further, it transpired that a few days before the onset of the problem he had watched *Murder on the Orient Express*. One of the final scenes in that film was a re-enacting of the murder where the murderers each stabbed the victim. That night James had a nightmare that he was being stabbed by huge chickens with long pointed beaks. This nightmare was so vivid that he had flashbacks of it during the day, when he would hyperventilate and feel very dizzy to the point of passing out. When he came round, the flashback image had gone and he felt better.

James was taught dream control. It was explained that the dreams were only made up in his mind so he could change them if he needed to. He was told that the chickens, however big they were in the dream, were really scared of him and if they came towards him he should shout at them and scare them away. This he practiced during hypnosis and he said, "They're getting smaller now anyway!"

He never had another 'fit' or nightmare after that one session.

This case highlights two points: firstly, the effectiveness of dream control, especially in children prone to nightmares; and, secondly, the gross misunderstanding that many of our colleagues have with regard to hypnosis. It remains incumbent upon us as hypnotherapists to move hypnotherapy out of the realms of the unknown to a more evidence based place within mainstream medicine.

References

Becker, P. M. (1993), Chronic insomnia: outcome of hypnotherapeutic intervention in six cases. *American Journal of Clinical Hypnosis*, 36, 98–105.

Borkovec, T. D. & Fowles, D. C. (1973), Controlled investigation of the effects of progressive and hypnotic relaxation on insomnia. *Journal of Abnormal Psychology*, 82, 153–8.

Brann, L., Mackrodt, K. & Joslin, M. (2007), Presentation at the joint conference of BSCAH, RSM and BSMDH, York, UK, May.

Graci, G. M. & Hardie, J. C. (2007), Evidenced-based hypnotherapy for the management of sleep disorders. *International Journal of Clinical Experimental Hypnosis*, 55 (3), 251–74.

Hall, H. (1999), Hypnosis and paediatrics, in Temes, R. (Ed.) *Medical hypnosis: an introduction and clinical guide*. Philadelphia, Churchill Livingstone. p. 79–93.

Hammond, D. C. (1990), *Handbook of hypnotic suggestions and metaphors*. New York: W. W. Norton.

Hublin, C., Kaprio, J., Partinen, M., Heikkil, K. & Koskenvuo, M. (1996), Daytime sleepiness in an adult, Finnish population. *Journal of Internal Medicine*, 239, 417–23.

Hublin, C., Kaprio, J., Partinen, M. & Koskenvuo, M. (2001), Insufficient sleep – a population-based study in adults. *Sleep*, 24, 392–400.

Hurwitz, T. D., Mahowald, M. W., Schenck, C. H., Schluter, J. L. & Bundlie S. R. (1991), A retrospective outcome study and review of hypnosis as treatment of adults with sleepwalking and sleep terror. *Journal of Nervous Mental Disorders*, 179, 228–33.

Ng, B. Y. & Lee, T. S. (2008), Hypnotherapy for sleep disorders. *Annals of the Academy Medicine, Singapore*, 37 (8), 683–8.

Stanley, N. (2009), Presentation at BSCAH Eastern Counties seminar, Norwich, autumn.

37

Performance Enhancement

Dr Barry Cripps

BSc BEd CPsychol CSci FBPsS, With contributions from Dr Geoff Ibbotson and Dr Ann Williamson

Introduction

This chapter addresses performance enhancement, primarily in sport. A case is presented demonstrating the use of integrated hypnosis in the treatment of exercise addiction. Clearly there are many other areas where performance enhancement is required such as in fear of public speaking, performing in an orchestra or singing in public, to name but three. The chapter goes on to describe a case where performance enhancement was used to facilitate an actress returning to the stage.

Outline of the Problem

Performance enhancement is also often used in supporting athletes in sport, helping to enhance their performance in some way and adding to and reinforcing the work done by other specialists in their sporting world.

Sport is a competitive, physical activity where a single athlete or a group of athletes attempts to engage in their game or activity and do better than their competitors. The term 'athlete' is used here as a generic term used to cover all sports people, not just field and track athletics. Athletes have always relied on trainers, coaches, technicians and

The Handbook of Contemporary Clinical Hypnosis: Theory and Practice, First Edition.
Edited by Les Brann, Jacky Owens and Ann Williamson.
© 2012 John Wiley & Sons, Ltd. Published 2015 by John Wiley & Sons, Ltd.

managers in order to support their endeavours and more recently have begun to enlist the services of the sport psychologist. Performance is also used generically to describe the activity of the athlete, whether in training or the gym, but mainly with regard to their competitive performance.

The perceptual motor skills in the aiming sports are, by and large, closed; they are repeated in a similar way over and over again. There are slight variations in the nature of the skills, but for example a golfer swings and hits the ball a number of times in order to complete their round. The nature of this hitting is very different depending where the ball lies on the course, the drive from the tee, the iron shot from the fairway, the pitch up on to the green, a pitch out of the sand bunker (hopefully not!), a chip and finally the putt to sink the ball into the hole (i.e. the target). The common factor is the swing, and golfers spend a great deal of time seeking to perfect their swing. In archery, depending on the round to be shot, an archer may shoot 144 arrows during a one-day competition, each shot using the same set of closed perceptual motor skills.

Hypnosis in sport is used as an adjunct to support other, mainly cognitive behavioural techniques such as concentration, focusing and self-talk, and to reinforce the work done by all the specialists in order to support the athlete and enhance their performance whatever the sport. Even when injured, hypnosis can facilitate the work of the physiotherapist in helping to focus and concentrate the resources of the mind and body towards a stress free recovery from injury (see later in this chapter on page 560).

Twenty years ago, sports psychologists were regarded with suspicion by most athletes and dismissed with comments such as *"There is nothing wrong with me, and I'm not going mad!"* and *"What's psychology got to do with getting the ball in the net?"*

The author's (BC) research and work with athletes in the 1980s suggested that all athletes experience anxiety, at some level, before they complete or indeed take part in training sessions. Researchers generally identified this phenomenon as performance arousal and were attracted by the early work of Yerkes and Dodson (1908; and see Figure 37.1).

Researchers such as Rushall (1992) demonstrated that when athletic performers and team players were able to control their levels of arousal and take a relaxed approach to their event, a 'successful' performance often ensued. Tension and anxiety could often lead to stress, breakdown and subsequent poor performance seen as failure in the athlete's eyes. Many sport psychology interventions, particularly in the aiming sports such as archery, shooting, snooker and golf, used the inverted U-shaped curve postulated by Yerkes and Dodson, in order to demonstrate that a level of optimal arousal could help athletes make a good start in their event.

Twenty years ago, in sport psychology, overcoming performance anxiety was seen to be a most important strategy for sport psychologists, coaches and athletes to focus on, in order to enhance their performance. Mental skills such as relaxation, concentration, mental rehearsal and imagery often provided a starting point for psychologists when working with athletes. In 1990 Jones and Hardy edited their seminal work, *Stress and Performance in Sport*, offering a critique of the often quoted inverted-U hypothesis. Together with others, notably Fazey and Hardy (1988), they suggested that it was important for performers to have multiple relaxation strategies so as to adjust their

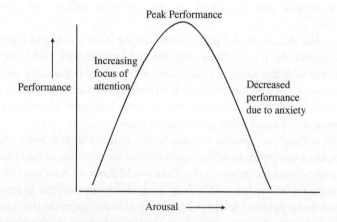

Figure 37.1 Performance–arousal curve.
Source: After Yerkes-Dodson (1908).
Note: The Yerkes-Dodson law is an empirical relationship between arousal and performance, originally developed by psychologists Robert M. Yerkes and John D. Dodson in 1908. The law dictates that performance increases with physiological or mental arousal, but only up to a point. When levels of arousal become too high, performance decreases. Difficult or intellectually demanding tasks may require a lower level of arousal (to facilitate concentration), whereas tasks demanding stamina or persistence may be performed better with higher levels of arousal (to increase motivation).
Because of task differences, the shape of the curve can be highly variable. For simple or well learned tasks, the relationship can be considered linear with improvements in performance as arousal increases. For complex, unfamiliar or difficult tasks, the relationship between arousal and performance becomes inverse, with declines in performance as arousal increases.

position regarding their cognitive anxiety by physiological arousal control as necessary. These researchers also suggested that it would be interesting to attempt to include other meta-cognitive variables such as self-confidence in their higher order catastrophe model of performance stress.

Research in sport psychology has moved on, and a most recent book by Lane (2008) deals with cognitive and affective factors such as mood, anxiety and self-confidence, managing psychological states like stress, imagery and sport performance. It also covers the scientific application of music in sport and exercise, leadership development in athletes and coaches, exercise addiction, physical activity and self-esteem as well as the placebo effect in sport and exercise. Hypnosis does not get a mention, the closest reference being to imagery, 'Using all the senses to recreate or create an experience in the mind'. To quote Virgil (70–19 BC), 'They are able because they see themselves as being able'. The way the author (BC) has used hypnosis in sport most successfully is to use ego boosting, almost reversing Virgil's quote, 'Being able to perform optimally because they have seen themselves do it'.

Work with about 20 archers and coaches for five squad weekends a year over 16 years provided a vast amount of data and experience to study performance anxiety, somatic and cognitive arousal and its effects on elite shooters before and during training and competition.

It was quite clear that successful performance on the archery field had a great deal to do with psychology and the 'mental game', and the archery fraternity readily recognized this. Working together with the national coaches and elite archery performers, techniques were devised for the control of performance anxiety in order to help archers make a good start in a performance and also be able to recover from a perceived 'disaster' like missing the target, a bow string breaking or some other performance upset.

In line with a theory of optimal arousal, it was quite clear that some archers needed winding up before a competition; whilst others needed the opposite, almost putting to sleep! Some of our most successful archers at that time would shoot more or less in a robotic state of mind, thinking about very little other than 'the middle of the middle' in archery terms, or scoring the maximum points of ten in the gold with as many arrows as they could. Many of the popular archery competitions, 'rounds' as they are called, require archers to shoot 144 arrows, from several different distances, in a one day competition. We constructed and worked together on five basic exercises, mental skills for the control of performance anxiety, namely, relaxation, breathing control (somatic), concentration, mental rehearsal (cognitive) and finally confidence boosting, with the objective of helping the archer make a good start. With certain archers, who responded well to suggestibility and had an open mind, a five part hypnotic induction was practiced and a self-hypnosis routine was recommended for use at any time, guided by a sound tape recording of the hypnosis session delivered on an individual basis.

The author (BC) regards hypnosis as the deepest, most powerful part of an intervention, and most archers took advantage of one hour hypnosis sessions, focused specifically on ego boosting with the objective of reducing levels of arousal, making a good start and so enhancing their performance.

Each archer had their own audio tape specifically focusing on their own anxieties, or particular performance changes. On occasions a group induction was sound taped for a very different purpose, aiming at sleeping soundly in the hot, double rooms in the Olympic village at the Barcelona Olympics (1992), entitled 'Sleeping in Barcelona'; it did not make the top ten in the charts, but it did help the archers get a reasonable night's sleep in the heat and stress of the Olympic village!

The most often stated difficulty athletes have before competition is their last minute loss of confidence. No matter at what level, whether local, national or international, most athletes tend to experience such a loss of confidence that comes out in self talk as: *"What if I fail . . . what if I mess it up completely . . . what if I drop the ball . . . miss the target . . . get out first ball . . . fall over on the ice . . . miss the penalty . . . fall off my horse . . . my horse refuses to jump?"* and so on. Athletes will often express a real sense of anxiety before competition, leading to perceived failure that consequently erodes their self confidence.

Elliot (2006) suggests that one explanation for last minute loss of confidence may lie in the approach/avoidance motivation theory. Elliot suggests that approach motivation is the energizing of behaviour by, or the direction of behaviour toward, positive stimuli (objects, events or possibilities), whereas avoidance motivation is the energization of behaviour by, or the direction of behaviour away from, negative stimuli (objects, events or possibilities). If so, we could assume that the athlete is motivated to perform because of the positive stimulation they will receive from participation and possible success, but at the same time they are afraid that they could receive negative stimuli by way of disappointment, boos from the crowd, criticism and possibly derision if they fail!

Many studies of performance anxiety suggest that the closer the start of the event becomes, the more athletes report increasing levels of arousal which could be explained by a greater emphasis on avoidance motivation accompanied by a consequent loss of confidence and feelings of failure. Competition can cause athletes to react physically (frequent visits to the toilet, feeling nauseous, hyperventilating and sweating) and mentally (feelings of panic, obsessive thoughts, indecision and defeatist self talk). Such states of increased arousal may not help certain athletes make a good start, and a poor start makes recovery more difficult.

The sport psychologist when helping athletes prepare for competition will often teach a series of mental skills in order to help the athlete distract themselves from negative thoughts and focus on positive thoughts and outcomes in order to give the athlete a good start. Such skills can involve relaxation, control of breathing, concentration, mental rehearsal and confidence-boosting exercises. When hypnosis is used, first of all guided by the psychologist, and then taught to the athlete for them to use themselves as self-hypnosis, the above mental skills can be supported through the athlete's own application of self-hypnosis, leading to performance enhancement.

Theory as to Why Hypnosis Might be Useful

When athletes work together with their coaches and psychologists, all three have a clear objective: to enhance the performance of the athlete. There is currently a debate within sport and exercise psychology challenging this objective (Brady & Maynard, 2010). In the author's (BC) view, this debate is an academic distraction to be largely ignored by practitioners. Since the author (BC) began practicing in occupational, sports and exercise psychology 30 years ago, it has been his understanding that when a sports client comes for consultation they seek help in some way, using his psychological expertise to enhance their performance at work or on the sports field. After the early days of the intervention (Steinberg & Cockerill, 1999) are over, work begins on helping athletes in some way enhance their performance. As time passes a meaningful and productive relationship is developed, based on facilitating the athlete's personal growth and reflexivity, counselling and referral if necessary to interdisciplinary support for help with diet and exercise. Most Olympic elite athletes will have a fairly sophisticated support team around them, of which the sport psychologist is but one member. The objective at all times is the health and wellbeing of the athlete, supported by parents, friends and professionals within the sport science, not forgetting the governing body structure to which they belong and from which they often receive financial support, and the enhancement of the athlete's performance.

Athletes are active people, they expect to do things and they expect the professionals working with them to ask them to do things; in short, they expect action. So, depending on the age and experience of each athlete they may need help with diary keeping, organizing themselves and their equipment and then teaching and practicing those mental skills which the research shows can help them make the most of their strengths such as relaxation, concentration, focusing, mental rehearsal or imagery, confidence boosting and so on. When, after careful discussion with the athlete and coach, the athlete is ready to accept learning and practicing a self-hypnosis routine, hypnosis is introduced. It has been said, 'Words are the most powerful drug the psychologist can apply', and hypnosis uses words as its communication medium.

Hypnosis is best used as an adjunct to the mental skill exercises, reinforcing Approach Motivation, addressing unconscious fears and containing positive affirmations for use as post-hypnotic suggestion (see page 23) in ego boosting. This leads to the maintenance of a high level of confidence whilst reducing performance anxiety and mitigating the possible presence of avoidance motivation.

The Published Evidence for the Use of Hypnosis in Sport

Much of the evidence for the use of hypnosis to enhance performance in sport is anecdotal. For example in 1956 at the Melbourne Olympics the Russians took 11 hypnotists to help athletes with visualization, relaxation and performance enhancement. These 11 hypnotists will have worked, in slightly different ways and with slightly different agendas, with their own athletes; and this poses a seemingly insuperable problem regarding researching the use of hypnosis on its own as a performance enhancement technique. In any intervention of a psychological nature with clients, there are so many variables that we cannot say that the performance of any athlete has been enhanced solely due to the effects of hypnosis.

'Hypnosis', then, is a generic term indicating an approach rather than a specific and replicable, experimental variable. Whilst there might be thousands of published studies claiming that hypnosis has brought about performance-enhancing changes in athletes, these cannot be scientifically controlled studies in the same way that we would conduct experiments in the laboratory. There are however, thousands of published case studies, where a hypnotist has, probably along with other cognitive-behavioural approaches, used their own hypnotic induction and protocol with an athlete whose performance has subsequently improved.

Mairs (1988) describes the use of hypnosis to enhance the performance of a sportsman (an archer) whereby he was trained to imagine observing himself going through the motions of loading (knocking!), aiming and firing (loosing!) as though he were coaching himself. This exercise helped the archer cope 'live' when anxieties and an irrational cognition were intrusive, threatening to upset his performance.

The Practical Evidence for the Successful Use of Hypnosis

The main evidence for the successful use of hypnosis the author (BC) will produce is his own work with the British Target Archery Pre-Olympic and Olympic Squads from 1980 to 1996. At the start of each winter closed season national squad training, the whole squad, manager, coaches, specialists and archers, set out their objectives for the next four years in order to complete an Olympic cycle. One of these objectives was always 'medals in Seoul (1988), Barcelona (1992), and Atlanta (1996)' and so on. For the next five squad training weekends, archers received the very best sport science advice from national coaches, a nutritionist, an exercise physiologist, a video camera expert, and the author (BC), as a British Association of Sport and Exercise Sciences accredited sport psychologist.

Sessions were with the whole group and also with individuals, and many of the individuals took advantage of hypnosis sessions, with a view to performance enhancement through ego boosting. Each archer received considerable focused support from each of the professionals mentioned above as well as receiving hypnosis from the author. As mentioned earlier, the hypnosis sessions were tape-recorded and each archer had a private, confidential copy of the session so that they could play it over and over to themselves whenever they felt the need. One medal winner, who now coaches a far eastern national squad, has recently asked for a copy of the induction protocol from 20 years ago because he found it so helpful. But of course, as UK archers gained more medals at Olympic Games, including Alison Williamson's bronze in Athens 2004, it would be an absolutely false claim to attribute hypnosis as the independent variable leading to success. What is legitimate to claim however is that hypnosis, as an adjunct to other psychological techniques, as well as specialist support from other branches of sport science, played its part in helping the athlete control their shooting under the stressful conditions of the Olympic archery field.

The Clinical Approaches Utilized within Hypnosis

A five part routine can be used as described below for athletes who participate in the aiming sports such as archery, golf, snooker and shooting in all its variations (other, more physical sports, notably team games, may require a different approach).

Induction

A five minute relaxation session focusing on a sound from outside the room, shifting to a sound inside the room emphasizing that "... *the sound of my voice, which will go with you,*" then concentrating on relaxation of muscle groups as in progressive muscle relaxation (PMR). The final part of the induction involves focusing on the eyelids:

I want you to notice and feel a part of the body that we do not often think about, your eyelids, and particularly the join between each eyelid, the place where the upper lid meets the bottom lid. Just imagine, and this is only imaginary, that your eyelids are so tightly shut that it would be difficult to open them. Of course, you know that you can open them at any time because you are in control of how your body feels. Now really believe that you cannot open your eyelids and notice that the more tightly shut your eyelids are, the more relaxed they become, and this is good because it shows you that you are in control of how your body feels as you will be in control on the shooting line. Now I want you to shift your attention from your eyelids down to your fingers and notice the position of your fingers and thumbs as they are resting in your lap. As we did with the eyelids I want you to imagine that your fingers are so heavy that it would be very difficult to move them, of course you know that you can move them at any time because you are in control of how your body feels; now, really believe that your fingers are so heavy that you could not move a finger. Notice the heavier your fingers become the more relaxed they are and this is good because it shows you that you are in control of how your body feels as you will be in control on the shooting line.

Deepening

This routine encourages the athlete to go deeper and deeper into hypnosis.

I want you now to go more deeply into hypnosis by counting down from nine to zero in three stages. So just imagine you can see a big, round figure nine, and when you can see it clearly take in a deep breath . . . breathe out slowly and see the figures ticking down in your mind, nine . . . eight . . . seven, down to the first level of deep relaxation. Now picture a large figure six in your mind and when you can see that clearly take in another deep breath. As you breathe out see the figures ticking down, six, five, four, down to the second level of deep relaxation. Finally, picture a figure three in your mind and when you can see that clearly, take in another deep breath. As you breathe out see the figures ticking down three, two, one and then zero. Here you are in the deepest state of relaxation that we call hypnosis. You have done this to yourself because you are in control, guided by me.

Special place

The supposition is that deep in our unconscious mind, that part of the mind that we talk to during hypnosis, there is a place, a feeling or an event that is special and unique to us and that by going there or recalling it, we are in a perfectly impregnable position, where nothing can harm us. Here we can be our new person, untouchable and unreachable by forces in the outside world. A couple of examples are described to the athlete such as a competitive cyclist whose special place was a ten mile training ride around High Wycombe, and a three day eventer whose special place was in a grass field, high up on her farm, lying down on her back in the summer and listening to the sounds of nature. At the same time the athlete is asked what they can see, hear and feel whilst they are in their special place. This uses visual perception, auditory perception and kinaesthetic awareness (i.e. three of the five perceptual senses) to reinforce the idea of the special place and make it more realistic for the participant. Athletes are usually very good at this exercise because they are used to tuning in to what is going on around them before concentrating solely on their event. Once safely in the special place, the client can begin to repeat their affirmations in order to become the new person, or act in new ways that we have just established; an explanation of these affirmations follows.

Affirmations

An affirmation is a positive statement about the self written in the present tense. Together with the athlete, five or six affirmations are written down focusing on ways to enhance their performance, words or feelings that they know will help them make a good start in their event by inducing confidence. A typical set of affirmations could be (in this case for a three day eventer):

- I'm here to beat them.
- I'm in control.
- I can do this.
- I do have good legs (meaning, strong legs to control the horse, not for fashion!).
- I've done this before.
- I'm reaching my goal.

The author (BC) would then say, *"These affirmations that we have written down for you will help you <u>think, feel and behave the way you want to</u>, long after the session has finished. They will help you <u>control</u> your feelings on the shooting/start line and give you a good, positive start."*

The affirmations are repeated three times, and the athlete is asked to silently say them over and over to themselves as the therapist repeats them.

The affirmations act as post-hypnotic suggestions in order to support the athlete, boost their ego, add self confidence and above all be in control of how they think, feel and act.

Re-alerting

Finally a gentle wake up to a count of nine is used as follows:

It is time to wake up now and we are going to come back to reality, to the here and now, to a count of nine. Count of one, two, three, just moving your toes and fingers, four, five, six, moving your elbows and knees, seven, eight, nine, just opening your eyes and giving a big stretch as if you have had a good night's sleep! Well done!

Upon 'coming back to the here and now', how the athlete experienced the session is discussed. This feedback is important because it tells the therapist what each individual likes or dislikes, and how much they understand the purpose of using the recorded session as their own application of self-hypnosis.

Most athletes appreciate the experience and understand that the routine is absolutely benign (i.e. if it does not work, no harm is done!).

A Case Study with Discussion and Commentary

This study was subject to peer review and reported in an occasional paper produced for the Sport and Exercise Psychology Section of the British Psychological Society, based on proceedings of a one day workshop at Warwick University. The full paper is available from the BPS or this author (BC), 'Exercise Addiction: Motivation for Participation in Sport and Exercise' (Annett et al., 1995).

This case study follows the life of a young mountain biker, John, from the age of 19, when he came fifth in the national championships, through to the present time. It is a study of intense dedication to sport, overtraining, physiological collapse and subsequent improving recovery which is now complete. It is a study in the now recognized syndrome of exercise addiction.

In an attempt to understand people's motivation for extremely strenuous sports (i.-e. marathon, triathlon), attention might be directed to the phenomenon of addiction to these types of exercises. Apparently, some people have become addicted to these activities, and their addiction provides an answer to the question why they take part. (Bakker et al., 1990)

John began mountain biking at the age of 16. His exercise history at school was positive, and he enjoyed a mixture of squash, cross-country running and his physical education lessons. After leaving school John went to a local college of further education embarking on a leisure and recreation course which he passed easily. His comments about himself at that age were *"Bright, brainy and well into sport"*. Sport made him popular among his peers, and in 1989 he won his first mountain bike event. He quickly rose up the ladder of the sport to become one of the top ten British juniors. When he was riding he was skilful, took risks and was, in his own words, 'reckless' on his bike. He began to obsessively dedicate himself to the sport, consequently cutting himself off from what would be considered to be the normal social development of a post-teenager.

John reported himself that his life had become very lonely, and soon he did not feel that he fitted in with his peer group. Whereas he was very comfortable in taking part in sport, he was not particularly comfortable at parties with his peers. John peaked early and took part in approximately 20 events throughout Europe. In 1992, when he was aged 20, he could only complete in about seven or eight events during the whole of that season. He found competition very hard indeed, and reports that his body was 'stressed out' at that time.

The next year, 1993, John came fifth in the nationals and reported that it was the first event he felt good riding in: *"I couldn't understand it, I felt my old self."* Towards the end of 1993, his performance faded off again. By September of that year, John had established enough of a reputation to go to the world championships in Canada. He says about that time that he knew he would not do well. He fell off in the downhill event and was concussed. Before this, he did not qualify in the cross country event because he said that his fatigue interrupted so much that he only did one lap.

John felt that maybe he could improve his performance by changing his diet, and so he stopped eating dairy products and began to eat a lot of carbohydrates. He came to see me in the middle of 1994 and reported that he felt normal, but not like an athlete. He had lost his motivation entirely and felt that he did not care at all for himself. He had stopped training properly and stopped doing a lot of stretching work which he had enjoyed.

John reported that his illness (i.e. his problem) began when he decided to 'go for it'. In 1990 he undertook a really strenuous 16 week training programme devised by an exercise physiologist. The programme included a gradual build up and taper down towards the racing season. This would appear to be a fairly reasonable but strenuous programme for an athlete aged around 25 to 30; for someone aged 18 plus, however, it might be considered by exercise physiologists to be rather heavy.

John reported that during the whole of this training period, he was not recovering and consequently felt tired. His sleeping patterns were irregular, and he often suffered from sore throats. Occasionally he reported that his heart was overworking, and his pulse rate would shoot up when he was doing mild exercise. John went to a specialist in sports physiology who diagnosed chronic fatigue syndrome and advised him to take the rest of the 1990 season off. In 1991 he started a gradual build up, and at first everything seemed all right. In 1992 he became seriously ill and suffered a high temperature for two weeks. His joints seized up, and the doctor diagnosed summer flu. John could not move, however, and suffered high temperatures.

When he recovered from this illness, he picked up a little and came fifth in the nationals in 1992; he actually felt good with no training! After the nationals, the next weekend, he went back to his old feelings of fatigue and reported that the race was such hard work even though he came third. (*Comment*: The author's [BC] subsequent experience with athletes with a propensity towards exercise addiction suggests that, after a fairly serious upper respiratory infection like influenza, if they resume heavy training too early their immune system can be affected leading possibly towards chronic fatigue syndrome, otherwise known as M.E.)

His training in 1993 went relatively well, although he was taking it easy, experiencing only the odd dry throat. In the middle of the season he rode in a 100 mile race and said he nearly died. His heart rate was high, and he never really recovered from that ride for the rest of the season. He got the shakes and shivers, and felt cold. At times he could hardly walk and felt completely wiped out even after 12 hours of sleep at night and two or three hours of sleep in the afternoon. Several of the local specialists were suggesting that John's difficulties were psychological, and so in the summer of 1994 he came to see the author (BC). An interesting observation: when all else fails, send in the shrink!

Presenting symptoms

- Constant feeling of tiredness and fatigue.
- John did not recover from exercise fast enough and certainly not before the next exercise session.
- Sleeping patterns were irregular.
- John reported a series of sore throats.

- During a race he started well but after a few laps he felt he had no power, it hurt and he loses everything and gives up. Sometimes he felt completely exhausted, even after 12 hours of sleep and a sleep during the day. He suffered from food allergies with nosebleeds and headaches after sugar, and high temperature and sleeplessness after wheat.
- His joints "seized up" after dairy products.
- Nuts, seeds and wheat gave him diarrhoea.

A haematology and biochemistry analysis reported all measures as in the normal range.

John's personality was measured using the Eysenck Personality Scales (EPQ-R). On this self report measure, John reported himself an Emotional (Neurotic) – Introvert. These scales include one for addiction measuring a certain extent of obsession. John's score for addiction was high, indicating that his personality could lead him towards sticking religiously to his training routine and possibly overtraining. The subsequent impact on his immune system, in the opinion of the author (BC), led to the development of the symptoms of exercise addiction.

Therapeutic intervention

A cognitive-behavioural approach was taken with John that looked at his whole life. A framework used the idea of two circles, rather like bicycle wheels, front wheel and back wheel. The front wheel represented his old circle of life, poor eating, not sticking to his regime, feelings of guilt, those feelings getting inside him, destroying everything else, not liking to be with people, disrupted sleep, mood swings and going into his shell wondering what people think of him. The rear wheel, where the power is applied, would replace the old circle of life and become his new circle of life, starting with eating well at breakfast, sticking to his regime, feeling good, becoming more carefree, feeling creative and positive, enjoying being with people, sleeping better, mood stabilizing and becoming much more sociable.

A daily schedule was drawn up starting at 7:15 A.M. involving work, rest, lunch relaxation, fun in the evenings, dinner, relaxation and more fun and early to bed at 9 P.M. His relaxation was cycling into town, going into the bike shop for a chat with mates, taking a walk, going swimming and being with his friends.

A hypnosis audio tape was made for him involving:

- Induction
- Deepening
- Special place imagery – at the coast on a beach in the Canary Islands, warm sand, with clear visual, auditory and kinaesthetic images.
- Affirmations: *"Feeling relaxed . . . be myself . . . have a laugh . . . feel positive . . . get on well with others . . . speak freely . . . joining . . . look to really enjoying the rest of the day."* These affirmations were repeated three times in order to reinforce the post-hypnotic suggestion that *"These suggestions will affect how you think, feel and act long after this session has finished and will go with you in order to support your new approach to life."*
- Re-alerting

John was asked to treat the tape like a bottle of antibiotic pills from his GP (i.e. play it once a day for 14 days, learn the routine and then play it whenever he felt a bit depressed).

A year later, John was seen informally and he reported in a verbatim interview:

Since I started working with you, I have been able to think more clearly about my life. I think about whom I am and what I want, and I am now able to focus on myself. I was at my lowest ebb physically. I had been to see everybody, and although things seemed to improve for a little while, nothing actually worked. I am now more positive, more determined and am back on track towards recovery. I actually played my self-hypnosis tape every day for four weeks (Comment: Obsessive behaviour! Addiction to the tape?) During those weeks I felt well, knew what I was doing and where I was going. I was able to think realistically. Now, in March 1995, my health is better, I have realistic goals, I can plan my life more effectively. My training is gradually increasing and my level of leisure cycling is nearly up to training. I go out running and swimming. For the first time I am beginning to think like a normal person.

John certainly appeared to be much less anxious and more positive, and his parents confirmed this. He now has a new job, is very active, has a serious relationship and is very happy.

Discussion

The intervention took what could be called an integrated life approach, that is to say three aspects of John's life were looked at: firstly, his own physical health and physiological functioning; secondly, his sport and, thirdly, his relationships with others. What was previously missing in John's life was an understanding of the importance of psychological well-being; it was quite clear that he was becoming seriously depressed. John has now added a psychological dimension to care for and monitor his health, relationships and sport which has made him a more tough-minded and hardy personality. Hypnosis was used as an adjunct to support this integrated life approach and as an adjunct to all of the therapeutic work and so enhanced John's performance in sport and indeed his everyday life.

By adopting a cognitive-behavioural approach and using the powerful conditioning of words in post-hypnotic suggestion, John is well on the way to recovery.

Use of Imagery

As well as the ego-boosting and affirmation techniques described above, there is also a place for using imagery. For example, a golfer might use imagery of his ball as much smaller than it is in reality and the hole in the green as much larger. Anchors generally (see page 145) and visualizations are very often used such as in the following case from contributor Dr G Ibbotson.

Peter was a cricketer whose bowling had declined markedly; he was having trouble 'letting the ball go'. He was taught to recall and visualize the best ball he had ever bowled, when he had bowled the opposition's best batsman with his first ball. He obviously could not make a physical anchor using his hands as he was bowling, so it was suggested that he anchored this by clenching the toes of his left foot. This anchor he activated as he planted his foot firmly on the ground and took his arm back to bowl.

One of the differences between a good and an elite athlete is not the power they put into their active muscles but how relaxed the antagonist muscles are, and hypnosis has been shown to help with this. It is interesting that visualizing doing an activity such as bending a finger or elbow has been shown to strengthen the relevant muscles even though no physical activity has taken place (Ranganathan et al., 2004). In Sweden, Unestahl et al. (1975) reported an interesting study which showed that PE students 'shooting' 30 hypnotic basket penalty shots a day made a significant improvement (compared with a control group) and improved as much as those making 30 physical training shots a day. This is of importance if an athlete is injured or unable to train as training in hypnosis rather than in reality may mean that muscles can maintain their strength.

Other Performance Anxieties

The term 'performance' can also be used generically to cover any important presentation activity required of us, for example a university lecturer delivering a series of lectures to say 150 undergraduates, a surgeon performing a delicate operation or a job applicant attending a selection interview or assessment centre, will all be included in this 'performance' category. So, performance is defined as the 'action or process of carrying out or accomplishing an action, task or function'. The action should be seen in terms of how successfully it was performed, and the audience, whether undergraduates, hospital patient or interview panel, could be asked how successful in their eyes the performance was conducted.

To demonstrate how hypnosis can be used, together with other performance-enhancing techniques, we will use as an example the case of Olivia (name and identification details changed), who returned successfully to the stage after a fairly protracted time working in film and television.

Olivia – a Return to the Stage

In Olivia's case the rendering of a dramatic role, requiring a high performance on stage in front of a live audience, after a long period in film and on television was her main concern and the reason she came for help.

Olivia talked about her last stage performance, eight years ago. It was a good performance, and at a personal level she wished to repeat that.

The diagnosis

Because of the magnitude of this next stage play, the whole arena and setting, the sheer size of the task sometimes filled Olivia with dread. This naturally occurring fear which at times can overcome us, quite often waking us in the small hours when our defences are down and indeed at other unguarded moments, was discussed. Olivia's main concerns were that she should not let the director or her fellow actors down and that she should perform optimally.

An approach was discussed covering two areas of performance psychology, a set of mental preparation skills for performance, and a self-hypnosis routine, all audio-recorded onto a CD with the objective of helping Olivia take control of her performance nerves just before she goes on stage. The purpose of the CD was to reinforce the learning and training of these valuable performance skills, and to use the performance affirmations as post-hypnotic suggestion to work on the unconscious and support her on stage. Eventually, once Olivia had selected and learned the most important exercises for her, the CD could be filed, to be brought out and used whenever a refresher is needed. She was also told that she could have a further session when she felt the need for a personal consultation.

Theory as to why hypnosis might be useful

It is now widely recognized amongst advocates of hypnosis that it is most effectively used in conjunction with other psychological techniques like progressive muscle relaxation, cognitive-behavioural therapy (CBT) approaches, and acting as an adjunct to these therapies. The purpose of the work with Olivia was to make sure that she got a good start on stage, after being cued, and moved confidently into her opening lines fully under control. The hypnosis protocol chosen contained affirmations which acted as post-hypnotic suggestion to support all the hard work that she, and indeed the whole cast, had put in under an internationally renowned stage director.

Published evidence

Gibson and Heap (1991) present 'a comprehensive range of the applications of hypnotic techniques in therapy for psychological disorders, and medical conditions where such techniques are a valuable adjunct' (back cover). They outline the obvious benefits of hypnosis whereby patients can experience quite profound depths of mental and physical relaxation and an enhanced disposition to respond automatically to suggestions administered by the hypnotist. In Olivia's case these suggestions, identified in preparation for the session as affirmations, helped Olivia be in control and make a good start in her performance. Once this good start had been made, all the training of the consummate professional, rehearsal and expert direction, would take over to enable her to let her do what she was very good at (i.e. acting).

The practical evidence for its successful use

As has been discussed previously, it is not possible to claim hypnosis as the independent variable in any experimental or therapeutic intervention because the stimulus material (the words and voice of the hypnotist) is never the same. What we do have, however, is practical evidence for the successful use of hypnosis in very many cases studies where patients and participants improve their 'performance' in some way.

Williamson (2004) and Kraft and Kraft (2004) describe working with patients whose driving performance had markedly declined, using self-hypnosis training together with dissociative imagery, and positive mental rehearsal. Systematic desensitization of driving scenarios in hypnosis, or 'virtual reality exposure therapy' relying on a computerized programme involving a sequence of driving scenarios, was also used. These patients reported complete recovery such that they could return to normal driving.

The clinical approaches utilized within hypnosis

Whether in sport or occupational psychology or in personal development with clients, during the early stages, as well as taking a full history, a psychologist may also use a personality questionnaire such as the Eysenck Cripps Cook Occupational Scales (ECCOS; Cook et al., 2007). This well known, valid and reliable personality questionnaire is of use to us in understanding a little about Olivia's personality, which can help and guide any coaching intervention.

Olivia reported herself to be of a Stable–Extravert disposition and not usually an anxious person. She would usually appear optimistic and emotionally stable and would come across as controlled and calm. This Extravert trait helped her make herself noticed in the workplace and set a pace for her natural tendency to want to keep moving and do things (an important indicator to the desired pace of any intervention and our work together). Olivia sought stimulation and change and avoided what she may have perceived as rather mundane and repetitive activities.

Olivia was a sociable person and cared for people in the organization to which she belonged (i.e. the theatre). She fitted readily into a team and was not a troublesome person. Olivia generally liked to be liked and accepted by others. Olivia could be a little bit impulsive and enjoyed taking certain calculated risks. She showed a normal level of awareness for others and was usually able to see their point of view and read their feelings. Finally, Olivia responded to the questionnaire in an open and honest way.

A measure of biofeedback looking at electro-dermal activity (EDA) through skin conductivity response (SCR), called 'relax-plus', was taken. Two sensors attached to the index finger of the non-dominant hand pick up the tiny positive and negative charges transmitted through the autonomic nervous system, to measure live, real time arousal response.

The personality measure (ECCOS, discussed above) measures the underlying personality trait of anxiety, which in Olivia's case was just below average. The graph exhibited by Olivia's state arousal using the biofeedback device showed her arousal system to be stable and under control. Even when anxiety-provoking cognitive events were quietly remembered, Olivia demonstrated that she was able to bring the biofeedback graph under control to reflect a stable arousal state.

These responses demonstrated that Olivia had an underlying stable, controlled personality trait and was able, when she wished, to control her level of state anxiety. Both these responses augured well for a stage performer.

Progressive muscle relaxation

Preparation for hypnosis involved the exercise of PMR (see page 114). The purpose of this exercise was to experience and train the body and mind to be able to relax at will, fully and deeply. This exercise for an actress can be practiced as a starting point before learning lines or rehearsing. It should not be used, however, before performance as it is too relaxing.

Breathing control

This exercise is an important crisis management exercise in order to prevent 'choking' and help bring the body back under control after a possible stressful moment. It is practiced by breathing in, holding the breath for a few seconds and then breathing out slowly, under control, to a self talk word such as *"Easy, easy ..."*

Concentration and focus

In the pre-performance hubbub of a stage play, in a large theatre, in front of an audience of hundreds, it is quite normal for negative self talk to intrude and concentration to wane. Levels of concentration were discussed; at level 3, normal everyday interaction with colleagues, level 2, sitting in the dressing room being made up, and level 1, just about to go on stage.

The immediate pre-performance level of concentration was level 1 and was accompanied by a self talk word, "REACH," indicating that Olivia should be heard, be seen and communicate fully through actions and words with her audience (i.e. to REACH them).

Imagery or mental rehearsal

Mental rehearsal is the practice of rehearsing the actions prior to going on to the stage so that at that important time, the mind is perfectly happy that everything had been learned, is in order, is known, is rehearsed and can be conducted faultlessly. Mental rehearsal can be practiced over and over again at any time in order to reinforce the actual start of the performance on stage. A routine list was made as follows:

- See yourself sitting in your dressing room.
- Knock-knock on the door, 'final call'.
- Get up and join the others.
- Go on to the stage wings.
- Listen to the play.
- At cue walk on, assisted by a gentle push from the stage manager!
- Opening words: *"How delightful to meet you ..."*

This routine was to be learned and practiced often.

Self-confidence anchor

This exercise involved programming a successful event in the past, a BAFTA ceremony, and visualizing, hearing and feeling that event as if Olivia was there at that time. At the point of feeling excited, the feelings were anchored to a clenched, dominant hand, calling a name for the feelings silently. This self-confidence exercise was practiced by reversing the process as follows:

- Clench the dominant hand.
- Call the name to yourself.
- Experience the feelings.
- Listen to the sounds.
- Visualize and experience the scene; remember the BAFTA event.
- GET up and go!

Self hypnosis

Self hypnosis involved five stages, which were audio-dubbed onto a CD:

- *Induction*: deeply relaxing, listening to sounds outside the room, inside the room, and then focusing on parts of the body, relaxing them more and more deeply, all the time repeating the phrase *"The more relaxed you become, the more in control you are."*
- *Deepening*: going more and more deeply into relaxation using the breathing in three stages, counting down, nine-eight-seven, six-five-four, three-two-one, *"arriving at the state of deep relaxation that we call hypnosis."*
- *Special place*: elicited beforehand but repeated here, at the top of a mountain in Norway, with her mother, seeing flowers and her mother, hearing birdsong, a waterfall and wild ponies and feeling bursting with happiness!
- *Affirmations*: in this special place *"Repeating the phrases that we wrote down earlier for you..."*:
    - *"I'm in control."*
    - *"I know my part."*
    - *"I love my audience."*
    - *"I trust my fellow actors."*
    - *"I am the luckiest person alive."*

This was followed by the post-hypnotic suggestion, "These phrases will affect you long after this session has finished, reinforcing your confidence and self belief, and setting you up for a good start to the performance."

Discussion and Commentary

What was so rewarding, as a teacher, psychologist and lifelong learner, was to meet and work with someone at the very top of her profession, still striving for perfection in her craft and understanding that her performance could be enhanced through the acquisition of performance skills. The culmination of the work with Olivia was an emotional and stupendous performance keeping a rapt and attentive audience completely absorbed for two and a half hours.

There follows a couple of short case examples where a quick resolution of performance anxiety was obtained using anchors (see page 145) and mental rehearsal.

Paula loved to sing as a hobby but was anxious about performing solo at a concert that the local operatic society was putting on for charity. In hypnosis Paula was asked to imagine a time when she had sung really well; when she felt elated and really pleased with how she had done. She anchored this to a simple pressing of her thumb and index finger of her right hand. She repeated this three times and still uses it to boost her confidence before performing.

Brian enjoyed singing and wanted to sing in his local pub but felt too anxious to do so. It was suggested that he stick a smiley face sticker on his microphone, and feelings of a successful rehearsal were anchored to this. He was then taught to do a repeated positive rehearsal in hypnosis using an image of his microphone to which he had stuck a smiley face, as well as rehearsing this in reality, so that when he did it as a performance he could readily access these good feelings.

So it can be seen from the examples given above that how the performer sees themselves generates either anxiety or a confident attitude. A positive attitude and a feeling of confidence together with being able to visualize their goal lead to a successful performance whether in sports, the performing arts or any other human activity.

References

Annett, J., Cripps, B. & Steinberg, H. (1995), *Exercise addiction: motivation for participation in sport and exercise*. London, Sport and Exercise Psychology Section of the British Psychological Society.

Bakker, F. C., Whiting, H. T. A. & Brug, H. V. D. (1990), *Sport psychology: concepts and applications*. Chichester, John Wiley and Sons, Ltd.

Brady, A. & Maynard, I. (2010), At an elite level the role of a sport psychologist is entirely about performance enhancement. *Sport and Exercise Psychology Review*, 6 (1), 59–66.

Cook, M., Cripps, B., Eysenck, H. J. & Eysenck, S. B. G. (2007), Technical manual to ECCOS, the Eysenck Cripps Cook Occupational Scales. http://www.eccos.co.uk

Elliot, A. J. (2006), The hierarchical model of approach-avoidance motivation. *Motivation and Emotion*, 30 (2), 111–16.

Fazey, J. A. & Hardy, L. (1988), *The inverted-U hypotheses: catastrophe for sports psychology*. British Association of Sports Sciences Monograph no. 1. Leeds, National Coaching Foundation.

Gibson, H. B. & Heap, M. (1991), *Hypnosis in therapy*. Hove, Lawrence Erlbaum.

Jones, G. J. & Hardy, L. (1990), *Stress and performance in sport*. Chichester, John Wiley & Sons, Ltd.

Kraft, T. & Kraft, D. (2004), Creating a virtual reality in hypnosis: a case of driving phobia. *Contemporary Hypnosis*, 21 (2), 79–85.

Lane, A. M. (2008), *Sport and exercise psychology: topics in applied psychology*. London, Hodder Education.

Mairs, D. (1988), Hypnosis in sport, in Heap, M. (Ed.) *Hypnosis: current clinical, experimental and forensic practices*. London, Croom Helm.

Ranganathan, V., Siemionow, V., Liu, J., Sahgal, V. & Yue, G. (2004), From mental power to muscle power – gaining strength by using the mind. *Neuropsychologia*, 42, 944–56.

Rushall, B. S. (1992), *Mental skills training for sports*. Canberra, Australian Coaching Council.

Steinberg, H. & Cockerill, I. (Eds.) (1999), *Sport psychology in practice: the early stages*. London, Sport and Exercise Psychology Section of the British Psychological Society.

Unestahl, L. E., Hultin, K. & Sundgren, B. (1975) Effekten av föreställningar under hypnos och avslappning på idrottsprestationer. *Högskolan i Örebro*, 1.

Williamson, A. (2004), A case of driving phobia treated with dissociative imagery. *Contemporary Hypnosis*, 21 (2), 86–92.

Yerkes, R. M. & Dodson, J. D. (1908), The relation of the strength of stimulus to rapidity of habit formation. *Journal of Comparative and Neurological Psychology*, 18, 459–82.

38

Informal Hypnotic Techniques

Dr Caron Moores, Dr Grahame Smith and Mr Martin Wall

A Co-Operative Project

The field of hypnosis is a collection of techniques in need of a unifying theory.

J Hall (1989)

Consider an alternative understanding and substitute 'free' for 'in need'. This freedom offers a huge opportunity to the flexible imaginative clinician; treatment need not be influenced and distorted by didactic theory. It is legitimate in tandem with all the adjunctive clinical skills, to use and trust the intuitive sense of the other, while monitoring the effect of interventions and dynamically modifying them as necessary.

Fifty years ago Shor (1959) spoke of 'the flesh and blood of hypnosis', and Mason (1960) called it 'the most fundamental of all hypnotic phenomena'. They were both responding to the relationship between clinician and therapist. The great value of the hypnotic project is that it is a co-operative venture between the participants.

The working hypothesis that informs this approach is that it is the patient's existential reality that is important, how they live and experience their lives emotionally and practically, each patient unique and fluid, changing with context and time. As Sartre (1943) so elegantly put it 'Existence precedes essence'. The endeavour is to find a resolution for the patient within their worldview (not necessarily the truth), rather than forming a diagnosis from a historically true narrative.

How can this briefly outlined philosophical position on the primacy of experience translate into practical therapy? Some research findings on the dynamics of hypnotic

The Handbook of Contemporary Clinical Hypnosis: Theory and Practice, First Edition.
Edited by Les Brann, Jacky Owens and Ann Williamson.
© 2012 John Wiley & Sons, Ltd. Published 2015 by John Wiley & Sons, Ltd.

inductions will serve to illustrate the nature of the processes being proposed (Banyai, 1998).

To briefly summarize this fascinating paper, Banyai and colleagues observed a series of subject and hypnotist pairs while they were inducing and testing hypnotic depth. After the event both subject and hypnotist were interviewed separately to record their experience of the session.

The data demonstrated a series of different styles of interaction; the primary two identified were maternal and paternal as predicted by Ferenczi (1965). Maternal can be likened to a physical organic style with an interactional synchrony between therapist and subject of overt (limb movement and postures) and covert (breathing and electromyography measurements) signifiers, plus a reliance on intuitive own body sensations to assess the state of the subject; it is a permissive approach.

The paternal style favours a cognitive rational involvement, thoughts rather than physical cues, an analysis of the subject's personality and pathology, invoked in an authoritarian manner. It has been the author's (MW) personal endeavour to have at his disposal both these styles so that he can adapt to the patient rather than the converse.

The value of brief informal interventions is in their subtlety and immediate effect, rather than dramatic, elaborate and profound reconstructions that can be achieved with more formal hypnotic therapy. The following narrative from a patient supervised recently will serve to illustrate some of the points raised.

The treatment was undertaken in a busy open clinic at a dental school with several active treatments underway and a queue of students waiting for their work in progress to be checked.

A patient the author (MW) had never met before was introduced by a student who had taken an excellent full history. The scheduled treatment plan was for the extraction of a carious tooth that had been giving the patient considerable pain resulting in loss of sleep and a considerable curtailment of daily activity.

The patient was obviously very anxious, and the author (MW) sensed from her continuing scanning of the clinic that she was somewhat overawed by the busyness around her. The author (MW) had the image of a lost soul tossed in the maelstrom of anxiety, pain and sleeplessness – an altered state waiting to be utilized.

After a brief conversation and with the benefit of the history, the words of the Navy hymn chimed in the author's (MW) mind.

> Eternal Father, strong to save,
> Whose arm hath bound the restless wave,
> Who biddest the mighty ocean deep
> Its own appointed limits keep. (W. Whiting 1825–1878)

Verbalization along the following lines served to engage the dissociated state and modify it into one of safety and empowerment.

You are safe now you have reached safety; here in this cubical it is calm and protected, like in a harbour safe from the storm. The activity outside (the cubical) *allows you to appreciate the calm and safety inside* (the cubical)."

Further verbalizations linked activity outside to calm and safety inside, along with continual reinforcement to encourage self praise at each stage.

You can begin to feel so pleased with yourself . . . so proud of your achievement.

The treatment was completed successfully by means of utilizing the patient's presenting symptoms and the patient's experiential reality.

To consider the theory that informed the intervention, both of Banyai's styles were involved. Intuitively and observationally (maternal), this patient need a secure controlled (paternal) approach. It is important to trust intuition but also to observe effect, and to be prepared to change and adapt as necessary.

The patient's overt symptoms were in response to the consequence of the pathology and pain, and conditioned by the context of a busy clinic with stressed staff movement and harsh lighting. The intervention was given in a paternal style with authority, conviction and a single-minded means to an end.

To understand the patient's experience within the cooperative nature of the hypnotic contract, it was instructive to read the comprehensive dental history taken by the student which referred to traumatic extractions in the past: the dentist had *". . . his knee on my chest"* the nurse was *". . . pinioning both my arms and legs."* Such statements are probably not historically true or indeed anatomically possible, however for the patient they were very definitely real, and it would have served no therapeutic purpose to challenge or disprove the narrative.

So in summary the author (MW) would not elevate this to a technique to be copied; it is in essence a plea to evolve your own techniques, tailored to your patient's and your own existential reality.

Are informal hypnotic techniques anything more than the good consultation skills we aspire to anyway? Maybe the answer is 'no': a good 'bedside manner' will incorporate many of the points we cultivate in hypnosis training. The works of Roger Neighbour (2005a, 2005b) made some techniques part of mainstream consultation skills. Rapport and good communication are pre-requisites for all helping styles. Maybe the answer is 'yes' in that techniques generated from hypnosis training are more experiential, utilize imagination and welcome or invite a shift of attention. We are intentionally using suggestibility. Understanding hypnosis enhances the skills of clinicians and opens up possibilities, but those trained in it do not 'own' hypnosis.

An anaesthetic colleague had a thoroughly engaging way of inserting IV 'Butterfly' needles in children. He would show the picture on the box, talk about butterflies and how one of these special ones would land on your hand. It might seem to give a tiny nip, but it would be no bother and you would see it growing a beautiful red tail. The staff were entranced as well as the patient, but he would not have professed to be using hypnosis.

It is easy to get bogged down in defining hypnosis and its induction. The author (GS) has used the working definition 'Hypnosis is an intentional shift in attention in which the mind is more receptive' since 1988. It owes much to Spiegel (1974) and Erickson (1958). It is handy in spite of its limitations, question begging nature and circularity.

In clinical situations the shift has often already occurred and is there for us to use. Patients have heightened focus and are receptive. A message can be delivered while they remain attentive, or 'hanging on every word'.

Consider 'breaking good news'. A patient has come for a result, perhaps chest X-rays or liver function. The doctor responds, *"Hmm ... I am rather concerned about your smoking and drinking ... I wonder how you feel about this,"* in the style of motivational interviewing. Of course, humanity demands swift progress to expression of pleasure that the result was normal (this time!). Such opportunities are lost when results are given less personally. Applications include dermatology, diabetes and sexual health. We should be prepared to examine our own reasons for any excess zeal or lack of it in suggesting life style changes to others.

Patients are often anxious or tense, and readily say 'yes' to an offer to show them 'the easy way' to cope with a procedure or to be able to relax more easily. This could be, for example, cool imagery for menopausal symptoms or skin irritation, such as mountain streams, the feel of a glass in your hand shaking the ice cubes, seeing the condensation and so on. 'Hairdresser' questions about holidays can be improved to evoke various sensory modalities. Similarly enquiry about pets can be guided to what it is like to stroke them (Olness & Kohen, 1996) and so on.

Minor changes of phraseology and tonality can be surprisingly effective. Try saying, *"Let yourself relax,"* rather than the oft heard *"Try to relax"* for abdominal examination. Be mindful of any need for a chaperone when utilizing suggestibility for procedures that could be deemed intimate.

For injections or venous access, the simple 'borrowed arm' dissociation is useful and can be employed as routine. It can be combined with imaginative involvement with a distraction.

A ten year old girl needed an orthopaedic procedure at short notice, requiring insertion of an 18 Gauge Venflon. Various conversational ploys drew a blank. She liked television. Did she watch *Strictly Come Dancing*? This met with vigorous affirmation. During the conversation, the author (GS) asked, *"Could we borrow your hand for now?"* and *"... just let it go and let me feel it."*

She was asked to name the judges and her favourite contestant. What was her dress like? She was to imagine being there at the studio seeing them in real life. She might notice me slipping something in the back of her hand, but it need not bother her. Her contestant had just finished to rapturous applause, and the judges did their catch phrases and held up the scores ... more applause.

The cannulation had been achieved with no reaction or distress. She was awarded ten all round for letting it be so easy. She examined the cannula with mild interest. A consultant anaesthetist remarked on the lack of fuss without the use of the usual bleb of local or of EMLA (eutectic mixture of local anaesthetic) cream.

The imagery does not need to be relaxing in the conventional sense. Indeed, when there is some sympathetic arousal and adrenalin flowing, it can be acknowledged. A needle phobic teenager (with whom the author [GS] had done two preparatory hypnosis sessions) accepted an injection as the whistle blew in a rugby match and went on to score a try with exhilaration and congratulation.

The capability to modify the experience of a symptom can be illustrated using a conversation about 'noticing' and 'not noticing' things via the various sensory modalities. Reference can be made to spectacles, jewellery and so on, having application for pain. Drawing attention increases awareness, whereas absorption in something else decreases it. The 'It's all in my mind, then?' tag can be dispelled, yet the use of the mind deployed to alleviate it.

The author's (GS) consulting room window looks out to a power station some three miles away. Often there are steam clouds and sun throwing the cooling towers into relief. In the foreground at 50 yards is an Italian restaurant. Also to be seen are rooftops, trees and aerials. The castle mound can be seen to the right. The window has bars dividing it into four panes. Looking through the window together opens up a wealth of themes of therapeutic value based on what we may notice or not notice. This can embrace perceptions of beauty, necessity, gustatory pleasure, history and power, right down to the bird mess on one window pane, a product of nature.

Physical techniques can be demonstrated briefly and effectively, for example hand on abdomen for 'chronic hyperventilation'. Inspired by the Papworth breathing exercises, yet one step removed from thinking about breathing, some physiological explanation and discussion of abdominal versus thoracic breathing are first given. The patient is invited to sit back and place the hand on their abdomen. The therapist does likewise. Both watch their hands. The knack of noticing hand movement is commented upon. *"I can see mine though it is a little jerky for the moment,"* then *"Ah yes . . . I can see you are getting that gentle movement now . . . just watching the hand. . . ."* Can the hand movement be felt? Maybe, but it is much easier to notice the relaxation. The patient may have closed their eyes by then, and will almost invariably note the relaxation. This can be extended to feeling a sensation of warmth between the hand and abdomen, with application for irritable bowel syndrome.

Mini-demonstrations of phenomena associated with hypnosis can be stand alone illustrations, or can be a prelude to more formal sessions. Much is just about possible within a standard ten minute slot.

Techniques broadly referred to as metaphor can be employed in normal consultations. An enuretic child may be asked to imagine a ship and its crew. The captain is always in charge and responsible, but the crew work as a team to ensure the normal running of the ship. The crew may sometimes have to wake the captain, according to how well practiced they are and how important it is. As they work more as a team, messages can be clearer and actions more efficient, and so on. The child's involvement can be tested by asking for details and nodding understanding.

Similarly, examples of training and teamwork for sport can be invoked.

Does the barber use hypnosis when positioning the customer's head? Not really, but, as in medicine, context, professional rapport and non-verbal communication are powerful

A dental colleague had a child who repeatedly put his hand to his mouth during examination and treatment. The dentist simply took his wrist and moved it out of the way, commenting that he was just attaching it to a brick on the floor. The hand remained immobile, and at the end he congratulated him while announcing that he was snipping the string.

factors. Sometimes the author (GS), in performing the ritual of taking the pulse, gives a barely perceptible twist and the patient's forearm remains suspended. Is this hypnosis? Perhaps it is a useful impromptu indication of possible responsiveness.

In informal hypnosis there is an ethical dilemma: when and where does the use of words become hypnosis? The words used during interventions with patients, and the 'authority' attributed to the speaker of those words, can affect the perception of discomfort by the patient. Words used in clinic prior to a procedure may act as suggestions to be acted upon at a later stage, and patients may subconsciously attribute authority to different professionals at different stages in their treatment.

A randomized controlled trial reported by Varelmann *et al.* (2010) compared the use of 'nice' (placebo) words, such as 'small pinch', versus harsh ('nocebo') words, such as 'big bee sting', prior to injection of local anaesthetic into the skin for placement of labour epidural catheters. A blinded observer obtained a visual analogue pain score immediately after the skin injection. They showed that pain scores were significantly reduced when placebo words were used versus nocebo words. Many anaesthetists tell the patient to expect a sharp scratch just prior to cannulation; it is the author's (CM) practice to talk about 'feeling some pushing'. Similarly with analgesia the author (CM) talks about "... *medicine to keep you comfortable afterwards*" rather than giving 'pain killers'.

Whilst in the anaesthetic room, prior to induction of anaesthesia, the patient's attention is usually focused on what the anaesthetist is saying. Anaesthetists are able to influence the post-operative course by the words they use. It is preferable for patients to wake up feeling comfortable and not feeling sick, so suggestions to this effect can be given as the induction agent is injected. Occasionally there is a specific problem that needs to be dealt with which only becomes apparent at the last minute. This is the grey area where usual anaesthetic patter may become 'hypnosis' as in the case example below.

Administration of intrathecal chemotherapy and bone marrow aspiration in children is undertaken under general anaesthesia as a day case procedure in the author's (CM) Hospital Trust. For logistical reasons (to ensure the smooth running of a very busy list), patients are assessed as 'fit for anaesthesia' by the oncology team in clinic, and the anaesthetic assessment is carried out in the anaesthetic room immediately prior to induction of anaesthesia. This is far from ideal as it leaves little time for discussion of the patient's worries or to build rapport, but as in the example below even a very short time can be used effectively.

A 14 year old boy, Michael, attended for lumbar puncture under general anaesthesia. He had had many previous anaesthetics without problem; but both he and his mum reported that he was always 'violent' post-operatively, so much so that he had required sedation in the recovery room on the past few occasions. They reported that on the last occasion Michael had not been given enough sedative and his aggressive behaviour had required him to be restrained; as he weighed 90 kg this had created a big problem for the recovery staff. There was no record on his previous anaesthetic chart of which drugs had been administered in recovery, but he had had a standard anaesthetic, exactly as had been planned on this occasion.

There was no time for a discussion of hypnotic techniques, for gaining of consent or for a formal hypnotic induction, but the author (CM) did have his undivided attention for the two minutes during which the anaesthetic drugs were being drawn up and his central venous line (CVL) cleaned prior to induction of anaesthesia. During this time Michael was told that today the anaesthetic being used would be the "... *calm anaesthetic medicine"* and that patients woke up very calmly in recovery with a big smile on their face after having this medicine. Anaesthesia was induced by injecting propofol, an intravenous induction agent, via his CVL slowly over 30 seconds. During the administration he was repeatedly told that he was having the 'calm medicine' and that he would be calm and smiling in recovery.

Michael woke up very calmly in recovery, and both he and his mum said that this was the best he had ever been. When he returned for the same procedure two months later (with the author [CM] again as anaesthetist), the accompanying nurse had sought out the previous anaesthetic chart (at Mum's request) to ask if he could have the 'smiley anaesthetic' again.

Bejenke (2007) reports the use of hypnosis with sedation for a hysterectomy with no perception of pain by the patient until she was moved into the recovery room, when there was acute onset of severe pain. She was moved back into theatre, at which point the pain eased, and further hypnosis was used to control the pain in the recovery room. It later emerged that the surgeon, in encouraging the use of hypnosis for the procedure, had 'confirmed' that she would feel no pain until she went into the recovery room. This is the state of affairs that surgeons are used to with general anaesthesia; patients are unconscious (and so pain free) during the procedure, but are often sore in the recovery room; his comment had permitted her to feel no pain during the procedure but to expect to be sore as she entered the recovery area. This highlights the fact that words used by people seen to be in a position of authority can greatly influence the outcome in a given situation.

An example of the power of words comes from the author's (CM) own hospital with the 'Nuss procedure' in which a U-shaped metal bar is placed within the chest cavity to correct pectus excavatum deformity. Pain control has been notoriously difficult in this group of patients despite the use of epidural analgesia combined with patient controlled analgesia with ketamine; it has since emerged that patients are routinely told by the surgeon in clinic that this is 'the most painful procedure known to man', and sure enough it is, despite the use of very good analgesic techniques.

The whole spectrum of mild to moderate psychological or psychiatric problems common in general practice have been given rather scant attention here. They often need more than these brief informal techniques. However, we should not miss the opportunity to use techniques acquired via hypnosis training in ordinary consultations. Often patients show affect, voice changes, catching the breath or frank tears. This is in a healing setting and a good professional relationship with all the common factors for therapeutic success and ingredients of hypnosis present. Here, the affect bridge (see page x) can be used without more ado. This has far better effect than handing the patient a tissue, a signal to stop and 'pull yourself together', however kindly meant.

Whether we are using hypnosis, and how explicit the induction is in these examples, is open to debate. Some colleagues may be uneasy about the ethical aspects of bypassing the traditional preparation of the patient and explanation of hypnosis. Indeed, using the term 'hypnosis' may improve results. In everyday practice, where rapport and trust are evident, the golden moment may be lost if we always divert to a formal explanation.

References

Banyai, E. I. (1998), The interactive nature of hypnosis: research evidence for a social-psychobiological model. *Contemporary Hypnosis*, 75 (1), 52–63.

Bejenke, C. (2007), Workshop given at the joint meeting of BSCAH, RSM and BSMDH Scotland, York, UK, May.

Erickson, M. H. (1958), Hypnosis in painful terminal illness. *American Journal of Clinical Hypnosis*, 1, 117–21.

Ferenczi, S. (1965), Introjektion und Uebertragung. Jahrbuch der Psychoanalyse 1909; 1: 422–57. Cited in Ferenczi, S. Comments on hypnosis (Translated by Jones, E.) in Shor, R. E.& Orne, M. T. (Eds.) *The nature of hypnosis: selected basic readings*. New York, Holt, Rinehart and Winston.

Hall, J. A. (1989), *Hypnosis: a Jungian perspective*. New York, Guilford Press.

Mason, A. A. (1960), *Hypnosis for medical and dental practitioners*. London, Camelot Press.

Neighbour, R. (2005a), *The inner apprentice*. Milton Keynes, Radcliffe.

Neighbour, R. (2005b), *The inner consultation*. Milton Keynes, Radcliffe.

Olness, K. & Kohen, D. (1996), *Hypnosis and hypnotherapy with children*, 3rd ed. New York, Guildford Press.

Sartre, J. P. (1943), *Being and nothingness*. New York, Washington Square Press.

Shor, R. E. (1959), Hypnosis and the concept of the generalised reality orientation. *American Journal of Psychotherapy*, 13, 582–602.

Spiegel, H. (1974), *Manual for hypnotic induction profile*. New York, Soni Medica.

Varelmann, D., Pancaro, C., Cappiello, E. C. & Camann, W. R. (2010), Nocebo-induced hyperalgesia during local anesthetic injection. *Anesthesia and Analgesia*, 110, 868–70.

39

Working Transculturally

Dr Geoff Ibbotson

Introduction

Cultures encompass customs, social interactions, beliefs, aspirations, perceptions of health, religious practice and styles of communication. It is all too easy to make judgements based purely on physical appearance and language and to be completely blind to cultural factors. In a similar way the use of politically correct speech confounds rather than resolves the problem. The politically correct phrases such as 'Caucasian' or 'Black' are unhelpful concepts because they divide people in a digital way whereas there are massive cultural differences within the classifications 'Caucasian' and 'Black'. The only way to approach the problem is to initially see the person as an individual and then to consider the context in which the person lived for their formative years, in order to develop an appreciation of their cultural experiences. Similarly, categorizing by language is an unhelpful approach. A French person and someone from the French Congo might speak a similar language, but clearly they are totally different culturally.

The Concepts of Family Relationships

As an example, the concept of relatives is totally different in the Chechyn culture from the traditional British understanding. Whilst blood relatives clearly exist, this is not taken into consideration as much as the classification of social contacts and relationships. A neighbour or a friend is classified and talked of as a cousin or a brother or sister (a brother or sister

The Handbook of Contemporary Clinical Hypnosis: Theory and Practice, First Edition.
Edited by Les Brann, Jacky Owens and Ann Williamson.
© 2012 John Wiley & Sons, Ltd. Published 2015 by John Wiley & Sons, Ltd.

being a closer friendship than a cousin). There are very deep obligations culturally which include providing needs such as food. It is an insult if a Chechyn person does not provide food to a visitor and similarly an insult if the visitor does not accept this hospitality.

Chechyns are Muslim, and Islam states that any other Muslim is their brother with all the associated obligations of hospitality. In certain situations the concepts of brotherhood are used in the United Kingdom in such circumstances as traditional trade unions or religious communities, but this is not common usage.

When working with one Chechyn family, there were considerable problems caused as a consequence of their different concept of relations. At the immigration hearing, the adjudicator was asking what relatives the family had. The first person to give evidence understood the western concept of relatives and replied. At a subsequent point in the hearing, the adjudicator questioned the son and he did not understand the western concept. When asked what relatives he had, he stated that all of his neighbours were cousins and he majored on social rather than blood relatives. This conflicting evidence caused the adjudicator, in the absence of explanation of the cultural differences, to reject the case as the evidence 'was not credible'. The author is pleased to report that eventually, after many years, the family were given indefinite leave to remain in the United Kingdom.

The young son of this family and the author were discussing the complexities of this concept of relatives. He said, *"We are brothers."* He went on to mischievously create a scenario. If he met a Chechyn girl outside Chechnya and she had needs, then she was, as a result of her needs, his cousin. As he developed a deeper relationship, she would become his sister. If he then married her, she would become his wife.

Respect for the culture is a pre-requisite for effective cross-cultural work. Questions regarding the cultural background of a patient give important information as to their beliefs and values as well as facilitating rapport.

The Muslim tradition puts responsibilities on the eldest son to provide materially and be in a leadership role for his family. If circumstances of illness or emotional distress prevent this obligation being met, then shame can confound the already fraught situation.

Interpreters

It is important to remember that it is not what you say, but how you say it! Our language expresses our conscious 'reality', whereas our internal imagery and our body language express our unconscious feelings. Natural rapport is a consequence of the unconscious interpretation of the body language expressed between individuals. Hence when using an interpreter, you can still ensure that you communicate non-verbally whilst leaving the verbal communication to the interpreter.

Normal good practice when working in NHS Mental Health Services is to use professional interpreters. The principle is good because the use of friends and family members to interpret is fraught with problems as the pre-existing relationship with the patient can seriously complicate progress. Also in cases where shame is an issue, then disclosure of content in these circumstances may be blocked.

The way agencies sort interpreters is clearly by language rather than by cultural background, knowledge and flexibility. It is not unusual for agencies, particularly with less common languages, to provide a person from another country. Whilst the linguistic match may be good and appropriate for translations of the written word, it is possible that this country has been in a state of war for a long time with the country of origin of the patient. Most patients are able to speak several languages or dialects, and it may be preferable to work using the second language of the patient if the cultural match is better. Sometimes the interpreter's perceptions will cause difficulties; for example in the experience of one editor (JO) some interpreters will not use the word 'cancer' and instead refer to 'microbes' which can lead to confusion.

Ideally one should have an opportunity to meet the interpreter alone prior to the arrival of the patient. In this way, rapport can be established and the function of the interpreter discussed. However this is not usually possible in NHS work due to financial and time constraints. It is most important at the end of the first session to establish that the interpreter and patient are comfortable with each other and prepared to work together. If this is the case, then the situation can be explained to the agency and an agreement made that the same interpreter will be used for all future sessions.

Such matters need to be discussed and agreed at the first session. Although professional interpreters understand the concepts of confidentiality, the ground rules may be different in different settings in which they work. Refugees and asylum seekers have often been in conflict with authorities, and it is vital that they understand your respect for them and the confidentiality of material discussed. The integrity of an interpreter is also paramount. It is most important that they are free of personal bias.

It is the author's experience that when working transculturally, one needs to work to different boundaries. In some cases patient and interpreter may wish to exchange telephone numbers and to communicate outside sessions, in such circumstances as reminding the patient just prior to the next appointment or communicating with the therapist if there are reasons why the patient cannot attend the next session.

Some interpreters are trained to talk in the first person when translating. This can be difficult for the therapist until they are familiar with this style.

Linear communication

Asylum seekers and refugees have often suffered interrogation and torture in their country of origin. Clearly this affects their attitudes towards authority and consequently the therapist. Hence it is necessary to adopt an open communication rather than an authoritarian approach. The process of interrogation and torture is usually linear. The roles are boss, torturer and victim. The paths of communication are that the boss only talks to the torturer, who then talks to the victim. The victim can only talk to the torturer.

The natural process when using an interpreter is also linear (i.e. therapist, interpreter and patient). However utilizing this style will mimic the torture experiences and will almost certainly cause problems.

Triangular communication

A safer style is to have a triangular approach with an even powerbase. At first this can be unusual to all three, but it has tremendous benefits. In this approach the chairs are in an equilateral triangle arrangement. The therapist faces the patient most of the time, facilitates body language communication with the patient and reads the body language as the conversation is translated. This gives the message that the important processing is communication with between the patient and therapist. The interpreter might at first feel left out of the communication but soon realizes that they should simply translate the auditory part of the communication.

Another very important role of the interpreter is to alert the therapist in situations where there is a cultural mismatch between the questions asked and the patient's cultural norms or with concepts such as 'family' relationships.

Questionnaires

The use of questionnaires in order to facilitate diagnoses such as post-traumatic stress disorder (PTSD) or to establish change in patients is an excellent practice when working with our native population. However their use in a transcultural situation is fraught with problems. Many questionnaires are available in a translated version as it is possible to simply translate the words of the questionnaire. The problem is with different cultural outlooks. Western populations express themselves in a feeling-focused way, but eastern cultures are more familiar with actions. Hence to ask *"How do you feel about this?"* is fine with westerners. With eastern cultures it is necessary to put things in a function focused or problem focused way such as *"How are you doing?"* or *"What do you need to do?"* (Summerfield, 2001).

The author finds the Psychological Outcome Profiles (PSYCHLOPS) questionnaire (Ashworth *et al.,* 2004) helpful because it focuses the therapy on the needs and goals of the patient, and the nature of the questionnaire is such that it can be used with those with poor English and from different cultural contexts (see page 586).

This difficulty with formal questionnaires does not, in any way, remove the need for enquiry at the end of each session as to how the patient saw the session and where there needs to be a change in direction or emphasis. Such an approach develops and strengthens the therapeutic alliance.

Eastern cultures often describe illness and the effects in a somatic idiom. There can often be non-specific symptoms such as weakness, headaches or pain in the heart described, and these can be very difficult to interpret if the health professional is of a western culture and training. However to label this as 'psychosomatic' or 'somatizing' is far too simplistic (Kirmayer & Young, 1998).

GPs are usually the ones who are asked to advise on appropriate treatment. If the patient does not speak English, then the provision of interpreters in these circumstances may be difficult. Given the 'pseudo-somatization', GPs may find it difficult to give appropriate treatment or make an appropriate referral. PTSD checklists may cause over-diagnosis because it is not possible to use a check-list to differentiate between normal and pathological distress following adverse life events (Summerfield, 2001).

Whilst it is easy to understand the prescription of psychoactive substances for poor sleep, distress and anxiety, they cannot address the social needs and the need for validation and connection.

Treatment

Our treatment approach in the United Kingdom tends to follow the medical model, and in these circumstances it is not the approach of choice. A study was carried out on survivors of a Bosnian concentration camp who were sent to Sweden. Half were sent to a place with temporary employment but no psychological services. The other half were sent to a place with psychological services but no work available. After a year it was seen that those who had the opportunity to work were doing better, whilst the other cohort were on indefinite sick leave (Eastmond, 1998).

Maslow's Hierarchy

No theory of psychology will ever be complete which does not centrally incorporate the concept that man has his future within him, dynamically active at the present moment.
Abraham Maslow (1968 p. 16)

Maslow classifies needs in a hierarchy that is usually shown as a pyramid. The lowest level comprises physiological needs for oxygen, food, water, sleep, sex and the elimination of body wastes. Next come safety needs for security, stability, predictability and order. The next level is belongingness and love which can be satisfied through intimacy with another person, association with a group or benevolence towards people in general. This is followed by esteem needs of self-esteem and respect from others. The highest level in the hierarchy is self-actualization, but Maslow estimates that this level is achieved by only 1% or 2% of the population. Such people have meta-needs that include truth, aliveness, uniqueness, perfection, justice and order, self sufficiency and meaningfulness (Maslow, 1943).

When working with a patient, it is not possible to work on higher levels until the first two levels are satisfied. This process can be called ' stabilization', and the interventions needed are social rather than medical; only when these needs have been satisfied can therapeutic work commence. The fact that the therapeutic alliance addresses the third level of needs demonstrates the harmonization between effective therapy and Maslow's concepts.

Many asylum seekers and refugees have been in conflict with the authorities for 'political activities'. It could be that activists are in fact self-actualizers attending to their meta-needs. The punitive response of imprisonment and torture removes the two lowest levels of needs and hence blocks the process of self-actualization.

The author has found in his department that transcultural patients were almost invariably passed over by therapists as they did not know what to do and were not prepared to work outside their comfort zone. When the author first started working transculturally, he had little insight into the difficulties and thought that he would simply need to use dissociated imagery such as the cinema technique (described on page 403) with the interpreter translating.

Here are the consequences of utilization of such a simplistic approach; this is shared to prevent others from falling into the same pit!

The author was working with an asylum seeker, Ahmed, with an interpreter who was also from the same area. The first two sessions went well, and so it was decided to use the cinema technique (see page 403) after explanation of the process. With more experience the author would realize that going for such an approach to deal with trauma was not appropriate in these circumstances. A 'safe place' for the patient to use as a safety anchor was being established, but Ahmed had great difficulty understanding the concept of a safe place as he had been persecuted all of his life and had never been able to feel safe. The author should have moved away from this approach at that time but failed to realize the possible complications and so decided to go on to the cinema. The author was observing the patient closely and not looking at the interpreter. As soon as the stage was reached where we were going to start work on a traumatic incident, the patient started to abreact. While attempting to deal with this, there was no response from the interpreter. He too was abreacting! The author had to deal with the interpreter's abreaction first and then continue to work with the patient. Having decided that the interpreter was more stable, dissociated imagery was used with him in order to resolve some of his past trauma. As for the patient he was taught the butterfly hug, an eye movement desensitization and reprocessing (EMDR) technique (Artigas & Jarero, 2000). Ahmed used this technique with good effect when he had flashbacks or when he woke up with nightmares. Ahmed also used imagery of a bonfire on which he could throw harmful events (and also people!). He found this very helpful and improved gradually.

There are several lessons to be learned from the handling of this patient.

- When working transculturally, it is not as simple as taking your normal approach and talking through an interpreter.
- When patients have complex traumatic backgrounds, one needs to work differently and at a much slower pace.

- It is important to be aware of other approaches such as the butterfly hug.
- However experienced you are in working with trauma, you are not always in control of the process.
- An expert is not someone who never makes mistakes but is rather a person who has made many mistakes and then hopefully learned from them.

An approach that the author uses very frequently in a transcultural setting is the use of metaphor (see page 58). The metaphor is set in the cultural context of the trauma and used to address the psychological needs of the patient. Here is an example of its use with a patient who had survived an armed kidnap attempt. The patient's uncle had previously been kidnapped and was not heard of again. The context was a situation in the Middle East where the important factors are:

- Whoever controls the water is in a position of power.
- In an open country situation, being higher than your adversary is a big advantage.
- Imagining being an eagle can be a very empowering experience.

Waseen was asked to imagine himself on a high ridge, overlooking a valley. He could see some people in the distance down in the valley, and as they came to a position below the patient he could see that they were the party who had attempted to kidnap him. Waseen shouted down to them that he was free and feeling good. He then took out a large water container and drank it so that they could see him. Waseen taunted them, shouting that he was high up in the cool breeze and they were in the stifling heat. He had ample water to drink, and they had none. To emphasize the point, Waseen even poured some on the ground so that they could see, shouting to them that he had more than enough water and they had none and were thirsty. After a few minutes, Waseen started rolling big rocks down the hill towards them and they had to dodge these. Waseen was then able to transform himself into an eagle, soar effortlessly on the thermals and dive down on them so that they had to scatter and hide.

This gave him control, payback and empowerment, and he enjoyed his 'homework' of soaring like an eagle whenever he wanted.

The use of metaphor requires the therapist to look for behaviour in the patient that links back to the traumatic experience and then present that metaphorically in order that the patient learns experientially and is able to develop a better response.

Antonije had been imprisoned and tortured in his own country for political reasons. He was behaving in a dysfunctional way in that he spent all his time in his bedroom, only coming out to wash. He did not associate with his family, who used to frequent the living room. On hearing this, the author realized that Antonije was probably living as he did when in prison in solitary confinement and feared contact with others as this usually preceded his being removed from his cell in order to be tortured. Antonije was therefore asked *"Who appointed you as your jailer?"* Antonije was silent for quite a time as he processed the question, and then his body language verified the validity of these assumptions. The interpreter was then asked to write out two sheets of paper in his language that stated, 'This is a bedroom, not a prison cell'. Antonije agreed that he would put these on the inside and outside of his bedroom door. When he returned two weeks later, he was looking much better and reported that he was functioning better. When asked if he was still reading the notices, he said that they were no longer there. On investigating further, Antonije reported that his sons had completely removed the door from his bedroom.

The principles of working transculturally can be summarized as:

- Address and understand the cultural differences – effectively using the interpreter in order to facilitate this process.
- Ensure that the lower level needs in Maslow's hierarchy are addressed and the patient is stable before attempting therapeutic interventions.
- Use a holistic rather than a medical model.
- Be prepared to step outside the traditional boundaries in order to address the needs of the patient.
- The use of metaphor usually reaps rich rewards.

Because of the potential difficulties, formal hypnotic techniques may not be appropriate in this group of patients. However exemplified in this chapter a less formal but still hypnotic approach of 'close your eyes and imagine' and the use of metaphor may prove useful. Transcultural situations should not be seen to preclude the use of more formal hypnosis, but the student would be well advised to be aware of possible pitfalls and tailor their approach accordingly.

References

Artigas, L. & Jarero, I. (2000), http://www.amamecrisis.com.mx/proing_butterfly.htm

Ashworth, M., Shepherd, M., Christey, J., Matthews, V., Wright, K., Parmentier, H., Robinson, S. & Godfrey, E. (2004), A client-centred psychometric instrument: the development of 'PSYCHLOPS' ('Psychological Outcome Profiles'). *Counselling and Psychotherapy Research*, 4, 27–33.

Eastmond, M. (1998), Nationalist discourses and the construction of difference: Bosnian Muslim refugees in Sweden. *Journal of Refugee Studies*, 11, 161–81.

Kirmayer, L. & Young, A. (1998), Culture and somatization: clinical, epidemiological and ethnographic perspectives. *Psychosomatic Medicine*, 60, 420–9.

Maslow, A. (1943), A theory of human motivation. *Psychological Review*, 50, 370–96.

Maslow, A. (1968), *Towards a psychology of being*. New York, Van Nostrand Reinhold.

Summerfield, D. (2001), Asylum-seekers, refugees and mental health services in the UK. *The Psychiatrist*, 25, 161–3.

40

Commissioning, Providing and Auditing a Hypnotherapy Service

Dr Les Brann

with contributions from Dr Ann Williamson

Competence of the Therapist

This chapter is written primarily to encourage the commissioning of hypnosis services. It provides an evidence base for GP consortia and other health care commissioners. The practical suggestions are also pertinent to the individual therapist setting up their own service.

This book is written by members of the British Society of Clinical & Academic Hypnosis (BSCAH) who follow the philosophy that hypnotherapy should only be carried out by those who are first and foremost qualified health professionals (for details, see their website: www.bscah.com). From that health professional base, hypnotherapy training, supervised clinical practice over two years, case reports and a viva voce examination lead to the gaining of the certificate of accreditation. This, we contend, is the minimum requirement for entry into the 'Referral List'. The BSCAH referral list is not meant as a list of recommended therapists, but simply a list of those members who have achieved this basic standard.

Even once accredited, the therapist is compelled to work within their field of competence. The acid test is to ask, *"Is this therapist competent to treat this condition without using hypnosis?"* For example it would be inappropriate to use hypnosis for

The Handbook of Contemporary Clinical Hypnosis: Theory and Practice, First Edition.
Edited by Les Brann, Jacky Owens and Ann Williamson.
© 2012 John Wiley & Sons, Ltd. Published 2015 by John Wiley & Sons, Ltd.

childbirth if the therapist had not had any training in obstetrics, but the midwife with hypnotherapy training would be ideally suited for this purpose.

Obtaining Patients

The therapist's field of competence will obviously dictate the patient group from which referrals will come. As hypnotherapy should be seen as only a part of the patient's overall care, the ideal route for referral is from the patient's GP or consultant responsible for the patient's medical management. For those referrals to be forthcoming the referrers need to know of the existence of the service, its referral criteria and, most importantly, from where the funding might come.

Providing a service through the NHS is difficult but not impossible and involves the preparation of a business plan and subsequent service specification. Currently it is the Primary Care Trusts (PCTs) that commission services, but this duty is soon to be transferred to GP consortia. Each PCT or consortia group will have their own business plan format but are likely to require the following:

- Identify the need:
  - What condition are you proposing to treat?
  - Will hypnotherapy be fulfilling an unmet need or be used as an alternative therapy to an existing treatment for this condition?
    - If an alternative therapy, what are the shortcomings of the existing service provision (e.g. lack of capacity, poor cost effectiveness or the need for patient choice)?
  - Quantify the need in terms of numbers of patients (be aware of backlogs)
- Why hypnosis?
  - Provide trial evidence showing the effectiveness of hypnotherapy for this condition
    - Provide outcome audit data to show effectiveness in a service provision setting
  - Provide comparative evidence showing hypnotherapy is at least as effective as, and preferably more effective than, the existing treatment model
    - The advantage of hypnotherapy may be by virtue of shorter treatment regimes and, therefore, cost
- Who will provide the therapy? Given the lack of regulation and the plethora of hypnosis 'qualifications', commissioning organizations are well advised to take note of our warnings to avoid running into governance issues and we therefore suggest the following:
  - Minimum qualifications:
    - Therapists must first and foremost be qualified health professionals
    - Hold the accreditation certificate from BSCAH or predecessor organizations (British Society of Medical & Dental Hypnosis [BSMDH] or British Society of Experimental & Clinical Hypnosis [BSECH])

- ○ Ideal qualifications:
    - ▪ The above accreditation plus postgraduate university diploma or masters degree in clinical hypnosis (previously from Sheffield University or University College London, and now currently from Stafford University)
    - ▪ European certificate of hypnosis
- Premises:
    - ○ Consulting rooms appropriately furnished and equipped
        - ▪ Comfortable chairs, couches and other facilities
        - ▪ Video capability
        - ▪ Secure records
        - ▪ Chaperone availability
    - ○ Disabled access
- Governance:
    - ○ Able to provide sufficient capacity to fulfil waiting times targets
    - ○ Collect data for outcome audit
    - ○ Undertake patient satisfaction survey
    - ○ Clinical supervision
    - ○ Continuing professional development
- Finance:
    - ○ Costs of the project, being aware of the need to take into account patients who fail to attend and cancellations

The above is only a guide but affords a template on which to work.

Following the acceptance of a business plan, more detailed work needs to be done in the form of a service specification. Such a document forms the basis of the legal contract and will detail the mechanics of the service, for example:

- Who can refer?
- What are the referral criteria?
- What is the administrative process for appointments?
- What is the audit requirement?
- What is the billing process?
- What is the process of communication between the therapist, the referrer and the patient's GP?

The workload for setting up an NHS service is enormous. Some therapists who are already working in an NHS department may simply be allowed to incorporate hypnotherapy into their day to day consultations without the need for a formal business plan, but the governance issues mentioned above are still likely to be required.

The setting up of a private clinic in some respects is less arduous, but details are equally important. The first essential is to ensure the safety of the patient, and this requires appropriate qualifications (see above) and valid indemnity insurance. When considering premises it is essential to have somebody else in the building to avoid opportunities for (malicious) claims of misconduct. Videoing the sessions is a better safeguard for the therapist and the patient. Keeping good records is also a prerequisite for good practice, and such records must be kept confidential and secure. Locked filing cabinets or password protected computer records are essential parts of the setting up process.

Outcome Audit

Clinical audit is not only good practice but also essential in cases where re-validation is required. Audit is helpful for the individual practitioner to identify which conditions respond best to their hypnotherapeutic intervention. Thus, when accepting referrals it is possible to give an honest idea of outcome. Some conditions, such as severe obsessive compulsive disorder (OCD), are difficult to treat using any treatment regime, and a poor outcome with hypnotherapy may be no worse than outcomes with other treatment modalities, so the use of hypnotherapy may still be a valid option. Poor outcomes may also be an indication of the therapist's learning needs and can therefore form the basis of their professional development plans.

Deciding what data to collect for audit purposes will differ between disciplines but are likely to include before and after therapy measures of the presenting symptom and of co-morbid conditions such as anxiety and depression. There are many questionnaires available and each discipline has its favourites, but the Measure Yourself Medical Outcome Profile (MYMOP) (Paterson, 1996; Paterson and Britten, 2000) is recommended as it is a patient centred questionnaire based on the symptoms that are troubling the patient most. Psychlops (Psychological Outcome Profiles) evolved from MYMOP and is more geared to psychological problems. It enquires about two problems (rather than symptoms) that trouble the patient, one thing they find hard to do and how they have felt during the previous week.

With MYMOP the patient lists and scores up to two (or more if required) symptoms, and each is measured independently, so whatever the symptom, improvements can be identified and measured. The questionnaire can be downloaded from the internet free of charge, although it is necessary to register that you are using it. This sort of questionnaire has advantages over conventional forms in that it deals with the problems that the patient has – for example the main symptom for a man with diarrhoea predominant irritable bowel syndrome (IBS) was 'fear' (of soiling himself). Conventionally, the clinician is likely to have recorded the problem in terms of frequency of bowel actions which, although linked, is significantly different from 'fear'.

An example of outcome data using MYMOP is presented in Table 40.1. These results were obtained from an average of 3.9 sessions per patient (*SD* 1.04).

Measurement of anxiety and depression can be achieved by any number of available questionnaires such as the Hospital Anxiety and Depression scale (HADs; Zigmond and Snaith, 1983). Examples of HADs outcome audit data are given in the relevant chapters.

Table 40.1   Example of MYMOP outcome audit

MYMOP SCORES	Before treatment	At follow-up	Change in score	
	Mean (SD)	Mean (SD)	Mean (SD)	Significance: *t*-test (effect size)
Symptom 1 $n = 135$	4.8 (1.03)	2.4 (1.39)	2.4 (1.59)	$P = 4.13 \times 10^{-36}$ (2.3)
Symptom 2 $n = 123$	4.5 (1.12)	2.2 (1.34)	2.3 (1.54)	$P = 6.12 \times 10^{-33}$ (2.0)
Activity $n = 122$	4.4 (1.30)	2.3 (1.58)	2.1 (1.65)	$P = 9.6 \times 10^{-27}$ (1.59)
Wellbeing $n = 135$	3.7 (1.37)	2.2 (1.27)	1.4 (1.55)	$P = 8.7 \times 10^{-20}$ (1.05)
MYMOP profile $n = 135$	4.3 (0.83)	2.3 (1.19)	2.03 (1.25)	$P = 1.8 \times 10^{-39}$ (2.4)

Source: Brann *et al.* (2010).

Because research evidence of efficacy does not guarantee effectiveness in day to day clinical practice, every practitioner should keep outcome data. Ideally this should extend to obtaining follow up data at appropriate intervals. Further to outcome audit we would also encourage all practitioners to consider undertaking research into all aspects of hypnosis but especially into outcomes as it is delivered in clinical practice.

Outcome audit tools need not be complex; simple analogue scales (such as the scaling question) can be used to record change. Specific areas may have their particular audit tool, for example the Impact of Event Scale (IES) which is useful in PTSD and measures how severely the traumatic incident affects the person emotionally and how much avoidance they display (Horowitz *et al.*, 1979).

Clinical Outcome Routine Evaluation (CORE; Barkham *et al.*, 1998; Evans *et al.*, 2000) measures psychological distress and consists of a 32 question patient questionnaire together with much other associated material which can be analysed and scored at a cost, although it is also possible to do this yourself. The author (AW) has found that the patient questionnaire, which is free to use, is a useful tool, and a simple spreadsheet tool has been developed to display outcomes (Ibbotson, 1997). The questionnaire measures four domains: wellbeing, problems, functioning and risk. The maximum score for any question is four, and the higher the score the worse the patient is emotionally. Averaging the initial and final scores across the four domains, a score greater than one is considered clinically abnormal. Reliable improvement is a reduction of the total initial score by anything greater than 0.5.

Having collected outcome data, it is preferable to present it in a form that is useful to both commissioners and clinical colleagues. Some form of statistical analysis to demonstrate clinical effectiveness is required such as effect size or *t*-test.

Other data of interest to commissioners and clinicians such as non-attendance and drop-out rates should also be collected. Lambert *et al.* (2004) showed that for psychological therapies, dropouts by the third visit average 47% and that this can account for a large percentage of mental health expenditure (Chasson, 2005).

Administration

Thus, providing a hypnotherapy service is more than simply agreeing to see a few patients. One other point worthy of consideration here is how long does each session need to be? There is no right answer and depends greatly on the sort of problem being treated. For example if hypnosis is being used as an adjunct to anaesthesia for day-case patients, ten or 15 minutes might be all that is available; yet if it is being used for anxiety or IBS, then sessions of about an hour are probably ideal. It should be remembered that such sessions require an enormous degree of concentration and five sessions in a day is probably all that the therapist should sensibly book.

Larger hypnotherapy units will also need to factor in administrative and secretarial time. Booking appointments and dealing with alterations, queries etc take considerable time. Writing back to the referrer is also essential and is probably best done once at the completion of therapy unless some major information surfaces that requires earlier correspondence. It is not necessary to detail the nuts and bolts of the hypnosis techniques but report the major theme of the therapy and the outcome.

The NHS needs accountability, measurable outcomes, efficient use of resources and a documented 'return on investment'. Practice based evidence can give this by having training and supervision targeted to outcomes of the individual therapists, by monitoring and real-time utilization of outcome data and by having treatment planning informed by local norms and outcome data.

References

Barkham, M., Evans, C., Margison, M., McGrath, G., Mellor-Clarke, J., Milne, D. & Connell, J. (1998), The rationale for developing & implementing core outcome batteries for routine use in service settings and psychotherapy outcome research. *Journal of Mental Health*, 7, 35–47.

Brann, L., Mackrodt, K. & Joslin, M. (2010), Outcome audit, Chelmsford Medical Hypnotherapy Unit. Paper presented at BSCAH Conference, Birmingham, UK.

British Society of Clinical & Academic Hypnosis (BSCAH) (N.d.), www.bscah.com

Chasson, G. (2005), Attrition in child treatment. *Psychotherapy Bulletin*, 40 (1), 4–7.

Evans, C., Mellor-Clark, J., Margison, F., Barkham, M., McGrath, G., Connell, J. & Audin, K. (2000), Clinical outcomes in routine evaluation: the CORE-OM. *Journal of Mental Health*, 9, 247–55.

Horowitz, M., Wilner, N. & Alvarez, W. (1979), Impact of Event Scale: a measure of subjective stress. *Psychosomatic Medicine*, 41 (3), 209–18.

Ibbotson, G. (1997), CORE spreadsheet tool. www.geofibbotson.co.uk

Lambert, M. J., Whipple, J. L., Hawkins, E. J., Vermeersch, D. A., Nielsen, S. L. & Smart, D. A. (2004), Is it time for clinicians routinely to track patient outcome: a meta-analysis. *Clinical Psychology*, 10, 288–301.

Paterson, C. (1996), Measuring outcome in primary care: a patient-generated measure, MYMOP, compared to the SF-36 health survey. *British Medical Journal* 312, 1016–20.

Paterson, C. & Britten, N. (2000), In pursuit of patient-centred outcomes: a qualitative evaluation of MYMOP, Measure Yourself Medical Outcome Profile. *Journal of Health Service Research & Policy*, 5 (1) 27–36.

Zigmond, A. S. & Snaith, R. P. (1983), The hospital anxiety and depression scale. *Acta Psychiatrica Scandinavia*, 67 (6), 361–70.

Appendix 1: Life History Inventory

Your name	
Your date of birth	

Wellbeing
How would you rate your feelings of wellbeing in these four periods of your life?

[Score 1 to 10 where 1 is excellent and 10 is very bad indeed]

Age 0 to 7	
Age 7 to 14	
Age 14 to 21	
After 21	

Your family of origin
How would you rate your relationships with your family throughout your life?

[Score 1 to 10 where 1 is excellent and 10 is very poor]

Score	

Partners, including long term boyfriends or girlfriends
How would you rate these relationships throughout your life?

[Score 1 to 10 where 1 is excellent and 10 is very poor]

Score	

Occupation
Are you in employment or full time education?

Yes	
No	

Is there anything else that you would like to express here?

The Handbook of Contemporary Clinical Hypnosis: Theory and Practice, First Edition.
Edited by Les Brann, Jacky Owens and Ann Williamson.
© 2012 John Wiley & Sons, Ltd. Published 2015 by John Wiley & Sons, Ltd.

To score:
To score add up the scores from the different domains but multiply the wellbeing scores as below.

Wellbeing
0–7 multiply score by 4:
7–14 multiply score by 3:
14–21 multiply score by 2:
Over 21 use original score:

Family of origin
Score:

Relationships
Score:

Occupation
Score 0 if in employment:
Score 10 if unemployed:

Total score:

If total score is below fifty then this indicates that the patient may be suitable for shorter therapy.

Appendix 2: What Goes in Must Come Out

The Handbook of Contemporary Clinical Hypnosis: Theory and Practice, First Edition.
Edited by Les Brann, Jacky Owens and Ann Williamson.
© 2012 John Wiley & Sons, Ltd. Published 2015 by John Wiley & Sons, Ltd.

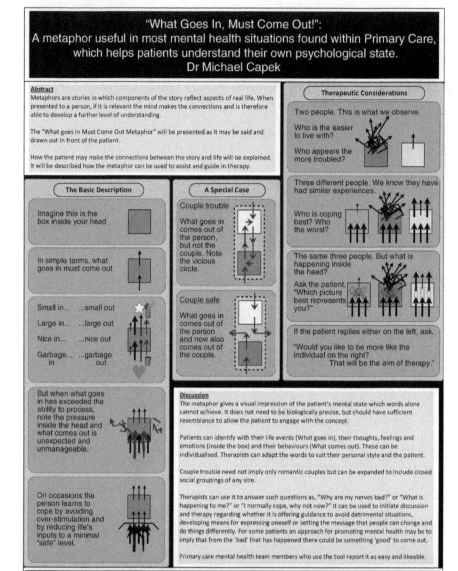

"What Goes In, Must Come Out!":
A metaphor useful in most mental health situations found within Primary Care, which helps patients understand their own psychological state.
Dr Michael Capek

Abstract

Metaphors are stories in which components of the story reflect aspects of real life. When presented to a person, if it is relevant the mind makes the connections and is therefore able to develop a further level of understanding.

The "What goes in Must Come Out Metaphor" will be presented as it may be said and drawn out in front of the patient.

How the patient may make the connections between the story and life will be explained. It will be described how the metaphor can be used to assist and guide in therapy.

Therapeutic Considerations

Two people. This is what we observe.

Who is the easier to live with?

Who appears the more troubled?

Three different people. We know they have had similar experiences.

Who is coping best? Who the worst?

The same three people. But what is happening inside the head?

Ask the patient, "Which picture best represents you?"

If the patient replies either on the left, ask.

"Would you like to be more like the individual on the right? That will be the aim of therapy."

The Basic Description

Imagine this is the box inside your head

In simple terms, what goes in must come out

Small in...   ...small out

Large in...   ...large out

Nice in...   ...nice out

Garbage...   ...garbage in   out

But when what goes in has exceeded the ability to process, note the pressure inside the head and what comes out is unexpected and unmanageable.

On occasions the person learns to cope by avoiding over-stimulation and by reducing life's inputs to a minimal "safe" level.

A Special Case

Couple trouble

What goes in comes out of the person, but not the couple. Note the vicious circle.

Couple safe

What goes in comes out of the person and now also comes out of the couple.

Discussion

The metaphor gives a visual impression of the patient's mental state which words alone cannot achieve. It does not need to be biologically precise, but should have sufficient resemblance to allow the patient to engage with the concept.

Patients can identify with their life events (What goes in), their thoughts, feelings and emotions (inside the box) and their behaviours (What comes out). These can be individualised. Therapists can adapt the words to suit their personal style and the patient.

Couple trouble need not imply only romantic couples but can be expanded to include closed social groupings of any size.

Therapists can use it to answer such questions as, "Why are my nerves bad?" or "What is happening to me?" or "I normally cope, why not now?" It can be used to initiate discussion and therapy regarding whether it is offering guidance to avoid detrimental situations, developing means for expressing oneself or setting the message that people can change and do things differently. For some patients an approach for promoting mental health may be to imply that from the 'bad' that has happened there could be something 'good' to come out.

Primary care mental health team members who use the tool report it as easy and likeable.

Dr Michael Capek (Affiliations)
GP, Northern Moor Medical Practice, Manchester 23
GPwSI in Mental Health to the Central Manchester Primary Care Mental Health Team
Council Member, BSCAH. (British Society of Clinical and Academic Hypnosis)
Contact: meycapek@doctors.org.uk

Glossary

Antabuse(disulfiram)	A drug used for the treatment of alcohol abuse or dependence by virtue of its action in producing intense nausea when taken with alcohol.
Apgar score	A score that is determined by evaluating a newborn baby on five simple criteria on a scale from zero to two, then summing up the five values thus obtained. The resulting Apgar score ranges from zero to 10. The five criteria are Appearance, Pulse, Grimace (Cry), Activity and Respiration.
Auditory evoked potential	An evoked potential measured following the delivery of an auditory stimulus.
Eidetic imagery	Visual or auditory imagery that is exceptionally vivid and allows for detailed recall of a previous experience.
Evoked potential	An electrical potential recorded from the nervous system of a human or other animal following the presentation of a stimulus and tends to range from less than a microvolt to several microvolts.
Fractionation	The term used for the deepening of the hypnotic state generated by repeatedly taking the patient in and out of hypnosis.
Functional Magnetic Resonance Imaging (fMRI)	A type of resonance imaging; a specialized MRI scan. It measures the changes in blood flow related to neural activity in the brain or spinal cord. Since the early 1990s, fMRI has come to dominate the brain mapping field due to its relatively low invasiveness, absence of radiation exposure and relatively wide availability.
Ipsative imagery	Ipsative (of the self) imagery is that used by patients to uniquely describe their symptoms; it is amenable to alteration in hypnosis.

The Handbook of Contemporary Clinical Hypnosis: Theory and Practice, First Edition.
Edited by Les Brann, Jacky Owens and Ann Williamson.
© 2012 John Wiley & Sons, Ltd. Published 2015 by John Wiley & Sons, Ltd.

Mandala	Sanskrit word for circle. Sacred art comprising circles and symmetry, comprising a metaphor for connection to the infinite.
Paradoxical response	This occurs when the intervention has the opposite effect to that which would normally be expected.
Perceptual positions	This is a neuro-linguistic programming and psychology term denoting that a complex system may look very different, and different information will be available, depending on how one looks at it and one's point of view. Three positions most commonly described are those of self, other and neutral observer.
Placebo effect	The measurable, observable or felt improvement in health or behaviour not attributable to a medication or invasive treatment that has been administered.
Positron emission tomography (PET)	A nuclear medicine imaging technique which produces a three-dimensional image or picture of functional processes in the body. The system detects pairs of gamma rays emitted indirectly by a positron-emitting radionuclide (tracer), which is introduced into the body on a biologically active molecule. Images of tracer concentration in three-dimensional or four-dimensional space (the fourth dimension being time) within the body are then reconstructed by computer analysis.
Pseudo-memory	A non-technical term to describe memory of events that did not occur. This term is often used interchangeably with *false memory*.
Repression	The unconscious exclusion of painful impulses, desires, memories or fears from the conscious mind. The level of 'forgetting' in repression can vary from a temporary abolition of uncomfortable thoughts to a high level of amnesia, where events that caused the anxiety are buried very deep. Repressed memories do not disappear. They can have an accumulative effect and reappear as unattributable anxiety or dysfunctional behaviour.
Schitzotypy	A psychological concept which describes a continuum of personality characteristics and experiences ranging from normal dissociative, imaginative states to more extreme states related to psychosis and, in particular, to schizophrenia.
Somnambulistic trance	A deep hypnotic state (literally, sleepwalking), generally accessible only to those who are more highly hypnotizable; suggestion may work more effectively at this level, but somnambulism is not required for a good therapeutic outcome

Trait anxiety   The tendency to experience anxiety. This is considered to be a characteristic of personality that endures over time and is manifest across a variety of situations.

Trance ratification   A perceived 'involuntary' action such as arm levitation which when experienced 'proves' to patients that they have been in hypnosis.

Transcranial magnetic stimulation (TMS)   A non-invasive method to cause depolarization in the neurons of the brain. TMS uses electromagnetic induction to induce weak electric currents using a rapidly changing magnetic field; this can cause activity in specific or general parts of the brain with minimal discomfort, allowing the functioning and interconnections of the brain to be studied.

Visual evoked potential   An evoked potential measured following the delivery of a visual stimulus.

Author Index

The Handbook of Contemporary Clinical Hypnosis: Theory and Practice, First Edition.
Edited by Les Brann, Jacky Owens and Ann Williamson.
© 2012 John Wiley & Sons, Ltd. Published 2015 by John Wiley & Sons, Ltd.

Subject Index

The Handbook of Contemporary Clinical Hypnosis: Theory and Practice, First Edition.
Edited by Les Brann, Jacky Owens and Ann Williamson.
© 2012 John Wiley & Sons, Ltd. Published 2015 by John Wiley & Sons, Ltd.